Houghton
Mifflin
Harcourt

Integrated
Mathematics 1

Volume 2

EDWARD B. BURGER

JULI K. DIXON

MATTHEW R. LARSON

STEVEN J. LEINWAND

Printed in the U.S.A.

ISBN 978-0-544-38976-2

4 5 6 7 8 9 10   0982   22 21 20 19 18 17 16 15

4500528120   B C D E F G

Authors

Timothy D. Kanold, Ph.D., is an award-winning international educator, author, and consultant. He is a former superintendent and director of mathematics and science at Adlai E. Stevenson High School District 125 in Lincolnshire, Illinois. He is a past president of the National Council of Supervisors of Mathematics (NCSM) and the Council for the Presidential Awardees of Mathematics (CPAM). He

has served on several writing and leadership commissions for NCTM during the past decade. He presents motivational professional development seminars with a focus on developing professional learning communities (PLC's) to improve the teaching, assessing, and learning of students. He has recently authored nationally recognized articles, books, and textbooks for mathematics education and school leadership, including *What Every Principal Needs to Know about the Teaching and Learning of Mathematics*.

Edward B. Burger, Ph.D., is the President of Southwestern University, a former Francis Christopher Oakley Third Century Professor of Mathematics at Williams College, and a former vice provost at Baylor University. He has authored or coauthored more than sixty-five articles, books, and video series; delivered over five hundred addresses and workshops throughout the world; and made more than fifty radio and

television appearances. He is a Fellow of the American Mathematical Society as well as having earned many national honors, including the Robert Foster Cherry Award for Great Teaching in 2010. In 2012, Microsoft Education named him a "Global Hero in Education."

Juli K. Dixon, Ph.D., is a Professor of Mathematics Education at the University of Central Florida. She has taught mathematics in urban schools at the elementary, middle, secondary, and post-secondary levels. She is an active researcher and speaker with numerous publications and conference presentations. Key areas of focus are deepening teachers' content knowledge and communicating and justifying

mathematical ideas. She is a past chair of the NCTM Student Explorations in Mathematics Editorial Panel and member of the Board of Directors for the Association of Mathematics Teacher Educators.

Matthew R. Larson, Ph.D., is the K-12 mathematics curriculum specialist for the Lincoln Public Schools and served on the Board of Directors for the National Council of Teachers of Mathematics from 2010 to 2013. He is a past chair of NCTM's Research Committee and was a member of NCTM's Task Force on Linking Research and Practice. He is the author of several books on implementing the Common Core Standards for Mathematics. He has taught mathematics at the secondary and college levels and held an appointment as an honorary visiting associate professor at Teachers College, Columbia University.

Steven J. Leinwand is a Principal Research Analyst at the American Institutes for Research (AIR) in Washington, D.C., and has over 30 years in leadership positions in mathematics education. He is past president of the National Council of Supervisors of Mathematics and served on the NCTM Board of Directors. He is the author of numerous articles, books, and textbooks and has made countless presentations with topics including student achievement, reasoning, effective assessment, and successful implementation of standards.

Exponential Relationships

MODULE 14

Geometric Sequences and Exponential Functions

Real-World Video 635
Are You Ready? 636

MODULE 15

Exponential Equations and Models

Real-World Video 707
Are You Ready? 708

UNIT 7

Volume 2

Transformations and Congruence

MODULE 16

Tools of Geometry

MODULE 17

Transformations and Symmetry

MODULE 18

Congruent Figures

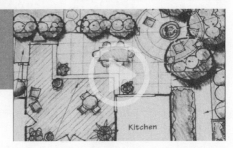

Real-World Video 883
Are You Ready? 884

© Houghton Mifflin Harcourt Publishing Company • Image Credit: ©Scott E. Feuer/Shutterstock

UNIT 8
Volume 2

Lines, Angles, and Triangles

MODULE 19

Lines and Angles

MODULE 20

Triangle Congruence Criteria

MODULE 21

Applications of Triangle Congruence

MODULE 22

Properties of Triangles

Special Segments in Triangles

Quadrilaterals and Coordinate Proof

MODULE 24

Properties of Quadrilaterals

MODULE 25

Coordinate Proof Using Slope and Distance

© Houghton Mifflin Harcourt Publishing Company • Image Credit:
©©Sportstock/iStockPhoto.com

Exponential Relationships

MATH IN CAREERS

Financial Research Analyst Financial research analysts perform quantitative analysis of market conditions. They use statistics and mathematical models to determine investment strategies and communicate findings.

If you are interested in a career as a financial research analyst, you should study these mathematical subjects:
- Algebra
- Business math
- Statistics
- Calculus
- Differential equations

Research other careers that require understanding how to calculate interest rates. Check out the career activity at the end of the unit to find out how **financial research analysts** use math.

Reading Start-Up

Vocabulary

Review Words

✔ explicit rule (*fórmula explícita*)
   exponent (*exponente*)
✔ linear function (*función lineal*)
✔ recursive rule (*fórmula recurrente*)
✔ sequence (*sucesión*)
✔ term (*término*)

Preview Words

   exponential decay (*decremento exponencial*)
   exponential function (*función exponencial*)
   exponential growth (*crecimiento exponencial*)

Visualize Vocabulary

Use the ✔ words to complete the Summary Triangle.

Write one word in each box.

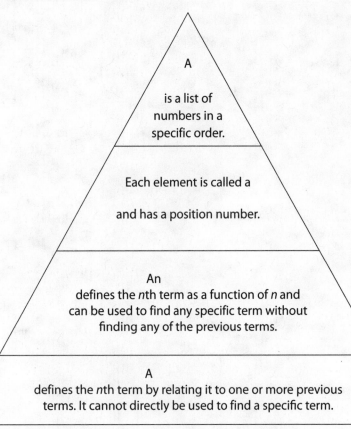

A _____ is a list of numbers in a specific order.

Each element is called a _____ and has a position number.

An _____ defines the *n*th term as a function of *n* and can be used to find any specific term without finding any of the previous terms.

A _____ defines the *n*th term by relating it to one or more previous terms. It cannot directly be used to find a specific term.

Understand Vocabulary

To become familiar with some of the vocabulary terms in this unit, consider the following. You may refer to the module, the glossary, or a dictionary.

1. A function of the form $y = a(b)^x$ is called an _____.

   When $b > 1$, the function represents _____.

   When $0 < b < 1$, the function represents _____.

Active Reading

Key-Term Fold Before beginning the unit, create a key-term fold note to help you organize what you learn. Write a vocabulary term on each tab of the key-term fold. Under each tab, write the definition of the term and an example of the term.

Geometric Sequences and Exponential Functions

Essential Question: How can you use geometric sequences and exponential functions to solve real-world problems?

REAL WORLD VIDEO
Pythons originally kept as pets but later released into the Florida ecosystem find themselves in an environment with no natural predators and prey ill-equipped to evade or defend itself. As a result, the python population can grow exponentially, causing havoc among local wildlife and pets.

MODULE PERFORMANCE TASK PREVIEW
What Does It Take to Go Viral?

You have just created a great video, and you share it with some of your friends. Then each of them shares it with the same number of their own friends. If this pattern continues, to how many friends should you show your video to make it go viral within a few days? Let's find out!

Are (YOU) Ready?

Complete these exercises to review skills you will need for this module.

• Online Homework
• Hints and Help
• Extra Practice

Exponents

Example 1　Evaluate $(-6)^3$.

$$(-6)^3 = (-6)(-6)(-6)$$

$$(-6)(-6)(-6) = -216$$

Write the base -6 multiplied by itself 3 times.

Multiply.

Evaluate each power.

1. 2^4

2. $(-3)^5$

3. 5^0

_____

_____

_____

Example 2　Simplify $x^3 \cdot x^5$.

$$x^3 \cdot x^5 = x^{3+5} = x^8$$

When multiplying numbers with the same base, add the exponents.

Simplify.

4. $x \cdot x^6$

5. $x^3y^2 \cdot y^4$

_____

_____

6. $3a^2b \cdot 5a^2b^4$

7. $4mno \cdot 7n^2o^2 \cdot mn$

_____

_____

Algebraic Expressions

Example 3　Evaluate $\frac{2}{3}x^2$ for $x = 6$.

$$\frac{2}{3}(6)^2$$

Substitute 6 for x.

$$\frac{2}{3}(36)$$

Evaluate the power.

$$24$$

Multiply.

Evaluate each expression for the given value of the variables.

8. $\frac{1}{2}x^3$ for $x = 4$

9. $\frac{3}{4}x^4$ for $x = -2$

_____

_____

10. $8x^2$ for $x = \frac{1}{2}$

11. $18x^3$ for $x = -\frac{1}{3}$

_____

_____

14.1 Understanding Geometric Sequences

Essential Question: How are the terms of a geometric sequence related?

⊘ Explore 1 Exploring Growth Patterns of Geometric Sequences

The sequence 3, 6, 12, 24, 48, … is a *geometric sequence*. In a **geometric sequence**, the ratio of successive terms is constant. The constant ratio is called the **common ratio**, often represented by *r*.

Ⓐ Complete each division.

$\dfrac{6}{3} = \boxed{}$ $\dfrac{12}{6} = \boxed{}$ $\dfrac{24}{12} = \boxed{}$ $\dfrac{48}{24} = \boxed{}$

Ⓑ The common ratio *r* for the sequence is _____.

Ⓒ Use the common ratio you found to identify the next term in the geometric sequence.

The next term is 48 · $\boxed{}$ = $\boxed{}$.

Reflect

1. Suppose you know the twelfth term in a geometric sequence. What do you need to know to find the thirteenth term? How would you use that information to find the thirteenth term?

_____

_____

_____

2. **Discussion** Suppose you know only that 8 and 128 are terms of a geometric sequence. Can you find the term that follows 128? If so, what is it?

_____

_____

_____

⊘ Explore 2 Comparing Growth Patterns of Arithmetic and Geometric Sequences

Recall that in arithmetic sequences, successive terms differ by the same nonzero number *d*, called the common difference. In geometric sequences, the ratio *r* of successive terms is constant. In this Explore, you will examine how the growth patterns in arithmetic and geometric sequences compare. In particular, you will look at the arithmetic sequence 3, 5, 7, … and the geometric sequence 3, 6, 12, … .

The tables shows the two sequences.

3, 5, 7, ...	
Term Number	**Term**
1	3
2	5
3	7
4	9
5	11

3, 6, 12, ...	
Term Number	**Term**
1	3
2	6
3	12
4	24
5	48

(A) The common difference d of the arithmetic sequence is $5 - 3 = 2$. The common ratio r of the geometric sequence is $\dfrac{6}{\boxed{}} = \boxed{}$.

(B) Complete the table. Find the differences of successive terms.

Arithmetic: 3, 5, 7, ...		
Term Number	**Term**	**Difference**
1	3	—
2	5	$5 - 3 = \boxed{}$
3	7	$7 - 5 = \boxed{}$
4	9	$9 - 7 = \boxed{}$
5	11	$11 - 9 = \boxed{}$

Geometric: 3, 6, 12, ...		
Term Number	**Term**	**Difference**
1	3	—
2	6	$6 - 3 = \boxed{}$
3	12	$12 - 6 = \boxed{}$
4	24	$24 - 12 = \boxed{}$
5	48	$48 - 24 = \boxed{}$

Ⓒ Compare the growth patterns of the sequences based on the tables.

_____

_____

_____

Ⓓ Graph both sequences in the same coordinate plane. Compare the growth patterns based on the graphs.

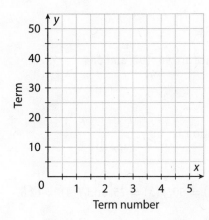

_____

_____

_____

Reflect

3. Which grows more quickly, the arithmetic sequence or the geometric sequence?

_____

_____

_____

🔑 Explain 1   Extending Geometric Sequences

In Explore 1, you saw that each term of a geometric sequence is the product of the preceding term and the common ratio. Given terms of a geometric sequence, you can use this relationship to write additional terms of the sequence.

Finding a Term of a Geometric Sequence
For $n \geq 2$, the nth term, $f(n)$, of a geometric sequence with common ratio r is $$f(n) = f(n-1)r.$$

Example 1 Find the common ratio r for each geometric sequence and use r to find the next three terms.

(A) 6, 12, 24, 48, …

$\frac{12}{6} = 2$, so the common ratio r is 2.

For this sequence, $f(1) = 6$, $f(2) = 12$, $f(3) = 24$, and $f(4) = 48$.

$f(4) = 48$, so $f(5) = 48(2) = 96$.

$f(5) = 96$, so $f(6) = 96(2) = 192$.

$f(6) = 192$, so $f(7) = 192(2) = 384$.

The next three terms of the sequence are 96, 192, and 384.

(B) 100, 50, 25, 12.5, …

$\frac{50}{\boxed{}} = \boxed{}$, so the common ratio r is _____.

For this sequence, $f(1) = 100$, $f(2) = 50$, $f(3) = 25$, and $f(4) = 12.5$.

$f(4) = 12.5$, so $f(5) = \boxed{} (0.5) = \boxed{}$.

$f(5) = \boxed{}$, so $f(6) = \boxed{} (0.5) = \boxed{}$.

$f(6) = \boxed{}$, so $f(7) = \boxed{} (0.5) = \boxed{}$.

The next three terms of the sequence are $\boxed{}$, $\boxed{}$, and $\boxed{}$.

Reflect

4. **Communicate Mathematical Ideas** A geometric sequence has a common ratio of 3. The 4th term is 54. What is the 5th term? What is the 3rd term?

_____

Your Turn

Find the common ratio r for each geometric sequence and use r to find the next three terms.

5. 5, 20, 80, 320, …

6. $9, -3, 1, -\frac{1}{3}, …$

© Houghton Mifflin Harcourt Publishing Company

Explain 2 · Recognizing Growth Patterns of Geometric Sequences in Context

You can find a term of a sequence by repeatedly multiplying the first term by the common ratio.

Example 2

(A) A bungee jumper jumps from a bridge. The table shows the bungee jumper's height above the ground at the top of each bounce. The heights form a geometric sequence. What is the bungee jumper's height at the top of the 5th bounce?

Bounce	Height (feet)
1	200
2	80
3	32

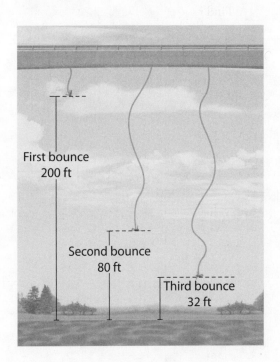

First bounce
200 ft

Second bounce
80 ft

Third bounce
32 ft

Find r.

$$\frac{80}{200} = 0.4 = r$$

$f(1) = 200$

$f(2) = 80$

$\quad = 200(0.4) \text{ or } 200(0.4)^1$

$f(3) = 32$

$\quad = 80(0.4)$

$\quad = 200(0.4)(0.4)$

$\quad = 200(0.4)^2$

In each case, to get $f(n)$, you multiply 200 by the common ratio, 0.4, $n-1$ times. That is, you multiply 200 by $(0.4)^{n-1}$.

The jumper's height on the 5th bounce is $f(5)$.

Multiply 200 by $(0.4)^{5-1} = (0.4)^4$.

$200(0.4)^4 = 200(0.0256)$

$\quad\quad\quad = 5.12$

The height of the jumper at the top of the 5th bounce is 5.12 feet.

Example 2

(B) A ball is dropped from a height of 144 inches. Its height on the 1st bounce is 72 inches. On the 2nd and 3rd bounces, the height of the ball is 36 inches and 18 inches, respectively. The heights form a geometric sequence. What is the height of the ball on the 6th bounce to the nearest tenth of an inch?

Find r.

$$\frac{36}{72} = \frac{1}{2} = r$$

$f(1) = \boxed{}$

$f(2) = \boxed{}$

$\qquad = 72\left(\boxed{}\right)$ or $72\left(\boxed{}\right)^1$

$f(3) = \boxed{}$

$\qquad = 36\left(\boxed{}\right)$

$\qquad = 72\left(\boxed{}\right)\left(\boxed{}\right)$

$\qquad = 72\left(\boxed{}\right)$

In each case, to get $f(n)$, you multiply 72 by the common ratio, _____, _____ times. That is, you

multiply 72 by _____.

The height of the ball on the 6th bounce is $f\left(\boxed{}\right)$.

Multiply 72 by _____ = _____.

The height of the ball at the top of the 6th bounce is about _____ inches.

7. Is it possible for a sequence that describes the bounce height of a ball to have a common ratio greater than 1?

_____

_____

8. **Physical Science** A ball is dropped from a height of 8 meters. The table shows the height of each bounce. The heights form a geometric sequence. How high does the ball bounce on the 4ᵗʰ bounce? Round your answer to the nearest tenth of a meter.

Bounce	Height (m)
1	6
2	4.5
3	3.375

Elaborate

9. Suppose all the terms of a geometric sequence are positive, and the common ratio r is between 0 and 1. Is the sequence increasing or decreasing? Explain.

_____

_____

_____

10. **Essential Question Check-In** If the common ratio of a geometric sequence is less than 0, what do you know about the signs of the terms of the sequence? Explain.

_____

_____

_____

☆ Evaluate: Homework and Practice

Find the common ratio r for each geometric sequence and use r to find the next three terms.

1. 5, 15, 45, 135 …

2. −2, 6, −18, 54 …

3. 4, 20, 100, 500, …

4. 8, 4, 2, 1, …

5. 72, −36, 18, −9, …

6. 200, −80, 32, −12.8, …

7. 10, 30, 90, 270, …

8. 5, 3, 1.8, 1.08, …

9. 18, 36, 72, 144

10. 243, 162, 108, 72, ...

Find the indicated term of each sequence by repeatedly multiplying the first term by the common ratio. Use a calculator.

11. 1, 8, 64, ...; 5th term

12. 16, −3.2, 0.64, ...; 7th term

13. −50, 15, −4.5, ...; 5th term

14. 3, −12, 48, ...; 6th term

Solve. You may use a calculator and round your answer to the nearest tenth of a unit if necessary.

15. Physical Science A ball is dropped from a height of 900 centimeters. The table shows the height of each bounce. The heights form a geometric sequence. How high does the ball bounce on the 5th bounce?

Bounce	Height (cm)
1	800
2	560
3	392

© Houghton Mifflin Harcourt Publishing Company

16. Leo's bank balances at the end of months 1, 2, and 3 are $1500, $1530, and $1560.60, respectively. The balances form a geometric sequence. What will Leo's balance be after 9 months?

17. Biology A biologist studying ants started on day 1 with a population of 1500 ants. On day 2, there were 3000 ants, and on day 3, there were 6000 ants. The increase in an ant population can be represented using a geometric sequence. What is the ant population on day 5?

18. Physical Science A ball is dropped from a height of 625 centimeters. The table shows the height of each bounce. The heights form a geometric sequence. How high does the ball bounce on the 8th bounce?

Bounce	Height (cm)
1	500
2	400
3	320

19. Finance The table shows the balance in an investment account after each month. The balances form a geometric sequence. What is the amount in the account after month 6?

Month	Amount ($)
1	1700
2	2040
3	2448

20. Biology A turtle population grows in a manner that can be represented by a geometric sequence. Given the table of values, determine the turtle population after 6 years.

Year	Number of Turtles
1	5
2	15
3	45

21. Consider the geometric sequence −8, 16, −32, ... Select all that apply.

a. The common ratio is 2.

b. The 5th term of the sequence is −128.

c. The 7th term is 4 times the 5th term.

d. The 8th term is 1024.

e. The 10th term is greater than the 9th term.

22. Justify Reasoning Suppose you are given a sequence with $r < 0$. What do you know about the signs of the terms of the sequence? Explain.

23. Critique Reasoning Miguel writes the following: 8, x, 8, x, … He tells Alicia that he has written a geometric sequence and asks her to identify the value of x. Alicia says the value of x must be 8. Miguel says that Alicia is incorrect. Who is right? Explain.

Lesson Performance Task

Multi-Step Gifford earns money by shoveling snow for the winter. He offers two payment plans: either pay $400 per week for the entire winter or pay $5 for the first week, $10 for the second week, $20 for the third week, and so on. Explain why each plan does or does not form a geometric sequence. Then determine the number of weeks after which the total cost of the second plan will exceed the total cost of the first plan.

14.2 Constructing Geometric Sequences

Essential Question: How do you write a geometric sequence?

Resource Locker

⊘ Explore 1 Understanding Recursive and Explicit Rules for Sequences

You learned previously that an explicit rule for a sequence defines the nth term as a function of n. A recursive rule defines the nth term of a sequence in terms of one or more previous terms.

You can use what you know to identify recursive and explicit rules for sequences, and identify whether the sequences are arithmetic, geometric, or neither.

A rule for the sequence 6, 9, 13.5,... is $f(n) = 6\left(\frac{3}{2}\right)^{n-1}$.

(A) The given rule is a(n) _____ rule because you do not need to know the

value of _____.

(B) The only unknown in the expression is _____, which

represents _____.

(C) The sequence is a(n) _____ sequence because each term is

the _____ of the previous term and $\frac{3}{2}$.

Reflect

1. **Discussion** How can you differentiate between a geometric sequence and an arithmetic sequence?

_____

_____

2. How can you tell by looking at a function rule for a sequence whether it is a recursive rule?

_____

_____

Constructing Recursive and Explicit Rules for Given Geometric Sequences

To write a recursive rule for a sequence, you need to know the first term, and a rule for successive terms.

Example 1 Write a recursive rule and an explicit rule for each geometric sequence.

Ⓐ Makers of Japanese swords in the 1400s repeatedly folded and hammered the metal to form layers. The folding process increased the strength of the sword.

The table shows how the number of layers depends on the number of folds.

Number of Folds	n	1	2	3	4	5
Number of Layers	$f(n)$	2	4	8	16	32

To write a recursive rule, find the common ratio by calculating the ratio of consecutive terms.

$\frac{4}{2} = 2$

The common ratio r is 2.

The first term is 2, so $f(1) = 2$.

All terms after the first term are the product of the previous term and the common ratio:

$f(2) = f(1) \cdot 2, f(3) = f(2) \cdot 2, f(4) = f(3) \cdot 2, \ldots$

State the recursive rule by providing the first term and the rule for successive terms.

$f(1) = 2$

$f(n) = f(n - 1) \cdot 2$ for $n \geq 2$

Write an explicit rule for the sequence by writing each term as the product of the first term and a power of the common ratio.

n	$f(n)$
1	$2(2)^0 = 2$
2	$2(2)^1 = 4$
3	$2(2)^2 = 8$
4	$2(2)^3 = 16$
5	$2(2)^4 = 32$

Generalize the results from the table: $f(n) = 2 \cdot 2^{n-1}$.

Ⓑ

n	1	2	3	4	5
f(n)	5	15	45	135	405

To write a recursive rule, find the common ratio by calculating the ratio of consecutive terms.

$$\frac{\boxed{}}{5} = \boxed{}$$

The common ratio r is _____.

The first term is _____. So, the recursive rule is:

$f(n) = f(n-1)\boxed{}$ for $n \geq 2$

Write an explicit rule for the sequence by writing each term as the product of the first term and a power of the common ratio.

n	f(n)
1	$5(3) = \boxed{}$
2	$5(3) = \boxed{}$
3	$5(3) = \boxed{}$
4	$5(3) = \boxed{}$
5	$5(3) = \boxed{}$

Generalize the results from the table: $f(n) = \boxed{}^{n-1}$.

Reflect

3. Explain why the sequence 5, 10, 20, 40, 80, … appears to be a geometric sequence.

_____

_____

4. Draw Conclusions How can you use properties of exponents to simplify the explicit rule $f(n) = 2 \cdot 2^{n-1}$?

_____

_____

651

Write a recursive rule and an explicit rule for each geometric sequence.

5.

n	1	2	3	4	5
$f(n)$	7	14	28	56	112

6. Write a recursive rule and an explicit rule for the geometric sequence 128, 32, 8, 2, 0.5, ...

✍ Explain 2 Deriving the General Forms of Geometric Sequence Rules

Example 2 Use each geometric sequence to help write a recursive rule and an explicit rule for any geometric sequence. For the general rules, the values of n are consecutive integers starting with 1.

Ⓐ 6, 24, 96, 384, 1536, …

Find the common ratio.

Numbers	**Algebra**
6, 24, 96, 384, 1536,…	$f(1), f(2), f(3), f(4), f(5),…$
Common ratio $= 4$	Common ratio $= r$

Write a recursive rule.

Numbers	**Algebra**
$f(1) = 6$ and	Given $f(1)$,
$f(n) = f(n-1) \cdot 4$ for $n \geq 2$	$f(n) = f(n-1) \cdot r$ for $n \geq 2$

Write an explicit rule.

Numbers	**Algebra**
$f(n) = 6 \cdot 4^{n-1}$	$f(n) = f(1) \cdot r^{n-1}$

(B) 4, 12, 36, 108, 324,...

Find the common ratio.

Numbers

4, 12, 36, 108, 324,...

Common ratio = ☐

Algebra

$f(1), f(2), f(3), f(4), f(5),...$

Common ratio = ☐

Write a recursive rule.

Numbers

$f(1) = $ ☐ and

$f(n) = f(n-1) \cdot$ ☐ for $n \geq$ ☐

Algebra

Given $f(1)$,

$f(n) = f(n-1) \cdot$ ☐ for $n \geq$ ☐

Write an explicit rule.

Numbers

$f(n) = $ ☐ $\cdot$ ☐$^{n-1}$

Algebra

$f(n) = f\left(\boxed{}\right) \cdot \boxed{}^{n-1}$

Reflect

7. **Discussion** The first term of a geometric sequence is 81 and the common ratio is $\frac{1}{3}$. Explain how the 4th term of the sequence can be determined.

_____

_____

8. What is the recursive rule for the sequence $f(n) = 5(4)^{n-1}$?

_____

_____

Your Turn

Use each geometric sequence to help write a recursive rule and an explicit rule for any geometric sequence.

9. 6, 12, 24, 48, 96,...

The explicit and recursive rules for a geometric sequence can also be written in subscript notation. In subscript notation, the subscript indicates the position of the term in the sequence. a_1, a_2, and a_3 are the first, second, and third terms of a sequence respectively. In general, a_n is the nth term of a sequence.

Example 3 Write an explicit rule for each sequence using subscript notation.

(A) **Photography** The shutter speed settings on a camera form a geometric sequence where a_n is the shutter speed in seconds and n is the setting number. The fifth setting on the camera is $\frac{1}{60}$ second and the seventh setting on the camera is $\frac{1}{15}$ second.

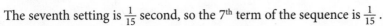

Identify the given terms in the sequence.

The fifth setting is $\frac{1}{60}$ second, so the 5th term of the sequence is $\frac{1}{60}$.

$$a_5 = \frac{1}{60}$$

The seventh setting is $\frac{1}{15}$ second, so the 7th term of the sequence is $\frac{1}{15}$.

$$a_7 = \frac{1}{15}$$

Find the common ratio.

$a_7 = a_6 \cdot r$	Write the recursive rule for a_7.
$a_6 = a_5 \cdot r$	Write the recursive rule for a_6.
$a_7 = a_5 \cdot r \cdot r$	Substitute the expression for a_6 into the rule for a_7.
$\frac{1}{15} = \frac{1}{60} \cdot r^2$	Substitute $\frac{1}{15}$ for a_7 and $\frac{1}{60}$ for a_5.
$4 = r^2$	Multiply both sides by 60.
$2 = r$	Definition of positive square root

Find the first term of the sequence.

$a_n = a_1 \cdot r^{n-1}$	Write the explicit rule.
$\frac{1}{60} = a_1 \cdot 2^{5-1}$	Substitute $\frac{1}{60}$ for a_n, 2 for r, and 5 for n.
$\frac{1}{60} = a_1 \cdot 16$	Simplify.
$\frac{1}{960} = a_1$	Divide both sides by 16.

Write the explicit rule.

$a_n = a_1 \cdot r^{n-1}$	Write the general rule.
$a_n = \frac{1}{960} \cdot (2)^{n-1}$	Substitute $\frac{1}{960}$ for a_1 and 2 for r.

(B) **Viral Video** You tell a number of friends about an interesting video you saw online. Each of those friends tells the same number of friends about it. This pattern continues, and there are no repeats in the people told. The numbers of people who hear about this video through you form a geometric sequence. There are 256 people at the fourth round and 4096 people at the sixth round.

Identify the given terms in the sequence.

The 4th term of the sequence is $\boxed{}$.

$a_4 = \boxed{}$

The 6th term of the sequence is $\boxed{}$.

$a_6 = \boxed{}$

Find the common ratio.

$a_6 = \boxed{} \cdot r$ Write the recursive rule for a_6.

$a_6 = \boxed{} \cdot r$ Write the recursive rule for a_5.

$a_6 = \boxed{} \cdot \boxed{} \cdot r$ Substitute the expression for a_5 into the rule for a_6.

$\boxed{} = \boxed{} \cdot r^2$ Substitute $\boxed{}$ for a_6 and $\boxed{}$ for a_4.

$\boxed{} = r^2$ Divide both sides by 256.

$\boxed{} = r$ Definition of positive square root.

Find the first term of the sequence.

$a_n = a_1 \cdot r^{n-1}$ Write the explicit rule.

$\boxed{} = a_1 \cdot \boxed{}^{-1}$ Substitute $\boxed{}$ for a_n, $\boxed{}$ for r, and $\boxed{}$ for n.

$\boxed{} = a_1 \cdot \boxed{}$ Simplify.

$\boxed{} = a_1$ Divide both sides by $\boxed{}$.

Write the explicit rule.

$a_n = a_1 \cdot r^{n-1}$ Write the general rule.

$a_n = \boxed{} \cdot \left(\boxed{} \right)^{n-1}$ Substitute $\boxed{}$ for a_1 and $\boxed{}$ for r.

Reflect

10. Finding the common ratio in the shutter speed example involved finding a square root. Why was the negative square root not considered?

_____

_____

Write an explicit rule for the sequence using subscript notation.

11. The third term of a geometric sequence is $\frac{1}{27}$ and the fifth term is $\frac{1}{243}$. All the terms of the sequence are positive.

💬 Elaborate

12. **What If** Suppose you are given the terms a_3 and a_6 of a geometric sequence. How can you find the common ratio r?

_____

13. If you know the second term and the common ratio of a geometric sequence, can you write an explicit rule for the sequence? If so, explain how.

_____

_____

_____

14. **Essential Question Check-In** How can you write the explicit rule for a geometric sequence if you know the recursive rule for the sequence?

_____

_____

• Online Homework
• Hints and Help
• Extra Practice

For each geometric sequence, write a recursive rule by finding the common ratio by calculating the ratio of consecutive terms. Write an explicit rule for the sequence by writing each term as the product of the first term and a power of the common ratio.

1.

n	1	2	3	4	5
a_n	2	6	18	54	162

2.

n	1	2	3	4	5
a_n	10	3	0.9	0.27	0.081

3.

n	1	2	3	4	5
a_n	5	20	80	320	1280

4.

n	1	2	3	4	5
a_n	6	−3	1.5	−0.75	0.375

5.

n	1	2	3	4	5
a_n	9	6	4	$2\frac{2}{3}$	$1\frac{7}{9}$

6.

n	1	2	3	4	5
a_n	−12	6	−3	1.5	−0.75

7.

n	1	2	3	4	5
a_n	4	24	144	864	5184

8.

n	1	2	3	4	5
a_n	10	5	2.5	1.25	0.625

9.

n	1	2	3	4	5
a_n	3	21	147	1029	7203

10.

n	1	2	3	4	5
a_n	8	72	648	5832	52,488

11.

n	1	2	3	4	5
a_n	6	30	150	750	3750

Use the geometric sequence to help write a recursive rule and an explicit rule for any geometric sequence. For the general rules, the values of n are consecutive integers starting with 1.

12. 5, 15, 45, 135, 405,…

13. 10, 40, 160, 640, 2,560,…

14. 5, 10, 20, 40, 80,…

15. 18, 90, 450, 2250, 11,250,…

Write an explicit rule for each geometric sequence using subscript notation. Use a calculator and round your answer to the nearest tenth if necessary.

16. The fifth term of the sequence is 5. The sixth term is 2.5.

17. The third term of the sequence is 120. The fifth term is 76.8.

18. The fourth term of the sequence is 216. The sixth term is 96.

19. **Sports** The numbers of teams in a single-elimination tennis tournament represents a geometric sequence where a_n is the number of teams competing and n is the round. There are 32 teams remaining in round 4 and 8 teams in round 6.

20. **Video Games** The number of points that a player must accumulate to reach the next level of a video game forms a geometric sequence where a_n is the number of points needed to complete level n. You need 20,000 points to complete level 3 and 8,000,000 points to compete level 5.

21. Conservation A state began an effort to increase the deer population. In year 2 of the effort, the deer population in a state forest was 1200. In year 4, the population was 1728.

22. Biology The growth of a local raccoon population approximates a geometric sequence where a_n is the number of raccoons in *a* given year and *n* is the year. After 6 years there are 45 raccoons and after 8 years there are 71 raccoons.

23. Chemistry A chemist measures the temperature in degrees Fahrenheit of a chemical compound every hour. The temperatures approximate a geometric sequence where a_n is the temperature at a given hour, and *n* is the hour. At hour 4, the temperature is 70 °F and at hour 6 the temperature is 80 °F.

24. Yusuf was asked to write a recursive rule for a sequence. Which of the following is an appropriate answer? Select all that apply.

    a. $f(n) = 11(5)^{n-1}$ **b.** $f(n) = 11f(n-1), f(1) = 555$ **c.** $f(n) = f(n-1) + 15, f(1) = 36$

    d. $f(n) = 12 + 19 \cdot f(n-1)$ **e.** $f(n) = -4\left(\frac{2}{3}\right)^{n-1}$

25. **Multi-Step** An economist predicts that the cost of food will increase by 4% per year for the next several years.

    a. Write an explicit rule for the sequence that gives the cost $f(n)$ in dollars of a box of cereal in year n that costs $3.20 in year 1. Justify your answer.

    b. What is the fourth term of the sequence? What does it represent in this situation? Justify your answer.

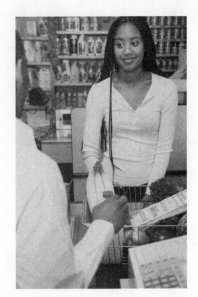

26. **Analyze Relationships** Suppose you know the 8th term of a geometric sequence and the common ratio r. How can you find the 3rd term of the sequence without writing a rule for the sequence? Explain.

27. **Explain the Error** Given that the second term of a sequence is 64 and the fourth term is 16, Francis wrote the explicit rule $a_n = 128 \cdot \left(\frac{1}{4}\right)^{n-1}$ for the sequence. Explain his error.

28. **Communicate Mathematical Ideas** Suppose you are given two terms of a geometric sequence like the ones in Example 3, except that both terms are negative. Explain how writing the explicit rule for the sequence would differ from the examples in this lesson.

Lesson Performance Task

The table shows how a population of rabbits has changed over time. Write an explicit rule for the geometric sequence described in the table. In what year will there be more than 5000 rabbits?

Time (years), n	Population, a_n
1	800
2	1200
3	1800
4	2700

14.3 Constructing Exponential Functions

Essential Question: What are discrete exponential functions and how do you represent them?

⊘ Explore   Understanding Discrete Exponential Functions

Recall that a discrete function has a graph consisting of isolated points.

(A) The table represents the cost of tickets to an annual event as a function of the number t of tickets purchased. Complete the table by *adding* 10 to each successive cost. Plot each ordered pair from the table.

Tickets t	Cost ($)	$(t, f(t))$
1	10	(1, 10)
2	20	(2, 20)
3	☐	$\left(3, \boxed{}\right)$
4	☐	$\left(4, \boxed{}\right)$
5	☐	$\left(5, \boxed{}\right)$

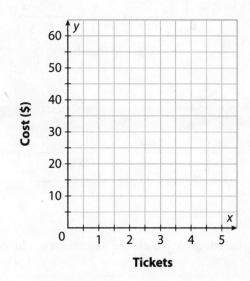

B The number of people attending an event doubles each year. The table represents the total attendance at each annual event as a function of the event number *n*. Complete the table by *multiplying* each successive attendance by 2. Plot each ordered pair from the table.

Event Number *n*	Attendance	$(n, g(n))$
1	20	(1, 20)
2	40	(2, 40)
3		$\left(3, \right)$
4		$\left(4, \right)$
5		$\left(5, \right)$

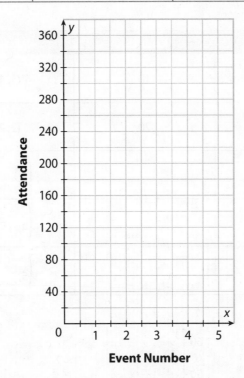

C Complete the table.

Function	Linear?	Discrete?
$f(t)$	Yes	
$g(n)$		

Reflect

1. **Communicate Mathematical Ideas** What are the limitations on the domains of these functions? Why?

_____

_____

⚙ Explain 1   Representing Discrete Exponential Functions

An **exponential function** is a function whose successive output values are related by a constant ratio. An exponential function can be represented by an equation of the form $f(x) = ab^x$, where a, b, and x are real numbers, $a \neq 0$, $b > 0$, and $b \neq 1$. The constant ratio is the base b.

When evaluating exponential functions, you will need to use the properties of exponents, including zero and negative exponents.

Recall that, for any nonzero number c:

$$c^0 = 1, c \neq 0$$

$$c^{-n} = \frac{1}{c^n}, c \neq 0.$$

Example 1   Complete the table for each function using the given domain. Then graph the function using the ordered pairs from the table.

(A) $f(x) = 3 \cdot \left(\frac{1}{2}\right)^x$ with a domain of $\left\{-1, 0, 1, 2, 3, 4\right\}$

$f(-1) = 3 \cdot \left(\frac{1}{2}\right)^{-1} = 3 \cdot \dfrac{1}{\left(\frac{1}{2}\right)} = 3 \cdot 2 = 6$

x	f(x)	(x, f(x))
−1		
0		
1		
2		
3		
4		

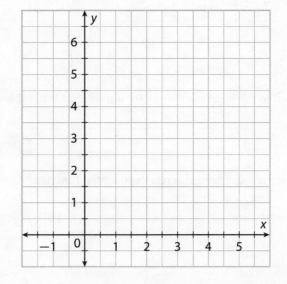

Ⓑ $f(x) = 3\left(\frac{4}{3}\right)^x$; domain $= \{-2, -1, 0, 1, 2, 3\}$

$$f(-2) = 3\left(\frac{4}{3}\right)^{-2} = 3 \cdot \dfrac{1}{\left(\dfrac{\boxed{}}{\boxed{}}\right)^{\boxed{2}}} = 3 \cdot \dfrac{\boxed{}^{2}}{\boxed{}^{2}} = 3 \cdot \dfrac{\boxed{}}{\boxed{}} = \dfrac{\boxed{}}{\boxed{}} = 1\dfrac{\boxed{}}{\boxed{}}$$

x	f(x)	(x, f(x))
−2	☐	$\left(-2, \boxed{}\right)$
−1	☐	$\left(-1, \boxed{}\right)$
0	☐	$\left(0, \boxed{}\right)$
1	☐	$\left(1, \boxed{}\right)$
2	☐	$\left(2, \boxed{}\right)$
3	$7\frac{1}{9}$	$\left(3, 7\frac{1}{9}\right)$

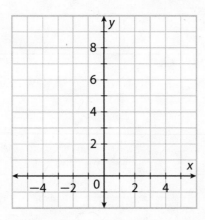

Reflect

2. **What If** What would happen to the function $f(x) = ab^x$ if a were 0? What if b were 1?

_____

_____

3. **Discussion** Why is a geometric sequence a discrete exponential function?

_____

_____

_____

Make a table for the function using the given domain. Then graph the function using the ordered pairs from the table.

4. $f(x) = 4\left(\dfrac{3}{2}\right)^x$; domain $= \left\{-3, -2, -1, 0, 1, 2\right\}$

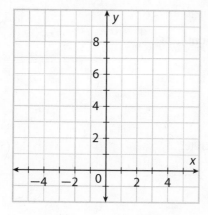

🎯 Explain 2   Constructing Exponential Functions from Verbal Descriptions

You can write an equation for an exponential function $f(x) = ab^x$ by finding or calculating the values of a and b.

The value of a is the value of the function when $x = 0$. The value of b is the common ratio of successive function values, $b = \dfrac{f(x+1)}{f(x)}$. For discrete functions with integer or whole number domains, these will be successive values of the function.

Example 2   Write an equation for the function.

Ⓐ   When a piece of paper is folded in half, the total thickness doubles. Suppose an unfolded piece of paper is 0.1 millimeter thick. The total thickness $t(n)$ of the paper is an exponential function of the number of folds n.

The value of a is the original thickness of the paper before any folds are made, or 0.1 millimeter.

Because the thickness doubles with each fold, the value of b (the constant ratio) is 2.

The equation for the function is $t(n) = 0.1(2)^n$.

B A savings account with an initial balance of $1000 earns 1% interest per month. That means that the account balance grows by a factor of 1.01 each month if no deposits or withdrawals are made. The account balance in dollars $B(t)$ is an exponential function of the time t in months after the initial deposit.

Let B represent the balance in dollars as a function of time t in months.

The value of a is the original balance, _____.

The value of b is the factor by which the balance changes every month, _____.

The equation for the function is $B(t) =$ _____.

Reflect

5. Why is the exponential function in the paper-folding example discrete?

_____

Your Turn

6. A piece of paper that is 0.2 millimeters thick is folded. Write an equation for the thickness t of the paper in millimeters as a function of the number n of folds.

⚷ Explain 3 ## Constructing Exponential Functions from Input-Output Pairs

You can use given two successive values of a discrete exponential function to write an equation for the function.

Example 3 **Write an equation for the function that includes the points.**

A (3, 12) and (4, 24)

Find b by dividing the function value of the second pair by the function value of the first: $b = \dfrac{24}{12} = 2$.

Evaluate the function for $x = 3$ and solve for a.

Write the general form. $\qquad\qquad f(x) = ab^x$

Substitute the value for b. $\qquad\qquad f(x) = a \cdot 2^x$

Substitute a pair of input-output values. $\quad 12 = a \cdot 2^3$

Simplify. $\qquad\qquad\qquad\qquad\qquad 12 = a \cdot 8$

Solve for a. $\qquad\qquad\qquad\qquad\quad a = \dfrac{3}{2}$

Use a and b to write an equation for the function. $\qquad f(x) = \dfrac{3}{2} \cdot 2^x$

© Houghton Mifflin Harcourt Publishing Company

(B) $(1, 3)$ and $\left(2, \dfrac{9}{4}\right)$

Find b by dividing the function value of the second pair by the first: $b = \dfrac{9}{4} \div 3 = \boxed{}$.

Write the general form. $\qquad f(x) = \boxed{}$

Substitute the value for b. $\qquad f(x) = a \cdot \boxed{}^{x}$

Substitute a pair of input-output values. $\qquad \boxed{} = a \cdot \left(\dfrac{3}{4}\right)^{\boxed{}}$

Simplify. $\qquad 3 = a \cdot \boxed{}$

Solve for a. $\qquad a = \boxed{}$

Use a and b to write an equation for the function. $\qquad f(x) = \boxed{}$

Your Turn

Write an equation for the function that includes the points.

7. $\left(-2, \dfrac{2}{5}\right)$ and $(-1, 2)$

💬 Elaborate

8. Explain why the following statement is true: For $0 < b < 1$ and $a > 0$, the function $f(x) = ab^x$ *decreases* as x increases.

_____

_____

_____

9. Explain why the following statement is true: For $b > 1$ and $a > 0$, the function $f(x) = ab^x$ *increases* as x increases.

_____

_____

_____

10. **Essential Question Check-In** What property do all pairs of adjacent points of a discrete exponential function share?

_____

© Houghton Mifflin Harcourt Publishing Company

Complete the table for each function using the given domain.
Then graph the function using the ordered pairs from the table.

1. $f(x) = \frac{1}{2} \cdot 4^x$; domain $= \{-2, -1, 0, 1, 2\}$.

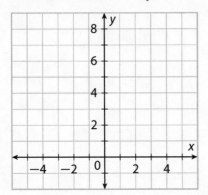

2. $f(x) = 9\left(\frac{1}{3}\right)^x$; domain $= \{0, 1, 2, 3, 4, 5\}$.

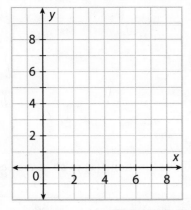

3. $f(x) = 6\left(\frac{2}{3}\right)^x$; domain $= \{-1, 0, 1, 2, 3, 4\}$.

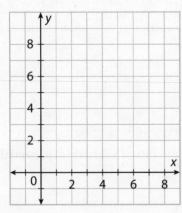

4. $f(x) = 6\left(\dfrac{4}{3}\right)^x$; domain $= \{-3, -2, -1, 0, 1\}$

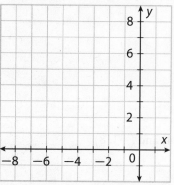

Write an equation for each function.

5. **Business** A recent trend in advertising is viral marketing. The goal is to convince viewers to share an amusing advertisement by e-mail or social networking. Imagine that the video is sent to 100 people on day 1. Each person agrees to send the video to 5 people the next day, and to request that each of those people send it to 5 people. The number of viewers $v(n)$ is an exponential function of the number n of days since the video was first shown.

6. A pharmaceutical company is testing a new antibiotic. The number of bacteria present in a sample when the antibiotic is applied is 100,000. Each hour, the number of bacteria present decreases by half. The number of bacteria remaining $r(n)$ is an exponential function of the number n of hours since the antibiotic was applied.

7. **Optics** A laser beam with an output of 5 milliwatts is directed into a series of mirrors. The laser beam loses 1% of its power every time it reflects off of a mirror. The power $p(n)$ is a function of the number of reflections.

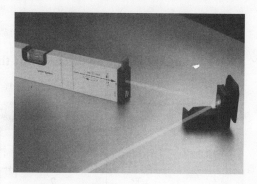

8. The NCAA basketball tournament begins with 64 teams, and after each round, half the teams are eliminated. The number of remaining teams $t(n)$ is an exponential function of the number n of rounds already played.

Write an equation for the function that includes the points.

9. $(2, 100)$ and $(3, 1000)$

10. $(-2, 4)$ and $(-1, 8)$

11. $\left(1, \dfrac{4}{5}\right)$ and $\left(2, \dfrac{2}{3}\right)$

12. $\left(-3, \dfrac{1}{16}\right)$ and $\left(-2, \dfrac{3}{8}\right)$

Use two points to write an equation for the function.

13.

x	f(x)
1	2
2	$\dfrac{2}{7}$
3	$\dfrac{2}{49}$
4	$\dfrac{2}{343}$

14.

x	f(x)
−4	0.53
−3	5.3
−2	53
−1	530

15.

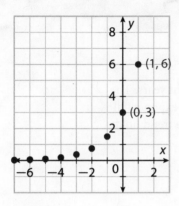

16.

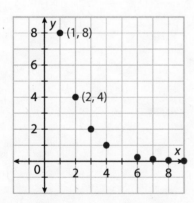

17. The height $h(n)$ of a bouncing ball is an exponential function of the number n of bounces. One ball is dropped and on the first bounce reaches a height of 6 feet. On the second bounce it reaches a height of 4 feet.

18. A child starts a playground swing from standing and doesn't use her legs to keep swinging. On the first swing she swings forward by 18 degrees, and on the second swing she only comes 13.5 degrees forward. The measure in degrees of the angle $m(n)$ is an exponential function of the number of swings.

19. Make a Prediction A town's population has been declining in recent years. The table shows the population since 1980. Is this data consistent with an exponential function? Explain. If so, predict the population for 2010 assuming the trend holds.

Year	Population
1980	5000
1990	4000
2000	3200
2010	

20. A piece of paper has a thickness of 0.15 millimeters. Write an equation to describe the thickness $t(n)$ of the paper when it is repeatedly folded in thirds.

© Houghton Mifflin Harcourt Publishing Company • Image Credits: ©Steve Hix/Somos Images/Corbis

21. Probability The probability of getting heads on a single coin flip is $\frac{1}{2}$. The probability of getting nothing but heads on a series of coin flips decreases by $\frac{1}{2}$ for each additional coin flip. Write an exponential function for the probability of getting all heads in a series of n coin flips.

22. Multipart Classification Determine whether each of the functions is exponential or not.

a. $f(x) = x^2$ ◯ Exponential ◯ Not exponential

b. $f(x) = 3 \cdot 2^x$ ◯ Exponential ◯ Not exponential

c. $f(x) = 3 \cdot \frac{1}{2} x$ ◯ Exponential ◯ Not exponential

d. $f(x) = 1.001^x$ ◯ Exponential ◯ Not exponential

e. $f(x) = 2 \cdot x^3$ ◯ Exponential ◯ Not exponential

f. $f(x) = \frac{1}{10} \cdot 5^x$ ◯ Exponential ◯ Not exponential

H.O.T. Focus on Higher Order Thinking

23. Explain the Error Biff observes that in every math test he has taken this year, he has scored 2 points higher than the previous test. His score on the first test was 56. He models his test scores with the exponential function $s(n) = 28 \cdot 2^n$ where $s(n)$ is the score on his nth test. Is this a reasonable model Explain.

24. Find the Error Kaylee needed to write the equation of an exponential function from points on the graph of the function. To determine the value of b, Kaylee chose the ordered pairs (1, 6) and (3, 54) and divided 54 by 6. She determined that the value of b was 9. What error did Kaylee make?

Lesson Performance Task

In ecology, an invasive species is a plant or animal species newly introduced to an ecosystem, often by human activity. Because invasive species often lack predators in their new habitat, their populations typically experience exponential growth. A small initial population grows to a large population that drastically alters an ecosystem. Feral rabbits that populate Australia and zebra mussels in the Great Lakes are two examples of problematic invasive species that grew exponentially from a small initial population.

An ecologist monitoring a local stream has been collecting samples of an unfamiliar fish species over the past four years and has summarized the data in the table.

Here are the results so far:

Year	Average Population Per Mile
2009	32
2010	48
2011	72
2012	108
2013	
2014	

a. Look at the data in the table and confirm that the growth pattern is exponential.

b. Write the equation that represents the average population per square meter as a function of years since 2009.

c. Predict the average populations expected for 2013 and 2014.

d. Graph the population versus time since 2009 and include the predicted values.

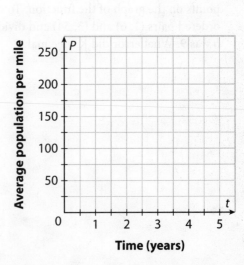

14.4 Graphing Exponential Functions

Essential Question: How do you graph an exponential function of the form $f(x) = ab^x$?

Resource Locker

⊘ Explore   Exploring Graphs of Exponential Functions

Exponential functions follow the general shape $y = ab^x$.

Ⓐ Graph the exponential functions on a graphing calculator, and match the graph to the correct function rule.

1. $y = 3(2)^x$

2. $y = 0.5(2)^x$

3. $y = 3(0.5)^x$

4. $y = -3(2)^x$

a.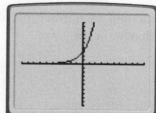

b.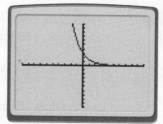

c.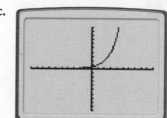

d.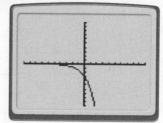

Ⓑ In all the functions 1–4 above, the base $b > 0$.

Use the graphs to make a conjecture: State the domain and range of $y = ab^x$ if $a > 0$.

_____

_____

Ⓒ In all the functions 1–4 above, the base $b > 0$.

Use the graphs to make a conjecture: State the domain and range of $y = ab^x$ if $a < 0$.

_____

_____

Ⓓ What is the y-intercept of $f(x) = 0.5(2)^x$?

_____

(E) Note the similarities between the *y*-intercept and *a*. What is their relationship?

_____

Reflect

1. **Discussion** What is the domain for any exponential function $y = ab^x$?

_____

2. **Discussion** Describe the values of *b* for all functions $y = ab^x$.

_____

🖉 Explain 1   Graphing Increasing Positive Exponential Functions

The symbol ∞ represents *infinity*. We can describe the *end behavior* of a function by describing what happens to the function values as *x* approaches positive infinity $(x \rightarrow \infty)$ and as *x* approaches negative infinity $(x \rightarrow -\infty)$.

Example 1   **Graph each exponential function. After graphing, identify *a* and *b*, the *y*-intercept, and the end behavior of the graph.**

(A) $f(x) = 2^x$

Choose several values of *x* and generate ordered pairs.

x	$f(x) = 2^x$
−1	0.5
0	1
1	2
2	4

Graph the ordered pairs and connect them with a smooth curve.

$a = 1$

$b = 2$

y-intercept: $(0, 1)$

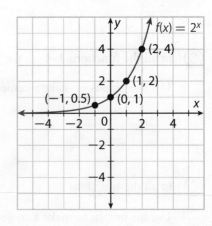

End Behavior: As *x*-values approach positive infinity $(x \rightarrow \infty)$, *y*-values approach positive infinity $(y \rightarrow \infty)$.
As *x*-values approach negative infinity $(x \rightarrow -\infty)$, *y*-values approach zero $(y \rightarrow 0)$.

Using symbols only, we say: As $x \rightarrow \infty, y \rightarrow \infty$, and as $x \rightarrow -\infty, y \rightarrow 0$.

Ⓑ $f(x) = 3(4)^x$

Choose several values of x and generate ordered pairs.

x	$f(x) = 3(4)^x$
−1	
0	
1	
2	

Graph the ordered pairs and connect them with a smooth curve.

$a = \boxed{}$

$b = \boxed{}$

y-intercept: $\left(\boxed{} , \boxed{}\right)$

End Behavior: As $x \to \infty$, $y \to \boxed{}$ and as $x \to -\infty$, $y \to \boxed{}$.

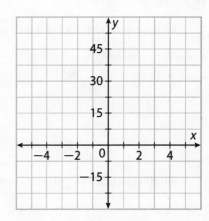

Reflect

3. If $a > 0$ and $b > 1$, what is the end behavior of the graph?

_____

_____

4. Describe the y-intercept of the exponential function $f(x) = ab^x$ in terms of a and b.

_____

Your Turn

5. Graph the exponential function $f(x) = 2(2)^x$

After graphing, identify a and b, the y-intercept, and the end behavior of the graph.

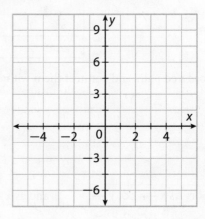

⚙ Explain 2 Graphing Decreasing Negative Exponential Functions

You can use end behavior to discuss the behavior of a graph.

Example 2 Graph each exponential function. After graphing, identify a and b, the y-intercept, and the end behavior of the graph. Use end behavior to discuss the behavior of the graph.

Ⓐ $f(x) = -2(3)^x$

Choose several values of x and generate ordered pairs.

x	$f(x) = -2(3)^x$
−1	−0.7
0	−2
1	−6
2	−18

Graph the ordered pairs and connect them with a smooth curve.

$a = -2$

$b = 3$

y-intercept: $(0, -2)$

End Behavior: As $x \to \infty$, $y \to -\infty$ and as $x \to -\infty$, $y \to 0$.

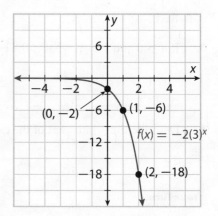

Ⓑ $f(x) = -3(4)^x$

Choose several values of x and generate ordered pairs.

x	$f(x) = -3(4)^x$
−1	
0	
1	
2	

Graph the ordered pairs and connect them with a smooth curve.

$a = \boxed{}$

$b = \boxed{}$

y-intercept: $\left(\boxed{}, \boxed{} \right)$

End Behavior: As $x \to \infty$, $y \to \boxed{}$ and as $x \to -\infty$, $y \to \boxed{}$.

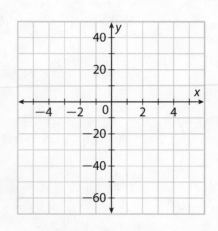

6. If $a < 0$ and $b > 1$, what is the end behavior of the graph?

_____

_____

7. Graph the exponential function. $f(x) = -3(3)^x$

After graphing, identify a and b, the y-intercept, and the end behavior of the graph.

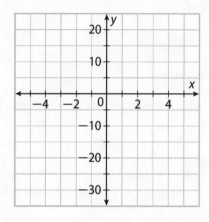

⚡ Explain 3 **Graphing Decreasing Positive Exponential Functions**

Example 3 **Graph each exponential function. After graphing, identify a and b, the y-intercept, and the end behavior of the graph.**

Ⓐ $f(x) = (0.5)^x$

Choose several values of x and generate ordered pairs.

x	$f(x) = (0.5)^x$
−1	2
0	1
1	0.5
2	0.25

Graph the ordered pairs and connect them with a smooth curve.

$a = 1$

$b = 0.5$

y-intercept: $(0, 1)$

End Behavior: As $x \to \infty$, $y \to 0$ and as $x \to -\infty$, $y \to \infty$.

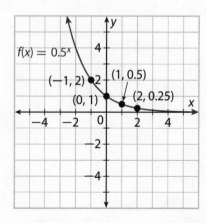

Ⓑ $f(x) = 2(0.4)^x$

Choose several values of x and generate ordered pairs.

x	$f(x) = 2(0.4)^x$
-1	
0	
1	
2	

Graph the ordered pairs and connect them with a smooth curve.

$a = \boxed{}$

$b = \boxed{}$

y-intercept: $\left(\boxed{} , \boxed{} \right)$

End Behavior: As $x \to \infty$, $y \to \boxed{}$ and as $x \to -\infty$, $y \to \boxed{}$.

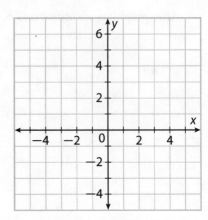

Reflect

8. If $a > 0$ and $0 < b < 1$, what is the end behavior of the graph?

_____

_____

Your Turn

9. Graph the exponential function. After graphing, identify a and b, the y-intercept, and the end behavior of the graph.

$f(x) = 3(0.5)^x$

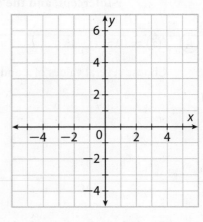

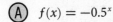

Explain 4 **Graphing Increasing Negative Exponential Functions**

Example 4 Graph each exponential function. After graphing, identify a and b, the y-intercept, and the end behavior of the graph.

(A) $f(x) = -0.5^x$

Choose several values of x and generate ordered pairs.

x	$f(x) = -0.5^x$
−1	−2
0	−1
1	−0.5
2	−0.25

Graph the ordered pairs and connect them with a smooth curve.

$a = -1$

$b = 0.5$

y-intercept: $(0, -1)$

End Behavior: As $x \to \infty$, $y \to 0$ and as $x \to -\infty$, $y \to -\infty$.

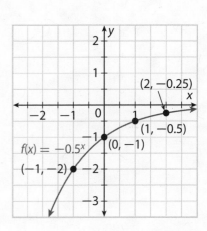

(B) $f(x) = -3(0.4)^x$

Choose several values of x and generate ordered pairs.

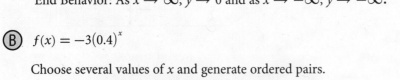

x	$f(x) = -3(0.4)^x$
−1	
0	
1	
2	

Graph the ordered pairs and connect them with a smooth curve.

$a = \boxed{}$

$b = \boxed{}$

y-intercept: $\left(\boxed{}, \boxed{} \right)$

End Behavior: As $x \to \infty$, $y \to \boxed{}$ and as $x \to -\infty$, $y \to \boxed{}$.

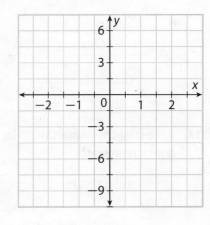

10. If $a < 0$ and $0 < b < 1$, what is the end behavior of the graph?

_____

_____

11. Graph the exponential function. After graphing, identify a and b, the y-intercept, and the end behavior of the graph. Use inequalities to discuss the behavior of the graph.

$$f(x) = -2(0.5)^x$$

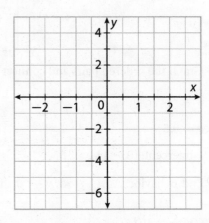

12. Why is $f(x) = 3(-0.5)^x$ not an exponential function?

_____

_____

_____

_____

_____

13. Essential Question Check-In When an exponential function of the form $f(x) = ab^x$ is graphed, what does a represent?

_____

_____

© Houghton Mifflin Harcourt Publishing Company

• Online Homework
• Hints and Help
• Extra Practice

State a, b, and the y-intercept then graph the function on a graphing calculator.

1. $f(x) = 2(3)^x$

2. $f(x) = -6(2)^x$

3. $f(x) = -5(0.5)^x$

4. $f(x) = 3(0.8)^x$

5. $f(x) = 6(3)^x$

6. $f(x) = -4(0.2)^x$

7. $f(x) = 7(0.9)^x$

8. $f(x) = -3(2)^x$

State a, b, and the y-intercept then graph the function and describe the end behavior of the graphs.

9. $f(x) = 3(3)^x$

10. $f(x) = 5(0.6)^x$

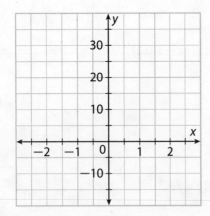

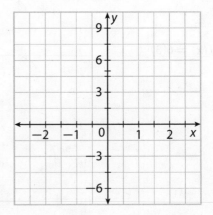

11. $f(x) = -6(0.7)^x$

12. $f(x) = -4(3)^x$

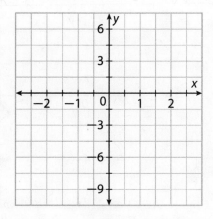

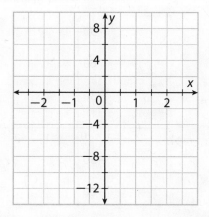

13. $f(x) = 5(2)^x$

14. $f(x) = -2(0.8)^x$

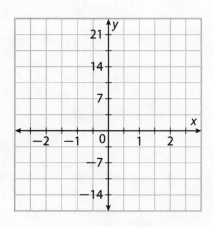

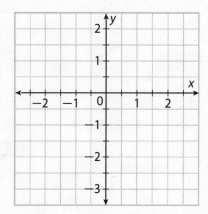

15. $f(x) = 9(3)^x$

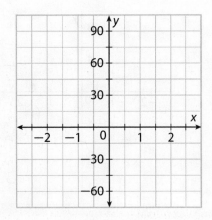

16. $f(x) = -5(2)^x$

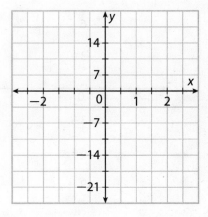

17. $f(x) = 7(0.4)^x$

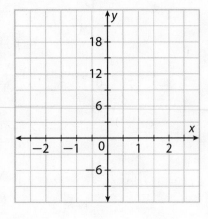

18. $f(x) = 6(2)^x$

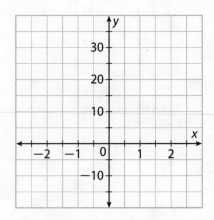

19. Identify the domain and range of each function. Make sure to provide these answers using inequalities.

   a. $f(x) = 3(2)^x$

   b. $f(x) = 7(0.4)^x$

   c. $f(x) = -2(0.6)^x$

   d. $f(x) = -3(4)^x$

   e. $f(x) = 2(22)^x$

20. **Statistics** In 2000, the population of Massachusetts was 6.3 million people and was growing at a rate of about 0.32% per year. At this growth rate, the function $f(x) = 6.3(1.0032)^x$ gives the population, in millions x years after 2000. Using this model, find the year when the population reaches 7 million people.

21. **Physics** A ball is rolling down a slope and continuously picks up speed. Suppose the function $f(x) = 1.2(1.11)^x$ describes the speed of the ball in inches per minute. How fast will the ball be rolling in 20 minutes? Round the answer to the nearest whole number.

H.O.T. Focus on Higher Order Thinking

22. **Draw Conclusions** Assume that the domain of the function $f(x) = 3(2)^x$ is the set of all real numbers. What is the range of the function?

23. **What If?** If $b = 1$ in an exponential function, what will the graph of b look like?

24. **Critical Thinking** Using the graph of an exponential function, how can b be found?

25. Critical Thinking Use the table to write the equation for the exponential function.

x	f(x)
−1	$\frac{4}{5}$
0	4
1	20
2	100

Lesson Performance Task

A pumpkin is being grown for a contest at the state fair. Its growth can be modeled by the equation $P = 25(1.56)^n$, where P is the weight of the pumpkin in pounds and n is the number of weeks the pumpkin has been growing. By what percentage does the pumpkin grow every week? After how many weeks will the pumpkin be 80 pounds?

After the pumpkin grows to 80 pounds, it grows more slowly. From then on, its growth can be modeled by $P = 25(1.23)^n$, where n is the number of weeks since the pumpkin reached 80 pounds. Estimate when the pumpkin will reach 150 pounds.

14.5 Transforming Exponential Functions

Essential Question: How does the graph of $f(x) = ab^x$ change when a and b are changed?

⊘ Explore   Changing the Value of b in $f(x) = b^x$

Investigate the effect of b on the function $f(x) = b^x$.

Ⓐ Complete the table of values for the functions $f_1(x) = 1.2^x$ and $f_2(x) = 1.5^x$. Use a calculator to find the values and round to the nearest thousandth if necessary.

x	$f_1(x) = 1.2^x$	$f_2(x) = 1.5^x$
−2	0.694	
−1		0.667
0		
1	1.2	1.5
2		

Ⓑ Select the option that makes the statement true.

$\big(f_1(x)/f_2(x)\big)$ increases more quickly as x increases.

$\big(f_1(x)/f_2(x)\big)$ approaches 0 more quickly as x decreases.

Ⓒ The y-intercept of $f_1(x)$ is [ ]. The y-intercept of $f_2(x)$ is [ ].

Ⓓ Fill in the table of values for the functions $f_3(x) = 0.6^x$ and $f_4(x) = 0.9^x$. Round to the nearest thousandth again.

x	$f_3(x) = 0.6^x$	$f_4(x) = 0.9^x$
−2	2.778	
−1		1.111
0		
1	0.6	0.9
2		

Ⓔ $\big(f_3(x)/f_4(x)\big)$ increases more quickly as x decreases.

$\big(f_3(x)/f_4(x)\big)$ approaches 0 more quickly as x increases.

Ⓕ The y-intercept of $f_3(x)$ is [ ]. The y-intercept of $f_4(x)$ is [ ].

1. Consider the function, $y = 1.3^x$. How will its graph compare with the graphs of $f_1(x)$ and $f_2(x)$? Discuss end behavior and the y-intercept.

_____

_____

_____

_____

⚷ Explain 1   Changing the Value of a in $f(x) = ab^x$ with $b > 1$

Multiplying a growing exponential function $(b > 1)$ by a constant a does not change the growth rate, but it does stretch or compress the graph vertically, and reflects the graph across the x-axis if $a < 0$.

A **vertical stretch** of a graph is a transformation that pulls the graph away from the x-axis. By multiplying the y-value of each (x, y) pair by a, where $|a| > 1$, the graph is stretched by a factor of $|a|$.

A **vertical compression** of a graph is a transformation that pushes the graph toward the x-axis. By multiplying the y-value of each (x, y) pair by a, where $|a| < 1$, the graph is compressed by a factor of $|a|$.

Example 1   Make a table of values for the function given. Then graph it on the same coordinate plane with the graph of $y = 1.5^x$. Describe the end behavior and find the y-intercept of each graph.

(A) $f(x) = 0.3(1.5)^x$

x	$f(x) = 0.3(1.5)^x$
−2	0.133
−1	0.2
0	0.3
1	0.45
2	0.675
3	1.013
4	1.519

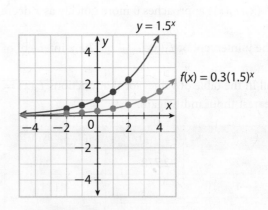

End Behavior:

$$f(x) \to \infty \text{ as } x \to \infty$$

$$f(x) \to 0 \text{ as } x \to -\infty$$

y-intercept: 0.3

Ⓑ $f(x) = -2(1.5)^x$

x	$f(x) = -2(1.5)^x$
−4	
−3	
−2	
−1	
0	
1	
2	

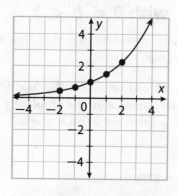

End Behavior:

$f(x) \rightarrow$ ⬜ as $x \rightarrow \infty$

$f(x) \rightarrow$ ⬜ as $x \rightarrow -\infty$

y-intercept: ⬜

Reflect

2. **Discussion** What can you say about the common behavior of graphs of the form $f(x) = ab^x$ with $b > 1$? What is different when a changes sign?

_____

_____

_____

Your Turn

Graph each function, and describe the end behavior and find the y-intercept of each graph.

3. $f(x) = -0.5(1.5)^x$

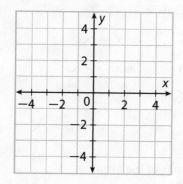

4. $f(x) = 4(1.5)^x$

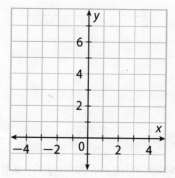

⚙ Explain 2 Changing the Value of a in $f(x) = ab^x$ with $0 < b < 1$

Multiplying a decaying exponential function $(b < 1)$ by a constant a does not change the growth rate, but it does stretch or compress the graph vertically.

Example 2 Make a table of values for the function given. Then graph it on the same coordinate plane with the graph of $y = 0.6^x$. Describe the end behavior and find the y-intercept of each graph.

Ⓐ $f(x) = -3(0.6)^x$

x	$f(x) = -3(0.6)^x$
−1	−5
0	−3
1	−1.8
2	−1.08
3	−0.648

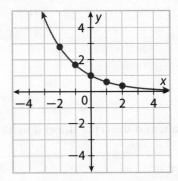

End behavior:

$f(x) \to 0$ as $x \to \infty$

$f(x) \to -\infty$ as $x \to -\infty$

y-intercept: −3

Ⓑ $f(x) = 0.5\,(0.6)^x$

x	$f(x) = 0.5(0.6)^x$
−4	
−3	
−2	
−1	
0	
1	
2	

End Behavior:

$f(x) \to$ ☐ as $x \to \infty$

$f(x) \to$ ☐ as $x \to -\infty$

y-intercept: ☐

Reflect

5. **Discussion** What can you say about the common behavior of graphs of the form $f(x) = ab^x$ with $0 < b < 1$? What is different when a changes sign?

_____

_____

_____

Your Turn

Graph each function, and describe its end behavior and *y*-intercept.

6. $f(x) = 2(0.6)^x$

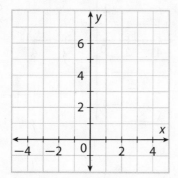

7. $f(x) = -0.25(0.6)^x$

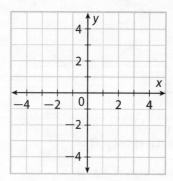

🔑 **Explain 3**   **Adding a Constant to an Exponential Function**

Adding a constant to an exponential function causes the graph of the function to translate up or down, depending on the sign of the constant.

Example 3   **Make a table of values for each function and graph them together on the same coordinate plane. Find the *y*-intercepts, and explain how they relate to the translation of the graph.**

Ⓐ $f(x) = 2^x$ and $g(x) = 2^x + 2$

x	$f(x) = 2^x$	$g(x) = 2^x + 2$
−2	0.25	2.25
−1	0.5	2.5
0	1	3
1	2	4
2	4	6

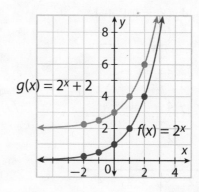

The *y*-intercept of $f(x)$ is 1.

The *y*-intercept of $g(x)$ is 3.

The *y*-intercept of $g(x)$ is 2 more than that of $f(x)$ because $g(x)$ is a vertical translation of $f(x)$ up by 2 units.

Ⓑ $f(x) = 0.7^x$ and $g(x) = 0.7^x - 3$

x	$f(x) = 0.7^x$	$g(x) = 0.7^x - 3$
−2		
−1		
0		
1		
2		

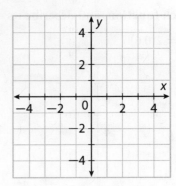

The y-intercept of $f(x)$ is ☐ .

The y-intercept of $g(x)$ is ☐ .

The y-intercept of $g(x)$ is 3 (more/less) than that of $f(x)$ because $g(x)$ is a vertical translation of $f(x)$ (up/down) by 3 units.

Reflect

8. What do you think will happen to the y-intercept of an exponential function with both a stretch and a translation, such as $f(x) = 3(0.7)^x + 2$?

_____

_____

Your Turn

Graph the functions together on the same coordinate plane. Find the y-intercepts, and explain how they relate to the translation of the graph.

9. $f(x) = 0.4^x$ and $g(x) = 0.4^x + 4$

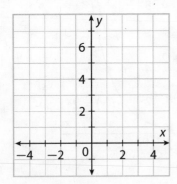

10. $f(x) = 2(1.5)^x$ and $g(x) = 2(1.5)^x - 3$

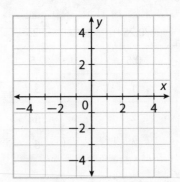

11. How do you determine the y-intercept of an exponential function $f(x) = ab^x + k$ that has been both stretched and translated?

_____

_____

12. Describe the end behavior of a translated exponential function $f(x) = b^x + k$ with $b > 1$ as x approaches $-\infty$.

_____

_____

13. **Essential Question Check-in** If a and b are positive real numbers and $b \neq 1$, how does the graph of $f(x) = ab^x$ change when b is changed?

_____

_____

⊛ Evaluate: Homework and Practice

- Online Homework
- Hints and Help
- Extra Practice

Exercises 1 and 2 refer to the functions $f_1(x) = 2.5^x$ and $f_2(x) = 3^x$.

1. Which function grows faster as x increases toward ∞?

2. Which function approaches 0 faster as x decreases toward $-\infty$?

Exercises 3 and 4 refer to the functions $f_1(x) = 0.5^x$ and $f_2(x) = 0.7^x$.

3. Which function grows faster as x decreases toward $-\infty$?

4. Which function approaches 0 faster as x increases toward ∞?

Label each of the following functions, $g(x)$, as a vertical stretch or a vertical compression of the parent function, $f(x)$, and tell whether it is reflected about the x-axis.

5. $g(x) = 0.7(0.5)^x$, $f(x) = 0.5^x$

6. $g(x) = -1.2(5)^x$, $f(x) = 5^x$

Label each of the following functions, $g(x)$, as a vertical stretch or a vertical compression of the parent function, $f(x)$, and tell whether it is reflected about the x-axis.

7.

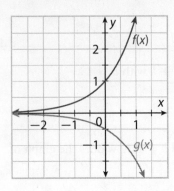

8.

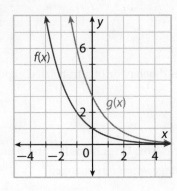

Find the y-intercept for each of the functions, $g(x)$, from Exercises 5–8.

9. $g(x) = 0.7(0.5)^x$

10. $g(x) = -1.2(5)^x$

11. Use $g(x)$ from Exercise 7.

12. Use $g(x)$ from Exercise 8.

Describe the translation of each of the functions, $g(x)$, compared to the parent function, $f(x)$.

13. $f(x) = 0.4^x, g(x) = 0.4^x + 5$

14. $f(x) = -2(1.5)^x, g(x) = -2(1.5)^x - 2$

15.

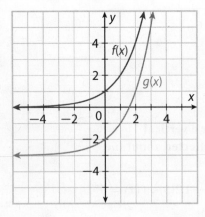

16.

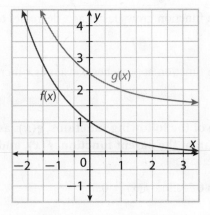

The height of the *n*th bounce of a bouncy ball dropped from a height of 10 feet can be characterized by a decaying exponential function, $h(n) = 10(0.8)^n$, where each bounce reaches 80% of the height of the previous bounce.

17. Write the new function if the ball is dropped from 5 feet.

18. What kind of transformation was that from the original function, $h(n) = 10(0.8)^n$?

19. Write the function that describes what happens if the ball is dropped from 10 feet above a table top that is at a height of 3 feet.

20. Biology Unrestrained growth of cells in a petri dish can be extremely rapid, with a single cell growing into a number of cells, *N*, given by the formula, $N(t) = 8^t$, after *t* hours.

   a. Write the formula for the number of cells in the petri dish when a culture is started with 50 isolated cells.

   b. How many cells do you expect after 3 hours?

A bank account with an initial deposit of $1000 and an interest rate of 5% increases by 5% each year. The balance (B) as a function of time in years (t) can be described by an exponential function: $B(t) = 1000(1.05)^t$.

21. What parameter of the exponential form $f(x) = ab^x + k$ represents the initial balance of $1000?

22. What is the y-intercept of $B(t)$?

23. What parameter would change if the interest rate were changed to 7%?

24. Which bank account balance grows faster, the one with 5% interest or the one with 7% interest?

25. What kind of transformation is represented by changing the initial balance to $500?

26. Match the graph to the characteristics of the function $f(x) = ab^x$.

1. $a < 0, b > 1$ **2.** $a > 0, b < 1$ **3.** $a > 0, b > 1$ **4.** $a < 0, b < 1$

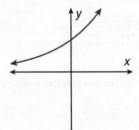

a.

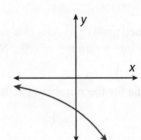

b.

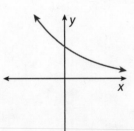

c.

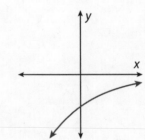

d.

27. Critical Thinking Describe how the graph of $f(x) = ab^x$ changes for a given positive value of a as you increase the value of b when $b > 1$. Discuss the rise and fall of the graph and the y-intercept.

28. Communicate Mathematical Ideas Consider the functions $f_1(x) = (1.02)^x$ and $f_2(x) = (1.03)^x$. Which function increases more quickly as x increases to the right of 0? How do the growth factors support your answer?

29. Communicate Mathematical Ideas Consider the function $f_1(x) = (0.94)^x$ and $f_2(x) = (0.98)^x$. Which function decreases more quickly as x increases to the right of 0? How do the growth factors support your answer?

Lesson Performance Task

A coffee shop serves two patrons cups of coffee. The initial temperature of the coffee is 170 °F. As the coffee sits in the 70 °F room, the temperature follows the pattern of a transformed exponential function. One patron leaves her coffee untouched, resulting in a slow cooling toward room temperature. The other patron is in a hurry and stirs her coffee, resulting in a faster cooling rate.

Both cups of coffee can be modeled with transformed exponential functions of the form $T(t) = ab^t + k$.

Each minute, the unstirred coffee gets 10% closer to room temperature, and the stirred coffee gets 20% closer. Find the functions $T_s(t)$ and $T_u(t)$ for the stirred and unstirred cups of coffee, fill in the table of values, and graph the functions. Determine how long it takes each cup to drop below 130 °F (don't try to solve the equations exactly, just use the table to answer to the nearest minute).

Time (minutes)	Temperature (°F, unstirred)	Temperature (°F, stirred)
0		
1		
2		
3		
4		
5		

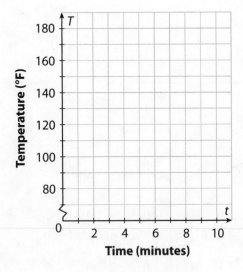

Geometric Sequences and Exponential Functions

Essential Question: How can you use geometric sequences and exponential functions to solve real-world problems?

Key Vocabulary

common ratio
(razón común)

explicit rule
(fórmula explícita)

exponential function
(función exponencial)

geometric sequence
(sucesión geométrica)

recursive rule
(fórmula recurrente)

KEY EXAMPLE   (Lesson 14.1)

Find the common ratio r for the geometric sequence 2, 6, 18, 54, … and use r to find the next three terms.

$\frac{6}{2} = 3$, so the common ratio r is 3.

For this sequence, $f(1) = 2$, $f(2) = 6$, $f(3) = 18$, and $f(4) = 54$.

$f(4) = 54$, so $f(5) = 54(3) = 162$.

$f(5) = 162$, so $f(6) = 162(3) = 486$.

$f(6) = 486$, so $f(7) = 486(3) = 1458$.

The next three terms of the sequence are 162, 486, and 1458.

KEY EXAMPLE   (Lesson 14.3)

Write an equation for the exponential function that includes the points $(2, 8)$ and $(3, 16)$.

Find b by dividing the function value of the second pair by the function value of the first: $b = \frac{16}{8} = 2$.

Evaluate the function for $x = 2$ and solve for a.

$f(x) = ab^x$	Write the general form.
$f(x) = a \cdot 2^x$	Substitute the value for b.
$8 = a \cdot 2^2$	Substitute a pair of input-output values.
$8 = a \cdot 4$	Simplify.
$a = 2$	Solve for a.
$f(x) = 2 \cdot 2^x$	Use a and b to write an equation for the function.

KEY EXAMPLE   (Lesson 14.5)

Describe the transformations of the function $g(x) = 2(3)^x + 5$ as compared to the parent function $f(x) = 3^x$.

a has changed from 1 to 2.

This corresponds to a vertical stretch by a factor of 2.

The constant has changed from 0 to 5.

This corresponds to a translation of 5 units up.

$g(x)$ has been stretched by a factor of 2 and translated 5 units up.

EXERCISES

Find the common ratio r for each geometric sequence and use r to find the next three terms. *(Lesson 14.1)*

1. 1701, 567, 189,...

2. 5, 20, 80,...

Write a recursive rule and an explicit rule for each geometric sequence. *(Lesson 14.2)*

3. 4, 12, 36, 108, 324,...

4. 6, 30, 150, 750, 3750,...

Write an equation for the exponential function that includes the pair of given points. *(Lesson 14.3)*

5. $(2, 16)$ and $(3, 32)$

6. $(2, 4)$ and $(3, 2)$

7. Find a, b, and the y-intercept for $f(x) = 5(2)^x$, and then describe its end behavior. *(Lesson 14.4)*

MODULE PERFORMANCE TASK

What Does It Take to Go Viral?

You want your newest video to be so popular that it gets more than 750,000 daily views within a week after you post it. You share it with friends and assume that each friend will share the video with the same number of people that you do, and so on. How can you determine the smallest number of friends you need to show your video to? What answer do you think would be too big? Too small?

Start by listing in the space below how you plan to tackle the problem. Then use your own paper to complete the task. Be sure to write down all your data and assumptions. Then use numbers, tables, or algebra to explain how you reached your conclusion.

(Ready) to Go On?

14.1–14.5 Geometric Sequences and Exponential Functions

- Online Homework
- Hints and Help
- Extra Practice

Write a recursive rule and an explicit rule for each geometric sequence, and then find the next three terms. *(Lessons 14.1, 14.2)*

1. 2, 8, 32,…

2. 1024, 512, 256,…

Write an equation for the exponential function that includes the pair of given points. Find *a*, *b*, and the *y*-intercept, and then graph the function and describe its end behavior. *(Lessons 14.3, 14.4)*

3. $(1, 12)$ and $(-1, 0.75)$

4. $(-1, -8)$ and $(1, -2)$

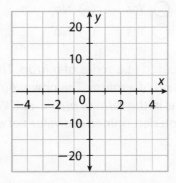

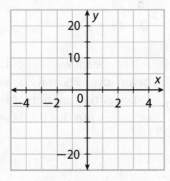

5. Describe the transformations of the function $g(x) = 0.25(5)^x - 2$ as compared to the parent function $f(x) = 5^x$. *(Lesson 14.5)*

ESSENTIAL QUESTION

6. How does the rate of change of an exponential function behave as the value of *x* increases?

Assessment Readiness

1. Consider the geometric sequence 6, 24, 96, 384, ….
   Choose True or False for each statement.

   A. The sixth term is 1536. ◯ True ◯ False

   B. The explicit rule is $f(n) = 6(4)^{n-1}$. ◯ True ◯ False

   C. The recursive rule is $f(1) = 4$; $f(n) = f(n-1) \cdot 6$. ◯ True ◯ False

2. Does the given system of equations have exactly one solution? Select Yes or No for each system.

   A. $\begin{cases} 3x-2y = 6 \\ 2x+ 2y = 14 \end{cases}$ ◯ Yes ◯ No

   B. $\begin{cases} y = -4x - 5 \\ y = -4x + 2 \end{cases}$ ◯ Yes ◯ No

   C. $\begin{cases} 5x - 3y = 15 \\ 5x + 3y = 15 \end{cases}$ ◯ Yes ◯ No

3. Is the given number a term in both the sequence $f(n) = f(n - 1) + 5$ and the sequence $f(n) = 3(2)^{n-1}$, if $f(1) = 3$? Select Yes or No for each number.

   A. 8 ◯ Yes ◯ No

   B. 18 ◯ Yes ◯ No

   C. 24 ◯ Yes ◯ No

   D. 48 ◯ Yes ◯ No

4. A laser beam with an output of 6 milliwatts is focused at a series of mirrors. The laser beam loses 2% of its power every time it reflects off of a mirror. The power $p(n)$ is an exponential function of the number of reflections in the form of $p(n) = ab^n$. Write the equation $p(n)$ for this laser beam. Explain how you determined the values of a and b.

Exponential Equations and Models

Essential Question: How can you use exponential equations to represent real-world situations?

REAL WORLD VIDEO
Scientists have found many ways to use radioactive elements that decay exponentially over time. Uranium-235 is used to power nuclear reactors, and scientists use Carbon-14 dating to calculate how long ago an organism lived.

MODULE PERFORMANCE TASK PREVIEW
Half-Life

Accidents at nuclear reactors like the one in Fukushima, Japan, in 2011 commonly release the radioactive isotopes iodine-131 and cesium-137. Iodine-131 often causes thyroid problems, whereas cesium-137 permeates the entire body and can cause death. Each isotope decays over time but at very different rates. How can you figure out the concentration of isotopes at a nuclear accident? Let's find out!

Are YOU Ready?

Complete these exercises to review skills you will need for this module.

Constant Rate of Change

Example 1   Tell if the rate of change is constant.

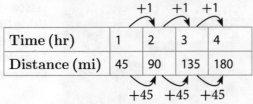

Time (hr)	1	2	3	4
Distance (mi)	45	90	135	180

$$\text{rate of change} = \frac{\text{change in miles}}{\text{change in hours}}$$

$$= \frac{45}{1}$$

The rate of change is constant.

Tell if the rate of change is constant.

1.

Age (mo)	3	6	9	12
Weight (lb)	12	16	18	20

2.

Hours	2	4	6	8
Pay ($)	16	32	48	64

Percent

Example 2   Write 7% as a decimal.

$$7\% = \frac{7}{100} = 0.07$$

Write the percent in the form $\frac{r}{100}$ and then write the decimal.

Write the percent as a decimal.

3. 21%

4. 3.5%

5. 108%

6. 0.25%

Exponents

Example 3   Find the value of $2(3)^4$.

$$2(3)^4 = 2(3 \cdot 3 \cdot 3 \cdot 3)$$

$$= 162$$

Write the power as a multiplication expression. Multiply.

Find the value.

7. $3(4)^2$

8. $24(0.5)^3$

9. $5(2)^5$

10. $350(0.1)^3$

15.1 Using Graphs and Properties to Solve Equations with Exponents

Essential Question: How can you solve equations involving variable exponents?

⊘ Explore 1   Solving Exponential Equations Graphically

In previous lessons, variables have been raised to rational exponents and you have seen how to simplify and solve equations containing these expressions. How do you solve an equation with a rational number raised to a variable? In certain cases, this is not a difficult task. If $2^x = 4$ it is easy to see that $x = 2$ since $2^2 = 4$. In other cases, like $3(2)^x = 96$, where would you begin? Let's find out.

(A) Solve for $3(2)^x = 96$ for x.

(B) Let $f(x) = 3(2)^x$. Complete the table for $f(x)$.

x	f(x)
1	6
2	
3	
4	
5	
6	
7	

(C) Using the table of values, graph $f(x)$ on the axes provided.

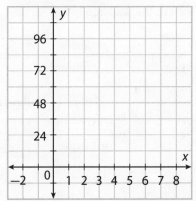

(D) Let $g(x) = 96$. Complete the table for $g(x)$.

x	g(x)
1	96
2	
3	
4	
5	
6	
7	96

(E) Using the table, graph $g(x)$ on the same axes as $f(x)$.

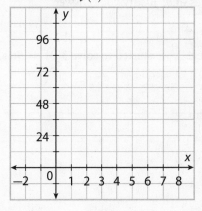

(F) The graphs intersect at point(s): ☐ This means that $f(x) = $ ☐ when $x = $ ☐ .

1. **Discussion** Consider the function $h(x) = -96$. Where do $f(x)$ and $h(x)$ intersect?

_____

_____

2. Divide the equation $3(2)^x = 96$ by 3 on both sides (an Algebraic Step) and utilize the same method as in Explore 1 to graph each side of the equation as a function. The point of intersection would be: [ ].

Is this the same point of intersection? Is this the same answer? Can this be done? Elaborate as to why or why not.

_____

_____

_____

⊘ Explore 2 Solving Exponential Equations Algebraically

Recall the example $2^x = 4$, with the solution $x = 2$. What about a slightly more complicated equation? Can an equation like $5(2)^x = 160$ be solved using algebra?

(A) Solve $5(2)^x = 160$ for x. The first step in isolating the term containing the variable

on one side of the equation is to _____.

$$\frac{5(2)^x}{\boxed{}} = \frac{160}{\boxed{}}$$

(B) Simplify.

$(2)^x = \boxed{}$

(C) Rewrite the right hand side as a power of 2.

$(2)^x = (2)^{\boxed{}}$

(D) Solve.

$x = \boxed{}$

Reflect

3. **Discussion** The last step of the solution process seems to imply that if $b^x = b^y$ then $x = y$. Is this true for all values of b? Justify your answer.

_____

4. In Reflect 2, we started to solve $3(2)^x = 96$ algebraically. Finish solving for x.

_____

_____

_____

_____

Solving the previous exponential equation for x used the idea that if $2^x = 2^5$, then $x = 5$. This will be a powerful tool for solving exponential equations if it can be generalized to if $b^x = b^y$ then $x = y$. However, there are values for which this is clearly not true. For example, $0^7 = 0^3$ but $7 \neq 3$. If the values of b are restricted, we get the following property.

Equality of Bases Property

Two powers with the same positive base other than 1 are equal if and only if the exponents are equal.

Algebraically, if $b > 0$ and, $b \neq 1$, then $b^x = b^y$ if and only if $x = y$.

Example 1 Solve by equating exponents and using the Equality of Bases Property.

Ⓐ $\quad \dfrac{2}{5}(5)^x = 250$

$\dfrac{5}{2} \cdot \dfrac{2}{5}(5)^x = 250 \cdot \dfrac{5}{2}$ Multiply both sides by $\dfrac{5}{2}$.

$\qquad\qquad 5^x = 625$ Simplify.

$\qquad\qquad 5^x = 5^4$ Rewrite the right side as a power of 5.

$\qquad\qquad\quad x = 4$ Equality of Bases Property.

Ⓑ $\quad 2\left(\dfrac{5}{3}\right)^x = \dfrac{250}{27}$

$\dfrac{2\left(\dfrac{5}{3}\right)^x}{\boxed{}} = \dfrac{\dfrac{250}{27}}{\boxed{}}$ Divide both sides by $\boxed{}$.

$\left(\dfrac{5}{3}\right)^x = \dfrac{\boxed{}}{27}$ Simplify.

$\left(\dfrac{5}{3}\right)^x = \boxed{}^{\,3}$ Rewrite the right side as a power of $\boxed{}$.

$\qquad\quad x = \boxed{}$ Equality of _____ Property.

Reflect

5. Suppose while solving an equation algebraically you are confronted with:

$5^x = 15$

$5^x = 5^{\square}$

Can you find x using the method in the examples above?

_____

Solve by equating exponents and using the Equality of Bases Property.

6. $\frac{2}{3}(3)^x = 18$

7. $\frac{3}{2}\left(\frac{4}{3}\right)^x = \frac{8}{3}$

🕐 **Explain 2** **Solving a Real-World Exponential Equation by Graphing**

Some equations cannot be solved using the method in the previous example because it isn't possible to write both sides of the equation as a whole number power of the same base. Instead, you can consider the expressions on either side of the equation as the rules for two different functions. You can then solve the original equation in one variable by graphing the two functions. The solution is the input value for the point where the two graphs intersect.

Example 2 **Solve by graphing two functions.**

An animal reserve has 20,000 elk. The population is increasing at a rate of 8% per year. There is concern that food will be scarce when the population has doubled. How long will it take for the population to reach 40,000?

🧩 **Analyze Information**

Identify the important information.

- The starting population is   20,000.

- The ending population is   _____.

- The growth rate is   _____.

🧩 **Formulate a Plan**

With the given situation and data there is enough information to write and solve an exponential model of the population as a function of time. Write the exponential equation and then solve it using a graphing calculator.

Set $f(x) =$ _____ and $g(x) =$ _____.

Input $Y_1 = f(x)$ and $Y_2 = g(x)$ into a graphing calculator, graph the functions,

and _____.

Solve

Write a function $P(t) = ab^t$, where $P(t)$ is the population and t is the number of years since the population was initially measured.

a represents _____

$a = \boxed{}$

b represents _____

$b = \boxed{}$

The function is $P(t) = \boxed{} \left(\boxed{} \right)^t$.

To find the time when the population is 40,000, set _____ or _____

equal to 40,000 and _____.

$40{,}000 = \boxed{} \left(\boxed{} \right)^t$.

Write functions for the expressions on either side of the equation.

$f(x) = $ _____

$g(x) = $ _____

Using a graphing calculator, set $Y_1 = f(x)$ and $Y_2 = g(x)$. View the graph.
Use the intersect feature on the CALC menu to find the intersection of the two graphs.

The approximate x-value where the graphs intersect is $\boxed{}$.

Therefore, the population will double in just a little over $\boxed{}$ years.

Justify and Evaluate

Check the solution by evaluating the function at $t = \boxed{}$.

$P \left(\boxed{} \right) = 20{,}000 \cdot \boxed{}$

$\qquad = 20{,}000 \cdot \left(\boxed{} \right)$

$\qquad = \boxed{}$

Since $\boxed{} \approx 40{,}000$, it _____ accurate to say the population will double

in _____ years.

This prediction _____ reasonable because $1.08^{\boxed{}} \approx \boxed{}$.

Solve using a graphing calculator.

8. There are 225 wolves in a state park. The population is increasing at the rate of 15% per year. You want to make a prediction for how long it will take the population to reach 500.

9. There are 175 deer in a state park. The population is increasing at the rate of 12% per year. You want to make a prediction for how long it will take the population to reach 300.

💬 Elaborate

10. Explain how you would solve $0.25 = 0.5^x$. Which method can always be used to solve an exponential equation?

_____

_____

_____

11. What would you do first to solve the equation $\frac{1}{4}(6)^x = 54$?

_____

12. How does isolating the power in an exponential equation like $\frac{1}{4}(6)^x = 54$ compare to isolating the variable in a linear equation?

_____

_____

13. Given a population decreasing by 1% per year, when will the population double? What will this type of situation look like when graphed on a calculator?

_____

_____

_____

_____

14. Solve $0.5 = 1.01^x$ graphically. Suppose this equation models the point where a population increasing at a rate of 1% per year is halved. When will the population be halved?

_____

_____

15. **Essential Question Check-In** How can you solve equations involving variable exponents?

_____

_____

1. Would it have been easier to find the solution to the equation in Explore 1, $3(2)^x = 96$, algebraically? Justify your answer. In general, if you can solve an exponential equation graphing by hand, why can you solve it algebraically?

2. The equation $2 = (1.01)^x$ models a population that has doubled. What is the rate of increase? What does x represent?

3. Can we solve equations using both algebraic and graphical methods?

Solve the given equation.

4. $4(2)^x = 64$

5. $7(3)^x = 63$

6. $\dfrac{6^x}{4} = 54$

7. $\left(\dfrac{1}{4}\right)\left(\dfrac{5}{6}\right)^x = \dfrac{75}{432}$

8. $2\left(\dfrac{7}{2}\right)^x = \dfrac{49}{2}$

9. $3(11)^x = 3993$

© Houghton Mifflin Harcourt Publishing Company

10. $2(9)^x = 162$

11. $2\left(\dfrac{1}{9}\right)^x = \dfrac{2}{81}$

12. $2\left(\dfrac{4}{13}\right)^x = \dfrac{32}{169}$

13. $\left(\dfrac{1}{2}\right)\left(\dfrac{2}{3}\right)^x = \left(\dfrac{1}{4}\right)\left(\dfrac{16}{27}\right)$

14. $(8)\left(\dfrac{2}{3}\right)^x = (4)\left(\dfrac{16}{27}\right)$

15. $\left(\dfrac{2}{5}\right)\left(\dfrac{2}{5}\right)^x = \dfrac{8}{125}$

16. $\left(\dfrac{2}{5}\right)^x\left(\dfrac{2}{5}\right)^x = \left(\dfrac{8}{125}\right)\left(\dfrac{8}{125}\right)$

17. There is a draught and the oak tree population is decreasing at the rate of 7% per year. If the population continues to decrease at the same rate, how long will it take for the population to be half of what it is?

18. An animal reserve has 40,000 elk. The population is increasing at a rate of 11% per year. How long will it take for the population to reach 80,000?

19. A lake has a small population of a rare endangered fish. The lake currently has a population of 10 fish. The number of fish is increasing at a rate of 4% per year. When will the population double? How long will it take the population to be 80 fish?

20. Tim has a savings account with the bank. The bank pays him 1% per year. He has $5000 and wonders when it will reach $5200. When will his savings reach $5200?

21. Tim is considering a different savings account that pays 1%, but this time it is compounded monthly.

(When interest is compounded monthly, the bank pays interest every month instead of every year. The function representing compounded interest is $S(t) = P\left(1 + \frac{r}{n}\right)^{nt}$, where P is the principal, or initial deposit in the account, r is the interest rate, n is the number of times the interest is compounded per year, t is the year, and $S(t)$ is the savings after t years.)

How many years will it take Tim to earn $200 at this bank? Should he switch?

22. Lisa has a credit card that charges 3% interest on a monthly balance. She buys a $200 bike and plans to pay for it by making monthly payments of $100. How many months will it take her to pay it off? Assume the first payment she makes is charged no interest because she paid it before the first bill.

23. Analyze Relationships A city has 175,000 residents. The population is increasing at the rate of 10% per year.

a. You want to make a prediction for how long it will take for the population to reach 300,000. Round your answer to the nearest tenth of a year.

b. Suppose there are 350,000 residents of another city. The population of this city is decreasing at a rate of 3% per year. Which city's population will reach 300,000 sooner? Explain.

24. Explain the Error Jean and Marco each solved the equation $9(3)^x = 729$. Whose solution is incorrect? Explain your reasoning. How could the person who is incorrect fix the work?

Jean	*Marco*
$9(3)^x = 729$	$9(3)^x = 729$
$\left(\dfrac{1}{9}\right) \cdot \cancel{9}(3)^x = \left(\dfrac{1}{9}\right) \cdot 729$	$3^2 \cdot (3)^x = 729$
$3^x = 81 = 3^4$	$3^{2+x} = 729 = 3^6$
$x = 4$	$x = 6$

25. Critical Thinking Without solving, state the column containing the equation with the greater solution for each pair of equations. Explain your reasoning.

$$\left(\dfrac{1}{3}\right)(3)^x = 243 \qquad\qquad \left(\dfrac{1}{3}\right)(9)^x = 243$$

Lesson Performance Task

A town has a population of 78,918 residents. The town council is offering a prize for the best prediction of how long it will take the population to reach 100,000. The population rate is increasing 6% per year. Find the best prediction in order to win the prize. Write an exponential equation in the form $y = ab^x$ and explain what a and b represent.

15.2 Modeling Exponential Growth and Decay

Essential Question: How can you use exponential functions to model the increase or decrease of a quantity over time?

⊘ Explore 1 Describing End Behavior of a Growth Function

When you graph a function $f(x)$ in a coordinate plane, the x-axis represents the independent variable and the y-axis represents the dependent variable. Therefore, the graph of $f(x)$ is the same as the graph of the equation $y = f(x)$. You will use this form when you use a calculator to graph functions.

Ⓐ Use a graphing calculator to graph the exponential growth function $f(x) = 200(1.10)^x$, using Y_1 for $f(x)$. Use a viewing window from −20 to 20 for x, with a scale of 2, and from −100 to 1000 for y, with a scale of 50. Sketch the curve on the axes provided.

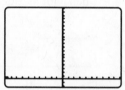

Ⓑ To describe the end behavior of the function, you describe the function values as x increases or decreases without bound. Using the TRACE feature, move the cursor to the right along the curve. Describe the end behavior as x increases without bound.

_____

_____

Ⓒ Using the TRACE feature, move the cursor to the left along the curve. Describe the end behavior as x decreases without bound.

_____

_____

Reflect

1. Describe the domain and range of the function using inequalities.

_____

2. Identify the y-intercept of the graph of the function.

_____

3. An asymptote of a graph is a line the graph approaches more and more closely. Identify an asymptote of this graph.

_____

4. **Discussion** Why is the value of the function always greater than 0?

_____

_____

⊘ Explore 2 Describing End Behavior of a Decay Function

Use the form from the first Explore exercise to graph another function on your calculator.

(A) Use a graphing calculator to graph the exponential decay function
$f(x) = 500(0.8)^x$, using Y_1 for $f(x)$. Use a viewing window from -10 to 10 for
x, with a scale of 1, and from -500 to 5000 for y, with a scale of 500. Sketch
the curve on the axes provided.

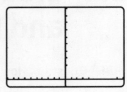

(B) Using the TRACE feature, move the cursor to the right along the curve.
Describe the end behavior as x increases without bound.

_____

_____

(C) Using the TRACE feature, move the cursor to the left along the curve. Describe the end
behavior as x decreases without bound.

_____

_____

Reflect

5. **Discussion** Describe the domain and range of the function using inequalities.

_____

_____

6. Identify the y-intercept of the graph of the function.

_____

_____

7. Identify an asymptote of this graph. Why is this line an asymptote?

_____

_____

⚙ Explain 1　Modeling Exponential Growth

Recall that a function of the form $y = ab^x$ represents exponential growth when $a > 0$ and $b > 1$. If b is replaced by $1 + r$ and x is replaced by t, then the function is the **exponential growth model** $y = a(1 + r)^t$, where a is the initial amount, the base $(1 + r)$ is the growth factor, r is the growth rate, and t is the time interval. The value of the model increases with time.

Example 1 Write an exponential growth function for each situation. Graph each function and state its domain, range and an asymptote. What does the y-intercept represent in the context of the problem?

(A) A painting is sold for $1800, and its value increases by 11% each year after it is sold. Find the value of the painting in 30 years.

Write the exponential growth function for this situation.

$$y = a(1 + r)^t$$

$$= 1800(1 + 0.11)^t$$

$$= 1800(1.11)^t$$

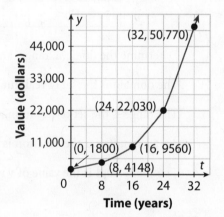

Find the value in 30 years.

$$y = 1800(1.11)^t$$

$$= 1800(1.11)^{30}$$

$$\approx 41,206.13$$

After 30 years, the painting will be worth approximately $41,206.

Create a table of values to graph the function.

t	y	(t, y)
0	1800	(0, 1800)
8	4148	(8, 4148)
16	9560	(16, 9560)
24	22,030	(24, 22,030)
32	50,770	(32, 50,770)

Determine the domain, range and an asymptote of the function.

The domain is the set of real numbers t such that $t \geq 0$.

The range is the set of real numbers y such that $y \geq 1800$.

An asymptote for the function is $y = 0$.

The y-intercept is the value of y when $t = 0$, which is the value of the painting when it was sold.

(B) A baseball trading card is sold for $2, and its value increases by 8% each year after it is sold. Find the value of the baseball trading card in 10 years.

Write the exponential growth function for this situation.

$y = a(1 + r)^t$

$= \boxed{}\left(1 + \boxed{}\right)^t$

$= \boxed{}\left(\boxed{}\right)^t$

Find the value in 10 years.

$y = a(1 + r)^t$

$= \boxed{}\left(\boxed{}\right)^t$

$= \boxed{}\left(\boxed{}\right)^{\boxed{}}$

$\approx \boxed{}$

After 10 years, the baseball trading card will be worth approximately $_____.

Create a table of values to graph the function.

t	y	(t, y)
0		
3		
6		
9		
12		

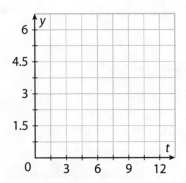

Determine the domain, range, and an asymptote of the function.

The domain is the set of real numbers t such that $t \geq \boxed{}$.

The range is the set of real numbers y such that $y \geq \boxed{}$.

An asymptote for the function is _____.

The y-intercept is the value of y when $t = 0$, which is the _____.

Reflect

8. Find a recursive rule that models the exponential growth of $y = 1800(1.11)^t$.

_____

9. Find a recursive rule that models the exponential growth of $y = 2(1.08)^t$.

_____

10. Write and graph an exponential growth function, and state the domain and range. Tell what the y-intercept represents. Sara sold a coin for $3, and its value increases by 2% each year after it is sold. Find the value of the coin in 8 years.

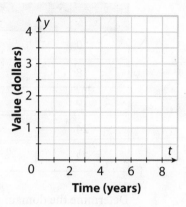

⚙ Explain 2   Modeling Exponential Decay

Recall that a function of the form $y = ab^x$ represents exponential decay when $a > 0$ and $0 < b < 1$. If b is replaced by $1 - r$ and x is replaced by t, then the function is the **exponential decay model** $y = a(1 - r)^t$, where a is the initial amount, the base $(1 - r)$ is the decay factor, r is the decay rate, and t is the time interval.

Example 2   Write an exponential decay function for each situation. Graph each function and state its domain and range. What does the y-intercept represent in the context of the problem?

Ⓐ The population of a town is decreasing at a rate of 3% per year. In 2005, there were 1600 people. Find the population in 2013.

Write the exponential decay function for this situation.

$$y = a(1 - r)^t$$
$$= 1600(1 - 0.03)^t$$
$$= 1600(0.97)^t$$

Find the value in 8 years.

$$y = 1600(0.97)^t$$
$$= 1600(0.97)^8$$
$$\approx 1254$$

After 8 years, the town's population will be about 1254 people.

Create a table of values to graph the function.

t	y	(t, y)
0	1600	(0, 1600)
8	1254	(8, 1254)
16	983	(16, 983)
24	770	(24, 770)
32	604	(32, 604)

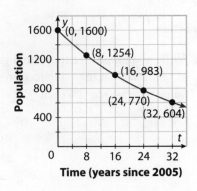

Determine the domain and range of the function.

The domain is the set of real numbers t such that $t \geq 0$. The range is the set of real numbers y such that $0 \leq y \leq 1600$.

The y-intercept is the value of y when $t = 0$, the number of people before it started to lose population.

B The value of a car is depreciating at a rate of 5% per year. In 2010, the car was worth $32,000. Find the value of the car in 2013.

Write the exponential decay function for this situation.

$y = a(1 - r)^t$

$= \boxed{} \left(1 - \boxed{} \right)^t$

$= \boxed{} \left(\boxed{} \right)^t$

Find the value in 3 years.

$y = a(1 - r)^t$

$= \boxed{} \left(\boxed{} \right)^t = \boxed{} \left(\boxed{} \right)^{\boxed{}} \approx \boxed{}$

After 3 years, the car's value will be $\boxed{}$.

Create a table of values to graph the function.

t	y	(t, y)
0		
1		
2		
3		

Determine the domain and range of the function.

The domain is the set of real numbers t such that $t \geq \boxed{}$
The range is the set of real numbers y such

that $\boxed{} \leq y \leq \boxed{}$.

The y-intercept, 32,000, is the value of y when $t = 0$, the _____ value of the car.

11. Find a recursive rule that models the exponential decay of $y = 1600(0.97)^t$.

_____

12. Find a recursive rule that models the exponential decay of $y = 32{,}000(0.95)^t$.

_____

Your Turn

13. The value of a boat is depreciating at a rate of 9% per year. In 2006, the boat was worth $17,800. Find the worth of the boat in 2013. Write an exponential decay function for this situation. Graph the function and state its domain and range. What does the y-intercept represent in the context of the problem?

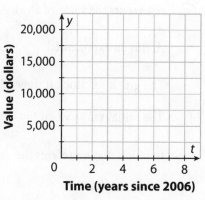

⚙ Explain 3 Comparing Exponential Growth and Decay

Graphs can be used to describe and compare exponential growth and exponential decay models over time.

Example 3 Use the graphs provided to write the equations of the functions. Then describe and compare the behaviors of both functions.

(A) The graph shows the value of two different shares of stock over the period of 4 years since they were purchased. The values have been changing exponentially.

The graph for Stock A shows that the value of the stock is decreasing as time increases.

The initial value, when $t = 0$, is 16. The value when $t = 1$ is 12. Since $12 \div 16 = 0.75$, the function that represents the value of Stock A after t years is $A(t) = 16(0.75)^t$. $A(t)$ is an exponential decay function.

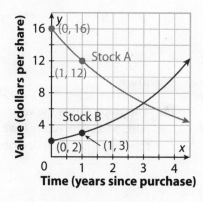

The graph for Stock B shows that the value of the stock is increasing as time increases.

The initial value, when $t = 0$, is 2. The value when $t = 1$ is 3. Since $3 \div 2 = 1.5$, the function that represents the value of Stock B after t years is $B(t) = 2(1.5)^t$. $B(t)$ is an exponential growth function.

The value of Stock A is going down over time. The value of Stock B is going up over time. The initial value of Stock A is greater than the initial value of Stock B. However, after about 3 years, the value of Stock B becomes greater than the value of Stock A.

B The graph shows the value of two different shares of stocks over the period of 4 years since they were purchased. The values have been changing exponentially.

The graph for Stock A shows that the value of the stock is

_____ as time increases.

The initial value, when $t = 0$, is ☐ . The value when $t = 1$

is ☐ . Since ☐ $\div$ ☐ $=$ ☐ , the function that

represents the value of Stock A after t years is $A(t) =$ ☐ $\left(\text{☐}\right)^t$.

$A(t)$ is an exponential _____ function.

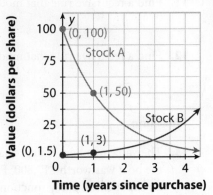

The graph for Stock B shows that the value of the stock is _____ as time increases.

The initial value, when $t = 0$, is ☐ . The value when $t = 1$ is ☐ . Since ☐ $\div$ ☐ $=$ ☐ , the

function that represents the value of Stock B after t years is $B(t) =$ ☐ (☐)t. $B(t)$ is an exponential

_____ function.

The value of Stock A is going _____ over time. The value of Stock B is going _____ over time.

The initial value of Stock A is _____ than the initial value of Stock B. However, after about ☐ years,

the value of Stock B becomes _____ than the value of Stock A.

Reflect

14. Discussion In the function $B(t) = 1.5(2)^t$, is it likely that the value of B can be accurately predicted in 50 years?

_____

_____

Your Turn

15. The graph shows the value of two different shares of stocks over the period of 4 years since they were purchased. The values have been changing exponentially. Use the graphs provided to write the equations of the functions. Then describe and compare the behaviors of both functions.

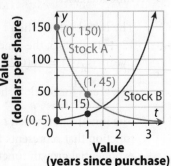

16. If $b > 1$ in a function of the form $y = ab^x$, is the function an example of exponential growth or an example of exponential decay?

_____

17. What is an asymptote of the function $y = 35(1.1)^x$?

_____

18. **Essential Question Check-In** What equation should be used when modeling an exponential function that models a decrease in a quantity over time?

_____

_____

 **Evaluate: Homework and Practice**

• Online Homework
• Hints and Help
• Extra Practice

Graph the function on a graphing calculator, and state its domain, range, end behavior, and an asymptote.

1. $f(x) = 300(1.16)^x$

2. $f(x) = 800(0.85)^x$

3. $f(x) = 65(1.64)^x$

4. $f(x) = 57(0.77)^x$

Write an exponential function to model each situation. Then find the value of the function after the given amount of time.

5. Annual sales for a company are $155,000 and increases at a rate of 8% per year for 9 years.

6. The value of a textbook is $69 and decreases at a rate of 15% per year for 11 years.

7. A new savings account is opened with $300 and gains 3.1% yearly for 5 years.

8. The value of a car is $7800 and decreases at a rate of 8% yearly for 6 years.

9. The starting salary at a construction company is fixed at $55,000 and increases at a rate of 1.8% yearly for 4 years.

10. The value of a piece of fine jewelry is $280 and decreases at a rate of 3% yearly for 7 years.

11. The population of a town is 24,000 and is increasing at a rate of 6% per year for 3 years.

12. The value of a new stadium is $3.4 million and decreases at a rate of 2.39% yearly for 10 years.

Write an exponential function for each situation. Graph each function and state its domain and range. Determine what the *y*-intercept represents in the context of the problem.

13. The value of a boat is depreciating at a rate of 7% per year. In 2004, the boat was worth $192,000. Find the value of the boat in 2013.

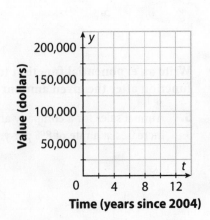

14. The value of a collectible baseball card is increasing at a rate of 0.5% per year. In 2000, the card was worth $1350. Find the value of the card in 2013.

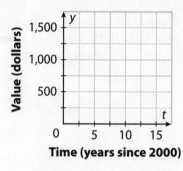

15. The value of an airplane is depreciating at a rate of 7% per year. In 2004, the airplane was worth $51.5 million. Find the value of the airplane in 2013.

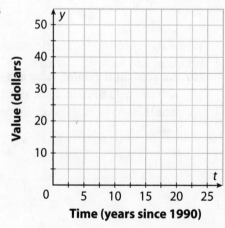

16. The value of a movie poster is increasing at a rate of 3.5% per year. In 1990, the poster was worth $20.25. Find the value of the poster in 2013.

17. The value of a couch is decreasing at a rate of 6.2% per year. In 2007, the couch was worth $1232. Find the value of the couch in 2014.

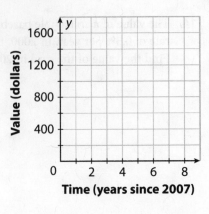

18. The population of a town is increasing at a rate of 2.2% per year. In 2001, the town had a population of 34,567. Find the population of the town in 2018.

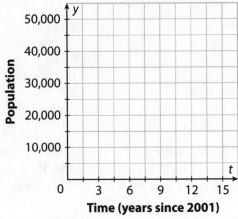

19. A house is losing value at a rate of 5.4% per year. In 2009, the house was value $131,000. Find the worth of the house in 2019.

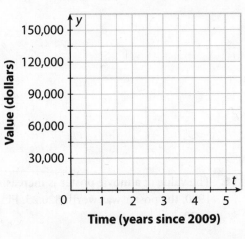

20. An account is gaining value at a rate of 4.94% per year. The account held $113 in 2005. What will the bank account hold in 2017?

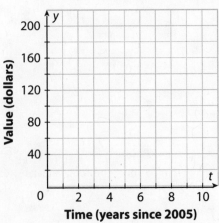

Use a calculator to graph the functions. Describe and compare each pair of functions.

21. $A(t) = 13(0.6)^t$ and $B(t) = 4(3.2)^t$

22. $A(t) = 9(0.4)^t$ and $B(t) = 0.6(1.4)^t$

23. $A(t) = 547(0.32)^t$ and $B(t) = 324(3)^t$

24. $A(t) = 2(0.6)^t$ and $B(t) = 0.2(1.4)^t$

25. Identify the y-intercept of each of the exponential functions.

    a. $3123(432{,}543)^x$ **d.** $76(89{,}047{,}832)^x$

    b. 0 **e.** 1

    c. $45(54)^x$

H.O.T.   **Focus on Higher Order Thinking**

26. Explain the Error A student was asked to find the value of a $2500 item after 4 years. The item was depreciating at a rate of 20% per year. What is wrong with the student's work?
$2500(0.2)^4$
$4

27. Make a Conjecture The value of a certain car can be modeled by the function $y = 18000(0.76)^t$, where t is time in years. Will the value of the function ever be 0?

28. Communicate Mathematical Ideas Explain how a graph of an exponential function may resemble the graph of a linear function.

Lesson Performance Task

Archeologists have several methods of determining the age of recovered artifacts. One method is radioactive dating.

All matter is made of atoms. Atoms, in turn, are made of protons, neutrons, and electrons. An "element" is defined as an atom with a given number of protons. Carbon, for example, has exactly 6 protons. Carbon atoms can, however, have different numbers of neutrons. These are known as "isotopes" of carbon. Carbon-12 has 6 neutrons, carbon-13 has 7 neutrons, and carbon-14 has 8 neutrons. All carbon-based life forms contain these different isotopes of carbon.

Carbon-12 and carbon-13 account for over 99% of all the carbon in living things. Carbon-14, however, accounts for approximately 1 part per trillion or 0.0000000001% of the total carbon in living things. More importantly, carbon-14 is unstable and has a half-life of approximately 5700 years. This means that, within the span of 5700 years, one-half of any amount of carbon will "decay" into another atom. In other words, if you had 10 g of carbon-14 today, only 5 g would remain after 5700 years.

But, as long as an organism is living, it keeps taking in and releasing carbon-14, so the level of it in the organism, as small as it is, remains constant. Once an organism dies, however, it no longer ingests carbon-14, so the level of carbon-14 in it drops due to radioactive decay. Because we know how much carbon-14 an organism had when it was alive, as well as how long it takes for that amount to become half of what it was, you can determine the age of the organism by comparing these two values.

Use the information presented to create a function that will model the amount of carbon-14 in a sample as a function of its age. Create the model $C(n)$ where C is the amount of carbon-14 in parts per quadrillion (1 part per trillion is 1000 parts per quadrillion) and n is the age of the sample in half-lives. Graph the model.

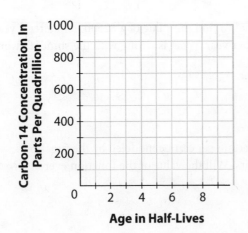

© Houghton Mifflin Harcourt Publishing Company • Image Credits: ©worker/Shutterstock

15.3 Using Exponential Regression Models

Essential Question: How can you use exponential regression to model data?

⊘ Explore 1 Fitting an Exponential Function to Data

One of the reasons data is valuable is that it allows us to make predictions for values that fall outside of the data set. In order to do this, the data needs to be synthesized into a function. An **exponential regression** is a graphing calculator tool used to generate an exponential equation that fits data exhibiting exponential growth or decay. The statistical tools on a graphing calculator offer several possible methods for finding a regression model for a set of data. Use a graphing calculator to find the exponential regression equation that models the data provided.

Number of Internet Hosts							
Years since 2001	0	1	2	3	4	5	6
Number (millions)	110	147	172	233	318	395	433

(A) Enter the data from the table on a graphing calculator, with years since 2001 in L1. Input the number of Internet hosts in L2. Create a scatter plot of the data on the calculator. Plot the data points on the given grid.

(B) Use the statistical calculation features of a graphing calculator to calculate the exponential regression equation for the data you entered into L1 and L2.

The exponential regression function is

_____.

(Round to three significant digits.)

(C) Graph the exponential regression equation with the data points on the calculator. Sketch a graph of the exponential regression equation on the grid with the data points that you plotted.

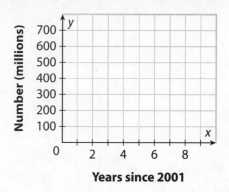

Years since 2001

Reflect

1. Discussion Which parameter, *a* or *b*, represents the initial value of the function? Explain how you know.

_____

_____

2. What is the growth rate of this exponential model?

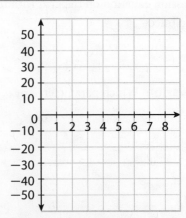

⊘ Explore 2 Plotting and Analyzing Residuals of Exponential Models

Recall that a residual is the difference between the actual y-value in the data set and the predicted y-value. Residuals can be used to assess how well a model fits a data set. If a model fits the data well, then the following are true.

- The numbers of positive and negative residuals are roughly equal.
- The residuals are randomly distributed about the x-axis on a residual plot.
- The absolute value of the residuals is small relative to the data values.

Ⓐ According to the data, in 2002 there were 147,000,000 Internet hosts. Find the y-value predicted by the model.

$y = ab^x \quad y = 113(1.27)^1 \quad y = \boxed{}$

The actual y-value from the data is _____.

Ⓑ Find the difference between the data y-value and the model's predicted y-value.

data $-$ model $= 147 - 143 = \boxed{}$

Ⓒ On your calculator, enter the regression equation as the rule for equation Y_1. Then view the table to find the y-values predicted by model (y_m). Complete the table.

	Number of Internet Hosts		
x	Actual y-value, y_d	Predicted y-value, y_m	Residual $y_d - y_m$
0	110	113	−3
1	147	143	
2	172		
3	233		
4	318		
5	395		
6	433		

Ⓓ Create a residual scatter plot by plotting the x-values and the residuals in the last column as the second coordinate.

3. **Multiple Representations** What does the residual plot reveal about the fit of the model? Does this agree with the correlation coefficient?

_____

_____

_____

4. **Look for Patterns** What can you infer about the accuracy of the model as it moves further away from the initial value? Explain.

_____

_____

🔑 Explain 1 Modeling with Exponential Functions

Exponential regression functions can be used to make predictions.

Example 1 Find an exponential regression function for the given data, and use the model to make predictions.

Ⓐ The table shows the population y of Middleton, where x is the number of years since the end of 2000.

Suppose Middleton's town council decides to build a new high school when its population exceeds 25,000.

When will the population likely exceed 25,000?

Years since 2000, x	Population, y
0	5,005
1	6,010
2	7,203
3	8,700
4	10,521
5	12,420
6	14,982
7	18,010

Enter the x-values into L1 and the y-values into L2 in a graphing calculator and view a scatter plot of the data.

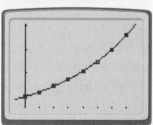

Find the exponential regression model and the regression coefficient for the data. Plot the regression function on the scatter plot.

$y = 5011(1.201)^x \quad r = 0.999$

Use the regression model to construct an equation in one variable to solve in order to determine the time x when the population will reach 25,000.

$25,000 = 5011(1.201)^x$

Enter $y = 25,000$ as Y_2 in the graphing calculator, and find the point of intersection.

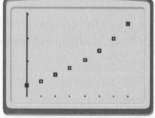

The intersection is at about $(8.792, 25,000)$. The population will reach 25,000 in about 9 years.

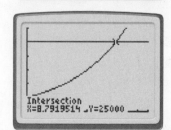

© Houghton Mifflin Harcourt Publishing Company

(B) The table shows the value of a car every year since it was purchased.

The owner plans to sell the car when it reaches 10% of its original value. How long will she have owned the car when she sells it?

Find the exponential regression model and the regression coefficient for the data. Round to four significant digits.

$y =$ ⬚ $r =$ ⬚

Use the regression model to construct an equation in one variable to solve in order to determine the time x when the value will reach 10% of the original value.

_____

The intersection is at _____. The car will have dropped to a value of $2500

after _____ years.

Age of Car, x	Value, y
0	$25,000.00
1	$21,462.50
2	$17,881.88
3	$15,506.66
4	$12,919.65
5	$11,203.56
6	$9,523.03
7	$7,934.28
8	$6,880.39
9	$5,732.52
10	$4,872.64

Reflect

5. Use the regression model to predict the population at the end of 2015 and at the end of 2030. Round to four significant digits. Which prediction is likely to be more accurate? Explain your reasoning.

_____

_____

_____

6. During what year does the population reach 25,000? Explain your reasoning.

_____

_____

7. Suppose the town will need a new high school already in place when the population reaches 25,000. How will the prediction above help the town make plans?

_____

_____

Create a model from the table of values and answer the questions.

8. The table shows the population of Arizona (in thousands) in each census from 1900–2000.

   Use the model to predict the census results from 2010 and compare the estimate to 6,392,017, the actual population according to the 2010 national census.

Years Since 1900 (x)	Population, (y)
0	123
10	204
20	334
30	436
40	499
50	750
60	1302
70	1771
80	2718
90	3665
100	5131

9. The table shows the population of box turtles in a Tennessee wildlife park over a period of 5 years.

   Use the model to predict the number of box turtles in the sixth year.

Year, (x)	Population, (y)
1	21
2	27
3	33
4	41
5	48

💬 Elaborate

10. What does a pattern in the plot of the regression data indicate?

    _____

    _____

11. **Discussion** While it is typically the best model for population growth, what are some factors that cause population growth to deviate from the exponential format?

    _____

    _____

    Essential Question Check-In What do the variables a and b represent in the regression equation $f(x) = ab^x$?

    _____

    _____

⭐ Evaluate: Homework and Practice

1. The concentration of ibuprofen in a person's blood was plotted each hour. An exponential model fit the data with $a = 400$ and $b = 0.71$. Interpret these parameters.

2. The table shows the temperature of a pizza over three-minute intervals after it is removed from the oven.

a. Find an exponential regression function for the data.

Time	Temperature
0	450
3	350
6	290
9	230
12	190
15	150
18	130
21	110

b. Complete the table to calculate the residuals. Plot the residuals on the scatter plot.

Time	Temperature	Predicted Temperature	Residual
0	450		
3	350		
6	290		
9	230		
12	190		
15	150		
18	130		
21	110		

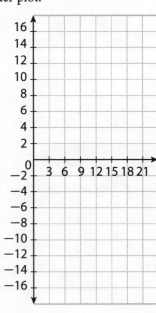

c. Graph y = 70 and the exponential regression function together with the graphing calculator, and find the intersection to predict how long it will take the pizza to cool down to 70° F.

For Exercises 3 and 4, use a graphing calculator to calculate the exponential regression equation, and use it to solve the problem.

3. The table shows the monthly membership in an online gaming club. When will there be more than 3000 members?

Month	Membership
0	2100
1	2163
2	2199
3	2249
4	2285
5	2329
6	2376
7	2415
8	2464
9	2514
10	2576

4. The table below shows a set of data that can be modeled with an exponential function. When will *y* be 6000?

x	y
0	15
1	22
2	34
3	50
4	75
5	113
6	170
7	258
8	388
9	575
10	857

5. A researcher is conducting an experiment on the rate that caffeine is eliminated from the body. Three volunteers are given four 8-ounce servings of coffee and asked to consume it as quickly as possible. The researchers then tested the caffeine remaining in each volunteer's blood every 20 minutes for 4 hours to determine the rate of elimination. The table gives the results in milligrams for the three volunteers.

Time (hr)	Student A (mg)	Student B (mg)	Student C (mg)
0	400	400	400
0.33	383	374	387
0.67	365	357	370
1.00	349	341	353
1.33	333	326	337
1.67	318	311	322
2.00	304	297	308
2.33	290	284	294
2.67	277	271	281
3.00	264	259	269
3.33	252	247	257
3.67	241	236	246
4.00	230	225	235

Find the hourly rate at which each student metabolizes caffeine and the time when each student will have 10 mg of caffeine in the blood.

6. The population of Boston, MA in thousands of people is given in the table below.

1990	572	2001	602
1991	561	2002	608
1992	552	2003	608
1993	552	2004	607
1994	551	2005	610
1995	558	2006	612
1996	556	2007	623
1997	556	2008	637
1998	555	2009	645
1999	555	2010	618
2000	590	2011	625

Find a model for the population of Boston as a function of years since 1990 using the even years and a model using the odd years. Compare the models.

Find an exponential model for the radioactive decay of the given isotope.

7. Nobelium-253

Minutes	Mass (grams)
0	10,000.00
1	6651.56
2	4424.33
3	2942.87
4	1957.47
5	1302.02
6	866.05
7	576.06
8	383.17
9	254.87
10	169.53

8. Manganese-52

Weeks	Mass (ounces)
0	200.00
1	83.97
2	35.26
3	14.80
4	6.22
5	2.61
6	1.10
7	0.46
8	0.19
9	0.08
10	0.03

Find an exponential model for the data in the given table.

9.

x	y
0	7
1	10.86
2	16.86
3	26.16
4	40.60
5	63
6	97.77
7	151.72
8	235.44
9	365.37
10	567

10.

x	y
0	2.6
1	3.91
2	5.88
3	8.85
4	13.31
5	20.01
6	30.1
7	45.27
8	68.10
9	102.42
10	154.05

11.

x	y
0	11
1	11.1
2	11.21
3	11.32
4	11.43
5	11.53
6	11.64
7	11.76
8	11.87
9	11.98
10	12.09

12.

x	y
0	4
1	7.36
2	13.54
3	24.92
4	45.85
5	84.36
6	155.23
7	285.62
8	525.54
9	966.99
10	1779.26

Lesson 3

13. The yearly profits of Company A are shown in the table. Use the information given to find a function P(t) that models the yearly profits P of the company as a function of t, the number of years since 1995.

Year	Profit (millions)
1995	5.00
1996	5.15
1997	5.30
1998	5.47
1999	5.63
2000	5.79
2001	5.97
2002	6.15
2003	6.33
2004	6.52
2005	6.71

14. Find the Error A student is doing homework and comes to the following question.

The table shows the balance in a student's savings account for 10 years. The student hasn't deposited or withdrawn any money over the time period. Find the exponential model for the student's balance as a function of time.

The student performs exponential regression on the data and compares the result with the answer in the back of the text.

The text gives the solution as $b(t) = 200(1.05)^t$, but the student's model is $b(t) = 190.48(1.05)^t$. Find the error in the student's calculations or explain why the student's model is correct.

Year	Balance
2001	$200.00
2002	$210.00
2003	$220.50
2004	$231.53
2005	$243.10
2006	$255.26
2007	$268.02
2008	$281.42
2009	$295.49
2010	$310.27

15. Determine whether each of the following represents an increasing exponential function, a decreasing exponential function, or a non-exponential function. Select the correct answer for each part.

a. $f(t) = \frac{1}{2}t^5$ ○ Increasing exponential   ○ Decreasing exponential   ○ Non-exponential

b.

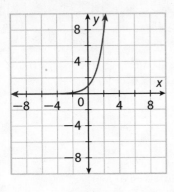

○ Increasing exponential   ○ Decreasing exponential   ○ Non-exponential

c.

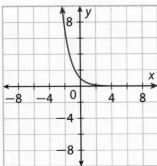

○ Increasing exponential   ○ Decreasing exponential   ○ Non-exponential

d. $f(x) = 20(0.85)^x$ ○ Increasing exponential   ○ Decreasing exponential   ○ Non-exponential

e. $f(x) = 7(1.16)^x$ ○ Increasing exponential   ○ Decreasing exponential   ○ Non-exponential

f.

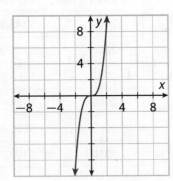

○ Increasing exponential   ○ Decreasing exponential   ○ Non-exponential

16. **Critique Reasoning** The absolute values of the residuals in Mark's regression model are less than 20. Working on a different data set, Sandy obtained residuals in the hundreds. This led Mark to conclude his data is a better fit than Sandy's. Explain why Mark is wrong to base his assessment of their regression models on the values of the residuals.

17. **Make a Conjecture** When Chris used exponential regression on the Arizona population data, he obtained the following results: $a = 186$, $b = 1.026$, $r = 0.813$, which differed from the given exponential regression function of $f(x) = 135.9(1.037)^x$. When he reviewed the data in his lists, he found he had entered a number incorrectly. Is it more likely that his error was in entering the last population value too high or too low? Justify your reasoning.

18. **Draw Conclusions** Madelyn has recorded the number of bacteria on her growth plate every hour for 3 hours. She finds that a linear model fits her data better than the expected exponential model. What should she do to improve her model?

Lesson Performance Task

A student with an interest-bearing savings account reports the yearly balance in her account in the following table.

Years Since Opening the Account	Balance
1	$6152.42
2	$6305.22
3	$6459.59
4	$6626.83
5	$6793.00
6	$6965.05
7	$7148.27
8	$7322.20
9	$7505.25
10	$7710.33
11	$7906.32
12	$8092.77

Perform an exponential regression on the data. Then estimate the amount of money the student placed in the account initially and the yearly interest rate.

15.4 Comparing Linear and Exponential Models

Essential Question: How can you recognize when to use a linear model or an exponential model?

Explore 1   Comparing Constant Change and Constant Percent Change

Suppose that you are offered a job that pays you $1000 the first month with a raise every month after that. You can choose a $100 raise or a 10% raise. Which option would you choose? What if the raise were 8%, 6%, or 4%?

(A) Find the monthly salaries for the first three months. Record the results in the table, rounded to the nearest dollar.

- For the $100 raise, enter 1000 into your graphing calculator, press ENTER, enter +100, press ENTER, and then press ENTER repeatedly.

- For the 10% raise, enter 1000, press ENTER, enter × 1.10, press ENTER, and then press ENTER repeatedly.

- For the other raises, multiply by 1.08, 1.06, or 1.04.

Monthly Salary after Indicated Monthly Raise					
Month	$100	10%	8%	6%	4%
0	$1000	$1000	$1000	$1000	$1000
1	$1100	$1100	$1080	$1060	$1040
2					
3					

(B) For each option, find how much the salary changes each month, both in dollars and as a percent of the previous month's salary. Round the each percent to the nearest whole number. Record the values in the table.

Change in Salary per Month for Indicated Monthly Raise										
Interval	$100		10%		8%		6%		4%	
	$	%	$	%	$	%	$	%	$	%
0 – 1	100	10	100	10	80	8	60	6	40	4
1 – 2	100			10		8		6		4
2 – 3	100			10		8		6		4

(C) Continue the calculations you did in Part A until you find the number of months it takes for each salary with a percent raise to exceed the salary with the $100 raise. Record the number of months in the table below.

Number of Months until Salary with Percent Raise Exceeds Salary with $100 Raise			
10%	8%	6%	4%
2			

Reflect

1. **Discussion** Compare and contrast the salary changes per month for the raise options. Explain the source of any differences.

_____

_____

2. **Discussion** Would you choose a constant change per month or a percent increase per month? What would you consider when deciding? Explain your reasoning.

_____

_____

⊘ Explore 2 Exploring How Linear and Exponential Functions Grow

Linear functions change by equal differences, while exponential functions change by equal factors. Now you will explore the proofs of these statements. $x_2 - x_1$ and $x_4 - x_3$ represent two intervals in the x-values of a function.

(A) Complete the proof that linear functions grow by equal differences over equal intervals.

Given: $x_2 - x_1 = x_4 - x_3$

   f is linear function of the form $f(x) = mx + b$.

Prove: $f(x_2) - f(x_1) = f(x_4) - f(x_3)$

Proof: 1. $x_2 - x_1 = x_4 - x_3$ Given

   2. $m(x_2 - x_1) = \boxed{} \, x_4 - x_3$ Multiplication Property of Equality

   3. $mx_2 - \boxed{} = mx_4 - \boxed{}$ Distributive Property

   4. $mx_2 + b - mx_1 - b =$ Addition & Subtraction Properties of Equality

     $mx_4 + \boxed{} - mx_3 - \boxed{}$

   5. $mx_2 + b - (mx_1 + b) =$ Distributive property

     $mx_4 + b - \left(\boxed{} \right)$

   6. $f(x_2) - f(x_1) = \left(\boxed{} \right)$ Definition of $f(x)$

© Houghton Mifflin Harcourt Publishing Company

(B) Complete the proof that exponential functions grow by equal factors over equal intervals.

Given: $x_2 - x_1 = x_4 - x_3$

g is an exponential function of the form $g(x) = ab^x$.

Prove: $\dfrac{g(x_2)}{g(x_1)} = \dfrac{g(x_4)}{g(x_3)}$

Proof: 1. $x_2 - x_1 = x_4 - x_3$ Given

2. $b^{(x_2 - x_1)} = b^{(x_4 - x_3)}$ If $x = y$, then $b^x = b^y$.

3. $\dfrac{b^{x_2}}{b^{x_1}} = \dfrac{b^{x_4}}{\boxed{}}$ Quotient of Powers Property

4. $\dfrac{ab^{x_2}}{ab^{x_1}} = \dfrac{ab^{x_4}}{\boxed{}}$ Multiplication Property of Equality

5. $\dfrac{g(x_2)}{g(x_1)} = \dfrac{gx_4}{\boxed{}}$ Definition of $g(x)$

3. In the previous proofs, what do $x_2 - x_1$ and $x_4 - x_3$ represent?

🔑 Explain 1   Comparing Linear and Exponential Functions

When comparing raises, a fixed dollar increase can be modeled by a linear function and a fixed percent increase can be modeled by an exponential function.

Example 1   Compare the two salary plans listed by using a graphing calculator. Will Job B ever have a higher monthly salary than Job A? If so, after how many months will this occur?

(A) • Job A: $1000 for the first month with a $100 raise every month thereafter

• Job B: $1000 for the first month with a 1% raise every month thereafter

Write the functions that represent the monthly salaries. Let t represent the number of elapsed months.

Job A: $S_A(t) = 1000 + 100t$ Job B: $S_B(t) = 1000(1.01)^t$

Graph the functions on a calculator using Y_1 for Job A and Y_2 for Job B. Estimate the number of months it takes for the salaries to become equal using the intersect feature of the calculator. At $x \approx 364$ months, the salaries are equal.

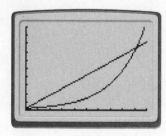
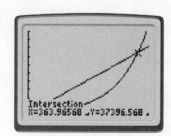

Go to the estimated intersection point in the table feature. Find the first *x*-value at which Y_2 exceeds Y_1. Job B will have a higher monthly salary than Job A after 364 months.

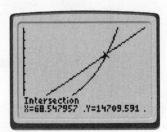

(B) • Job A: $1000 for the first month with a $200 raise every month thereafter

• Job B: $1000 for the first month with a 4% raise every month thereafter

Write the functions that represent the monthly salaries. Let *t* represent the number of elapsed months.

Job A: $S_A(t) = \boxed{} + \boxed{} \, t$ Job B: $S_B(t) = \boxed{} \left(\boxed{} \right)^t$

Graph the functions on a calculator and use this graph to estimate the number of months it takes for the salaries to become equal.

At $x \approx \boxed{}$ months, the salaries are equal.

Job B will have a higher salary than Job A after $\boxed{}$ months.

Reflect

4. In Example 1A, which job offers a monthly salary that reflects a constant change, and which offers a monthly salary that reflects a constant percent change?

_____

_____

5. Describe an exponential increase in terms of multiplication.

_____

_____

Your Turn

6. • Job A: $2000 for the first month with a $300 raise every month thereafter

• Job B: $1500 for the first month with a 5% raise every month thereafter

⊘ Explain 2 Choosing between Linear and Exponential Models

Both linear equations and exponential equations and their graphs can model real-world situations. Determine whether the dependent variable appears to change by a common difference or a common ratio to select the correct model.

Example 2 Determine whether each situation is better described by an increasing or decreasing function, and whether a linear or exponential regression should be used. Then find a regression equation for each situation by using a graphing calculator.

Ⓐ A gas has an initial pressure of 165 torr. Its pressure was then measured every 5 seconds for 25 seconds.

Pressure over Time		Change per Interval	
Time (s)	Pressure (torr)	Difference $P(t_n) - P(t_n - 1)$	Factor $\dfrac{P(t_n)}{P(t_n - 1)}$
0	165		
5	153	−12	0.93
10	142	−11	0.93
15	129	−13	0.91
20	116	−13	0.90
25	102	−14	0.88

The dependent variable is pressure, and it is decreasing while the number of seconds is increasing. This means that the function is decreasing.

Note that because the factor changes are relatively close to equal while the difference changes are not, an exponential regression model should be used.

Perform the exponential regression analysis and evaluate the fit.

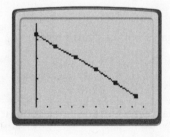
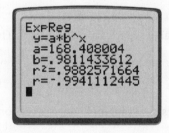

Note that the *r*-value suggests a good fit.

Generate a Residual Plot
for the data.

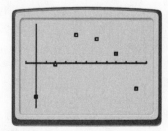

The analysis of residuals suggests a good fit.

(B) A closed container holding an unspecified gas has an initial pressure of 44 torr. The container was then placed over a flame and its pressure was measured every 5 minutes for 25 minutes.

Pressure over Time		Change per Interval	
Time (min)	Pressure (torr)	Difference $P(t_n) - P(t_n - 1)$	Factor $\dfrac{P(t_n)}{P(t_n - 1)}$
0	44		
5	49		
10	60		
15	72		
20	90		
25	105		

Is the function increasing or decreasing? Explain. _____

_____

Which changes are closer to being equal, the differences or the factors? _____

Which type of regressions should be used? _____

Perform the regression analysis and evaluate the fit.

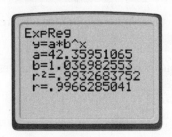
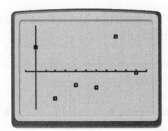

Note that the *r*-value suggests a _____ fit. The analysis of residuals suggests a _____ fit.

Reflect

7. What would the residual plot look like if an exponential regression was not a good fit for a function?

_____

_____

Determine whether this situation is better described by an increasing or decreasing function, and whether a linear or exponential regression should be used. Then find a regression equation.

8. A barrel of gasoline has an initial pressure of 432 torr. Its pressure was then measured every 5 minutes for 25 minutes.

Pressure over Time		Change per Interval	
Time (min)	Pressure (torr)	Difference $P(t_n) - P(t_n - 1)$	Factor $\dfrac{P(t_n)}{P(t_n - 1)}$
0	432		
5	454		
10	499		
15	534		
20	582		
25	611		

🗨 Elaborate

9. In the long term, which type of raise will guarantee a larger paycheck: a fixed raise or a percentage raise?

_____

10. What type of function is typically represented by a linear function?

_____

_____

11. Essential Question Check-In An exponential growth model is appropriate when the increase per

successive interval _____.

State whether each situation is best represented by an exponential or linear function. Then write an exponential or linear function for the model and state whether the model is increasing or decreasing.

1. Enrollment at a school is initially 454 students and grows by 3% per year.

2. A salesperson initially earns $50,434 dollars per year and receives a yearly raise of $675.

3. A customer borrows $450 at 5% interest compounded annually.

4. A wildlife park has 35 zebras and sends 1 zebra to another wildlife park each year.

5. The value of a house is $546,768 and decreases by 3% each year.

6. The population of a town is 66,666 people and decreases by 160 people each year.

7. A business has a total income of $236,000 and revenues go up by 6.4% per year.

Use a graphing calculator to answer each question.

8. **Statistics** Companies A and B each have 100 employees. If Company A increases its workforce by 31 employees each month and Company B increases its workforce by an average of 10% each month, when will Company B have more employees than Company A?

9. **Finance** Employees A and B each initially earn $18.00 per hour. If Employee A receives a $1.50 per hour raise each year and Employee B receives a 4% raise each year, when will Employee B make more per hour than Employee A?

10. **Finance** Account A and B each start out with $400. If Account A earns $45 each year and Account B earns 5% of its value each year, when will Account B have more money than Account A?

11. **Finance** Stock A starts out with $900 and gains $50 each month. Stock B starts out with $800 and gains 11% each month. When will Stock B be worth more money than Stock A?

12. Finance Accounts A and B both start out with $800. If Account A earns $110 per year and Account B earns 3% of its value each year, when will Account B have more money than Account A?

13. Finance Two factory workers, A and B, each earn $24.00 per hour. If Employee A receives a $0.75 per hour raise each year and Employee B receives 1.9% raise each year, when will Employee B make more per hour than Employee A?

14. Statistics Two car manufacturers, A and B, each have 500 employees. If Manufacturer A increases its workforce by 15 employees each month and Manufacturer B increases its workforce by 1% each month, when will Manufacturer B have more employees?

15. Finance Stock A is initially worth $1300 and loses $80 each month. Stock B is initially worth $400 and gains 9.5% each month. When will Stock B be worth more than Stock A?

Biology Each table shows an animal population's change over time. Determine whether each situation is best described by an increasing or decreasing function and whether a linear or exponential regression should be used. Then find a regression equation for each situation. Evaluate the fit.

16.

x	y	difference $y_2 - y_1$	factor $\frac{y_2}{y_1}$
1	49		
2	58		
3	70		
4	83		
5	101		

17.

x	y	difference $y_2 - y_1$	factor $\frac{y_2}{y_1}$
1	31		
2	32		
3	34		
4	35		
5	37		

18.

x	y	difference $y_2 - y_1$	factor $\frac{y_2}{y_1}$
1	46		
2	61		
3	83		
4	107		
5	143		

19.

x	y	difference $y_2 - y_1$	factor $\frac{y_2}{y_1}$
1	22		
2	35		
3	60		
4	104		
5	189		

20. Using the given exponential functions, state *a* and *b*.

   a. $y = 3(4)^x$ **b.** $y = -5(8)^x$ **c.** $y = 4(0.6)^x$

   d. $y = -5(0.9)^x$ **e.** $y = 2^x$

21. Suppose that you are offered a job that pays you $2000 the first month with a raise every month after that. You can choose a $400 raise or a 15% raise. Which option would you choose? What if the raise were 10%, 8%, or 5%?

Monthly Salary after Indicated Monthly Raise					
Month	$400	15%	10%	8%	5%
0	$2000	$2000	$2000	$2000	$2000
1	$2400	$2300	$2200	$2160	$2100
2					
3					

Change in Salary per Month for Indicated Monthly Raise										
Interval	$400		15%		10%		8%		5%	
	$	%	$	%	$	%	$	%	$	%
0–1	400	20	300	15	200	10	160	8	100	5
1–2	400			15		10		8		5
2–3	400			15		10		8		5

Number of Months until Salary with Percent Raise Exceeds Salary with $400 Raise			
15%	10%	8%	5%
5			

22. Draw Conclusions Liam would like to put $6000 in savings for a 5-year period. Should he choose a simple interest account that pays an interest rate of 5% of the principal (initial amount) each year or a compounded interest account that pays an interest rate of 1.5% of the total account value each month?

23. Critical Thinking Why will an exponential growth function always eventually exceed a linear growth function?

24. Explain the Error JoAnn analyzed the following data showing the number of cells in a bacteria culture over time.

Time (min)	0	6.9	10.8	13.5	15.7	17.4
Cells	8	16	24	32	40	48

She concluded that since the number of cells showed a constant change and the time did not, neither a linear function nor an exponential function modeled the number of cells over time well. Was she correct?

Lesson Performance Task

Two major cities each have a population of 25,000 people.
The population of City A increases by about 150 people per year.
The population of City B increases by about 0.5% per year.

a. Find the population increase for each city for the first
5 years. Round to the nearest whole number, if necessary.
Then compare the changes in the populations of each city
per year.

b. Will City B ever have a larger population than City A? If
so, what year will this occur?

Exponential Equations and Models

Essential Question: How can you use exponential equations to represent real-world situations?

KEY EXAMPLE   *(Lesson 15.2)*

A comic book is sold for \$3, and its value increases by 6% each year after it is sold. Write an exponential growth function to find the value of the comic book in 25 years. Then graph it and state its domain and range. What does the *y*-intercept represent?

Write the exponential growth function for this situation.

$$y = a(1 + r)^t$$
$$= 3(1 + 0.06)^t$$
$$= 3(1.06)^t$$

Find the value in 25 years.

$$y = 3(1.06)^t$$
$$= 3(1.06)^{25}$$
$$\approx 12.88$$

After 25 years, the comic book will be worth approximately \$12.88.

Create a table of values to graph the function.

t	y	(t, y)
0	3	(0, 3)
5	4.01	(5, 4.01)
10	5.37	(10, 5.37)
15	7.19	(15, 7.19)
20	9.62	(20, 9.62)
25	12.88	(25, 12.88)
30	17.23	(30, 17.23)

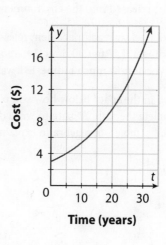

The domain is the set of real numbers t such that $t \geq 0$.

The range is the set of real numbers y such that $y \geq 3$.

The *y*-intercept is the value of y when $t = 0$, which is the time when the comic book was sold.

EXERCISES

Solve each equation for _x_. *(Lesson 15.1)*

1. $3(2)^x = 96$

2. $\dfrac{5^x}{25} = 25$

3. The value of a textbook is \$120 and decreases at a rate of 12% per year. Write a function to model the situation, and then find the value of the textbook after 9 years. *(Lesson 15.2)*

Find an exponential model for the data in the given table. *(Lesson 15.3)*

4.

x	0	1	2	3	4	5	6	7	8	9	10
y	9	12.85	16.89	28.15	42.58	65.1	99.34	153	237.6	339.2	478.61

State whether each situation is best represented by an exponential or linear function. Then write an exponential or linear function for the model and state whether the model is increasing or decreasing. *(Lesson 15.4)*

5. A customer borrows \$950 at 6% interest compounded annually.

6. The population of a town is 8548 people and decreases by 90 people each year.

MODULE PERFORMANCE TASK

Half-Life

The half-life of iodine-131 is 8 days, and the half-life of cesium-137 is 30 years. Both of these isotopes can be released into the environment during a nuclear accident.

Suppose that a nuclear reactor accident released 100 grams of cesium-137 and an unknown amount of iodine-131. After 40 days the amount of iodine-131 is equal to the amount of cesium-137. About how much iodine-131 was released by the accident?

Start by listing in the space below how you plan to tackle the problem. Then use your own paper to complete the task. Be sure to write down all your data and assumptions. Then use numbers, graphs, tables, or algebra to explain how you reached your conclusion.

© Houghton Mifflin Harcourt Publishing Company

(Ready) to Go On?

15.1–15.4 Exponential Equations and Models

- Online Homework
- Hints and Help
- Extra Practice

1. Mike has a savings account with the bank. The bank pays him annual interest of 1.5%. He has $4000 and wonders how much he will have in the account in 5 years. Write an exponential function to model the situation and then find how much he will have. *(Lesson 15.1)*

State each function's domain, range, and end behavior. *(Lesson 15.2)*

2. $f(x) = 900(0.65)^x$

3. $f(x) = 400(1.23)^x$

4. The table shows the temperature of a pizza over three-minute intervals after it is removed from the oven.

Time, (x)	0	4	8	12	16
Temperature, (y)	450	340	240	190	145

Create a model describing the data and use it to predict the temperature after 20 minutes. *(Lesson 15.3)*

5. Account A and B each start out with $600. If Account A earns $50 each year and Account B earns 6% of its value each year, after how many years will Account B have more money than Account A? *(Lesson 15.4)*

ESSENTIAL QUESTION

6. How can you identify an exponential equation?

© Houghton Mifflin Harcourt Publishing Company

Assessment Readiness

1. Consider the end behavior of $f(x) = 75(1.25)^x$. Select True or False for each statement.

   A. As $x \to -\infty, y \to -\infty$. ○ True ○ False

   B. As $x \to -\infty, y \to 0$. ○ True ○ False

   C. As $x \to \infty, y \to \infty$. ○ True ○ False

2. An engineer took the following measurements: 3.22 cm, 14.1 cm, 18 cm, and 24.025 cm. Choose True or False for each statement.

   A. The most precise measurement has 4 significant digits. ○ True ○ False

   B. Written using the correct number of significant digits, the sum of the measurements should be rounded to the ones place. ○ True ○ False

   C. The least precise measurement has 2 significant digits. ○ True ○ False

3. Solve $36(3)^x = 4$. What is the value of x? Explain how you got your answer.

4. Consider the following situation: enrollment at a school is initially 322 students and grows by 4% per year. Write an equation to represent this situation, and use it to predict the number of students at the school in 5 years.

Assessment Readiness

- Online Homework
- Hints and Help
- Extra Practice

1. Is the given equation equivalent to $V = IR$?

   A. $R = IV$ ○ Yes   ○ No

   B. $R = \dfrac{V}{I}$ ○ Yes   ○ No

   C. $I = \dfrac{V}{R}$ ○ Yes   ○ No

2. Consider the graph of $16x - 2y = 48$. Select True or False for each statement.

   A. The slope is 8.   ○ True   ○ False

   B. The y-intercept is 4.   ○ True   ○ False

   C. The x-intercept is 3.   ○ True   ○ False

3. Consider the sequence 8, 4, 0, −4,…. Determine if each statement is True or False.

   A. It is a geometric sequence.   ○ True   ○ False

   B. The fifth term is −8.   ○ True   ○ False

   C. $f(10) = -28$.   ○ True   ○ False

4. Write an explicit and recursive rule for the geometric sequence −5, 10, −20, 40,… and use it to find the 12th term of the sequence. Is each statement correct?

   A. The recursive rule is $f(1) = -2$;   ○ Yes   ○ No
   $f(n) = 5 \cdot f(n - 1)$.

   B. The explicit rule is   ○ Yes   ○ No
   $f(n) = -5(-2)^{n-1}$.

   C. The 12th term is −20,480.   ○ Yes   ○ No

5. Consider the end behavior of $f(x) = -6\left(\dfrac{1}{2}\right)^x$. Is each statement True or False?

   A. As $x \rightarrow -\infty$, $y \rightarrow -\infty$ ○ True   ○ False

   B. As $x \rightarrow \infty$, $y \rightarrow 0$ ○ True   ○ False

   C. As $x \rightarrow \infty$, $y \rightarrow -\infty$ ○ True   ○ False

6. Solve each equation. Is the given solution correct?

A. $5(2x - 7) = -6x - 27; x = \frac{1}{2}$ ⭕ Yes ⭕ No

B. $6 - \frac{2}{3}x = -2x - 2; x = -3$ ⭕ Yes ⭕ No

C. $9p = 3(4 - p) + 12; p = 12$ ⭕ Yes ⭕ No

7. Describe the end behavior of $y = -2(3)^{-x}$.

8. Graph $f(x) = 4\left(\frac{1}{2}\right)^x$. What are the domain and range of the function?

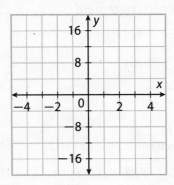

9. Solve $3(16)^{\frac{x}{4}} = 192$ for x. Show your work.

Performance Tasks

★**10.** Francesca invents the recursive rule $f(1) = 3$, $f(n) = f(n - 1) \cdot f(n - 1)$. Write the first four terms of the sequence. Is the sequence geometric? Explain why or why not.

★★**11.** Billy earns money by mowing lawns for the summer. He offers two payment plans.

> **Plan 1:** Pay $250 for the entire summer.
> **Plan 2:** Pay $1 the first week, $2 the second week, $4 the third week, and so on.

A. Do the payments for Plan 2 form a geometric sequence? Explain.

B. If you were one of Billy's customers, which plan would you choose? (Assume that the summer is 10 weeks long.) Explain your choice.

★★★**12.** As a promotion, a clothing store draws the name of one of its customers each week. The prize is a coupon for the store. If the winner is not present at the drawing, he or she cannot claim the prize, and the amount of the coupon increases for the following week's drawing. The function $f(x) = 20(1.2)^x$ gives the amount of the coupon in dollars after x weeks of the prize going unclaimed.

A. What is the amount of the coupon after 2 weeks of the prize going unclaimed?

B. After how many weeks of the prize going unclaimed will the amount of the coupon be greater than $100?

C. What is the original amount of the coupon?

D. Find the percent increase each week.

E. Do you think it would be wise for the owner of the store to set a limit on the number of weeks a prize can go unclaimed? Why or why not?

Financial Research Analyst The graph shows the value of two different shares of stock over the period of four years since they were purchased. The values have been changing exponentially.

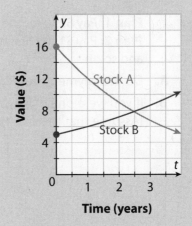

a. For Stock A, which model fits the graph, exponential growth or exponential decay? Find the initial value and the growth or decay factor.

b. For Stock B, which model fits the graph, exponential growth or exponential decay? Find the initial value and the growth or decay factor.

c. According to the graph, after how many years was the value of Stock A about equal to the value of Stock B? What was that value?

d. After how many years was the value of Stock A about twice the value of Stock B? Explain how you found your answer.

UNIT 7

Transformations and Congruence

MODULE 16
Tools of Geometry

MODULE 17
Transformations and Symmetry

MODULE 18
Congruent Figures

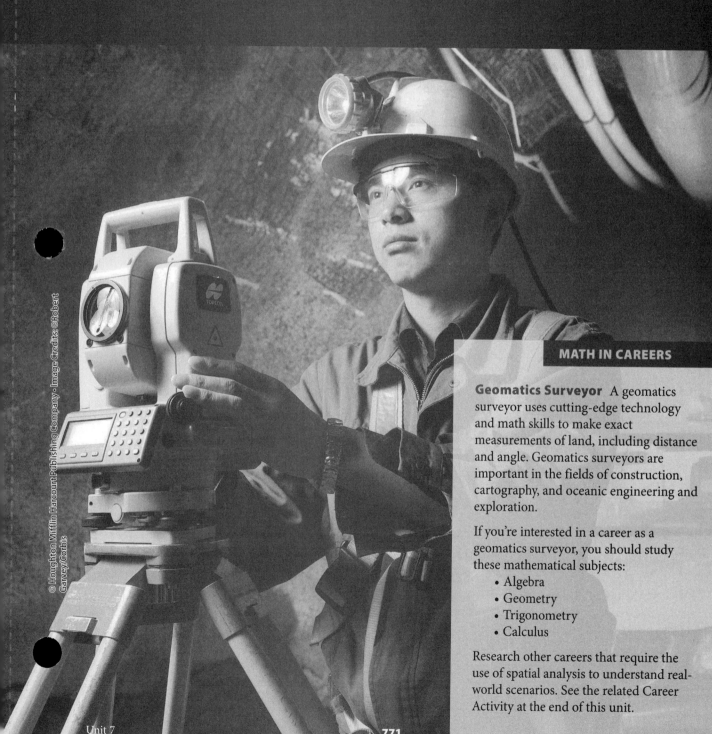

© Houghton Mifflin Harcourt Publishing Company • Image Credits: ©Robert Garvey/Corbis

MATH IN CAREERS

Geomatics Surveyor A geomatics surveyor uses cutting-edge technology and math skills to make exact measurements of land, including distance and angle. Geomatics surveyors are important in the fields of construction, cartography, and oceanic engineering and exploration.

If you're interested in a career as a geomatics surveyor, you should study these mathematical subjects:
• Algebra
• Geometry
• Trigonometry
• Calculus

Research other careers that require the use of spatial analysis to understand real-world scenarios. See the related Career Activity at the end of this unit.

Reading Start-Up

Vocabulary

Review Words

✔ midpoint *(punto medio)*

✔ angle *(ángulo)*

✔ transformation *(transformación)*

✔ complementary angle *(ángulo complementario)*

✔ supplementary angle *(ángulo suplementario)*

✔ acute angle *(ángulo agudo)*

✔ obtuse angle *(ángulo obtuso)*

Preview Words

angle bisector *(bisectriz de un ángulo)*

vertex *(vértice)*

collinear *(colineales)*

postulate *(postulado)*

Visualize Vocabulary

Use the ✔ words to complete the chart. You may put more than one word in each box.

Angle	Description	Example		
	Angle whose measure is less than 90°	40°	50°	140°
	Angle whose measure is greater than 90°	110°	None	70°

Understand Vocabulary

Complete the sentences using the preview words.

1. A(n) _____ is a ray that divides an angle into two angles that both have the same measure.

2. The common endpoint of two rays that form an angle is the _____ of the angle.

3. Points that lie on the same line are _____ .

Active Reading

Booklet Before beginning each module, create a booklet to help you organize what you learn. As you study each lesson, draw the different graphical concepts that you learn and write their definitions.

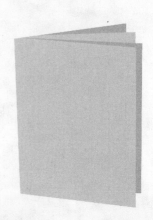

Tools of Geometry

Essential Question: How can you use the tools of geometry to solve real-world problems?

REAL WORLD VIDEO
Check out how the tools of geometry can be used to solve real-world problems, such as planning a park fountain's location to be the same distance from the park's three entrances.

MODULE PERFORMANCE TASK PREVIEW

How Far Is It?

How does your cellphone know how far away the nearest restaurant is? In this module, you'll explore how apps and search engines use GPS coordinates to calculate distances. So enter your present location and let's find out!

Complete these exercises to review skills you will need for this module.

Algebraic Representations of Transformations

Example 1

Shift $y = \sqrt{x}$ horizontally 2 units to the right.

$(0, 0)$ to $(2, 0)$	Write the starting point and its transformation.
$y - 0 = \sqrt{x - 2}$	Use the transformed point to write the equation.
$y = \sqrt{x - 2}$	Simplify.

• Online Homework
• Hints and Help
• Extra Practice

Transform the equations.

1. Shift $y = 5x$ 3 units up.

2. Stretch $y = 5x$ vertically about the fixed x-axis by a factor of 2.

3. Shift $y = 5\sqrt{x} + 3$ horizontally 2 units to the right and stretch by a factor of 3. (Stretch vertically about the fixed $y = 3$ line.)

Angle Relationships

Example 2

Find the angle complementary to the given angle, $75°$.

$x + 75° = 90°$	Write as an equation.
$x = 90° - 75°$	Solve for x.
$x = 15°$	

Find the complementary angle.

4. $20°$ _____

5. $35°$ _____

6. $67°$ _____

Find the supplementary angle.

7. $80°$ _____

8. $65°$ _____

9. $34°$ _____

Distance and Midpoint Formulas

Example 3

Find the distance between $(2, 3)$ and $(5, 7)$.

$\sqrt{(5 - 2)^2 + (7 - 3)^2}$	Apply the distance formula.
$= \sqrt{9 + 16}$	Simplify each square.
$= 5$	Add and find the square root.

Find each distance and midpoint for the given points.

10. The points $(6, 14)$ and $(1, 2)$ Distance _____   Midpoint _____

11. The points $(4, 6)$ and $(19, 14)$ Distance _____   Midpoint _____

16.1 Segment Length and Midpoints

Essential Question: How do you draw a segment and measure its length?

Resource
Locker

Explore Exploring Basic Geometric Terms

In geometry, some of the names of figures and other terms will already be familiar from everyday life. For example, a *ray* like a beam of light from a spotlight is both a familiar word and a geometric figure with a mathematical definition.

The most basic figures in geometry are *undefined terms*, which cannot be defined using other figures. The terms *point*, *line*, and *plane* are undefined terms. Although they do not have formal definitions, they can be described as shown in the table.

Undefined Terms		
Term	**Geometric Figure**	**Ways to Name the Figure**
A **point** is a specific location. It has no dimension and is represented by a dot.	• *P*	point *P*
A **line** is a connected straight path. It has no thickness and it continues forever in both directions.	*A* *B* *ℓ*	line *ℓ*, line *AB*, line *BA*, $\overleftrightarrow{AB}$, or $\overleftrightarrow{BA}$
A **plane** is a flat surface. It has no thickness and it extends forever in all directions.	*X* *Z* *R* *Y*	plane *R* or plane *XYZ*

In geometry, the word *between* is another undefined term, but its meaning is understood from its use in everyday language. You can use undefined terms as building blocks to write definitions for defined terms, as shown in the table.

Defined Terms		
Term	**Geometric Figure**	**Ways to Name the Figure**
A **line segment** (or *segment*) is a portion of a line consisting of two points (called **endpoints**) and all points between them.	*C* *D*	segment *CD*, segment *DC*, $\overline{CD}$, or $\overline{DC}$
A **ray** is a portion of a line that starts at a point (the *endpoint*) and continues forever in one direction.	*P* *Q*	ray *PQ* or $\overrightarrow{PQ}$

You can use points to sketch lines, segments, rays, and planes.

(A) Draw two points *J* and *K*. Then draw a line through them. (Remember that a line shows arrows at both ends.)

(B) Draw two points *J* and *K* again. This time, draw the line segment with endpoints *J* and *K*.

(C) Draw a point *K* again and draw a ray from endpoint *K*. Plot a point *J* along the ray.

(D) Draw three points *J*, *K*, and *M* so that they are not all on the same line. Then draw the plane that contains the three points. (You might also put a script letter such as $\mathcal{B}$ on your plane.)

(E) Give a name for each of the figures you drew. Then use a circle to choose whether the type of figure is an undefined term or a defined term.

Point _____   undefined term/defined term

Line _____   undefined term/defined term

Segment _____   undefined term/defined term

Ray _____   undefined term/defined term

Plane _____   undefined term/defined term

Reflect

1. In Step C, would $\overrightarrow{JK}$ be the same ray as $\overrightarrow{KJ}$? Why or why not?

_____

2. In Step D, when you name a plane using 3 letters, does the order of the letters matter?

_____

3. **Discussion** If $\overleftrightarrow{PQ}$ and $\overleftrightarrow{RS}$ are different names for the same line, what must be true about points *P*, *Q*, *R*, and *S*?

_____

🔑 Explain 1   Constructing a Copy of a Line Segment

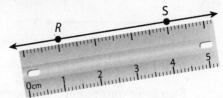

The distance along a line is undefined until a unit distance, such as 1 inch or 1 centimeter, is chosen. You can use a ruler to find the distance between two points on a line. The distance is the absolute value of the difference of the numbers on the ruler that correspond to the two points. This distance is the length of the segment determined by the points.

In the figure, the length of $\overline{RS}$, written RS (or SR), is the distance between R and S.

$$RS = |4 - 1| = |3| = 3 \text{ cm} \quad \text{or} \quad SR = |1 - 4| = |-3| = 3 \text{ cm}$$

Points that lie in the same plane are **coplanar**. Lines that lie in the same plane but do not intersect are **parallel**. Points that lie on the same line are **collinear**. The *Segment Addition Postulate* is a statement about collinear points. A **postulate** is a statement that is accepted as true without proof. Like undefined terms, postulates are building blocks of geometry.

Postulate 1: Segment Addition Postulate

Let A, B, and C be collinear points. If B is between A and C, then $AB + BC = AC$.

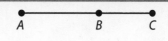

A *construction* is a geometric drawing that produces an accurate representation without using numbers or measures. One type of construction uses only a compass and straightedge. You can construct a line segment whose length is equal to that of a given segment using these tools along with the Segment Addition Postulate.

Example 1   Use a compass and straightedge to construct a segment whose length is $AB + CD$.

Ⓐ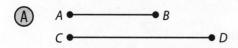

Step 1 Use the straightedge to draw a long line segment. Label an endpoint X. (See the art drawn in Step 4.)

Step 2 To copy segment AB, open the compass to the distance AB.

Step 3 Place the compass point on X, and draw an arc. Label the point Y where the arc and the segment intersect.

Step 4 To copy segment CD, open the compass to the distance CD. Place the compass point on Y, and draw an arc. Label the point Z where this second arc and the segment intersect.

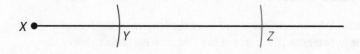

$\overline{XZ}$ is the required segment.

© Houghton Mifflin Harcourt Publishing Company

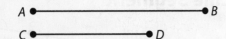

(B)

Step 1 Use the straightedge to draw a long line segment. Label an endpoint X.

Step 2 To copy segment AB, open the compass to the distance AB.

Step 3 Place the compass point on X, and draw an arc. Label the point Y where the arc and the segment intersect.

Step 4 To copy segment CD, open the compass to the distance CD. Place the compass point on Y, and draw an arc. Label the point Z where this second arc and the segment intersect.

Reflect

4. **Discussion** Look at the line and ruler above Example 1. Why does it not matter whether you find the distance from R to S or the distance from S to R?

_____

_____

_____

5. In Part B, how can you check that the length of $\overline{YZ}$ is the same as the length of $\overline{CD}$?

_____

Your Turn

6. Use a ruler to draw a segment PQ that is 2 inches long. Then use your compass and straightedge to construct a segment MN with the same length as $\overline{PQ}$.

⚙ Explain 2   Using the Distance Formula on the Coordinate Plane

The Pythagorean Theorem states that $a^2 + b^2 = c^2$, where a and b are the lengths of the legs of a right triangle and c is the length of the hypotenuse. You can use the Distance Formula to apply the Pythagorean Theorem to find the distance between points on the coordinate plane.

The Distance Formula

The distance between two points (x_1, y_1) and (x_2, y_2) on the coordinate plane is $\sqrt{(x_2 - x_1)^2 + (y_2 - y_1)^2}$.

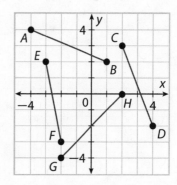

Example 2 Determine whether the given segments have the same length. Justify your answer.

(A) $\overline{AB}$ and $\overline{CD}$

Write the coordinates of the endpoints.	$A(-4, 4)$, $B(1, 2)$, $C(2, 3)$, $D(4, -2)$
Find the length of $\overline{AB}$.	$AB = \sqrt{\left(1 - (-4)\right)^2 + (2 - 4)^2}$
Simplify the expression.	$= \sqrt{5^2 + (-2)^2} = \sqrt{29}$
Find the length of $\overline{CD}$.	$CD = \sqrt{(4 - 2)^2 + (-2 - 3)^2}$
Simplify the expression.	$= \sqrt{2^2 + (-5)^2} = \sqrt{29}$

So, $AB = CD = \sqrt{29}$. Therefore, $\overline{AB}$ and $\overline{CD}$ have the same length.

(B) $\overline{EF}$ and $\overline{GH}$

Write the coordinates of the endpoints. $E(-3, 2)$, $F\left(\boxed{}, \boxed{}\right)$, $G(-2, -4)$, $H\left(\boxed{}, \boxed{}\right)$

Find the length of $\overline{EF}$. $EF = \sqrt{\left(\boxed{} - (-3)\right)^2 + \left(\boxed{} - 2\right)^2}$

Simplify the expression. $= \sqrt{\left(\boxed{}\right)^2 + \left(\boxed{}\right)^2} = \sqrt{\boxed{}}$

Find the length of $\overline{GH}$. $GH = \sqrt{\left(\boxed{} - (-2)\right)^2 + \left(\boxed{} - (-4)\right)^2}$

Simplify the expression. $= \sqrt{\left(\boxed{}\right)^2 + \left(\boxed{}\right)^2} = \sqrt{\boxed{}}$

So, _____. Therefore, _____

© Houghton Mifflin Harcourt Publishing Company

7. Consider how the Distance Formula is related to the Pythagorean Theorem. To use the Distance Formula to find the distance from $U(-3, -1)$ to $V(3, 4)$, you write $UV = \sqrt{\left(3 - (-3)\right)^2 + \left(4 - (-1)\right)^2}$. Explain how $\left(3 - (-3)\right)$ in the Distance Formula is related to a in the Pythagorean Theorem and how $\left(4 - (-1)\right)$ in the Distance Formula is related to b in the Pythagorean Theorem.

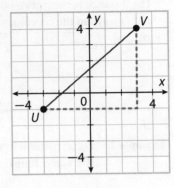

_____

_____

_____

_____

8. Determine whether $\overline{JK}$ and $\overline{LM}$ have the same length. Justify your answer.

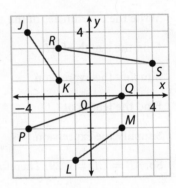

🔑 Explain 3 Finding a Midpoint

The **midpoint** of a line segment is the point that divides the segment into two segments that have the same length. A line, ray, or other figure that passes through the midpoint of a segment is a **segment bisector**.

In the figure, the tick marks show that $PM = MQ$. Therefore, M is the midpoint of $\overline{PQ}$ and line ℓ bisects $\overline{PQ}$.

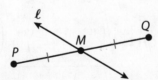

You can use paper folding as a method to construct a bisector of a given segment and locate the midpoint of the segment.

Example 3 Use paper folding to construct a bisector of each segment.

(A)

Step 1 Use a compass and straightedge to copy $\overline{AB}$ on a piece of paper.

Step 2 Fold the paper so that point B is on top of point A.

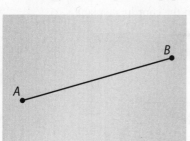

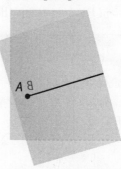

Step 3 Open the paper. Label the point where the crease intersects the segment as point M.

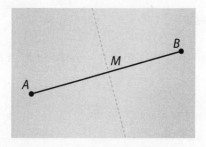

Point M is the midpoint of $\overline{AB}$ and the crease is a bisector of $\overline{AB}$.

(B) **Step 1** Use a compass and straightedge to copy $\overline{JK}$ on a piece of paper.

Step 2 Fold the paper so that point K is on top of point _____.

Step 3 Open the paper. Label the point where the crease intersects the segment as point N.

Point N is the _____ of $\overline{JK}$ and the crease is a _____ of $\overline{JK}$.

Step 4 Make a sketch of your paper folding construction or attach your folded piece of paper.

Reflect

9. Explain how you could use paper folding to divide a line segment into four segments of equal length.

_____

_____

_____

10. Explain how to use a ruler to check your construction in Part B.

_____

_____

⚙ Explain 4 **Finding Midpoints on the Coordinate Plane**

You can use the *Midpoint Formula* to find the midpoint of a segment on the coordinate plane.

The Midpoint Formula

The midpoint M of $\overline{AB}$ with endpoints $A(x_1, y_1)$ and $B(x_2, y_2)$ is given by $M\left(\dfrac{x_1 + x_2}{2}, \dfrac{y_1 + y_2}{2}\right)$.

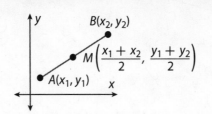

Example 4 Show that each statement is true.

Ⓐ If $\overline{PQ}$ has endpoints $P(-4, 1)$ and $Q(2, -3)$, then the midpoint M of $\overline{PQ}$ lies in Quadrant III.

Use the Midpoint Formula to find the midpoint of $\overline{PQ}$. $\qquad M\left(\dfrac{-4 + 2}{2}, \dfrac{1 + (-3)}{2}\right) = M(-1, -1)$
Substitute the coordinates, then simplify.

So M lies in Quadrant III, since the x- and y-coordinates are both negative.

Ⓑ If $\overline{RS}$ has endpoints $R(3, 5)$ and $S(-3, -1)$, then the midpoint M of $\overline{RS}$ lies on the y-axis.

Use the Midpoint Formula to find the midpoint of $\overline{RS}$. $\qquad M\left(\dfrac{3 + \boxed{}}{2}, \dfrac{5 + \boxed{}}{2}\right) = M\left(\boxed{}, \boxed{}\right)$
Substitute the coordinates, then simplify.

So M lies on the y-axis, since _____.

Your Turn

Show that each statement is true.

11. If $\overline{AB}$ has endpoints $A(6, -3)$ and $B(-6, 3)$, then the midpoint M of $\overline{AB}$ is the origin.

12. If $\overline{JK}$ has endpoints $J(7, 0)$ and $K(-5, -4)$, then the midpoint M of $\overline{JK}$ lies in Quadrant IV.

13. Explain why the Distance Formula is not needed to find the distance between two points that lie on a horizontal or vertical line.

_____

_____

_____

14. When you use the Distance Formula, does the order in which you subtract the x- and y-coordinates matter? Explain.

_____

_____

15. When you use the Midpoint Formula, can you take either point as (x_1, y_1) or (x_2, y_2)? Why or why not?

_____

_____

16. Essential Question Check-In What is the difference between finding the length of a segment that is drawn on a sheet of blank paper and a segment that is drawn on a coordinate plane?

_____

_____

 ☆ Evaluate: Homework and Practice

- Online Homework
- Hints and Help
- Extra Practice

Write the term that is suggested by each figure or description. Then state whether the term is an undefined term or a defined term.

1.

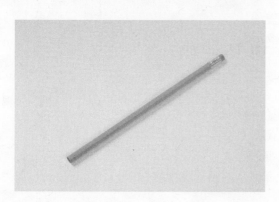

2.

3.

4.

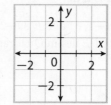

Use a compass and straightedge to construct a segment whose length is $AB + CD$.

5.
   A •————————• B
   C •————————• D

6. A •————————• B
   C •—————• D

Copy each segment onto a sheet of paper. Then use paper folding to construct a bisector of the segment.

7. A •————————————• B

8.
   L
   K

Determine whether the given segments have the same length. Justify your answer.

9. $\overline{AB}$ and $\overline{BC}$

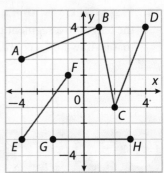

10. $\overline{EF}$ and $\overline{GH}$

11. $\overline{AB}$ and $\overline{CD}$

12. $\overline{BC}$ and $\overline{EF}$

Show that each statement is true.

13. If $\overline{DE}$ has endpoints $D(-1, 6)$ and $E(3, -2)$, then the midpoint M of $\overline{DE}$ lies in Quadrant I.

14. If $\overline{ST}$ has endpoints $S(-6, -1)$ and $T(0, 1)$, then the midpoint M of $\overline{ST}$ lies in on the x-axis.

Show that each statement is true.

15. If $\overline{JK}$ has endpoints $J(-2, 3)$ and $K(6, 5)$, and $\overline{LN}$ has endpoints $L(0, 7)$ and $N(4, 1)$, then $\overline{JK}$ and $\overline{LN}$ have the same midpoint.

16. If $\overline{GH}$ has endpoints $G(-8, 1)$ and $H(4, 5)$, then the midpoint M of $\overline{GH}$ lies on the line $y = -x + 1$.

Use the figure for Exercises 17 and 18.

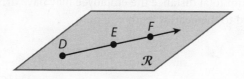

17. Name two different rays in the figure.

18. Name three different segments in the figure.

Sketch each figure.

19. two rays that form a straight line and that intersect at point P

20. two line segments that both have a midpoint at point M

21. Draw and label a line segment, $\overline{JK}$, that is 3 inches long. Use a ruler to draw and label the midpoint M of the segment.

22. Draw the segment PQ with endpoints $P(-2, -1)$ and $Q(2, 4)$ on the coordinate plane. Then find the length and midpoint of $\overline{PQ}$.

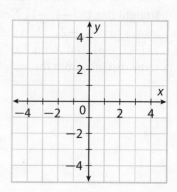

23. Multi-Step The sign shows distances from a rest stop to the exits for different towns along a straight section of highway. The state department of transportation is planning to build a new exit to Freestone at the midpoint of the exits for Roseville and Edgewood. When the new exit is built, what will be the distance from the exit for Midtown to the exit for Freestone?

Midtown	17 mi
Roseville	35 mi
Edgewood	59 mi

24. On a town map, each unit of the coordinate plane represents 1 mile. Three branches of a bank are located at $A(-3, 1)$, $B(2, 3)$, and $C(4, -1)$. A bank employee drives from Branch A to Branch B and then drives halfway to Branch C before getting stuck in traffic. What is the minimum total distance the employee may have driven before getting stuck in traffic? Round to the nearest tenth of a mile.

25. A city planner designs a park that is a quadrilateral with vertices at $J(-3, 1)$, $K(1, 3)$, $L(5, -1)$, and $M(-1, -3)$. There is an entrance to the park at the midpoint of each side of the park. A straight path connects each entrance to the entrance on the opposite side. Assuming each unit of the coordinate plane represents 10 meters, what is the total length of the paths to the nearest meter?

26. Communicate Mathematical Ideas A video game designer places an anthill at the origin of a coordinate plane. A red ant leaves the anthill and moves along a straight line to $(1, 1)$, while a black ant leaves the anthill and moves along a straight line to $(-1, -1)$. Next, the red ant moves to $(2, 2)$, while the black ant moves to $(-2, -2)$. Then the red ant moves to $(3, 3)$, while the black ant moves to $(-3, -3)$, and so on. Explain why the red ant and the black ant are always the same distance from the anthill.

27. Which of the following points are more than 5 units from the point $P(-2, -2)$? Select all that apply.

A. $A(1, 2)$

B. $B(3, -1)$

C. $C(2, -4)$

D. $D(-6, -6)$

E. $E(-5, 1)$

H.O.T. Focus on Higher Order Thinking

28. Analyze Relationships Use a compass and straightedge to construct a segment whose length is $AB - CD$. Use a ruler to check your construction.

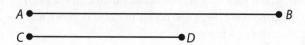

29. Critical Thinking Point M is the midpoint of $\overline{AB}$. The coordinates of point A are $(-8, 3)$ and the coordinates of M are $(-2, 1)$. What are the coordinates of point B?

30. Make a Conjecture Use a compass and straightedge to copy $\overline{AB}$ so that one endpoint of the copy is at point X. Then repeat the process three more times, making three different copies of $\overline{AB}$ that have an endpoint at point X. Make a conjecture about the set of all possible copies of $\overline{AB}$ that have an endpoint at point X.

$X \bullet$

Lesson Performance Task

A carnival ride consists of four circular cars—*A*, *B*, *C*, and *D*—each of which spins about a point at its center. The center points of cars *A* and *B* are attached by a straight beam, as are the center points of cars *C* and *D*. The two beams are attached at their midpoints by a rotating arm. The figure shows how the beams and arm can rotate.

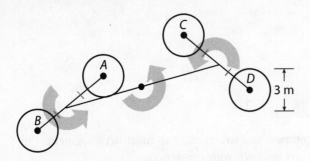

A plan for the ride uses a coordinate plane in which each unit represents one meter. In the plan, the center of car *A* is $(-6, -1)$, the center of car *B* is $(-2, -3)$, the center of car *C* is $(3, 4)$, and the center of car *D* is $(5, 0)$. Each car has a diameter of 3 meters.

The manager of the carnival wants to place a fence around the ride. Describe the shape and dimensions of a fence that will be appropriate to enclose the ride. Justify your answer.

16.2 Angle Measures and Angle Bisectors

Resource Locker

Essential Question: How is measuring an angle similar to and different from measuring a line segment?

🧭 Explore   Constructing a Copy of an Angle

Start with a point *X* and use a compass and straightedge to construct a copy of ∠*S*.

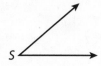

•
X

(A) Use a straightedge to draw a ray with endpoint *X*.

(B) Place the point of your compass on *S* and draw an arc that intersects both sides of the angle. Label the points of intersection *T* and *U*.

(D) Place the point of the compass on *T* and open it to the distance *TU*.

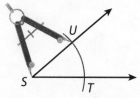

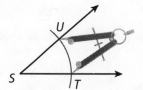

(C) Without adjusting the compass, place the point of the compass on *X* and draw an arc that intersects the ray. Label the intersection *Y*.

(E) Without adjusting the compass, place the point of the compass on *Y* and draw an arc. Label the intersection with the first arc *Z*.

(F) Use a straightedge to draw $\overrightarrow{XZ}$.
∠*X* is a copy of ∠*S*.

Reflect

1. If you could place the angle you drew on top of ∠*S* so that $\overrightarrow{XY}$ coincides with $\overrightarrow{ST}$, what would be true about $\overrightarrow{XZ}$? Explain.

_____

_____

2. **Discussion** Is it possible to do the construction with a compass that is stuck open to a fixed distance? Why or why not?

_____

_____

An **angle** is a figure formed by two rays with the same endpoint.
The common endpoint is the **vertex** of the angle.
The rays are the **sides** of the angle.

Example 1 Draw or name the given angle.

 ∠*PQR*

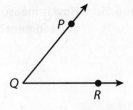

When an angle is named with three letters, the middle letter is the vertex. So, the vertex of angle ∠*PQR* is point *Q*.

The sides of the angle are two rays with common endpoint *Q*. So, the sides of the angle are $\vec{QP}$ and $\vec{QR}$.

Draw and label the angle as shown.

(B)

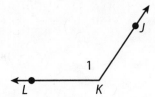

The vertex of the angle shown is point ☐ . A name for the angle is ∠☐ .

The vertex must be in the middle, so two more names for the angle are ∠☐☐☐

and ∠☐☐☐ .

The angle is numbered, so another name is ∠☐ .

Reflect

3. Without seeing a figure, is it possible to give another name for ∠*MKG*?
If so, what is it? If not, why not?

Your Turn

Use the figure for 4–5.

4. Name ∠2 in as many different ways as possible.

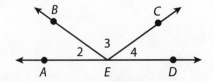

5. Use a compass and straightedge to copy ∠*BEC*.

⚙ Explain 2 Measuring Angles

The distance around a circular arc is undefined until a measurement unit is chosen. **Degrees** (°) are a common measurement unit for circular arcs. There are 360° in a circle, so an angle that measures 1° is $\frac{1}{360}$ of a circle. The measure of an angle is written m∠A or m∠PQR.

You can classify angles by their measures.

Classifying Angles			
Acute Angle	**Right Angle**	**Obtuse Angle**	**Straight Angle**

$0° < m∠A < 90°$	$m∠A = 90°$	$90° < m∠A < 180°$	$m∠A = 180°$

Example 2 Use a protractor to draw an angle with the given measure.

Ⓐ 53°

Step 1 Use a straightedge to draw a ray, $\overrightarrow{XY}$.

Step 2 Place your protractor on point X as shown. Locate the point along the edge of the protractor that corresponds to 53°. Make a mark at this location and label it point Z.

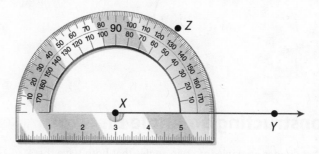

Step 3 Draw $\overrightarrow{XZ}$. m∠ZXY = 53°.

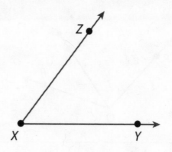

Ⓑ 138°

Step 1 Use a straightedge to draw a ray, $\overrightarrow{AB}$.

Step 2 Place your protractor on point A so that $\overrightarrow{AB}$ is at zero.

Step 3 Locate the point along the edge of the protractor that corresponds to 138°.
Make a mark at this location and label it point C.

Step 4 Draw $\overrightarrow{AC}$. m∠CAB = 138°.

Reflect

6. Explain how you can use a protractor to check that the angle you constructed
in the Explore is a copy of the given angle.

Your Turn

**Each angle can be found in the rigid frame of the bicycle.
Use a protractor to find each measure.**

7.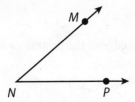

8.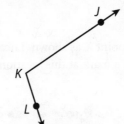

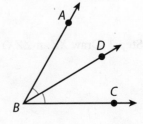

🔧 Explain 3 Constructing an Angle Bisector

An **angle bisector** is a ray that divides an angle into two angles that both have the
same measure. In the figure, $\overrightarrow{BD}$ bisects ∠ABC, so m∠ABD = m∠CBD. The arcs
in the figure show equal angle measures.

Postulate 2: Angle Addition Postulate

If S is in the interior of ∠PQR, then
m∠PQR = m∠PQS + m∠SQR.

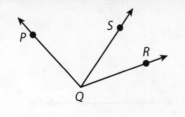

© Houghton Mifflin Harcourt Publishing Company • Image Credits: ©Gena73/
Shutterstock

Example 3 Use a compass and straightedge to construct the bisector of the given angle. Check that the measure of each of the new angles is one-half the measure of the given angle.

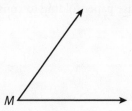

Ⓐ

Step 1 Place the point of your compass on point *M*. Draw an arc that intersects both sides of the angle. Label the points of intersection *P* and *Q*.

Step 2 Place the point of the compass on *P* and draw an arc in the interior of the angle.

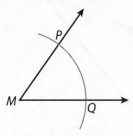

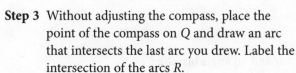

Step 3 Without adjusting the compass, place the point of the compass on *Q* and draw an arc that intersects the last arc you drew. Label the intersection of the arcs *R*.

Step 4 Use a straightedge to draw $\overrightarrow{MR}$.

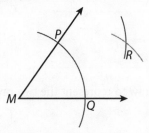

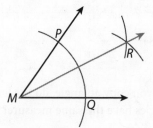

Step 5 Measure with a protractor to confirm that m∠*PMR* = m∠*QMR* = $\frac{1}{2}$m∠*PMQ*.

$27° = 27° = \frac{1}{2}(54°)$✓

Ⓑ

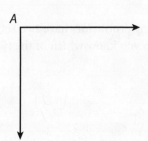

Step 1 Draw an arc centered at *A* that intersects both sides of the angle. Label the points of intersection *B* and *C*.

Step 2 Draw an arc centered at *B* in the interior of the angle.

Step 3 Without adjusting the compass, draw an arc centered at *C* that intersects the last arc you drew. Label the intersection of the arcs *D*.

Step 4 Draw $\overrightarrow{AD}$.

Step 5 Check that m∠*BAD* = m∠*CAD* = $\frac{1}{2}$m∠*BAC*.

9. **Discussion** Explain how you could use paper folding to construct the bisector of an angle.

_____

_____

Use a compass and straightedge to construct the bisector of the given angle. Check that the measure of each of the new angles is one-half the measure of the given angle.

10.

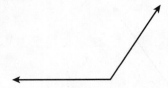

11.

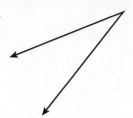

💬 Elaborate

12. What is the relationship between a segment bisector and an angle bisector?

_____

_____

13. When you copy an angle, do the lengths of the segments you draw to represent the two rays affect whether the angles have the same measure? Explain.

_____

_____

_____

14. **Essential Question Check-In** Many protractors have two sets of degree measures around the edge. When you measure an angle, how do you know which of the two measures to use?

_____

_____

_____

☆ Evaluate: Homework and Practice

- Online Homework
- Hints and Help
- Extra Practice

Use a compass and straightedge to construct a copy of each angle.

1.

2.

3.

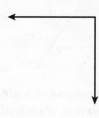

Draw an angle with the given name.

4. ∠JWT

5. ∠NBQ

Name each angle in as many different ways as possible.

6.

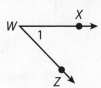

7.

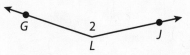

Use a protractor to draw an angle with the given measure.

8. 19°

9. 100°

Use a protractor to find the measure of each angle.

10.

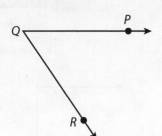

11.

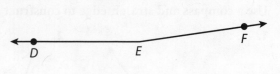

Use a compass and straightedge to construct the bisector of the given angle. Check that the measure of each of the new angles is one-half the measure of the given angle.

12.

13.

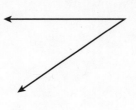

14.

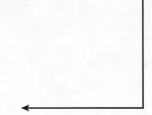

Use the Angle Addition Postulate to find the measure of each angle.

15. ∠BXC

16. ∠BXE

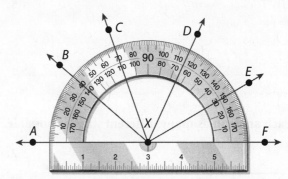

Use a compass and straightedge to copy each angle onto a separate piece of paper. Then use paper folding to construct the angle bisector.

17.

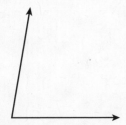

18.

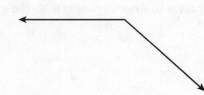

19. Use a compass and straightedge to construct an angle whose measure is
m∠A + m∠B. Use a protractor to check your construction.

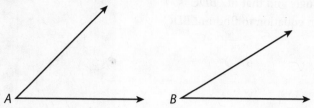

20. Find the value of *x*, given
that m∠PQS = 112°.

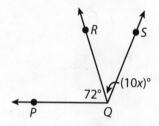

21. Find the value of *y*, given
that m∠KLM = 135°.

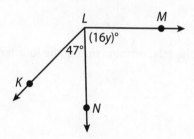

22. Multi-Step The figure shows a map of five streets that meet at Concord Circle. The
measure of the angle formed by Melville Road and Emerson Avenue is 118°.
The measure of the angle formed by Emerson Avenue and Thoreau Street is 134°.
Hawthorne Lane bisects the angle formed by Melville Road and Emerson Avenue.
Dickinson Drive bisects the angle formed by Emerson Avenue and Thoreau Street.
What is the measure of the angle formed by Hawthorne Lane and Dickinson Drive?
Explain your reasoning.

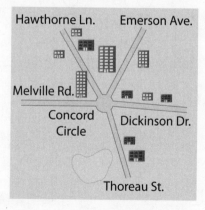

23. Represent Real-World Problems A carpenter is building a rectangular bookcase with diagonal braces across the back, as shown. The carpenter knows that ∠ADC is a right angle and that m∠BDC is 32° greater than m∠ADB. Write and solve an equation to find m∠BDC and m∠ADB.

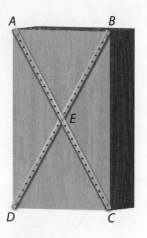

24. Describe the relationships among the four terms.

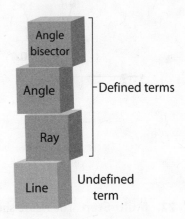

25. Determine whether each of the following pairs of angles have equal measures. Select the correct answer for each lettered part.

A. ∠KJL and ∠LJM   ○ Yes   ○ No

B. ∠MJP and ∠PJR   ○ Yes   ○ No

C. ∠LJP and ∠NJR   ○ Yes   ○ No

D. ∠MJK and ∠PJR   ○ Yes   ○ No

E. ∠KJR and ∠MJP   ○ Yes   ○ No

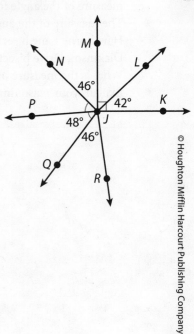

26. Make a Conjecture A rhombus is a quadrilateral with four sides of equal length. Use a compass and straightedge to bisect one of the angles in each of the rhombuses shown. Then use your results to state a conjecture.

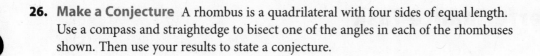

27. What If? What happens if you perform the steps for constructing an angle bisector when the given angle is a straight angle? Does the construction still work? If so, explain why and show a sample construction. If not, explain why not.

28. Critical Thinking Use a compass and straightedge to construct an angle whose measure is $m\angle A - m\angle B$. Use a protractor to check your construction.

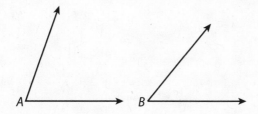

29. Communicate Mathematical Ideas Explain the steps for using a compass and straightedge to construct an angle with $\frac{1}{4}$ the measure of a given angle. Then draw an angle and show the construction.

Lesson Performance Task

A store sells custom-made stands for tablet computers. When an order comes in, the customer specifies the angle at which the stand should hold the tablet. Then an employee bends a piece of aluminum to the correct angle to make the stand. The figure shows the templates that the employee uses to make a 60° stand and a 40° stand.

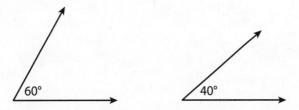

The store receives an order for a 50° stand. The employee does not have a template for a 50° stand and does not have a protractor. Can the employee use the existing templates and a compass and straightedge to make a template for a 50° stand? If so, explain how and show the steps the employee should use. If not, explain why not.

16.3 Representing and Describing Transformations

Essential Question: How can you describe transformations in the coordinate plane using algebraic representations and using words?

Explore   Performing Transformations Using Coordinate Notation

A **transformation** is a function that changes the position, shape, and/or size of a figure. The inputs of the function are points in the plane; the outputs are other points in the plane. A figure that is used as the input of a transformation is the **preimage**. The output is the **image**. Translations, reflections, and rotations are three types of transformations. The decorative tiles shown illustrate all three types of transformations.

You can use *prime notation* to name the image of a point. In the diagram, the transformation *T* moves point *A* to point *A'* (read "A prime"). You can use function notation to write $T(A) = A'$. Note that a transformation is sometimes called a *mapping*. Transformation *T* maps *A* to *A'*.

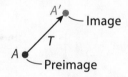

Coordinate notation is one way to write a rule for a transformation on a coordinate plane. The notation uses an arrow to show how the transformation changes the coordinates of a general point, (x, y).

Find the unknown coordinates for each transformation and draw the image. Then complete the description of the transformation and compare the image to its preimage.

Ⓐ $(x, y) \rightarrow (x - 4, y - 3)$

Preimage (x, y)		Rule $(x, y) \rightarrow (x - 4, y - 3)$		Image $(x - 4, y - 3)$
$A(0, 4)$	$\rightarrow$	$A'(0 - 4, 4 - 3)$	$=$	$A'(-4, 1)$
$B(3, 0)$	$\rightarrow$	$B'(3 - 4, 0 - 3)$	$=$	$B'(\boxed{}, \boxed{})$
$C(0, 0)$	$\rightarrow$	$C'(0 - 4, 0 - 3)$	$=$	$C'(\boxed{}, \boxed{})$

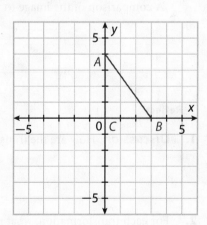

The transformation is a translation 4 units (left/right)

and 3 units (up/down).

A comparison of the image to its preimage shows that

_____

Ⓑ $(x, y) \rightarrow (-x, y)$

Preimage (x, y)	Rule $(x, y) \rightarrow (-x, y)$		Image $(-x, y)$
$R(-4, 3) \rightarrow$	$R'(-(-4), 3)$	$=$	$R'(\boxed{}, \boxed{})$
$S(-1, 3) \rightarrow$	$S'(-(-1), 3)$	$=$	$S'(\boxed{}, \boxed{})$
$T(-4, 1) \rightarrow$	$T'(-(-4), 1)$	$=$	$T'(\boxed{}, \boxed{})$

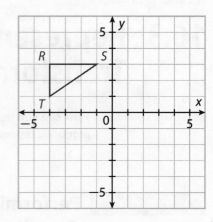

The transformation is a reflection across the (x-axis/y-axis).

A comparison of the image to its preimage shows that

_____

_____ .

Ⓒ $(x, y) \rightarrow (2x, y)$

Preimage (x, y)	Rule $(x, y) \rightarrow (2x, y)$		Image $(2x, y)$
$J(\boxed{}, \boxed{}) \rightarrow$	$J'(2 \cdot \boxed{}, \boxed{})$	$=$	$J'(\boxed{}, \boxed{})$
$K(\boxed{}, \boxed{}) \rightarrow$	$K'(2 \cdot \boxed{}, \boxed{})$	$=$	$K'(\boxed{}, \boxed{})$
$L(\boxed{}, \boxed{}) \rightarrow$	$L'(2 \cdot \boxed{}, \boxed{})$	$=$	$L'(\boxed{}, \boxed{})$

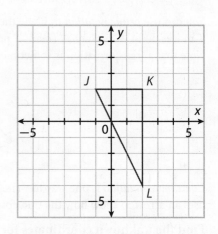

The transformation is a (horizontal/vertical) stretch by a

factor of _____.

A comparison of the image to its preimage shows that

_____

_____ .

Reflect

1. **Discussion** How are the transformations in Steps A and B different from the transformation in Step C?

_____

_____

2. For each transformation, what rule could you use to map the image back to the preimage?

_____

_____

⚙ Explain 1 Describing Rigid Motions Using Coordinate Notation

Some transformations preserve length and angle measure, and some do not. A **rigid motion** (or *isometry*) is a transformation that changes the position of a figure without changing the size or shape of the figure. Translations, reflections, and rotations are rigid motions.

Properties of Rigid Motions	
• Rigid motions preserve distance.	• Rigid motions preserve collinearity.
• Rigid motions preserve angle measure.	• Rigid motions preserve parallelism.
• Rigid motions preserve betweenness.	

If a figure is determined by certain points, then its image after a rigid motion is determined by the images of those points. This is true because of the betweenness and collinearity properties of rigid motions. For example, suppose $\triangle ABC$ is determined by its vertices, points A, B, and C. You can find the image of $\triangle ABC$ by finding the images of points A, B, and C and connecting them with segments.

Example 1 Use coordinate notation to write the rule that maps each preimage to its image. Then identify the transformation and confirm that it preserves length and angle measure.

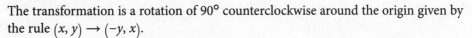

(A)
Preimage		Image
$A(1, 2)$	$\rightarrow$	$A'(-2, 1)$
$B(4, 2)$	$\rightarrow$	$B'(-2, 4)$
$C(3, -2)$	$\rightarrow$	$C'(2, 3)$

Look for a pattern in the coordinates.

The *x*-coordinate of each image point is the opposite of the *y*-coordinate of its preimage.

The *y*-coordinate of each image point equals the *x*-coordinate of its preimage.

The transformation is a rotation of 90° counterclockwise around the origin given by the rule $(x, y) \rightarrow (-y, x)$.

Find the length of each side of $\triangle ABC$ and $\triangle A'B'C'$. Use the Distance Formula as needed.

$$AB = 3$$

$$BC = \sqrt{(3-4)^2 + (-2-2)^2}$$
$$= \sqrt{17}$$

$$AC = \sqrt{(3-1)^2 + (-2-2)^2}$$
$$= \sqrt{20}$$

$$A'B' = 3$$

$$B'C' = \sqrt{(2-(-2))^2 + (3-4)^2}$$
$$= \sqrt{17}$$

$$A'C' = \sqrt{(2-(-2))^2 + (3-1)^2}$$
$$= \sqrt{20}$$

Since $AB = A'B'$, $BC = B'C'$, and $AC = A'C'$, the transformation preserves length.

Find the measure of each angle of $\triangle ABC$ and $\triangle A'B'C'$. Use a protractor.

$m\angle A = 63°$, $m\angle B = 76°$, $m\angle C = 41°$ $m\angle A' = 63°$, $m\angle B' = 76°$, $m\angle C' = 41°$

Since $m\angle A = m\angle A'$, $m\angle B = m\angle B'$, and $m\angle C = m\angle C'$, the transformation preserves angle measure.

(B)

Preimage		Image
$P(-3, -1)$	$\rightarrow$	$P'(-3, 1)$
$Q(3, -1)$	$\rightarrow$	$Q'(3, 1)$
$R(1, -4)$	$\rightarrow$	$R'(1, 4)$

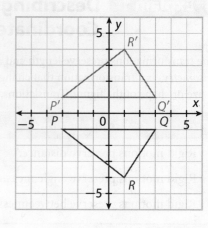

Look for a pattern in the coordinates.

The x-coordinate of each image point

_____ the x-coordinate of its preimage.

The y-coordinate of each image point

_____ the y-coordinate of its preimage.

The transformation is a _____

given by the rule _____.

Find the length of each side of $\triangle PQR$ and $\triangle P'Q'R'$.

$PQ = \boxed{}$

$QR = \sqrt{\left(1 - \boxed{}\right)^2 + \left(-4 - \boxed{}\right)^2}$

$= \sqrt{\boxed{}}$

$PR = \sqrt{\left(1 - \boxed{}\right)^2 + \left(-4 - \boxed{}\right)^2}$

$= \sqrt{\boxed{}} = \boxed{}$

$P'Q' = \boxed{}$

$Q'R' = \sqrt{\left(1 - \boxed{}\right)^2 + \left(4 - \boxed{}\right)^2}$

$= \sqrt{\boxed{}}$

$P'R' = \sqrt{\left(1 - \boxed{}\right)^2 + \left(4 - \boxed{}\right)^2}$

$= \sqrt{\boxed{}} = \boxed{}$

Since _____, the transformation preserves length.

Find the measure of each angle of $\triangle PQR$ and $\triangle P'Q'R'$. Use a protractor.

$m\angle P = \boxed{}$, $m\angle Q = \boxed{}$, $m\angle R = \boxed{}$ $m\angle P' = \boxed{}$, $m\angle Q' = \boxed{}$, $m\angle R' = \boxed{}$

Since _____, the transformation preserves angle measure.

Reflect

3. How could you use a compass to test whether corresponding lengths in a preimage and image are the same?

_____

_____

_____

4. Look back at the transformations in the Explore. Classify each transformation as a rigid motion or not a rigid motion.

_____

Use coordinate notation to write the rule that maps each preimage to its image. Then identify the transformation and confirm that it preserves length and angle measure.

5.

Preimage		Image
$D(-4, 4)$	$\rightarrow$	$D'(4, -4)$
$E(2, 4)$	$\rightarrow$	$E'(-2, -4)$
$F(-4, 1)$	$\rightarrow$	$F'(4, -1)$

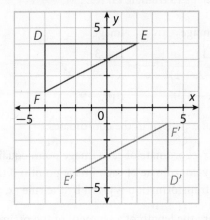

6.

Preimage		Image
$S(-3, 4)$	$\rightarrow$	$S'(-2, 2)$
$T(2, 4)$	$\rightarrow$	$T'(3, 2)$
$U(-2, 0)$	$\rightarrow$	$U'(-1, -2)$

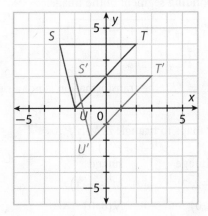

🔑 Explain 2 Describing Nonrigid Motions Using Coordinate Notation

Transformations that stretch or compress figures are not rigid motions because they do not preserve distance.

The view in the fun house mirror is an example of a vertical stretch.

Example 2 Use coordinate notation to write the rule that maps each preimage to its image. Then confirm that the transformation is not a rigid motion.

(A) $\triangle JKL$ maps to triangle $\triangle J'K'L'$.

Preimage		Image
$J(4, 1)$	$\rightarrow$	$J'(4, 3)$
$K(-2, -1)$	$\rightarrow$	$K'(-2, -3)$
$L(0, -3)$	$\rightarrow$	$L'(0, -9)$

Look for a pattern in the coordinates.

The x-coordinate of each image point equals the x-coordinate of its preimage.
The y-coordinate of each image point is 3 times the y-coordinate of its preimage.
The transformation is given by the rule $(x, y) \rightarrow (x, 3y)$.

Compare the length of a segment of the preimage to the length of the corresponding segment of the image.

$$JK = \sqrt{(-2 - 4)^2 + (-1 - 1)^2} \qquad J'K' = \sqrt{(-2 - 4)^2 + (-3 - 3)^2}$$

$$= \sqrt{40} \qquad\qquad\qquad\qquad = \sqrt{72}$$

Since $JK \neq J'K'$, the transformation is not a rigid motion.

(B) $\triangle MNP$ maps to triangle $\triangle M'N'P'$.

Preimage		Image
$M(-2, 2)$	$\rightarrow$	$M'(-4, 1)$
$N(4, 0)$	$\rightarrow$	$N'(8, 0)$
$P(-2, -2)$	$\rightarrow$	$P'(-4, -1)$

The x-coordinate of each image point is _____ the x-coordinate of its preimage.

The y-coordinate of each image point is _____ the y-coordinate of its preimage.

The transformation is given by the rule _____.

Compare the length of a segment of the preimage to the length of the corresponding segment of the image.

$$MN = \sqrt{(x_2 - x_1)^2 + (y_2 - y_1)^2} \qquad M'N' = \sqrt{(x_2 - x_1)^2 + (y_2 - y_1)^2}$$

$$= \sqrt{\left(4 - \boxed{}\right)^2 + \left(0 - \boxed{}\right)^2} \qquad = \sqrt{\left(\boxed{} - \boxed{}\right)^2 + \left(\boxed{} - \boxed{}\right)^2}$$

$$= \sqrt{\boxed{}^2 + \boxed{}^2} \qquad\qquad = \sqrt{\boxed{}^2 + \boxed{}^2}$$

$$= \sqrt{\boxed{}} \qquad\qquad\qquad = \sqrt{\boxed{}}$$

Since _____, the transformation is not a rigid motion.

7. How could you confirm that a transformation is not a rigid motion by using a protractor?

_____

_____

_____

Your Turn

Use coordinate notation to write the rule that maps each preimage to its image. Then confirm that the transformation is not a rigid motion.

8. $\triangle ABC$ maps to triangle $\triangle A'B'C'$.

Preimage		Image
$A(2, 2)$	$\rightarrow$	$A'(3, 3)$
$B(4, 2)$	$\rightarrow$	$B'(6, 3)$
$C(2, -4)$	$\rightarrow$	$C'(3, -6)$

9. $\triangle RST$ maps to triangle $\triangle R'S'T'$.

Preimage		Image
$R(-2, 1)$	$\rightarrow$	$R'(-1, 3)$
$S(4, 2)$	$\rightarrow$	$S'(2, 6)$
$T(2, -2)$	$\rightarrow$	$T'(1, -6)$

💬 Elaborate

10. Critical Thinking To confirm that a transformation is not a rigid motion, do you have to check the length of every segment of the preimage and the length of every segment of the image? Why or why not?

_____

_____

_____

_____

11. Make a Conjecture A polygon is transformed by a rigid motion. How are the perimeters of the preimage polygon and the image polygon related? Explain.

_____

_____

_____

12. Essential Question Check-In How is coordinate notation for a transformation, such as $(x, y) \rightarrow (x + 1, y - 1)$, similar to and different from algebraic function notation, such as $f(x) = 2x + 1$?

_____

_____

_____

• Online Homework
• Hints and Help
• Extra Practice

Draw the image of each figure under the given transformation.
Then describe the transformation in words.

1. $(x, y) \rightarrow (-x, -y)$

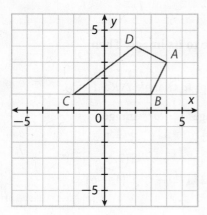

2. $(x, y) \rightarrow (x + 5, y)$

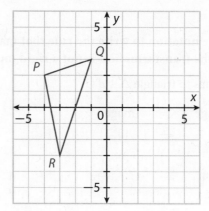

3. $(x, y) \rightarrow \left(x, \frac{1}{3}y\right)$

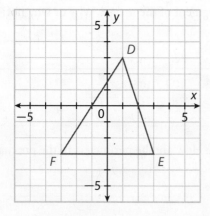

4. $(x, y) \rightarrow (y, x)$

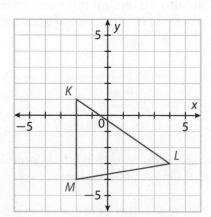

Use coordinate notation to write the rule that maps each preimage to its image. Then identify the transformation and confirm that it preserves length and angle measure.

5.

Preimage		Image
$A(-4, 4)$	$\rightarrow$	$A'(4, 4)$
$B(-1, 2)$	$\rightarrow$	$B'(2, 1)$
$C(-4, 1)$	$\rightarrow$	$C'(1, 4)$

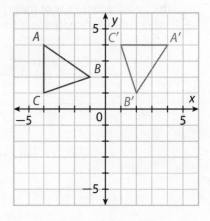

6.

Preimage		Image
$J(0, 3)$	$\rightarrow$	$J'(-3, 0)$
$K(4, 3)$	$\rightarrow$	$K'(-3, -4)$
$L(2, 1)$	$\rightarrow$	$L'(-1, -2)$

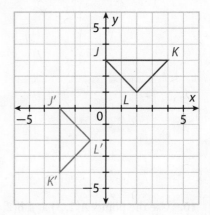

Use coordinate notation to write the rule that maps each preimage to its image. Then confirm that the transformation is not a rigid motion.

7. $\triangle ABC$ maps to triangle $\triangle A'B'C'$.

Preimage		Image
$A(6, 6)$	$\rightarrow$	$A'(3, 3)$
$B(4, -2)$	$\rightarrow$	$B'(2, -1)$
$C(0, 0)$	$\rightarrow$	$C'(0, 0)$

8. $\triangle FGH$ maps to triangle $\triangle F'G'H'$.

Preimage		Image
$F(-1, 1)$	$\rightarrow$	$F'(-2, 1)$
$G(1, -1)$	$\rightarrow$	$G'(2, -1)$
$H(-2, -2)$	$\rightarrow$	$H'(-4, -2)$

9. **Analyze Relationships** A mineralogist is studying a quartz crystal. She uses a computer program to draw a side view of the crystal, as shown. She decides to make the drawing 50% wider, but to keep the same height. Draw the transformed view of the crystal. Then write a rule for the transformation using coordinate notation. Check your rule using the original coordinates.

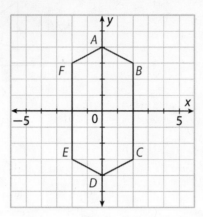

10. Use the points $A(2, 3)$ and $B(2, -3)$.

   a. Describe segment AB and find its length.

   b. Describe the image of segment AB under the transformation $(x, y) \rightarrow (x, 2y)$.

   c. Describe the image of segment AB under the transformation $(x, y) \rightarrow (x + 2, y)$.

   d. Compare the two transformations.

11. Use the points $H(-4, 1)$ and $K(4, 1)$.

    a. Describe segment HK and find its length.

    b. Describe the image of segment HK under the transformation $(x, y) \rightarrow (-y, x)$.

    c. Describe the image of segment HK under the transformation $(x, y) \rightarrow (2x, y)$.

    d. Compare the two transformations.

12. Make a Prediction A landscape architect designs a flower bed that is a quadrilateral, as shown in the figure. The plans call for a light to be placed at the midpoint of the longest side of the flower bed. The architect decides to change the location of the flower bed using the transformation $(x, y) \rightarrow (x, -y)$. Describe the location of the light in the transformed flower bed. Then make the required calculations to show that your prediction is correct.

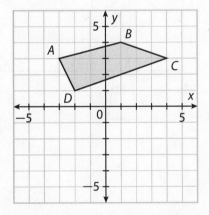

13. Multiple Representations If a transformation moves points only up or down, how do the coordinates of the point change? What can you conclude about the coordinate notation for the transformation?

14. Match each transformation with the correct description.

A. $(x, y) \rightarrow (3x, y)$ _____ dilation with scale factor 3

B. $(x, y) \rightarrow (x + 3, y)$ _____ translation 3 units up

C. $(x, y) \rightarrow (x, 3y)$ _____ translation 3 units right

D. $(x, y) \rightarrow (x, y + 3)$ _____ horizontal stretch by a factor of 3

E. $(x, y) \rightarrow (3x, 3y)$ _____ vertical stretch by a factor of 3

Draw the image of each figure under the given transformation. Then describe the transformation as a rigid motion or not a rigid motion. Justify your answer.

15. $(x, y) \rightarrow (2x + 4, y)$

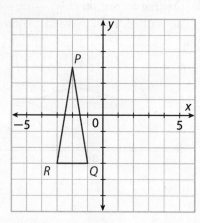

16. $(x, y) \rightarrow (0.5x, y - 4)$

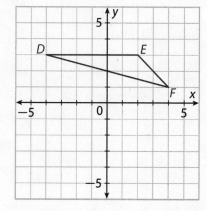

17. **Explain the Error** A student claimed that the transformation $(x, y) \rightarrow (3x, y)$ is a rigid motion because the segment joining $(5, 0)$ to $(5, 2)$ is transformed to the segment joining $(15, 0)$ to $(15, 2)$, and both of these segments have the same length. Explain the student's error.

18. **Critical Thinking** Write a rule for a transformation that maps $\triangle STU$ to $\triangle S'T'U'$.

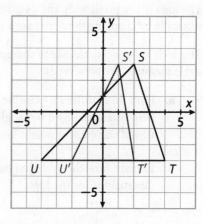

19. **Justify Reasoning** Consider the transformation given by the rule $(x, y) \rightarrow (0, 0)$. Describe the transformation in words. Then explain whether or not the transformation is a rigid motion and justify your reasoning.

20. **Communicate Mathematical Ideas** One of the properties of rigid motions states that rigid motions preserve parallelism. Explain what this means, and give an example using a specific figure and a specific rigid motion. Include a graph of the preimage and image.

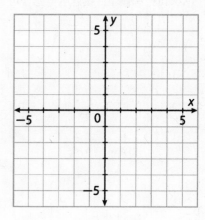

Lesson Performance Task

A Web designer has created the logo shown here for Matrix Engineers.

The logo is 100 pixels wide and 24 pixels high. Images placed in Web pages can be stretched horizontally and vertically by changing the dimensions in the code for the Web page.

The Web designer would like to change the dimensions of the logo so that lengths are increased or decreased but angle measures are preserved.

a. Find three different possible sets of dimensions for the width and height so that lengths are changed but angle measures are preserved. The dimensions must be whole numbers of pixels. Justify your choices.

b. Explain how the Web designer can use transformations to find additional possible dimensions for the logo.

16.4 Reasoning and Proof

Essential Question: How do you go about proving a statement?

🧭 Explore   Exploring Inductive and Deductive Reasoning

A **conjecture** is a statement that is believed to be true. You can use *inductive* or *deductive* reasoning to show, or *prove*, that a conjecture is true. **Inductive reasoning** is the process of reasoning that a rule or statement is true because specific cases are true. **Deductive reasoning** is the process of using logic to draw conclusions.

Complete the steps to make a conjecture about the sum of three consecutive counting numbers.

Ⓐ   Write a sum to represent the first three consecutive counting numbers, starting with 1.

_____

Ⓑ   Is the sum divisible by 3?

_____

Ⓒ   Write the sum of the next three consecutive counting numbers, starting with 2.

_____

Ⓓ   Is the sum divisible by 3?

_____

Ⓔ   Complete the conjecture:

The _____ of three consecutive counting numbers is divisible by _____.

Recall that postulates are statements you accept are true. A **theorem** is a statement that you can prove is true using a series of logical steps. The steps of deductive reasoning involve using appropriate undefined words, defined words, mathematical relationships, postulates, or other previously-proven theorems to prove that the theorem is true.

Use deductive reasoning to prove that the sum of three consecutive counting numbers is divisible by 3.

Ⓕ   Let the three consecutive counting numbers be represented by n, $n + 1$, and ⬚.

Ⓖ   The sum of the three consecutive counting numbers can be written as $3n +$ ⬚.

Ⓗ The expression $3n + 3$ can be factored as $3\left(\boxed{}\right)$.

Ⓘ The expression $3(n + 1)$ is divisible by $\boxed{}$ for all values of n.

Ⓙ Recall the conjecture in Step E: The sum of three consecutive counting numbers is divisible by 3.

Look at the steps in your deductive reasoning. Is the conjecture true or false? _____

Reflect

1. **Discussion** A **counterexample** is an example that shows a conjecture to be false. Do you think that counterexamples are used mainly in inductive reasoning or in deductive reasoning?

_____

_____

2. Suppose you use deductive reasoning to show that an angle is not acute. Can you conclude that the angle is obtuse? Explain.

_____

_____

_____

⚒ Explain 1 Introducing Proofs

A **conditional statement** is a statement that can be written in the form "If p, then q" where p is the *hypothesis* and q is the *conclusion*. For example, in the conditional statement "If $3x - 5 = 13$, then $x = 6$," the hypothesis is "$3x - 5 = 13$" and the conclusion is "$x = 6$."

Most of the Properties of Equality can be written as conditional statements. You can use these properties to solve an equation like "$3x - 5 = 13$" to prove that "$x = 6$."

Properties of Equality	
Addition Property of Equality	If $a = b$, then $a + c = b + c$.
Subtraction Property of Equality	If $a = b$, then $a - c = b - c$.
Multiplication Property of Equality	If $a = b$, then $ac = bc$.
Division Property of Equality	If $a = b$ and $c \neq 0$, then $\frac{a}{c} = \frac{b}{c}$.
Reflexive Property of Equality	$a = a$
Symmetric Property of Equality	If $a = b$, then $b = a$.
Transitive Property of Equality	If $a = b$ and $b = c$, then $a = c$.
Substitution Property of Equality	If $a = b$, then b can be substituted for a in any expression.

© Houghton Mifflin Harcourt Publishing Company

Example 1 Use deductive reasoning to solve the equation. Use the Properties of Equality to justify each step.

(A) $14 = 3x - 4$

$14 = 3x - 4$

$18 = 3x$ Addition Property of Equality

$6 = x$ Division Property of Equality

$x = 6$ Symmetric Property of Equality

(B) $9 = 17 - 4x$

$9 = 17 - 4x$

$\boxed{} = -4x$ _____ Property of Equality

$\boxed{} = -4x$

$\boxed{} = x$ _____ Property of Equality

$x = \boxed{}$ _____ Property of Equality

Your Turn

Write each statement as a conditional.

3. All zebras belong to the genus *Equus*.

4. The bill will pass if it gets two-thirds of the vote in the Senate.

5. Use deductive reasoning to solve the equation $3 - 4x = -5$.

6. Identify the Property of Equality that is used in each statement.

If $x = 2$, then $2x = 4$.	
$5 = 3a$; therefore, $3a = 5$.	
If $T = 4$, then $5T + 7$ equals 27.	
If $9 = 4x$ and $4x = m$, then $9 = m$.	

⚙ Explain 2 Using Postulates about Segments and Angles

Recall that two angles whose measures add up to 180° are called *supplementary angles*. The following theorem shows one type of supplementary angle pair, called a *linear pair*. A **linear pair** is a pair of adjacent angles whose non-common sides are opposite rays. You will prove this theorem in an exercise in this lesson.

The Linear Pair Theorem

If two angles form a linear pair, then they are supplementary.

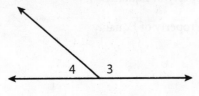

$m\angle 3 + m\angle 4 = 180°$

You can use the Linear Pair Theorem, as well as the Segment Addition Postulate and Angle Addition Postulate, to find missing values in expressions for segment lengths and angle measures.

Example 2 Use a postulate or theorem to find the value of x in each figure.

Ⓐ Given: $RT = 5x - 12$

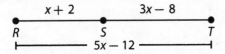

Use the Segment Addition Postulate.

$$RS + ST = RT$$

$$(x + 2) + (3x - 8) = 5x - 12$$

$$4x - 6 = 5x - 12$$

$$6 = x$$

$$x = 6$$

© Houghton Mifflin Harcourt Publishing Company

Ⓑ Given: m∠RST = (15x − 10)°

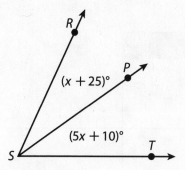

R

P

(x + 25)°

(5x + 10)°

S   T

Use the _____ Postulate.

$$m\angle RST = m\angle \boxed{} + m\angle \boxed{}$$

$$(15x - 10)° = \boxed{}° + \boxed{}°$$

$$15x - 10 = \boxed{}$$

$$\boxed{} x = \boxed{}$$

$$x = \boxed{}$$

Reflect

7. **Discussion** The Linear Pair Theorem uses the terms *opposite rays* as well as *adjacent angles*. Write a definition for each of these terms. Compare your definitions with your classmates.

_____

_____

_____

Your Turn

8. Two angles *LMN* and *NMP* form a linear pair. The measure of ∠*LMN* is twice the measure of ∠*NMP*. Find m∠*LMN*.

Postulates about points, lines, and planes help describe geometric figures.

Postulates about Points, Lines, and Planes

Through any two points, there is exactly one line.

Through any three noncollinear points, there is exactly one plane containing them.

If two points lie in a plane, then the line containing those points lies in the plane.

If two lines intersect, then they intersect in exactly one point.

If two planes intersect, then they intersect in exactly one line.

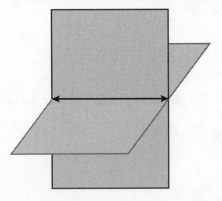

Example 3 Use each figure to name the results described.

Ⓐ

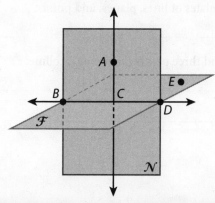

Description	Example from the figure
the line of intersection of two planes	Possible answer: The two planes intersect in line *BD*.
the point of intersection of two lines	The line through point *A* and the line through point *B* intersect at point *C*.
three coplanar points	Possible answer: The points *B, D,* and *E* are coplanar.
three collinear points	The points *B, C,* and *D* are collinear.

Ⓑ

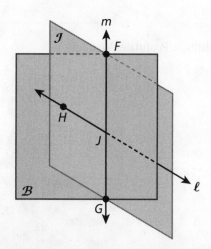

Description	Example from the figure
the line of intersection of two planes	
the point of intersection of two lines	
three coplanar points	
three collinear points	

9. Find examples in your classroom that illustrate the postulates of lines, planes, and points.

_____

10. Draw a diagram of a plane with three collinear points and three points that are noncollinear.

_____

💬 Elaborate

11. What is the difference between a postulate and a definition? Give an example of each.

_____

_____

_____

_____

_____

12. Give an example of a diagram illustrating the Segment Addition Postulate. Write the Segment Addition Postulate as a conditional statement.

13. Explain why photographers often use a tripod when taking pictures.

_____

_____

_____

14. Essential Question Check-In What are some of the reasons you can give in proving a statement using deductive reasoning?

_____

_____

Explain why the given conclusion uses inductive reasoning.

1. Find the next term in the pattern: 3, 6, 9.
The next term is 12 because the previous terms are multiples of 3.

2. $3 + 5 = 8$ and $13 + 5 = 18$, therefore the sum of two odd numbers is an even number.

3. My neighbor has two cats and both cats have yellow eyes.
Therefore when two cats live together, they will both have yellow eyes.

4. It always seems to rain the day after July 4th.

Give a counterexample for each conclusion.

5. If x is a prime number, then $x + 1$ is not a prime number.

6. The difference between two even numbers is positive.

7. Points A, B, and C are noncollinear, so therefore they are noncoplanar.

8. The square of a number is always greater than the number.

In Exercises 9–12 use deductive reasoning to write a conclusion.

9. If a number is divisible by 2, then it is even.
The number 14 is divisible by 2.

Use deductive reasoning to write a conclusion.

10. If two planes intersect, then they intersect in exactly one line.
Planes ℜ and ℑ intersect.

11. Through any three noncollinear points, there is exactly one plane containing them.
Points W, X, and Y are noncollinear.

12. If the sum of the digits of an integer is divisible by 3, then the number is divisible by 3.
The sum of the digits of 46,125 is 18, which is divisible by 3.

Identify the hypothesis and conclusion of each statement.

13. If the ball is red, then it will bounce higher.

14. If a plane contains two lines, then they are coplanar.

15. If the light does not come on, then the circuit is broken.

16. You must wear your jacket if it is cold outside.

Use a definition, postulate, or theorem to find the value of x in the figure described.

17. Point E is between points D and F. If $DE = x - 4$, $EF = 2x + 5$, and $DF = 4x - 8$, find x.

18. Y is the midpoint of $\overline{XZ}$. If $XZ = 8x - 2$ and $YZ = 2x + 1$, find x.

19. $\overrightarrow{SV}$ is an angle bisector of $\angle RST$. If $m\angle RSV = (3x + 5)°$ and $m\angle RST = (8x - 14)°$, find x.

20. $\angle ABC$ and $\angle CBD$ are a linear pair. If $m\angle ABC = m\angle CBD = 3x - 6$, find x.

Use the figure for Exercises 21 and 22.

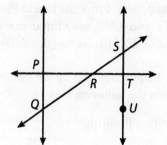

21. Name three collinear points.

22. Name two linear pairs.

Explain the error in each statement.

23. Two planes can intersect in a single point.

24. Three points have to be collinear.

25. A line is contained in exactly one plane

26. If $x^2 = 25$, then $x = 5$.

H.O.T. Focus on Higher Order Thinking

27. **Analyze Relationships** What is the greatest number of intersection points 4 coplanar lines can have? What is the greatest number of planes determined by 4 noncollinear points? Draw diagrams to illustrate your answers.

28. Justify Reasoning Prove the Linear Pair Theorem.
Given: $\angle MJK$ and $\angle MJL$ are a linear pair of angles.
Prove: $\angle MJK$ and $\angle MJL$ are supplementary.

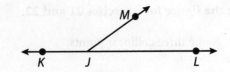

Complete the proof by writing the missing reasons.
Choose from the following reasons.

Angle Addition Postulate   Definition of linear pair

Substitution Property of Equality   Given

Statements	Reasons
1. $\angle MJK$ and $\angle MJL$ are a linear pair.	1.
2. $\overrightarrow{JL}$ and $\overrightarrow{JK}$ are opposite rays.	2.
3. $\overrightarrow{JL}$ and $\overrightarrow{JK}$ form a straight line.	3. Definition of opposite rays
4. $m\angle LJK = 180°$	4. Definition of straight angle
5. $m\angle MJK + m\angle MJL = m\angle LJK$	5.
6. $m\angle MJK + m\angle MJL = 180°$	6.
7. $\angle MJK$ and $\angle MJL$ are supplementary.	7. Definition of supplementary angles

Lesson Performance Task

If two planes intersect, then they intersect in exactly one line.

Find a real-world example that illustrates the postulate above. Then formulate a conjecture by completing the following statement:

If three planes intersect, then _____.

Justify your conjecture with real-world examples or a drawing.

Tools of Geometry

Essential Question: How can you use tools of geometry to solve real-world problems?

KEY EXAMPLE   *(Lesson 16.1)*

Find the midpoint of $(5, 6)$ and $(1, 3)$.

$\left(\dfrac{5 + 1}{2}, \dfrac{6 + 3}{2}\right)$ Apply the midpoint formula.

$= \left(\dfrac{6}{2}, \dfrac{9}{2}\right)$ Simplify the numerators.

$= \left(3, \dfrac{9}{2}\right)$ Simplify.

KEY EXAMPLE   *(Lesson 16.2)*

The ray $\overrightarrow{BD}$ is the angle bisector of $\angle ABC$ and $m\angle ABC = 40°$. Find $m\angle ABD$.

$\overrightarrow{BD}$ is the angle bisector of $\angle ABC$ so it divides the angle into two angles of equal measure.

Then $m\angle ABD + m\angle DBC = m\angle ABC$ and $m\angle ABD = m\angle DBC$.

So, $2 \cdot m\angle ABD = m\angle ABC$.

$m\angle ABD = 20°$ Substitute the angles and simplify.

KEY EXAMPLE   *(Lesson 16.3)*

Use the rule $(x, y) \rightarrow (x + 1, 2y)$ and the points of a triangle, $A(1, 2)$, $B(2, 4)$, and $C(2, 2)$ to find the image. Determine whether this is a rigid motion.

$A'\big(1 + 1, 2(2)\big)$, $B'\big(2 + 1, 2(4)\big)$, $C'\big(2 + 1, 2(2)\big)$ Use the transformation rule.

$A'(2, 4)$, $B'(3, 8)$, $C'(3, 4)$ Simplify.

$A'B' = \sqrt{(3 - 2)^2 + (8 - 4)^2}$ Use the distance formula to find the distance between A' and B'.

$= \sqrt{17} \approx 4.1$ Simplify.

$AB = \sqrt{(2 - 1)^2 + (4 - 2)^2}$ Use the distance formula to find the distance between A and B.

$= \sqrt{5} \approx 2.2$ Simplify.

The image is not a rigid motion because the side lengths are not equal.

Key Vocabulary

point *(punto)*
line *(línea)*
plane *(plano)*
line segment *(segmento de línea)*
endpoints *(punto final)*
ray *(rayo)*
coplanar *(coplanares)*
parallel *(paralelo)*
collinear *(colineales)*
postulate *(postulado)*
midpoint *(punto medio)*
segment bisector *(segmento bisectriz)*
angle *(ángulo)*
vertex *(vértice)*
side *(lado)*
degrees *(grados)*
angle bisector *(bisectriz de un ángulo)*
transformation *(transformación)*
preimage *(preimagen)*
image *(imagen)*
rigid motion *(movimiento rígido)*
conjecture *(conjetura)*
inductive reasoning *(razonamiento inductivo)*
deductive reasoning *(razonamiento deductivo)*
theorem *(teorema)*
counterexample *(contraejemplo)*
conditional statement *(sentencia condicional)*
linear pair *(par lineal)*

© Houghton Mifflin Harcourt Publishing Company

EXERCISES

Find the midpoint of the pairs of points. *(Lesson 16.1)*

1. $(4, 7)$ and $(2, 9)$ _____

2. $(5, 5)$ and $(-1, 3)$ _____

Find the measure of the angle formed by the angle bisector. *(Lesson 16.2)*

3. The ray $\overrightarrow{BD}$ is the angle bisector of $\angle ABC$ and $m\angle ABC = 110°$. Find $m\angle ABD$. _____

Use the rule $(x, y) \rightarrow (3x, 2y)$ to find the image for the preimage defined by the points. Determine whether the transformation is a rigid motion. *(Lesson 16.3)*

4. $A(3, 5)$, $B(5, 3)$, $C(2, 2)$

The points of the image are _____.

The image _____ a rigid motion.

Determine whether the conjecture uses inductive or deductive reasoning. *(Lesson 16.4)*

5. The child chose Rock in all four games of Rock-Paper-Scissors. The child always chooses Rock.

MODULE PERFORMANCE TASK

How Far Is It?

Many smartphone apps and online search engines will tell you the distances to nearby restaurants from your current location. How do they do that? Basically, they use latitude and longitude coordinates from GPS to calculate the distances. Let's explore how that works for some longer distances.

The table lists latitude and longitude for four state capitals. Use an app or search engine to find the latitude and longitude for your current location, and record them in the last line of the table.

- Which of the state capitals do you think is nearest to you? Which is farthest away? Use the distance formula to calculate your distance from each of the cities in degrees. Then convert each distance to miles.

- Use an app or search engine to find the distance between your location and each of the capital cities. How do these distances compare with the ones you calculated? How might you account for any differences?

City	Latitude	Longitude
Austin, TX	30.31° N	97.76° W
Columbus, OH	39.98° N	82.99° W
Nashville, TN	36.17° N	86.78 ° W
Sacramento, CA	38.57° N	121.5° W
Your Location		

16.1–16.4 Tools of Geometry

• Online Homework
• Hints and Help
• Extra Practice

Use a definition, postulate, or theorem to find the value desired.

1. Point M is the midpoint between points $A(-5, 4)$ and $B(-1, -6)$. Find the location of M. *(Lesson 16.1)*

Given triangle EFG, graph its image $E'F'G'$ and confirm that the transformation preserves length and angle measure. *(Lessons 16.1, 16.3)*

2. $(x, y) \rightarrow (x - 1, y + 5)$

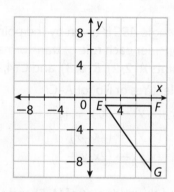

Find the measure of the angle formed by the angle bisector. *(Lesson 16.2)*

3. The ray $\overrightarrow{GJ}$ is the angle bisector of $\angle FGH$ and $m\angle FGH = 75°$. Find $m\angle FGJ$.

4. The ray $\overrightarrow{XZ}$ is the angle bisector of $\angle WXY$ and $m\angle WXY = 155°$. Find $m\angle YXZ$.

ESSENTIAL QUESTION

5. When is a protractor preferred to a ruler when finding a measurement?

Assessment Readiness

1. For two angles, $\angle ABC$ and $\angle DBC$, m$\angle ABC = 30°$ and $\angle DBC$ is its complement. Ray $\overrightarrow{BE}$ is the angle bisector of $\angle ABD$. Consider each angle. Does the angle have a measure of 45°?

   Select Yes or No for A–C.

   A. $\angle DBC$ ◯ Yes   ◯ No

   B. $\angle ABE$ ◯ Yes   ◯ No

   C. $\angle DBE$ ◯ Yes   ◯ No

2. The line $y = \sqrt{x}$ is transformed into $y = \sqrt{5x}$. Choose True or False for each statement.

   A. A dilation can be used to obtain this transformation.   ◯ True   ◯ False

   B. A rotation can be used to obtain this transformation.   ◯ True   ◯ False

   C. A translation can be used to obtain this transformation.   ◯ True   ◯ False

3. Triangle ABC is given by the points $A(1, 1)$, $B(3, 2)$, and $C(2, 3)$. Consider each rule of transformation. Does the rule result in an image with points $A'(2, 2)$, $B'(6, 3)$, and $C'(4, 4)$?

   Select Yes or No for A–C.

   A. $(x, y) \rightarrow (x, y + 1)$ ◯ Yes   ◯ No

   B. $(x, y) \rightarrow (2x, 2y)$ ◯ Yes   ◯ No

   C. $(x, y) \rightarrow (2x, y + 1)$ ◯ Yes   ◯ No

4. Find the midpoint of $(4, 5)$ and $(-2, 12)$. Show your work.

Transformations and Symmetry

Essential Question: How can you use transformations to solve real-world problems?

REAL WORLD VIDEO
Check out how transformations can be used to cut patterns out of fabric as efficiently as possible.

MODULE PERFORMANCE TASK PREVIEW

Animating Digital Images

In this module, you will use transformations to create a simple animation of a bird in flight. How do computer animators use translations, rotations, and reflections? Let's find out.

Are YOU Ready?

Complete these exercises to review the skills you will need for this module.

Properties of Reflections

Example 1 A figure in the first quadrant is reflected over the *x*-axis. What quadrant is the image in?

The image is in the fourth quadrant. A figure drawn on tracing paper can be reflected across the *x*-axis by folding the paper along the axis.

Find the quadrant of each image.

1. The image from reflecting a figure in the first quadrant over the *y*-axis _____

2. The image from reflecting a figure in the second quadrant over the *x*-axis _____

Properties of Rotations

Example 2 A figure in the first quadrant is rotated 90° counterclockwise around the origin. What quadrant is the image in?

The image is in the second quadrant. In the second quadrant, each point of the figure forms a clockwise 90° angle around the origin with its corresponding point in the original figure.

Find the quadrant of each image.

3. The image from rotating a figure in the third quadrant 180° clockwise _____

4. The image from rotating a figure in the first quadrant 360° clockwise _____

Properties of Translations

Example 3 A figure in the first quadrant is translated up 3 units and to the right 1 unit. What quadrant is the image in?

The image is in the first quadrant. A translation only moves the image in a direction; the image is not reflected or rotated.

Answer each question.

5. A figure in the first quadrant is translated down and to the right. Is it known what quadrant the image is in?

_____

6. A figure is translated 3 units up and 2 units left. How large is the image in comparison to the figure?

_____

17.1 Translations

Essential Question: How do you draw the image of a figure under a translation?

Resource Locker

⊘ Explore Exploring Translations

A translation slides all points of a figure the same distance in the same direction.

You can use tracing paper to model translating a triangle.

(A) First, draw a triangle on lined paper. Label the vertices *A*, *B*, and *C*. Then draw a line segment *XY*. An example of what your drawing may look like is shown.

(B) Use tracing paper to draw a copy of triangle *ABC*. Then copy $\overline{XY}$ so that the point *X* is on top of point *A*. Label the point made from *Y* as *A'*.

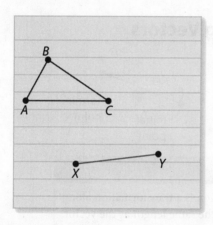

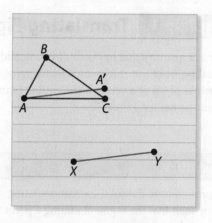

(C) Using the same piece of tracing paper, place *A'* on *A* and draw a copy of △*ABC*. Label the corresponding vertices *B'* and *C'*. An example of what your drawing may look like is shown.

(D) Use a ruler to draw line segments from each vertex of the preimage to the corresponding vertex on the new image.

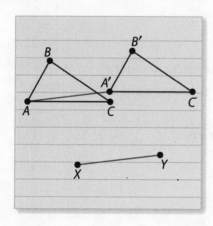

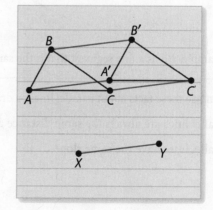

Ⓔ Measure the distances *AA'*, *BB'*, *CC'*, and *XY*. Describe how *AA'*, *BB'*, and *CC'* compare to the length *XY*.

_____

_____

Reflect

1. Are *BB'*, *AA'*, and *CC'* parallel, perpendicular, or neither? Describe how you can check that your answer is reasonable.

_____

_____

_____

2. How does the angle *BAC* relate to the angle *B'A'C'*? Explain.

_____

_____

_____

🔑 Explain 1   Translating Figures Using Vectors

A **vector** is a quantity that has both direction and magnitude.
The **initial point** of a vector is the starting point.
The **terminal point** of a vector is the ending point. The vector shown may be named $\overrightarrow{EF}$ or $\vec{v}$.

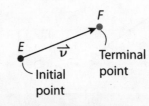

Translation

It is convenient to describe translations using vectors. A **translation** is a transformation along a vector such that the segment joining a point and its image has the same length as the vector and is parallel to the vector.

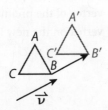

For example, *BB'* is a line segment that is the same length as and is parallel to vector $\vec{v}$.

You can use these facts about parallel lines to draw translations.

• Parallel lines are always the same distance apart and never intersect.

• Parallel lines have the same slope.

Example 1 Draw the image of △*ABC* after a translation along $\vec{v}$.

Ⓐ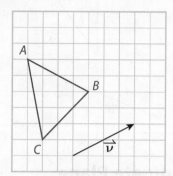

Draw a copy of $\vec{v}$ with its initial point at vertex *A* of △*ABC*. The copy must be the same length as $\vec{v}$, and it must be parallel to $\vec{v}$. Repeat this process at vertices *B* and *C*.

Draw segments to connect the terminal points of the vectors. Label the points *A'*, *B'*, and *C'*. △*A'B'C'* is the image of △*ABC*.

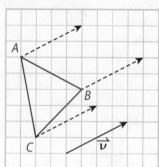

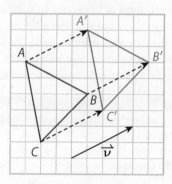

Ⓑ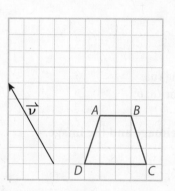

Draw a vector from the vertex *A* that is the same length as and _____ vector $\vec{v}$. The terminal point *A'* will be _____ units up and 3 units _____.

Draw three more vectors that are parallel from _____, _____, and _____ with terminal points *B'*, *C'*, and *D'*.

Draw segments connecting *A'*, *B'*, *C'*, and *D'* to form _____.

Reflect

3. How is drawing an image of quadrilateral *ABCD* like drawing an image of △*ABC*? How is it different?

_____

_____

_____

_____

4. Draw the image of △ABC after a translation along $\vec{v}$.

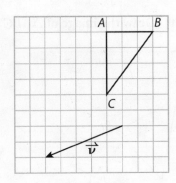

✏ Explain 2 Drawing Translations on a Coordinate Plane

A vector can also be named using component form, $\langle a, b \rangle$, which specifies the horizontal change a and the vertical change b from the initial point to the terminal point. The component form for $\overrightarrow{PQ}$ is $\langle 5, 3 \rangle$.

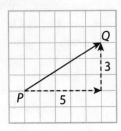

You can use the component form of the vector to draw coordinates for a new image on a coordinate plane. By using this vector to move a figure, you are moving the x-coordinate 5 units to the right. So, the new x-coordinate would be 5 greater than the x-coordinate in the preimage. Using this vector you are also moving the y-coordinate up 3 units. So, the new y-coordinate would be 3 greater than the y-coordinate in the preimage.

Rules for Translations on a Coordinate Plane	
Translation a units to the right	$\langle x, y \rangle \rightarrow \langle x + a, y \rangle$
Translation a units to the left	$\langle x, y \rangle \rightarrow \langle x - a, y \rangle$
Translation b units up	$\langle x, y \rangle \rightarrow \langle x, y + b \rangle$
Translation b units down	$\langle x, y \rangle \rightarrow \langle x, y - b \rangle$

So, when you move an image to the right a units and up b units, you use the rule $\langle x, y \rangle \rightarrow \langle x + a, y + b \rangle$ which is the same as moving the image along vector $\langle a, b \rangle$.

Example 2 Calculate the vertices of the image figure. Graph the preimage and the image.

Ⓐ Preimage coordinates: $(-2, 1)$, $(-3, -2)$, and $(-1, -2)$. Vector: $\langle 4, 6 \rangle$

Predict which quadrant the new image will be drawn in: 1st quadrant.

Use a table to record the new coordinates. Use vector components to write the transformation rule.

Then use the preimage coordinates to draw the preimage, and use the image coordinates to draw the new image.

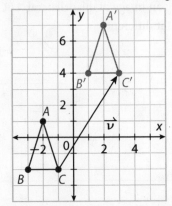

Preimage coordinates (x, y)	Image $(x + 4, y + 6)$
$(-2, 1)$	$(2, 7)$
$(-3, -2)$	$(1, 4)$
$(-1, -2)$	$(3, 4)$

B Preimage coordinates: $A(3, 0)$, $B(2, -2)$, and $C(4, -2)$. Vector $\langle -2, 3 \rangle$

Prediction: The image will be in Quadrant _____.

Preimage coordinates (x, y)	Image $\left(x - \boxed{}, y + \boxed{} \right)$	
(3, 0)	$\left(\boxed{}, \boxed{} \right)$	
(2, -2)	$\left(\boxed{}, \boxed{} \right)$	
(4, -2)	$\left(\boxed{}, \boxed{} \right)$	

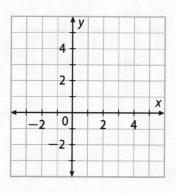

Your Turn

Draw the preimage and image of each triangle under a translation along $\langle -4, 1 \rangle$.

5. Triangle with coordinates:
$A(2, 4)$, $B(1, 2)$, $C(4, 2)$.

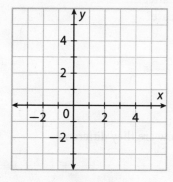

6. Triangle with coordinates:
$P(2, -1)$, $Q(2, -3)$, $R(4, -3)$.

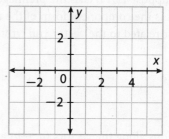

🔑 Explain 3 Specifying Translation Vectors

You may be asked to specify a translation that carries a given figure onto another figure.
You can do this by drawing the translation vector and then writing it in component form.

Example 3 Specify the component form of the vector that maps $\triangle ABC$ to $\triangle A'B'C'$.

A

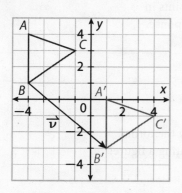

Determine the components of $\vec{v}$.

The horizontal change from the initial point $(-4, 1)$ to the terminal point $(1, -3)$ is $1 - (-4) = 5$.

The vertical change from the initial point $(-4, 1)$ to the terminal point $(1, -3)$ is $-3 - 1 = -4$

Write the vector in component form.

$$\vec{v} = \langle 5, -4 \rangle$$

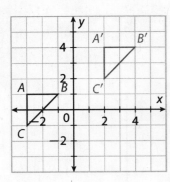

Ⓑ Draw the vector $\vec{v}$ from a vertex of $\triangle ABC$ to its image in $\triangle A'B'C'$.

Determine the components of $\vec{v}$.

The horizontal change from the initial point $(-3, 1)$ to the terminal point $(2, 4)$ is _____ – _____ = _____.

The vertical change from the initial point to the terminal point is _____ – _____ = _____

Write the vector in component form. $\vec{v} = \left\langle \boxed{}, \boxed{} \right\rangle$

Reflect

7. What is the component form of a vector that translates figures horizontally? Explain.

_____

_____

Your Turn

8. In Example 3A, suppose $\triangle A'B'C'$ is the preimage and $\triangle ABC$ is the image after translation. What is the component form of the translation vector in this case? How is this vector related to the vector you wrote in Example 3A?

💬 Elaborate

9. How are translations along the vectors $\langle a, -b \rangle$ and $\langle -a, b \rangle$ similar and how are they different?

_____

_____

10. A translation along the vector $\langle -2, 7 \rangle$ maps point P to point Q. The coordinates of point Q are $(4, -1)$. What are the coordinates of point P? Explain your reasoning.

_____

_____

11. A translation along the vector $\langle a, b \rangle$ maps points in Quadrant I to points in Quadrant III. What can you conclude about a and b? Justify your response.

_____

_____

_____

12. Essential Question Check-In How does translating a figure using the formal definition of a translation compare to the previous method of translating a figure?

_____

_____

☆ Evaluate: Homework and Practice

• Online Homework
• Hints and Help
• Extra Practice

Draw the image of △ABC after a translation along $\vec{v}$.

1.

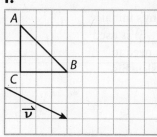

2.

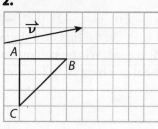

3.

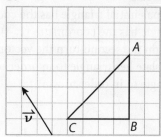

4. Line segment $\overline{XY}$ was used to draw a copy of △ABC. $\overline{XY}$ is 3.5 centimeters long. What is the length of $AA' + BB' + CC'$?

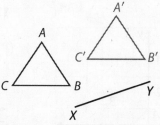

Draw the preimage and image of each triangle under the given translation.

5. Triangle: $A(-3, -1)$;
$B(-2, 2)$; $C(0, -1)$;
Vector: $\langle 3, 2 \rangle$

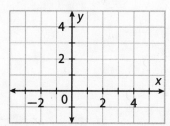

6. Triangle: $P(1, -3)$;
$Q(3, -1)$; $R(4, -3)$;
Vector: $\langle -1, 3 \rangle$

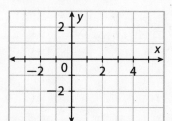

7. Triangle: $X(0, 3)$;
$Y(-1, 1)$; $Z(-3, 4)$;
Vector: $\langle 4, -2 \rangle$

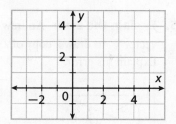

8. Find the coordinates of the image under the transformation $\langle 6, -11 \rangle$.

$(x, y) \rightarrow$ $(2, -3) \rightarrow$

$(3, 1) \rightarrow$ $(4, -3) \rightarrow$

9. Name the vector. Write it in component form.

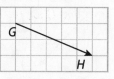

10. Match each set of coordinates for a preimage with the coordinates of its image after applying the vector $\langle 3, -8 \rangle$. Indicate a match by writing a letter for a preimage on the line in front of the corresponding image.

A. $(1, 1)$; $(10, 1)$; $(6, 5)$ _____ $(6, -10)$; $(6, -4)$; $(9, -3)$

B. $(0, 0)$; $(3, 8)$; $(4, 0)$; $(7, 8)$ _____ $(1, -6)$; $(5, -6)$; $(-1, -8)$; $(7, -8)$

C. $(3, -2)$; $(3, 4)$; $(6, 5)$ _____ $(4, -7)$; $(13, -7)$; $(9, -3)$

D. $(-2, 2)$; $(2, 2)$; $(-4, 0)$; $(4, 0)$ _____ $(3, -8)$; $(6, 0)$; $(7, -8)$; $(10, 0)$

11. **Persevere in Problem Solving** Emma and Tony are playing a game. Each draws a triangle on a coordinate grid. For each turn, Emma chooses either the horizontal or vertical value for a vector in component form. Tony chooses the other value, alternating each turn. They each have to draw a new image of their triangle using the vector with the components they chose and using the image from the prior turn as the preimage. Whoever has drawn an image in each of the four quadrants first wins the game.

Emma's initial triangle has the coordinates $(-3, 0)$, $(-4, -2)$, $(-2, -2)$ and Tony's initial triangle has the coordinates $(2, 4)$, $(2, 2)$, $(4, 3)$. On the first turn the vector $\langle 6, -5 \rangle$ is used and on the second turn the vector $\langle -10, 8 \rangle$ is used. What quadrant does Emma need to translate her triangle to in order to win? What quadrant does Tony need to translate his triangle to in order to win?

Specify the component form of the vector that maps each figure to its image.

12.

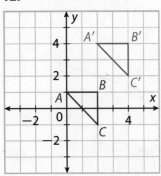

13.

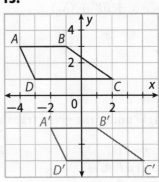

14.

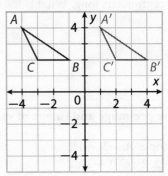

15. **Explain the Error** Andrew is using vector $\vec{v}$ to draw a copy of $\triangle ABC$. Explain his error.

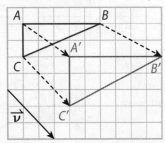

16. **Explain the Error** Marcus was asked to identify the vector that maps $\triangle DEF$ to $\triangle D'E'F'$. He drew a vector as shown and determined that the component form of the vector is $\langle 3, 1 \rangle$. Explain his error.

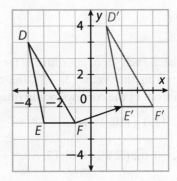

17. **Algebra** A cartographer is making a city map. Line *m* represents Murphy Street. The cartographer translates points on line *m* along the vector $\langle 2, -2 \rangle$ to draw Nolan Street. Draw the line for Nolan Street on the coordinate plane and write its equation. What is the image of the point $(0, 3)$ in this situation?

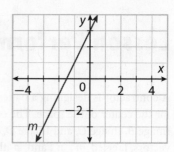

18. **Represent Real-World Problems** A builder is trying to level out some ground with a front-end loader. He picks up some excess dirt at (9, 16) and then maneuvers through the job site along the vectors $\langle -6, 0 \rangle$, $\langle 2, 5 \rangle$, $\langle 8, 10 \rangle$ to get to the spot to unload the dirt. Find the coordinates of the unloading point. Find a single vector from the loading point to the unloading point.

19. **Look for a Pattern** A checker player's piece begins at *K* and, through a series of moves, lands on *L*. What translation vector represents the path from *K* to *L*?

20. **Represent Real-World Problems** A group of hikers walks 2 miles east and then 1 mile north. After taking a break, they then hike 4 miles east to their final destination. What vector describes their hike from their starting position to their final destination? Let 1 unit represent 1 mile.

21. **Communicate Mathematical Ideas** In a quilt pattern, a polygon with vertices $(-4, -2)$, $(-3, -1)$, $(-2, -2)$, and $(-3, -3)$ is translated repeatedly along the vector $\langle 2, 2 \rangle$. What are the coordinates of the third polygon in the pattern? Explain how you solved the problem.

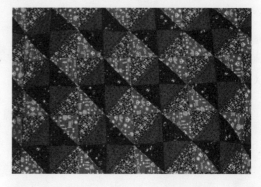

Lesson Performance Task

A contractor is designing a pattern for tiles in an entryway, using a sun design called Image *A* for the center of the space. The contractor wants to duplicate this design three times, labeled Image *B*, Image *C*, and Image *D*, above Image *A* so that they do not overlap. Identify the three vectors, labeled $\vec{m}$, $\vec{n}$, and $\vec{p}$ that could be used to draw the design, and write them in component form. Draw the images on grid paper using the vectors you wrote.

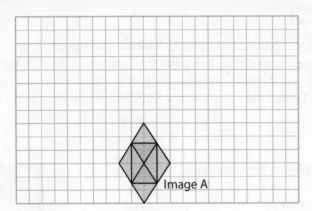

Image A

17.2 Reflections

Essential Question: How do you draw the image of a figure under a reflection?

⊘ Explore   Exploring Reflections

Use tracing paper to explore reflections.

(A) Draw and label a line ℓ on tracing paper. Then draw and label a quadrilateral *ABCD* with vertex *C* on line ℓ.

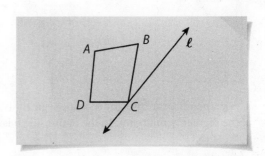

(B) Fold the tracing paper along line ℓ. Trace the quadrilateral. Then unfold the paper and draw the image of the quadrilateral. Label it *A′ B′ C′ D′*.

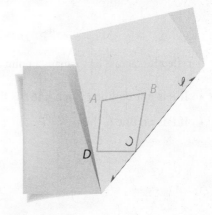

(C) Draw segments to connect each vertex of quadrilateral *ABCD* with its image. Use a protractor to measure the angle formed by each segment and line ℓ. What do you notice?

_____

(D) Use a ruler to measure each segment and the two shorter segments formed by its intersection with line ℓ. What do you notice?

_____

Reflect

1. In this activity, the fold line (line ℓ) is the line of reflection. What happens when a point is located on the line of reflection?

_____

_____

2. Discussion A student claims that a figure and its reflected image always lie on opposite sides of the line of reflection. Do you agree? Why or why not?

_____

_____

_____

🔑 Explain 1   Reflecting Figures Using Graph Paper

Perpendicular lines are lines that intersect at right angles. In the figure, line ℓ is perpendicular to line m. The right angle mark in the figure indicates that the lines are perpendicular.

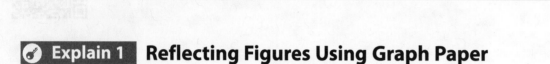

The **perpendicular bisector** of a line segment is a line perpendicular to the segment at the segment's midpoint. In the figure, line n is the perpendicular bisector of $\overline{AB}$.

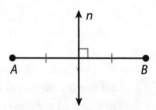

A **reflection** across line ℓ maps a point P to its image P'.

- If P is not on line ℓ, then line ℓ is the perpendicular bisector of $\overline{PP'}$.
- If P is on line ℓ, then $P = P'$.

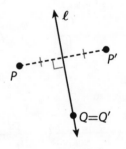

Example 1   Draw the image of $\triangle ABC$ after a reflection across line ℓ.

(A) **Step 1** Draw a segment with an endpoint at vertex A so that the segment is perpendicular to line ℓ and is bisected by line ℓ. Label the other endpoint of the segment A'.

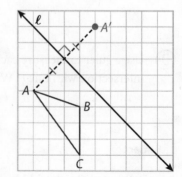

Step 2 Repeat Step 1 at vertices *B* and *C*.

Step 3 Connect points *A'*, *B'*, and *C'*.
△*A'B'C'* is the image of △*ABC*.

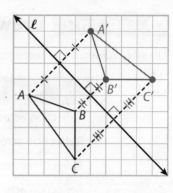

(B) Draw the image of △*ABC* after a reflection across line ℓ.

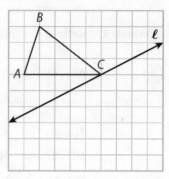

Step 1 Draw a segment with an endpoint at vertex *A* so that the segment is perpendicular to line ℓ and is bisected by line ℓ. Label the other endpoint of the segment *A'*.

Step 2 Repeat Step 1 at vertex *B*.

Notice that *C* and *C'* are the same point because *C* is on the line of reflection.

Step 3 Connect points *A'*, *B'*, and *C'*. △*A'B'C'* is the image of △*ABC*.

Reflect

3. How can you check that you drew the image of the triangle correctly?

_____

_____

_____

4. In Part A, how can you tell that $\overline{AA'}$ is perpendicular to line ℓ?

_____

_____

_____

Your Turn

Draw the image of △*ABC* after a reflection across line ℓ.

5.

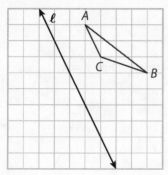

6.

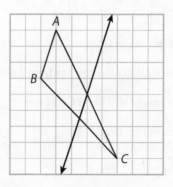

⚙ Explain 2 Drawing Reflections on a Coordinate Plane

The table summarizes coordinate notation for reflections on a coordinate plane.

Rules for Reflections on a Coordinate Plane	
Reflection across the x-axis	$(x, y) \rightarrow (x, -y)$
Reflection across the y-axis	$(x, y) \rightarrow (-x, y)$
Reflection across the line $y = x$	$(x, y) \rightarrow (y, x)$
Reflection across the line $y = -x$	$(x, y) \rightarrow (-y, -x)$

Example 2 Reflect the figure with the given vertices across the given line.

Ⓐ $M(1, 2)$, $N(1, 4)$, $P(3, 3)$; y-axis

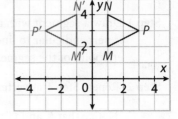

Step 1 Find the coordinates of the vertices of the image.

$A(x, y) \rightarrow A'(-x, y)$.

$M(1, 2) \rightarrow M'(-1, 2)$

$N(1, 4) \rightarrow N'(-1, 4)$

$P(3, 3) \rightarrow P'(-3, 3)$

Step 2 Graph the preimage.

Step 3 Predict the quadrant in which the image will lie. Since $\triangle MNP$ lies in Quadrant I and the triangle is reflected across the y-axis, the image will lie in Quadrant II.

Graph the image.

Ⓑ $D(2, 0)$, $E(2, 2)$, $F(5, 2)$, $G(5, 1)$; $y = x$

Step 1 Find the coordinates of the vertices of the image.

$A(x, y) \rightarrow A' \left(\boxed{} , \boxed{} \right)$

$D(2, 0) \rightarrow D' \left(\boxed{} , \boxed{} \right)$

$E(2, 2) \rightarrow E' \left(\boxed{} , \boxed{} \right)$

$F(5, 2) \rightarrow F' \left(\boxed{} , \boxed{} \right)$

$G(5, 1) \rightarrow G' \left(\boxed{} , \boxed{} \right)$

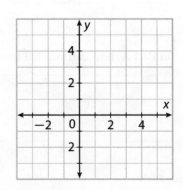

Step 2 Graph the preimage.

Step 3 Since $DEFG$ lies in Quadrant I and the quadrilateral is reflected across the line $y = x$,

the image will lie in Quadrant _____.

Graph the image.

7. How would the image of △MNP be similar to and different from the one you drew in Part A if the triangle were reflected across the x-axis?

_____

_____

8. A classmate claims that the rule $(x, y) \rightarrow (-x, y)$ for reflecting a figure across the y-axis only works if all the vertices are in the first quadrant because the values of x and y must be positive. Explain why this reasoning is not correct.

_____

_____

_____

Your Turn

Reflect the figure with the given vertices across the given line.

9. S(3, 4), T(3, 1), U(−2, 1), V(−2, 4); x-axis

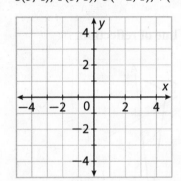

10. A(−4, −2), B(−1, −1), C(−1, −4); y = −x

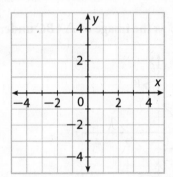

🔑 **Explain 3**   **Specifying Lines of Reflection**

Example 3   Given that △A′B′C′ is the image of △ABC under a reflection, draw the line of reflection.

Ⓐ Draw the segments $\overline{AA'}$, $\overline{BB'}$, and $\overline{CC'}$.

Find the midpoint of each segment.

The midpoint of $\overline{AA'}$ is $\left(\dfrac{-3 + 5}{2}, \dfrac{3 + (-1)}{2} \right) = (1, 1)$.

The midpoint of $\overline{BB'}$ is $\left(\dfrac{-2 + 2}{2}, \dfrac{0 + (-2)}{2} \right) = (0, -1)$.

The midpoint of $\overline{CC'}$ is $\left(\dfrac{-5 + 3}{2}, \dfrac{-1 + (-5)}{2} \right) = (-1, -3)$.

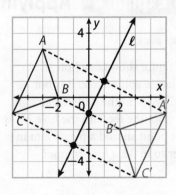

Plot the midpoints. Draw line ℓ through the midpoints.

Line ℓ is the line of reflection.

© Houghton Mifflin Harcourt Publishing Company

Ⓑ Draw $\overline{AA'}$, $\overline{BB'}$, and $\overline{CC'}$. Find the midpoint of each segment.

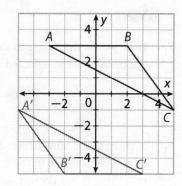

The midpoint of $\overline{AA'}$ is $\left(\dfrac{\boxed{} + \boxed{}}{2}, \dfrac{\boxed{} + \boxed{}}{2}\right) = \left(\boxed{}, \boxed{}\right)$.

The midpoint of $\overline{BB'}$ is $\left(\dfrac{\boxed{} + \boxed{}}{2}, \dfrac{\boxed{} + \boxed{}}{2}\right) = \left(\boxed{}, \boxed{}\right)$.

The midpoint of $\overline{CC'}$ is $\left(\dfrac{\boxed{} + \boxed{}}{2}, \dfrac{\boxed{} + \boxed{}}{2}\right) = \left(\boxed{}, \boxed{}\right)$.

Plot the midpoints. Draw line ℓ through the midpoints. Line ℓ is the line of reflection.

Reflect

11. How can you use a ruler and protractor to check that line ℓ is the line of reflection?

_____

_____

Your Turn

Given that $\triangle A'B'C'$ is the image of $\triangle ABC$ under a reflection, draw the line of reflection.

12.

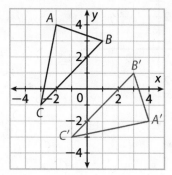

13.

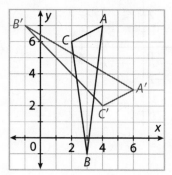

🔑 **Explain 4** **Applying Reflections**

Example 4

The figure shows one hole of a miniature golf course. It is not possible to hit the ball in a straight line from the tee T to the hole H. At what point should a player aim in order to make a hole in one?

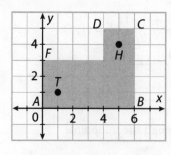

Understand the Problem

The problem asks you to locate point X on the wall of the miniature golf hole so that the ball can travel in a straight line from T to X and from X to H.

Make a Plan

In order for the ball to travel directly from T to X to H, the angle of the ball's path as it hits the wall must equal the angle of the ball's path as it leaves the wall. In the figure, m∠1 must equal m∠2.

Let H' be the reflection of point H across $\overline{BC}$.

Reflections preserve angle measure, so m∠2 = m∠ ☐ . Therefore, m∠1 is equal to

m∠2 when m∠1 is equal to m∠3. This occurs when T, ☐ , and H' are collinear.

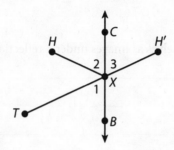

Solve

Reflect H across $\overline{BC}$ to locate H'.

The coordinates of H' are (☐ , ☐).

Draw $\overline{TH'}$ and locate point X where $\overline{TH'}$ intersects $\overline{BC}$.

The coordinates of point X are (☐ , ☐).

The player should aim at this point.

Look Back

To check that the answer is reasonable, plot point X using the coordinates you found. Then use a protractor to check that the angle of the ball's path as it hits the wall at point X is equal to the angle of the ball's path as it leaves the wall from point X.

Reflect

14. Is there another path the ball can take to hit a wall and then travel directly to the hole? Explain.

_____

_____

© Houghton Mifflin Harcourt Publishing Company

15. Cara is playing pool. She wants to use the cue ball C to hit the ball at point A without hitting the ball at point B. To do so, she has to bounce the cue ball off the side rail and into the ball at point A. Find the coordinates of the exact point along the side rail that Cara should aim for.

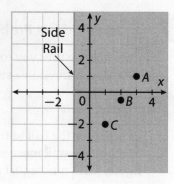

💬 Elaborate

16. Do any points in the plane have themselves as images under a reflection? Explain.

_____

_____

_____

_____

_____

17. If you are given a figure and its image under a reflection, how can you use paper folding to find the line of reflection?

_____

_____

_____

_____

_____

18. **Essential Question Check-In** How do you draw the image of a figure under a reflection across the x-axis?

_____

_____

_____

_____

• Online Homework
• Hints and Help
• Extra Practice

Use tracing paper to copy each figure and line ℓ. Then fold the paper to draw and label the image of the figure after a reflection across line ℓ.

1.

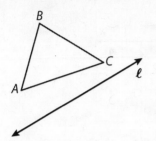

2.

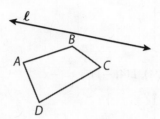

3.

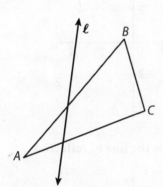

4.

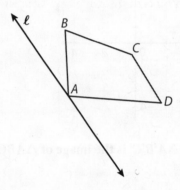

Draw the image of △ABC after a reflection across line ℓ.

5.

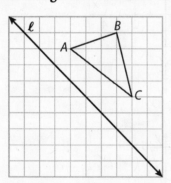

6.

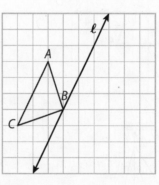

7.

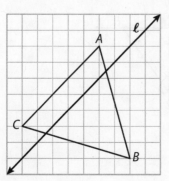

8.

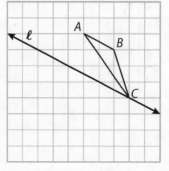

Reflect the figure with the given vertices across the given line.

9. $P(-2, 3)$, $Q(4, 3)$, $R(-1, 0)$, $S(-4, 1)$; x-axis

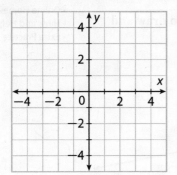

10. $A(-3, -3)$, $B(1, 3)$, $C(3, -1)$; y-axis

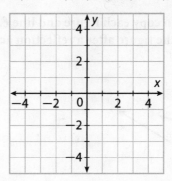

11. $J(-1, 2)$, $K(2, 4)$, $L(4, -1)$; $y = -x$

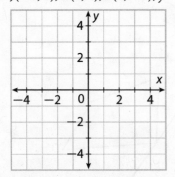

12. $D(-1, 1)$, $E(3, 2)$, $F(4, -1)$, $G(-1, -3)$; $y = x$

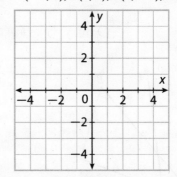

Given that $\triangle A'B'C'$ **is the image of** $\triangle ABC$ **under a reflection, draw the line of reflection.**

13.

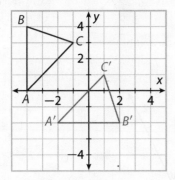

14.

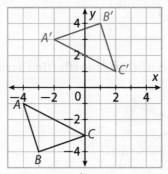

15.

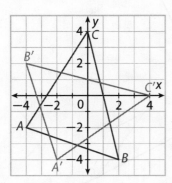

16.

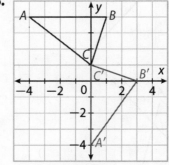

17. Jamar is playing a video game. The object of the game is to roll a marble into a target. In the figure, the shaded rectangular area represents the video screen and the striped rectangle is a barrier. Because of the barrier, it is not possible to roll the marble M directly into the target T. At what point should Jamar aim the marble so that it will bounce off a wall and roll into the target?

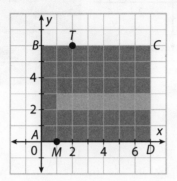

18. A trail designer is planning two trails that connect campsites A and B to a point on the river, line ℓ. She wants the total length of the trails to be as short as possible. At what point should the trails meet the river?

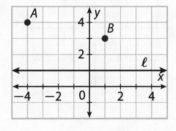

Algebra In the figure, point K is the image of point J under a reflection across line ℓ. Find each of the following.

19. JM

20. y

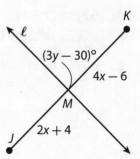

21. Make a Prediction Each time Jenny presses the tab key on her keyboard, the software reflects the logo she is designing across the x-axis. Jenny's cat steps on the keyboard and presses the tab key 25 times. In which quadrant does the logo end up? Explain.

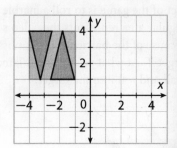

22. Multi-Step Write the equation of the line of reflection.

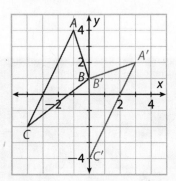

23. Communicate Mathematical Ideas
The figure shows rectangle *PQRS* and its image after a reflection across the *y*-axis. A student said that *PQRS* could also be mapped to its image using the translation $(x, y) \rightarrow (x + 6, y)$. Do you agree? Explain why or why not.

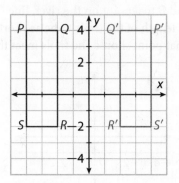

24. Which of the following transformations map △*ABC* to a triangle that intersects the *x*-axis? Select all that apply.

A. $(x, y) \rightarrow (-x, y)$

B. $(x, y) \rightarrow (x, -y)$

C. $(x, y) \rightarrow (y, x)$

D. $(x, y) \rightarrow (-y, -x)$

E. $(x, y) \rightarrow (x, y + 1)$

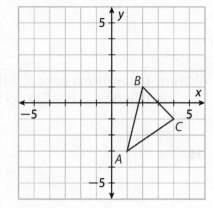

25. Explain the Error $\triangle M'N'P'$ is the image of $\triangle MNP$. Casey draws $\overline{MM'}$, $\overline{NN'}$, and $\overline{PP'}$. Then she finds the midpoint of each segment and draws line ℓ through the midpoints. She claims that line ℓ is the line of reflection. Do you agree? Explain.

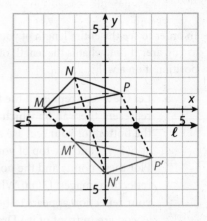

26. Draw Conclusions Plot the images of points D, E, F, and G after a reflection across the line $y = 2$. Then write an algebraic rule for the reflection.

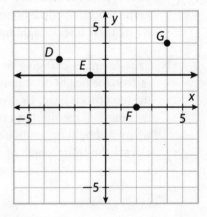

27. Critique Reasoning Mayumi wants to draw the line of reflection for the reflection that maps $\triangle ABC$ to $\triangle A'B'C'$. She claims that she just needs to draw the line through the points X and Y. Do you agree? Explain.

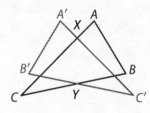

28. Justify Reasoning Point Q is the image of point P under a reflection across line ℓ. Point R lies on line ℓ. What type of triangle is $\triangle PQR$? Justify your answer.

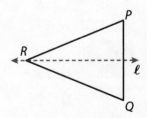

Lesson Performance Task

In order to see the entire length of your body in a mirror, do you need a mirror that is as tall as you are? If not, what is the length of the shortest mirror you can use, and how should you position it on a wall?

a. Let the *x*-axis represent the floor and let the *y*-axis represent the wall on which the mirror hangs. Suppose the bottom of your feet are at $F(3, 0)$, your eyes are at $E(3, 7)$, and the top of your head is at $H(3, 8)$. Plot these points and the points that represent their reflection images. (*Hint:* When you look in a mirror, your reflection appears to be as far behind the mirror as you are in front of it.) Draw the lines of sight from your eyes to the reflection of the top of your head and to the reflection of the bottom of your feet. Determine where these lines of sight intersect the mirror.

b. Experiment by changing your distance from the mirror, the height of your eyes, and/or the height of the top of your head. Use your results to determine the length of the shortest mirror you can use and where it should be positioned on the wall so that you can see the entire length of your body in the mirror.

© Houghton Mifflin Harcourt Publishing Company • Image Credits: ©Eric Camden/Houghton Mifflin Harcourt

17.3 Rotations

Essential Question: How do you draw the image of a figure under a rotation?

⊙ Explore   Exploring Rotations

You can use geometry software or an online tool to explore rotations.

(A) Draw a triangle and label the vertices
A, *B*, and *C*. Then draw a point *P*.
Mark *P* as a center. This will allow
you to rotate figures around point *P*.

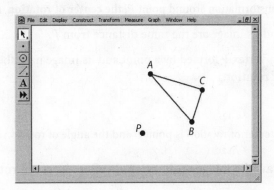

(B) Select △*ABC* and rotate it 90° around
point *P*. Label the image of △*ABC* as
△*A'B'C'*. Change the shape, size, or
location of △*ABC* and notice how
△*A'B'C'* changes.

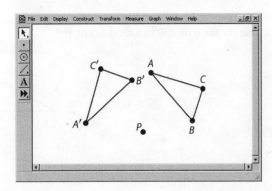

(C) Draw ∠*APA'*, ∠*BPB'*, and ∠*CPC'*. Measure these angles. What do you notice? Does this
relationship remain true as you move point *P*? What happens if you change the size and
shape of △*ABC*?

_____

_____

(D) Measure the distance from *A* to *P* and the distance from *A'* to *P*. What do you notice? Does
this relationship remain true as you move point *P*? What happens if you change the size and
shape of △*ABC*?

_____

_____

1. What can you conclude about the distance of a point and its image from the center of rotation?

_____

2. What are the advantages of using geometry software or an online tool rather than tracing paper or a protractor and ruler to investigate rotations?

_____

_____

⚙ Explain 1 Rotating Figures Using a Ruler and Protractor

A **rotation** is a transformation around point *P*, the **center of rotation**, such that the following is true.

- Every point and its image are the same distance from *P*.

- All angles with vertex *P* formed by a point and its image have the same measure. This angle measure is the **angle of rotation**.

In the figure, the center of rotation is point *P* and the angle of rotation is 110°.

Example 1 **Draw the image of the triangle after the given rotation.**

Ⓐ Counterclockwise rotation of 150° around point *P*

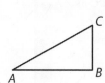

Step 1 Draw $\overline{PA}$. Then use a protractor to draw a ray that forms a 150° angle with $\overline{PA}$.

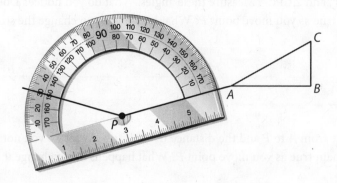

Step 2 Use a ruler to mark point A' along the ray so that $PA' = PA$.

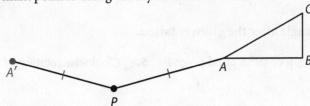

Step 3 Repeat Steps 1 and 2 for points B and C to locate points B' and C'. Connect points A', B', and C' to draw $\triangle A'B'C'$.

Ⓑ Clockwise rotation of 75° around point Q

Step 1 Draw $\overline{QD}$. Use a protractor to draw a ray forming a clockwise 75° angle with $\overline{QD}$.

Step 2 Use a ruler to mark point D' along the ray so that $QD' = QD$.

Step 3 Repeat Steps 1 and 2 for points E and F to locate points E' and F'. Connect points D', E', and F' to draw $\triangle D'E'F'$.

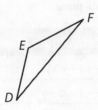

Reflect

3. How could you use tracing paper to draw the image of $\triangle ABC$ in Part A?

_____

_____

_____

_____

Draw the image of the triangle after the given rotation.

4. Counterclockwise rotation of 40° around point *P* **5.** Clockwise rotation of 125° around point *Q*

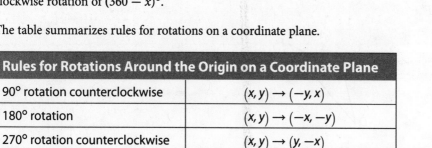

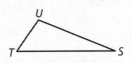

🗝 Explain 2 **Drawing Rotations on a Coordinate Plane**

You can rotate a figure by more than 180°. The diagram shows counterclockwise rotations of 120°, 240°, and 300°. Note that a rotation of 360° brings a figure back to its starting location.

When no direction is specified, you can assume that a rotation is counterclockwise. Also, a counterclockwise rotation of *x*° is the same as a clockwise rotation of (360 − *x*)°.

The table summarizes rules for rotations on a coordinate plane.

Rules for Rotations Around the Origin on a Coordinate Plane	
90° rotation counterclockwise	$(x, y) \rightarrow (-y, x)$
180° rotation	$(x, y) \rightarrow (-x, -y)$
270° rotation counterclockwise	$(x, y) \rightarrow (y, -x)$
360° rotation	$(x, y) \rightarrow (x, y)$

Example 2 Draw the image of the figure under the given rotation.

(A) Quadrilateral *ABCD*; 270°

The rotation image of (x, y) is (y, −x).

Find the coordinates of the vertices of the image.

$A(0, 2) \rightarrow A'(2, 0)$

$B(1, 4) \rightarrow B'(4, -1)$

$C(4, 2) \rightarrow C'(2, -4)$

$D(3, 1) \rightarrow D'(1, -3)$

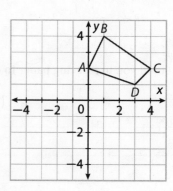

Predict the quadrant in which the image will lie. Since quadrilateral *ABCD* lies in Quadrant I and the quadrilateral is rotated counterclockwise by 270°, the image will lie in Quadrant IV.

Plot *A'*, *B'*, *C'*, and *D'* to graph the image.

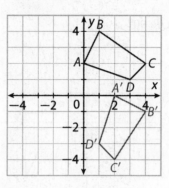

(B) △*KLM*; 180°

The rotation image of (x, y) is ($\boxed{}$, $\boxed{}$).

Find the coordinates of the vertices of the image.

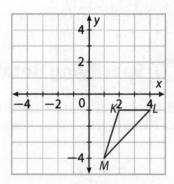

$K(2, -1) \rightarrow K'\left(\boxed{}, \boxed{}\right)$

$L(4, -1) \rightarrow L'\left(\boxed{}, \boxed{}\right)$

$M(1, -4) \rightarrow M'\left(\boxed{}, \boxed{}\right)$

Predict the quadrant in which the image will lie. Since △*KLM* lies in Quadrant ____ and

the triangle is rotated by 180°, the image will lie in Quadrant ____.

Plot *K'*, *L'*, and *M'* to graph the image.

Reflect

6. **Discussion** Suppose you rotate quadrilateral *ABCD* in Part A by 810°. In which quadrant will the image lie? Explain.

_____

_____

_____

Draw the image of the figure under the given rotation.

7. △PQR; 90°

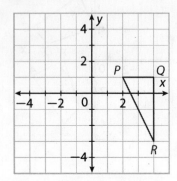

8. Quadrilateral DEFG; 270°

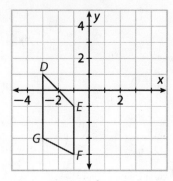

🔑 Explain 3 Specifying Rotation Angles

Example 3 Find the angle of rotation and direction of rotation in the given figure.
Point P is the center of rotation.

Ⓐ

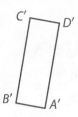

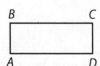

Draw segments from the center of rotation to a vertex and
to the image of the vertex.

Measure the angle formed by the segments. The angle
measure is 80°.

Compare the locations of the preimage and image to find
the direction of the rotation.

The rotation is 80° counterclockwise.

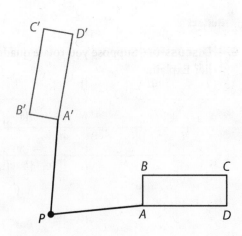

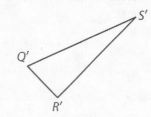

Draw segments from the center of rotation to a vertex and to the image of the vertex.

Measure the angle formed by the segments.

The angle measure is [ ]°.

The rotation is [ ]° (clockwise/counterclockwise).

9. **Discussion** Does it matter which points you choose when you draw segments from the center of rotation to points of the preimage and image? Explain.

_____

_____

10. In Part A, is a different angle of rotation and direction possible? Explain.

_____

_____

Your Turn

Find the angle of rotation and direction of rotation in the given figure. Point _P_ is the center of rotation.

11.

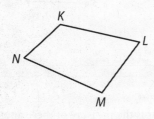

12. If you are given a figure, a center of rotation, and an angle of rotation, what steps can you use to draw the image of the figure under the rotation?

_____

_____

_____

_____

13. Suppose you are given $\triangle DEF$, $\triangle D'E'F'$, and point P. What are two different ways to prove that a rotation around point P cannot be used to map $\triangle DEF$ to $\triangle D'E'F'$?

_____

_____

14. **Essential Question Check-In** How do you draw the image of a figure under a counterclockwise rotation of 90° around the origin?

_____

_____

_____

⭐ Evaluate: Homework and Practice

• Online Homework
• Hints and Help
• Extra Practice

1. Alberto uses geometry software to draw $\triangle STU$ and point P, as shown. He marks P as a center and uses the software to rotate $\triangle STU$ 115° around point P. He labels the image of $\triangle STU$ as $\triangle S'T'U'$.

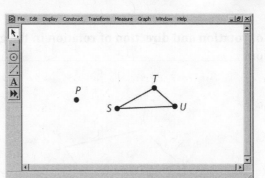

Which three angles must have the same measure? What is the measure of these angles?

Draw the image of the triangle after the given rotation.

2. Counterclockwise rotation of 30° around point *P*

3. Clockwise rotation of 55° around point *J*

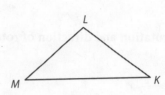

4. Counterclockwise rotation of 90° around point *P*

P •

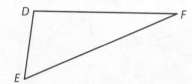

Draw the image of the figure under the given rotation.

5. △*ABC*; 270°

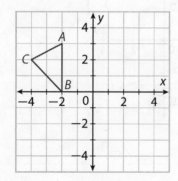

6. △*RST*; 90°

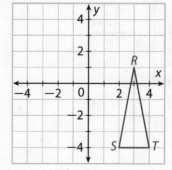

7. Quadrilateral *EFGH*; 180°

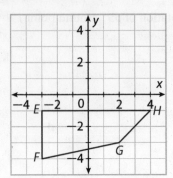

8. Quadrilateral *PQRS*; 270°

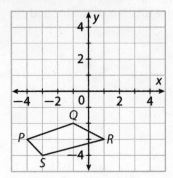

Find the angle of rotation and direction of rotation in the given figure. Point *P* is the center of rotation.

9.

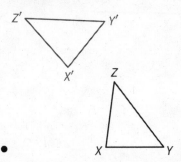

10.

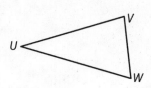

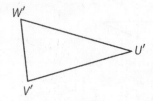

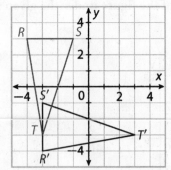

Write an algebraic rule for the rotation shown. Then describe the transformation in words.

11.

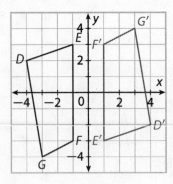

12.

_____

_____

_____

_____

13. Vanessa used geometry software to apply a transformation to △ABC, as shown. According to the software, m∠APA′ = m∠BPB′ = m∠CPC′. Vanessa said this means the transformation must be a rotation. Do you agree? Explain.

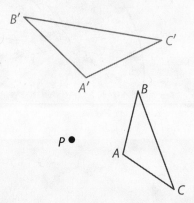

_____

_____

_____

_____

14. Make a Prediction In which quadrant will the image of △FGH lie after a counterclockwise rotation of 1980°? Explain how you made your prediction.

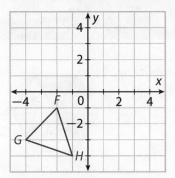

_____

_____

_____

_____

15. Critical Thinking The figure shows the image of △MNP after a counterclockwise rotation of 270°. Draw and label △MNP.

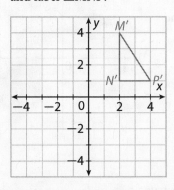

_____

_____

_____

_____

16. Multi-Step Write the equation of the image of line ℓ after a clockwise rotation of 90°. (*Hint*: To find the image of line ℓ, choose two or more points on the line and find the images of the points.)

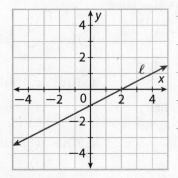

_____

_____

_____

_____

17. A Ferris wheel has 20 cars that are equally spaced around the circumference of the wheel. The wheel rotates so that the car at the bottom of the ride is replaced by the next car. By how many degrees does the wheel rotate?

_____

_____

_____

18. The Skylon Tower, in Niagara Falls, Canada, has a revolving restaurant 775 feet above the falls. The restaurant makes a complete revolution once every hour. While a visitor was at the tower, the restaurant rotated through 135°. How long was the visitor at the tower?

_____

_____

_____

19. Amani plans to use drawing software to make the design shown here. She starts by drawing Triangle 1. Explain how she can finish the design using rotations.

_____

_____

_____

20. An animator is drawing a scene in which a ladybug moves around three mushrooms. The figure shows the starting position of the ladybug. The animator rotates the ladybug 180° around mushroom *A*, then 180° around mushroom *B*, and finally 180° around mushroom *C*. What are the final coordinates of the ladybug?

_____

_____

_____

21. Determine whether each statement about the rotation $(x, y) \rightarrow (y, -x)$ is true or false. Select the correct answer for each lettered part.

a. Every point in Quadrant I is mapped to a point in Quadrant II. ◯ True ◯ False

b. Points on the *x*-axis are mapped to points on the *y*-axis. ◯ True ◯ False

c. The origin is a fixed point under the rotation. ◯ True ◯ False

d. The rotation has the same effect as a 90° clockwise rotation. ◯ True ◯ False

e. The angle of rotation is 180°. ◯ True ◯ False

f. A point on the line $y = x$ is mapped to another point on the line $y = x$. ◯ True ◯ False

22. Communicate Mathematical Ideas Suppose you are given a figure and a center of rotation *P*. Describe two different ways you can use a ruler and protractor to draw the image of the figure after a 210° counterclockwise rotation around *P*.

_____

_____

_____

23. Explain the Error Kevin drew the image of △*ABC* after a rotation of 85° around point *P*. Explain how you can tell from the figure that he made an error. Describe the error.

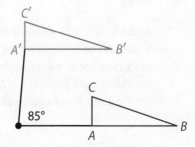

_____

_____

_____

24. Critique Reasoning Isabella said that all points turn around the center of rotation by
the same angle, so all points move the same distance under a rotation. Do you agree with Isabella's statement? Explain.

_____

_____

_____

25. Look for a Pattern Isaiah uses software to draw △*DEF* as shown. Each time he presses the left arrow key, the software rotates the figure on the screen 90° counterclockwise. Explain how Isaiah can determine which quadrant the triangle will lie in if he presses the left arrow key *n* times.

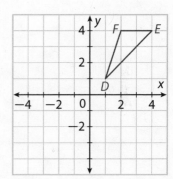

_____

_____

Lesson Performance Task

A tourist in London looks up at the clock in Big Ben tower and finds that it is exactly 8:00. When she looks up at the clock later, it is exactly 8:10.

a. Through what angle of rotation did the minute hand turn? Through what angle of rotation did the hour hand turn?

b. Make a table that shows different amounts of time, from 5 minutes to 60 minutes, in 5-minute increments. For each number of minutes, provide the angle of rotation for the minute hand of a clock and the angle of rotation for the hour hand of a clock.

17.4 Investigating Symmetry

Essential Question: How do you determine whether a figure has line symmetry or rotational symmetry?

◉ Explore 1 Identifying Line Symmetry

A figure has **symmetry** if a rigid motion exists that maps the figure onto itself. A figure has **line symmetry** (or *reflectional symmetry*) if a reflection maps the figure onto itself. Each of these lines of reflection is called a **line of symmetry**.

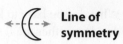

You can use paper folding to determine whether a figure has line symmetry.

Ⓐ Trace the figure on a piece of tracing paper.

Ⓑ If the figure can be folded along a straight line so that one half of the figure exactly matches the other half, the figure has line symmetry. The crease is the line of symmetry. Place your shape against the original figure to check that each crease is a line of symmetry.

Ⓒ Sketch any lines of symmetry on the figure.

The figure has _____ line of symmetry.

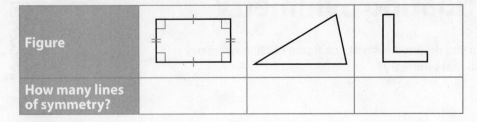

(D) Draw the lines of symmetry, if any, on each figure and tell the total number of lines of symmetry each figure has.

Figure			
How many lines of symmetry?			

Reflect

1. What do you have to know about any segments and angles in a figure to decide whether the figure has line symmetry?

_____

_____

2. What figure has an infinite number of lines of symmetry? _____

3. **Discussion** A figure undergoes a rigid motion, such as a rotation. If the figure has line symmetry, does the image of the figure have line symmetry as well? Give an example.

_____

_____

⊙ Explore 2 Identifying Rotational Symmetry

A figure has **rotational symmetry** if a rotation maps the figure onto itself. The **angle of rotational symmetry**, which is greater than 0° but less than or equal to 180°, is the smallest angle of rotation that maps a figure onto itself.

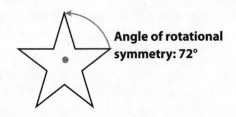

Angle of rotational symmetry: 72°

An angle of rotational symmetry is a fractional part of 360°. Notice that every time the 5-pointed star rotates $\frac{360°}{5} = 72°$, the star coincides with itself. The angles of rotation for the star are 72°, 144°, 216°, and 288°. If a copy of the figure rotates to exactly match the original, the figure has rotational symmetry.

(A) Trace the figure onto tracing paper. Hold the center of the traced figure against the original figure with your pencil. Rotate the traced figure counterclockwise until it coincides again with the original figure beneath.

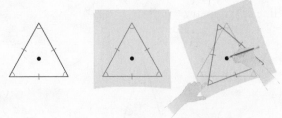

By how many degrees did you rotate the figure? _____

What are all the angles of rotation? _____

Ⓑ Determine whether each figure has rotational symmetry. If so, identify all the angles of rotation less than 360°.

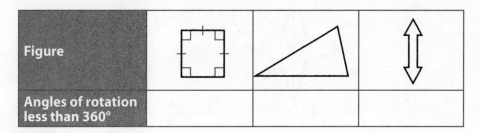

Figure			
Angles of rotation less than 360°			

Reflect

4. What figure is mapped onto itself by a rotation of any angle? _____

5. Discussion A figure is formed by line *l* and line *m*, which intersect at an angle of 60°. Does the figure have an angle of rotational symmetry of 60°? If not, what is the angle of rotational symmetry?

_____

_____

🔑 Explain 1 Describing Symmetries

A figure may have line symmetry, rotational symmetry, both types of symmetry, or no symmetry.

Example 1 Describe the symmetry of each figure. Draw the lines of symmetry, name the angles of rotation, or both if the figure has both.

Ⓐ

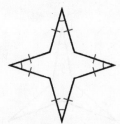

Step 1 Begin by finding the line symmetry of the figure. Look for matching halves of the figure. For example, you could fold the left half over the right half, and fold the top half over the bottom half. Draw one line of symmetry for each fold. Notice that the lines intersect at the center of the figure.

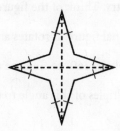

Step 2 Now look for other lines of symmetry. The two diagonals also describe matching halves. The figure has a total of 4 lines of symmetry.

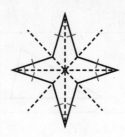

Step 3 Next, look for rotational symmetry. Think of the figure rotated about its center until it matches its original position. The angle of rotational symmetry of this figure is $\frac{1}{4}$ of 360°, or 90°.

The other angles of rotation for the figure are the multiples of 90° that are less than 360°. So the angles of rotation are 90°, 180°, and 270°.

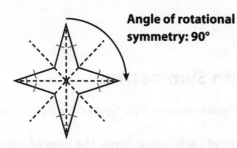

Angle of rotational symmetry: 90°

Number of lines of symmetry: 4   Angles of rotation: 90°, 180°, 270° _____

Ⓑ

Step 1 Look for lines of symmetry. One line divides the figure into left and right halves. Draw this line on the figure. Then draw similar lines that begin at the other vertices of the figure.

Step 2 Now look for rotational symmetry. Think of the figure rotating about its

center until it matches the original figure. It rotates around the circle by a

fraction of _____. Multiply by 360° to find the angle of rotation,

which is _____. Find multiples of this angle to find other angles

of rotation.

Number of lines of symmetry: _____   Angles of rotation: _____

Describe the type of symmetry for each figure. Draw the lines of symmetry, name the angles of rotation, or both if the figure has both.

6. Figure *ABCD*

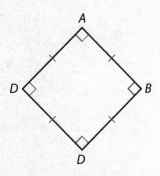

Types of symmetry: _____

Number of lines of symmetry: _____

Angles of rotation: _____

7. Figure *EFGHI*

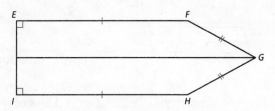

Types of symmetry: _____

Number of lines of symmetry: _____

Angles of rotation: _____

8. Figure *KLNPR*

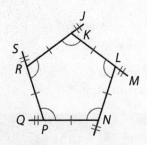

Types of symmetry: _____

Number of lines of symmetry: _____

Angles of rotation: _____

9. Figure *TUVW*

Types of symmetry: _____

Number of lines of symmetry: _____

Angles of rotation: _____

 Elaborate

10. How are the two types of symmetry alike? How are they different?

_____

_____

11. **Essential Question Check-In** How do you determine whether a figure has line symmetry or rotational symmetry?

_____

_____

_____

_____

• Online Homework
• Hints and Help
• Extra Practice

Draw all the lines of symmetry for the figure, and give the number of lines of symmetry. If the figure has no line symmetry, write zero.

1.

Lines of symmetry: _____

2.

Lines of symmetry: _____

3.

Lines of symmetry: _____

For the figures that have rotational symmetry, list the angles of rotation less than 360°. For figures without rotational symmetry, write "no rotational symmetry."

4.

Angles of rotation: _____

5.

Angles of rotation: _____

6.

Angles of rotation: _____

In the tile design shown, identify whether the pattern has line symmetry, rotational symmetry, both line and rotational symmetry, or no symmetry.

7.

8.

For figure *ABCDEF* shown here, identify the image after each transformation described. For example, a reflection across $\overline{AD}$ has an image of figure *AFEDCB*. In the figure, all the sides are the same length and all the angles are the same measure.

9. Reflection across $\overline{CF}$

Figure _____

10. rotation of 240° clockwise, or 120° counterclockwise

Figure _____

11. reflection across the line that connects the midpoint of $\overline{BC}$ and the midpoint of $\overline{EF}$

Figure _____

In the space provided, sketch an example of a figure with the given characteristics.

12. no line symmetry; angle of rotational symmetry: 180°

13. one line of symmetry; no rotational symmetry

14. Describe the line and rotational symmetry in this figure.

15. **Communicate Mathematical Ideas** How is a rectangle similar to an ellipse? Use concepts of symmetry in your answer.

16. **Explain the Error** A student was asked to draw all of the lines of symmetry on each figure shown. Identify the student's work as correct or incorrect. If incorrect, explain why.

a.

b.

c.

Lesson Performance Task

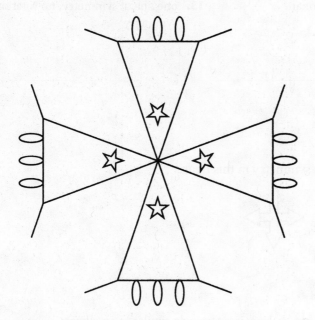

Use symmetry to design a work of art. Begin by drawing one simple geometric figure, such as a triangle, square, or rectangle, on a piece of construction paper. Then add other lines or two-dimensional shapes to the figure. Next, make identical copies of the figure, and then arrange them in a symmetric pattern.

Evaluate the symmetry of the work of art you created. Rotate it to identify an angle of rotational symmetry. Compare the line symmetry of the original figure with the line symmetry of the finished work.

© Houghton Mifflin Harcourt Publishing Company

Transformations and Symmetry

Essential Question: How can you use transformations to solve real-world problems?

KEY EXAMPLE   *(Lesson 17.1)*

Translate the square $ABCD$ along the vector $\langle 2, 1 \rangle$.

$A(1, 2), B(3, 2), C(1, 4), D(3, 4)$.

$(x, y) \rightarrow (x + a, y + b)$ Write the rule for translation along the vector $\langle a, b \rangle$.

$A(1, 2) \rightarrow A'(1 + 2, 2 + 1)$ Apply the rule to each point.

$B(3, 2) \rightarrow B'(3 + 2, 2 + 1)$

$C(1, 4) \rightarrow C'(1 + 2, 4 + 1)$

$D(3, 4) \rightarrow D'(3 + 2, 4 + 1)$

$A'(3, 3), B'(5, 3),$ Now simplify.

$C'(3, 5), D'(5, 5)$

KEY EXAMPLE   *(Lesson 17.2)*

Determine the vertices of the image of $\triangle ABC$.

$A(2, 3), B(3, 4),$ and $C(3, 1)$ reflected across the line $y = x$.

$(x, y) \rightarrow (y, x)$ Write the rule for reflection across the line $y = x$.

$A(2, 3), A'(3, 2)$ Apply the rule to each point.

$B(3, 4), B'(4, 3)$

$C(3, 1), C'(1, 3)$

KEY EXAMPLE   *(Lesson 17.3)*

Determine the vertices of the image of $\triangle DFE$.

$D(1, 2), F(2, 2),$ and $E(2, 0)$, rotated 270° counterclockwise about the origin.

$(x, y) \rightarrow (y, -x)$ Write the rule for a rotation 270° counterclockwise.

$D(1, 2), \rightarrow D'(2, -1)$ Apply the rule to each point.

$F(2, 2), \rightarrow F'(2, -2)$

$E(2, 0), \rightarrow E'(0, -2)$

Key Vocabulary

vector *(vector)*

initial point *(punto inicial)*

terminal point *(punto terminal)*

translation *(translación)*

perpendicular lines *(líneas perpendiculares)*

perpendicular bisector *(mediatriz)*

reflection *(reflexión)*

rotation *(rotación)*

center of rotation *(centro de rotación)*

angle of rotation *(ángulo de rotación)*

symmetry *(simetría)*

line symmetry *(simetría de línea)*

line of symmetry *(línea de simetría)*

rotational symmetry *(simetría rotacional)*

angle of rotational symmetry *(ángulo de simetría rotacional)*

EXERCISES

Translate each figure along each vector. *(Lesson 17.1)*

1. The line segment determined by $A(4, 7)$ and $B(2, 9)$ along $\langle 0, -2 \rangle$.

   The endpoints of the image are _____.

2. The triangle determined by $A(-3, 2)$, $B(4, 4)$, and $C(1, 1)$ along $\langle -1, -3 \rangle$.

   The vertices of the image are _____.

Determine the vertices of each image. *(Lesson 17.2)*

3. The image of the rectangle *ABCD* reflected across the line $y = -x$.

   $A(-3, 2)$, $B(3, 2)$, $C(-3, -3)$, $D(3, -3)$

   The vertices of the image are _____.

4. The image of the polygon *ABCDE* reflected across the *x*-axis.

   $A(-1, -1)$, $B(0, 1)$, $C(4, 2)$, $D(6, 0)$, $E(3, -3)$

   The vertices of the image are _____.

Determine the vertices of the image. *(Lesson 17.3)*

5. The figure defined by $A(3, 5)$, $B(5, 3)$, $C(2, 2)$ rotated 180° counterclockwise about the origin.

   The points of the image are _____.

MODULE PERFORMANCE TASK

Animating Digital Images

A computer animator is designing an animation in which a bird flies off its perch, swoops down and to the right, and then flies off the right side of the screen. The graph shows the designer's preliminary sketch, using a triangle to represent the bird in its initial position (top) and one intermediate position.

Plan a series of rotations and translations to animate the flight of the bird. Sketch each rotation and translation on a graph and label the coordinates of the triangle's vertices at each position. If you wish, you can test out how well your animation works by making a flipbook of your graphs.

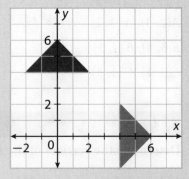

(Ready) to Go On?

17.1–17.4 Transformations and Symmetry

- Online Homework
- Hints and Help
- Extra Practice

1. Line segment $\overline{YZ}$ was used to translate *ABCDE*. $\overline{YZ}$ is 6.2 inches long. What is the length of $AA' + BB' + CC' + DD' + EE'$? *(Lesson 17.1)*

Given figure *FGHI* and its image *F'G'H'I'*, answer the following. *(Lesson 17.2, 17.3)*

2a. Write an algebraic rule for the rotation shown and then describe the rotation in words.

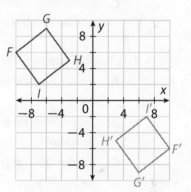

2b. Tell whether the figure *FGHI* has line symmetry, rotational symmetry, both types of symmetry, or no symmetry. If the figure has line symmetry, record the number. If the figure has rotational symmetry, list the angles of rotation that are less than 360°.

Types of symmetry	Number of lines of symmetry	Angles of rotation

3. Given triangle *ABC* with $A(-2, 4)$, $B(-2, 1)$, and $C(-4, 0)$, and its image *A'B'C'* with $A'(2, 0)$, $B'(-1, 0)$, and $C'(-2, -2)$, find the line of reflection. *(Lesson 17.2)*

Essential Question

4. In which situations are translations useful for transformations? Reflections? Rotations?

MODULE 17
MIXED REVIEW

Assessment Readiness

1. Triangle *ABC* is given by the points *A*(−1, 5), *B*(0, 3), and *C*(2, 4). It is reflected over the line *y* = −2*x* − 2. Does the image contain each of the points?

   Select Yes or No for A–C.

   A. *A'*(−5, 3) ○ Yes ○ No
   B. *B'*(−4, 6) ○ Yes ○ No
   C. *C'*(−6, 0) ○ Yes ○ No

2. A triangle, △*ABC*, is rotated 90° counterclockwise, reflected across the *x*-axis, and then reflected across the *y*-axis. Choose True or False for each statement.

   A. Rotating △*ABC* 180° clockwise is an equivalent transformation. ○ True ○ False
   B. Rotating △*ABC* 270° counterclockwise is an equivalent transformation. ○ True ○ False
   C. Reflecting △*ABC* across the *y*-axis is an equivalent transformation. ○ True ○ False

3. Choose True or False for each statement about equilateral triangles.

   A. An equilateral triangle has 3 equal angle measures. ○ True ○ False
   B. An equilateral triangle has 3 equal side measures. ○ True ○ False
   C. An equilateral triangle has 3 lines of symmetry. ○ True ○ False

4. A line segment with points *P*(1, 2) and *Q*(4, 3) is reflected across the line *y* = *x*. What are the new coordinates of the points of the line segment?

5. Draw on the figure all lines of symmetry and explain why those lines are the lines of symmetry. Give all angles of rotational symmetry less than 360°.

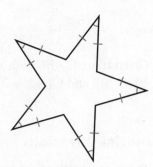

Study Guide Review

Congruent Figures

Essential Question: How can you use congruency to solve real-world problems?

REAL WORLD VIDEO
Check out how landscape architects use transformations of geometric shapes to design green space for parks and homes.

MODULE PERFORMANCE TASK PREVIEW

Jigsaw Puzzle

In this module, you will use congruency and a series of transformations to solve a portion of a jigsaw puzzle. What is some of the basic geometry behind a jigsaw puzzle? Let's get started on finding out how all the pieces fit together!

Are (YOU) Ready?

Complete these exercises to review skills you will need for this module.

Properties of Reflections

Example 1

Find the points that define the reflection of the figure given by $A(1, 1)$, $B(2, 3)$, and $C(3, 1)$ across the y-axis.

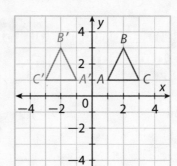

Use the rules for reflections on a coordinate plane. For a reflection across the y-axis:

$(x, y) \rightarrow (-x, y)$

$A(1, 1) \rightarrow A'(-1, 1)$, $B(2, 3) \rightarrow B'(-2, 3)$,

$C(3, 1) \rightarrow C'(-3, 1)$

Find the vertices of the reflected figure.

1. $\triangle ABC$ reflected across the x-axis _____

2. $\triangle ABC$ reflected across $y = x$ _____

Properties of Rotations

Example 2

Find the vertices of $\triangle ABC$ rotated 90° counterclockwise around the origin.

$(x, y) \rightarrow (-y, x)$ Write the rule for rotation.

$A(1, 1) \rightarrow A'(-1, 1)$, $B(2, 3) \rightarrow B'(-3, 2)$,

$C(3, 1) \rightarrow C'(-1, 3)$ Apply the rule.

Find the vertices of the rotated figure.

3. $\triangle ABC$ rotated 180° around the origin _____

Properties of Translations

Example 3

Calculate the vertices of the image of $\triangle ABC$ translated using the rule $(x, y) \rightarrow (x + 2, y + 1)$.

$A(1, 1) \rightarrow A'(3, 2)$, $B(2, 3) \rightarrow B'(4, 4)$,

$C(3, 1) \rightarrow C'(5, 2)$ Apply the rule.

Calculate the vertices of the image.

4. $\triangle ABC$ translated using the rule $(x, y) \rightarrow (x - 2, y + 2)$ _____

18.1 Sequences of Transformations

Essential Question: What happens when you apply more than one transformation to a figure?

Explore Combining Rotations or Reflections

A transformation is a function that takes points on the plane and maps them to other points on the plane. Transformations can be applied one after the other in a sequence where you use the image of the first transformation as the preimage for the next transformation.

Find the image for each sequence of transformations.

(A) Using geometry software, draw a triangle and label the vertices *A*, *B*, and *C*. Then draw a point outside the triangle and label it *P*.

Rotate △*ABC* 30° around point *P* and label the image as △*A'B'C'*. Then rotate △*A'B'C'* 45° around point *P* and label the image as △*A"B"C"*. Sketch your result.

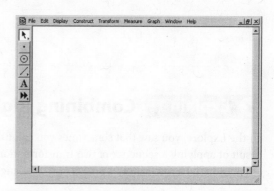

(B) Make a conjecture regarding a single rotation that will map △*ABC* to △*A"B"C"*. Check your conjecture, and describe what you did.

_____

_____

(C) Using geometry software, draw a triangle and label the vertices *D*, *E*, and *F*. Then draw two intersecting lines and label them *j* and *k*.

Reflect △*DEF* across line *j* and label the image as △*D'E'F'*. Then reflect △*D'E'F'* across line *k* and label the image as △*D"E"F"*. Sketch your result.

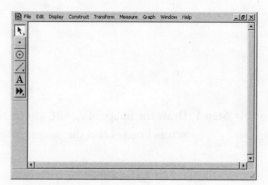

(D) Consider the relationship between △*DEF* and △*D"E"F"*. Describe the single t ransformation that maps △*DEF* to △*D"E"F"*. How can you check that you are correct?

_____

_____

1. Repeat Step A using other angle measures. Make a conjecture about what single transformation will describe a sequence of two rotations about the same center.

   _____

   _____

2. Make a conjecture about what single transformation will describe a sequence of three rotations about the same center.

   _____

   _____

3. **Discussion** Repeat Step C, but make lines j and k parallel instead of intersecting. Make a conjecture about what single transformation will now map $\triangle DEF$ to $\triangle D''E''F''$. Check your conjecture and describe what you did.

   _____

   _____

   _____

🔑 Explain 1 Combining Rigid Transformations

In the Explore, you saw that sometimes you can use a single transformation to describe the result of applying a sequence of two transformations. Now you will apply sequences of rigid transformations that cannot be described by a single transformation.

Example 1 Draw the image of $\triangle ABC$ after the given combination of transformations.

Ⓐ Reflection over line ℓ then translation along $\overrightarrow{v}$

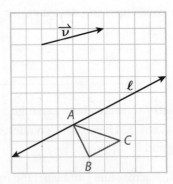

Step 1 Draw the image of $\triangle ABC$ after a reflection across line ℓ. Label the image $\triangle A'B'C'$.

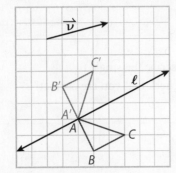

Step 2 Translate $\triangle A'B'C'$ along $\overrightarrow{v}$. Label this image $\triangle A''B''C''$.

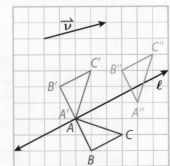

Ⓑ 180° rotation around point P, then translation along $\vec{v}$, then reflection across line ℓ

Apply the rotation. Label the image $\triangle A'B'C'$.

Apply the translation to $\triangle A'B'C'$. Label the image $\triangle A''B''C''$.

Apply the reflection to $\triangle A''B''C''$. Label the image $\triangle A'''B'''C'''$.

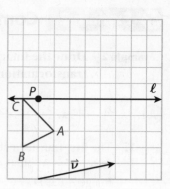

Reflect

4. Are the images you drew for each example the same size and shape as the given preimage? In what ways do rigid transformations change the preimage?

_____

_____

_____

5. Does the order in which you apply the transformations make a difference? Test your conjecture by performing the transformations in Part B in a different order.

_____

_____

_____

6. For Part B, describe a sequence of transformations that will take $\triangle A''B''C''$ back to the preimage.

_____

_____

_____

Your Turn

Draw the image of the triangle after the given combination of transformations.

7. Reflection across ℓ then 90° rotation around point P

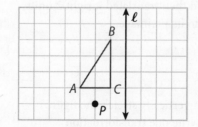

8. Translation along $\vec{v}$ then 180° rotation around point P then translation along $\vec{u}$

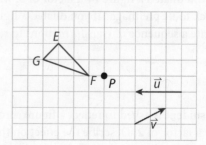

⚙ Explain 2   Combining Nonrigid Transformations

Example 2   Draw the image of the figure in the plane after the given combination of transformations.

Ⓐ $(x, y) \rightarrow \left(\dfrac{3}{2}x, \dfrac{3}{2}y\right) \rightarrow (-x, y) \rightarrow (x + 1, y - 2)$

1. The first transformation is a dilation by a factor of $\dfrac{3}{2}$. Apply the dilation. Label the image $A'B'C'D'$.

2. Apply the reflection of $A'B'C'D'$ across the y-axis. Label this image $A''B''C''D''$.

3. Apply the translation of $A''B''C''D''$. Label this image $A'''B'''C'''D'''$.

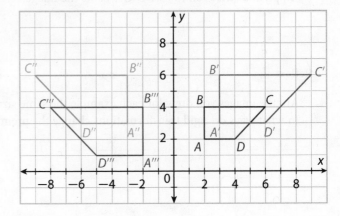

Ⓑ $(x, y) \rightarrow (3x, y) \rightarrow \left(\dfrac{1}{2}x, -\dfrac{1}{2}y\right)$

1. The first transformation is a [horizontal/vertical] stretch by a factor of _____.

   Apply the stretch. Label the image _____.

2. The second transformation is a dilation by a factor of _____ combined with a reflection.

   Apply the transformation to _____. Label the image _____.

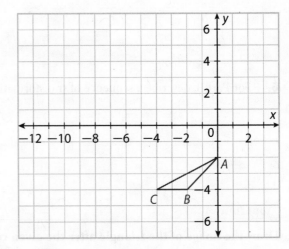

Reflect

9. If you dilated a figure by a factor of 2, what transformation could you use to return the figure back to its preimage? If you dilated a figure by a factor of 2 and then translated it right 2 units, write a sequence of transformations to return the figure back to its preimage.

_____

_____

10. A student is asked to reflect a figure across the y-axis and then vertically stretch the figure by a factor of 2. Describe the effect on the coordinates. Then write one transformation using coordinate notation that combines these two transformations into one.

_____

_____

Your Turn

Draw the image of the figure in the plane after the given combination of transformations.

11. $(x, y) \rightarrow (x - 1, y - 1) \rightarrow (3x, y) \rightarrow (-x, -y)$ **12.** $(x, y) \rightarrow \left(\frac{3}{2}x, -2y\right) \rightarrow (x - 5, y + 4)$

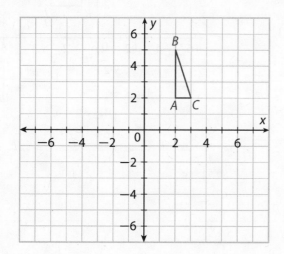

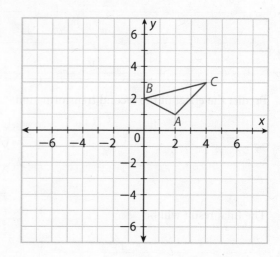

🔑 Explain 3   Predicting the Effect of Transformations

Example 3   Predict the result of applying the sequence of transformations to the given figure.

Ⓐ $\triangle LMN$ is translated along the vector $\langle -2, 3 \rangle$, reflected across the y-axis, and then reflected across the x-axis.

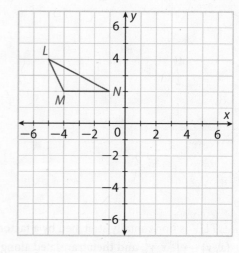

Predict the effect of the first transformation: A translation along the vector $\langle -2, 3 \rangle$ will move the figure left 2 units and up 3 units. Since the given triangle is in Quadrant II, the translation will move it further from the x- and y-axes. It will remain in Quadrant II.

Predict the effect of the second transformation: Since the triangle is in Quadrant II, a reflection across the y-axis will change the orientation and move the triangle into Quadrant I.

Predict the effect of the third transformation: A reflection across the x-axis will again change the orientation and move the triangle into Quadrant IV. The two reflections are the equivalent of rotating the figure 180° about the origin.

The final result will be a triangle the same shape and size as $\triangle LMN$ in Quadrant IV. It has been rotated 180° about the origin and is farther from the axes than the preimage.

Square *HIJK* is rotated 90° clockwise about the origin and then dilated by a factor of 2, which maps $(x, y) \rightarrow (2x, 2y)$.

Predict the effect of the first transformation: _____

_____

_____

Predict the effect of the second transformation: _____

_____

_____

The final result will be _____

_____

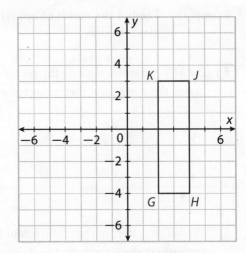

Your Turn

Predict the result of applying the sequence of transformations to the given figure.

13. Rectangle *GHJK* is reflected across the *y*-axis and translated along the vector $\langle 5, 4 \rangle$.

14. △*TUV* is horizontally stretched by a factor of $\frac{3}{2}$, which maps $(x, y) \rightarrow \left(\frac{3}{2}x, y\right)$, and then translated along the vector $\langle 2, 1 \rangle$.

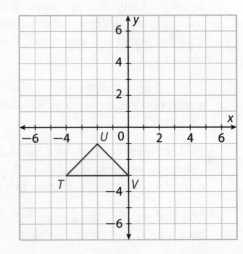

15. Discussion How many different sequences of rigid transformations do you think you can find to take a preimage back onto itself? Explain your reasoning.

_____

_____

_____

_____

_____

16. Is there a sequence of a rotation and a dilation that will result in an image that is the same size and position as the preimage? Explain your reasoning.

_____

_____

_____

_____

_____

17. Essential Question Check-In In a sequence of transformations, the order of the transformations can affect the final image. Describe a sequence of transformations where the order does not matter. Describe a sequence of transformations where the order does matter.

_____

_____

_____

_____

_____

☆ Evaluate: Homework and Practice

• Online Homework
• Hints and Help
• Extra Practice

Draw and label the final image of △ABC after the given sequence of transformations.

1. Reflect △ABC over the y-axis and then translate by ⟨2, −3⟩.

2. Rotate △ABC 90 degrees clockwise about the origin and then reflect over the x-axis.

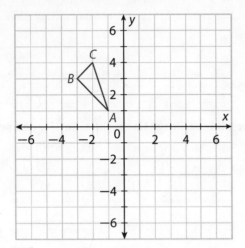

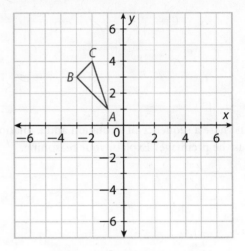

3. Translate △ABC by ⟨4, 4⟩, rotate 90 degrees counterclockwise around A, and reflect over the y-axis.

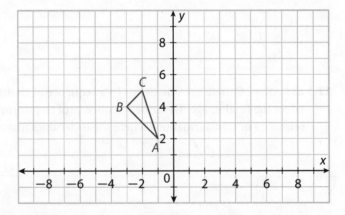

4. Reflect △ABC over the x-axis, translate by ⟨−3, −1⟩, and rotate 180 degrees around the origin.

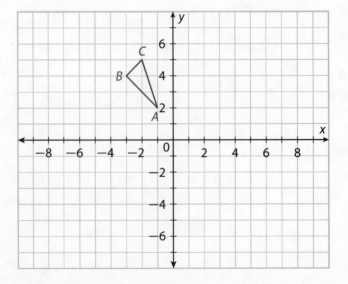

Draw and label the final image of △ABC after the given sequence of transformations.

5. $(x, y) \rightarrow \left(x, \frac{1}{3}y\right) \rightarrow (-2x, -2y)$

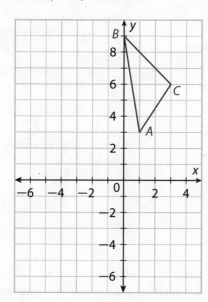

6. $(x, y) \rightarrow \left(-\frac{3}{2}x, \frac{2}{3}y\right) \rightarrow (x + 6, y - 4) \rightarrow \left(\frac{2}{3}x, -\frac{3}{2}y\right)$

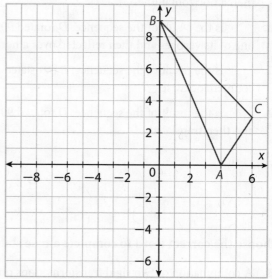

Predict the result of applying the sequence of transformations to the given figure.

7. △ABC is translated along the vector $\langle -3, -1 \rangle$, reflected across the x-axis, and then reflected across the y-axis.

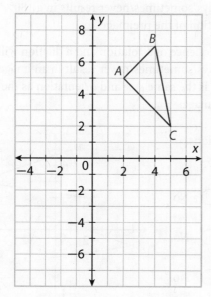

8. △ABC is translated along the vector $\langle -1, -3 \rangle$, rotated 180° about the origin, and then dilated by a factor of 2.

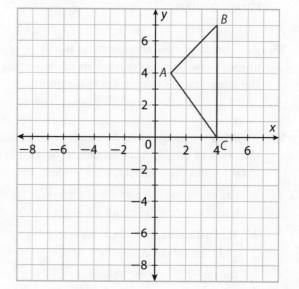

In Exercises 9–12, use the diagram. Fill in the blank with the letter of the correct image described.

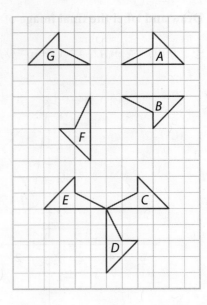

9. _____ is the result of the sequence: *G* reflected over a vertical line and then a horizontal line.

10. _____ is the result of the sequence: *D* rotated 90° clockwise around one of its vertices and then reflected over a horizontal line.

11. _____ is the result of the sequence: *E* translated and then rotated 90° counterclockwise.

12. _____ is the result of the sequence: *D* rotated 90° counterclockwise and then translated.

Choose the correct word to complete a true statement.

13. A combination of two rigid transformations on a preimage will always/sometimes/never produce the same image when taken in a different order.

14. A double rotation can always/sometimes/never be written as a single rotation.

15. A sequence of a translation and a reflection always/sometimes/never has a point that does not change position.

16. A sequence of a reflection across the *x*-axis and then a reflection across the *y*-axis always/sometimes/never results in a 180° rotation of the preimage.

17. A sequence of rigid transformations will always/sometimes/never result in an image that is the same size and orientation as the preimage.

18. A sequence of a rotation and a dilation will always/sometimes/never result in an image that is the same size and orientation as the preimage.

19. △*QRS* is the image of △*LMN* under a sequence of transformations. Can each of the following sequences be used to create the image, △*QRS*, from the preimage, △*LMN*? Select yes or no.

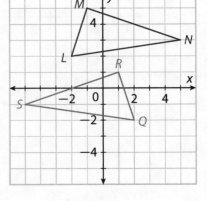

   a. Reflect across the *y*-axis and then translate along the vector ⟨0, −4⟩. ◯ Yes ◯ No

   b. Translate along the vector ⟨0, −4⟩ and then reflect across the *y*-axis. ◯ Yes ◯ No

   c. Rotate 90° clockwise about the origin, reflect across the *x*-axis, and then rotate 90° counterclockwise about the origin. ◯ Yes ◯ No

   d. Rotate 180° about the origin, reflect across the *x*-axis, and then translate along the vector ⟨0, −4⟩. ◯ Yes ◯ No

20. A teacher gave students this puzzle: "I had a triangle with vertex *A* at (1, 4) and vertex *B* at (3, 2). After two rigid transformations, I had the image shown. Describe and show a sequence of transformations that will give this image from the preimage."

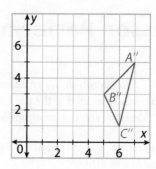

21. Analyze Relationships What two transformations would you apply to △*ABC* to get △*DEF*? How could you express these transformations with a single mapping rule in the form of $(x, y) \rightarrow (?, ?)$?

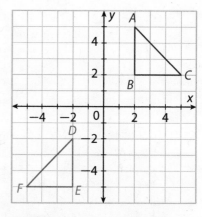

22. Multi-Step Muralists will often make a scale drawing of an art piece before creating the large finished version. A muralist has sketched an art piece on a sheet of paper that is 3 feet by 4 feet.

a. If the final mural will be 39 feet by 52 feet, what is the scale factor for this dilation?

b. The owner of the wall has decided to only give permission to paint on the lower half of the wall. Can the muralist simply use the transformation $(x, y) \rightarrow \left(x, \frac{1}{2}y\right)$ in addition to the scale factor to alter the sketch for use in the allowed space? Explain.

23. Communicate Mathematical Ideas As a graded class activity, your teacher asks your class to reflect a triangle across the *y*-axis and then across the *x*-axis. Your classmate gets upset because he reversed the order of these reflections and thinks he will have to start over. What can you say to your classmate to help him?

Lesson Performance Task

The photograph shows an actual snowflake. Draw a detailed sketch of the "arm" of the snowflake located at the top left of the photo (10:00 on a clock face). Describe in as much detail as you can any translations, reflections, or rotations that you see.

Then describe how the entire snowflake is constructed, based on what you found in the design of one arm.

18.2 Proving Figures are Congruent Using Rigid Motions

Essential Question: How can you determine whether two figures are congruent?

🧭 Explore   Confirming Congruence

Two plane figures are congruent if and only if one can be obtained from the other by a sequence of rigid motions (that is, by a sequence of reflections, translations, and/or rotations).

A landscape architect uses a grid to design the landscape around a mall. Use tracing paper to confirm that the landscape elements are congruent.

(A) Trace planter *ABCD*. Describe a transformation you can use to move the tracing paper so that planter *ABCD* is mapped onto planter *EFGH*. What does this confirm about the planters?

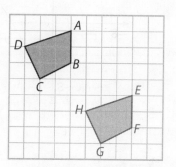

_____

_____

_____

(B) Trace pools *JKLM* and *NPQR*. Fold the paper so that pool *JKLM* is mapped onto pool *NPQR*. Describe the transformation. What does this confirm about the pools?

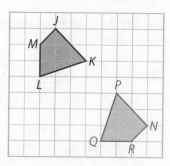

_____

_____

_____

(C) Determine whether the lawns are congruent. Is there a rigid transformation that maps $\triangle LMN$ to $\triangle DEF$? What does this confirm about the lawns?

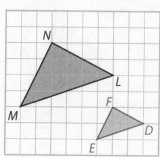

_____

_____

_____

Reflect

1. How do the sizes of the pairs of figures help determine if they are congruent?

_____

_____

Example 1 Use the definition of congruence to decide whether the two figures are congruent. Explain your answer.

Ⓐ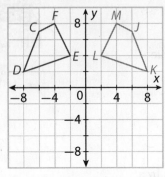

The two figures appear to be the same size and shape, so look for a rigid transformation that will map one to the other.

You can map CDEF onto JKLM by reflecting CDEF over the y-axis. This reflection is a rigid motion that maps CDEF to JKLM, so the two figures are congruent.

The coordinate notation for the reflection is $(x, y) \rightarrow (-x, y)$.

Ⓑ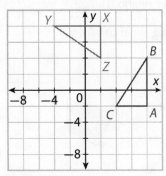

The two figures appear to be the same/different.

You can map $\triangle ABC$ to $\triangle XYZ$

by _____.

This is/is not a rigid motion that maps $\triangle ABC$ to $\triangle XYZ$, so the two figures are/are not congruent.

The coordinate notation for the rotation is _____.

Your Turn

Use the definition of congruence to decide whether the two figures are congruent. Explain your answer.

2.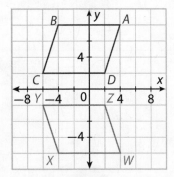

3.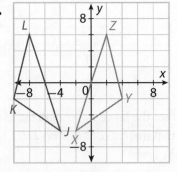

⚙ Explain 2 Finding a Sequence of Rigid Motions

The definition of congruence tells you that when two figures are known to be congruent, there must be some sequence of rigid motions that maps one to the other.

Example 2 The figures shown are congruent. Find a sequence of rigid motions that maps one figure to the other. Give coordinate notation for the transformations you use.

Ⓐ $\triangle ABC \cong \triangle PQR$

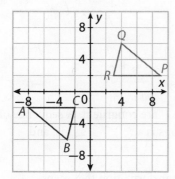

Map $\triangle ABC$ to $\triangle PQR$ with a rotation of 180° around the origin, followed by a horizontal translation.

Rotation: $(x, y) \rightarrow (-x, -y)$

Translation: $(x, y) \rightarrow (x + 1, y)$

Ⓑ $ABCD \cong JKLM$

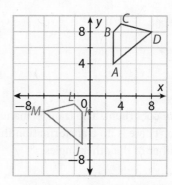

Map $ABCD$ to $JKLM$ with a

_____,

followed by a _____.

_____: $(x, y) \rightarrow$ _____

_____: $(x, y) \rightarrow$ _____

Reflect

4. How is the orientation of the figure affected by a sequence of transformations?

_____

_____

Your Turn

The figures shown are congruent. Find a sequence of rigid motions that maps one figure to the other. Give coordinate notation for the transformations you use.

5. $JKLM \cong WXYZ$

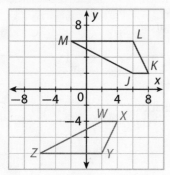

6. $ABCDE \cong PQRST$

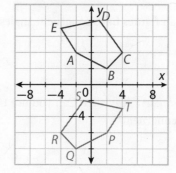

⚙ Explain 3 Investigating Congruent Segments and Angles

Congruence can refer to parts of figures as well as whole figures. Two angles are congruent if and only if one can be obtained from the other by rigid motions (that is, by a sequence of reflections, translations, and/or rotations.) The same conditions are required for two segments to be congruent to each other.

Example 3 Determine which angles or segments are congruent. Describe transformations that can be used to verify congruence.

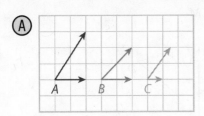

(A)

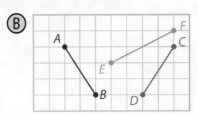

(B)

∠A and ∠C are congruent. The transformation is a translation. There is no transformation that maps ∠B to either of the other angles.

$\overline{AB}$ and _____ are congruent. A sequence of transformations is a _____ and a translation.

There is no transformation that maps _____ to either of the other segments.

Your Turn

7. Determine which segments and which angles are congruent. Describe transformations that can be used to show the congruence.

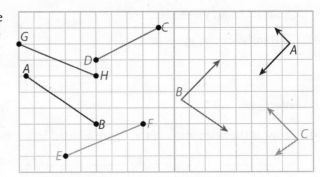

💬 Elaborate

8. Can you say two angles are congruent if they have the same measure but the segments that identify the rays that form the angle are different lengths?

9. **Discussion** Can figures have congruent angles but not be congruent figures?

10. **Essential Question Check-In** Can you use transformations to prove that two figures are not congruent?

• Online Homework
• Hints and Help
• Extra Practice

Use the definition of congruence to decide whether the two figures are congruent. Explain your answer. Give coordinate notation for the transformations you use.

1.

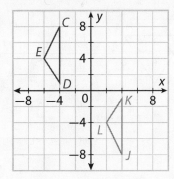

2.

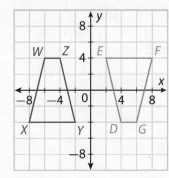

3.

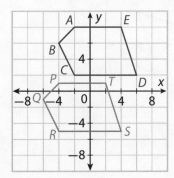

4.

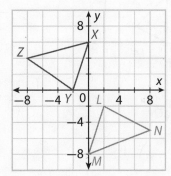

5.

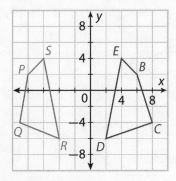

The figures shown are congruent. Find a sequence of rigid motions that maps one figure to the other. Give coordinate notation for the transformations you use.

6. $RSTU \cong WXYZ$

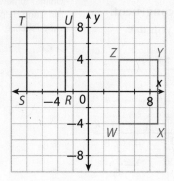

7. $\triangle ABC \cong \triangle DEF$

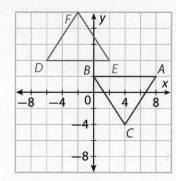

8. $DEFGH \cong PQRST$

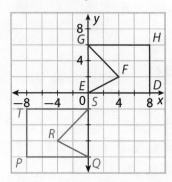

9. $\triangle CDE \cong \triangle WXY$

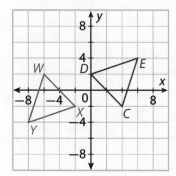

Determine which of the angles are congruent. Which transformations can be used to verify the congruence?

10.

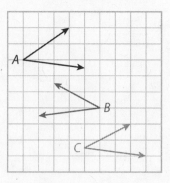

11.

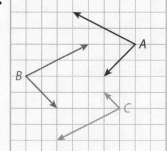

Determine which of the segments are congruent. Which transformations can be used to verify the congruence?

12.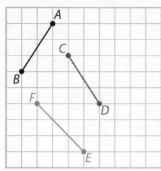

13.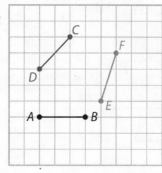

Use the definition of congruence to decide whether the two figures are congruent. Explain your answer. Give coordinate notation for the transformations you use.

14.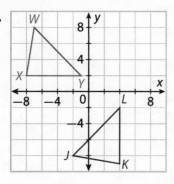

15.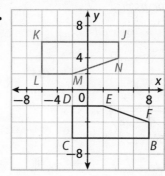

16.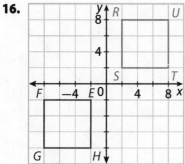

17.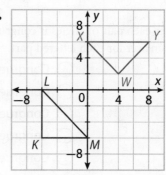

The figures shown are congruent. Find a sequence of transformations for the indicated mapping. Give coordinate notation for the transformations you use.

18. Map *DEFGH* to *PQRST*.

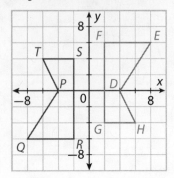

19. Map *JKLM* to *WXYZ*.

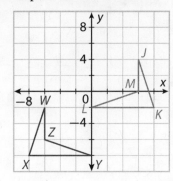

20. Map *ABCDEF* to *PQRSTU*.

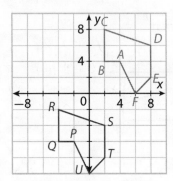

21. Map △*DEF* to △*KLM*.

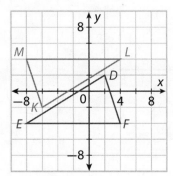

22. Determine whether each pair of angles is congruent or not congruent.
Select the correct answer for each lettered part.

    a. ∠A and ∠B   ○ Congruent   ○ Not congruent

    b. ∠A and ∠C   ○ Congruent   ○ Not congruent

    c. ∠B and ∠C   ○ Congruent   ○ Not congruent

    d. ∠B and ∠D   ○ Congruent   ○ Not congruent

    e. ∠C and ∠D   ○ Congruent   ○ Not congruent

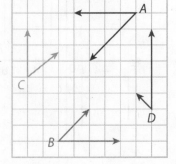

23. If *ABCD* and *WXYZ* are congruent, then *ABCD* can be mapped to *WXYZ* using a rotation and a translation. Determine whether the statement is true or false. Then explain your reasoning.

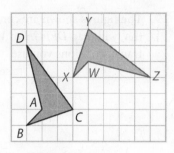

24. Which segments are congruent? Which are not congruent? Explain.

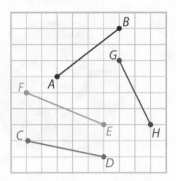

25. Which angles are congruent? Which are not congruent? Explain.

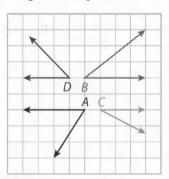

26. The figures shown are congruent. Find a sequence of transformations that will map *CDEFG* to *QRSTU*. Give coordinate notation for the transformations you use.

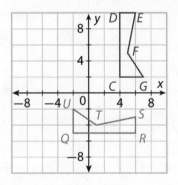

27. The figures shown are congruent. Find a sequence of transformations that will map △*LMN* to △*XYZ*. Give coordinate notation for the transformations you use.

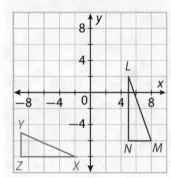

28. Which sequence of transformations does not map a figure onto a congruent figure? Explain.

A. Rotation of 180° about the origin, reflection across the *x*-axis, horizontal translation $(x, y) \rightarrow (x + 4, y)$

B. Reflection across the *y*-axis, combined translation $(x, y) \rightarrow (x - 5, y + 2)$

C. Rotation of 180° about the origin, reflection across the *y*-axis, dilation $(x, y) \rightarrow (2x, 2y)$

D. Counterclockwise rotation of 90° about the origin, reflection across the *y*-axis, combined translation $(x, y) \rightarrow (x - 11, y - 12)$

29. The figures shown are congruent. Find a sequence of transformations that will map *DEFGH* to *VWXYZ*. Give coordinate notation for the transformations you use.

30. How can you prove that two arrows in the recycling symbol are congruent to each other?

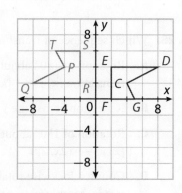

31. The city of St. Louis was settled by the French in the mid 1700s and joined the United States in 1803 as part of the Louisiana Purchase. The city flag reflects its French history by featuring the fleur-de-lis. How can you prove that the left and right petals are congruent to each other?

32. **Draw Conclusions** Two students are trying to show that the two figures are congruent. The first student decides to map *CDEFG* to *PQRST* using a rotation of 180° around the origin, followed by the translation $(x, y) \rightarrow (x, y + 6)$. The second student believes the correct transformations are a reflection across the *y*-axis, followed by the vertical translation $(x, y) \rightarrow (x, y - 2)$. Are both students correct, is only one student correct, or is neither student correct?

© Houghton Mifflin Harcourt Publishing Company • Image Credits: ©ImageClub/Getty Images; ©Atlaspix/Shutterstock

33. Justify Reasoning Two students are trying to show that the two figures are congruent. The first student decides to map *DEFG* to *RSTU* using a rotation of 180° about the origin, followed by the vertical translation $(x, y) \rightarrow (x, y + 4)$. The second student uses a reflection across the *x*-axis, followed by the vertical translation $(x, y) \rightarrow (x, y + 4)$, followed by a reflection across the *y*-axis. Are both students correct, is only one student correct, or is neither student correct?

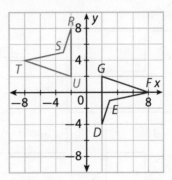

34. Look for a Pattern Assume the pattern of congruent squares shown in the figure continues forever.

Write rules for rigid motions that map square 0 onto square 1, square 0 onto square 2, and square 0 onto square 3.

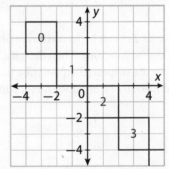

Write a rule for a rigid motion that maps square 0 onto square *n*.

35. Analyze Relationships Suppose you know that $\triangle ABC$ is congruent to $\triangle DEF$ and that $\triangle DEF$ is congruent to $\triangle GHJ$. Can you conclude that $\triangle ABC$ is congruent to $\triangle GHJ$? Explain.

36. Communicate Mathematical Ideas Ella plotted the points $A(0, 0)$, $B(4, 0)$, and $C(0, 4)$. Then she drew $\overline{AB}$ and $\overline{AC}$. Give two different arguments to explain why the segments are congruent.

Lesson Performance Task

The illustration shows how nine congruent shapes can be fitted together to form a larger shape. Each of the shapes can be formed from Shape #1 through a combination of translations, reflections, and/or rotations.

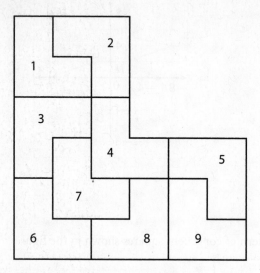

Describe how each of Shapes 2–9 can be formed from Shape #1 through a combination of translations, reflections, and/or rotations. Then design a figure like this one, using a least eight congruent shapes. Number the shapes. Then describe how each of them can be formed from Shape #1 through a combination of translations, reflections, and/or rotations.

© Houghton Mifflin Harcourt Publishing Company

18.3 Corresponding Parts of Congruent Figures Are Congruent

Essential Question: What can you conclude about two figures that are congruent?

⊘ Explore   Exploring Congruence of Parts of Transformed Figures

You will investigate some conclusions you can make when you know that two figures are congruent.

(A) Fold a sheet of paper in half. Use a straightedge to draw a triangle on the folded sheet. Then cut out the triangle, cutting through both layers of paper to produce two congruent triangles. Label them △ABC and △DEF, as shown.

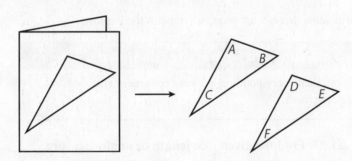

(B) Place the triangles next to each other on a desktop. Since the triangles are congruent, there must be a sequence of rigid motions that maps △ABC to △DEF. Describe the sequence of rigid motions.

_____

(C) The same sequence of rigid motions that maps △ABC to △DEF maps parts of △ABC to parts of △DEF. Complete the following.

$\overline{AB} \rightarrow$ ☐ $\overline{BC} \rightarrow$ ☐ $\overline{AC} \rightarrow$ ☐

$A \rightarrow$ ☐ $B \rightarrow$ ☐ $C \rightarrow$ ☐

(D) What does Step C tell you about the corresponding parts of the two triangles? Why?

_____

_____

1. If you know that △$ABC \cong$ △DEF, what six congruence statements about segments and angles can you write? Why?

_____

_____

_____

2. Do your findings in this Explore apply to figures other than triangles? For instance, if you know that quadrilaterals *JKLM* and *PQRS* are congruent, can you make any conclusions about corresponding parts? Why or why not?

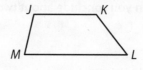 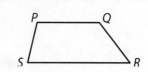

_____

_____

_____

🔑 Explain 1   Corresponding Parts of Congruent Figures Are Congruent

The following true statement summarizes what you discovered in the Explore.

Corresponding Parts of Congruent Figures Are Congruent
If two figures are congruent, then corresponding sides are congruent and corresponding angles are congruent.

Example 1   △$ABC \cong$ △DEF. **Find the given side length or angle measure.**

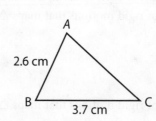 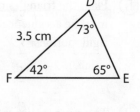

(A) DE

 Step 1 Find the side that corresponds to $\overline{DE}$.

   Since △$ABC \cong$ △DEF, $\overline{AB} \cong \overline{DE}$.

 Step 2 Find the unknown length.

   $DE = AB$, and $AB = 2.6$ cm,
   so $DE = 2.6$ cm.

(B) $m\angle B$

 Step 1 Find the angle that corresponds to $\angle B$.

   Since △$ABC \cong$ △DEF, $\angle B \cong \angle \boxed{}$.

 Step 2 Find the unknown angle measure.

   $m\angle B = m\angle \boxed{}$, and $m\angle \boxed{} = \boxed{}°$, so $m\angle B = \boxed{}°$.

Reflect

3. **Discussion** The triangles shown in the figure are congruent. Can you conclude that $\overline{JK} \cong \overline{QR}$? Explain.

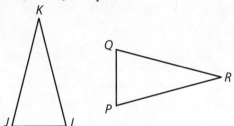

_____

_____

_____

_____

Your Turn

$\triangle STU \cong \triangle VWX$. Find the given side length or angle measure.

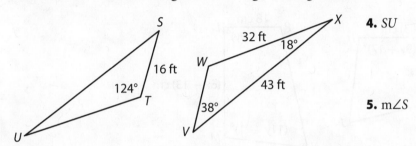

4. SU

5. $m\angle S$

⚙️ Explain 2 Applying the Properties of Congruence

Rigid motions preserve length and angle measure. This means that congruent segments have the same length, so $\overline{UV} \cong \overline{XY}$ implies $UV = XY$ and vice versa. In the same way, congruent angles have the same measure, so $\angle J \cong \angle K$ implies $m\angle J = m\angle K$ and vice versa.

Properties of Congruence	
Reflexive Property of Congruence	$\overline{AB} \cong \overline{AB}$
Symmetric Property of Congruence	If $\overline{AB} \cong \overline{CD}$, then $\overline{CD} \cong \overline{AD}$.
Transitive Property of Congruence	If $\overline{AB} \cong \overline{CD}$ and $\overline{CD} \cong \overline{EF}$, then $\overline{AB} \cong \overline{EF}$.

Example 2 $\triangle ABC \cong \triangle DEF$. Find the given side length or angle measure.

(A) AB

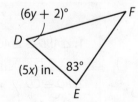

Since $\triangle ABC \cong \triangle DEF$, $\overline{AB} \cong \overline{DE}$.
Therefore, $AB = DE$.

Write an equation. $3x + 8 = 5x$

Subtract $3x$ from each side. $8 = 2x$

Divide each side by 2. $4 = x$

So, $AB = 3x + 8 = 3(4) + 8 = 12 + 8 = 20$ in.

Ⓑ m∠D

Since △ABC ≅ △DEF, ∠ ☐ ≅ ∠D. Therefore, m∠ ☐ = m∠D.

Write an equation. $5y + ☐ = ☐ + 2$

Subtract 5y from each side. $11 = ☐ + 2$

Subtract 2 from each side. $☐ = ☐$

So, m∠D = $(6y + 2)° = (6 · ☐ + 2)° = ☐°$.

Your Turn

Quadrilateral *GHJK* ≅ quadrilateral *LMNP*. Find the given side length or angle measure.

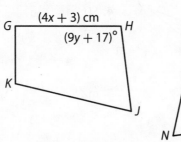
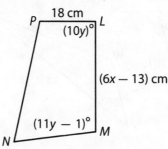

6. *LM*

7. m∠H

🔑 Explain 3   Using Congruent Corresponding Parts in a Proof

Example 3   Write each proof.

Ⓐ Given: △ABD ≅ △ACD

Prove: D is the midpoint of $\overline{BC}$.

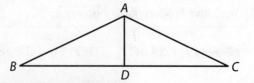

Statements	Reasons
1. △ABD ≅ △ACD	1. Given
2. $\overline{BD} ≅ \overline{CD}$	2. Corresponding parts of congruent figures are congruent.
3. D is the midpoint of $\overline{BC}$.	3. Definition of midpoint.

Ⓑ Given: Quadrilateral *JKLM* ≅ quadrilateral *NPQR*; ∠*J* ≅ ∠*K*

Prove: ∠*J* ≅ ∠*P*

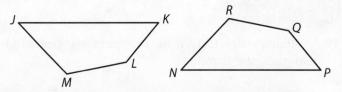

Statements	Reasons
1. Quadrilateral *JKLM* ≅ quadrilateral *NPQR*	1.
2. ∠*J* ≅ ∠*K*	2.
3. ∠*K* ≅ ∠*P*	3.
4. ∠*J* ≅ ∠*P*	4.

Your Turn

Write each proof.

8. Given: △*SVT* ≅ △*SWT*
   Prove: $\overline{ST}$ bisects ∠*VSW*.

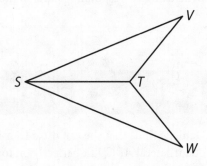

9. Given: Quadrilateral *ABCD* ≅ quadrilateral *EFGH*;
   $\overline{AD}$ ≅ $\overline{CD}$
   Prove: $\overline{AD}$ ≅ $\overline{GH}$

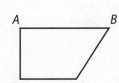
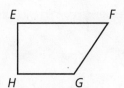

10. A student claims that any two congruent triangles must have the same perimeter. Do you agree? Explain.

_____

_____

11. If △PQR is a right triangle and △PQR ≅ △XYZ, does △XYZ have to be a right triangle? Why or why not?

_____

_____

_____

12. **Essential Question Check-In** Suppose you know that pentagon ABCDE is congruent to pentagon FGHJK. How many additional congruence statements can you write using corresponding parts of the pentagons? Explain.

_____

_____

☆ Evaluate: Homework and Practice

- Online Homework
- Hints and Help
- Extra Practice

1. Danielle finds that she can use a translation and a reflection to make quadrilateral ABCD fit perfectly on top of quadrilateral WXYZ. What congruence statements can Danielle write using the sides and angles of the quadrilaterals? Why?

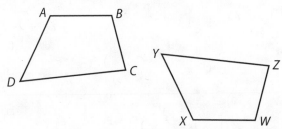

△DEF ≅ △GHJ. **Find the given side length or angle measure.**

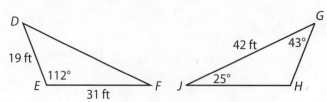

2. JH

3. m∠D

***KLMN ≅ PQRS*.** Find the given side length or angle measure.

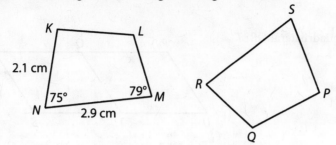

4. m∠R

5. PS

△*ABC* ≅ △*TUV*. Find the given side length or angle measure.

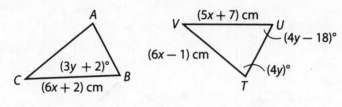

6. BC

7. m∠U

***DEFG ≅ KLMN*.** Find the given side length or angle measure.

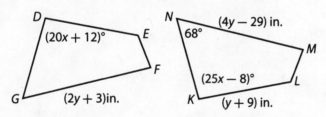

8. FG

9. m∠D

10. $\overline{GH}$ ≅ _____

11. ∠J ≅ _____

12. GJ = _____

13. m∠G = _____

Write each proof.

14. Given: Quadrilateral $PQTU \cong$ quadrilateral $QRST$
Prove: $\overline{QT}$ bisects $\overline{PR}$.

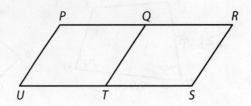

15. Given: $\triangle ABC \cong \triangle ADC$

Prove: $\overline{AC}$ bisects $\angle BAD$ and $\overline{AC}$ bisects $\angle BCD$.

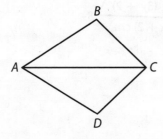

16. Given: Pentagon $ABCDE \cong$ pentagon $FGHJK$; $\angle D \cong \angle E$
Prove: $\angle D \cong \angle K$

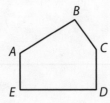 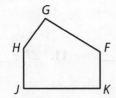

$\triangle GHJ \cong \triangle PQR$ and $\triangle PQR \cong \triangle STU$. **Complete the following using a side or angle of $\triangle STU$. Justify your answers.**

$\triangle ABC \cong \triangle DEF$. **Find the given side length or angle measure.**

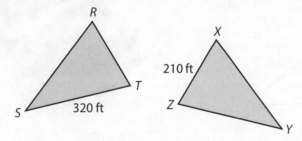

17. m∠D

18. m∠C

19. The figure shows the dimensions of two city parks, where $\triangle RST \cong \triangle XYZ$ and $\overline{YX} \cong \overline{YZ}$. A city employee wants to order new fences to surround both parks. What is the total length of the fences required to surround the parks?

20. A tower crane is used to lift steel, concrete, and building materials at construction sites. The figure shows part of the horizontal beam of a tower crane, in which $\triangle ABG \cong \triangle BCH \cong \triangle HGB$

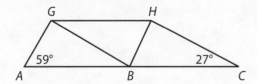

a. Is it possible to determine m∠GBH? If so, how? If not, why not?

b. A member of the construction crew claims that $\overline{AC}$ is twice as long as $\overline{AB}$. Do you agree? Explain.

21. Multi-Step A company installs triangular pools at hotels. All of the pools are congruent and $\triangle JKL \cong \triangle MNP$ in the figure. What is the perimeter of each pool?

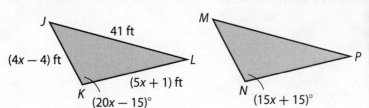

22. Kendall and Ava lay out the course shown below for their radio-controlled trucks. In the figure, $\triangle ABD \cong \triangle CBD$. The trucks travel at a constant speed of 15 feet per second. How long does it take a truck to travel on the course from A to B to C to D? Round to the nearest tenth of a second.

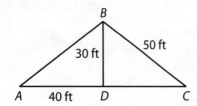

23. $\triangle MNP \cong \triangle QRS$. Determine whether each statement about the triangles is true or false. Select the correct answer for each lettered part.

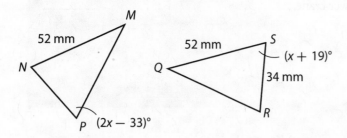

a. $\triangle QRS$ is isosceles. ○ True ○ False

b. $\overline{MP}$ is longer than $\overline{MN}$. ○ True ○ False

c. $m\angle P = 52°$ ○ True ○ False

d. The perimeter of $\triangle QRS$ is 120 mm. ○ True ○ False

e. $\angle M \cong \angle Q$ ○ True ○ False

24. Justify Reasoning Given that $\triangle ABC \cong \triangle DEF$, $AB = 2.7$ ft, and $AC = 3.4$ ft, is it possible to determine the length of $\overline{EF}$? If so, find the length and justify your steps. If not, explain why not.

25. Explain the Error A student was told that $\triangle GHJ \cong \triangle RST$ and was asked to find GH. The student's work is shown below. Explain the error and find the correct answer.

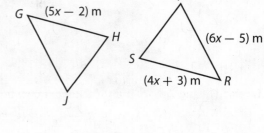

Student's Work
$5x - 2 = 6x - 5$
$-2 = x - 5$
$3 = x$
$GH = 5x - 2 = 5(3) - 2 = 13$ m

26. Critical Thinking In $\triangle ABC$, $m\angle A = 55°$, $m\angle B = 50°$, and $m\angle C = 75°$. In $\triangle DEF$, $m\angle E = 50°$, and $m\angle F = 65°$. Is it possible for the triangles to be congruent? Explain.

27. Analyze Relationships $\triangle PQR \cong \triangle SQR$ and $\overline{RS} \cong \overline{RT}$. A student said that point R appears to be the midpoint of $\overline{PT}$. Is it possible to prove this? If so, write the proof. If not, explain why not.

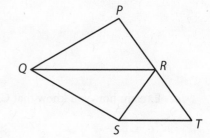

Lesson Performance Task

The illustration shows a "Yankee Puzzle" quilt.

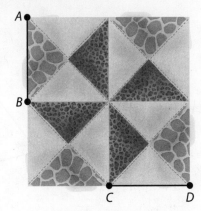

a. Use the idea of congruent shapes to describe the design of the quilt.

b. Explain how the triangle with base $\overline{AB}$ can be transformed to the position of the triangle with base $\overline{CD}$.

c. Explain how you know that $CD = AB$.

Congruent Figures

Essential Question: How can you use congruency to solve real-world problems?

KEY EXAMPLE *(Lesson 18.1)*

Write the vertices of the image of the figure given by
$A(2, 1)$, $B(3, 3)$, $C(2, 4)$ after the transformations.

$(x, y) \rightarrow (x + 1, y + 2) \rightarrow (3x, y)$

$A(2, 1) \rightarrow A'(3, 3)$

$B(3, 3) \rightarrow B'(4, 5)$ Apply the transformations in order to each point. Apply the first transformation.

$C(2, 4) \rightarrow C'(3, 6)$

$A'(3, 3) \rightarrow A''(9, 3)$ Apply the second transformation.

$B'(4, 5) \rightarrow B''(12, 5)$

$C'(3, 6) \rightarrow C''(9, 6)$

The image of the transformed figure is determined by the points
$A''(9, 3)$, $B''(12, 5)$, $C''(9, 6)$.

KEY EXAMPLE *(Lesson 18.2)*

Determine whether a triangle $\triangle ABC$ is congruent to its image after the transformations
$(x, y) \rightarrow (x + 1, y + 2) \rightarrow (2x, y)$.

The transformation $(x, y) \rightarrow (x + 1, y + 2)$ is a translation, which is a rigid motion, so after this transformation the image is congruent. The transformation $(x, y) \rightarrow (2x, y)$ is a dilation, which is not a rigid motion, so the image from this transformation is not congruent.

After the transformations, the image is not congruent to $\triangle ABC$ because one of the transformations is not a rigid motion.

KEY EXAMPLE *(Lesson 18.3)*

Find the angle in $\triangle DFE$ congruent to $\angle A$ and the side congruent to $\overline{BC}$ when
$\triangle ABC \cong \triangle DFE$.

Since $\triangle ABC \cong \triangle DFE$, and corresponding parts of congruent figures are congruent, $\angle A \cong \angle D$ and $\overline{BC} \cong \overline{FE}$.

EXERCISES

Write the vertices of the image of the figure after the transformations. *(Lesson 18.1)*

1. The figure given by $A(1, -2)$, $B(2, 5)$, $C(-3, 7)$, and the transformations

$(x, y) \rightarrow (x, y - 1) \rightarrow (-y, 2x)$ _____.

Find the rigid motions to transform one figure into its congruent figure. *(Lesson 18.2)*

2. In the figure, $\triangle ABC \cong \triangle DEF$.

The rigid motions to transform from $\triangle ABC \cong \triangle DEF$ are

_____.

Find the congruent parts. *(Lesson 18.3)*

3. Given $\triangle ABC \cong \triangle DEF$, $\angle A \cong$ _____.

4. Given $\triangle ABC \cong \triangle DEF$, $\overline{CA} \cong$ _____.

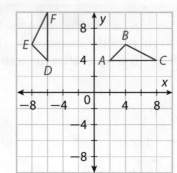

MODULE PERFORMANCE TASK

Jigsaw Puzzle

A popular pastime, jigsaw puzzles are analogous to the series of transformations that can be performed to move one figure onto another congruent figure.

In the photo, identify at least three pieces that would likely fit into one of the empty spaces in the puzzle. Describe the rotations and translations necessary to move the piece to its correct position in the puzzle.

© Houghton Mifflin Harcourt Publishing Company • Image Credits: ©Hitdelight/Shutterstock

(Ready) to Go On?

18.1–18.3 Congruent Figures

- Online Homework
- Hints and Help
- Extra Practice

Predict the results of the transformations. *(Lesson 18.1)*

1. Triangle △*ABC* is in the first quadrant and translated along ⟨2, 1⟩ and reflected across the *x*-axis.

Which quadrant will the triangle be in after the first transformation? _____

Which quadrant will the triangle be in after the second transformation? _____

Determine whether the triangles are congruent using rigid motions. *(Lesson 18.2)*

2. Using the graph with △*ABC*, △*DEF*, and △*PQR*:

A. Determine whether △*ABC* is congruent to △*DEF*.

B. Determine whether △*DEF* is congruent to △*PQR*.

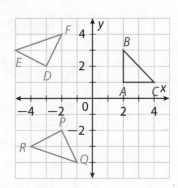

Find the congruent parts of the triangles. *(Lesson 18.3)*

3. List all of the pairs of congruent sides for two congruent triangles △*ABC* and △*DEF*.

ESSENTIAL QUESTION

4. How can you determine whether a figure is congruent to another figure?

Assessment Readiness

1. A line segment with points $R(3, 5)$ and $S(5, 5)$ is reflected across the line $y = -x$ and translated 2 units down. Determine whether each choice is a coordinate of the image of the line segment. Select Yes or No for A–C.

   A. $R'(-5, -3)$ ○ Yes ○ No

   B. $R'(-5, -5)$ ○ Yes ○ No

   C. $S'(-5, -7)$ ○ Yes ○ No

2. The polygon *ABCD* is congruent to *PQRS*. The measure of angle *B* is equal to 65°. Choose True or False for each statement.

   A. The supplement of angle *Q* measures 115°. ○ True ○ False

   B. Angle *Q* measures 115°. ○ True ○ False

   C. The supplement of angle *B* measures 115°. ○ True ○ False

3. Triangle *LMN* is a right triangle. The measure of angle *L* is equal to 35°. Triangle *LMN* is congruent to △*PRQ* with right angle *R*. Choose True or False for each statement.

   A. The measure of angle *Q* is 55°. ○ True ○ False

   B. The measure of angle *R* is 90°. ○ True ○ False

   C. The measure of angle *P* is 35°. ○ True ○ False

4. The two triangles, △*ABC* and △*DEF*, are congruent. Which side is congruent to $\overline{CA}$? Which side is congruent to $\overline{BA}$?

• Online Homework
• Hints and Help
• Extra Practice

1. Consider each expression. If $x = -2$, is the value of the expression a positive number? Select Yes or No.

   A. $-2(x - 2)^2$ ○ Yes   ○ No

   B. $-3x(5 - 4x)$ ○ Yes   ○ No

   C. $x^3 + 6x$ ○ Yes   ○ No

2. A bedroom is shaped like a rectangular prism. The floor has a length of 4.57 meters and a width of 4.04 meters. The height of the room is 2.3 meters.

   Choose True or False for each statement.

   A. The perimeter of the floor with the correct number of significant digits is 17.22 meters.   ○ True   ○ False

   B. The area of the floor with the correct number of significant digits is 18.46 square meters.   ○ True   ○ False

   C. The volume of the room with the correct number of significant digits is 42 cubic meters.   ○ True   ○ False

3. Does the ray $\overrightarrow{BD}$ bisect $\angle ABC$?

   Select Yes or No for each pair of angles.

   A. $m\angle ABC = 60°$, $m\angle ABD = 30°$ ○ Yes   ○ No

   B. $m\angle ABC = 96°$, $m\angle ABD = 47°$ ○ Yes   ○ No

   C. $m\angle ABC = 124°$, $m\angle ABD = 62°$ ○ Yes   ○ No

4. Is the point C the midpoint of the line $\overline{AB}$?

   Select Yes or No for each statement.

   A. $A(1, 2)$, $B(3, 4)$, and $C(2, 3)$ ○ Yes   ○ No

   B. $A(-1, 2)$, $B(3, -1)$, and $C(1, 0)$ ○ Yes   ○ No

   C. $A(-3, 0)$, $B(-1, 5)$, and $C(-2, 2)$ ○ Yes   ○ No

5. Is $\overline{RS}$ a translation of $\overline{DF}$?

   Select Yes or No for each statement.

   A. $R(2, 2)$, $S(5, 2)$, and $D(3, 3)$, $F(5, 3)$ ○ Yes   ○ No

   B. $R(-1, 3)$, $S(2, -2)$, and $D(-4, 2)$, $F(-1, -3)$ ○ Yes   ○ No

   C. $R(5, -3)$, $S(2, 2)$, and $D(1, -4)$, $F(-1, -3)$ ○ Yes   ○ No

6. Does the shape have rotational symmetry?

Select Yes or No for each statement.

   A. A square   ◯ Yes   ◯ No

   B. A trapezoid   ◯ Yes   ◯ No

   C. A right triangle   ◯ Yes   ◯ No

7. Determine whether each image of $\triangle ABC$, with $A(1, 3)$, $B(2, 3)$, $C(4, 5)$, can be formed with only the given transformation. Select True or False for each statement.

   A. $A'(2, 4)$, $B'(3, 4)$, $C'(5, 6)$ is formed
by translation.   ◯ True   ◯ False

   B. $A'(-1, 3)$, $B'(-2, 3)$, $C'(-4, 5)$ is formed
by rotation.   ◯ True   ◯ False

   C. $A'(1, -5)$, $B'(2, -3)$, $C'(4, -1)$ is formed
by reflection.   ◯ True   ◯ False

8. For $\triangle DEF$, with $D(2, 2)$, $E(3, 5)$, $F(4, 3)$, and $\triangle D'E'F'$, with $D'(4, 2)$, $E'(3, 5)$, $F'(2, 3)$, determine whether the image can be formed with the sequence of transformations. Select True or False for each statement.

   A. The image is formed by a reflection
followed by a translation.   ◯ True   ◯ False

   B. The image is formed by a rotation
followed by a reflection.   ◯ True   ◯ False

   C. The image is formed by two consecutive
reflections.   ◯ True   ◯ False

9. Use the figure to answer the questions below.

   A. What is a specific series of rigid transformations
that maps $\triangle ABC$ to $\triangle DEF$?

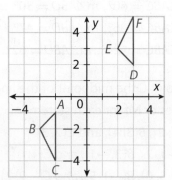

   B. List all congruent pairs of angles and sides for the
two figures.

Performance Tasks

★**10.** A student has drawn a figure of a square *PQRS* with points $P(-5, 5)$, $Q(1, 5)$, $R(1, -1)$, and $S(-5, -1)$. For the next assignment, the teacher wants students to inscribe another square, but with sides of length $\sqrt{18}$, in the square. How would a student find the correct square? What are the vertices of the inscribed square?

★★**11.** A square table is set with four identical place settings, one on each side of the table. Each setting consists of a plate and spoon. Choose one as the original place setting. What transformation describes the location of each of the other three? Express your answer in terms of degrees, lines of reflection, or directions from the original place setting.

★★★**12.** In spherical geometry, the plane is replaced by the surface of a sphere. In this context, straight lines are defined as great circles, which are circles that have the same center as the sphere. They are the largest possible circles on the surface of the sphere.

A. On a globe, lines of longitude run north and south. In spherical geometry, are lines of longitude straight lines? Are any lines of longitude parallel (nonintersecting)?

B. Lines of latitude run east and west. In spherical geometry, are lines of latitude straight lines? Are any lines of latitude parallel (nonintersecting)?

C. In general, in how many places does a pair of straight lines intersect in spherical geometry?

Geomatics Surveyor A geomatics surveyor is surveying a piece of land of length 400 feet and width 300 feet. Standing at one corner, he finds that the elevation of the opposite corner is 50 feet greater than his elevation. Find the distance between the surveyor and the middlemost point of the piece of land (ignoring elevation), the elevation of the middlemost point in comparison to his location (assuming that the elevation increases at a constant rate), and the distance between the surveyor and the middlemost point of the piece of land considering its elevation.

UNIT 8

Lines, Angles, and Triangles

MATH IN CAREERS

Architect An architect is responsible for designing spaces where people work and live. In addition to a keen eye for detail and strong artistic skills, architects use mathematics to create spaces that are both functional and aesthetically pleasing.

If you're interested in a career as an architect, you should study these mathematical subjects:

- Algebra
- Geometry
- Trigonometry

Research other careers that require the use of spatial analysis to understand real-world scenarios. See the related Career Activity at the end of this unit.

© Houghton Mifflin Harcourt Publishing Company•Image Credits: ©Ocean/Corbis

Reading Start-Up

Vocabulary

Review Words

✔ adjacent angles (*ángulos adyacentes*)

✔ parallel lines (*líneas paralelas*)

✔ congruence (*congruencia*)

✔ vertical angles (*ángulos verticales*)

✔ complementary angles (*ángulos complementarios*)

✔ supplementary angles (*ángulos suplementarios*)

✔ transversal (*transversal*)

Preview Words

indirect proof (*demostración indirecta*)

hypotenuse (*hipotenusa*)

legs (*catetos*)

interior angle (*ángulo interior*)

exterior angle (*ángulo exterior*)

isosceles triangle (*triángulo isósceles*)

equilateral triangle (*triángulo equilátero*)

circumscribe (*circunscribir*)

inscribed (*apuntado*)

Visualize Vocabulary

Use the ✔ words to complete the case diagram. Write the review words in the bubbles and draw a picture to illustrate each case.

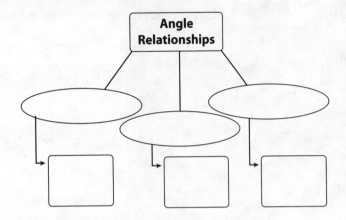

Understand Vocabulary

Complete the sentences using the preview words.

1. A(n) _____ has three sides with the same length.

2. A circle is _____ in a polygon if each side of the polygon is tangent to the circle.

3. The _____ of a right triangle is the longest side of the triangle.

Active Reading

Key-Term Fold While reading each module, create a key-term fold to help you organize vocabulary words. Write vocabulary terms on one side and definitions on the other side. Place a special emphasis on learning and speaking the English word while discussing the unit.

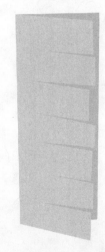

© Houghton Mifflin Harcourt Publishing Company

Lines and Angles

Essential Question: How can you use parallel and perpendicular lines to solve real-world problems?

REAL WORLD VIDEO
Check out how properties of parallel and perpendicular lines and angles can be used to create real-world illusions in a mystery spot building.

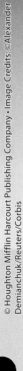

© Houghton Mifflin Harcourt Publishing Company • Image Credits: ©Alexander Demianchuk/Reuters/Corbis

MODULE PERFORMANCE TASK PREVIEW

Mystery Spot Building

In this module, you will use properties of parallel lines and angles to analyze the strange happenings in a mystery spot building. With a little bit of geometry, you'll be able to figure out whether mystery spot buildings are "on the up-and-up!"

Complete these exercises to review skills you will need for this module.

Angle Relationships

Example 1

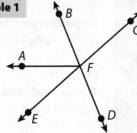

The measure of ∠AFB is 70° and the measure of ∠AFE is 40°. Find the measure of angle ∠BFE.

- Online Homework
- Hints and Help
- Extra Practice

m∠BFE = m∠AFB + m∠AFE   Angle Addition Postulate

m∠BFE = 70° + 40°   Substitute.

m∠BFE = 110°   Solve for m∠BFE.

Find the measure of the angle in the image from the example.

1. The measure of ∠BFE is 110°. Find m∠EFD.

m∠EFD = _____

2. The measure of ∠BFE is 110°. Find m∠BFC.

m∠BFC = _____

Parallel Lines Cut by a Transversal

Example 2   The measure of ∠7 is 110°. Find m∠3. Assume $p \parallel q$.

m∠3 = m∠7   Corresponding Angles Theorem

m∠3 = 110°   Substitute.

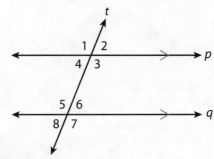

Find the measure of the angle in the image from the example. Assume $p \parallel q$.

3. The measure of ∠3 is 110°. Find m∠1.   m∠1 = _____

4. The measure of ∠3 is 110°. Find m∠6.   m∠6 = _____

Writing Equations of Parallel, Perpendicular, Vertical, and Horizontal Lines

Example 3   Find the line parallel to $y = 2x + 7$ that passes through the point $(3, 6)$.

$(y - y_1) = m(x - x_1)$ Use point-slope form.

$(y - 6) = 2(x - 3)$ Substitute for m, x_1, y_1. Parallel lines have the same slope, so $m = 2$.

$y - 6 = 2x - 6$ Simplify.

$y = 2x$ Solve for y.

Find the equation of the line described.

5. Perpendicular to $y = 3x + 5$; passing through the point $(-6, -4)$ _____

6. Parallel to the x-axis; passing through the point $(4, 1)$ _____

19.1 Angles Formed by Intersecting Lines

Essential Question: How can you find the measures of angles formed by intersecting lines?

⊙ Explore 1 Exploring Angle Pairs Formed by Intersecting Lines

When two lines intersect, like the blades of a pair of scissors, a number of angle pairs are formed. You can find relationships between the measures of the angles in each pair.

(A) Using a straightedge, draw a pair of intersecting lines like the open scissors. Label the angles formed as 1, 2, 3, and 4.

(B) Use a protractor to find each measure.

Angle	Measure of Angle
m∠1	
m∠2	
m∠3	
m∠4	
m∠1 + m∠2	
m∠2 + m∠3	
m∠3 + m∠4	
m∠1 + m∠4	

You have been measuring *vertical angles* and *linear pairs* of angles. When two lines intersect, the angles that are opposite each other are **vertical angles**. Recall that a *linear pair* is a pair of adjacent angles whose non-common sides are opposite rays. So, when two lines intersect, the angles that are on the same side of a line form a linear pair.

Reflect

1. Name a pair of vertical angles and a linear pair of angles in your diagram in Step A.

_____

2. Make a conjecture about the measures of a pair of vertical angles.

_____

3. Use the Linear Pair Theorem to tell what you know about the measures of angles that form a linear pair.

_____

_____

⊘ Explore 2 Proving the Vertical Angles Theorem

The conjecture from the Explore about vertical angles can be proven so it can be stated as a theorem.

The Vertical Angles Theorem
If two angles are vertical angles, then the angles are congruent.   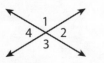 $\angle 1 \cong \angle 3$ and $\angle 2 \cong \angle 4$

You have written proofs in two-column and paragraph proof formats. Another type of proof is called a *flow proof*. A **flow proof** uses boxes and arrows to show the structure of the proof. The steps in a flow proof move from left to right or from top to bottom, shown by the arrows connecting each box. The justification for each step is written below the box. You can use a flow proof to prove the Vertical Angles Theorem.

Follow the steps to write a Plan for Proof and a flow proof to prove the Vertical Angles Theorem.

Given: $\angle 1$ and $\angle 3$ are vertical angles.

Prove: $\angle 1 \cong \angle 3$

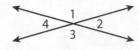

© Houghton Mifflin Harcourt Publishing Company

(A) Complete the final steps of a Plan for Proof:

Because ∠1 and ∠2 are a linear pair and ∠2 and ∠3 are a linear pair, these pairs of angles are supplementary. This means that m∠1 + m∠2 = 180° and m∠2 + m∠3 = 180°. By the Transitive Property, m∠1 + m∠2 = m∠2 + m∠3. Next:

_____

(B) Use the Plan for Proof to complete the flow proof. Begin with what you know is true from the Given or the diagram. Use arrows to show the path of the reasoning. Fill in the missing statement or reason in each step.

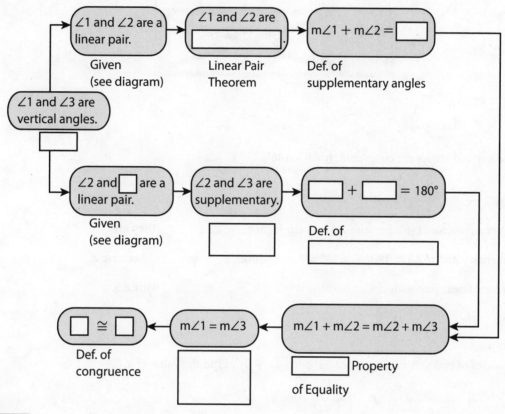

Reflect

4. **Discussion** Using the other pair of angles in the diagram, ∠2 and ∠4, would a proof that ∠2 ≅ ∠4 also show that the Vertical Angles Theorem is true? Explain why or why not.

_____

_____

5. Draw two intersecting lines to form vertical angles. Label your lines and tell which angles are congruent. Measure the angles to check that they are congruent.

_____

_____

🎸 Explain 1 Using Vertical Angles

You can use the Vertical Angles Theorem to find missing angle measures in situations involving intersecting lines.

Example 1 Cross braces help keep the deck posts straight. Find the measure of each angle.

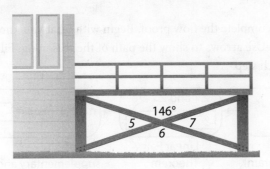

(A) ∠6

   Because vertical angles are congruent, m∠6 = 146°.

(B) ∠5 and ∠7

   From Part A, m∠6 = 146°. Because ∠5 and ∠6 form a _____, they are

   supplementary and m∠5 = 180° − 146° = ☐. m∠☐ = ☐ because ∠☐

   also forms a linear pair with ∠6, or because it is a _____ with ∠5.

Your Turn

6. The measures of two vertical angles are 58° and $(3x + 4)$°. Find the value of x.

7. The measures of two vertical angles are given by the expressions $(x + 3)$° and $(2x − 7)$°. Find the value of x. What is the measure of each angle?

⚙ Explain 2   Using Supplementary and Complementary Angles

Recall what you know about complementary and supplementary angles. **Complementary angles** are two angles whose measures have a sum of 90°. **Supplementary angles** are two angles whose measures have a sum of 180°. You have seen that two angles that form a linear pair are supplementary.

Example 2   Use the diagram below to find the missing angle measures. Explain your reasoning.

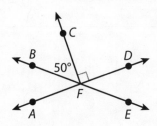

(A)   Find the measures of ∠AFC and ∠AFB.

∠AFC and ∠CFD are a linear pair formed by an intersecting line and ray,
$\overleftrightarrow{AD}$ and $\overrightarrow{FC}$, so they are supplementary and the sum of their measures is 180°. By the diagram, m∠CFD = 90°, so m∠AFC = 180° − 90° = 90° and ∠AFC is also a right angle.

Because together they form the right angle ∠AFC, ∠AFB and ∠BFC are complementary and the sum of their measures is 90°. So, m∠AFB = 90° − m∠BFC = 90° − 50° = 40°.

(B)   Find the measures of ∠DFE and ∠AFE.

∠BFA and ∠DFE are formed by two _____ and are opposite each other,

so the angles are _____ angles. So, the angles are congruent. From Part A

m∠AFB = 40°, so m∠DFE = ☐ also.

Because ∠BFA and ∠AFE form a linear pair, the angles are _____ and the sum

of their measures is ☐. So, m∠AFE = ☐ − m∠BFA = ☐ − ☐ = ☐.

Reflect

8.   In Part A, what do you notice about right angles ∠AFC and ∠CFD? Make a conjecture about right angles.

_____

_____

You can represent the measures of an angle and its complement as $x°$ and $(90 - x)°$. Similarly, you can represent the measures of an angle and its supplement as $x°$ and $(180 - x)°$. Use these expressions to find the measures of the angles described.

9. The measure of an angle is equal to the measure of its complement.

10. The measure of an angle is twice the measure of its supplement.

Elaborate

11. Describe how proving a theorem is different than solving a problem and describe how they are the same.

_____

_____

_____

12. **Discussion** The proof of the Vertical Angles Theorem in the lesson includes a Plan for Proof. How are a Plan for Proof and the proof itself the same and how are they different?

_____

_____

_____

13. Draw two intersecting lines. Label points on the lines and tell what angles you know are congruent and which are supplementary.

_____

_____

_____

14. **Essential Question Check-In** If you know that the measure of one angle in a linear pair is 75°, how can you find the measure of the other angle?

_____

_____

⭐ Evaluate: Homework and Practice

Use this diagram and information for Exercises 1–4.

Given: m∠*AFB* = m∠*EFD* = 50°

    Points *B*, *F*, *D* and points *E*, *F*, *C* are collinear.

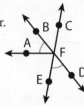

1. Determine whether each pair of angles is a pair of vertical angles, a linear pair of angles, or neither. Select the correct answer for each lettered part.

   A. ∠*BFC* and ∠*DFE*   ◯ Vertical   ◯ Linear Pair   ◯ Neither

   B. ∠*BFA* and ∠*DFE*   ◯ Vertical   ◯ Linear Pair   ◯ Neither

   C. ∠*BFC* and ∠*CFD*   ◯ Vertical   ◯ Linear Pair   ◯ Neither

   D. ∠*AFE* and ∠*AFC*   ◯ Vertical   ◯ Linear Pair   ◯ Neither

   E. ∠*BFE* and ∠*CFD*   ◯ Vertical   ◯ Linear Pair   ◯ Neither

   F. ∠*AFE* and ∠*BFC*   ◯ Vertical   ◯ Linear Pair   ◯ Neither

2. Find m∠*AFE*.   **3.** Find m∠*DFC*.

4. Find m∠*BFC*.

5. **Represent Real-World Problems** A sprinkler swings back and forth between *A* and *B* in such a way that ∠1 ≅ ∠2, ∠1 and ∠3 are complementary, and ∠2 and ∠4 are complementary. If m∠1 = 47.5°, find m∠2, m∠3, and m∠4.

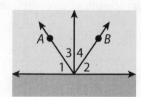

Determine whether each statement is true or false. If false, explain why.

6. If an angle is acute, then the measure of its complement must be greater than the measure of its supplement.

7. A pair of vertical angles may also form a linear pair.

8. If two angles are supplementary and congruent, the measure of each angle is 90°.

9. If a ray divides an angle into two complementary angles, then the original angle is a right angle.

You can represent the measures of an angle and its complement as $x°$ and $(90 - x)°$. Similarly, you can represent the measures of an angle and its supplement as $x°$ and $(180 - x)°$. Use these expressions to find the measures of the angles described.

10. The measure of an angle is three times the measure of its supplement.

11. The measure of the supplement of an angle is three times the measure of its complement.

12. The measure of an angle increased by 20° is equal to the measure of its complement.

Write a plan for a proof for each theorem.

13. If two angles are congruent, then their complements are congruent.

   Given: $\angle ABC \cong \angle DEF$

   Prove: The complement of $\angle ABC \cong$ the complement of $\angle DEF$.

14. If two angles are congruent, then their supplements are congruent.

   Given: $\angle ABC \cong \angle DEF$

   Prove: The supplement of $\angle ABC \cong$ the supplement of $\angle DEF$.

15. Justify Reasoning Complete the two-column proof for the theorem "If two angles are congruent, then their supplements are congruent."

Statements	Reasons
1. ∠ABC ≅ ∠DEF	1. Given
2. The measure of the supplement of ∠ABC = 180° − m∠ABC.	2. Definition of the _____ of an angle
3. The measure of the supplement of ∠DEF = 180° − m∠DEF.	3. _____
4. _____	4. If two angles are congruent, their measures are equal.
5. The measure of the supplement of ∠DEF = 180° − m∠ABC.	5. Substitution Property of _____
6. The measure of the supplement of ∠ABC = the measure of the supplement of ∠DEF.	6. _____
7. The supplement of ∠ABC ≅ the supplement of _____.	7. If the measures of the supplements of two angles are equal, then supplements of the angles are congruent.

16. Probability The probability P of choosing an object at random from a group of objects is found by the fraction $P(\text{event}) = \dfrac{\text{Number of favorable outcomes}}{\text{Total number of outcomes}}$. Suppose the angle measures 30°, 60°, 120°, and 150° are written on slips of paper. You choose two slips of paper at random.

a. What is the probability that the measures you choose are complementary?

b. What is the probability that the measures you choose are supplementary?

17. Communicate Mathematical Ideas Write a proof of the Vertical Angles Theorem in paragraph proof form.

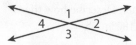

Given: ∠2 and ∠4 are vertical angles.

Prove: ∠2 ≅ ∠4

18. Analyze Relationships If one angle of a linear pair is acute, then the other angle must be obtuse. Explain why.

19. Critique Reasoning Your friend says that there is an angle whose measure is the same as the measure of the sum of its supplement and its complement. Is your friend correct? What is the measure of the angle? Explain your friend's reasoning.

20. Critical Thinking Two statements in a proof are:

$$m\angle A = m\angle B$$

$$m\angle B = m\angle C$$

What reason could you give for the statement $m\angle A = m\angle C$? Explain your reasoning.

Lesson Performance Task

The image shows the angles formed by a pair of scissors. When the scissors are closed, m∠1 = 0°. As the scissors are opened, the measures of all four angles change in relation to each other. Describe how the measures change as m∠1 increases from 0° to 180°.

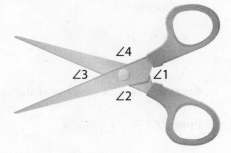

19.2 Transversals and Parallel Lines

Essential Question: How can you prove and use theorems about angles formed by transversals that intersect parallel lines?

🧭 Explore   Exploring Parallel Lines and Transversals

A **transversal** is a line that intersects two coplanar lines at two different points. In the figure, line *t* is a transversal. The table summarizes the names of angle pairs formed by a transversal.

Angle Pair	Example
Corresponding angles lie on the same side of the transversal and on the same sides of the intersected lines.	∠1 and ∠5
Same-side interior angles lie on the same side of the transversal and between the intersected lines.	∠3 and ∠6
Alternate interior angles are nonadjacent angles that lie on opposite sides of the transversal between the intersected lines.	∠3 and ∠5

Recall that parallel lines lie in the same plane and never intersect. In the figure, line ℓ is parallel to line *m*, written ℓ∥*m*. The arrows on the lines also indicate that they are parallel.

ℓ∥*m*

When parallel lines are cut by a transversal, the angle pairs formed are either congruent or supplementary. The following postulate is the starting point for proving theorems about parallel lines that are intersected by a transversal.

Same-Side Interior Angles Postulate

If two parallel lines are cut by a transversal, then the pairs of same-side interior angles are supplementary.

Follow the steps to illustrate the postulate and use it to find angle measures.

(A) Draw two parallel lines and a transversal, and number the angles formed from 1 to 8.

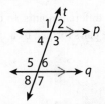

(B) Identify the pairs of same-side interior angles.

_____

(C) What does the postulate tell you about these same-side interior angle pairs?

_____

(D) If $m\angle 4 = 70°$, what is $m\angle 5$? Explain.

_____

_____

Reflect

1. Explain how you can find $m\angle 3$ in the diagram if $p \parallel q$ and $m\angle 6 = 61°$.

_____

_____

2. **What If?** If $m \parallel n$, how many pairs of same-side interior angles are shown in the figure? What are the pairs?

_____

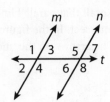

Explain 1 Proving that Alternate Interior Angles are Congruent

Other pairs of angles formed by parallel lines cut by a transversal are alternate interior angles.

Alternate Interior Angles Theorem

If two parallel lines are cut by a transversal, then the pairs of alternate interior angles have the same measure.

To prove something to be true, you use definitions, properties, postulates, and theorems that you already know.

Example 1 **Prove the Alternate Interior Angles Theorem.**

Given: $p \parallel q$

Prove: $m\angle 3 = m\angle 5$

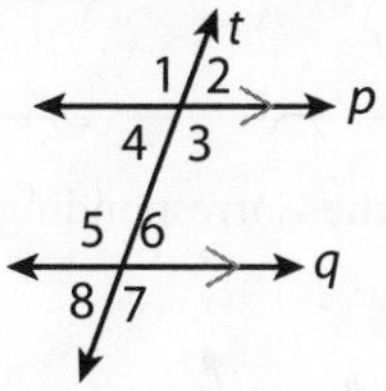

Complete the proof by writing the missing reasons. Choose from the following reasons. You may use a reason more than once.

- Same-Side Interior Angles Postulate
- Given
- Definition of supplementary angles
- Subtraction Property of Equality
- Substitution Property of Equality
- Linear Pair Theorem

Statements	Reasons
1. $p \parallel q$	
2. $\angle 3$ and $\angle 6$ are supplementary.	
3. $m\angle 3 + m\angle 6 = 180°$	
4. $\angle 5$ and $\angle 6$ are a linear pair.	
5. $\angle 5$ and $\angle 6$ are supplementary.	
6. $m\angle 5 + m\angle 6 = 180°$	
7. $m\angle 3 + m\angle 6 = m\angle 5 + m\angle 6$	
8. $m\angle 3 = m\angle 5$	

Reflect

3. In the figure, explain why $\angle 1$, $\angle 3$, $\angle 5$, and $\angle 7$ all have the same measure.

4. Suppose m∠4 = 57° in the figure shown. Describe two different ways to determine *m∠6*.

_____

_____

_____

Explain 2 ## Proving that Corresponding Angles are Congruent

Two parallel lines cut by a transversal also form angle pairs called corresponding angles.

Corresponding Angles Theorem
If two parallel lines are cut by a transversal, then the pairs of corresponding angles have the same measure.

Example 2 Complete a proof in paragraph form for the Corresponding Angles Theorem.

Given: $p\|q$

Prove: m∠4 = m∠8

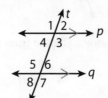

By the given statement, $p\|q$. ∠4 and ∠6 form a pair of _____.

So, using the Alternate Interior Angles Theorem, _____.

∠6 and ∠8 form a pair of vertical angles. So, using the Vertical Angles Theorem,

_____. Using the _____

in m∠4 = m∠6, substitute _____ for m∠6. The result is _____.

Reflect

5. Use the diagram in Example 2 to explain how you can prove the Corresponding Angles Theorem using the Same-Side Interior Angles Postulate and a linear pair of angles.

_____

_____

_____

6. Suppose m∠4 = 36°. Find m∠5. Explain.

_____

_____

_____

Explain 3   Using Parallel Lines to Find Angle Pair Relationships

You can apply the theorems and postulates about parallel lines cut by a transversal to solve problems.

Example 3   Find each value. Explain how to find the values using postulates, theorems, and algebraic reasoning.

(A) In the diagram, roads *a* and *b* are parallel. Explain how to find the measure of ∠VTU.

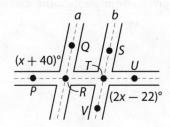

It is given that m∠PRQ = $(x + 40)°$ and m∠VTU = $(2x − 22)°$. m∠PRQ = m∠RTS by the Corresponding Angles Theorem and m∠RTS = m∠VTU by the Vertical Angles Theorem. So, m∠PRQ = m∠VTU, and $x + 40 = 2x − 22$. Solving for *x*, $x + 62 = 2x$, and $x = 62$. Substitute the value of *x* to find m∠VTU: m∠VTU = $(2(62) − 22)° = 102°$.

(B) In the diagram, roads *a* and *b* are parallel. Explain how to find the measure of m∠WUV.

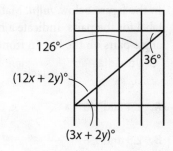

It is given that m∠PRS = $(9x)°$ and m∠WUV = $(22x + 25)°$.

m∠PRS = m∠RUW by the _____.

∠RUW and _____ are supplementary angles.

So, m∠RUW + m∠WUV = _____. Solving for *x*, $31x + 25 = 180$,

and _____. Substitute the value of *x* to find _____;

m∠WUV = $(22(5) + 25)°$ _____.

Your Turn

7. In the diagram of a gate, the horizontal bars are parallel and the vertical bars are parallel. Find *x* and *y*. Name the postulates and/or theorems that you used to find the values.

_____

_____

_____

8. How is the Same-Side Interior Angles Postulate different from the two theorems in the lesson (Alternate Interior Angles Theorem and Corresponding Angles Theorem)?

_____

_____

9. **Discussion** Look at the figure below. If you know that p and q are parallel, and are given one angle measure, can you find all the other angle measures? Explain.

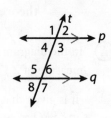

_____

_____

_____

_____

10. **Essential Question Check-In** Why is it important to establish the Same-Side Interior Angles Postulate before proving the other theorems?

_____

_____

_____

⭐ Evaluate: Homework and Practice

• Online Homework
• Hints and Help
• Extra Practice

1. In the figure below, $m \| n$. Match the angle pairs with the correct label for the pairs. Indicate a match by writing the letter for the angle pairs on the line in front of the corresponding labels.

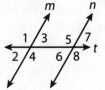

A. ∠4 and ∠6   _____ Corresponding Angles

B. ∠5 and ∠8   _____ Same-Side Interior Angles

C. ∠2 and ∠6   _____ Alternate Interior Angles

D. ∠4 and ∠5   _____ Vertical Angles

2. Complete the definition: A _____ is a line that intersects two coplanar lines at two different points.

Use the figure to find angle measures. In the figure, $p \parallel q$.

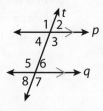

3. Suppose $m\angle 4 = 82°$. Find $m\angle 5$.

4. Suppose $m\angle 3 = 105°$. Find $m\angle 6$.

5. Suppose $m\angle 3 = 122°$. Find $m\angle 5$.

6. Suppose $m\angle 4 = 76°$. Find $m\angle 6$.

7. Suppose $m\angle 5 = 109°$. Find $m\angle 1$.

8. Suppose $m\angle 6 = 74°$. Find $m\angle 2$.

Use the figure to find angle measures. In the figure, $m \parallel n$ and $x \parallel y$.

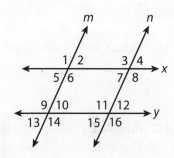

9. Suppose $m\angle 5 = 69°$. Find $m\angle 10$.

10. Suppose $m\angle 9 = 115°$. Find $m\angle 6$.

11. Suppose $m\angle 12 = 118°$. Find $m\angle 7$.

12. Suppose $m\angle 4 = 72°$. Find $m\angle 11$.

13. Suppose $m\angle 4 = 114°$. Find $m\angle 14$.

14. Suppose $m\angle 5 = 86°$. Find $m\angle 12$.

15. Ocean waves move in parallel lines toward the shore. The figure shows the path that a windsurfer takes across several waves. For this exercise, think of the windsurfer's wake as a line. If $m\angle 1 = (2x + 2y)°$ and $m\angle 2 = (2x + y)°$, find x and y. Explain your reasoning.

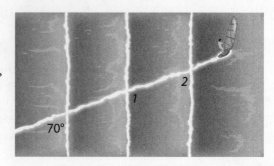

In the diagram of movie theater seats, the incline of the floor, f, is parallel to the seats, s.

16. If $m\angle 1 = 60°$, what is x?

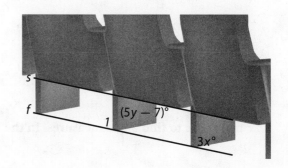

17. If $m\angle 1 = 68°$, what is y?

18. Complete a proof in paragraph form for the Alternate Interior Angles Theorem.

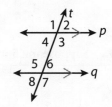

Given: $p \parallel q$

Prove: $m\angle 3 = m\angle 5$

It is given that $p \parallel q$, so using the Same-Side Interior Angles Postulate, $\angle 3$ and $\angle 6$

are _____. So, the sum of their measures is _____ and $m\angle 3 + m\angle 6 = 180°$.

You can see from the diagram that $\angle 5$ and $\angle 6$ form a line, so they are a _____,

which makes them _____. Then $m\angle 5 + m\angle 6 = 180°$. Using the

Substitution Property of Equality, you can substitute _____ in $m\angle 3 + m\angle 6 = 180°$ with

$m\angle 5 + m\angle 6$. This results in $m\angle 3 + m\angle 6 = m\angle 5 + m\angle 6$. Using the Subtraction Property

of Equality, you can subtract _____ from both sides. So, _____.

19. Write a proof in two-column form for the Corresponding Angles Theorem.

Given: $p \parallel q$

Prove: $m\angle 1 = m\angle 5$

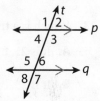

Statements	Reasons

20. Explain the Error Angelina wrote a proof in paragraph form to prove that the measures of corresponding angles are congruent. Identify her error, and describe how to fix the error.

Angelina's proof:

I am given that $p \parallel q$. $\angle 1$ and $\angle 4$ are supplementary angles because they form a linear pair, so $m\angle 1 + m\angle 4 = 180°$. $\angle 4$ and $\angle 8$ are also supplementary because of the Same-Side Interior Angles Postulate, so $m\angle 4 + m\angle 8 = 180°$. You can substitute $m\angle 4 + m\angle 8$ for $180°$ in the first equation above. The result is $m\angle 1 + m\angle 4 = m\angle 4 + m\angle 8$. After subtracting $m\angle 4$ from each side, I see that $\angle 1$ and $\angle 8$ are corresponding angles and $m\angle 1 = m\angle 8$.

21. Counterexample Ellen thinks that when two lines that are not parallel are cut by a transversal, the measures of the alternate interior angles are the same. Write a proof to show that she is correct or use a counterexample to show that she is incorrect.

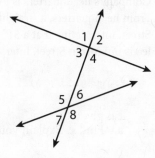

Analyzing Mathematical Relationships Use the diagram of a staircase railing for Exercises 22 and 23. $\overline{AG} \parallel \overline{CJ}$ and $\overline{AD} \parallel \overline{FJ}$. Choose the best answer.

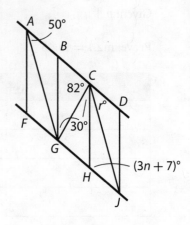

22. Which is a true statement about the measure of $\angle DCJ$?

A. It is 30°, by the Alternate Interior Angles Theorem.

B. It is 30°, by the Corresponding Angles Theorem.

C. It is 50°, by the Alternate Interior Angles Theorem.

D. It is 50°, by the Corresponding Angles Theorem.

23. Which is a true statement about the value of *n*?

A. It is 25, by the Alternate Interior Angles Theorem.

B. It is 25, by the Same-Side Interior Angles Postulate.

C. It is 35, by Alternate Interior Angles Theorem.

D. It is 35, by the Same-Side Interior Angles Postulate.

Lesson Performance Task

Washington Street is parallel to Lincoln Street. The Apex Company's headquarters is located between the streets. From headquarters, a straight road leads to Washington Street, intersecting it at a 51° angle. Another straight road leads to Lincoln Street, intersecting it at a 37° angle.

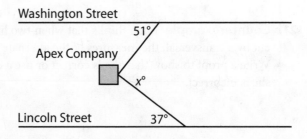

a. Find *x*. Explain your method.

b. Suppose that another straight road leads from the opposite side of headquarters to Washington Street, intersecting it at a $y°$ angle, and another straight road leads from headquarters to Lincoln Street, intersecting it at a $z°$ angle. Find the measure of the angle *w* formed by the two roads. Explain how you found *w*.

19.3 Proving Lines are Parallel

Essential Question: How can you prove that two lines are parallel?

⊘ Explore   Writing Converses of Parallel Line Theorems

You form the **converse** of and if-then statement "if *p*, then *q*" by swapping *p* and *q*.
The converses of the postulate and theorems you have learned about lines cut by a transversal
are true statements. In the Explore, you will write specific cases of each of these converses.

The diagram shows two lines cut by a transversal *t*. Use the diagram and the given statements
in Steps A–D. You will complete the statements based on your work in Steps A–D.

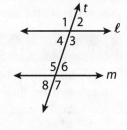

Statements	
lines ℓ and *m* are parallel	∠4 ≅ ∠ ☐
∠6 and ∠ ☐ are supplementary	∠ ☐ ≅ ∠7

(A) Use two of the given statements together to complete a statement about the diagram using
the Same-Side Interior Angles Postulate.

By the postulate: If _____, then ∠6 and ∠ ☐
are supplementary.

(B) Now write the converse of the Same-Side Interior Angles Postulate using the diagram and
your statement in Step A.

By its converse: If _____,

then _____.

(C) Repeat to illustrate the Alternate Interior Angles Theorem and its converse using the
diagram and the given statements.

By the theorem: If _____, then ∠4 ≅ ∠ ☐ .

By its converse: If _____,

then _____.

(D) Use the diagram and the given statements to illustrate the Corresponding Angles Theorem
and its converse.

By the theorem: If _____, then ∠ ☐ ≅ ∠7.

By its converse: _____.

Reflect

1. How do you form the converse of a statement?

_____

_____

2. What kind of angles are ∠4 and ∠6 in Step C? What does the converse you wrote in Step C mean?

_____

_____

🔧 Explain 1 Proving that Two Lines are Parallel

The converses from the Explore can be stated formally as a postulate and two theorems. (You will prove the converses of the theorems in the exercises.)

> **Converse of the Same-Side Interior Angles Postulate**
>
> If two lines are cut by a transversal so that a pair of same-side interior angles are supplementary, then the lines are parallel.

> **Converse of the Alternate Interior Angles Theorem**
>
> If two lines are cut by a transversal so that any pair of alternate interior angles are congruent, then the lines are parallel.

> **Converse of the Corresponding Angles Theorem**
>
> If two lines are cut by a transversal so that any pair of corresponding angles are congruent, then the lines are parallel.

You can use these converses to decide whether two lines are parallel.

Example 1 A mosaic designer is using quadrilateral-shaped colored tiles to make an ornamental design. Each tile is congruent to the one shown here.

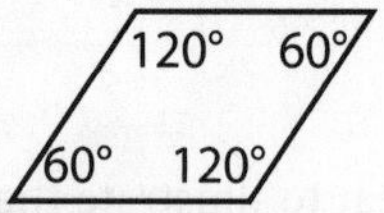

The designer uses the colored tiles to create the pattern shown here.

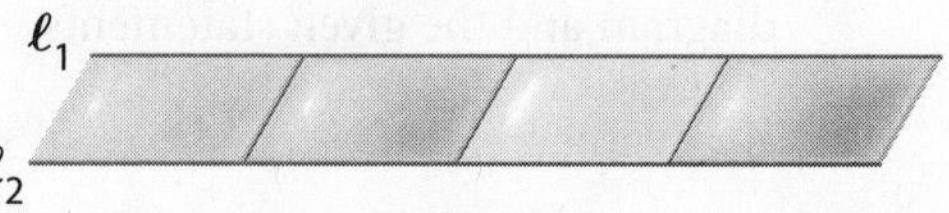

(A) Use the values of the marked angles to show that the two lines ℓ_1 and ℓ_2 are parallel.

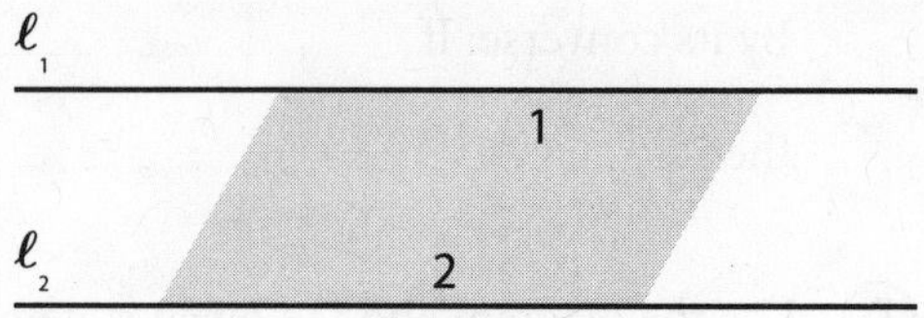

Measure of ∠1: 120° Measure of ∠2: 60°

Relationship between the two angles: They are supplementary.

Conclusion: $\ell_1 \parallel \ell_2$ by the Converse of the Same-Side Interior Angles Postulate.

(B) Now look at this situation. Use the values of the marked angles to show that the two lines are parallel.

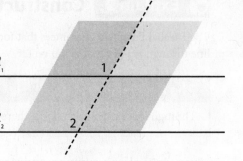

Measure of ∠1: _____   Measure of ∠2: _____

Relationship between the two

angles: _____

Conclusion:

_____

Reflect

3. **What If?** Suppose the designer had been working with this basic shape instead. Do you think the conclusions in Parts A and B would have been different? Why or why not?

_____

_____

Your Turn

Explain why the lines are parallel given the angles shown. Assume that all tile patterns use this basic shape.

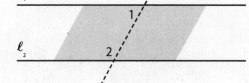

4.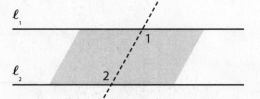

5.

⏱ Explain 2 Constructing Parallel Lines

The Parallel Postulate guarantees that for any line ℓ, you can always construct a parallel line through a point that is not on ℓ.

The Parallel Postulate
Through a point P not on line ℓ, there is exactly one line parallel to ℓ.

Example 2 Use a compass and straightedge to construct parallel lines.

Ⓐ Construct a line m through a point P not on a line ℓ so that m is parallel to ℓ.

Step 1 Draw a line ℓ and a point P not on ℓ.

P

ℓ

Step 2 Choose two points on ℓ and label them Q and R. Use a straightedge to draw $\overleftrightarrow{PQ}$.

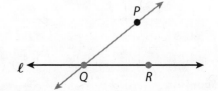

Step 3 Use a compass to copy $\angle PQR$ at point P, as shown, to construct line m.

line m ∥ line ℓ

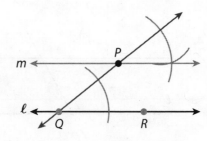

Ⓑ In the space provided, follow the steps to construct a line r through a point G not on a line s so that r is parallel to s.

Step 1 Draw a line s and a point G not on s.

Step 2 Choose two points on s and label them E and F. Use a straightedge to draw $\overleftrightarrow{GE}$.

Step 3 Use a compass to copy $\angle GEF$ at point G. Label the side of the angle as line r.
line r ∥ line s

© Houghton Mifflin Harcourt Publishing Company

6. **Discussion** Explain how you know that the construction in Part A or Part B produces a line passing through the given point that is parallel to the given line.

_____

_____

_____

Your Turn

7. Construct a line m through P parallel to line ℓ.

• P

![pencil icon] **Explain 3** ## Using Angle Pair Relationships to Verify Lines are Parallel

When two lines are cut by a transversal, you can use relationships of pairs of angles to decide if the lines are parallel.

Example 3 Use the given angle relationships to decide whether the lines are parallel. Explain your reasoning.

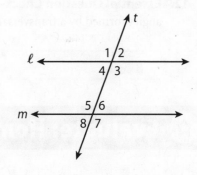

(A) $\angle 3 \cong \angle 5$

Step 1 Identify the relationship between the two angles.
$\angle 3$ and $\angle 5$ are congruent alternate interior angles.

Step 2 Are the lines parallel? Explain.
Yes, the lines are parallel by the Converse of the Alternate Interior Angles Theorem.

(B) $m\angle 4 = (x + 20)°$, $m\angle 8 = (2x + 5)°$, and $x = 15$.

Step 1 Identify the relationship between the two angles.

$m\angle 4 = (x + 20)°$ $m\angle 8 = (2x + 5)°$

$= \left(\boxed{} + 20\right)° = \boxed{}$ $= \left(2 \cdot \boxed{} + 5\right)° = \boxed{}$

So, _____ and _____ are _____ angles.

Step 2 Are the lines parallel? Explain.

_____

Identify the type of angle pair described in the given
condition. How do you know that lines ℓ and m are parallel?

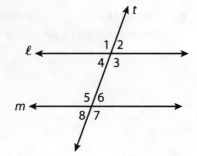

8. $m\angle 3 + m\angle 6 = 180°$

_____

_____

9. $\angle 2 \cong \angle 6$

_____

_____

💬 Elaborate

10. How are the converses in this lesson different from the postulate/theorems in the previous lesson?

_____

_____

11. What If? Suppose two lines are cut by a transversal such that alternate interior angles are both congruent
and supplementary. Describe the lines.

_____

_____

12. Essential Question Check-In Name two ways to test if a pair of lines is parallel, using the interior
angles formed by a transversal crossing the two lines.

_____

_____

☆ Evaluate: Homework and Practice

• Online Homework
• Hints and Help
• Extra Practice

The diagram shows two lines cut by a transversal t. Use the diagram
and the given statements in Exercises 1–3 on the facing page.

Statements
lines ℓ and m are parallel
$m\angle \boxed{} + m\angle 3 = 180°$
$\angle 1 \cong \angle \boxed{}$
$\angle \boxed{} \cong \angle 6$

1. Use two of the given statements together to complete statements about the diagram to illustrate the Corresponding Angles Theorem. Then write its converse.

   By the theorem: If _____, then ∠1 ≅ ∠☐ .

   By its converse: _____

2. Use two of the given statements together to complete statements about the diagram to illustrate the Same-Side Interior Angles Postulate. Then write its converse.

   By the postulate: If _____, then m∠☐ + m∠3 = 180°.

   By its converse: _____

3. Use two of the given statements together to complete statements about the diagram to illustrate the Alternate Interior Angles Theorem. Then write its converse.

   By the theorem: If _____, then ∠☐ ≅ ∠6.

   By its converse: _____

4. **Matching** Match the angle pair relationship on the left with the name of a postulate or theorem that you could use to prove that lines ℓ and m in the diagram are parallel.

   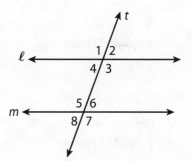

   A. ∠2 ≅ ∠6

   B. ∠3 ≅ ∠5

   C. ∠4 and ∠5 are supplementary.

   D. ∠4 ≅ ∠8

   E. m∠3 + m∠6 = 180°

   F. ∠4 ≅ ∠6

   _____ Converse of the Corresponding Angles Theorem

   _____ Converse of the Same-Side Interior Angles Postulate

   _____ Converse of the Alternate Interior Angles Theorem

Use the diagram for Exercises 5–8.

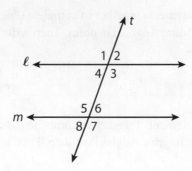

5. What must be true about ∠7 and ∠3 for the lines to be parallel? Name the postulate or theorem.

6. What must be true about ∠6 and ∠3 for the lines to be parallel? Name the postulate or theorem.

7. Suppose m∠4 = $(3x + 5)°$ and m∠5 = $(x + 95)°$, where $x = 20$. Are the lines parallel? Explain.

8. Suppose m∠3 = $(4x + 12)°$ and m∠7 = $(80 − x)°$, where $x = 15$. Are the lines parallel? Explain.

Use a converse to answer each question.

9. What value of x makes the horizontal parts of the letter Z parallel?

10. What value of x makes the vertical parts of the letter N parallel?

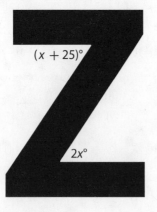

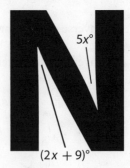

11. Engineering An overpass intersects two lanes of a highway. What must the value of x be to ensure the two lanes are parallel?

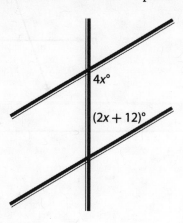

$4x°$

$(2x + 12)°$

12. A trellis consists of overlapping wooden slats. What must the value of x be in order for the two slats to be parallel?

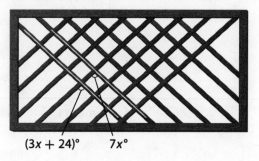

$(3x + 24)°$ $7x°$

13. Construct a line parallel to ℓ that passes through P.

ℓ

P

14. Communicate Mathematical Ideas In Exercise 13, how many parallel lines can you draw through P that are parallel to ℓ? Explain.

15. Justify Reasoning Write a two-column proof of the Converse of the Alternate Interior Angles Theorem.

Given: lines ℓ and m are cut by a transversal t; $\angle 1 \cong \angle 2$

Prove: $\ell \parallel m$

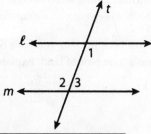

Statements	Reasons

16. Justify Reasoning Write a two-column proof of the Converse of the Corresponding Angles Theorem.

Given: lines ℓ and m are cut by a transversal t; $\angle 1 \cong \angle 2$

Prove: $\ell \parallel m$

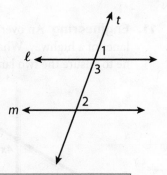

Statements	Reasons

Lesson Performance Task

In the last lesson, you saw a street map of a section of Harlem in New York City. The map is shown here. Draw a sketch of the rectangle bounded by West 111th Street and West 121st Street in one direction and Eighth Avenue and Lenox Avenue in the other. Include all the streets and avenues that run between sides of the rectangle. Show St. Nicholas Avenue as a diagonal of the rectangle.

Now imagine that you have been given the job of laying out these streets and avenues on a bare plot of land. Explain in detail how you would do it.

19.4 Perpendicular Lines

Essential Question: What are the key ideas about perpendicular bisectors of a segment?

(Ⓢ) Explore **Constructing Perpendicular Bisectors and Perpendicular Lines**

You can construct geometric figures without using measurement tools like a ruler or a protractor. By using geometric relationships and a compass and a straightedge, you can construct geometric figures with greater precision than figures drawn with standard measurement tools.

In Steps A–C, construct the perpendicular bisector of $\overline{AB}$.

Ⓐ Place the point of the compass at point *A*. Using a compass setting that is greater than half the length of $\overline{AB}$, draw an arc.

Ⓑ Without adjusting the compass, place the point of the compass at point *B* and draw an arc intersecting the first arc in two places. Label the points of intersection *C* and *D*.

Ⓒ Use a straightedge to draw $\overleftrightarrow{CD}$, which is the perpendicular bisector of $\overline{AB}$.

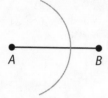

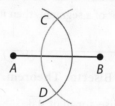

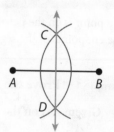

In Steps D–E, construct a line perpendicular to a line ℓ that passes through some point *P* that is not on ℓ.

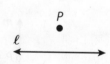

Ⓓ Place the point of the compass at *P*. Draw an arc that intersects line ℓ at two points, *A* and *B*.

Ⓔ Use the methods in Steps A–C to construct the perpendicular bisector of $\overline{AB}$.

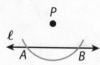

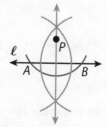

Because it is the perpendicular bisector of $\overline{AB}$, then the constructed line through *P* is perpendicular to line ℓ.

1. In Step A of the first construction, why do you open the compass to a setting that is greater than half the length of $\overline{AB}$?

_____

2. **What If?** Suppose Q is a point *on* line ℓ. Is the construction of a line perpendicular to ℓ through Q any different than constructing a perpendicular line through a point P *not* on the line, as in Steps D and E?

_____

_____

_____

🔑 Explain 1   Proving the Perpendicular Bisector Theorem Using Reflections

You can use reflections and their properties to prove a theorem about perpendicular bisectors. These theorems will be useful in proofs later on.

Perpendicular Bisector Theorem
If a point is on the perpendicular bisector of a segment, then it is equidistant from the endpoints of the segment.

Example 1   Prove the Perpendicular Bisector Theorem.

Given: P is on the perpendicular bisector m of $\overline{AB}$.

Prove: $PA = PB$

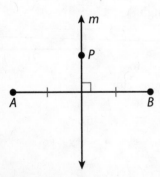

Consider the reflection across _____. Then the reflection

of point P across line m is also _____ because point P lies

on _____, which is the line of reflection.

Also, the reflection of _____ across line m is B by the definition

of _____.

Therefore, $PA = PB$ because _____ preserves distance.

3. **Discussion** What conclusion can you make about $\triangle KLJ$ in the diagram using the Perpendicular Bisector Theorem?

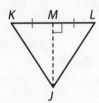

_____

_____

Use the diagram shown. $\overline{BD}$ is the perpendicular bisector of $\overline{AC}$.

4. Suppose $ED = 16$ cm and $DA = 20$ cm. Find DC.

5. Suppose $EC = 15$ cm and $BA = 25$ cm. Find BC.

🔑 Explain 2 Proving the Converse of the Perpendicular Bisector Theorem

The converse of the Perpendicular Bisector Theorem is also true. In order to prove the converse, you will use an *indirect proof* and the *Pythagorean Theorem*.

In an **indirect proof**, you assume that the statement you are trying to prove is false. Then you use logic to lead to a contradiction of given information, a definition, a postulate, or a previously proven theorem. You can then conclude that the assumption was false and the original statement is true.

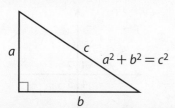

Recall that the Pythagorean Theorem states that for a right triangle with legs of length a and b and a hypotenuse of length c, $a^2 + b^2 = c^2$.

Converse of the Perpendicular Bisector Theorem

If a point is equidistant from the endpoints of a segment, then it lies on the perpendicular bisector of the segment.

Example 2 Prove the Converse of the Perpendicular Bisector Theorem

Given: $PA = PB$

Prove: P is on the perpendicular bisector m of $\overline{AB}$.

Step A: Assume what you are trying to prove is false.

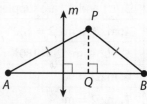

Assume that P is *not* on the perpendicular bisector m of _____.
Then, when you draw a perpendicular line from P to the line containing A and B,

it intersects $\overline{AB}$ at point Q, which is not the _____ of $\overline{AB}$.

Step B: Complete the following to show that this assumption leads to a contradiction.

$\overline{PQ}$ forms two right triangles, $\triangle AQP$ and _____.

So, $AQ^2 + QP^2 = PA^2$ and $BQ^2 + QP^2 = \boxed{}$ by the _____ Theorem.

Subtract these equations:

$AQ^2 + QP^2 = PA^2$

$\underline{BQ^2 + QP^2 = PB^2}$

$AQ^2 - BQ^2 = PA^2 - PB^2$

However, $PA^2 - PB^2 = 0$ because _____.

Therefore, $AQ^2 - BQ^2 = 0$. This means that $AQ^2 = BQ^2$ and $AQ = BQ$. This contradicts the fact that Q is not the midpoint of $\overline{AB}$. Thus, the initial assumption must be incorrect, and P must lie on the _____ of $\overline{AB}$.

6. In the proof, once you know $AQ^2 = BQ^2$, why can you conclude that $AQ = BQ$?

_____

Your Turn

7. $\overline{AD}$ is 10 inches long. $\overline{BD}$ is 6 inches long. Find the length of $\overline{AC}$.

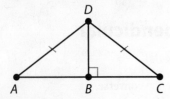

Explain 3   Proving Theorems about Right Angles

The symbol $\perp$ means that two figures are perpendicular. For example, $\ell \perp m$ or $\overleftrightarrow{XY} \perp \overline{AB}$.

Example 3   Prove each theorem about right angles.

(A) If two lines intersect to form one right angle, then they are perpendicular
and they intersect to form four right angles.

Given: $m\angle 1 = 90°$ **Prove:** $m\angle 2 = 90°$, $m\angle 3 = 90°$, $m\angle 4 = 90°$

Statement	Reason
1. $m\angle 1 = 90°$	**1.** Given
2. $\angle 1$ and $\angle 2$ are a linear pair.	**2.** Given
3. $\angle 1$ and $\angle 2$ are supplementary.	**3.** Linear Pair Theorem
4. $m\angle 1 + m\angle 2 = 180°$	**4.** Definition of supplementary angles
5. $90° + m\angle 2 = 180°$	**5.** Substitution Property of Equality
6. $m\angle 2 = 90°$	**6.** Subtraction Property of Equality
7. $m\angle 2 = m\angle 4$	**7.** Vertical Angles Theorem
8. $m\angle 4 = 90°$	**8.** Substitution Property of Equality
9. $m\angle 1 = m\angle 3$	**9.** Vertical Angles Theorem
10. $m\angle 3 = 90°$	**10.** Substitution Property of Equality

(B) If two intersecting lines form a linear pair of angles with equal measures, then the lines are
perpendicular.

Given: $m\angle 1 = m\angle 2$ **Prove:** $\ell \perp m$

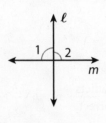

By the diagram, $\angle 1$ and $\angle 2$ form a linear pair so $\angle 1$ and $\angle 2$ are supplementary

by the _____. By the definition of supplementary angles,

$m\angle 1 + m\angle 2 =$ _____. It is also given that _____,

so $m\angle 1 + m\angle 1 = 180°$ by the _____. Adding

gives $2 \cdot m\angle 1 = 180°$, and $m\angle 1 = 90°$ by the Division Property of Equality. Therefore,

$\angle 1$ is a right angle and $\ell \perp m$ by the _____.

8. State the converse of the theorem in Part B. Is the converse true?

_____

_____

Your Turn

9. Given: $b \parallel d$, $c \parallel e$, $m\angle 1 = 50°$, and $m\angle 5 = 90°$. Use the diagram to find $m\angle 4$.

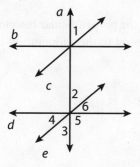

Elaborate

10. Discussion Explain how the converse of the Perpendicular Bisector Theorem justifies the compass-and-straightedge construction of the perpendicular bisector of a segment.

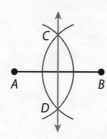

_____

_____

_____

11. Essential Question Check-In How can you construct perpendicular lines and prove theorems about perpendicular bisectors?

_____

_____

_____

_____

1. How can you construct a line perpendicular to line ℓ that passes through point *P* using paper folding?

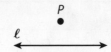

2. **Check for Reasonableness** How can you use a ruler and a protractor to check the construction in Elaborate Exercise 11?

3. Describe the point on the perpendicular bisector of a segment that is closest to the endpoints of the segment.

4. **Represent Real-World Problems** A field of soybeans is watered by a rotating irrigation system. The watering arm, $\overline{CD}$, rotates around its center point. To show the area of the crop of soybeans that will be watered, construct a circle with diameter *CD*.

Use the diagram to find the lengths. $\overline{BP}$ is the perpendicular bisector of $\overline{AC}$. $\overline{CQ}$ is the perpendicular bisector of $\overline{BD}$. $AB = BC = CD$.

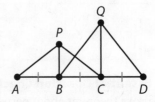

5. Suppose $AP = 5$ cm. What is the length of $\overline{PC}$?

6. Suppose $AP = 5$ cm and $BQ = 8$ cm. What is the length of $\overline{QD}$?

7. Suppose $AC = 12$ cm and $QD = 10$ cm. What is the length of $\overline{QC}$?

8. Suppose $PB = 3$ cm and $AD = 12$ cm . What is the length of $\overline{PC}$?

Given: $PA = PC$ and $BA = BC$. Use the diagram to find the lengths or angle measures described.

9. Suppose m∠2 = 38°. Find m∠1.

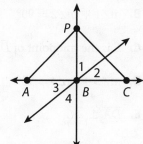

10. Suppose $PA = 10$ cm and $PB = 6$ cm. What is the length of $\overline{AC}$?

11. Find m∠3 + m∠4.

Given: $m \parallel n$, $x \parallel y$, and $y \perp m$. Use the diagram to find the angle measures.

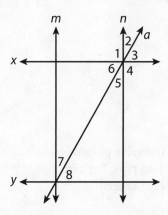

12. Suppose m∠7 = 30°. Find m∠3.

13. Suppose m∠1 = 90°. What is m∠2 + m∠3 + m∠5 + m∠6?

Use this diagram of trusses for a railroad bridge in Exercise 14.

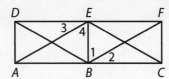

14. Suppose $\overline{BE}$ is the perpendicular bisector of $\overline{DF}$. Which of the following statements do you know are true? Select all that apply. Explain your reasoning.

   A. $BD = BF$

   B. $m\angle 1 + m\angle 2 = 90°$

   C. E is the midpoint of $\overline{DF}$.

   D. $m\angle 3 + m\angle 4 = 90°$

   E. $\overline{DA} \perp \overline{AC}$

15. **Algebra** Two lines intersect to form a linear pair with equal measures. One angle has the measure $2x°$ and the other angle has the measure $(20y - 10)°$. Find the values of x and y. Explain your reasoning.

16. **Algebra** Two lines intersect to form a linear pair of congruent angles. The measure of one angle is $(8x + 10)°$ and the measure of the other angle is $\left(\frac{15y}{2}\right)°$. Find the values of x and y. Explain your reasoning.

H.O.T.   Focus on Higher Order Thinking

17. **Communicate Mathematical Ideas** The valve pistons on a trumpet are all perpendicular to the lead pipe. Explain why the valve pistons must be parallel to each other.

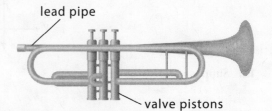

lead pipe

valve pistons

18. Justify Reasoning Prove the theorem: In a plane, if a transversal is perpendicular to one of two parallel lines, then it is perpendicular to the other.

Given: $\overline{RS} \perp \overline{CD}$ and $\overline{AB} \parallel \overline{CD}$ Prove: $\overline{RS} \perp \overline{AB}$

Statements	Reasons

19. Analyze Mathematical Relationships Complete the indirect proof to show that two supplementary angles cannot both be obtuse angles.

Given: $\angle 1$ and $\angle 2$ are supplementary.

Prove: $\angle 1$ and $\angle 2$ cannot both be obtuse.

Assume that two supplementary angles *can* both be obtuse angles. So, assume that

$\angle 1$ and $\angle 2$ _____. Then m$\angle 1 > 90°$ and m$\angle 2 > \boxed{}$

by _____. Adding the two inequalities,

m$\angle 1 +$ m$\angle 2 > \boxed{}$. However, by the definition of supplementary angles,

_____. So m$\angle 1 +$ m$\angle 2 > 180°$ contradicts the given information.

This means the assumption is _____, and therefore

_____.

Lesson Performance Task

A utility company wants to build a wind farm to provide electricity to the towns of Acton, Baxter, and Coleville. Because of concerns about noise from the turbines, the residents of all three towns do not want the wind farm built close to where they live. The company comes to an agreement with the residents to build the wind farm at a location that is equally distant from all three towns.

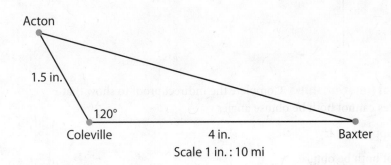

Scale 1 in. : 10 mi

a. Use the drawing to draw a diagram of the locations of the towns using a scale of 1 in. : 10 mi. Draw the 4-inch and 1.5-inch lines with a 120° angle between them. Write the actual distances between the towns on your diagram.

b. Estimate where you think the wind farm will be located.

c. Use what you have learned in this lesson to find the exact location of the wind farm. What is the approximate distance from the wind farm to each of the three towns?

19.5 Equations of Parallel and Perpendicular Lines

Essential Question: How can you find the equation of a line that is parallel or perpendicular to a given line?

⊘ Explore   Exploring Slopes of Lines

Recall that the *slope* of a straight line in a coordinate plane is the ratio of the *rise* to the *run*. In the figure, the slope of $\overline{AB}$ is $\frac{\text{rise}}{\text{run}} = \frac{4}{8} = \frac{1}{2}$.

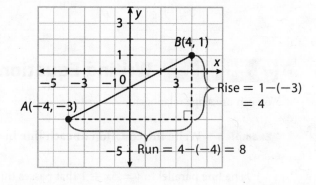

(A) Graph the equations $y = 2(x + 1)$ and $y = 2x - 3$.

(B) What do you notice about the graphs of the two lines? About the slopes of the lines?

_____

The graphs of $x + 3y = 22$ and $y = 3x - 14$ are shown.

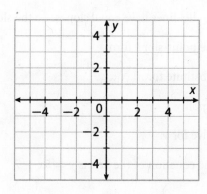

(C) Use a protractor. What is the measure of the angle formed by the intersection of the lines. What does that tell you about the lines?

_____

(D) What are the slopes of the two lines? How are they related?

_____

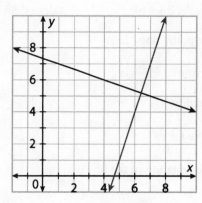

(E) Complete the statements: If two nonvertical lines

are _____, then they have equal slopes. If two nonvertical lines are perpendicular,

then the product of their slopes is _____.

Reflect

1. Your friend says that if two lines have opposite slopes, they are perpendicular. He uses the slopes 1 and −1 as examples. Do you agree with your friend? Explain.

_____

_____

_____

2. The frets on a guitar are all perpendicular to one of the strings. Explain why the frets must be parallel to each other.

_____

_____

_____

🔧 Explain 1 Writing Equations of Parallel Lines

You can use slope relationships to write an equation of a line parallel to a given line.

Example 1 Write the equation of each line in slope-intercept form.

(A) The line parallel to $y = 5x + 1$ that passes through $(-1, 2)$

Parallel lines have equal slopes. So the slope of the required line is 5.

Use point-slope form.	$y - y_1 = m(x - x_1)$
Substitute for m, x_1, y_1.	$y - 2 = 5\big(x - (-1)\big)$
Simplify.	$y - 2 = 5x + 5$
Solve for y.	$y = 5x + 7$

The equation of the line is $y = 5x + 7$.

(B) The line parallel to $y = -3x + 4$ that passes through $(9, -6)$

Parallel lines have $\boxed{}$ slopes. So the slope of the required line is $\boxed{}$.

Use point-slope form.	$y - y_1 = m(x - x_1)$
Substitute for m, x_1, y_1.	$y - \boxed{} = \boxed{}\left(x - \boxed{}\right)$
Simplify.	$y + 6 = \boxed{}\, x + \boxed{}$
Solve for y.	$y = \boxed{}\, x + \boxed{}$

The equation of the line is $\boxed{}$.

3. What is the equation of the line through a given point and parallel to the *x*-axis? Why?

_____

_____

Your Turn

Write the equation of each line in slope-intercept form.

4. The line parallel to $y = -x$ that passes through $(5, 2.5)$

5. The line parallel to $y = \frac{3}{2}x + 4$ that passes through $(-4, 0)$

🔑 Explain 2   Writing Equations of Perpendicular Lines

You can use slope relationships to write an equation of a line perpendicular to a given line.

Example 2   **Write the equation of each line in slope-intercept form.**

Ⓐ The line perpendicular to $y = 4x - 2$ that passes through $(3, -1)$

Perpendicular lines have slopes that are opposite reciprocals, which means that the product of the slopes will be -1. So the slope of the required line is $-\frac{1}{4}$.

$$y - y_1 = m(x - x_1) \qquad \text{Use point-slope form.}$$

$$y - (-1) = -\frac{1}{4}(x - 3) \qquad \text{Substitute for } m, x_1, y_1.$$

$$y + 1 = -\frac{1}{4}x + \frac{3}{4} \qquad \text{Simplify.}$$

$$y = -\frac{1}{4}x - \frac{1}{4} \qquad \text{Solve for } y.$$

The equation of the line is $y = -\frac{1}{4}x - \frac{1}{4}$.

Ⓑ The line perpendicular to $y = -\frac{2}{5}x + 12$ that passes through $(-6, -8)$

The product of the slopes of perpendicular lines is $\boxed{}$. So the slope of the required line is $\boxed{}$.

$$y - y_1 = m(x - x_1) \qquad \text{Use point-slope form.}$$

$$y - \boxed{} = \boxed{}\left(x - \boxed{}\right) \qquad \text{Substitute for } m, x_1, y_1.$$

$$y + 8 = \boxed{}\,x + \boxed{} \qquad \text{Simplify.}$$

$$y = \boxed{}\,x + \boxed{} \qquad \text{Solve for } y.$$

The equation of the line is y $\boxed{}$.

6. A carpenter's square forms a right angle. A carpenter places the square so that one side is parallel to an edge of a board, and then draws a line along the other side of the square. Then he slides the square to the right and draws a second line. Why must the two lines be parallel?

_____

_____

_____

_____

Your Turn

Write the equation of each line in slope-intercept form.

7. The line perpendicular to $y = \frac{3}{2}x + 2$ that passes through $(3, -1)$

8. The line perpendicular to $y = -4x$ that passes through $(0, 0)$

💬 Elaborate

9. Discussion Would it make sense to find the equation of a line parallel to a given line, and through a point on the given line? Explain.

_____

_____

10. Would it make sense to find the equation of a line perpendicular to a given line, and through a point on the given line? Explain.

_____

11. Essential Question Check-In How are the slopes of parallel lines and perpendicular lines related? Assume the lines are not vertical.

_____

• Online Homework
• Hints and Help
• Extra Practice

Use the graph for Exercises 1–4.

1. A line with a positive slope is parallel to one of the lines shown. What is its slope?

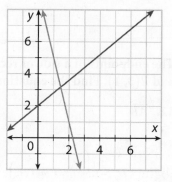

2. A line with a negative slope is perpendicular to one of the lines shown. What is its slope?

3. A line with a positive slope is perpendicular to one of the lines shown. What is its slope?

4. A line with a negative slope is parallel to one of the lines shown. What is its slope?

Find the equation of the line that is parallel to the given line and passes through the given point.

5. $y = -3x + 1;\ (9, 0)$

6. $y = 0.6x - 3;\ (-2, 2)$

7. $y = 5(x + 1);\ \left(\frac{1}{2}, -\frac{1}{2}\right)$

Find the equation of the line that is perpendicular to the given line and passes through the given point.

8. $y = 10x;\ (1, -3)$

9. $y = -\frac{1}{3}x - 5;\ (12, 0)$

10. $y = \frac{5x + 1}{3};\ (1, 1)$

11. Determine whether the lines are parallel. Use slope to explain your answer.

_____

_____

_____

_____

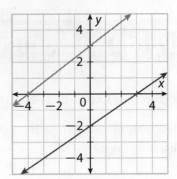

The endpoints of a side of rectangle $ABCD$ in the coordinate plane are at $A(1, 5)$ and $B(3, 1)$. Find the equation of the line that contains the given segment.

12. $\overline{AB}$

13. $\overline{BC}$

14. $\overline{AD}$

15. $\overline{CD}$ if point C is at $(7, 3)$

16. A well is to be dug at the location shown in the diagram. Use the diagram for parts (a–c).

    a. Find the equation that represents the road.

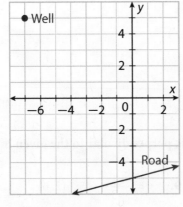

    b. A path is to be made from the road to the well. Describe how this should be done to minimize the length of the path.

    c. Find the equation of the line that contains the path.

© Houghton Mifflin Harcourt Publishing Company • Image Credits: ©Gary S. Chapman/Photographer's Choice RF/Getty Images

17. Use the graph for parts (a–c),

    a. Find the equation of the perpendicular bisector of the segment. Explain your method.

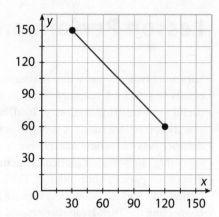

    b. Find the equation of the line that is parallel to the segment, but has the same y-intercept as the equation you found in part **a**.

    c. What is the relationship between the two lines you found in parts (a) and (b)?

18. Line m is perpendicular to $x - 3y = -1$ and passes through $(1, 5)$. What is the slope of line m?

  A. -3 **B.** $\dfrac{1}{3}$ **C.** 3 **D.** 5

19. Determine whether each pair of lines are parallel, perpendicular, or neither. Select the correct answer for each lettered part.

    a. $x - 2y = 12$; $y = x + 5$ ◯ Parallel   ◯ Perpendicular   ◯ Neither

    b. $\dfrac{1}{5}x + y = 8$; $y = -5x$ ◯ Parallel   ◯ Perpendicular   ◯ Neither

    c. $3x - 2y = 12$; $3y = -2x + 5$ ◯ Parallel   ◯ Perpendicular   ◯ Neither

    d. $y = 3x - 1$; $15x - 5y = 10$ ◯ Parallel   ◯ Perpendicular   ◯ Neither

    e. $7y = 4x + 1$; $14x + 8y = 10$ ◯ Parallel   ◯ Perpendicular   ◯ Neither

H.O.T. Focus on Higher Order Thinking

20. Communicate Mathematical Ideas Two lines in the coordinate plane have opposite slopes, are parallel, and the sum of their y-intercepts is 10. If one of the lines passes through $(5, 4)$, what are the equations of the lines?

21. Explain the Error Alan says that two lines in the coordinate plane are perpendicular if and only if the slopes of the lines are m and $\frac{1}{m}$. Identify and correct two errors in Alan's statement.

22. Analyze Relationships Two perpendicular lines have opposite y-intercepts. The equation of one of these lines is $y = mx + b$. Express the x-coordinate of the intersection point of the lines in terms of m and b.

Lesson Performance Task

Surveyors typically use a unit of measure called a rod, which equals $16\frac{1}{2}$ feet. (A rod may seem like an odd unit, but it's very useful for measuring sections of land, because an acre equals exactly 160 square rods.) A surveyor was called upon to find the distance between a new interpretive center at a park and the park entrance. The surveyor plotted the points shown on a coordinate grid of the park in units of 1 rod. The line between the Interpretive Center and Park Headquarters forms a right angle with the line connecting the Park Headquarters and Park Entrance.

What is the distance, in feet, between the Interpretive Center and the park entrance? Explain the process you used to find the answer.

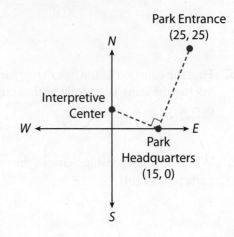

Essential Question: How can you use parallel and perpendicular lines to solve real-world problems?

Key Vocabulary

vertical angles
  (ángulos verticales)
complementary angles
  (ángulos complementarios)
supplementary angles
  (ángulos suplementarios)
transversal *(transversal)*
indirect proof *(prueba
  indirecta)*

KEY EXAMPLE   *(Lesson 19.1)*

Find m$\angle ABD$ given that m$\angle CBE = 40°$ and the angles are formed by the intersection of the lines $\overleftrightarrow{AC}$ and $\overleftrightarrow{DE}$ at point B.

When two lines intersect, they form two pairs of vertical angles at their intersection. Note that $\angle ABD$ and $\angle CBE$ are vertical angles and $\angle DBC$ and $\angle ABE$ are vertical angles.

$\angle ABD \cong \angle CBE$ Vertical Angles Theorem

m$\angle ABD =$ m$\angle CBE = 40°$ Definition of congruence of angles

KEY EXAMPLE   *(Lesson 19.2)*

Find m$\angle APD$ given that $\overleftrightarrow{AB}$ intersects the parallel lines $\overleftrightarrow{DE}$ and $\overleftrightarrow{FG}$ at the points P and Q, respectively, and m$\angle AQF = 70°$.

When a transversal intersects two parallel lines, it forms a series of angle pairs. Note that $\angle APD$ and $\angle AQF$ are a pair of corresponding angles.

m$\angle APD =$ m$\angle AQF$ Corresponding Angles Theorem

m$\angle APD = 70°$ Substitute the known angle measure.

KEY EXAMPLE   *(Lesson 19.3)*

Determine whether the lines $\overleftrightarrow{DE}$ and $\overleftrightarrow{FG}$ are parallel given that $\overleftrightarrow{AB}$ intersects them at the points P and Q, respectively, m$\angle APE = 60°$, and m$\angle BQF = 60°$.

Lines $\overleftrightarrow{AB}$ and $\overleftrightarrow{DE}$ intersect, so they create two pairs of vertical angles. The angle which is the opposite of $\angle APE$ is $\angle DPB$, so they are called vertical angles.

$\angle APE \cong \angle DPB$ Vertical Angles Theorem

m$\angle APE =$ m$\angle DPB$ Definition of congruence

m$\angle DPB = 60°$ Substitute the known angle measure.

m$\angle BQF =$ m$\angle DPB = 60°$

$\angle BQF \cong \angle DPB$ Definition of congruence

Thus, the lines $\overleftrightarrow{DE}$ and $\overleftrightarrow{FG}$ are parallel by the converse of the Corresponding Angles Theorem because their corresponding angles are congruent.

EXERCISES

Find the angle measure.

1. m∠ABD given that m∠CBD = 40° and the angles are formed by the intersection of the lines $\overleftrightarrow{AC}$ and $\overleftrightarrow{DE}$ at point B. *(Lesson 19.1)*

2. m∠BPE given that $\overleftrightarrow{AB}$ intersects the parallel lines $\overleftrightarrow{DE}$ and $\overleftrightarrow{FG}$ at the points P and Q, respectively, and m∠AQF = 45°. *(Lesson 19.2)*

Determine whether the lines are parallel. *(Lesson 19.3)*

3. $\overleftrightarrow{DE}$ and $\overleftrightarrow{FG}$, given that $\overleftrightarrow{AB}$ intersects them at the points P and Q, respectively, m∠APD = 60°, and m∠BQG = 120°.

Find the distance and angle formed from the perpendicular bisector. *(Lesson 19.4)*

4. Find the distance of point D from B given that D is the point at the perpendicular bisector of the line segment $\overline{AB}$, $\overleftrightarrow{DE}$ intersects $\overline{AB}$, and AD = 3. Find m∠ADE.

Find the equation of the line. *(Lesson 19.5)*

5. Perpendicular to $y = \frac{2}{3}x + 2$ and passes through the point $(3, 4)$.

MODULE PERFORMANCE TASK

Mystery Spot Geometry

Inside mystery spot buildings, some odd things can appear to occur. Water can appear to flow uphill, and people can look as if they are standing at impossible angles. That is because there is no view of the outside, so the room appears to be normal.

The illustration shows a mystery spot building constructed so that the floor is at a 25° angle with the ground.

View from outside

View from inside

- A table is placed in the room with its legs perpendicular to the floor and the tabletop perpendicular to the legs. Sketch or describe the relationship of the tabletop to the floor, walls, and ceiling of the room. What would happen if a ball were placed on the table?
- A chandelier hangs from the ceiling of the room. How does it appear to someone inside? How does it appear to someone standing outside of the room?

Use your own paper to complete the task. Use sketches, words, or geometry to explain how you reached your conclusions.

(Ready) to Go On?

19.1–19.5 Lines and Angles

- Online Homework
- Hints and Help
- Extra Practice

Find the measure of each angle. Assume lines $\overleftrightarrow{GB}$ and $\overleftrightarrow{FC}$ are parallel.
(Lessons 19.1, 19.2)

1. The measure of ∠*WOX* is 70°. Find m∠*YOZ*.

2. The measure of ∠*AXB* is 40°. Find m∠*FZE*.

3. The measure of ∠*XWO* is 70°. Find m∠*OYC*.

4. The measure of ∠*BXO* is 110°. Find m∠*OZF*.

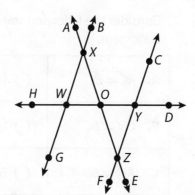

Use the diagram to find lengths. $\overline{PB}$ is the perpendicular bisector of $\overline{AC}$. $\overline{QC}$ is the perpendicular bisector of $\overline{BD}$. $AB = BC = CD$. *(Lesson 19.4)*

5. Given $BD = 24$ and $PC = 13$, find PB.

6. Given $QB = 23$ and $BC = 12$, find QD.

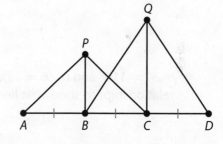

Find the equation of each line. *(Lessons 19.5)*

7. The line parallel to $y = -\frac{3}{7}x + 5$ and passing through the point $(-7, -1)$

8. The line perpendicular to $y = \frac{1}{5}x + 3$ and passing through the point $(2, 7)$

9. The perpendicular bisector to the line segment between $(-3, 8)$ and $(9, 4)$

ESSENTIAL QUESTION

10. Say you want to create a ladder. Which lines should be parallel or perpendicular to each other?

Assessment Readiness

1. Consider each equation. Is it the equation of a line that is parallel or perpendicular to $y = 3x + 2$?
Select Yes or No for A–C.

   A. $y = -\frac{1}{3}x - 8$ ○ Yes ○ No

   B. $y = 3x - 10$ ○ Yes ○ No

   C. $y = 2x + 4$ ○ Yes ○ No

2. Consider the following statements about $\triangle ABC$. Choose True or False for each statement.

A. $AC = BC$	○ True	○ False
B. $CD = BC$	○ True	○ False
C. $AD = BD$	○ True	○ False

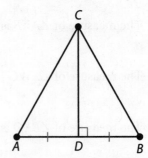

3. The measure of angle 3 is 130° and the measure of angle 4 is 50°. State two different relationships that can be used to prove m∠1 = 130°.

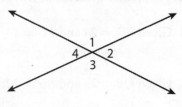

4. m∠1 = 110° and m∠6 = 70°. Use angle relationships to show that lines m and n are parallel.

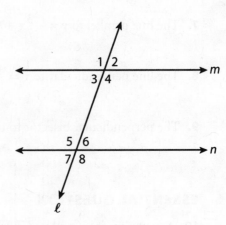

Triangle Congruence Criteria

Essential Question: How can you use triangle congruence to solve real-world problems?

REAL WORLD VIDEO
Take a look at some of the geometry involved in the engineering marvels of the Golden Gate Bridge in San Francisco.

MODULE PERFORMANCE TASK PREVIEW

Golden Gate Triangles

In this module, you will explore congruent triangles in the trusses of the lower deck of the Golden Gate Bridge. How can you use congruency to help figure out how far apart the two towers of the bridge are? Let's find out.

Are YOU Ready?

Angle Relationships

Example 1 Line segments $\overline{AB}$ and $\overline{DC}$ are parallel. Find the measure of angle $\angle CDE$.

$m\angle CDE = m\angle ABE$ Equate alternate interior angles.

$m\angle CDE = 33°$ Substitute.

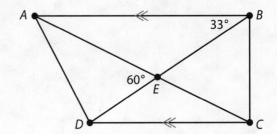

Find each angle in the image from the example.

1. $m\angle BEC$

2. $m\angle BAE$

Congruent Figures

Example 2 Find the length DF. Assume $\triangle DEF \cong \triangle GHJ$.

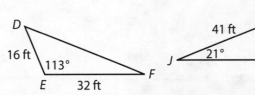

Since $\triangle DEF \cong \triangle GHJ$, the sides $\overline{DF}$ and $\overline{GJ}$ are congruent, or $\overline{DF} \cong \overline{GJ}$. Thus, $DF = GJ$. Since $GJ = 41$ ft, length DF must also be 41 ft.

Use the figure from the example to find the given side length or angle measure. Assume $\triangle DEF \cong \triangle GHJ$.

3. Find $m\angle GHJ$.

4. Find the length GH.

5. Find $m\angle FDE$.

6. Find the length HJ.

20.1 Exploring What Makes Triangles Congruent

Essential Question: How can you show that two triangles are congruent?

⊘ Explore   Transforming Triangles with Congruent Corresponding Parts

You can apply what you've learned about corresponding parts of congruent figures to write the following true statement about triangles.

If two triangles are congruent, then the corresponding parts of the triangles are congruent.

The statement is sometimes referred to as *CPCTC*. The converse of CPCTC can be stated as follows.

If all corresponding parts of two triangles are congruent, then the triangles are congruent.

Use a straightedge and tracing paper to explore this converse statement.

(A) Trace the angles and segments shown to draw △*ABC*. Repeat the process to draw △*DEF* on a separate piece of tracing paper. Label the triangles.

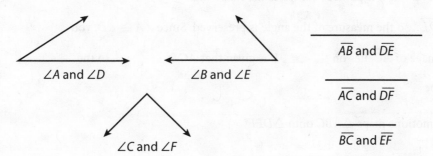

∠*A* and ∠*D*   ∠*B* and ∠*E* $\overline{AB}$ and $\overline{DE}$

∠*C* and ∠*F* $\overline{AC}$ and $\overline{DF}$

$\overline{BC}$ and $\overline{EF}$

(B) What must you do to show that the triangles are congruent?

_____

(C) Flip the piece of tracing paper with △*ABC* and arrange the two triangles on a desk as shown in the figure. Then move the tracing paper with △*ABC* so that point *A* maps to point *D*. Name the rigid motion that you used.

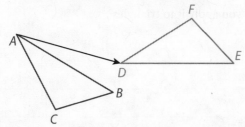

_____

Ⓓ Name a rigid motion you can use to map point B to point E. How can you be sure the image of B is E?

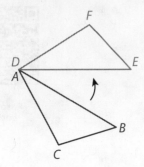

_____

_____

Ⓔ Name a rigid motion you can use to map point C to point F.

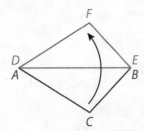

_____

Ⓕ To show that the image of point C is point F, complete the following.

∠A is reflected across $\overleftrightarrow{DE}$, so the measure of the angle is preserved. Since ∠A ≅ ∠D, you

can conclude that the image of $\overrightarrow{AC}$ lies on _____. It is given that $\overline{AC}$ ≅ _____, so the

image of point C must be _____.

Ⓖ What sequence of rigid motions maps △ABC onto △DEF?

_____

_____

Reflect

1. **Discussion** Is there another sequence of rigid motions that maps △ABC onto △DEF? Explain.

_____

_____

2. **Discussion** Is the converse of CPCTC always true when you apply it to triangles? Explain why or why not based on the results of the Explore.

_____

_____

_____

⚙ Explain 1 **Deciding If Triangles are Congruent by Comparing Corresponding Parts**

A **biconditional** is a statement that can be written in the form "*p* if and only if *q*." You can combine what you learned in the Explore with the fact that corresponding parts of congruent triangles are congruent to write the following true biconditional.

> *Two triangles are congruent if and only if corresponding pairs of sides and corresponding pairs of angles are congruent.*

To decide whether two triangles are congruent, you can compare the corresponding parts. If they are congruent, the triangles are congruent. If any of the corresponding parts are not congruent, then the triangles are not congruent.

Example 1 Determine whether the given triangles are congruent. Explain.

(A)

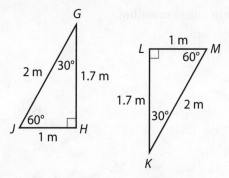

Compare corresponding sides to decide if they are congruent.

$GH = KL = 1.7$ m, $HJ = LM = 1$ m, and $GJ = KM = 2$ m.

So, $\overline{GH} \cong \overline{KL}$, $\overline{HJ} \cong \overline{LM}$, and $\overline{GJ} \cong \overline{KM}$.

Compare corresponding angles to decide if they are congruent.

$m\angle G = m\angle K = 30°$, $m\angle H = m\angle L = 90°$, and $m\angle J = m\angle M = 60°$.

So, $\angle G \cong \angle K$, $\angle H \cong \angle L$, and $\angle J \cong \angle M$.

$\triangle GHJ \cong \triangle KLM$ because all pairs of corresponding parts are congruent.

(B)

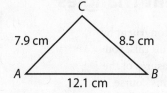 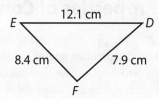

Compare corresponding sides to decide if they are congruent.

$AB = \boxed{} = \boxed{}$ cm, so $\overline{AB} \cong \boxed{}$. $AC = \boxed{} = \boxed{}$ cm, so $\overline{AC} \cong \boxed{}$.

However, $BC \neq \boxed{}$, so $\overline{BC}$ is not congruent to $\boxed{}$.

The triangles are not congruent because _____

_____

© Houghton Mifflin Harcourt Publishing Company

3. **Critique Reasoning** The **contrapositive** of a conditional statement "if *p*, then *q*" is the statement "If not *q*, then not *p*." The contrapositive of a true statement is always true. Janelle says that you can justify Part B using the contrapositive of CPCTC. Is this accurate? Explain your reasoning.

_____

_____

_____

_____

Your Turn

Determine whether the given triangles are congruent. Explain your reasoning.

4.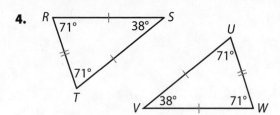

5.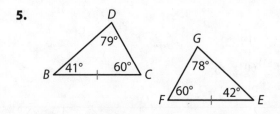

🔧 Explain 2   Applying Properties of Congruent Triangles

Triangles are part of many interesting designs. You can ensure that triangles are congruent by making corresponding sides congruent and corresponding angles congruent. To do this, you may have to use the Triangle Sum Theorem, which states that the sum of the measures of the angles of a triangle is 180°. You will explore this theorem in more detail later in this course.

Example 2 Find the value of the variable that results in congruent triangles.

  A

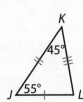 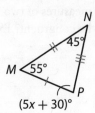

Step 1 Identify corresponding angles.

∠M corresponds to ∠J, because they have the same measure and they are formed by congruent corresponding sides. Similarly, ∠N corresponds to ∠K. So, ∠P corresponds to ∠L.

Step 2 Find m∠L.

Triangle Sum Theorem	$m\angle J + m\angle K + m\angle L = 180°$
Substitute.	$55° + 45° + m\angle L = 180°$
Simplify.	$100° + m\angle L = 180°$
Subtract 100° from each side.	$m\angle L = 80°$

Step 3 Write an equation to find the value of x.

Set corresponding measures equal.	$m\angle P = m\angle L$
Substitute.	$5x + 30 = 80$
Subtract 30 from each side.	$5x = 50$
Divide each side by 5.	$x = 10$

B

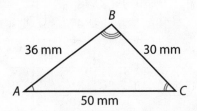 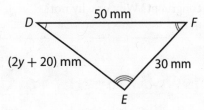

Step 1 Identify corresponding sides, beginning with side $\overline{DE}$.

$\angle A \cong \angle \boxed{}$, $\angle B \cong \angle \boxed{}$, and , $\angle C \cong \angle \boxed{}$, so $\overline{DE}$ corresponds to $\boxed{}$.

Step 2 Write an equation to find the value of y.

Set corresponding measures equal.	$DE = \boxed{}$ mm
Substitute.	$2y + 20 = \boxed{}$
Subtract 20 from each side.	$2y = \boxed{}$
Divide each side by 2.	$y = \boxed{}$

6. The measures of two angles of △QRS are 18° and 84°. The measures of two angles of △TUV are 18° and 76°. Is it possible for the triangles to be congruent? Explain.

_____

_____

_____

Your Turn

Find the value of the variable that results in congruent triangles.

7.

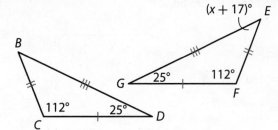

8.

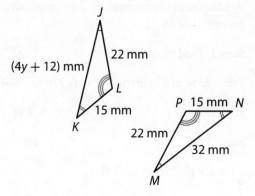

💬 Elaborate

9. All three angles of △ABC measure 60° and all three sides are 4 inches long. All three angles of △PQR measure 60° and all three sides are 4 inches long. Can you conclude that the triangles are congruent? Why or why not?

_____

_____

_____

10. Use the concept of rigid motion to explain why two triangles cannot be congruent if any pair of corresponding parts is not congruent.

_____

_____

_____

11. Essential Question Check-In △PQR and △STU have six pairs of congruent corresponding parts and △PQR can be mapped onto △STU by a translation followed by a rotation. How are the triangles related? Explain your reasoning.

_____

_____

☆ Evaluate: Homework and Practice

1. Describe a sequence of rigid motions that maps △MNP onto △MQR to show that △MNP ≅ △MQR.

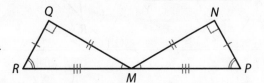

Determine whether the given triangles are congruent. Explain your reasoning.

2.

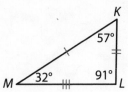

3.

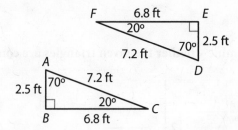

4.

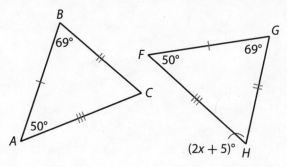

5.

Find the value of the variable that results in congruent triangles.

6.

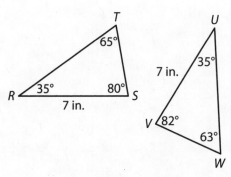

7.

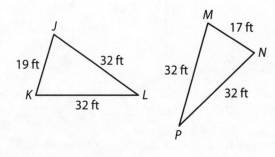

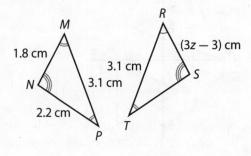

8.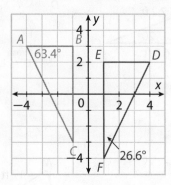

9.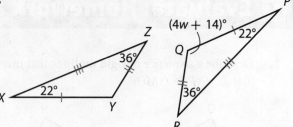

Determine whether the given triangles are congruent. Explain.

10.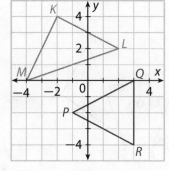

11.

12.

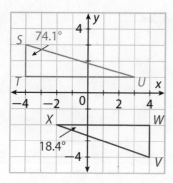

13.

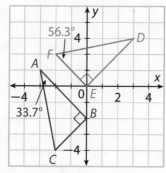

14. △*FGH* represents an artist's initial work on a design for a new postage stamp. What must be the values of *x*, *y*, and *z* in order for the artist's stamp to be congruent to △*ABC*?

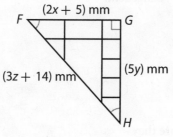
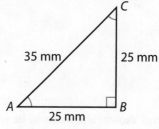

15. Multi-Step Find the values of the variables that result in congruent triangles.

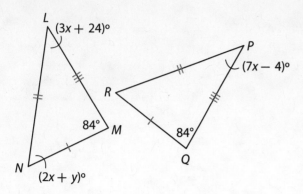

Determine whether each statement is always, sometimes, or never true. Explain your reasoning.

16. If △*ABC* has angles that measure 10° and 40°, and △*DEF* has angles that measure 40° and 120°, then △*ABC* ≅ △*DEF*.

17. Two triangles with different perimeters are congruent.

18. If △*JKL* ≅ △*MNP*, then m∠*L* = m∠*N*.

19. Two triangles that each contain a right angle are congruent.

20. Tenaya designed the earrings shown. She wants to be sure they are congruent. She knows that the three pairs of corresponding angles are congruent. What additional measurements should she make? Explain.

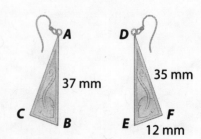

© Houghton Mifflin Harcourt Publishing Company

21. Determine whether △*JKL* and △*PQR* are congruent or not congruent based on the given information. Select the correct answer for each lettered part.

    a. m∠*J* = m∠*K* = m∠*L* = 60°, m∠*P* = m∠*Q* = m∠*R* = 60°,
      JK = *KL* = *JL* = 1.2 cm, *PQ* = *QR* = *PR* = 1.5 cm   ◯ Congruent ◯ Not congruent

    b. m∠*J* = 48°, m∠*K* = 93°, m∠*P* = 48°, m∠*R* = 39°,
      $\overline{JK} \cong \overline{PQ}$, $\overline{KL} \cong \overline{QR}$, $\overline{JL} \cong \overline{PR}$ ◯ Congruent ◯ Not congruent

    c. ∠*J* ≅ ∠*P*, ∠*K* ≅ ∠*Q*, ∠*L* ≅ ∠*R*,
      JK = *PQ* = 22 in., *KL* = *QR* = 34 in., *JL* = *PR* = 28 in. ◯ Congruent ◯ Not congruent

    d. m∠*J* = 51°, m∠*K* = 77°, m∠*P* = 51°, m∠*R* = 53°   ◯ Congruent ◯ Not congruent

    e. m∠*J* = 45°, m∠*K* = 80°, m∠*Q* = 80°, m∠*R* = 55°,
      JK = *PQ* = 1.5 mm, *KL* = *QR* = 1.3 mm, *JL* = *PR* = 1.8 mm ◯ Congruent ◯ Not congruent

H.O.T. **Focus on Higher Order Thinking**

22. Counterexamples Isaiah says it is not necessary to check all six pairs of congruent corresponding parts to decide whether two triangles are congruent. He says that it is enough to check that the corresponding angles are congruent. Sketch a counterexample. Explain your counterexample.

23. Critique Reasoning Kelly was asked to determine whether △*KLN* is congruent to △*MNL*. She noted that $\overline{KL} \cong \overline{MN}$, $\overline{KN} \cong \overline{ML}$, and that the three pairs of corresponding angles are congruent. She said that this is only five pairs of congruent corresponding parts, so it is not possible to conclude that △*KLN* is congruent to △*MNL*. Do you agree? Explain.

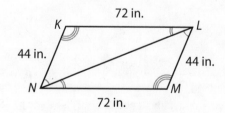

24. Analyze Relationships David uses software to draw two triangles. He finds that he can use a rotation and a reflection to map one triangle onto the other, and he finds that the image of vertex *D* is vertex *L*, the image of vertex *V* is vertex *C*, and the image of vertex *W* is vertex *Y*. In how many different ways can David write a congruence statement for the triangles? Explain.

Lesson Performance Task

For Kenny's science project, he is studying whether honeybees favor one color of eight-petal flowers over other colors. For his display, he is making eight-petal flowers from paper in various colors. For each flower, he'll cut out eight triangles like the one in the figure.

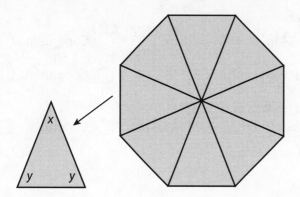

a. Find *x*, the measure in degrees of the top angle of each triangle. Explain how you found *x*.

b. Find *y*, the measure in degrees of the two base angles of each triangle. Explain how you found *y*.

c. Explain how Kenny could confirm that one of his triangles is congruent to the other seven.

© Houghton Mifflin Harcourt Publishing Company

20.2 ASA Triangle Congruence

Essential Question: What does the ASA Triangle Congruence Theorem tell you about triangles?

Resource Locker

⊘ Explore 1 Drawing Triangles Given Two Angles and a Side

You have seen that two triangles are congruent if they have six pairs of congruent corresponding parts. However, it is not always possible to check all three pairs of corresponding sides and all three pairs of corresponding angles. Fortunately, there are shortcuts for determining whether two triangles are congruent.

(A) Draw a segment that is 4 inches long. Label the endpoints *A* and *B*.

(B) Use a protractor to draw a 30° angle so that one side is $\overline{AB}$ and its vertex is point *A*.

(C) Use a protractor to draw a 40° angle so that one side is $\overline{AB}$ and its vertex is point *B*. Label the point where the sides of the angles intersect as point *C*.

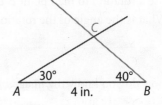

(D) Put your triangle and a classmate's triangle beside each other. Is there a sequence of rigid motions that maps one to the other? What does this tell you about the triangles?

_____

Reflect

1. In a polygon, the side that connects two consecutive angles is the *included side* of those two angles. Describe the triangle you drew using the term *included side*. Be as precise as possible.

_____

_____

2. **Discussion** Based on your results, how can you decide whether two triangles are congruent without checking that all six pairs of corresponding sides and corresponding angles are congruent?

_____

_____

⊙ Explore 2 Justifying ASA Triangle Congruence

Explain the results of Explore 1 using transformations.

Ⓐ Use tracing paper to make two copies of the triangle from Explore 1 as shown. Identify the corresponding parts you know to be congruent and mark these congruent parts on the figure.

$\angle A \cong$ _____

$\angle B \cong$ _____

$\overline{AB} \cong$ _____

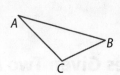 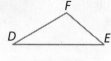

Ⓑ What can you do to show that these triangles are congruent?

_____

Ⓒ Translate △ABC so that point A maps to point D. What translation vector did you use?

_____

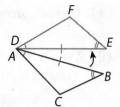

Ⓓ Use a rotation to map point B to point E. What is the center of the rotation? What is the angle of the rotation?

_____

Ⓔ How do you know the image of point B is point E?

_____

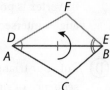

Ⓕ What rigid motion do you think will map point C to point F?

_____

Ⓖ To show that the image of point C is point F, notice that $\angle A$ is reflected across $\overleftrightarrow{DE}$, so the measure of the angle is preserved. Since $\angle A \cong \angle D$ you can conclude that the image of $\overline{AC}$ lies on _____. In particular, the image of point C must lie on _____. By similar reasoning, the image of $\overline{BC}$ lies on _____ and the image of point C must lie on _____. The only point that lies on both $\overline{DF}$ and $\overline{EF}$ is _____.

Ⓗ Describe the sequence of rigid motions used to map △ABC to △DEF.

_____

Reflect

3. **Discussion** Arturo said the argument in the activity works for any triangles with two pairs of congruent corresponding angles, and it is not necessary for the included sides to be congruent. Do you agree? Explain.

_____

_____

⚙ Explain 1 | Deciding Whether Triangles Are Congruent Using ASA Triangle Congruence

You can state your findings about triangle congruence as a theorem. This theorem can help you decide whether two triangles are congruent.

ASA Triangle Congruence Theorem

If two angles and the included side of one triangle are congruent to two angles and the included side of another triangle, then the triangles are congruent.

Example 1 Determine whether the triangles are congruent. Explain your reasoning.

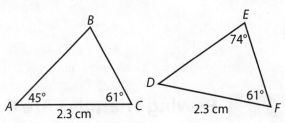

(A) **Step 1** Find m∠D.

$$m\angle D + m\angle E + m\angle F = 180°$$

$$m\angle D + 74° + 61° = 180°$$

$$m\angle D + 135° = 180°$$

$$m\angle D = 45°$$

Step 2 Compare the angle measures and side lengths.

m∠A = m∠D = 45°, AC = DF = 2.3 cm, and m∠C = m∠F = 61°

So, ∠A ≅ ∠D, $\overline{AC} \cong \overline{DF}$, and ∠C ≅ ∠F.

∠A and ∠C include side $\overline{AC}$, and ∠D and ∠F include side $\overline{DF}$.

So, △ABC ≅ △DEF by the ASA Triangle Congruence Theorem.

(B) **Step 1** Find m∠P.

$$m\angle M + m\angle N + m\angle P = 180°$$

$$\boxed{}° + \boxed{}° + m\angle P = 180°$$

$$\boxed{}° + m\angle P = 180°$$

$$m\angle P = \boxed{}°$$

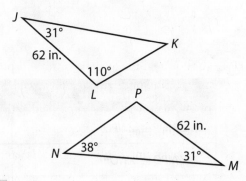

Step 2 Compare the angle measures and side lengths.

None of the angles in △MNP has a measure of $\boxed{}$.
Therefore, there | is/is not | a sequence of rigid motions that maps △MNP onto △JKL, and △MNP | is/is not | congruent to △JKL.

Reflect

4. In Part B, do you need to find m∠K? Why or why not?

_____

_____

© Houghton Mifflin Harcourt Publishing Company

Determine whether the triangles are congruent. Explain your reasoning.

5.

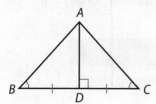

6.

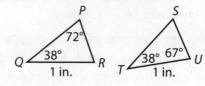

🔧 **Explain 2** **Proving Triangles Are Congruent Using ASA Triangle Congruence**

The ASA Triangle Congruence Theorem may be used as a reason in a proof.

Example 2   Write each proof.

Ⓐ   Given: $\angle MQP \cong \angle NPQ$, $\angle MPQ \cong \angle NQP$

Prove: $\triangle MQP \cong \triangle NPQ$

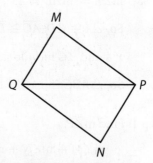

Statements	Reasons
1. $\angle MQP \cong \angle NPQ$	1. Given
2. $\angle MPQ \cong \angle NQP$	2. Given
3. $\overline{QP} \cong \overline{QP}$	3. Reflexive Property of Congruence
4. $\triangle MQP \cong \triangle NPQ$	4. ASA Triangle Congruence Theorem

Ⓑ Given: $\angle A \cong \angle C$, E is the midpoint of $\overline{AC}$.

Prove: $\triangle AEB \cong \triangle CED$

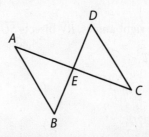

Statements	Reasons
1. $\angle A \cong \angle C$	1.
2. E is the midpoint of $\overline{AC}$.	2.
3. $\overline{AE} \cong \overline{CE}$	3.
4. $\angle AEB \cong \angle CED$	4.
5. $\triangle AEB \cong \triangle CED$	5.

Reflect

7. In Part B, suppose the length of $\overline{AB}$ is 8.2 centimeters. Can you determine the length of any other segments in the figure? Explain.

_____

Your Turn

Write each proof.

8. Given: $\angle JLM \cong \angle KML$, $\angle JML \cong \angle KLM$

Prove: $\triangle JML \cong \triangle KLM$

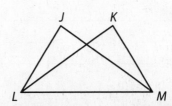

Statements	Reasons

9. Given: ∠S and ∠U are right angles, $\overline{RV}$ bisects $\overline{SU}$.

   Prove: △RST ≅ △VUT

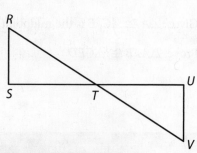

Statements	Reasons

💬 **Elaborate**

10. Discussion Suppose you and a classmate both draw triangles with a 30° angle, a 70° angle, and a side that is 3 inches long. How will they compare? Explain your reasoning.

_____

_____

_____

11. Discussion How can a diagram show you that corresponding parts of two triangles are congruent without providing specific angle measures or side lengths?

_____

_____

_____

12. Essential Question Check-In What must be true in order for you to use the ASA Triangle Congruence Theorem to prove that triangles are congruent?

_____

_____

1. Natasha draws a segment $\overline{PQ}$ that is 6 centimeters long. She uses a protractor to draw a 60° angle so that one side is $\overline{PQ}$ and its vertex is point P. Then she uses a protractor to draw an 35° angle so that one side is $\overline{PQ}$ and its vertex is point Q.

a. Draw a triangle following the instructions that Natasha used. Label the vertices and the known side and angle measures.

b. Will there be a sequence of rigid motions that will map your triangle onto Natasha's triangle? Explain.

2. Tomas drew two triangles, as shown, so that $\angle B \cong \angle E$, $\overline{BC} \cong \overline{EC}$, and $\angle ACB \cong \angle DCE$. Describe a sequence of one or more rigid motions Tomas can use to show that $\triangle ABC \cong \triangle DEC$.

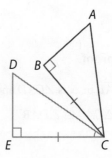

Determine whether the triangles are congruent. Explain your reasoning.

3.

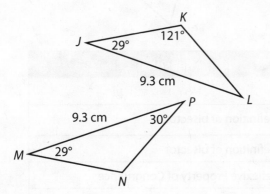

4.

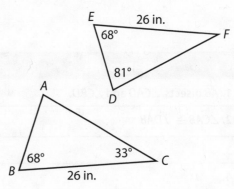

Determine whether the triangles are congruent. Explain your reasoning.

5.

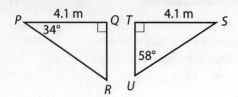

6.

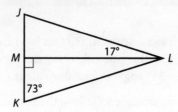

Write each proof.

7.   **Given:** $\overline{AB}$ bisects $\angle CAD$ and $\angle CBD$.

   Prove: $\triangle CAB \cong \triangle DAB$

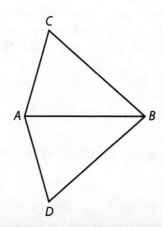

Statements	Reasons
1. $\overline{AB}$ bisects $\angle CAD$ and $\angle CBD$.	1.
2. $\angle CAB \cong \angle DAB$	2. Definition of bisector
3.	3. Definition of bisector
4.	4. Reflexive Property of Congruence
5. $\triangle CAB \cong \triangle DAB$	5.

8. Given: $\overline{AB}$ is parallel to $\overline{CD}$, $\angle ACB \cong \angle CAD$.

   Prove: $\triangle ABC \cong \triangle CDA$

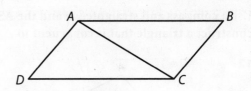

9. Given: $\angle H \cong \angle J$, G is the midpoint of $\overline{HJ}$, $\overline{FG}$ is perpendicular to $\overline{HJ}$.

   Prove: $\triangle FGH \cong \triangle FGJ$

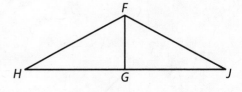

10. The figure shows quadrilateral $PQRS$. What additional information do you need in order to conclude that $\triangle SPR \cong \triangle QRP$ by the ASA Triangle Congruence Theorem? Explain.

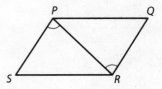

11. Communicate Mathematical Ideas In the figure, $\overline{WX}$ is parallel to $\overline{LM}$.

   a. Describe a sequence of two rigid motions that maps $\triangle LMN$ to $\triangle WXY$.

   b. How can you be sure that point N maps to point Y?

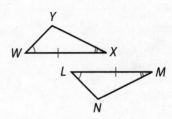

Use a compass and straightedge and the ASA Triangle Congruence Theorem to construct a triangle that is congruent to △ABC.

12.

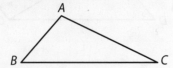

13.

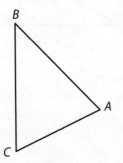

14. Multi-Step For what values of the variables is △QPR congruent to △SPR? In this case, what is m∠Q?

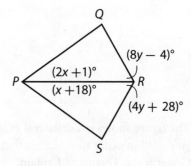

Write each proof.

15. Given: $\angle A \cong \angle E$, C is the midpoint of $\overline{AE}$.

Prove: $\overline{AB} \cong \overline{ED}$

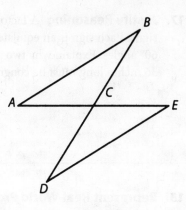

16. The figure shows $\triangle GHJ$ and $\triangle PQR$ on a coordinate plane.

a. Explain why the triangles are congruent using the ASA Triangle Congruence Theorem.

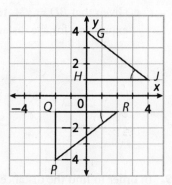

b. Explain why the triangles are congruent using rigid motions.

17. Justify Reasoning A factory makes triangular traffic signs. Each sign is an equilateral triangle with three 60° angles. Explain why two signs that each have a side 36 inches long must be congruent.

18. Represent Real-World Problems Rob is making the kite shown in the figure.

a. Can Rob conclude that △ABD ≅ △ACD? Why or why not?

b. Rob says that AB = AC and BD = CD. Do you agree? Explain.

c. Given that BD = x + 15 cm and AB = x cm, write an expression for the distance around the kite in centimeters.

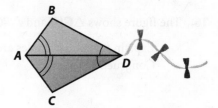

19. In order to find the distance across a canyon, Mariela sites a tree across the canyon (point A) and locates points on her side of the canyon as shown. Explain how she can use this information to find the distance AB across the canyon.

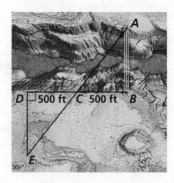

20. Determine whether each of the following provides enough information to prove that $\triangle SQP \cong \triangle SQR$. Select the correct answer for each lettered part.

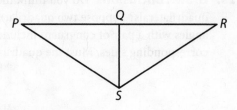

a. Q is the midpoint of $\overline{PR}$. ◯ Yes ◯ No

b. $\angle P \cong \angle R$ ◯ Yes ◯ No

c. $\angle SQP$ is a right angle, $\angle PSQ \cong \angle RSQ$ ◯ Yes ◯ No

d. $\angle SQP$ is a right angle, $m\angle P = 32°$, $m\angle RSQ = 58°$. ◯ Yes ◯ No

e. $\angle P \cong \angle R$, $\angle PSQ \cong \angle RSQ$ ◯ Yes ◯ No

H.O.T.   Focus on Higher Order Thinking

21. Counterexamples Jasmine said that the ASA Triangle Congruence Theorem works for quadrilaterals. That is, if two angles and the included side of one quadrilateral are congruent to two angles and the included side of another quadrilateral, then the quadrilaterals are congruent. Sketch and mark a figure of two quadrilaterals as a counterexample to show that Jasmine is incorrect.

22. Critique Reasoning $\triangle ABC$ and $\triangle DEF$ are both right angles and both triangles contain a 30° angle. Both triangles have a side that is 9.5 mm long. Yoshio claims that he can use the ASA Triangle Congruence Theorem to show that the triangles are congruent. Do you agree? Explain.

23. Draw Conclusions Do you think there is an ASAS Congruence Theorem for quadrilaterals? Suppose two quadrilaterals have a pair of congruent consecutive angles with a pair of congruent included sides and an additional pair of congruent corresponding sides. Must the quadrilaterals be congruent? Justify your response.

Lesson Performance Task

The flag of the Congo Republic consists of green and red right triangles separated by a yellow parallelogram. Construct an argument to prove that $\triangle BAF \cong \triangle EDC$.

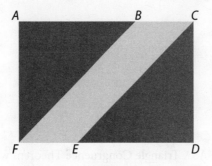

20.3 SAS Triangle Congruence

Essential Question: What does the SAS Triangle Congruence Theorem tell you about triangles?

Resource Locker

⊘ Explore 1 | Drawing Triangles Given Two Sides and an Angle

You know that when all corresponding parts of two triangles are congruent, then the triangles are congruent. Sometimes you can determine that triangles are congruent based on less information.

For this activity, cut two thin strips of paper, one 3 in. long and the other 2.5 in. long.

3 in.   2.5 in.

Ⓐ On a sheet of paper use a straightedge to draw a horizontal line. Arrange the 3 in. strip to form a 45° angle, as shown. Next, arrange the 2.5 in. strip to complete the triangle. How many different triangles can you form? Support your answer with a diagram.

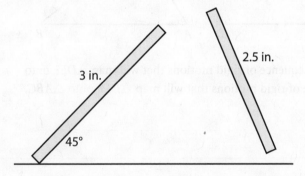

3 in.

2.5 in.

45°

Ⓑ Now arrange the two strips of paper to form a 45° angle so that the angle is *included* between the two consecutive sides, as shown. With this arrangement, can you construct more than one triangle? Why or why not?

_____

_____

_____

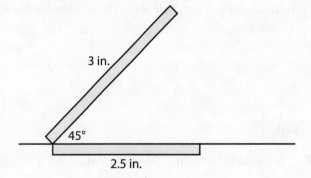

3 in.

45°

2.5 in.

© Houghton Mifflin Harcourt Publishing Company

1. **Discussion** If two triangles have two pairs of congruent corresponding sides and one pair of congruent corresponding angles, under what conditions can you conclude that the triangles must be congruent? Explain.

_____

_____

⊘ Explore 2 Justifying SAS Triangle Congruence

You can explain the results of Explore 1 using transformations.

Ⓐ Construct △*DEF* by copying ∠*A*, side $\overline{AB}$, and side $\overline{AC}$. Let point *D* correspond to point *A*, point *E* correspond to point *B*, and point *F* correspond to point *C*, and place point *E* on the segment shown.

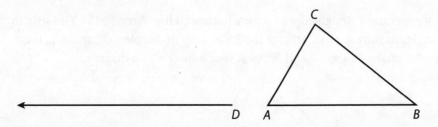

Ⓑ The diagram illustrates one step in a sequence of rigid motions that will map △*DEF* onto △*ABC*. Describe a complete sequence of rigid motions that will map △*DEF* onto △*ABC*.

_____

_____

_____

_____

_____

Ⓒ What can you conclude about the relationship between △*ABC* and △*DEF*? Explain your reasoning.

_____

_____

2. Is it possible to map △*DEF* onto △*ABC* using a single rigid motion? If so, describe the rigid motion.

_____

_____

⊘ Explain 1 Deciding Whether Triangles are Congruent Using SAS Triangle Congruence

What you explored in the previous two activities can be summarized in a theorem. You can use this theorem and the definition of congruence in terms of rigid motions to determine whether two triangles are congruent.

SAS Triangle Congruence Theorem

If two sides and the included angle of one triangle are congruent to two sides and the included angle of another triangle, then the triangles are congruent.

Example 1 Determine whether the triangles are congruent. Explain your reasoning.

Ⓐ Look for congruent corresponding parts.

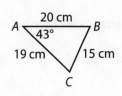
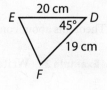

- Sides $\overline{DE}$ and $\overline{DF}$ do not correspond to side $\overline{BC}$, because they are not 15 cm long.
- $\overline{DE}$ corresponds to $\overline{AB}$, because $DE = AB = 20$ cm.
- $\overline{DF}$ corresponds to $\overline{AC}$, because $DF = AC = 19$ cm.
- $\angle A$ and $\angle D$ must be corresponding angles, but they don't have the same measure.

The triangles are not congruent, because there is no sequence of rigid motions that maps $\triangle ABC$ onto $\triangle DEF$.

Ⓑ

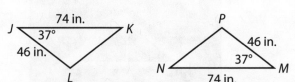

Look for congruent corresponding parts.

- $\overline{JL}$ corresponds to _____, because $JL =$ _____ = _____ in.

- _____ corresponds to MN, because _____ = $MN = 74$ in.

- _____ corresponds to _____, because _____ = _____ = _____.

Two sides and the included angle of $\triangle JKL$ are congruent to two sides and the included angle

and of _____. $\triangle JKL \cong$ _____ by the _____.

3. Determine whether the triangles are congruent. Explain your reasoning.

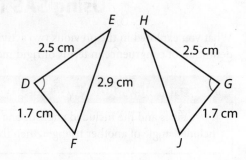

⏣ Explain 2 Proving Triangles Are Congruent Using SAS Triangle Congruence

Theorems about congruent triangles can be used to show that triangles in real-world objects are congruent.

Example 2 Write each proof.

Ⓐ Write a proof to show that the two halves of a triangular window are congruent if the vertical post is the perpendicular bisector of the base.

Given: $\overline{BD}$ is the perpendicular bisector of $\overline{AC}$.
Prove: $\triangle BDA \cong \triangle BDC$

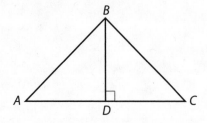

It is given that $\overline{BD}$ is the perpendicular bisector of $\overline{AC}$. By the definition of a perpendicular bisector, $AD = CD$, which means $\overline{AD} \cong \overline{CD}$, and $\overline{BD} \perp \overline{AC}$, which means $\angle BDA$ and $\angle BDC$ are congruent right angles. In addition, $\overline{BD} \cong \overline{BD}$ by the reflexive property of congruence. So two sides and the included angle of $\triangle BDA$ are congruent to two sides and the included angle of $\triangle BDC$. The triangles are congruent by the SAS Triangle Congruence Theorem.

Ⓑ Given: $\overline{CD}$ bisects $\overline{AE}$ and $\overline{AE}$ bisects $\overline{CD}$
Prove: $\triangle ABC \cong \triangle EBD$

It is given that $\overline{CD}$ bisects $\overline{AE}$ and $\overline{AE}$ bisects $\overline{CD}$. So by the definition

of a bisector, $AB = EB$ and _____, which makes $\overline{AB} \cong \overline{EB}$

and _____. $\angle ABC \cong$ _____ because they are

_____. So two sides and the _____ angle of $\triangle ABC$

are congruent to two sides and the _____ angle of $\triangle EBD$. The

triangles are congruent by the _____.

4. Given: $\overline{AB} \cong \overline{AD}$ and $\angle 1 \cong \angle 2$

   Prove: $\triangle BAC \cong \triangle DAC$

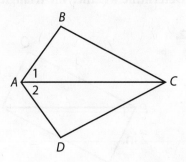

💬 Elaborate

5. Explain why the corresponding angles must be *included* angles in order to use the SAS Triangle Congruence Theorem.

   _____

   _____

6. Jeffrey draws $\triangle PQR$ and $\triangle TUV$. He uses a translation to map point P to point T and point R to point V as shown. What should be his next step in showing the triangles are congruent? Why?

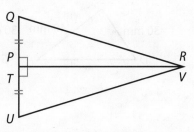

   _____

   _____

7. **Essential Question Check-In** If two triangles share a common side, what else must be true for the SAS Triangle Congruence Theorem to apply?

   _____

   _____

⭐ Evaluate: Homework and Practice

- Online Homework
- Hints and Help
- Extra Practice

1. Sarah performs rigid motions mapping point A to point D and point B to point E, as shown. Does she have enough information to confirm that the triangles are congruent? Explain your reasoning.

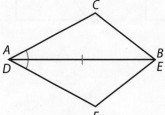

Determine whether the triangles are congruent. Explain your reasoning.

2.

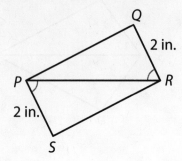

3.

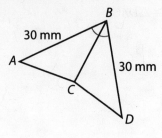

4.

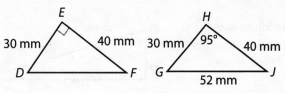

5.

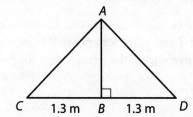

Find the value of the variable that results in congruent triangles. Explain.

6.

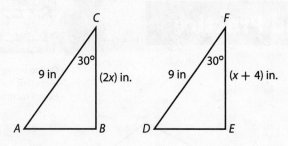

7.

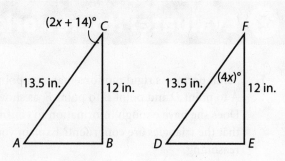

8. Given that polygon *ABCDEF* is a regular hexagon, prove that $\overline{AC} \cong \overline{AE}$.

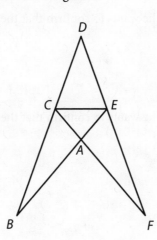

Statements	Reasons

9. A product designer is designing an easel with extra braces as shown in the diagram. Prove that if $\overline{BD} \cong \overline{FD}$ and $\overline{CD} \cong \overline{ED}$, then the braces $\overline{BE}$ and $\overline{FC}$ are also congruent.

10. An artist is framing a large picture and wants to put metal poles across the back to strengthen the frame as shown in the diagram. If the metal poles are both the same length and they bisect each other, prove that $\overline{AB} \cong \overline{CD}$ and $\overline{AD} \cong \overline{CB}$.

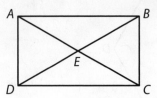

11. The figure shows a side panel of a skateboard ramp. Kalim wants to confirm that the right triangles in the panel are congruent.

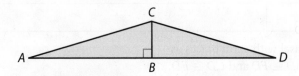

a. What measurements should Kalim take if he wants to confirm that the triangles are congruent by SAS? Explain.

b. What measurements should Kalim take if he wants to confirm that the triangles are congruent by ASA? Explain.

12. Which of the following are reasons that justify why the triangles are congruent? Select all that apply.

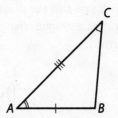 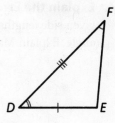

A. SSA Triangle Congruence Theorem

B. SAS Triangle Congruence Theorem

C. ASA Triangle Congruence Theorem

D. Converse of CPCTC

E. CPCTC

13. Multi-Step Refer to the following diagram to answer each question.

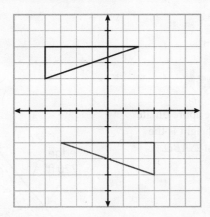

a. Use a triangle congruence theorem to explain why these triangles are congruent.

b. Describe a sequence of rigid motions to map the top triangle onto the bottom triangle to confirm that they are congruent.

14. Explain the Error Mark says that the diagram confirms that a given angle and two given side lengths determine a unique triangle even if the angle is not an included angle. Explain Marc's error.

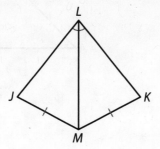

15. Justify Reasoning The opposite sides of a rectangle are congruent. Can you conclude that a diagonal of a rectangle divides the rectangle into two congruent triangles? Justify your response.

Lesson Performance Task

The diagram of the Great Pyramid at Giza gives the approximate lengths of edge $\overline{AB}$ and slant height $\overline{AC}$. The slant height is the perpendicular bisector of $\overline{BD}$. Find the perimeter of $\triangle ABD$. Explain how you found the answer.

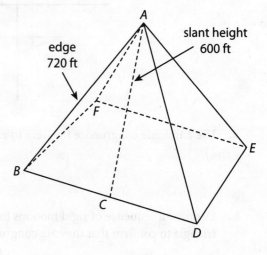

edge 720 ft

slant height 600 ft

20.4 SSS Triangle Congruence

Essential Question: What does the SSS Triangle Congruence Theorem tell you about triangles?

⊘ Explore Constructing Triangles Given Three Side Lengths

Two triangles are congruent if and only if a rigid motion transformation maps one triangle onto the other triangle. Many theorems can also be used to identify congruent triangles.

Follow these steps to construct a triangle with sides of length 5 in., 4 in., and 3 in. Use a ruler, compass, and either tracing paper or a transparency.

Ⓐ Use a ruler to draw a line segment of length 5 inches. Label the endpoints *A* and *B*.

Ⓑ Open a compass to 4 inches. Place the point of the compass on *A*, and draw an arc as shown.

Ⓒ Now open the compass to 3 inches. Place the point of the compass on *B*, and draw a second arc.

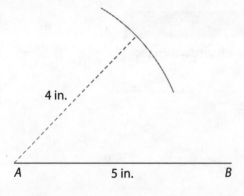

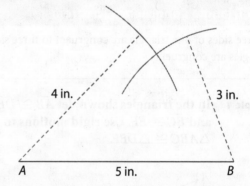

Ⓓ Next, find the intersection of the two arcs. Label the intersection C. Draw $\overline{AC}$ and $\overline{BC}$. Label the side lengths on the figure.

Ⓔ Repeat steps A through D to draw △*DEF* on a separate piece of tracing paper. The triangle should have sides with the same lengths as △*CAB*. Start with a segment that is 4 in. long. Label the endpoints *D* and *E* as shown.

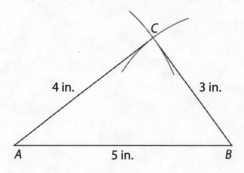

(F) Compare △*CAB* and △*DEF*. Are they congruent? How do you know?

_____

_____

Reflect

1. **Discussion** When you construct △*CAB*, how do you know that the intersection of the two arcs is a distance of 4 inches from *A* and 3 inches from *B*?

_____

_____

2. Compare your triangles to those made by other students. Are they all congruent? Explain.

_____

_____

⚲ Explain 1 Justifying SSS Triangle Congruence

You can use rigid motions and the converse of the Perpendicular Bisector Theorem to justify this theorem.

SSS Triangle Congruence Theorem

If three sides of one triangle are congruent to three sides of another triangle, then the triangles are congruent.

Example 1 In the triangles shown, let $\overline{AB} \cong \overline{DE}$, $\overline{AC} \cong \overline{DF}$, and $\overline{BC} \cong \overline{EF}$. Use rigid motions to show that △*ABC* ≅ △*DEF*.

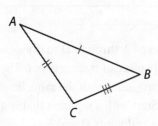
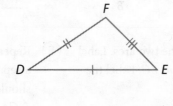

© Houghton Mifflin Harcourt Publishing Company

(A) Transform △*ABC* by a translation along $\overrightarrow{AD}$ followed by a rotation about point *D*, so that $\overline{AB}$ and $\overline{DE}$ coincide. The segments coincide because they are the same length.

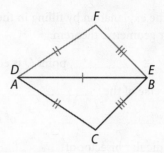

Does a reflection across $\overline{AB}$ map point *C* to point *F*? To show this, notice that $DC = DF$, which means that point *D* is equidistant from point *C* and point *F*.

Therefore, point *D* lies on the perpendicular bisector of $\overline{CF}$ by the converse of the perpendicular bisector theorem. Because $EC = EF$, point *E* also lies on the perpendicular bisector of $\overline{CF}$.

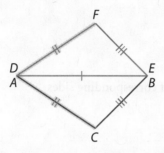

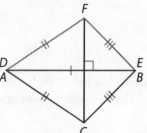

Since point *D* and point *E* both lie on the perpendicular bisector of $\overline{CF}$ and there is a unique line through any two points, $\overleftrightarrow{DE}$ is the perpendicular bisector of $\overline{CF}$. By the definition of reflection, the image of point *C* must be point *F*. Therefore, △*ABC* is mapped onto △*DEF* by a translation, followed by a rotation, followed by a reflection, and the two triangles are congruent.

(B) Show that △*ABC* ≅ △*PQR*.

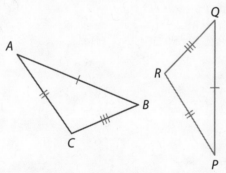

Triangle *ABC* is transformed by a sequence of rigid motions to form the figure shown below. Identify the sequence of rigid motions. (You will complete the proof on the following page.)

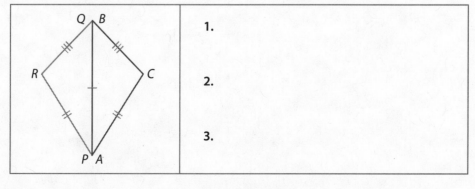

1.

2.

3.

Complete the explanation by filling in the blanks with the name of a point, line segment, or geometric theorem.

Because $\overline{QR} \cong$ _____, point Q is equidistant from _____ and _____. Therefore, by the converse of the _____ Theorem, point Q lies on the

_____ of $\overline{RC}$. Similarly, $\overline{PR} \cong$ _____. So point _____ lies on

the perpendicular bisector of _____. Because two points determine a line, the line $\overleftrightarrow{PQ}$ is

the _____.

By the definition of reflection, the image of point C must be point _____. Therefore,

$\triangle ABC \cong \triangle PQR$ because $\triangle ABC$ is mapped to _____ by a translation, a rotation,

and a _____.

Reflect

3. Can you conclude that two triangles are congruent if two pairs of corresponding sides are congruent? Explain your reasoning and include an example.

_____

_____

_____

Your Turn

4. Use rigid motions and the converse of the perpendicular bisector theorem to explain why $\triangle ABC \cong \triangle ADC$.

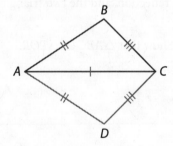

Proving Triangles Are Congruent Using SSS Triangle Congruence

You can apply the SSS Triangle Congruence Theorem to confirm that triangles are congruent. Remember, if any one pair of corresponding parts of two triangles is not congruent, then the triangles are not congruent.

Example 2 Prove that the triangles are congruent or explain why they are not congruent.

(A) $AB = DE = 1.7$ m, so $\overline{AB} \cong \overline{DE}$.

BC = EF = 2.4 m, so $\overline{BC} \cong \overline{EF}$.

AC = DF = 2.3 m, so $\overline{AC} \cong \overline{DF}$.

The three sides of $\triangle ABC$ are congruent to the three sides of $\triangle DEF$.

$\triangle ABC \cong \triangle DEF$ by the SSS Triangle Congruence Theorem.

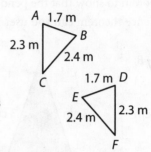

(B) DE = _____ = 20 cm, so _____.

DH = _____ = 12 cm, so _____.

EH = _____ = 24 cm, so _____.

The three sides of $\triangle DEH$ are congruent to

the three sides of _____, so the two triangles are

congruent by _____.

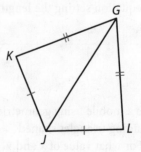

Your Turn

Prove that the triangles are congruent or explain why they are not congruent.

5.

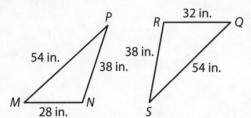

6.

_____

_____

_____

🛠 Explain 3 Applying Triangle Congruence

You can use the SSS Triangle Congruence Theorem and other triangle congruence theorems to solve many real-world problems that involve congruent triangles.

Example 3 Find the value of x for which you can show the triangles are congruent.

Ⓐ Lexi bought matching triangular pendants for herself and her mom in the shapes shown. For what value of x can you use a triangle congruence theorem to show that the pendants are congruent? Which triangle congruence theorem can you use? Explain.

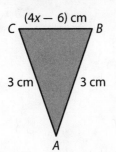 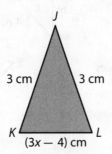 

$\overline{AB} \cong \overline{JK}$ and $\overline{AC} \cong \overline{JL}$, because they have the same measure. So, if $\overline{BC} \cong \overline{KL}$, then $\triangle ABC \cong \triangle JKL$ by the SSS Triangle Congruence Theorem. Write an equation setting the lengths equal and solve for x. $4x - 6 = 3x - 4$; $x = 2$

Ⓑ Adeline made a design using triangular tiles as shown. For what value of x can you use a triangle congruence theorem to show that the tiles are congruent? Which triangle congruence theorem can you use? Explain.

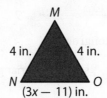 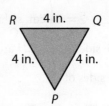

Notice that $\overline{PQ} \cong \overline{MN}$ and _____ $\cong \overline{MO}$, because they have the same measure.

If $\overline{NO} \cong \overline{QR}$, then $\triangle MNO \cong$ _____ by the _____ Triangle Congruence Theorem.

Write an equation setting the lengths equal and solve for x.

_____

Your Turn

7. Craig made a mobile using geometric shapes including triangles shaped as shown. For what value of x and y can you use a triangle congruence theorem to show that the triangles are congruent? Which triangle congruence theorem can you use? Explain.

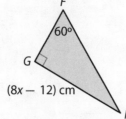 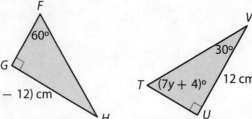

8. An isosceles triangle has two sides of equal length. If we ask everyone in class to construct an isosceles triangle that has one side of length 8 cm and another side of length 12 cm, how many sets of congruent triangles might the class make?

_____

_____

_____

9. **Essential Question Check-In** How do you explain the SSS Triangle Congruence Theorem?

_____

_____

_____

_____

_____

_____

⭐ Evaluate: Homework and Practice

- Online Homework
- Hints and Help
- Extra Practice

Use a compass and a straightedge to complete the drawing of △DEF so that it is congruent to △ABC.

1.

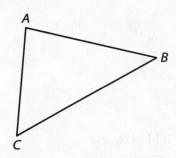
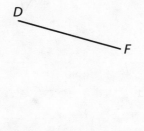

On a separate piece of paper, use a compass and a straightedge to construct two congruent triangles with the given side lengths. Label the lengths of the sides.

2. 3 in., 3.5 in., 4 in.

3. 3 cm, 11 cm, 12 cm

Identify a sequence of rigid motions that maps one side of △ABC onto one side of △DEF.

4.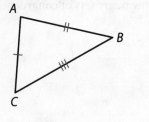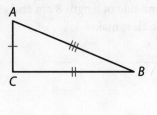

_____

_____

_____

5.

_____

_____

_____

6.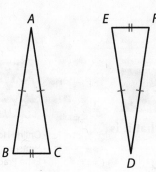

_____

_____

_____

7.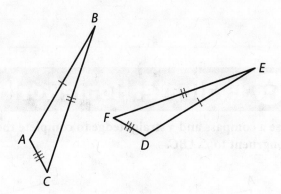

_____

_____

_____

In each figure, identify the perpendicular bisector and the line segment it bisects, and explain how to use the information to show that the two triangles are congruent.

8.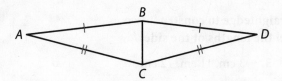

_____

_____

_____

9.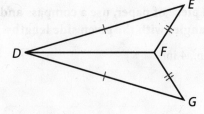

_____

_____

_____

Prove that the triangles are congruent or explain why this is not possible.

10.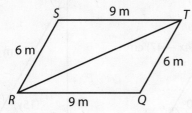

_____

_____

_____

_____

11.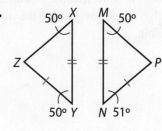

_____

_____

_____

_____

12.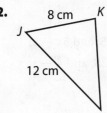

_____

_____

13.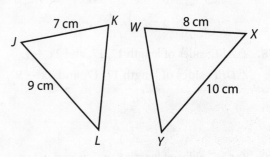

_____

_____

_____

_____

14. Carol bought two chairs with triangular backs. For what value of x can you use a triangle congruence theorem to show that the triangles are congruent? Which triangle congruence theorem can you use? Explain.

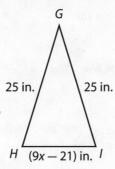

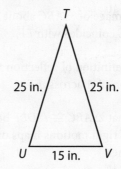

_____

_____

15. For what values of x and y can you use a triangle congruence theorem to show that the triangles are congruent? Which triangle congruence theorem can you use? Explain.

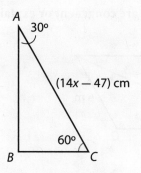
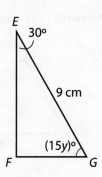

Find all possible solutions for x such that $\triangle ABC$ is congruent to $\triangle DEF$. One or more of the problems may have no solution.

16. $\triangle ABC$: sides of length 6, 8, and x.
$\triangle DEF$: sides of length 6, 9, and $x - 1$.

17. $\triangle ABC$: sides of length 3, $x + 1$, and 14.
$\triangle DEF$: sides of length 13, $x - 9$, and $2x - 6$

18. $\triangle ABC$: sides of length 17, 17, and $2x + 1$.
$\triangle DEF$: sides of length 17, 17, and $3x - 9$

19. $\triangle ABC$: sides of length 19, 25, and $5x - 2$.
$\triangle DEF$: sides of length 25, 28, and $4 - y$

20. $\triangle ABC$: sides of length 8, $x - y$, and $x + y$
$\triangle DEF$: sides of length 8, 15, and 17

21. $\triangle ABC$: sides of length 9, x, and $2x - y$
$\triangle DEF$: sides of length 8, 9, and $2y - x$

22. These statements are part of an explanation for the SSS Triangle Congruence Theorem. Write the numbers 1 to 6 to place these strategies in a logical order. The statements refer to triangles ABC and DEF shown here.

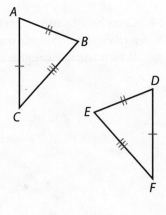

_____ Rotate the image of $\triangle ABC$ about E, so that the image of $\overline{BC}$ coincides with $\overline{EF}$.

_____ Apply the definition of reflection to show D is the reflection of A across $\overrightarrow{EF}$.

_____ Conclude that $\triangle ABC \cong \triangle DEF$ because a sequence of rigid motions maps one triangle onto the other.

_____ Translate $\triangle ABC$ along $\overrightarrow{BE}$.

_____ Define $\overrightarrow{EF}$ as the perpendicular bisector of the line connecting D and the image of A.

_____ Identify E, and then F, as equidistant from D and the image of A.

23. Determine whether the given information is sufficient to guarantee that two triangles are congruent. Select the correct answer for each lettered part.

A. The triangles have three pairs of congruent corresponding angles.

◯ sufficient   ◯ not sufficient

B. The triangles have three pairs of congruent corresponding sides.

◯ sufficient   ◯ not sufficient

C. The triangles have two pairs of congruent corresponding sides and one pair of congruent corresponding angles.

◯ sufficient   ◯ not sufficient

D. The triangles have two pairs of congruent corresponding angles and one pair of congruent corresponding sides.

◯ sufficient   ◯ not sufficient

E. Two angles and the included side of one triangle are congruent to two angles and the included side of the other triangle.

◯ sufficient   ◯ not sufficient

F. Two sides and the included angle of one triangle are congruent to two sides and the included angle of the other triangle.

◯ sufficient   ◯ not sufficient

24. Make a Conjecture Does a version of SSS congruence apply to quadrilaterals? Provide an example to support your answer.

_____

_____

25. Are two triangles congruent if all pairs of corresponding angles are congruent? Support your answer with an example.

_____

_____

_____

_____

26. Explain the Error Ava wants to know the distance *JK* across a pond. She locates points as shown. She says that the distance across the pond must be 160 ft by the SSS Triangle Congruence Theorem. Explain her error.

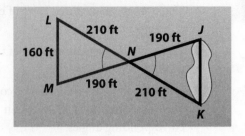

_____

_____

27. Analyze Relationships Write a proof.

Given: ∠BFC ≅ ∠ECF, ∠BFC ≅ ∠ECF

$\overline{AB} \cong \overline{DE}$, $\overline{EF} \cong \overline{DC}$

Prove: △ABF ≅ △DEC

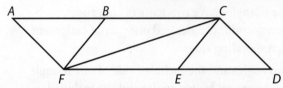

Statements	Reasons

Lesson Performance Task

Mike and Michelle each hope to get a contract with the city to build benches for commuters to sit on while waiting for buses. The benches must be stable so that they don't collapse, and they must be attractive. Their designs are shown. Judge the two benches on stability and attractiveness. Explain your reasoning.

Mike

Michelle

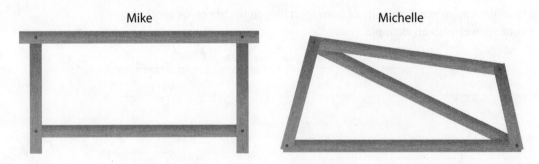

Triangle Congruence Criteria

Essential Question: How can you use triangle congruence criteria to solve real-world problems?

KEY EXAMPLE   (Lesson 20.1)

Triangle $\triangle ABC$ is congruent to $\triangle DEF$. Given that $AB = 7$ and $DE = 5y - 3$, find y.

$\overline{AB} \cong \overline{DE}$	Corresponding parts of congruent triangles are congruent.
$AB = DE$	Definition of congruent sides
$5y - 3 = 7$	Write the equation.
$5y = 10$	Add 3 to each side.
$y = 2$	Divide each side by 5.

KEY EXAMPLE   (Lesson 20.2)

Given: $\overline{AB} \cong \overline{BC} \cong \overline{CD} \cong \overline{DA}$

$m\angle DAB = m\angle ABC = m\angle BCD$
$= m\angle ADC = 90°$

$\angle EDC \cong \angle ECD$

Prove: E is the midpoint of $\overline{AB}$.

$m\angle DAB = m\angle ABC$	Given
$\angle DAB \cong \angle ABC$	Definition of congruent sides.
$\angle EDC \cong \angle ECD$	Given
$m\angle ADC = m\angle BCD$	Given
$m\angle ADC - m\angle ECD = m\angle BCD - \angle ECD$	Subtraction property of equality.
$\angle ADE \cong \angle BCE$	
$AD \cong BC$	Given
$\triangle ADE \cong \triangle BCE$	ASA Triangle Congruence Theorem.
$AE = EB$	CPCT

Therefore, E is the midpoint of $\overline{AB}$ by the definition of midpoint.

KEY EXAMPLE   (Lesson 20.3)

Determine whether the triangles are congruent. Explain your reasoning.

It is given that $\overline{AB} \cong \overline{AD}$ and $\angle BAC \cong \angle DAC$. By the reflexive property of congruence, $\overline{AC} \cong \overline{AC}$. Since two sides and an included angle of each triangle are congruent, $\triangle BAC \cong \triangle DAC$ by the SAS Triangle Congruence Theorem.

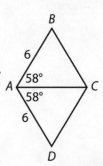

EXERCISES

Solve for *y* given each set of constraints. *(Lesson 20.1)*

1. Given $\triangle PQR \cong \triangle DEF$, $PQ = 15$, $QR = 10$, $RP = 8$, and $EF = 6y + 4$. _____

2. Given $\triangle PQR \cong \triangle ABC$, $m\angle P = 60°$, $m\angle Q = 40°$, and $m\angle C = (7y + 10)°$. _____

Determine whether the triangles are congruent.
Explain your reasoning. *(Lesson 20.3)*

3.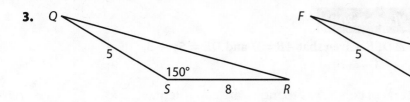

4. Barbara and Sherwin want to use the SSS Triangle Congruence Theorem to see if their triangular slices of watermelon are congruent. They each measure two sides of their slices. Barbara measures sides of lengths 7 inches and 6 inches, while Sherwin measures sides of lengths 8 inches and 5 inches. Do they need to measure the third sides of their slices to determine whether they are congruent? If so, what must the side lengths be for the slices to be congruent? Explain. *(Lesson 20.4)*

MODULE PERFORMANCE TASK

Golden Gate Triangles

The Golden Gate Bridge in San Francisco is famous worldwide. The suspension bridge spans the Golden Gate strait with suspension cables attached to two towers that are 4200 feet apart. The bridge also uses trusses, support structures formed by triangles, to help support the weight of the towers and the rest of the bridge.

Use visual evidence from the photo to estimate how many isosceles triangles can be found between the two towers.

Use your own paper to complete the task. Be sure to write down all your data and assumptions. Then use graphs, numbers, words, or algebra to explain how you reached your conclusion.

© Houghton Mifflin Harcourt Publishing Company • Image Credits: ©Radius Images/Corbis

20.1–20.4 Triangle Congruence Criteria

- Online Homework
- Hints and Help
- Extra Practice

1. $\triangle ABC \cong \triangle EDF$. Determine the value of x. *(Lesson 20.1)*

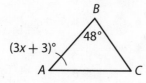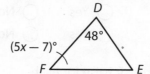

2. Plot point F so that $\triangle ABC \cong \triangle FGH$. Identify a sequence of rigid motions that maps $\triangle ABC$ onto $\triangle FGH$ and use a theorem to explain why the triangles are congruent. *(Lessons 20.1, 20.4)*

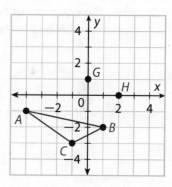

ESSENTIAL QUESTION

3. How can you tell that triangles are congruent without knowing the lengths of all sides and the measures of all angles?

Assessment Readiness

1. Two triangles, △ABC and △XYZ, are congruent. The measure of angle C, m∠C, is equal to 81°. The measure of angle X, m∠X, is equal to 56°.

   Select Yes or No for A–C.

   A. Does m∠A = 99°?   ○ Yes   ○ No

   B. Does m∠B = 43°?   ○ Yes   ○ No

   C. Are ∠A and ∠Z congruent?   ○ Yes   ○ No

2. Look at the triangles to the right. Choose True or False for each of the statements about them.

   A. A value of x = 16 results in congruent triangles.   ○ True   ○ False

   B. A value of x = 27 results in congruent triangles.   ○ True   ○ False

   C. A value of x = 31 does not result in congruent triangles.   ○ True   ○ False

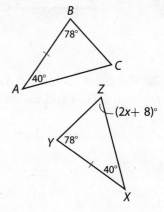

3. Write the equation of one line that is perpendicular to and one line that is parallel to y = 7x + 9.

4. In the figure, segment $\overline{AB}$ is parallel to $\overline{CD}$, $\overline{XY}$ is the perpendicular bisector of $\overline{AB}$, and E is the midpoint of $\overline{XY}$. Prove that △AEB ≅ △CED.

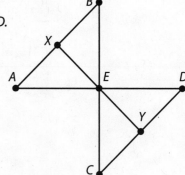

Applications of Triangle Congruence

Essential Question: How can you use applications of triangle congruence to solve real-world problems?

REAL WORLD VIDEO
A geodesic dome encloses the greatest volume of space for a given surface area. Check out how applications of triangles are involved in the design of geodesic domes.

MODULE PERFORMANCE TASK PREVIEW

Geodesic Domes

In this module, you will use a three-dimensional shape called an icosahedron to explore the geometry of a geodesic dome. Let's dive in and find out what triangles have to do with icosahedrons and geodesic domes.

Complete these exercises to review the skills you will need for this module.

• Online Homework
• Hints and Help
• Extra Practice

Distance Formula

Example 1 Find the distance between $(1, -6)$ and $(-1, -2)$.

$\sqrt{(-1-1)^2 + (-2-(-6))^2}$

$= \sqrt{4 + 16}$ Apply the distance formula.

$= \sqrt{20}$ Simplify each square.

Simplify.

Find the distance between the given points.

1. The points $(-1, 2)$ and $(2, -2)$ _____

2. The points $(-5, 21)$ and $(0, 19)$_____

Congruent Figures

Example 2 Determine whether the triangles are congruent. Explain your reasoning.

Step 1: Find m∠R.

$m\angle R + m\angle P + m\angle Q = 180°$

$m\angle R + 58° + 43° = 180°$

$m\angle R = 79°$

So, $\triangle QPR \cong \triangle TSU$ by the ASA Triangle Congruence Theorem.

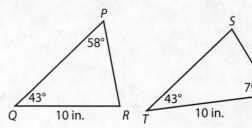

3. Determine whether the triangles are congruent. Explain your reasoning.

_____

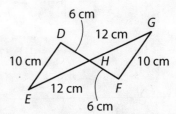

Angle Theorems for Triangles

Example 3 Given $a = 7$ cm and $b = 5$ cm, find the missing length.

$a^2 + b^2 = c^2$ Pythagorean Theorem

$(7)^2 + (5)^2 = c^2$ Substitute $a = 7$ and $b = 5$.

$c = \sqrt{49 + 25}$ Solve for c.

$c = \sqrt{74}$ cm   Simplify.

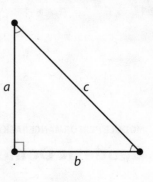

Use the given values to find the missing lengths in the figure from the example.

4. $c = 13$ cm and $b = 5$ cm

$a =$ _____

5. $c = 7$ cm and $a = 6$ cm

$b =$ _____

21.1 Justifying Constructions

Essential Question: How can you be sure that the result of a construction is valid?

✦ Explore 1   Using a Reflective Device to Construct a Perpendicular Line

You have constructed a line perpendicular to a given line through a point not on the line using a compass and straightedge. You can also use a reflective device to construct perpendicular lines.

(A) **Step 1** Place the reflective device along line ℓ. Look through the device to locate the image of point P on the opposite side of line ℓ. Draw the image of point P and label it P'.

    Step 2 Use a straightedge to draw $\overleftrightarrow{PP'}$.

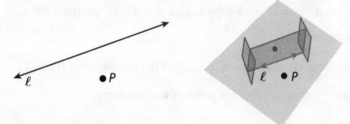

Explain why $\overleftrightarrow{PP'}$ is perpendicular to line ℓ.

_____

_____

(B) Place the reflective device so that it passes through point Q and is approximately perpendicular to line m. Adjust the angle of the device until the image of line m coincides with line m. Draw a line along the reflective device and label it line n. Explain why line n is perpendicular to line m.

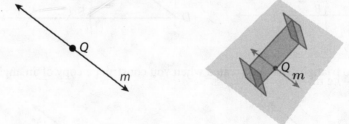

_____

_____

_____

Reflect

1. How can you check that the lines you drew are perpendicular to lines ℓ and m?

_____

_____

2. Use the reflective device to draw two points on line ℓ that are reflections of each other. Label the points X and X'. What is true about PX and PX'? Why? Use a ruler to check your prediction.

_____

_____

3. Describe how to construct a perpendicular bisector of a line segment using paper folding. Use a rigid motion to explain why the result is a perpendicular bisector.

_____

_____

_____

⊘ Explore 2 **Justifying the Copy of an Angle Construction**

You have seen how to construct a copy of an angle, but how do you know that the copy must be congruent to the original? Recall that to construct a copy of an angle A, you use these steps.

> **Step 1** Draw a ray with endpoint D.
>
> **Step 2** Draw an arc that intersects both rays of ∠A. Label the intersections B and C.
>
> **Step 3** Draw the same arc on the ray. Label the point of intersection E.
>
> **Step 4** Set the compass to the length BC.
>
> **Step 5** Place the compass at E and draw a new arc. Label the intersection of the new arc F. Draw $\overline{DF}$. ∠D is congruent to ∠A.

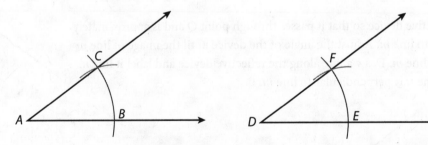

(A) Sketch and name the two triangles that are created when you construct a copy of an angle.

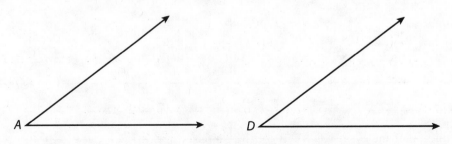

Ⓑ What segments do you know are congruent? Explain how you know.

_____

_____

_____

Ⓒ Are the triangles congruent? How do you know?

_____

Reflect

4. Discussion Suppose you used a larger compass setting to create $\overline{AB}$ than another student when copying the same angle. Will your copied angles be congruent?

_____

_____

5. Does the justification above for constructing a copy of an angle work for obtuse angles?

_____

_____

_____

🔑 **Explain 1** **Proving the Angle Bisector and Perpendicular Bisector Constructions**

You have constructed angle bisectors and perpendicular bisectors. You now have the tools you need to prove that these compass and straightedge constructions result in the intended figures.

Example 1 **Prove two bisector constructions.**

Ⓐ You have used the following steps to construct an angle bisector.

Step 1 Draw an arc intersecting the sides of the angle. Label the intersections B and C.

Step 2 Draw intersecting arcs from B and C. Label the intersection of the arcs as D.

Step 3 Use a straightedge to draw $\overline{AD}$.

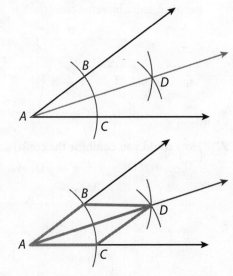

Prove that the construction results in the angle bisector.

The construction results in the triangles ABD and ACD. Because the same compass setting was used to create them, $\overline{AB} \cong \overline{AC}$ and $\overline{BD} \cong \overline{CD}$. The segment $\overline{AD}$ is congruent to itself by the Reflexive Property of Congruence. So, by the SSS Triangle Congruence Theorem, $\triangle ABD \cong \triangle ACD$.

Corresponding parts of congruent figures are congruent, so $\angle BAD \cong \angle DAC$.

By the definition of angle bisector, $\overrightarrow{AD}$ is the angle bisector of $\angle A$.

(B) You have used the following steps to construct a perpendicular bisector.

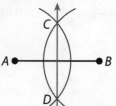

Step 1 Draw an arc centered at *A*.

Step 2 Draw an arc with the same diameter centered at *B*. Label the intersections *C* and *D*.

Step 3 Draw $\overline{CD}$.

Prove that the construction results in the perpendicular bisector.

The point *C* is equidistant from the endpoints of _____ , so by the _____

_____ Theorem, it lies on the _____ of $\overline{AB}$. The point *D* is also equidistant

from the endpoints of _____, so it also lies on the _____ of $\overline{AB}$. Two points

determine a line, so _____

Reflect

6. In Part B, what can you conclude about the measures of the angles made by the intersection of $\overline{AB}$ and $\overline{CD}$?

_____

_____

7. **Discussion** A classmate claims that in the construction shown in Part B, $\overline{AB}$ is the perpendicular bisector of $\overline{CD}$. Is this true? Justify your answer.

_____

_____

Your Turn

8. The construction in Part B is also used to construct the midpoint *R* of $\overline{MN}$. How is the proof of this construction different from the proof of the perpendicular bisector construction in Part B?

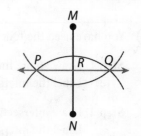

_____

_____

_____

_____

9. How could you combine the constructions in Example 1 to construct a 45° angle?

_____

_____

_____

_____

10. Describe how you can construct a line that is parallel to a given line using the construction of a perpendicular to a line.

_____

_____

11. Use a straightedge and a piece of string to construct an equilateral triangle that has *AB* as one of its sides. Then explain how you know your construction works. (*Hint*: Consider an arc centered at *A* with radius *AB* and an arc centered at *B* with radius *AB*.)

_____

_____

_____

A ●————————————————● B

12. Essential Question Check-In Is a construction something that must be proven? Explain.

_____

_____

_____

⭐ Evaluate: Homework and Practice

- Online Homework
- Hints and Help
- Extra Practice

1. Julia is given a line ℓ and a point *P* not on line ℓ. She is asked to use a reflective device to construct a line through *P* that is perpendicular to line ℓ. She places the device as shown in the figure. What should she do next to draw the required line?

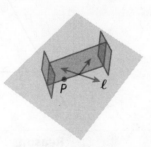

2. Describe how to construct a copy of a segment. Explain how you know that the segments are congruent.

Complete the proof of the construction of a segment bisector.

3. **Given:** the construction of the segment bisector of $\overline{AB}$

Prove: $\overline{CD}$ bisects $\overline{AB}$

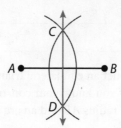

Statements	Reasons
1. $AC = \underline{\hspace{1cm}}$ and $AD = \underline{\hspace{1cm}}$.	**1.** Same compass setting used
2. C is on the perpendicular bisector of $\overline{AB}$.	**2.** _____ _____
3. D is on the perpendicular bisector of $\overline{AB}$.	**3.** _____ _____
4. _____ is the perpendicular bisector of $\overline{AB}$.	**4.** Through any two points, there is exactly one line.
5. _____	**5.** Definition of _____

4. Complete the proof of the construction of a congruent angle.

Given: the construction of $\angle CAB$ given $\angle HFG$

Prove: $\angle CAB \cong \angle HFG$

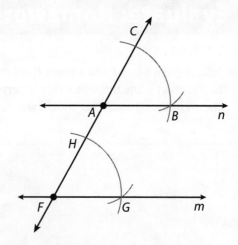

Statements	Reasons
1. $FG = FH = \underline{\hspace{1cm}} = AC$	**1.** same compass setting
2. $GH = CB$	**2.** _____
3. $\triangle FGH \cong \triangle ABC$	**3.** _____
4. $\angle CAB \cong \angle HFG$	**4.** _____

To construct a line through the given point P, parallel to line ℓ, you use the following steps.

Step 1 Choose a point Q on line ℓ and draw $\overline{QP}$.

Step 2 Construct an angle congruent to ∠1 at P.

Step 3 Construct the line through the given point, parallel to the line shown.

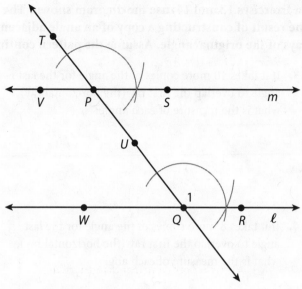

Describe the relationship between the given angles or segments. Justify your answer.

5. ∠TPS and ∠UQR

6. ∠SPU and ∠RQU

7. ∠VPU and ∠UQR

8. ∠TPS and ∠WQU

9. $\overline{QU}$ and $\overline{PS}$

10. $\overline{QU}$ and $\overline{PT}$

11. To construct a line through the given point P, parallel to line ℓ, you use the following steps.

Step 1 Draw line m through P and intersecting line ℓ.

Step 2 Construct an angle congruent to ∠1 at P.

Step 3 Construct the line through the given point, parallel to the line shown.

How do you know that lines ℓ and n are parallel? Explain.

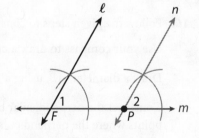

12. Construct an angle whose measure is $\frac{1}{4}$ the measure of ∠Z. Justify the construction.

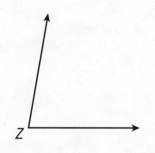

In Exercises 13 and 14, use the diagram shown. The diagram shows the result of constructing a copy of an angle adjacent to one of the rays of the original angle. Assume the pattern continues.

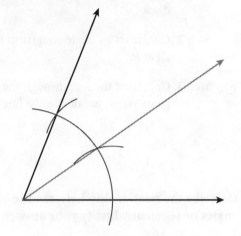

13. If it takes 10 more copies of the angle for the last angle to overlap the first ray (the horizontal ray), what is the measure of each angle?

14. If it takes 8 more copies of the angle for the last angle to overlap the first ray (the horizontal ray), what is the measure of each angle?

15. Sonia draws a segment on a piece of paper. She wants to find three points that are equidistant from the endpoints of the segment. Explain how she can use paper folding to help her locate the three points.

In Exercises 16–18, a polygon is inscribed in a circle if all of the polygon's vertices lie on the circle.

16. Follow the given steps to construct a square inscribed in a circle.

Use your compass to draw a circle. Mark the center.

Draw a diameter, $\overline{AB}$, using a straightedge.

Construct the perpendicular bisector of $\overline{AB}$. Label the points where the perpendicular bisector intersects the circle as C and D.

Use the straightedge to draw $\overline{AC}$, $\overline{CB}$, $\overline{BD}$, and $\overline{DA}$.

17. Suppose you are given a piece of tracing paper with a circle on it and you do not have a compass. How can you use paper folding to inscribe a square in the circle?

18. Follow the given steps to construct a regular hexagon inscribed in a circle.

Tie a pencil to one end of the string.

Mark a point *O* on your paper. Place the string on point *O* and hold it down with your finger. Pull the string taut and draw a circle. Mark and label a point *A*.

Hold the point on the string that you placed on point *O*, and move it to point *A*. Pull the string taut and draw an arc that intersects the circle. Label the point as *B*.

Hold the point on the string that you placed on point *A*, and move it to point *B*. Draw an arc to locate point *C* on the circle. Repeat to locate points *D*, *E*, and *F*. Use your straightedge to draw *ABCDEF*.

19. Your teacher constructed the figure shown. It shows the construction of line *PT* through point *P* and parallel to line *AB*.

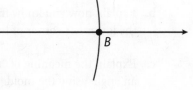

a. Compass settings of length *AB* and *AP* were used in the construction. Complete the statements:

With the compass set to length *AP*, an arc was drawn with the compass point at point ___.

With the compass set to length ___, an arc was drawn with the compass point at point ___.

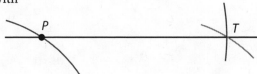

The two arcs intersect at point ___.

b. Write two congruence statements involving segments in the construction.

c. Write a proof that the construction is true. That is, given the construction, prove $\overline{PT} \| \overline{AB}$. (*Hint*: Draw segments to create two congruent triangles.)

23. Use the segments shown. Construct and label a segment, $\overline{XY}$, whose length is the average of the lengths of $\overline{AB}$ and $\overline{CD}$. Justify the method you used.

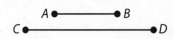

Lesson Performance Task

A plastic "mold" for copying a 30° angle is shown here.

a. If you drew a 30°—60°—90° triangle using the mold, how would you know that your triangle and the mold were congruent?

b. Explain how you know that any angle you would draw using the lower left corner of the mold would measure 30°.

c. Explain the meaning of "tolerance" in the context of drawing an angle using the mold.

21.2 AAS Triangle Congruence

Essential Question: What does the AAS Triangle Congruence Theorem tell you about two triangles?

Explore   Exploring Angle-Angle-Side Congruence

If two angles and a non-included side of one triangle are congruent to the corresponding angles and side of another triangle, are the triangles congruent?

In this activity you'll be copying a side and two angles from a triangle.

(A) Use a compass and straightedge to copy segment *AC*. Label it as segment *EF*.

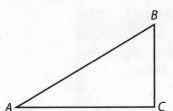

(B) Copy ∠*A* using $\overline{EF}$ as a side of the angle.

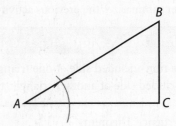

(C) On a separate transparent sheet or a sheet of tracing paper, copy ∠*B*. Label its vertex *G*. Make the rays defining ∠*G* longer than their corresponding sides on △*ABC*.

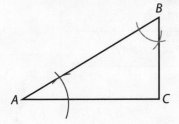

(D) Now overlay the ray from ∠*E* with the ray from ∠*G* to form a triangle. Make sure that side $\overline{EF}$ maintains the length you defined for it.

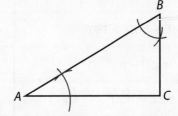

Ⓔ How many triangles can you construct?

_____

Ⓕ Copy all of △EFG to the transparency. Then overlay it on △ABC. Are the triangles congruent? How do you know?

_____

Reflect

1. Suppose you had started this activity by copying segment BC and then angles A and C. Would your results have been the same? Why or why not?

_____

2. Compare your results to those of your classmates. Does this procedure work with any triangle?

_____

🔑 **Explain 1** **Justifying Angle-Angle-Side Congruence**

The following theorem summarizes the previous activity.

Angle-Angle-Side (AAS) Congruence Theorem

If two angles and a non-included side of one triangle are congruent to the corresponding angles and non-included side of another triangle, then the triangles are congruent.

Prove the AAS Congruence Theorem.

Given: $\angle A \cong \angle D$, $\angle C \cong \angle F$, $\overline{BC} \cong \overline{EF}$

Prove: $\triangle ABC \cong \triangle DEF$

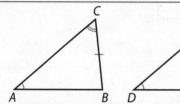

Statements	Reasons
1. $\angle A \cong \angle D$, $\angle C \cong \angle \boxed{}$, $\overline{BC} \cong \overline{EF}$	1. Given
2. $m\angle A + m\angle B + m\angle C = 180°$	2.
3. $m\angle B = 180° - m\angle A - m\angle \boxed{}$	3. Subtraction Property of Equality
4. $m\angle \boxed{} + m\angle E + m\angle F = 180°$	4. Triangle Sum Theorem
5. $m\angle E = 180° - m\angle D - m\angle \boxed{}$	5. Subtraction Property of Equality
6. $m\angle A = m\angle D$, $m\angle C = m\angle F$	6.
7. $m\angle E = 180° - m\angle A - m\angle C$	7.
8. $m\angle \boxed{} \cong m\angle B$	8. Transitive Property of Equality
9. $\angle B \cong m\angle E$	9.
10. $\triangle ABC \cong \triangle DEF$	10. Triangle Congruence Theorem

3. **Discussion** The Third Angles Theorem says "If two angles of one triangle are congruent to two angles of another triangle, then the third pair of angles are congruent." How could using this theorem simplify the proof of the AAS Congruence Theorem?

_____

_____

_____

4. Could the AAS Congruence Theorem be used in the proof? Explain.

_____

_____

_____

🔑 Explain 2 Using Angle-Angle-Side Congruence

Example 2 Use the AAS Theorem to prove the given triangles are congruent.

Ⓐ Given: $\overline{AC} \cong \overline{EC}$ and $m \| n$

Prove: $\triangle ABC \cong \triangle EDC$

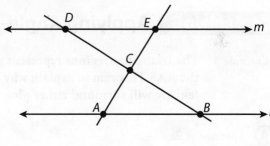

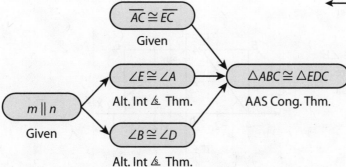

Ⓑ Given: $\overline{CB} \| \overline{ED}$, $\overline{AB} \| \overline{CD}$, and $\overline{CB} \cong \overline{ED}$.

Prove: $\triangle ABC \cong \triangle CDE$

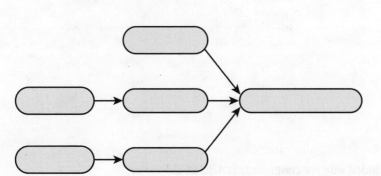

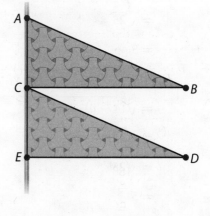

5. Given: $\angle ABC \cong \angle DEF$, $\overline{BC} \parallel \overline{EF}$, $\overline{AC} \cong \overline{DF}$. Use the AAS Theorem to prove the triangles are congruent.

Write a paragraph proof.

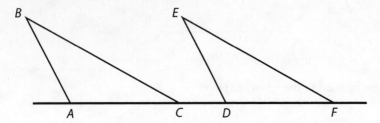

🔧 Explain 3 Applying Angle-Angle-Side Congruence

Example 3 The triangular regions represent plots of land. Use the AAS Theorem to explain why the same amount of fencing will surround either plot.

Ⓐ Given: $\angle A \cong \angle D$

It is given that $\angle A \cong \angle D$. Also, $\angle B \cong \angle E$ because both are right angles. Compare AC and DF using the Distance Formula.

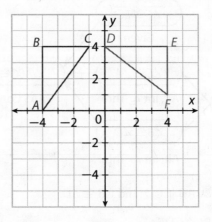

$AC = \sqrt{(x_1 - x_2)^2 + (y_1 - y_2)^2}$

$\quad = \sqrt{\left(-1 - (-4)\right)^2 + (4 - 0)^2}$

$\quad = \sqrt{3^2 + 4^2}$

$\quad = \sqrt{25}$

$\quad = 5$

$DF = \sqrt{(x_1 - x_2)^2 + (y_1 - y_2)^2}$

$\quad = \sqrt{(4 - 0)^2 + (1 - 4)^2}$

$\quad = \sqrt{4^2 + (-3)^2}$

$\quad = \sqrt{25}$

$\quad = 5$

Because two angles and a non-included side are congruent, $\triangle ABC \cong \triangle DEF$ by AAS. Therefore the triangles have the same perimeter and the same amount of fencing is needed.

B Given: $\angle P \cong \angle Z$, $\angle Q \cong \angle X$

It is given that $\angle P \cong \angle Z$ and $\angle Q \cong \angle X$.

Compare YZ and _____ using the distance formula.

$YZ = \sqrt{(x_1 - x_2)^2 + (y_1 - y_2)^2}$

$ = \sqrt{\left(\boxed{} - (-1)\right)^2 + \left(\boxed{} - (-2)\right)^2}$

$ = \sqrt{\left(\boxed{}\right)^2 + \left(\boxed{}\right)^2}$

$ = \sqrt{\boxed{} + \boxed{}}$

$ = \sqrt{\boxed{}}$

$\underline{} = \sqrt{(x_1 - x_2)^2 + (y_1 - y_2)^2}$

$ = \sqrt{\left(\boxed{} - 0\right)^2 + \left(\boxed{} - 0\right)^2}$

$ = \sqrt{\left(\boxed{}\right)^2 + \left(\boxed{}\right)^2}$

$ = \sqrt{\boxed{} + \boxed{}}$

$ = \sqrt{\boxed{}}$

Because two angles and a non-included side are congruent, $\triangle XYZ \cong \triangle \boxed{}$ by

AAS. Therefore the triangles have the same perimeter and the same amount of fencing is needed.

Reflect

6. Explain how you could have avoided using the distance formula in Example 2B.

_____

_____

_____

Refer to the diagram to answer the questions.

Given: ∠A ≅ ∠D and ∠B ≅ ∠E

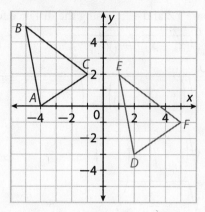

7. Show that the two triangles are congruent using the AAS Theorem. Use the distance formula to compare *BC* and *EF*.

8. Show that the two triangles are congruent using the AAS Theorem. Use the distance formula to compare *AC* and *DF*.

9. Two isosceles triangles share a side. With which diagram can the AAS Theorem be used to show the triangles are congruent? Explain.

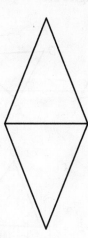
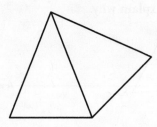

_____

_____

_____

10. What must be true of the right triangles in the roof truss to use the AAS Congruence Theorem to prove the two triangles are congruent? Explain.

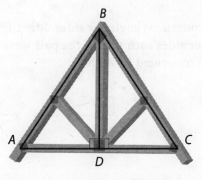

_____

_____

_____

11. **Essential Question Check-In** You know that a pair of triangles has two pairs of congruent corresponding angles. What other information do you need to show that the triangles are congruent?

_____

_____

_____

• Online Homework
• Hints and Help
• Extra Practice

Decide whether you have enough information to determine that the triangles are congruent. If they are congruent, explain why.

1.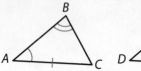

2.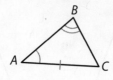

3.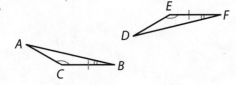

4.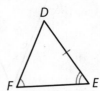

5.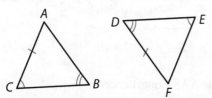

6.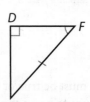

Each diagram shows two triangles with two congruent angles or sides. Identify one additional pair of corresponding angles or sides such that, if the pair were congruent, the two triangles could be proved congruent by AAS.

7.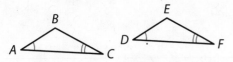

8.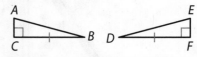

9.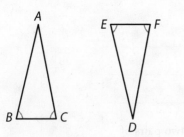

10.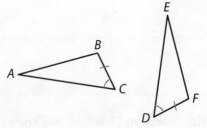

11.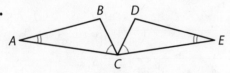

12.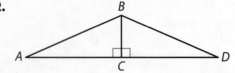

13. Complete the proof.

Given: $\angle B \cong \angle D$, $\overleftrightarrow{AC}$ bisects $\angle BCD$.

Prove: $\triangle ABC \cong \triangle ADC$

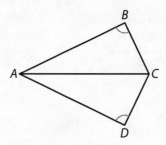

Statements	Reasons
1. $\overline{AC} \cong \overline{AC}$	1.
2. $\overleftrightarrow{AC}$ bisects $\angle BCD$.	2. Given
3.	3. Definition of angle bisector
4.	4. Given
5. $\triangle ABC \cong \triangle ADC$	5.

14. Write a two-column proof or a paragraph proof.

Given: $\overline{AB} \parallel \overline{DE}$, $\overline{CB} \cong \overline{CD}$.

Prove: $\triangle ABC \cong \triangle EDC$

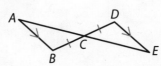

Each diagram shows $\triangle ABC$ and $\triangle DEF$ on the coordinate plane, with $\angle A \cong \angle E$, and $\angle C \cong \angle F$. Identify whether the two triangles are congruent. If they are not congruent, explain how you know. If they are congruent, find the length of each side of each triangle.

15.

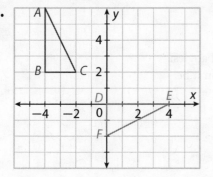

16.

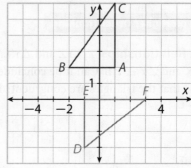

17.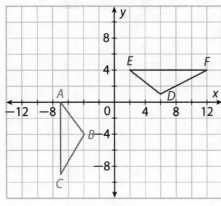

18.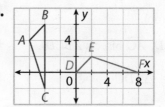

19.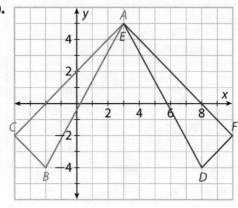

20.

21. Which theorem or postulate can be used to prove that the triangles are congruent? Select all that apply.

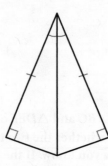

   A. ASA   **B.** SAS   **C.** SSS   **D.** AAS

H.O.T.   **Focus on Higher Order Thinking**

22. Analyze Relationships △XYZ and △KLM have two congruent angles: ∠X ≅ ∠K and ∠Y ≅ ∠L. Can it be concluded that ∠Z ≅ ∠M? Can it be concluded that the triangles are congruent? Explain.

23. Communicate Mathematical Ideas △GHJ and △PQR have two congruent angles: ∠G ≅ ∠P and ∠H ≅ ∠Q. If $\overline{HJ}$ is congruent to one of the sides of △PQR, are the two triangles congruent? Explain.

24. **Make a Conjecture** Combine the theorems of ASA Congruence and AAS Congruence into a single statement that describes a condition for congruency between triangles.

25. **Justify Reasoning** Triangles *ABC* and *DEF* are constructed with the following angles: m∠*A* = 35°, m∠*B* = 45°, m∠*D* = 65°, m∠*E* = 45°. Also, *AC* = *DF* = 12 units. Are the two triangles congruent? Explain.

26. **Justify Reasoning** Triangles *ABC* and *DEF* are constructed with the following angles: m∠*A* = 65°, m∠*B* = 60°, m∠*D* = 65°, m∠*F* = 55°. Also, *AB* = *DE* = 7 units. Are the two triangles congruent? Explain.

27. **Algebra** A bicycle frame includes △*VSU* and △*VTU*, which lie in intersecting planes. From the given angle measures, can you conclude that △*VSU* ≅ △*VTU*? Explain.

$$m\angle VUS = (7y - 2)° \qquad m\angle VUT = \left(5\frac{1}{2}x - \frac{1}{2}\right)°$$

$$m\angle USV = 5\frac{2}{3}y° \qquad m\angle UTV = (4x + 8)°$$

$$m\angle SVU = (3y - 6)° \qquad m\angle TVU = 2x°$$

Lesson Performance Task

A mapmaker has successfully mapped Carlisle Street and River Avenue, as shown in the diagram. The last step is to map Beacon Street correctly. To save time, the mapmaker intends to measure just one more angle or side of the triangle.

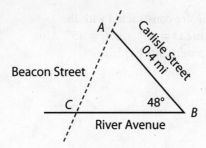

a. Which angle(s) or side(s) could the mapmaker measure to be sure that only one triangle is possible? For each angle or side that you name, justify your answer.

b. Suppose that instead of measuring the length of Carlisle Street, the mapmaker measured ∠A and ∠C along with ∠B. Would the measures of the three angles alone assure a unique triangle? Explain.

21.3 HL Triangle Congruence

Essential Question: What does the HL Triangle Congruence Theorem tell you about two triangles?

Explore Is There a Side-Side-Angle Congruence Theorem?

You have already seen several theorems for proving that triangles are congruent. In this Explore, you will investigate whether there is a SSA Triangle Congruence Theorem.

Follow these steps to draw $\triangle ABC$ such that m$\angle A = 30°$, $AB = 6$ cm, and $BC = 4$ cm. The goal is to determine whether two side lengths and the measure of a non-included angle (SSA) determine a unique triangle.

Ⓐ Use a protractor to draw a large 30° angle on a separate sheet of paper. Label it $\angle A$.

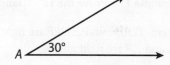

Ⓑ Use a ruler to locate point B on one ray of $\angle A$ so that $AB = 6$ cm.

Ⓒ Now draw $\overline{BC}$ so that $BC = 4$ cm. To do this, open a compass to a distance of 4 cm. Place the point of the compass on point B and draw an arc. Plot point C where the arc intersects the side of $\angle A$. Draw $\overline{BC}$ to complete $\triangle ABC$.

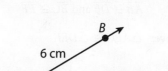

Ⓓ What do you notice? Is it possible to draw only one $\triangle ABC$ with the given side length? Explain.

_____

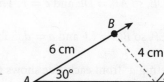

Reflect

1. Do you think that SSA is sufficient to prove congruence? Why or why not?

_____

_____

2. **Discussion** Your friend said that there is a special case where SSA can be used to prove congruence. Namely, when the non-included angle was a right angle. Is your friend right? Explain.

_____

_____

_____

🎷 Explain 1 Justifying the Hypotenuse-Leg Congruence Theorem

In a right triangle, the side opposite the right angle is the **hypotenuse**.
The two sides that form the sides of the right angle are the **legs**.

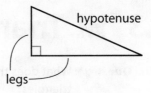

You have learned four ways to prove that triangles are congruent.

- Angle-Side-Angle (ASA) Congruence Theorem
- Side-Angle-Side (SAS) Congruence Theorem
- Side-Side-Side (SSS) Congruence Theorem
- Angle-Angle-Side (AAS) Congruence Theorem

The Hypotenuse-Leg (HL) Triangle Congruence Theorem is a special case of AAS that allows you to show that two right triangles are congruent.

Hypotenuse-Leg (HL) Triangle Congruence Theorem

If the hypotenuse and a leg of a right triangle are congruent to the hypotenuse and a leg of another right triangle, then the triangles are congruent.

Example 1 Prove the HL Triangle Congruence Theorem.

Given: $\triangle ABC$ and $\triangle DEF$ are right triangles;
$\angle C$ and $\angle F$ are right angles.

$\overline{AB} \cong \overline{DE}$ and $\overline{BC} \cong \overline{EF}$

Prove: $\triangle ABC \cong \triangle DEF$

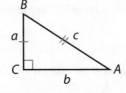
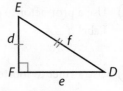

By the Pythagorean Theorem, $a^2 + b^2 = c^2$ and $\boxed{}^2 + \boxed{}^2 = f^2$. It is given that

$\overline{AB} \cong \overline{DE}$, so $AB = DE$ and $c = f$. Therefore, $c^2 = f^2$ and $a^2 + b^2 = \boxed{}^2 + \boxed{}^2$. It is given that

$\overline{BC} \cong \overline{EF}$, so $BC = EF$ and $a = d$. Substituting a for d in the above equation, $a^2 + b^2 = \boxed{}^2 + \boxed{}^2$.

Subtracting a^2 from each side shows that $b^2 = \boxed{}^2$, and taking the square root of each side, $b = \boxed{}$.

This shows that $\overline{AC} \cong \boxed{}$.

Therefore, $\triangle ABC \cong \triangle DEF$ by _____.

Your Turn

3. Determine whether there is enough information to prove that
   triangles $\triangle VWX$ and $\triangle YXW$ are congruent. Explain.

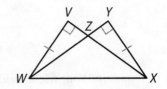

🛠 Explain 2 | Applying the HL Triangle Congruence Theorem

Example 2 Use the HL Congruence Theorem to prove that the triangles are congruent.

Ⓐ Given: ∠P and ∠R are right angles. $\overline{PS} \cong \overline{RQ}$

Prove: △PQS ≅ △RSQ

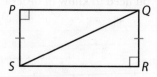

Statements	Reasons
1. ∠P and ∠R are right angles.	1. Given
2. $\overline{PS} \cong \overline{RQ}$	2. Given
3. $\overline{SQ} \cong \overline{SQ}$	3. Reflexive Property of Congruence
4. △PQS ≅ △RSQ	4. HL Triangle Congruence Theorem

Ⓑ Given: ∠J and ∠L are right angles. K is the midpoint of $\overline{JL}$ and $\overline{MN}$.

Prove: △JKN ≅ △LKM

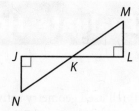

Statements	Reasons
1. ∠J and ∠L are right angles.	1.
2. K is the midpoint of $\overline{JL}$ and $\overline{MN}$.	2.
3. $\overline{JK} \cong \overline{LK}$ and $\overline{MK} \cong \overline{NK}$	3.
4. △JKN ≅ △LKM	4.

Reflect

4. Is it possible to write the proof in Part B without using the HL Triangle Congruence Theorem? Explain.

_____

_____

_____

Your Turn

Use the HL Congruence Theorem to prove that the triangles are congruent.

5. Given: ∠CAB and ∠DBA are right angles. $\overline{AD} \cong \overline{BC}$

Prove: △ABC ≅ △BAD

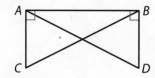

6. You draw a right triangle with a hypotenuse that is 5 inches long. A friend also draws a right triangle with a hypotenuse that is 5 inches long. Can you conclude that the triangles are congruent using the HL Congruence Theorem? If not, what else would you need to know in order to conclude that the triangles are congruent?

_____

_____

_____

7. Essential Question Check-In How is the HL Triangle Congruence Theorem similar to and different from the ASA, SAS, SSS, and AAS Triangle Congruence Theorems?

_____

_____

_____

⭐ Evaluate: Homework and Practice

- Online Homework
- Hints and Help
- Extra Practice

1. Tyrell used geometry software to construct ∠*ABC* so that m∠*ABC* = 20°. Then he dragged point *A* so that *AB* = 6 cm. He used the software's compass tool to construct a circle centered at point *A* with radius 3 cm. Based on this construction, is there a unique △*ABC* with m∠*ABC* = 20°, *AB* = 6 cm, and *AC* = 3 cm? Explain.

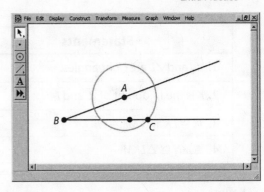

Determine whether enough information is given to prove that the triangles are congruent. Explain your answer.

2. △*ABC* and △*DCB*

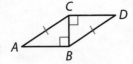

3. △*PQR* and △*STU*

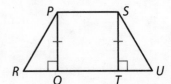

4. △GKJ and △JHG

5. △EFG and △SQR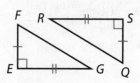

Write a two-column proof, using the HL Congruence Theorem, to prove that the triangles are congruent.

6. Given: ∠A and ∠B are right angles. $\overline{AB} \cong \overline{DC}$
Prove: △ABC ≅ △DCB

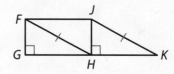

7. Given: ∠FGH and ∠JHK are right angles.
H is the midpoint of $\overline{GK}$. $\overline{FH} \cong \overline{JK}$
Prove: △FGH ≅ △JHK

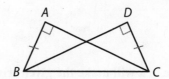

8. Given: $\overline{MP}$ is perpendicular to $\overline{QR}$.
N is the midpoint of $\overline{MP}$. $\overline{QP} \cong \overline{RM}$
Prove: △MNR ≅ △PNQ

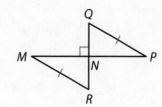

9. Given: $\angle ADC$ and $\angle BDC$ are right angles. $\overline{AC} \cong \overline{BC}$
   Prove: $\overline{AD} \cong \overline{BD}$

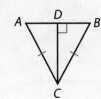

Algebra What value of *x* will make the given triangles congruent? Explain.

10. $\triangle JKL$ and $\triangle JKM$

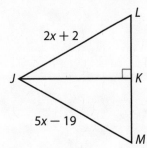

11. $\triangle ABC$ and $\triangle ABD$

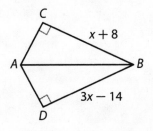

12. $\triangle STV$ and $\triangle UVT$

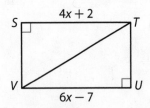

13. $\triangle MPQ$ and $\triangle PMN$

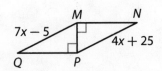

Algebra Use the HL Triangle Congruence Theorem to show that △*ABC* ≅ △*DEF*.
(*Hint*: Use the Distance Formula to show that appropriate sides are congruent. Use the slope formula to show that appropriate angles are right angles.)

14.

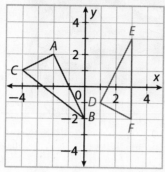

15.

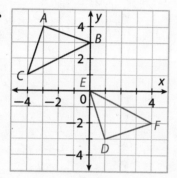

16. Communicate Mathematical Ideas A vertical tower is supported by two guy wires, as shown. The guy wires are both 58 feet long. Is it possible to determine the distance from the bottom of guy wire $\overline{AB}$ to the bottom of the tower? If so, find the distance. If not, explain why not.

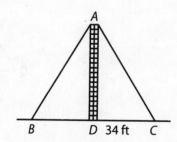

17. A carpenter built a truss, as shown, to support the roof of a doghouse.

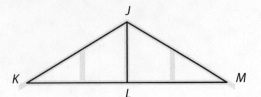

a. The carpenter knows that $\overline{KJ} \cong \overline{MJ}$. Can the carpenter conclude that $\triangle KJL \cong \triangle MJL$? Why or why not?

b. **What If?** Suppose the carpenter also knows that $\angle JLK$ is a right angle. Can the carpenter now conclude that $\triangle KJL \cong \triangle MJL$? Explain.

18. Counterexamples Denise said that if two right triangles share a common hypotenuse, then the triangles must be congruent. Sketch a figure that serves as a counterexample to show that Denise's statement is not true.

19. Multi-Step The front of a tent is covered by a triangular flap of material. The figure represents the front of the tent, with $\overline{PS} \perp \overline{QR}$ and $\overline{PQ} \cong \overline{PR}$. Jonah needs to determine the perimeter of $\triangle PQR$ so that he can replace the zipper on the tent. Find the perimeter. Explain your steps.

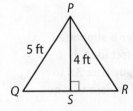

20. A student is asked to write a two-column proof for the following.

Given: ∠ABC and ∠DCB are right angles. $\overline{AC} \cong \overline{BD}$

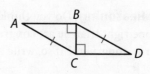

Prove: $\overline{AB} \cong \overline{DC}$

Assuming the student writes the proof correctly, which of the following will appear as a statement or reason in the proof? Select all that apply.

A. ASA Triangle Congruence Theorem

B. $\overline{BC} \cong \overline{BC}$

C. ∠A ≅ ∠D

D. Reflexive Property of Congruence

E. CPCTC

F. HL Triangle Congruence Theorem

H.O.T. Focus on Higher Order Thinking

21. Analyze Relationships Is it possible for a right triangle with a leg that is 10 inches long and a hypotenuse that is 26 inches long to be congruent to a right triangle with a leg that is 24 inches long and a hypotenuse that is 26 inches long? Explain.

22. Communicate Mathematical Ideas In the figure, $\overline{JK} \cong \overline{LM}$, $\overline{JM} \cong \overline{LK}$, and ∠J and ∠L are right angles. Describe how you could use three different congruence theorems to prove that △JKM ≅ △LMK.

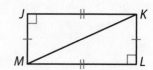

23. Justify Reasoning Do you think there is an LL Triangle Congruence Theorem? That is, if the legs of one right triangle are congruent to the legs of another right triangle, are the triangles necessarily congruent? If so, write a proof of the theorem. If not, provide a counterexample.

Lesson Performance Task

The figure shows kite *ABCD*.

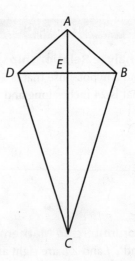

a. What would you need to know about the relationship between $\overline{AC}$ and $\overline{DB}$ in order to prove that $\triangle ADE \cong \triangle ABE$ and $\triangle CDE \cong \triangle CBE$ by the HL Triangle Congruence Theorem?

b. Can you prove that $\triangle ADC$ and $\triangle ABC$ are congruent using the HL Triangle Congruence Theorem? Explain why or why not.

c. How can you prove that the two triangles named in Part b are in fact congruent, even without the additional piece of information?

Applications of Triangle Congruence

Essential Question: How can you use triangle congruence to solve real-world problems?

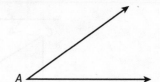

KEY EXAMPLE *(Lesson 21.1)*

Construct the bisector of the angle shown.

Place the point of the compass at *A* and draw an arc intersecting the sides of the angle. Label its points of intersection as *B* and *C*.

Use the same compass setting to draw intersecting arcs from *B* and *C*. Label the intersection of the arcs as point *D*.

Use a straight edge to draw $\overrightarrow{AD}$.

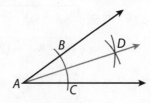

KEY EXAMPLE *(Lesson 21.2)*

Construct the line through the given point, parallel to the line shown.

Use a straightedge to draw $\overleftrightarrow{AC}$.

Copy $\angle CAB$. Start by constructing a pair of arcs.

Then construct the pair of arc intersections.

Draw line ℓ through *C* and the arc intersection. This line is parallel to *m*.

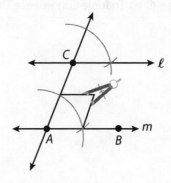

(Lesson 21.3)

The triangular regions represent plots of land. Use the AAS Theorem to explain why the same amount of fencing will surround either plot.

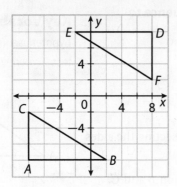

Given: $\angle B \cong \angle E$

$\angle A \cong \angle D$ Both right angles

Compare AC and DF using the distance formula.

$$AC = \sqrt{(x_1 - x_2)^2 + (y_1 - y_2)^2} \qquad DF = \sqrt{(x_1 - x_2)^2 + (y_1 - y_2)^2}$$

$$= \sqrt{(-8 - (-8))^2 + (-2 - (-8))^2} \qquad = \sqrt{(8 - 8)^2 + (2 - 8)^2}$$

$$= \sqrt{0 + 36} \qquad\qquad\qquad\qquad\qquad = \sqrt{0 + 36}$$

$$= 6 \qquad\qquad\qquad\qquad\qquad\qquad\quad = 6$$

Because two angles and a nonincluded side are congruent, $\triangle ABC \cong \triangle DEF$ by AAS. Therefore the triangles have the same perimeter by CPCTC and the same amount of fencing is needed.

(Lesson 21.3)

Write the given proof.

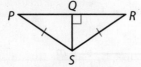

Given: $\overline{PS} \cong \overline{SR}$

Prove: $\triangle PQS \cong \triangle RQS$

Statements	Reasons
1. $\angle PQS$ and $\angle RQS$ are right angles.	1. Given
2. $\overline{PS} \cong \overline{SR}$	2. Given
3. $\overline{SQ} \cong \overline{SQ}$	3. Reflexive Property of Congruence
4. $\triangle PQS \cong \triangle RQS$	4. HL Triangle Congruence Theorem

EXERCISES

Refer to the diagram, which shows isosceles triangle *ABC* to find the measure of the angle. $\overline{AD}$ and $\overline{CD}$ **are angle bisectors.** *(Lesson 21.1)*

1. m∠*BAC* _____

2. m∠*ADC* _____

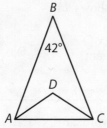

Identify the sides or angles that need to be congruent in order to make the given triangles congruent by AAS. *(Lesson 21.2)*

3.

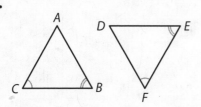

4.

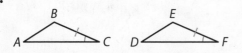

Determine whether the two triangles are congruent or not by the HL Theorem. Show all work. *(Lesson 21.3)*

5.

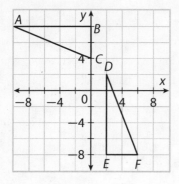

Geodesic Dome Design

A geodesic dome is derived from a 20-sided structure called an icosahedron, made of equilateral triangles. The illustration shows an icosahedron with the length of one side of a triangle labeled.

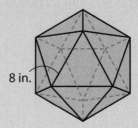

8 in.

Are all of the triangles that make up the icosahedron congruent? How can you find the total surface area of the icosahedron?

Use the space below to complete the task. Be sure to write down all your data and assumptions. Then use graphs, numbers, words, or algebra to explain how you reached your conclusion.

21.1–21.3 Applications of Triangle Congruence

- Online Homework
- Hints and Help
- Extra Practice

Given the figure below, answer the following.

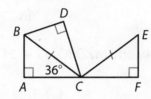

1. Given: $\angle A \cong \angle D$, $\overline{BC}$ bisects $\angle ACD$. Prove: $\triangle ABC \cong \triangle DBC$ *(Lesson 21.2)*

2. Given: $\angle A$ and $\angle F$ are right angles, C is the midpoint of $\overline{AF}$, $\overline{BC} \cong \overline{EC}$. Prove: $\triangle ABC \cong \triangle FEC$ *(Lesson 21.3)*

3. Given: $\overline{BC}$ bisects $\angle ACD$ and m$\angle ACB$ is 36°. Find m$\angle BCD$. *(Lesson 21.1)*

ESSENTIAL QUESTION

4. When given two sides and an angle of two triangles are equal, when can it be proven and when can't it be proven that the two triangles are congruent?

Assessment Readiness

1. Which of these are theorems that can be used to prove two triangles are congruent?

   Select Yes or No for A–C.

   A. SSA   ◯ Yes   ◯ No

   B. AAS   ◯ Yes   ◯ No

   C. SAS   ◯ Yes   ◯ No

2. Line $\overleftrightarrow{BD}$ bisects $\angle ABC$, $m\angle ABD = 4x$, and $m\angle DBC = x + 36$. Choose True or False for each statement.

   A. $m\angle ABC = 48°$ ◯ True   ◯ False

   B. $m\angle ABC = 96°$ ◯ True   ◯ False

   C. $m\angle DBC = 48°$ ◯ True   ◯ False

3. Given $\triangle GHI$ and $\triangle JKL$, $GI = 5$, $HI = 4$, $JK = 4$, and $JL = 5$, what else do you need to know to prove the two triangles are congruent using HL?

4. Given: $\overline{AB} \cong \overline{BC}$, $\overline{BD}$ is the perpendicular bisector of $\overline{AC}$
   Prove: $\triangle ABD \cong \triangle CBD$

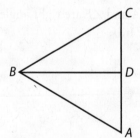

Properties of Triangles

Essential Question: How can you use properties of triangles to solve real-world problems?

UNITED STATES

FEDERAL TRADE COMMISSION BUILDING

REAL WORLD VIDEO
Check out some of the famous buildings and landmarks in the Federal Triangle area of Washington, DC.

MODULE PERFORMANCE TASK PREVIEW

The Federal Triangle

Is the Federal Triangle really a triangle? In this module, you will use a map of the Federal Triangle to explore the geometric properties of the entire area. Time to "capitalize" on your geometry knowledge!

Complete these exercises to review the skills you will need for this module.

Solving Systems of Inequalities

Example 1   Solve the given system of inequalities. $\begin{cases} x + 7 > 2 \\ 3 + x < 9 \end{cases}$

$x + 7 > 2$ $3 + x < 9$ **Separate inequalities**

$x > 2 - 7$ $x < 9 - 3$ **Solve for** x.

$x > -5$ $x < 6$ **Simplify.**

                $-5 < x < 6$ **Combine solved inequalities.**

The solutions to the system are all values greater than -5 and less than 6.

Solve each system of inequalities.

1. $\dfrac{AB + 176}{3} < 116$ **2.** $n + 14 > 16$

$248 + AB > 368$ $2(n + 68) < 148$

_____   _____

Angle Relationships

Example 2   Find the measure of $\angle x$.

$m\angle x + 72° = 180°$ **Definition of supplementary angles**

$m\angle x = 180° - 72°$ **Solve for** $m\angle x$.

$m\angle x = 108°$ **Simplify.**

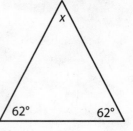

Find the measure of each angle in the image from the example.

3. $m\angle y =$ _____   **4.** $m\angle z =$ _____

Angle Theorems for Triangles

Example 3   Find the missing angle.

$62° + 62° + m\angle x = 180°$ **Triangle Sum Theorem**

$m\angle x = 180° - 62° - 62°$ **Solve for** $m\angle x$.

$m\angle x = 56°$ **Simplify.**

Find the missing angles in the given triangles.

5.

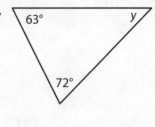

$y =$ _____

6.

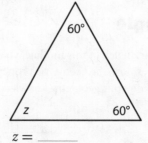

$z =$ _____

22.1 Interior and Exterior Angles

Essential Question: What can you say about the interior and exterior angles of a triangle and other polygons?

⊘ Explore 1 Exploring Interior Angles in Triangles

You can find a relationship between the measures of the three angles of a triangle. An **interior angle** is an angle formed by two sides of a polygon with a common vertex. So, a triangle has three interior angles.

(A) Use a straightedge to draw a large triangle on a sheet of paper and cut it out. Tear off the three corners and rearrange the angles so their sides are adjacent and their vertices meet at a point.

(B) What seems to be true about placing the three interior angles of a triangle together?

_____

(C) Make a conjecture about the sum of the measures of the interior angles of a triangle.

_____

_____

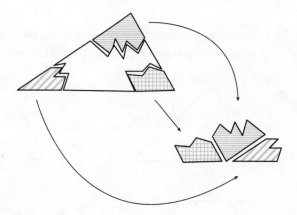

interior angles

The conjecture about the sum of the interior angles of a triangle can be proven so it can be stated as a theorem. In the proof, you will add an *auxiliary line* to the triangle figure. An **auxiliary line** is a line that is added to a figure to aid in a proof.

The Triangle Sum Theorem
The sum of the angle measures of a triangle is 180°.

(D) Fill in the blanks to complete the proof of the Triangle Sum Theorem.

Given: △ABC

Prove: $m\angle 1 + m\angle 2 + m\angle 3 = 180°$

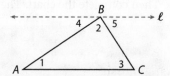

Statements	Reasons
1. Draw line ℓ through point *B* parallel to $\overline{AC}$.	**1.** Parallel Postulate
2. $m\angle 1 = m\angle$ _____ and $m\angle 3 = m\angle$ _____	**2.**
3. $m\angle 4 + m\angle 2 + m\angle 5 = 180°$	**3.** Angle Addition Postulate and definition of straight angle
4. $m\angle$ _____ $+ m\angle 2 + m\angle$ _____ $= 180°$	**4.**

1. Explain how the Parallel Postulate allows you to add the auxiliary line into the triangle figure.

_____

_____

2. What does the Triangle Sum Theorem indicate about the angles of a triangle that has three angles of equal measure? How do you know?

_____

_____

⊘ Explore 2 Exploring Interior Angles in Polygons

To determine the sum of the interior angles for any polygon, you can use what you know about the Triangle Sum Theorem by considering how many triangles there are in other polygons. For example, by drawing the diagonal from a vertex of a quadrilateral, you can form two triangles. Since each triangle has an angle sum of 180°, the quadrilateral must have an angle sum of 180° + 180° = 360°.

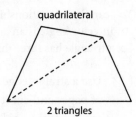
quadrilateral

2 triangles

(A) Draw the diagonals from any one vertex for each polygon. Then state the number of triangles that are formed. The first two have already been completed.

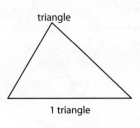
triangle

1 triangle

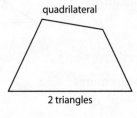
quadrilateral

2 triangles

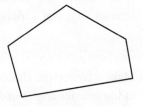

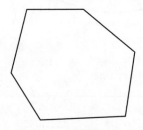

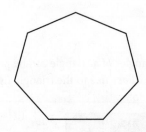

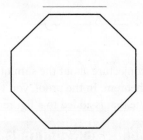

(B) For each polygon, identify the number of sides and triangles, and determine the angle sums. Then complete the chart. The first two have already been done for you.

Polygon	Number of Sides	Number of Triangles	Sum of Interior Angle Measures
Triangle	3	1	(1)180° = 180°
Quadrilateral	4	2	(2)180° = 360°
Pentagon			(___) 180° = _____
Hexagon			(___) 180° = _____
Decagon			(___) 180° = _____

(C) Do you notice a pattern between the number of sides and the number of triangles? If *n* represents the number of sides for any polygon, how can you represent the number of triangles? _____

(D) Make a conjecture for a rule that would give the sum of the interior angles for any *n*-gon.

Sum of interior angle measures = _____

Reflect

3. In a regular hexagon, how could you use the sum of the interior angles to determine the measure of each interior angle?

_____

_____

4. How might you determine the number of sides for a polygon whose interior angle sum is 3240°?

_____

🔑 Explain 1   Using Interior Angles

You can use the angle sum to determine the unknown measure of an angle of a polygon when you know the measures of the other angles.

Polygon Angle Sum Theorem

The sum of the measures of the interior angles of a convex polygon with *n* sides is $(n - 2)180°$.

Example 1   Determine the unknown angle measures.

(A) For the nonagon shown, find the unknown angle measure $x°$.

First, use the Polygon Angle Sum Theorem to find the sum of the interior angles:

$n = 9$

$(n - 2)180° = (9 - 2)180° = (7)180° = 1260°$

Then solve for the unknown angle measure, $x°$:

$125 + 130 + 172 + 98 + 200 + 102 + 140 + 135 + x = 1260$

$$x = 158$$

The unknown angle measure is 158°.

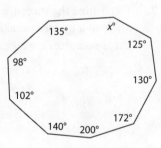

(B) Determine the unknown interior angle measure of a convex octagon in which the measures of the seven other angles have a sum of 940°.

$n = \boxed{}$

$\text{Sum} = \left(\boxed{} - 2 \right) 180° = \left(\boxed{} \right) 180° = \boxed{}$

$\boxed{} + x = \boxed{}$

$x = \boxed{}$

The unknown angle measure is _____.

Reflect

5. How might you use the Polygon Angle Sum Theorem to write a rule for determining the measure of each interior angle of any regular convex polygon with n sides?

_____

_____

Your Turn

6. Determine the unknown angle measures in this pentagon.

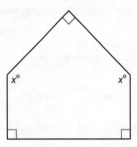

7. Determine the measure of the fourth interior angle of a quadrilateral if you know the other three measures are 89°, 80°, and 104°.

8. Determine the unknown angle measures in a hexagon whose six angles measure 69°, 108°, 135°, 204°, $b°$, and $2b°$.

⏺ Explain 2　Proving the Exterior Angle Theorem

An **exterior angle** is an angle formed by one side of a polygon and the extension of an adjacent side. Exterior angles form linear pairs with the interior angles.

A **remote interior angle** is an interior angle that is not adjacent to the exterior angle.

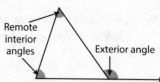

Example 2　Follow the steps to investigate the relationship between each exterior angle of a triangle and its remote interior angles.

Step 1　Use a straightedge to draw a triangle with angles 1, 2, and 3. Line up your straightedge along the side opposite angle 2. Extend the side from the vertex at angle 3. You have just constructed an exterior angle. The exterior angle is drawn *supplementary* to its adjacent interior angle.

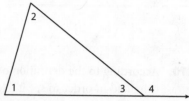

Step 2　You know the sum of the measures of the interior angles of a triangle.

$$m\angle 1 + m\angle 2 + m\angle 3 = \boxed{}°$$

Since an exterior angle is supplementary to its adjacent interior angle, you also know:

$$m\angle 3 + m\angle 4 = \boxed{}°$$

Make a conjecture: What can you say about the measure of the exterior angle and the measures of its remote interior angles?

Conjecture: _____

_____

The conjecture you made in Step 2 can be formally stated as a theorem.

Exterior Angle Theorem
The measure of an exterior angle of a triangle is equal to the sum of the measures of its remote interior angles.

Step 3　Complete the proof of the Exterior Angle Theorem.

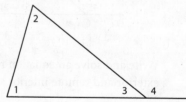

∠4 is an exterior angle. It forms a linear pair with interior angle ∠3. Its remote interior angles are ∠1 and ∠2.

By the _____, $m\angle 1 + m\angle 2 + m\angle 3 = 180°$.

Also, $m\angle 3 + m\angle 4 =$ _____ because they are supplementary and make a straight angle.

By the Substitution Property of Equality, then, $m\angle 1 + m\angle 2 + m\angle 3 = m\angle\_\_\_\_ + m\angle\_\_\_\_$.

Subtracting m∠3 from each side of this equation leaves _____.

This means that the measure of an exterior angle of a triangle is equal to the sum of the measures of the remote interior angles.

9. Discussion Determine the measure of each exterior angle. Add them together. What can you say about their sum? Explain.

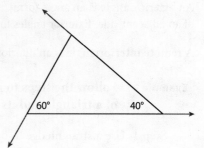

_____

_____

_____

_____

10. According to the definition of an exterior angle, one of the sides of the triangle must be extended in order to see it. How many ways can this be done for any vertex? How many exterior angles is it possible to draw for a triangle? for a hexagon?

_____

_____

🗝 Explain 3 Using Exterior Angles

You can apply the Exterior Angle Theorem to solve problems with unknown angle measures by writing and solving equations.

Example 3 Determine the measure of the specified angle.

(A) Find m∠B.

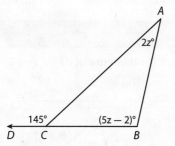

(B) Find m∠PRS.

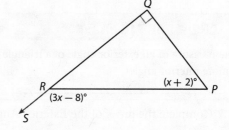

Write and solve an equation relating the exterior and remote interior angles.

$145 = 2z + 5z - 2$

$145 = 7z - 2$

$z = 21$

Now use this value for the unknown to evaluate the expression for the required angle.

$m\angle B = (5z - 2)° = (5(21) - 2)°$

$= (105 - 2)°$

$= 103°$

Write an equation relating the exterior and remote interior angles.

_____

Solve for the unknown.   _____

_____

_____

Use the value for the unknown to evaluate the expression for the required angle.

_____

Determine the measure of the specified angle.

11. Determine m∠N in △MNP.

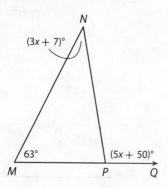

12. If the exterior angle drawn measures 150°, and the measure of ∠D is twice that of ∠E, find the measure of the two remote interior angles.

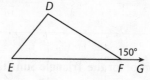

💬 Elaborate

13. In your own words, state the Polygon Angle Sum Theorem. How does it help you find unknown angle measures in polygons?

_____

_____

_____

14. When will an exterior angle be acute? Can a triangle have more than one acute exterior angle? Describe the triangle that tests this.

_____

_____

15. **Essential Question Check-In** Summarize the rules you have discovered about the interior and exterior angles of triangles and polygons.

_____

_____

_____

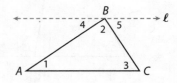

1. Consider the Triangle Sum Theorem in relation to a right triangle. What conjecture can you make about the two acute angles of a right triangle? Explain your reasoning.

2. Complete a flow proof for the Triangle Sum Theorem.

Given △ABC

Prove m∠1 + m∠2 + m∠3 = 180°

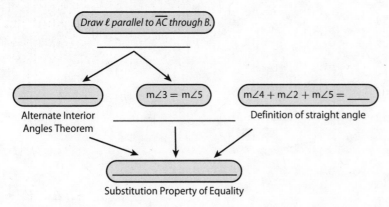

3. Given a polygon with 13 sides, find the sum of the measures of its interior angles.

4. A polygon has an interior angle sum of 3060°. How many sides must the polygon have?

5. Two of the angles in a triangle measure 50° and 27°. Find the measure of the third angle.

Solve for the unknown angle measures of the polygon.

6. A pentagon has angle measures of 100°, 105°, 110° and 115°. Find the fifth angle measure.

7. The measures of 13 angles of a 14-gon add up to 2014°. Find the fourteenth angle measure?

8. Determine the unknown angle measures for the quadrilateral in the diagram.

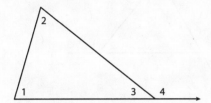

9. The cross-section of a beehive reveals it is made of regular hexagons. What is the measure of each angle in the regular hexagon?

10. Create a flow proof for the Exterior Angle Theorem.

Find the value of the variable to find the unknown angle measure(s).

11. Find *w* to find the measure of the exterior angle.

12. Find *x* to find the measure of the remote interior angle.

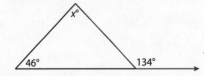

13. Find m∠H.

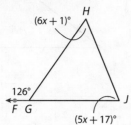

(6x + 1)° H

126°
F G J

(5x + 17)°

14. Determine the measure of the indicated exterior angle in the diagram.

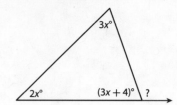

3x°

2x°   (3x + 4)° ?

15. Match each angle with its corresponding measure, given m∠1 = 130° and m∠7 = 70°. Indicate a match by writing the letter for the angle on the line in front of the corresponding angle measure.

A. m∠2   _____ 50°

B. m∠3   _____ 60°

C. m∠4   _____ 70°

D. m∠5   _____ 110°

E. m∠6   _____ 120°

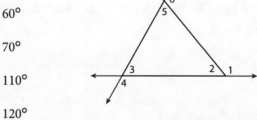

7
6
5

3   2 1
4

16. The map of France commonly used in the 1600s was significantly revised as a result of a triangulation survey. The diagram shows part of the survey map. Use the diagram to find the measure of ∠KMJ .

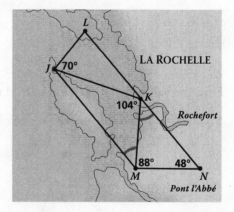

L

J 70°   LA ROCHELLE

K
104°
Rochefort

88° 48°
M   N
Pont l'Abbé

17. An artistic quilt is being designed using computer software. The designer wants to use regular octagons in her design. What interior angle measures should she set in the computer software to create a regular octagon?

18. A ladder propped up against a house makes a 20° angle with the wall. What would be the ladder's angle measure with the ground facing away from the house?

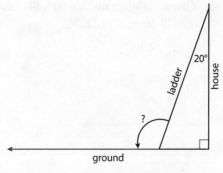

19. Photography The aperture of a camera is made by overlapping blades that form a regular decagon.

a. What is the sum of the measures of the interior angles of the decagon?

b. What would be the measure of each interior angle? each exterior angle?

c. Find the sum of all ten exterior angles.

20. Determine the measure of ∠UXW in the diagram.

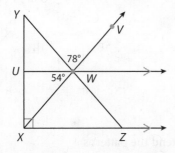

21. Determine the measures of angles x, y, and z.

22. Given the diagram in which $\overrightarrow{BD}$ bisects $\angle ABC$ and $\overrightarrow{CD}$ bisects $\angle ACB$, what is m$\angle BDC$?

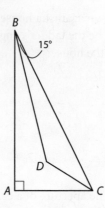

23. **What If?** Suppose you continue the congruent angle construction shown here. What polygon will you construct? Explain.

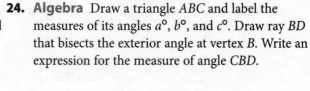

24. **Algebra** Draw a triangle ABC and label the measures of its angles $a°$, $b°$, and $c°$. Draw ray BD that bisects the exterior angle at vertex B. Write an expression for the measure of angle CBD.

25. **Look for a Pattern** Find patterns within this table of data and extend the patterns to complete the remainder of the table. What conjecture can you make about polygon exterior angles from Column 5?

Column 1 Number of Sides	Column 2 Sum of the Measures of the Interior Angles	Column 3 Average Measure of an Interior Angle	Column 4 Average Measure of an Exterior Angle	Column 5 Sum of the Measures of the Exterior Angles
3	180°	60°	120°	120°(3) =
4	360°	90°	90°	90°(4) =
5	540°	108°		
6		120°		

Conjecture:

26. Explain the Error Find and explain what this student did incorrectly when solving the following problem.

What type of polygon would have an interior angle sum of 1260°?

$$1260 = (n - 2)180$$
$$7 = n - 2$$
$$5 = n$$

The polygon is a pentagon.

H.O.T. Focus on Higher Order Thinking

27. Communicate Mathematical Ideas Explain why if two angles of one triangle are congruent to two angles of another triangle, then the third pair of angles are also congruent.

Given: $\angle L \cong \angle R$, $\angle M \cong \angle S$

Prove: $\angle N \cong \angle T$

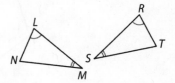

28. Analyze Relationships Consider a right triangle. How would you describe the measures of its exterior angles? Explain.

29. Look for a Pattern In investigating different polygons, diagonals were drawn from a vertex to break the polygon into triangles. Recall that the number of triangles is always two less than the number of sides. But diagonals can be drawn from all vertices. Make a table where you compare the number of sides of a polygon with how many diagonals can be drawn (from all the vertices). Can you find a pattern in this table?

Lesson Performance Task

You've been asked to design the board for a new game called Pentagons. The board consists of a repeating pattern of regular pentagons, a portion of which is shown in the illustration. When you write the specifications for the company that will make the board, you include the measurements of ∠BAD, ∠ABC, ∠BCD and ∠ADC. Find the measures of those angles and explain how you found them.

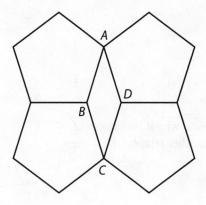

22.2 Isosceles and Equilateral Triangles

Essential Question: What are the special relationships among angles and sides in isosceles and equilateral triangles?

◎ Explore   Investigating Isosceles Triangles

An **isosceles triangle** is a triangle with at least two congruent sides.

The congruent sides are called the **legs** of the triangle.

The angle formed by the legs is the **vertex angle**.

The side opposite the vertex angle is the **base**.

The angles that have the base as a side are the **base angles**.

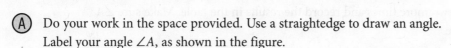

In this activity, you will construct isosceles triangles and investigate other potential characteristics/properties of these special triangles.

Ⓐ   Do your work in the space provided. Use a straightedge to draw an angle. Label your angle ∠A, as shown in the figure.

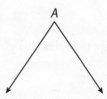

Ⓑ   Using a compass, place the point on the vertex and draw an arc that intersects the sides of the angle. Label the points *B* and *C*.

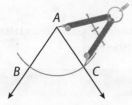

(C) Use the straightedge to draw line segment $\overline{BC}$.

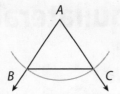

(D) Use a protractor to measure each angle. Record the measures in the table under the column for Triangle 1.

	Triangle 1	Triangle 2	Triangle 3	Triangle 4
m∠A				
m∠B				
m∠C				

(E) Repeat steps A–D at least two more times and record the results in the table. Make sure ∠A is a different size each time.

Reflect

1. How do you know the triangles you constructed are isosceles triangles?

2. **Make a Conjecture** Looking at your results, what conjecture can be made about the base angles, ∠B and ∠C?

✪ Explain 1   Proving the Isosceles Triangle Theorem and Its Converse

In the Explore, you made a conjecture that the base angles of an isosceles triangle are congruent. This conjecture can be proven so it can be stated as a theorem.

Isosceles Triangle Theorem

If two sides of a triangle are congruent, then the two angles opposite the sides are congruent.

This theorem is sometimes called the Base Angles Theorem and can also be stated as "Base angles of an isosceles triangle are congruent."

Example 1 Prove the Isosceles Triangle Theorem and its converse.

Step 1 Complete the proof of the Isosceles Triangle Theorem.

Given: $\overline{AB} \cong \overline{AC}$

Prove: $\angle B \cong \angle C$

Statements	Reasons
1. $\overline{BA} \cong \overline{CA}$	1. Given
2. $\angle A \cong \angle A$	2.
3. $\overline{CA} \cong \overline{BA}$	3. Symmetric Property of Equality
4. $\triangle BAC \cong \triangle CAB$	4.
5.	5. CPCTC

Step 2 Complete the statement of the Converse of the Isosceles Triangle Theorem.

If two _____ of a _____ are congruent, then the two _____ opposite

those _____ are _____ .

Step 3 Complete the proof of the Converse of the Isosceles Triangle Theorem.

Given: $\angle B \cong \angle C$

Prove: $\overline{AB} \cong \overline{AC}$

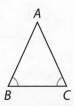

Statements	Reasons
1. $\angle ABC \cong \angle ACB$	1. Given
2.	2. Reflexive Property of Congruence
3. $\angle \quad \cong \angle ABC$	3. Symmetric Property of Equality
4. $\triangle ABC \cong \triangle$	4.
5. $\overline{AB} \cong \overline{AC}$	5.

Reflect

3. **Discussion** In the proofs of the Isosceles Triangle Theorem and its converse, how might it help to sketch a reflection of the given triangle next to the original triangle, so that vertex *B* is on the right?

_____

_____

Proving the Equilateral Triangle Theorem and Its Converse

An **equilateral triangle** is a triangle with three congruent sides.

An **equiangular triangle** is a triangle with three congruent angles.

Equilateral Triangle Theorem
If a triangle is equilateral, then it is equiangular.

Example 2 Prove the Equilateral Triangle Theorem and its converse.

Step 1 Complete the proof of the Equilateral Triangle Theorem.

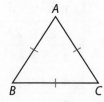

Given: $\overline{AB} \cong \overline{AC} \cong \overline{BC}$
Prove: $\angle A \cong \angle B \cong \angle C$

Given that $\overline{AB} \cong \overline{AC}$ we know that $\angle B \cong \angle$ _____ by the

_____.

It is also known that $\angle A \cong \angle B$ by the Isosceles Triangle Theorem, since _____.

Therefore, $\angle A \cong \angle C$ by _____.

Finally, $\angle A \cong \angle B \cong \angle C$ by the _____ Property of Congruence.

The converse of the Equilateral Triangle Theorem is also true.

Converse of the Equilateral Triangle Theorem
If a triangle is equiangular, then it is equilateral.

Step 2 Complete the proof of the Converse of the Equilateral Triangle Theorem.

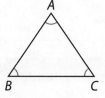

Given: $\angle A \cong \angle B \cong \angle C$

Prove: $\overline{AB} \cong \overline{AC} \cong \overline{BC}$

Because $\angle B \cong \angle C$, $\overline{AB} \cong$ ☐ by the

_____.

$\overline{AC} \cong \overline{BC}$ by the Converse of the Isosceles Triangle Theorem because

☐ $\cong \angle B$.

Thus, by the Transitive Property of Congruence, _____, and therefore, $\overline{AB} \cong \overline{AC} \cong \overline{BC}$.

Reflect

4. To prove the Equilateral Triangle Theorem, you applied the theorems of isosceles triangles. What can be concluded about the relationship between equilateral triangles and isosceles triangles?

© Houghton Mifflin Harcourt Publishing Company

🎸 Explain 3   Using Properties of Isosceles and Equilateral Triangles

You can use the properties of isosceles and equilateral triangles to solve problems involving these theorems.

Example 3   Find the indicated measure.

Ⓐ Katie is stitching the center inlay onto a banner that she created to represent her new tutorial service. It is an equilateral triangle with the following dimensions in centimeters. What is the length of each side of the triangle?

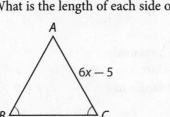

To find the length of each side of the triangle, first find the value of x.

$\overline{AC} \cong \overline{BC}$	Converse of the Equilateral Triangle Theorem
$AC = BC$	Definition of congruence
$6x - 5 = 4x + 7$	Substitution Property of Equality
$x = 6$	Solve for x.

Substitute 6 for x into either $6x - 5$ or $4x + 7$.

$$6(6) - 5 = 36 - 5 = 31 \quad \text{or} \quad 4(6) + 7 = 24 + 7 = 31$$

So, the length of each side of the triangle is 31 cm.

Ⓑ m∠T

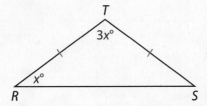

To find the measure of the vertex angle of the triangle, first find the value of _____.

$m\angle R = m\angle S = x°$		Theorem
$m\angle R + m\angle S + \boxed{} = 180°$		Triangle Sum Theorem
$x + x + 3x = 180$		Substitution Property of Equality
$\boxed{} = 180$		Addition Property of Equality
$x = \boxed{}$	$\boxed{}$	Property of Equality

So, $m\angle T = 3x° = 3\left(\boxed{}\right)° = \boxed{}°$.

5. Find m∠P.

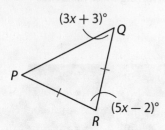

6. Katie's tutorial service is going so well that she is having shirts made with the equilateral triangle emblem. She has given the t-shirt company these dimensions. What is the length of each side of the triangle in centimeters?

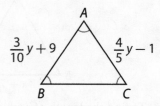

Elaborate

7. **Discussion** Consider the vertex and base angles of an isosceles triangle. Can they be right angles? Can they be obtuse? Explain.

_____

_____

_____

_____

_____

8. **Essential Question Check-In** Discuss how the sides of an isosceles triangle relate to its angles.

_____

_____

_____

1. Use a straightedge. Draw a line. Draw an acute angle with vertex *A* along the line. Then use a compass to copy the angle. Place the compass point at another point *B* along the line and draw the copied angle so that the angle faces the original angle. Label the intersection of the angle sides as point *C*. Look at the triangle you have formed. What is true about the two base angles of $\triangle ABC$? What do you know about $\overline{CA}$ and $\overline{CB}$? What kind of triangle did you form? Explain your reasoning.

2. Prove the Isosceles Triangle Theorem as a paragraph proof.

   Given: $\overline{AB} \cong \overline{AC}$

   Prove: $\angle B \cong \angle C$

3. Complete the flow proof of the Equilateral Triangle Theorem.

   Given: $\overline{AB} \cong \overline{AC} \cong \overline{BC}$

   Prove: $\angle A \cong \angle B \cong \angle C$

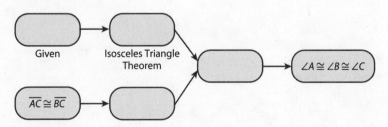

Find the measure of the indicated angle.

4. m∠A

5. m∠R

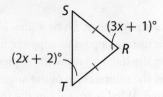

6. m∠O

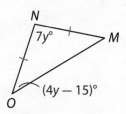

7. m∠E

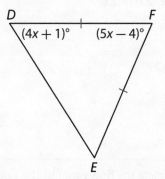

Find the length of the indicated side.

8. $\overline{DE}$

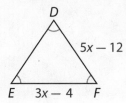

9. $\overline{KL}$

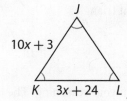

10. $\overline{AB}$

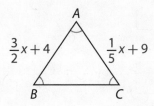

11. $\overline{BC}$

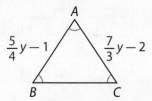

12. Given $\triangle JKL$ with m$\angle J = 63°$ and m$\angle L = 54°$, is the triangle an acute, isosceles, obtuse, or right triangle?

13. Find x. Explain your reasoning. The horizontal lines are parallel.

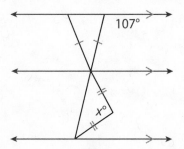

14. Summarize Complete the diagram to show the cause and effect of the theorems covered in the lesson. Explain why the arrows show the direction going both ways.

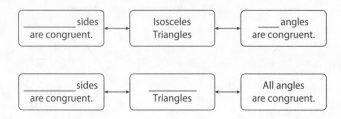

15. A plane is flying parallel to the ground along $\overrightarrow{AC}$. When the plane is at A, an air-traffic controller in tower T measures the angle to the plane as 40°. After the plane has traveled 2.4 miles to B, the angle to the plane is 80°. How can you find BT?

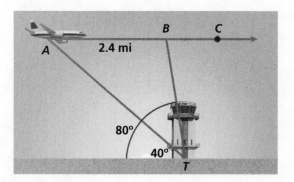

16. John is building a doghouse. He decides to use the roof truss design shown. If m∠DBF = 35°, what is the measure of the vertex angle of the isosceles triangle?

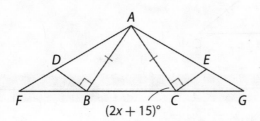

17. The measure of the vertex angle of an isosceles triangle is 12 more than 5 times the measure of a base angle. Determine the sum of the measures of the base angles.

18. Justify Reasoning Determine whether each of the following statements is true or false. Select the correct answer for each lettered part. Explain your reasoning.

    a. All isosceles triangles have at least two acute angles.   ◯ True ◯ False

    b. If the perimeter of an equilateral triangle is P, then the length of each of its sides is $\frac{P}{3}$.   ◯ True ◯ False

    c. All isosceles triangles are equilateral triangles.   ◯ True ◯ False

    d. If you know the length of one of the legs of an isosceles triangle, you can determine its perimeter.   ◯ True ◯ False

    e. The exterior angle of an equilateral triangle is obtuse.   ◯ True ◯ False

19. Critical Thinking Prove $\angle B \cong \angle C$, given point M is the midpoint of $\overline{BC}$.

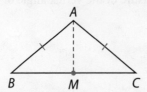

Statements	Reasons

20. Given that $\triangle ABC$ is an isosceles triangle and $\overline{AD}$ and $\overline{CD}$ are angle bisectors, what is m$\angle ADC$?

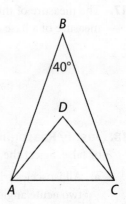

21. Analyze Relationships Isosceles right triangle ABC has a right angle at B and $\overline{AB} \cong \overline{CB}$. $\overline{BD}$ bisects angle B, and point D is on $\overline{AC}$. If $\overline{BD} \perp \overline{AC}$, describe triangles ABD and CBD. Explain. HINT: Draw a diagram.

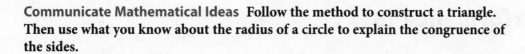

Communicate Mathematical Ideas Follow the method to construct a triangle. Then use what you know about the radius of a circle to explain the congruence of the sides.

22. Construct an isosceles triangle. Explain how you know that two sides are congruent.
   • Use a compass to draw a circle. Mark two different points on the circle.
   • Use a straightedge to draw a line segment from the center of the circle to each of the two points on the circle (radii).
   • Draw a line segment (chord) between the two points on the circle.

I know two sides are congruent because _____

_____

_____

23. Construct an equilateral triangle. Explain how you know the three sides are congruent.
   • Use a compass to draw a circle.
   • Draw another circle of the same size that goes through the center of the first circle. (Both should have the same radius length.)
   • Mark one point where the circles intersect.
   • Use a straightedge to draw line segments connecting both centers to each other and to the intersection point.

I know the three sides are congruent because _____

_____

_____

_____

_____

Lesson Performance Task

The control tower at airport *A* is in contact with an airplane flying at point *P*, when it is
5 miles from the airport, and 30 seconds later when it is at point *Q*, 4 miles from the airport.
The diagram shows the angles the plane makes with the ground at both times. If the plane flies
parallel to the ground from *P* to *Q* at constant speed, how fast is it traveling?

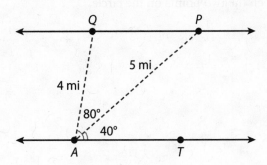

22.3 Triangle Inequalities

Essential Question: How can you use inequalities to describe the relationships among side lengths and angle measures in a triangle?

Resource
Locker

⊘ Explore   Exploring Triangle Inequalities

A triangle can have sides of different lengths, but are there limits to the lengths of any of the sides?

(A) Consider a △ABC where you know two side lengths, AB = 4 inches and BC = 2 inches. On a separate piece of paper, draw $\overline{AB}$ so that it is 4 inches long.

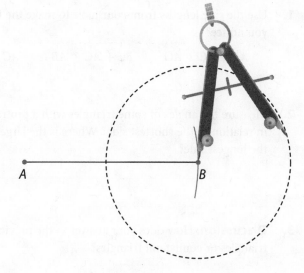

(B) To determine all possible locations for C with $\overline{BC}$ = 2 inches, set your compass to 2 inches. Draw a circle with center at B.

(C) Choose and label a final vertex point C so it is located on the circle. Using a straightedge, draw the segments to form a triangle.

Are there any places on the circle where point C cannot lie? Explain.

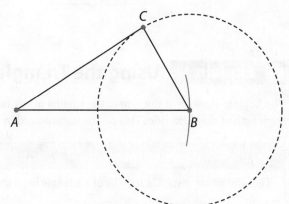

_____

_____

_____

(D) Measure and record the lengths of the three sides of your triangle.

(E) The figures below show two other examples of $\triangle ABC$ that could have been formed. What are the values that $\overline{AC}$ approaches when point C approaches $\overline{AB}$?

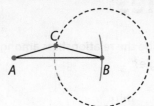 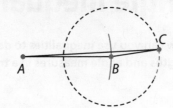

Reflect

1. Use the side lengths from your table to make the following comparisons. What do you notice?

$$AB + BC \; ? \; AC \qquad BC + AC \; ? \; AB \qquad AC + AB \; ? \; BC$$

2. Measure the angles of some triangles with a protractor. Where is the smallest angle in relation to the shortest side? Where is the largest angle in relation to the longest side?

3. **Discussion** How does your answer to the previous question relate to isosceles triangles or equilateral triangles?

🔑 Explain 1 Using the Triangle Inequality Theorem

The Explore shows that the sum of the lengths of any two sides of a triangle is greater than the length of the third side. This can be summarized in the following theorem.

Triangle Inequality Theorem

The sum of any two side lengths of a triangle is greater than the third side length.

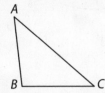

$$AB + BC > AC$$

$$BC + AC > AB$$

$$AC + AB > BC$$

To be able to form a triangle, each of the three inequalities must be true. So, given three side lengths, you can test to determine if they can be used as segments to form a triangle. To show that three lengths cannot be the side lengths of a triangle, you only need to show that one of the three triangle inequalities is false.

Example 1 Use the Triangle Inequality Theorem to tell whether a triangle can have sides with the given lengths. Explain.

Ⓐ 4, 8, 10

$$4 + 8 \overset{?}{>} 10 \qquad 4 + 10 \overset{?}{>} 8 \qquad 8 + 10 \overset{?}{>} 4$$

$$12 > 10 \checkmark \qquad 14 > 8 \checkmark \qquad 18 > 4 \checkmark$$

Conclusion: The sum of each pair of side lengths is greater than the third length. So, a triangle can have side lengths of 4, 8, and 10.

Ⓑ 7, 9, 18

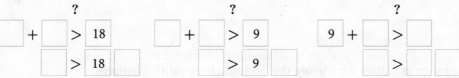

Conclusion:

_____

Reflect

4. Can an isosceles triangle have these side lengths? Explain. 5, 5, 10

_____

_____

5. How do you know that the Triangle Inequality Theorem applies to all equilateral triangles?

_____

_____

Your Turn

Determine if a triangle can be formed with the given side lengths. Explain your reasoning.

6. 12 units, 4 units, 17 units

7. 24 cm, 8 cm, 30 cm

Finding Possible Side Lengths in a Triangle

From the Explore, you have seen that if given two side lengths for a triangle, there are an infinite number of side lengths available for the third side. But the third side is also restricted to values determined by the Triangle Inequality Theorem.

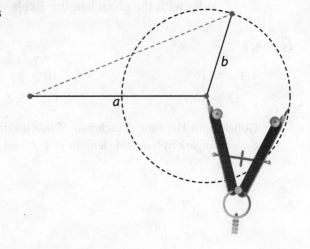

Example 2   Find the range of values for x using the Triangle Inequality Theorem.

(A)   Find possible values for the length of the third side using the Triangle Inequality Theorem.

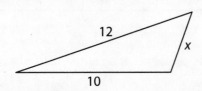

$$x + 10 > 12 \qquad\qquad x + 12 > 10 \qquad\qquad 10 + 12 > x$$
$$x > 2 \qquad\qquad\qquad x > -2 \qquad\qquad\quad 22 > x$$

$$2 < x < 22$$

Ignore the inequality with a negative value, since a triangle cannot have a negative side length. Combine the other two inequalities to find the possible values for x.

(B)

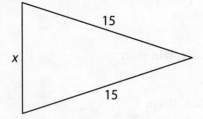

$$\boxed{} < x < \boxed{}$$

Reflect

8. **Discussion** Suppose you know that the length of the base of an isosceles triangle is 10, but you do not know the lengths of its legs. How could you use the Triangle Inequality Theorem to find the range of possible lengths for each leg? Explain.

_____

_____

_____

_____

Your Turn

Find the range of values for *x* using the Triangle Inequality Theorem.

9.

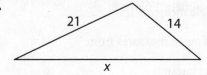

10.

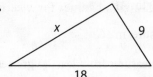

🔑 **Explain 3**   **Ordering a Triangle's Angle Measures Given Its Side Lengths**

From the Explore Step D, you can see that changing the length of $\overline{AC}$ also changes the measure of $\angle B$ in a predictable way.

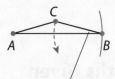

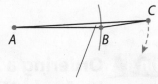

As side *AC* gets shorter, m∠*B* approaches 0°   As side *AC* gets longer, m∠*B* approaches 180°

Side-Angle Relationships in Triangles
If two sides of a triangle are not congruent, then the larger angle is opposite the longer side.

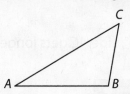

$AC > BC$
m∠B > m∠A

Example 3   **For each triangle, order its angle measures from least to greatest.**

Ⓐ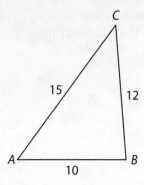

Longest side length: *AC*

Greatest angle measure: m∠*B*

Shortest side length: *AB*

Least angle measure: m∠*C*

Order of angle measures from least to greatest:
m∠*C*, m∠*A*, m∠*B*

Ⓑ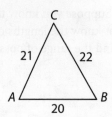

Longest side length: _____

Greatest angle measure: _____

Shortest side length: _____

Least angle measure: _____

Order of angle measures from

least to greatest: _____

For each triangle, order its angle measures from least to greatest.

11.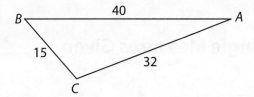

12.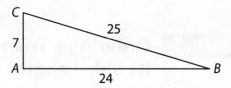

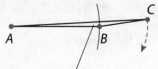 **Explain 4**   **Ordering a Triangle's Side Lengths Given Its Angle Measures**

From the Explore Step D, you can see that changing the the measure of ∠*B* also changes length of $\overline{AC}$ in a predictable way.

As m∠*B* approaches 0°, side *AC* gets shorter   As m∠*B* approaches 180°, side *AC* gets longer

---

Angle-Side Relationships in Triangles

If two angles of a triangle are not congruent, then the longer side is opposite the larger angle.

© Houghton Mifflin Harcourt Publishing Company

Example 4 For each triangle, order the side lengths from least to greatest.

(A)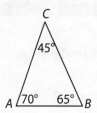

Greatest angle measure: m∠B

Longest side length: *AC*

Least angle measure: m∠A

Shortest side length: *BC*

Order of side lengths from least to greatest: *BC, AB, AC*

(B)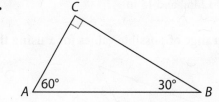

Greatest angle measure: _____

Longest side length: _____

Least angle measure: _____

Shortest side length: _____

Order of side lengths from least

to great: _____

Your Turn

For each triangle, order the side lengths from least to greatest.

13.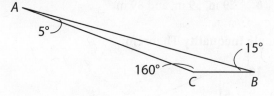

14.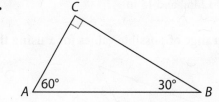

💬 Elaborate

15. When two sides of a triangle are congruent, what can you conclude about the angles opposite those sides?

_____

16. What can you conclude about the side opposite the obtuse angle in an obtuse triangle?

_____

17. **Essential Question Check-In** Suppose you are given three values that could represent the side lengths of a triangle. How can you use one inequality to determine if the triangle exists?

_____
_____

• Online Homework
• Hints and Help
• Extra Practice

Use a compass and straightedge to decide whether each set of lengths can form a triangle.

1. 7 cm, 9 cm, 18 cm

2. 2 in., 4 in., 5 in.

3. 1 in., 2 in., 10 in.

4. 9 cm, 10 cm, 11 cm

Determine whether a triangle can be formed with the given side lengths.

5. 10 ft, 3 ft, 15 ft

6. 12 in., 4 in., 15 in.

7. 9 in., 12 in., and 18 in.

8. 29 m, 59 m, and 89 m

Find the range of possible values for *x* using the Triangle Inequality Theorem.

9.

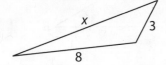

10.

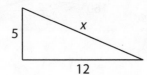

11. A triangle with side lengths 22.3, 27.6, and *x*

12. **Analyze Relationships** Suppose a triangle has side lengths AB, BC, and x, where $AB = 2 \cdot BC$. Find the possible range for x in terms of BC.

For each triangle, write to order the angle measures from least to greatest.

13.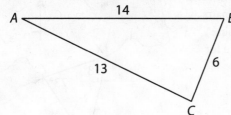

14.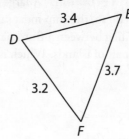

15. **Analyze Relationships** Suppose a triangle has side lengths *PQ*, *QR*, and *PR*, where *PR* = 2*PQ* = 3*QR*. Write the angle measures in order from least to greatest.

For each triangle, write the side lengths in order from least to greatest.

16.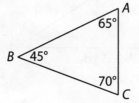

17.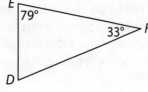

18. In △*JKL*, m∠*J* = 53°, m∠*K* = 68°, and m∠*L* = 59°.

19. In △*PQR*, m∠*P* = 102° and m∠*Q* = 25°.

20. **Represent Real-World Problems** Rhonda is traveling from New York City to Paris and is trying to decide whether to fly via Frankfurt or to get a more expensive direct flight. Given that it is 3,857 miles from New York City to Frankfurt and another 278 miles from Frankfurt to Paris, what is the range of possible values for the direct distance from New York City to Paris?

21. Represent Real-World Problems A large ship is sailing between three small islands. To do so, the ship must sail between two pairs of islands, avoiding sailing between a third pair. The safest route is to avoid the closest pair of islands. Which is the safest route for the ship?

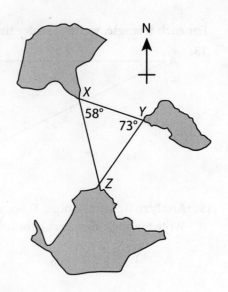

22. Represent Real-World Problems A hole on a golf course is a dogleg, meaning that it bends in the middle. A golfer will usually start by driving for the bend in the dogleg (from A to B), and then using a second shot to get the ball to the green (from B to C). Sandy believes she may be able to drive the ball far enough to reach the green in one shot, avoiding the bend (from A direct to C). Sandy knows she can accurately drive a distance of 250 yd. Should she attempt to drive for the green on her first shot? Explain.

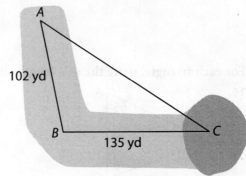

23. Represent Real-World Problems Three cell phone towers form a triangle, $\triangle PQR$. The measure of $\angle Q$ is 10° less than the measure of $\angle P$. The measure of $\angle R$ is 5° greater than the measure of $\angle Q$. Which two towers are closest together?

24. Algebra In $\triangle PQR$, $PQ = 3x + 1$, $QR = 2x - 2$, and $PR = x + 7$. Determine the range of possible values of x.

25. In any triangle ABC, suppose you know the lengths of $\overline{AB}$ and $\overline{BC}$, and suppose that $AB > BC$. If x is the length of the third side, $\overline{AC}$, use the Triangle Inequality Theorem to prove that $AB - BC < x < AB + BC$. That is, x must be between the difference and the sum of the other two side lengths. Explain why this result makes sense in terms of the constructions shown in the figure.

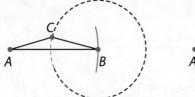
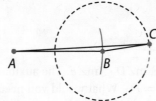

26. Given the information in the diagram, prove that $m\angle DEA < m\angle ABC$.

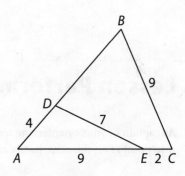

27. An isosceles triangle has legs with length 11 units. Which of the following could be the perimeter of the triangle? Choose all that apply. Explain your reasoning.

   a. 22 units

   b. 24 units

   c. 34 units

   d. 43 units

   e. 44 units

H.O.T. Focus on Higher Order Thinking

28. Communicate Mathematical Ideas Given the information in the diagram, prove that $PQ < PS$.

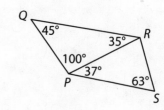

29. Justify Reasoning In obtuse $\triangle ABC$, $m\angle A < m\angle B$. The auxiliary line segment $\overline{CD}$ perpendicular to $\overrightarrow{AB}$ (extended beyond B) creates right triangles ADC and BDC. Describe how you could use the Pythagorean Theorem to prove that $BC < AC$.

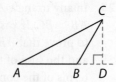

30. Make a Conjecture In acute $\triangle DEF$, $m\angle D < m\angle E$. The auxiliary line segment $\overline{FG}$ creates $\triangle EFG$, where $EF = FG$. What would you need to prove about the points D, G, and E to prove that $\angle DGF$ is obtuse, and therefore that $EF < DF$? Explain.

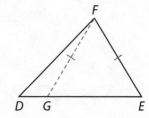

Lesson Performance Task

As captain of your orienteering team, it's your job to map out the shortest distance from point A to point H on the map. Justify each of your decisions.

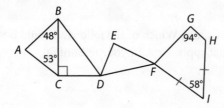

Properties of Triangles

Essential Question: How can you use the properties of triangles to solve real-world problems?

KEY EXAMPLE (Lesson 22.1)

Determine the measure of the fifth interior angle of a pentagon if you know the other four measures are 100°, 50°, 158°, and 147°.

$\text{Sum} = (5 - 2)180° = 540°$	Apply the Polygon Angle Sum Theorem.
$100 + 50 + 158 + 147 + x = 540$	Set the sum of the angle measures equal to 540.
$455 + x = 540$	Solve for x.
$x = 85$	

KEY EXAMPLE (Lesson 22.2)

Given an isosceles triangle $\triangle ABC$ with $\overline{AB} \cong \overline{AC}$, $AB = 4x + 3$, and $AC = 8x - 13$, find AB.

$\overline{AB} \cong \overline{AC}$	Given
$4x + 3 = 8x - 13$	Substitution
$x = 4$	Solve for x.
$AB = 4(4) + 3$	Substitute the value of x into AB.
$AB = 19$	Simplify.

KEY EXAMPLE (Lesson 22.3)

Given a triangle with sides 7, 12, and x, find the range of values for x.

According to the Triangle Inequality Theorem, the sum of any two side lengths of a triangle is greater than the third side length

$7 + 12 > x$	$7 + x > 12$	$x + 12 > 7$	Apply the Triangle Inequality Theorem.
$19 > x$	$x > 5$	$x > -5$	Simplify.
$5 < x < 19$			Combine the inequalities together.

Find how many sides a polygon has with the given interior angle sum. *(Lesson 22.1)*

1. 2700° _____

2. 1800° _____

Find the sum of interior angles a polygon has with the given number of sides.
(Lesson 22.1)

3. 3 _____

4. 19 _____

Given an isosceles triangle $\triangle DEF$ with $\overline{DE} \cong \overline{DF}$, $DE = 26$, and $m\angle F = 45°$, find the desired measurements. *(Lesson 22.2)*

5. $\overline{DF}$ _____

6. $m\angle D$ _____

Determine whether a triangle can have sides with the given lengths. *(Lesson 22.3)*

7. 5 mi, 19 mi, 15 mi _____

8. 4 ft, 3 ft, 10 ft _____

Find the range of the unknown side of a triangle with the given sides. *(Lesson 22.3)*

9. 5 mi, 19 mi, x mi _____

10. 4 ft, 3 ft, x ft _____

MODULE PERFORMANCE TASK

What's Up in the Federal Triangle?

The diagram shows a schematic of the Federal Triangle, an area located in Washington, DC. The area is bounded by Constitution Avenue on the south and Pennsylvania Avenue on the north and extends from 12th Street on the west to just past 6th Street on the east.

Is the shape of the Federal Triangle a triangle? How many sides does the Federal Triangle have? What is the actual shape of the Federal Triangle? What is the sum of the internal angles of the Federal Triangle? What portion of the area is actually a triangle?

Do some research and find the lengths of each side. Find the perimeter and area of the Federal Triangle. Find the area of the portion of the Federal Triangle that is a triangle.

Federal Triangle

22.1–22.3 Properties of Triangles

- Online Homework
- Hints and Help
- Extra Practice

Determine whether a triangle can be formed with the given side lengths. If the side lengths can form a triangle, determine if they will form an isosceles triangle, equilateral triangle, or neither. *(Lessons 22.2, 22.3)*

1. 3 mi, 8 mi, 3 mi

2. 7 cm, 7cm, 7cm

3. 4 ft, 4 ft, 2 ft

4. 20 m, 30 m, 10 m

5. 3 m, 4 m, 5 m

6. 26 yd, 26 yd, 26 yd

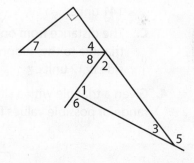

Use the figure to answer the following. *(Lesson 22.1)*

7. Given $m\angle 2 = 76°$, $m\angle 1 = 3 \cdot m\angle 3$, and $\angle 4 \cong \angle 8$, find $m\angle 1$, $m\angle 3$, $m\angle 4$, $m\angle 5$, $m\angle 6$, $m\angle 7$, and $m\angle 8$.

ESSENTIAL QUESTION

8. Is it possible for one angle of a triangle to be 180°? If so, demonstrate with an example. If not, explain why not.

Assessment Readiness

1. Two angles in a triangle have measurements of 34° and 84°.

   Select Yes or No for A–C.

   A. Does the third angle measure 62°? ◯ Yes ◯ No

   B. Could a triangle congruent to this one contain an angle of 75°? ◯ Yes ◯ No

   C. Is this triangle congruent to a right triangle? ◯ Yes ◯ No

2. Consider the following statements about a seven-sided polygon. Choose True or False for each statement.

   A. Each interior angle measures 135°. ◯ True ◯ False

   B. The sum of the measures of the interior angles is 1260°. ◯ True ◯ False

   C. The sum of the measures of the interior angles is 900°. ◯ True ◯ False

3. $\triangle ABC$ is an equilateral triangle, $AB = 4x + 45$, and $BC = 6x - 3$. Choose True or False for each statement.

   A. $x = 24$ ◯ True ◯ False

   B. The length of one side of the triangle is 141 units. ◯ True ◯ False

   C. The distance from one vertex of the triangle to the midpoint of an adjacent side is 12 units. ◯ True ◯ False

4. Given a triangle with a side of length 6 and another side of length 13, find the range of possible values for the third side, x.

5. Given $\triangle DEF$, with $DE = 3EF$ and $DF = 4DE$, explain how to write the sides and angles in order of least to greatest.

© Houghton Mifflin Harcourt Publishing Company

Special Segments in Triangles

Essential Question: How can you use special segments in triangles to solve real-world problems?

REAL WORLD VIDEO
Check out how the properties of triangles can be used by architects and urban planners to solve problems involving the positioning of landmarks.

MODULE PERFORMANCE TASK PREVIEW

Where Is the Heart of the Texas Triangle?

The Texas Triangle is a region with the cities of Dallas, Houston, and San Antonio as the vertices of the triangle. In this module, you will use theorems about triangles to explore the geometry of the region and locate its center.

Are (YOU) Ready?

Complete these exercises to review the skills you will need for this module.

Distance and Midpoint Formulas

Example 1   Find the midpoint between $(7, 1)$ and $(-4, 8)$.

$$\left(\frac{x_1 + x_2}{2}, \frac{y_1 + y_2}{2}\right)$$ Midpoint Formula

$$\left(\frac{7 + (-4)}{2}, \frac{1 + 8}{2}\right)$$ Substitute.

$$\left(\frac{3}{2}, \frac{9}{2}\right)$$ Simplify.

Find each midpoint for the given points.

1. $(2, 3)$ and $(14, 9)$ _____

2. $(-4, 7)$ and $(-1, -11)$ _____

Angle Theorems for Triangles

Example 2   Given that $m\angle a = 72°$ and $m\angle c = 48°$, find the missing angle.

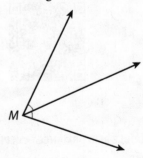

$m\angle a + m\angle b + m\angle c = 180°$ Triangle Sum Theorem

$72° + m\angle b + 48° = 180°$ Substitute.

$m\angle b + 120° = 180°$ Simplify.

$m\angle b = 60°$ Solve for $m\angle b$.

Find the missing angle in the figure from the example for the given values.

3. $m\angle b = 66°$ and $m\angle c = 75°$

_____

4. $m\angle a = 103°$ and $m\angle c = 49°$

_____

Geometric Drawings

Example 3   Use a compass and straightedge to construct the bisector of the given angle.

Angle with Bisector

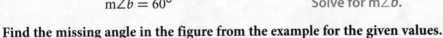

Use a compass and straightedge to construct the bisector of the given angle.

5.

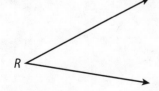

23.1 Perpendicular Bisectors of Triangles

Essential Question: How can you use perpendicular bisectors to find the point that is equidistant from all the vertices of a triangle?

⊘ Explore   Constructing a Circumscribed Circle

A circle that contains all the vertices of a polygon is **circumscribed** about the polygon. In the figure, circle C is circumscribed about △XYZ, and circle C is called the **circumcircle** of △XYZ. The center of the circumcircle is called the **circumcenter** of the triangle.

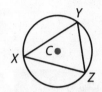

In the following activity, you will construct the circumcircle of △PQR. Copy the triangle onto a separate piece of paper.

Ⓐ The circumcircle will pass through P, Q, and R. So, the center of the circle must be equidistant from all three points. In particular, the center must be equidistant from Q and R.

The set of points that are equidistant from Q and R is called the _____ of $\overline{QR}$.
Use a compass and straightedge to construct the set of points.

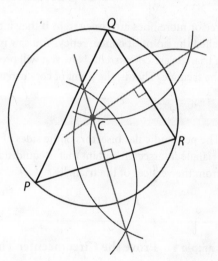

Ⓑ The center must also be equidistant from P and R. The set of points that are equidistant from P and R is called the _____ of $\overline{PR}$. Use a compass and straightedge to construct the set of points.

Ⓒ The center must lie at the intersection of the two sets of points you constructed. Label the point C. Then place the point of your compass at C and open it to distance CP. Draw the circumcircle.

1. **Make a Prediction** Suppose you started by constructing the set of points equidistant from P and Q and then constructed the set of points equidistant from Q and R. Would you have found the same center? Check by doing this construction.

    _____

    _____

    _____

2. Can you locate the circumcenter of a triangle without using a compass and straightedge? Explain.

    _____

    _____

    _____

🔑 Explain 1 Proving the Concurrency of a Triangle's Perpendicular Bisectors

Three or more lines are **concurrent** if they intersect at the same point. The point of intersection is called the **point of concurrency**. You saw in the Explore that the three perpendicular bisectors of a triangle are concurrent. Now you will prove that the point of concurrency is the circumcenter of the triangle. That is, the point of concurrency is equidistant from the vertices of the triangle.

Circumcenter Theorem

The perpendicular bisectors of the sides of a triangle intersect at a point that is equidistant from the vertices of the triangle.

$$PA = PB = PC$$

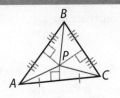

Example 1 **Prove the Circumcenter Theorem.**

Given: Lines ℓ, m, and n are the perpendicular bisectors of $\overline{AB}$, $\overline{BC}$, and $\overline{AC}$, respectively. P is the intersection of ℓ, m, and n.

Prove: $PA = PB = PC$

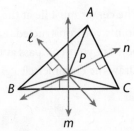

P is the intersection of ℓ, m, and n. Since P lies on the _____

of $\overline{AB}$, $PA = PB$ by the _____ Theorem. Similarly, P lies on

the _____ of $\overline{BC}$, so _____ $= PC$. Therefore, $PA =$ _____ $=$ _____

by the _____ Property of Equality.

3. **Discussion** How might you determine whether the circumcenter of a triangle is always inside the triangle? Make a plan and then determine whether the circumcenter is always inside the triangle.

_____

_____

_____

_____

✏ Explain 2 Using Properties of Perpendicular Bisectors

You can use the Circumcenter Theorem to find segment lengths in a triangle.

Example 2 $\overline{KZ}$, $\overline{LZ}$, and $\overline{MZ}$ are the perpendicular bisectors of $\triangle GHJ$. Use the given information to find the length of each segment. Note that the figure is not drawn to scale.

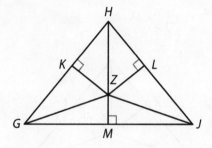

(A) Given: $ZM = 7$, $ZJ = 25$, $HK = 20$

Find: ZH and HG

Z is the circumcenter of $\triangle GHJ$, so $ZG = ZH = ZJ$.

$ZJ = 25$, so $ZH = 25$.

K is the midpoint of $\overline{GH}$, so $HG = 2 \cdot KH = 2 \cdot 20 = 40$.

(B) Given: $ZH = 85$, $MZ = 13$, $HG = 136$

Find: KG and ZJ

K is the _____ of $\overline{HG}$, so $KG = \boxed{}\,HG = \boxed{} \cdot \boxed{} = \boxed{}$.

Z is the _____ of $\triangle GHJ$, so $ZG = \underline{\quad} = \underline{\quad}$.

$ZH = \underline{\quad}$, so $ZJ = \underline{\quad}$.

4. In △ABC, ∠ACB is a right angle and D is the
    circumcenter of the triangle. If CD = 6.5,
    what is AB? Explain your reasoning.

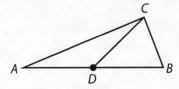

_____

_____

Your Turn

$\overline{KZ}$, $\overline{LZ}$, and $\overline{MZ}$ are the perpendicular bisectors of △GHJ. Copy the sketch and label
the given information. Use that information to find the length of each segment. Note
that the figure is not drawn to scale.

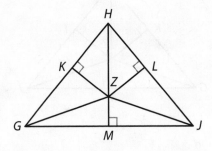

5. Given: ZG = 65, HL = 63, ZL = 16
    Find: GK and ZJ

6. Given: ZM = 25, ZH = 65, GJ = 120
    Find: GM and ZG

⚙ Explain 3 Finding a Circumcenter on a Coordinate Plane

Given the vertices of a triangle, you can graph the triangle and use the graph to find the circumcenter of the triangle.

Example 3 Graph the triangle with the given vertices and find the circumcenter of the triangle.

(A) $R(-6, 0)$, $S(0, 4)$, $O(0, 0)$

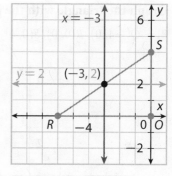

Step 1: Graph the triangle.

Step 2: Find equations for two perpendicular bisectors.

Side $\overline{RO}$ is on the x-axis, so its perpendicular bisector is vertical:

the line $x = -3$.

Side $\overline{SO}$ is on the y-axis, so its perpendicular bisector

is horizontal: the line $y = 2$.

Step 3: Find the intersection of the perpendicular bisectors.

The lines $x = -3$ and $y = 2$ intersect at $(-3, 2)$.

$(-3, 2)$ is the circumcenter of $\triangle ROS$.

(B) $A(-1, 5)$, $B(5, 5)$, $C(5, -1)$

Step 1 Graph the triangle.

Step 2 Find equations for two perpendicular bisectors.

Side $\overline{AB}$ is _____, so its perpendicular bisector

is vertical.

The perpendicular bisector of $\overline{AB}$ is the line _____.

Side $\overline{BC}$ is _____, so the perpendicular bisector of

$\overline{BC}$ is horizontal the line _____.

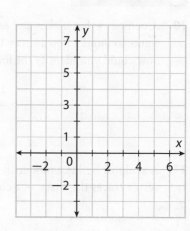

Step 3 Find the intersection of the perpendicular bisectors.

The lines _____ and _____ intersect at _____.

_____ is the circumcenter of $\triangle ABC$.

7. Draw Conclusions Could a vertex of a triangle also be its circumcenter?
If so, provide an example. If not, explain why not.

_____

_____

Graph the triangle with the given vertices and find the circumcenter of the triangle.

8. $Q(-4, 0), R(0, 0), S(0, 6)$

9. $K(1, 1), L(1, 7), M(6, 1)$

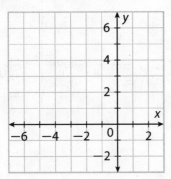

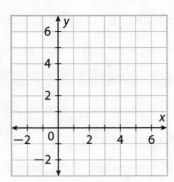

Elaborate

10. A company that makes and sells bicycles has its largest stores in three cities. The company
wants to build a new factory that is equidistant from each of the stores. Given a map,
how could you identify the location for the new factory?

_____

_____

_____

11. A sculptor builds a mobile in which a triangle rotates around its circumcenter. Each
vertex traces the shape of a circle as it rotates. What circle does it trace? Explain.

_____

_____

12. What If? Suppose you are given the vertices of a triangle *PQR*. You plot the points in a coordinate plane and notice that $\overline{PQ}$ is horizontal but neither of the other sides is vertical. How can you identify the circumcenter of the triangle? Justify your reasoning.

_____

_____

_____

_____

13. Essential Question Check-In How is the point that is equidistant from the three vertices of a triangle related to the circumcircle of the triangle?

_____

☆ Evaluate: Homework and Practice

- Online Homework
- Hints and Help
- Extra Practice

Construct the circumcircle of each triangle. Label the circumcenter *P*.

1.

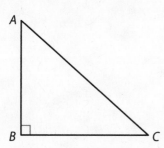

2.

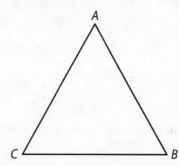

3.

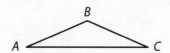

4.

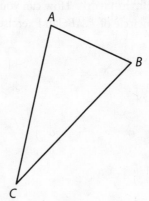

Complete the proof of the Circumcenter Theorem.

Use the diagram for Exercise 5–8. $\overline{ZD}$, $\overline{ZE}$, and $\overline{ZF}$ are the perpendicular bisectors of $\triangle ABC$. Use the given information to find the length of each segment. Note that the figure is not drawn to scale.

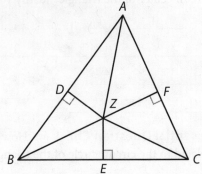

5. Given: $DZ = 40$, $ZA = 85$, $FC = 77$

Find: ZC and AC

6. Given: $FZ = 36$, $ZA = 85$, $AB = 150$

Find: AD and ZB

7. Given: $AZ = 85$, $ZE = 51$

Find: BC

(*Hint*: Use the Pythagorean Theorem.)

8. **Analyze Relationships** How can you write an algebraic expression for the radius of the circumcircle of $\triangle ABC$ in Exercises 6–8? Explain.

Complete the proof of the Circumcenter Theorem.

9. **Given:** Lines ℓ, m, and n are the perpendicular bisectors of $\overline{AB}$, $\overline{BC}$, and $\overline{AC}$, respectively. P is the intersection of ℓ, m, and n.

Prove: $PA = PB = PC$

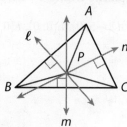

Statements	Reasons
1. Lines ℓ, m, and n are the perpendicular bisectors of $\overline{AB}$, $\overline{BC}$, and $\overline{AC}$.	1.
2. P is the intersection of ℓ, m, and n.	2.
3. $PA = $ _____	3. P lies on the perpendicular bisector of $\overline{AB}$.
4. _____ $= PC$	4. P lies on the perpendicular bisector of $\overline{BC}$.
5. $PA = $ _____ $= $ _____	5.

10. $\overline{PK}$, $\overline{PL}$, and $\overline{PM}$ are the perpendicular bisectors of sides $\overline{AB}$, $\overline{BC}$, and $\overline{AC}$. Tell whether the given statement is justified by the figure. Select the correct answer for each lettered part.

a. $AK = KB$ ◯ Justified ◯ Not Justified
b. $PA = PB$ ◯ Justified ◯ Not Justified
c. $PM = PL$ ◯ Justified ◯ Not Justified
d. $BL = \frac{1}{2}BC$ ◯ Justified ◯ Not Justified
e. $PK = KD$ ◯ Justified ◯ Not Justified

Graph the triangle with the given vertices and find the circumcenter of the triangle.

11. $D(-5, 0)$, $E(0, 0)$, $F(0, 7)$

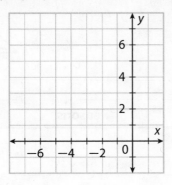

12. $Q(3, 4)$, $R(7, 4)$, $S(3, -2)$

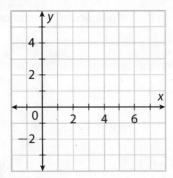

13. Represent Real-World Problems For the next Fourth of July, the towns of Ashton, Bradford, and Clearview will launch a fireworks display from a boat in the lake. Draw a sketch to show where the boat should be positioned so that it is the same distance from all three towns. Justify your sketch.

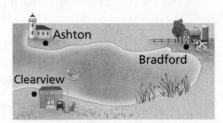

H.O.T. Focus on Higher Order Thinking

14. Analyze Relationships Explain how can you draw a triangle *JKL* whose circumcircle has a radius of 8 centimeters.

15. Persevere in Problem Solving $\overline{ZD}$, $\overline{ZE}$ and $\overline{ZF}$ are the perpendicular bisectors of $\triangle ABC$, which is not drawn to scale.

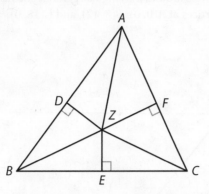

a. Suppose that $ZB = 145$, $ZD = 100$, and $ZF = 17$. How can you find AB and AC?

b. Find AB and AC.

c. Can you find BC? If so, explain how and find BC. If not, explain why not.

16. Multiple Representations Given the vertices $A(-2, -2)$, $B(4, 0)$, and $C(4, 4)$ of a triangle, the graph shows how you can use a graph and construction to locate the circumcenter P of the triangle. You can draw the perpendicular bisector of $\overline{CB}$ and construct the perpendicular bisector of $\overline{AB}$. Consider how you could identify P algebraically.

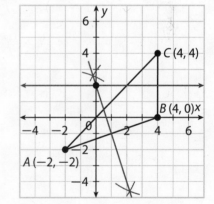

a. The perpendicular bisector of $\overline{AB}$ passes through its midpoint. Use the Midpoint Formula to find the midpoint of $\overline{AB}$.

b. What is the slope m of the perpendicular bisector of $\overline{AB}$? Explain how you found it.

c. Write an equation of the perpendicular bisector of $\overline{AB}$ and explain how you can use it find P.

Lesson Performance Task

A landscape architect wants to plant a circle of flowers around a triangular garden. She has sketched the triangle on a coordinate grid with vertices at $A(0, 0)$, $B(8, 12)$, and $C(18, 0)$.

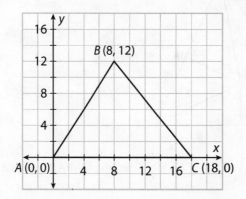

Explain how the architect can find the center of the circle that will circumscribe triangle ABC. Then find the radius of the circumscribed circle.

23.2 Angle Bisectors of Triangles

Essential Question: How can you use angle bisectors to find the point that is equidistant from all the sides of a triangle?

Resource Locker

⊘ Explore Investigating Distance from a Point to a Line

Use a ruler, a protractor, and a piece of tracing paper to investigate points on the bisector of an angle.

Ⓐ Use the ruler to draw a large angle on tracing paper. Label it ∠ABC. Fold the paper so that $\overrightarrow{BC}$ coincides with $\overrightarrow{BA}$. Open the paper. The crease is the bisector of ∠ABC. Plot a point P on the bisector.

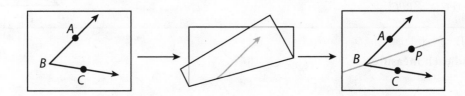

Ⓑ Use the ruler to draw several different segments from point P to $\overrightarrow{BA}$. Measure the lengths of the segments. Then measure the angle each segment makes with $\overrightarrow{BA}$. What do you notice about the shortest segment you can draw from point P to $\overrightarrow{BA}$?

_____

Ⓒ Draw the shortest segment you can from point P to $\overrightarrow{BC}$. Measure its length. How does its length compare with the length of the shortest segment you drew from point P to $\overrightarrow{BA}$?

_____

Reflect

1. Suppose you choose a point Q on the bisector of ∠XYZ and you draw the perpendicular segment from Q to $\overrightarrow{YX}$ and the perpendicular segment from Q to $\overrightarrow{YZ}$. What do you think will be true about these segments?

_____

2. Discussion What do you think is the best way to measure the distance from a point to a line? Why?

_____

_____

Explain 1   Applying the Angle Bisector Theorem and Its Converse

The **distance from a point to a line** is the length of the perpendicular segment from the point to the line. You will prove the following theorems about angle bisectors and the sides of the angle they bisect in Exercises 16 and 17.

Angle Bisector Theorem

If a point is on the bisector an of angle, then it is equidistant from the sides of the angle.

$\angle APC \cong \angle BPC$, so $AC = BC$.

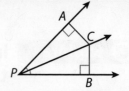

Converse of the Angle Bisector Theorem

If a point in the interior of an angle is equidistant from the sides of the angle, then it is on the bisector of the angle.

$AC = BC$, so $\angle APC \cong \angle BPC$

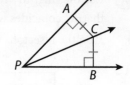

Example 1   Find each measure.

(A)   *LM*

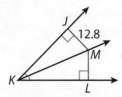

$\overrightarrow{KM}$ is the bisector of $\angle JKL$, so $LM = JM = 12.8$.

(B)   m$\angle ABD$, given that m$\angle ABC = 112°$

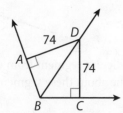

Since $AD = DC$, $\overrightarrow{AD} \perp \overrightarrow{BA}$, and $\overline{DC} \perp \overrightarrow{BC}$, you know that $\overrightarrow{BD}$

bisects $\angle ABC$ by the _____ Theorem.

So, m$\angle ABD = \frac{1}{2}$m$\angle$_____ = ☐°.

Reflect

3.   In the Converse of the Angle Bisector Theorem, why is it important to say that the point must be in the *interior* of the angle?

_____

_____

Find each measure.

4. *QS*

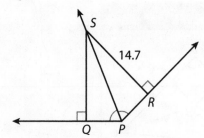

5. m∠*LJM*, given that m∠*KJM* = 29°

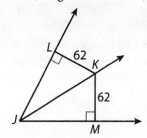

🔘 Explain 2 Constructing an Inscribed Circle

A circle is **inscribed** in a polygon if each side of the polygon is tangent to the circle. In the figure, circle *C* is inscribed in quadrilateral *WXYZ* and this circle is called the **incircle (inscribed circle)** of the quadrilateral.

In order to construct the incircle of a triangle, you need to find the center of the circle. This point is called the **incenter** of the triangle.

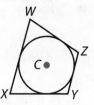

Example 2 **Use a compass and straightedge to construct the inscribed circle of △*PQR*.**

Step 1 The center of the inscribed circle must be equidistant from $\overline{PQ}$ and $\overline{PR}$. What is the set of points equidistant

from $\overline{PQ}$ and $\overline{PR}$? _____
Construct this set of points.

Step 2 The center must also be equidistant from $\overline{PR}$ and $\overline{QR}$. What is the set of points equidistant from $\overline{PR}$ and $\overline{QR}$?

_____ Construct this set of points.

Step 3 The center must lie at the intersection of the two sets of points you constructed. Label this point *C*.

Step 4 Place the point of your compass at *C* and open the compass until the pencil just touches a side of △*PQR*. Then draw the inscribed circle.

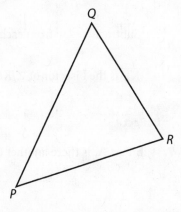

Reflect

6. Suppose you started by constructing the set of points equidistant from $\overline{PR}$ and $\overline{QR}$, and then constructed the set of points equidistant from $\overline{QR}$ and $\overline{QP}$. Would you have found the same center point? Check by doing this construction.

⚙ Explain 3 Using Properties of Angle Bisectors

As you have seen, the angle bisectors of a triangle are concurrent. The point of concurrency is the incenter of the triangle.

Incenter Theorem

The angle bisectors of a triangle intersect at a point that is equidistant from the sides of the triangle.

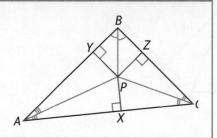

$$PX = PY = PZ$$

Example 3 $\overline{JV}$ and $\overline{KV}$ are angle bisectors of $\triangle JKL$. Find each measure.

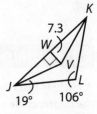

(A) the distance from V to $\overline{KL}$

V is the incenter of $\triangle JKL$. By the Incenter Theorem, V is equidistant from the sides of $\triangle JKL$. The distance from V to $\overline{JK}$ is 7.3. So the distance from V to $\overline{KL}$ is also 7.3.

(B) m∠VKL

$\overline{JV}$ is the bisector of $\angle \boxed{}$. $\qquad$ m∠KJL = 2 $\left(\boxed{}\right) = \boxed{}$

Triangle Sum Theorem $\qquad\qquad$ $\boxed{} + \boxed{} +$ m∠JKL = 180°

Subtract $\boxed{}$ from each side. $\qquad$ m∠JKL = $\boxed{}$

$\overline{KV}$ is the bisector of $\angle JKL$. $\qquad$ m∠VKL = $\frac{1}{2}\left(\boxed{}\right) = \boxed{}$

Reflect

7. In Part A, is there another distance you can determine? Explain.

_____

Your Turn

$\overline{QX}$ and $\overline{RX}$ are angle bisectors of $\triangle PQR$. Find each measure.

8. the distance from X to $\overline{PQ}$

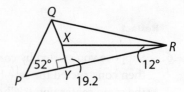

9. m∠PQX

10. *P* and *Q* are the circumcenter and incenter of $\triangle RST$, but not necessarily in that order. Which point is the circumcenter? Which point is the incenter? Explain how you can tell without constructing any bisectors.

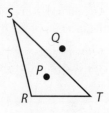

_____

_____

11. Complete the table by filling in the blanks to make each statement true.

	Circumcenter	Incenter
Definition	The point of concurrency of the _____	The point of concurrency of the _____
Distance	Equidistant from the _____	Equidistant from the _____
Location (Inside, Outside, On)	Can be _____ the triangle	Always _____ the triangle

12. **Essential Question Check-In** How do you know that the intersection of the bisectors of the angles of a triangle is equidistant from the sides of the triangle?

_____

_____

☆ Evaluate: Homework and Practice

• Online Homework
• Hints and Help
• Extra Practice

1. Use a compass and straightedge to investigate points on the bisector of an angle. On a separate piece of paper, draw a large angle *A*.

   a. Construct the bisector of $\angle A$.

   b. Choose a point on the angle bisector you constructed. Label it *P*. Construct a perpendicular through *P* to each side of $\angle A$.

   c. Explain how to use a compass to show that *P* is equidistant from the sides of $\angle A$.

Find each measure.

2. *VP*

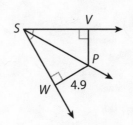

3. m$\angle LKM$, given that m$\angle JKL = 63°$

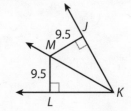

4. *AD*

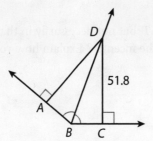

51.8

5. m∠*HFJ*, given that m∠*GFJ* = 45°

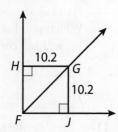

10.2

10.2

Construct an inscribed circle for each triangle.

6.

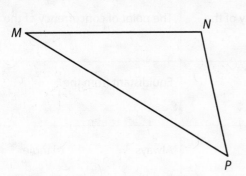

7.

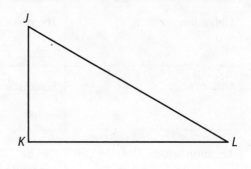

$\overline{CF}$ and $\overline{EF}$ are angle bisectors of △*CDE*. Find each measure.

8. the distance from *F* to $\overline{CD}$

9. m∠*FED*

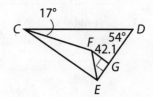

17°

54°

42.1

$\overline{TJ}$ and $\overline{SJ}$ are angle bisectors of △*RST*. Find each measure.

10. the distance from *J* to $\overline{RS}$

11. m∠*RTJ*

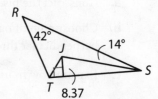

42°

14°

8.37

Find each measure.

12. *BC*

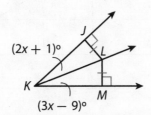

13. *VY*

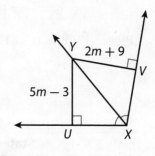

14. m∠*JKL*

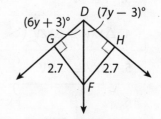

15. m∠*GDF*

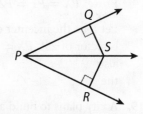

16. Complete the following proof of the Angle Bisector Theorem.

Given: $\overrightarrow{PS}$ bisects ∠*QPR*.

$\overline{SQ} \perp \overrightarrow{PQ}, \overline{SR} \perp \overrightarrow{PR}$

Prove: $SQ = SR$

Statements	Reasons
1. $\overrightarrow{PS}$ bisects ∠*QPR*. $\overline{SQ} \perp \overrightarrow{PQ}, \overline{SR} \perp \overrightarrow{PR}$	1.
2. ∠*QPS* ≅ ∠*RPS*	2.
3. ∠*SQP* and ∠*SRP* are right angles.	3. Definition of perpendicular
4. ∠*SQP* ≅ ∠*SRP*	4. All right angles are congruent.
5.	5. Reflexive Property of Congruence
6.	6. AAS Triangle Congruence Theorem
7. $\overline{SQ} \cong \overline{SR}$	7.
8. $SQ = SR$	8. Congruent segments have the same length.

17. Complete the following proof of the Converse of the Angle Bisector Theorem.

Given: $\overrightarrow{VX} \perp \overrightarrow{YX}$, $\overrightarrow{VZ} \perp \overrightarrow{YZ}$, $VX = VZ$.

Prove: $\overrightarrow{YV}$ bisects $\angle XYZ$.

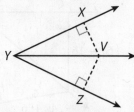

Statements	Reasons
1. $\overrightarrow{VX} \perp \overrightarrow{YX}$, $\overrightarrow{VZ} \perp \overrightarrow{YZ}$, $VX = VZ$	**1.**
2. $\angle VXY$ and $\angle VZY$ are right angles.	**2.**
3. $\overline{YV} \cong \overline{YV}$	**3.**
4. $\triangle YXV \cong \triangle YZV$	**4.**
5. $\angle XYV \cong \angle ZYV$	**5.**
6.	**8.**

18. Complete the following proof of the Incenter Theorem.

Given: $\overrightarrow{AP}, \overrightarrow{BP}$, and $\overrightarrow{CP}$ bisect $\angle A$, $\angle B$ and $\angle C$, respectively. $\overline{PX} \perp \overline{AC}$, $\overline{PY} \perp \overline{AB}$, $\overline{PZ} \perp \overline{BC}$

Prove: $PX = PY = PZ$

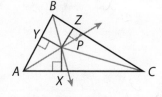

Let P be the incenter of $\triangle ABC$. Since P lies on the bisector of $\angle A$, $PX = PY$ by the _____ Theorem. Similarly, P also _____, so $PY = PZ$. Therefore, $PX = PY = PZ$, by the _____.

19. A city plans to build a firefighter's monument in a triangular park between three streets. Draw a sketch on the figure to show where the city should place the monument so that it is the same distance from all three streets. Justify your sketch.

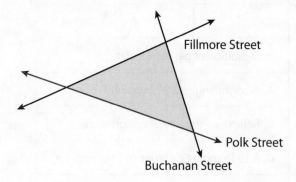

Fillmore Street

Polk Street

Buchanan Street

© Houghton Mifflin Harcourt Publishing Company • Image Credits: ©Pep Roig/ Alamy

20. A school plans to place a flagpole on the lawn so that it is equidistant from Mercer Street and Houston Street. They also want the flagpole to be equidistant from a water fountain at W and a bench at B. Find the point F where the school should place the flagpole. Mark the point on the figure and explain your answer.

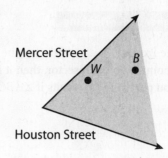

Mercer Street

W B

Houston Street

21. P is the incenter of $\triangle ABC$. Determine whether each statement is true or false. Select the correct answer for each lettered part.

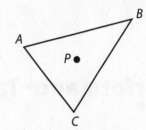

A B

P

C

a. Point P must lie on the perpendicular bisector of $\overline{BC}$. ◯ True ◯ False

b. Point P must lie on the angle bisector of $\angle C$. ◯ True ◯ False

c. If AP is 23 mm long, then CP must be 23 mm long. ◯ True ◯ False

d. If the distance from point P to $\overline{AB}$ is x, then the distance from point P to $\overline{BC}$ must be x. ◯ True ◯ False

e. The perpendicular segment from point P to $\overline{AC}$ is longer than the perpendicular segment from point P to $\overline{BC}$. ◯ True ◯ False

22. What If? In the Explore, you constructed the angle bisector of acute $\angle ABC$ and found that if a point is on the bisector, then it is equidistant from the sides of the angle. Would you get the same results if $\angle ABC$ were a straight angle? Explain.

23. Explain the Error A student was asked to draw the incircle for $\triangle PQR$. He constructed angle bisectors as shown. Then he drew a circle through points J, K, and L. Describe the student's error.

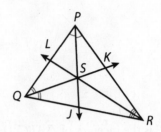

Lesson Performance Task

Teresa has just purchased a farm with a field shaped like a right triangle. The triangle has the measurements shown in the diagram. Teresa plans to install central pivot irrigation in the field. In this type of irrigation, a circular region of land is irrigated by a long arm of sprinklers—the radius of the circle—that rotates around a central pivot point like the hands of a clock, dispensing water as it moves.

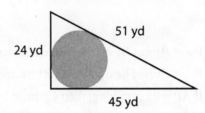

  a. Describe how she can find where to locate the pivot.

  b. Find the area of the irrigation circle. To find the radius, r, of a circle inscribed in a triangle with sides of length a, b, and c, you can use the formula $r = \dfrac{\sqrt{k(k-a)(k-b)(k-c)}}{k}$, where $k = \frac{1}{2}(a + b + c)$.

  c. About how much of the field that *not* be irrigated?

23.3 Medians and Altitudes of Triangles

Essential Question: How can you find the balance point or *center of gravity* of a triangle?

Resource Locker

⊘ Explore   Finding the Balance Point of a Triangle

If a triangle were cut out of a sheet of wood or paper, the triangle could be balanced around exactly one point inside the triangle.

A **median** of a triangle is a segment whose endpoints are a vertex of a triangle and the midpoint of the opposite side.

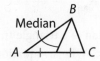

Every triangle has three distinct medians. You can use construction tools to show that the intersection of the three medians is the balance point of the triangle.

(A) Draw a large triangle on a sheet of construction paper. Label the vertices *A*, *B*, and *C*.

(B) Find the midpoint of the side opposite *A*, which is $\overline{BC}$. You may use a compass to find points equidistant to *B* and *C* and then draw the perpendicular bisector. Or you can use paper folding or a ruler. Write the label *X* for the midpoint.

(C) Draw a segment to connect *A* and *X*. The segment is one of the three medians of the triangle.

(D) Repeat Steps B and C, this time to draw the other two medians of the triangle. Write the label *Y* for the midpoint of the side opposite point *B*, and the label *Z* for the midpoint of the side opposite point *C*. Write the label *P* for the intersection of the three medians.

(E) Use a ruler to measure the lengths of each median and the subsegments defined by *P* in your triangle. Record your measurements in the table.

Median $\overline{AX}$:	AX = _____	AP = _____	PX = _____
Median $\overline{BY}$:	BY = _____	BP = _____	PY = _____
Median $\overline{CZ}$:	CZ = _____	CP = _____	PZ = _____

(F) What pattern do you observe in the measurements?

_____

_____

(G) Let *AX* be the length of any median of a triangle from a vertex *A*, and let *P* be the intersection of the three medians. Write an equation to describe the relationship between *AP* and *PX*.

(H) Let *AX* be the length of any median of a triangle from a vertex *A*, and let *P* be the intersection of the three medians. Write an equation to show the relationship between *AX* and *AP*.

(I) Cut out the triangle, and then punch a very small hole through *P*. Stick a pencil point through the hole, and then try to spin the triangle around the pencil point. How easily does it spin? Repeat this step with another point in the triangle, and compare the results.

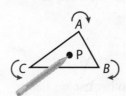

_____

_____

Reflect

1. Why is "balance point" a descriptive name for point *P*, the intersection of the three medians?

_____

_____

2. **Discussion** By definition, median $\overline{AX}$ intersects $\triangle ABC$ at points *A* and *X*. Could it intersect the triangle at a third point? Explain why or why not.

_____

_____

_____

✏️ Explain 1   Using the Centroid Theorem

The intersection of the three medians of a triangle is the *centroid* of the triangle. The centroid is always inside the triangle and divides each median by the same ratio.

Centroid Theorem

The centroid theorem states that the **centroid** of a triangle is located $\frac{2}{3}$ of the distance from each vertex to the midpoint of the opposite side.

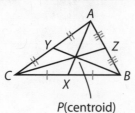

$$AP = \frac{2}{3}AX \qquad\qquad BP = \frac{2}{3}BY \qquad\qquad CP = \frac{2}{3}CZ$$

Example 1   Use the Centroid Theorem to find the length.

$AF = 9$, and $CE = 7.2$

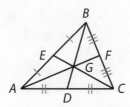

(A)   *AG*

Centroid Theorem	$AG = \frac{2}{3}AF$
Substitute 9 for *AF*.	$AG = \frac{2}{3}(9)$
Simplify.	$AG = 6$

Ⓑ *GE*

Centroid Theorem	$CG = \frac{2}{3}$ _____
Substitute for the given value.	$CG = \frac{2}{3}$ _____
Simplify.	$CG =$ _____
Segment Addition Postulate	$CG +$ _____ $= CE$
Subtraction Property of Equality	$GE = CE -$ _____
Substitute for the value of CG.	$GE = 7.2 -$ _____
Simplify.	$GE =$ _____

Reflect

3. To find the centroid of a triangle, how many medians of the triangle must you construct?

_____

4. Compare the lengths of $\overline{CG}$ and $\overline{GE}$ in Part B. What do you notice?

_____

5. **Make a Conjecture** The three medians of $\triangle FGH$ divide the triangle into six smaller triangles. Is it possible for the six smaller triangles to be congruent to one another? If yes, under what conditions?

_____

_____

Your Turn

6. Vertex L is 8 units from the centroid of $\triangle LMN$. Find the length of the median that has one endpoint at L.

7. Let P be the centroid of $\triangle STU$, and let $\overline{SW}$ be a median of $\triangle STU$. If $SW = 18$, find SP and PW.

8. In $\triangle ABC$, the median $\overline{AD}$ is perpendicular to $\overline{BC}$. If $AD = 21$ feet, describe the position of the centroid of the triangle.

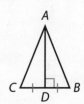

⚙ Explain 2　Finding the Intersection of Medians of a Triangle

When a triangle is plotted on the coordinate plane, the medians can be graphed and the location of the centroid can be identified.

Example 2　Find the coordinates of the centroid of the triangle shown on the coordinate plane.

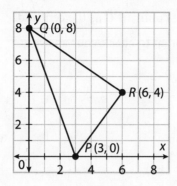

⚙ Analyze Information

What does the problem ask you to find? _____

What information does the graph provide that will help you find the answer?

_____

⚙ Formulate a Plan

The centroid is the _____ of the medians of the triangle. Begin by

calculating the _____ of one side of the triangle. Then draw a line to connect

that point to a _____. You need to draw only _____ medians to find the centroid.

⚙ Solve

Find and plot midpoints.

Let M be the midpoint of $\overline{QR}$.

$$M = \left(\frac{0+6}{2}, \frac{8+4}{2}\right) = \text{_____}$$

Let N be the midpoint of $\overline{QP}$.

$$N = \left(\frac{0+3}{2}, \frac{8+0}{2}\right) = \text{_____}$$

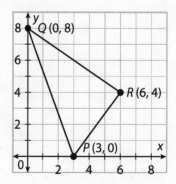

Draw the medians and identify equations.

Draw a segment to connect M and _____.

The segment is a median and is described by the equation _____.

Draw a segment to connect N and _____.

The segment is also a median and is described by the equation _____.

Find the centroid.

Identify the intersection of the two medians, which is (_____). Label it C.

The answer seems reasonable because it is positioned in the middle of the triangle. To check it, find the midpoint of $\overline{RP}$, which is _____. Label the midpoint L, and draw the third median, which is _____. The slope of the third median is

$\dfrac{2-8}{4.5-0} = -\dfrac{4}{3}$, and the equation that describes it is $y = -\dfrac{4}{3}x +$ ___ . It intersects the

other two medians at (_____), which confirms C as the centroid.

You can also apply the Centroid Theorem to check your answer.

$RC = \dfrac{2}{3}RN$

$RN =$ _____

$RC =$ _____

Substitute values into the first equation:

$3 = \dfrac{2}{3}$ _____

The equality is true, which confirms the answer.

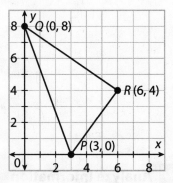

Your Turn

Find the centroid of the triangles with the given vertices. Show your work and check your answer.

9. $P(-1, 7)$, $Q(9, 5)$, $R(4, 3)$

10. $A(-6, 0)$, $B(0, 12)$, $C(6, 0)$

🔑 Explain 3 Finding the Orthocenter of a Triangle

Like the centroid, the *orthocenter* is a point that characterizes a triangle. This point involves the *altitudes* of the triangle rather than the medians.

An **altitude** of a triangle is a perpendicular segment from a vertex to the line containing the opposite side. Every triangle has three altitudes. An altitude can be inside, outside, or on the triangle.

In the diagram of $\triangle ABC$, the three altitudes are $\overline{AX}$, $\overline{BZ}$, and $\overline{CY}$. Notice that two of the altitudes are outside the triangle.

The length of an altitude is often called the height of a triangle.

The **orthocenter** of a triangle is the intersection (or point of concurrency) of the lines that contain the altitudes. Like the altitudes themselves, the orthocenter may be inside, outside, or on the triangle. Notice that the lines containing the altitudes are concurrent at P. The orthocenter of this triangle is P.

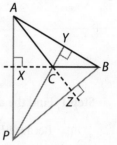

Example 3 **Find the orthocenter of the triangle by graphing the perpendicular lines to the sides of the triangle.**

Ⓐ **Step 1** Draw the triangle. Choose one vertex and then find and graph the equation of the line containing the altitude from that vertex.

Triangle with vertices $O(0, 0)$, $P(2, 6)$, and $Q(8, 0)$

Choose P. The side opposite P is $\overline{OQ}$, which is horizontal, so the altitude is vertical. The altitude is a segment of the line $x = 2$.

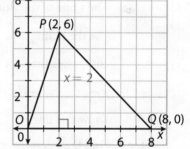

Step 2 Repeat Step 1 with a second vertex.

Choose O, the origin. The altitude that contains O is perpendicular to $\overline{PQ}$. Calculate the slope of $\overline{PQ}$ as $\frac{y_2 - y_1}{x_2 - x_1} = \frac{6 - 0}{2 - 8} = -1$.

Since the slope of the altitude is the opposite reciprocal of the slope of $\overline{PQ}$, the slope of the altitude is 1. The altitude is a segment of the line that passes through the origin and has a slope of 1. The equation of the line is $y = x$.

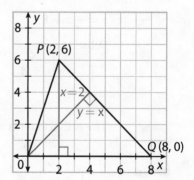

Step 3 Find the intersection of the two lines.

The orthocenter is the intersection of the two lines that contain the altitudes. The lines $x = 2$ and $y = x$ intersect at $(2, 2)$, which is the orthocenter.

© Houghton Mifflin Harcourt Publishing Company

Ⓑ

Step 1 Find the altitude that contains vertex A.

Because $\overline{BC}$ is vertical, the altitude through A is a _____ segment. The equation of the

line that contains the segment is $y =$ _____ . Draw this line.

Step 2 Find the altitude that contains vertex C.

First, calculate the slope of $\overline{AB}$. The slope is $\dfrac{6 - \rule{1cm}{0.4pt}}{6 - \rule{1cm}{0.4pt}}$, which equals _____ .

The slope of the altitude to $\overline{AB}$ is the _____ of 1, which is -1.

Use the point-slope form to find the equation of the line that has a slope of -1

and passes through _____:

$y -$ _____ $= -1(x -$ _____$)$, which simplifies to $y = -x + 8$.

Draw this line.

Step 3 Find the intersection of the two lines.

$y = -1$

$y = -x + 8$

Substitute for y:

_____ $= -x + 8$

$x =$ _____

The orthocenter is at (_____).

Reflect

11. Could the orthocenter of a triangle be concurrent with one of its vertices?
If yes, provide an example. If not, explain why not.

_____

_____

12. An altitude is defined to be a perpendicular segment from a vertex to the line containing
the opposite side. Why are the words "the line containing" important in this definition?

_____

_____

1158

Find the orthocenter for the triangles described by each set of vertices.

13. $Q(4, -3)$, $R(8, 5)$, $S(8, -8)$

14. $K(2, -2)$, $L(4, 6)$, $M(8, -2)$

 **Elaborate**

15. Could the centroid of a triangle be coincident with the orthocenter? If so, give an example.

_____

_____

16. Describe or sketch an example in which the orthocenter P of $\triangle ABC$ is far away from the triangle. That is, PA, PB, and PC are each greater than the length of any side of the triangle.

_____

_____

_____

17. A sculptor is assembling triangle-shaped pieces into a mobile. Describe circumstances when the sculptor would need to identify the centroid and orthocenter of each triangle.

_____

_____

_____

_____

18. **Essential Question Check-In** How can you find the centroid, or balance point, of a triangle?

_____

✪ Evaluate: Homework and Practice

• Online Homework
• Hints and Help
• Extra Practice

Use a compass and a straightedge to draw the medians and identify the centroid of the triangle. Label the centroid P.

1.

2.

3. **Critique Reasoning** Paul draws △ABC and the medians from vertices A and B. He finds that the medians intersect at a point, and he labels this point X. Paul claims that point X lies outside △ABC. Do you think this is possible? Explain.

4. For △ABC and its medians, match the segment on the left with its length.

A. AM	_____	1.5
B. AP	_____	2
C. PM	_____	2.5
D. BK	_____	3
E. BP	_____	4
F. PK	_____	4.5
G. CL	_____	5
H. CP	_____	6
I. PL	_____	7.5

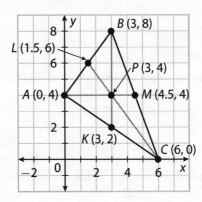

The diagram shows △*FGH*, its medians, centroid *P*, and the lengths of some of the subsegments. Apply the Centroid Theorem to find other lengths.

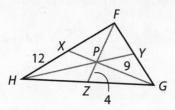

5. *FH* **6.** *PF* **7.** *GX*

The diagram shows △*XYZ*, which has side lengths of 8 inches, 12 inches, and 15 inches. The diagram also shows the medians, centroid *P*, and the lengths of some of the subsegments. Apply the Centroid Theorem to find other lengths.

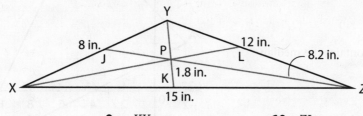

8. *LY* **9.** *KY* **10.** *ZJ*

11. The diagram shows △*ABC*, its medians, centroid *P*, and the lengths of some of the subsegments as expressions of variables *x* and *y*. Apply the Centroid Theorem to solve for the variables and to find other lengths.

a. *x*

b. *y*

c. *BP*

d. *BD*

e. *CP*

f. *PE*

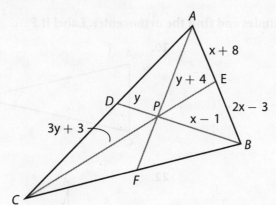

12. Draw the medians from A to $\overline{BC}$ and from C to $\overline{AB}$.

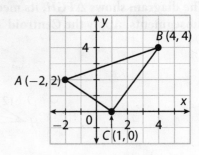

The vertices of a triangle are $A(-2, 3)$, $B(5, 10)$, and $C(12, -4)$. Find the coordinates or equations for each feature of the triangle.

13. the coordinates of the midpoint of $\overline{AC}$

14. the coordinates of the midpoint of $\overline{BC}$

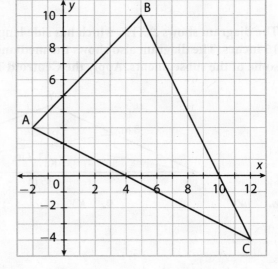

15. the equation of the line that contains the median through point B

16. the equation of the line that contains the median through point A

17. the coordinates of the intersection of the two medians

18. the coordinates of the center of balance of the triangle

For each triangle, draw the three altitudes and find the orthocenter. Label it P.

19.

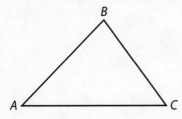

20.

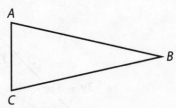

21.

22.

Find the orthocenter of each triangle with the given vertices.

23. For each t$A(2, 2)$, $B(2, 10)$, $C(4, 2)$

24. $A(2, 5)$, $B(10, -3)$, $C(4, 5)$

25. $A(9, 3)$, $B(9, -1)$, $C(6, 0)$

26. Draw Conclusions Triangles ABC, DBE, and FBG are all symmetric about the y–axis. Show that each triangle has the same centroid. What are the coordinates of the centroid?

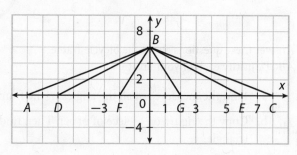

27. Analyze Relationships Triangle ABC is plotted on the coordinate plane. $\overline{AB}$ is horizontal, meaning it is parallel to the x-axis. $\overline{BC}$ is vertical, meaning it is parallel to the y-axis. Based on this information, can you determine the location of the orthocenter? Explain.

28. What if? The equilateral triangle shown here has its orthocenter and centroid at the origin. Suppose the triangle is stretched by moving *A* up the *y*-axis, while keeping *B* and *C* stationary. Describe and compare the changes to the centroid and the orthocenter of the triangle.

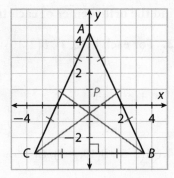

29. What If? The diagram shows right triangle *ABC* on the coordinate plane, and it shows the three medians and centroid *P*. How does the position of the centroid change when the triangle is stretched by moving *B* to the right along the *x*-axis, and keeping *A* and *C* stationary? How does the orthocenter change?

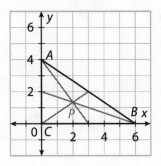

Lesson Performance Task

A bicycle frame consists of two adjacent triangles. The diagram shows some of the dimensions of the two triangles that make up the frame.

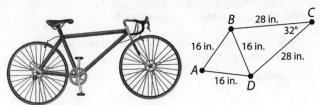

Answer these questions about the bicycle frame *ABCD*. Justify each of your answers.

a. Find the measures of all the angles in the frame.

b. Copy the figure on a piece of paper. Then find the center of gravity of each triangle.

c. Estimate the center of gravity of the entire frame and show it on your diagram.

d. Explain how you could modify the frame to lower its center of gravity and improve stability.

23.4 Midsegments of Triangles

Essential Question: How are the segments that join the midpoints of a triangle's sides related to the triangle's sides?

Resource
Locker

⊘ Explore   Investigating Midsegments of a Triangle

The **midsegment** of a triangle is a line segment that connects the midpoints of two sides of the triangle. Every triangle has three midsegments. Midsegments are often used to add rigidity to structures. In the support for the garden swing shown, the crossbar $\overline{DE}$ is a midsegment of △ABC

You can use a compass and straightedge to construct the midsegments of a triangle.

(A) Sketch a scalene triangle and label the vertices A, B, and C.

(B) Use a compass to find the midpoint of $\overline{AB}$. Label the midpoint D.

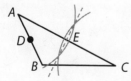

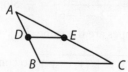

(C) Use a compass to find the midpoint of $\overline{AC}$. Label the midpoint E.

(D) Use a straightedge to draw $\overline{DE}$. $\overline{DE}$ is one of the midsegments of the triangle.

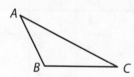

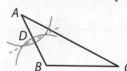

(E) Repeat the process to find the other two midsegments of △ABC. You may want to label the midpoint of $\overline{BC}$ as F.

© Houghton Mifflin Harcourt Publishing Company

1. Use a ruler to compare the length of $\overline{DE}$ to the length of $\overline{BC}$. What does this tell you about $\overline{DE}$ and $\overline{BC}$?

_____

2. Use a protractor to compare m∠ADE and m∠ABC. What does this tell you about $\overline{DE}$ and $\overline{BC}$? Explain.

_____

3. Compare your results with your class. Then state a conjecture about a midsegment of a triangle.

_____

_____

🔑 Explain 1   Describing Midsegments on a Coordinate Grid

You can confirm your conjecture about midsegments using the formulas for the midpoint, slope, and distance.

Example 1   Show that the given midsegment of the triangle is parallel to the third side of the triangle and is half as long as the third side.

Ⓐ   The vertices of $\triangle GHI$ are $G(-7, -1)$, $H(-5, 5)$, and $I(1, 3)$. J is the midpoint of $\overline{GH}$, and K is the midpoint of $\overline{IH}$. Show that $\overline{JK} \parallel \overline{GI}$ and $JK = \frac{1}{2}GI$. Sketch $\overline{JK}$.

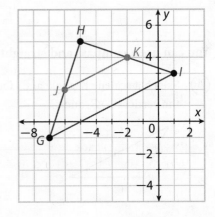

Step 1   Use the midpoint formula, $\left(\dfrac{x_1 + x_2}{2}, \dfrac{y_1 + y_2}{2}\right)$, to find the coordinates of J and K.

The midpoint of $\overline{GH}$ is $\left(\dfrac{-7 - 5}{2}, \dfrac{-1 + 5}{2}\right) = (-6, 2)$. Graph and label this point J.

The midpoint of $\overline{IH}$ is $\left(\dfrac{-5 + 1}{2}, \dfrac{5 + 3}{2}\right) = (-2, 4)$. Graph and label this point K. Use a straightedge to draw $\overline{JK}$.

Step 2   Use $\left(\dfrac{y_2 - y_1}{x_2 - x_1}\right)$ to compare the slopes of $\overline{JK}$ and $\overline{GI}$.

Slope of $\overline{JK} = \dfrac{4 - 2}{-2 - (-6)} = \dfrac{1}{2}$ Slope of $\overline{GI} = \dfrac{3 - (-1)}{1 - (-7)} = \dfrac{1}{2}$

Since the slopes are the same, $\overline{JK} \parallel \overline{GI}$.

Step 3   Use $\sqrt{(x_2 - x_1)^2 + (y_2 - y_1)^2}$ to compare the lengths of $\overline{JK}$ and $\overline{GI}$.

$JK = \sqrt{(-2 - (-6))^2 + (4 - 2)^2} = \sqrt{20} = 2\sqrt{5}$

$GI = \sqrt{(1 - (-7))^2 + (3 - (-1))^2} = \sqrt{80} = 4\sqrt{5}$

Since $2\sqrt{5} = \frac{1}{2}(4\sqrt{5})$, $JK = \frac{1}{2}GI$.

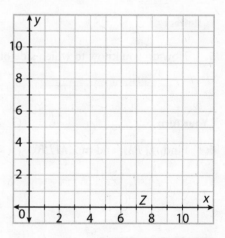

Ⓑ The vertices of △LMN are L(2, 7), M(10, 9), and N(8, 1). P is the midpoint of $\overline{LM}$, and Q is the midpoint of $\overline{MN}$.

Show that $\overline{PQ} \parallel \overline{LN}$ and $PQ = \frac{1}{2}LN$. Sketch $\overline{PQ}$.

Step 1 The midpoint of $\overline{LM} = \dfrac{2 + \boxed{}}{2}, \dfrac{7 + \boxed{}}{2} = \left(\boxed{}, \boxed{}\right)$.
Graph and label this point P.

The midpoint of $\overline{NM} = \left(\dfrac{\boxed{} + \boxed{}}{2}, \dfrac{\boxed{} + \boxed{}}{2} \right)$

$= \left(\boxed{}, \boxed{}\right)$. Graph and label this point Q. Use a straightedge to draw $\overline{PQ}$.

Step 2 Slope of $\overline{PQ} = \dfrac{5 - 8}{9 - \boxed{}} = \boxed{}$ Slope of $\overline{LN} = \dfrac{\boxed{} - \boxed{}}{\boxed{} - \boxed{}} = \boxed{}$

Since the slopes are the same, $\overline{PQ}$ and $\overline{LN}$ are _____.

Step 3 $PQ = \sqrt{\left(\boxed{} - 6\right)^2 + (5 - 8)^2} = \sqrt{\boxed{} + 9} = \sqrt{18} = 3\sqrt{2}$

$LN = \sqrt{\left(\boxed{} - \boxed{}\right)^2 + \left(\boxed{} - \boxed{}\right)^2} = \sqrt{\boxed{} + \boxed{}} = \sqrt{\boxed{}} = 6\sqrt{\boxed{}}$

Since $\boxed{}\sqrt{\boxed{}} = \frac{1}{2}\left(\boxed{}\sqrt{\boxed{}}\right)$, $\boxed{} = \frac{1}{2}\boxed{}$.

The length of $\overline{PQ}$ is _____ the length of $\overline{LN}$.

Your Turn

4. The vertices of △XYZ are X(3, 7), Y(9, 11), and Z(7, 1). U is the midpoint of $\overline{XY}$, and W is the midpoint of $\overline{XZ}$. Show that $\overline{UW} \parallel \overline{YZ}$ and $UW = \frac{1}{2}YZ$. Sketch △XYZ and $\overline{UW}$.

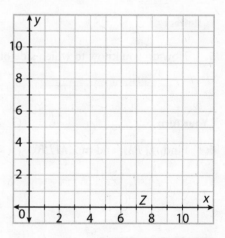

⊘ Explain 2   Using the Triangle Midsegment Theorem

The relationship you have been exploring is true for the three midsegments of every triangle.

Triangle Midsegment Theorem

The segment joining the midpoints of two sides of a triangle is parallel to the third side, and its length is half the length of that side.

You explored this theorem in Example 1 and will be proving it later in this course.

Example 2   Use triangle *RST*.

(A) Find *UW*.

By the Triangle Midsegment Theorem, the length of midsegment $\overline{UW}$ is half the length of $\overline{ST}$.

$UW = \frac{1}{2}ST$

$UW = \frac{1}{2}(10.2)$

$UW = 5.1$

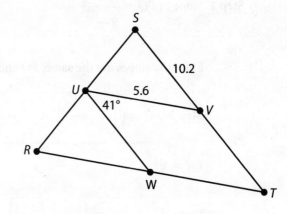

(B) Complete the reasoning to find m ∠*SVU*.

_____ $\overline{UW}\|\overline{ST}$

_____   m ∠*SVU* = m ∠*VUW*

Substitute ____ for _____   m ∠*SVU* = ☐

Reflect

5. How do you know to which side of a triangle a midsegment is parallel?

_____

Your Turn

6. Find *JL*, *PM*, and m ∠*MLK*.

_____

_____

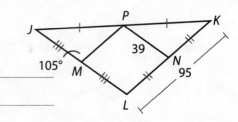

💬 Elaborate

7. Discussion Explain why $\overline{XY}$ is NOT a midsegment of the triangle.

_____

8. Essential Question Check–In Explain how the perimeter of $\triangle DEF$ compares to that of $\triangle ABC$.

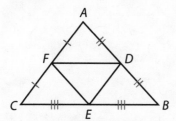

_____

⭐ Evaluate: Homework and Practice

• Online Homework
• Hints and Help
• Extra Practice

1. Use a compass and a ruler or geometry software to construct an obtuse triangle. Label the vertices. Choose two sides and construct the midpoint of each side; then label and draw the midsegment. Describe the relationship between the length of the midsegment and the length of the third side.

2. The vertices of $\triangle WXY$ are $W(-4, 1)$, $X(0, -5)$, and $Y(4, -1)$. A is the midpoint of $\overline{WY}$, and B is the midpoint of $\overline{XY}$. Show that $\overline{AB} \parallel \overline{WX}$ and $AB = \frac{1}{2} WX$.

3. The vertices of $\triangle FGH$ are $F(-1, 1)$, $G(-5, 4)$, and $H(-5, -2)$. X is the midpoint of $\overline{FG}$, and Y is the midpoint of $\overline{FH}$. Show that $\overline{XY} \parallel \overline{GH}$ and $XY = \frac{1}{2}GH$.

4. One of the vertices of $\triangle PQR$ is $P(3, -2)$. The midpoint of $\overline{PQ}$ is $M(4, 0)$. The midpoint of $\overline{QR}$ is $N(7, 1)$. Show that $\overline{MN} \parallel \overline{PR}$ and $MN = \frac{1}{2}PR$.

5. One of the vertices of $\triangle ABC$ is $A(0, 0)$. The midpoint of $\overline{AC}$ is $J\left(\frac{3}{2}, 2\right)$. The midpoint of $\overline{BC}$ is $K(4, 2)$. Show that $\overline{JK} \parallel \overline{BA}$ and $JK = \frac{1}{2} BA$.

Find each measure.

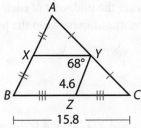

6. XY

7. BZ

8. AX

9. $m\angle YZC$

10. $m\angle BXY$

Algebra Find the value of n in each triangle.

11.

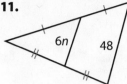

6n 48

12.

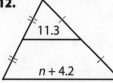

11.3

n + 4.2

13.

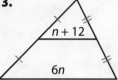

n + 12

6n

14.

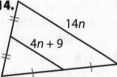

14n

4n + 9

15. Line segment XY is a midsegment of $\triangle MNP$. Determine whether each of the following statements is true or false. Select the correct answer for each lettered part.

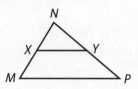

a. $MP = 2XY$ ◯ True   ◯ False

b. $MP = \frac{1}{2}XY$ ◯ True   ◯ False

c. $MX = XN$ ◯ True   ◯ False

d. $MX = \frac{1}{2}NX$ ◯ True   ◯ False

e. $NX = YN$ ◯ True   ◯ False

f. $XY = \frac{1}{2}MP$ ◯ True   ◯ False

16. What do you know about two of the midsegments in an isosceles triangle? Explain.

17. Suppose you know that the midsegments of a triangle are all 2 units long. What kind of triangle is it?

18. In $\triangle ABC$, m$\angle A = 80°$, m$\angle B = 60°$, m$\angle C = 40°$. The midpoints of $\overline{AB}$, $\overline{BC}$, and $\overline{AC}$ are D, E, and F, respectively. Which midsegment will be the longest? Explain how you know.

19. **Draw Conclusions** Carl's Construction is building a pavilion with an A-frame roof at the local park. Carl has constructed two triangular frames for the front and back of the roof, similar to $\triangle ABC$ in the diagram. The base of each frame, represented by $\overline{AC}$, is 36 feet long. He needs to insert a crossbar connecting the midpoints of $\overline{AB}$ and $\overline{BC}$, for each frame. He has 32 feet of timber left after constructing the front and back triangles. Is this enough to construct the crossbar for both the front and back frame? Explain.

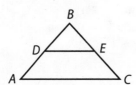

20. **Critique Reasoning** Line segment AB is a midsegment in $\triangle PQR$. Kayla calculated the length of $\overline{AB}$. Her work is shown below. Is her answer correct? If not, explain her error.

$$2(QR) = AB$$
$$2(25) = AB$$
$$50 = AB$$

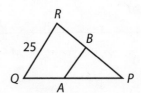

21. Using words or diagrams, tell how to construct a midsegment using only a straightedge and a compass.

22. **Multi-Step** A city park will be shaped like a right triangle, and there will be two pathways for pedestrians, shown by $\overline{VT}$ and $\overline{VW}$ in the diagram. The park planner only wrote two lengths on his sketch as shown. Based on the diagram, what will be the lengths of the two pathways?

23. **Communicate Mathematical Ideas** $\triangle XYZ$ is the midsegment of $\triangle PQR$. Write a congruence statement involving all four of the smaller triangles. What is the relationship between the area of $\triangle XYZ$ and $\triangle PQR$?

24. Copy the diagram shown. $\overline{AB}$ is a midsegment of $\triangle XYZ$. $\overline{CD}$ is a midsegment of $\triangle ABZ$.

    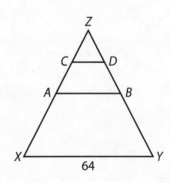

    a. What is the length of $\overline{AB}$? What is the ratio of AB to XY?

    b. What is the length of $\overline{CD}$? What is the ratio of CD to XY?

    c. Draw $\overline{EF}$ such that points E and F are $\frac{3}{4}$ the distance from point Z to points X and Y. What is the ratio of EF to XY? What is the length of $\overline{EF}$?

    d. Make a conjecture about the length of non-midsegments when compared to the length of the third side.

Lesson Performance Task

The figure shows part of a common roof design using very strong and stable triangular *trusses*. Points *B*, *C*, *D*, *F*, *G*, and *I* are midpoints of $\overline{AC}$, $\overline{AE}$, $\overline{CE}$, $\overline{GE}$, $\overline{HE}$ and $\overline{AH}$ respectively. What is the total length of all the stabilizing bars inside $\triangle AEH$? Explain how you found the answer.

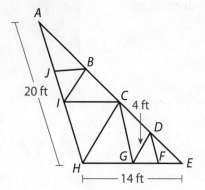

Special Segments in Triangles

Essential Question: How can you use special segments in triangles to solve real-world problems?

Key Vocabulary

altitude of a triangle
(altura de un triángulo)

centroid of a triangle
(centroide de un triángulo)

circumcenter of a triangle
(circuncentro de un triángulo)

circumscribed circle
(círculo circunscrito)

concurrent *(concurrente)*

distance from a point to a line
(distancia desde un punto hasta una línea)

equidistant *(equidistante)*

incenter of a triangle
(incentro de un triángulo)

inscribed circle
(círculo inscrito)

median of a triangle
(mediana de un triángulo)

midsegment of a triangle
(segmento medio de un triángulo)

orthocenter of a triangle
(ortocentro de un triángulo)

point of concurrency
(punto de concurrencia)

KEY EXAMPLE   *(Lesson 23.1)*

$\overline{DE}$ is a midsegment of $\triangle ABC$, and it is parallel to $\overline{AC}$. If the length of $\overline{BD}$ is 5 and the length of $\overline{EC}$ is 3, find the lengths of $\overline{DA}$ and $\overline{BE}$.

$\overline{DE}$ is a midsegment of $\triangle ABC$, so $\overline{BD}$ is half of $\overline{BA}$. $\overline{DA}$ is the other half of $\overline{BA}$. So, $DA = BD = 5$.

$\overline{DE}$ is a midsegment of $\triangle ABC$, so $\overline{EC}$ is half of $\overline{BC}$. $\overline{BE}$ is the other half of $\overline{BC}$. So, $EC = BE = 3$.

KEY EXAMPLE   *(Lesson 23.2)*

Find the coordinates of the centroid of the triangle.

Coordinates: $A(-1, 2)$, $B(3, 6)$, $C(4, 2)$

Centroid:

$M_{AB} = \left(\dfrac{-1 + 3}{2}, \dfrac{2 + 6}{2}\right) = (1, 4)$ Midpoint of $\overline{AB}$

$m = \dfrac{2 - 4}{4 - 1} = -\dfrac{2}{3}$ Slope of line passing through midpoint and C

$y - 4 = -\dfrac{2}{3}(x - 1)$ Find the equation of the median.

$y = -\dfrac{2}{3}x + \dfrac{14}{3}$

$M_{AC} = \left(\dfrac{-1 + 4}{2}, \dfrac{2 + 2}{2}\right) = \left(\dfrac{3}{2}, 2\right)$ Midpoint of $\overline{AC}$

$m = \dfrac{6 - 2}{3 - \dfrac{3}{2}} = \dfrac{8}{3}$ Slope of line passing through midpoint and B

$y - 6 = \dfrac{8}{3}(x - 3)$ Find the equation of the median.

$y = \dfrac{8}{3}x - 2$

$-\dfrac{2}{3}x + \dfrac{14}{3} = \dfrac{8}{3}x - 2$ Set the equations equal to each other to find the intersection.

$x = 2$

$y = \dfrac{8}{3}(2) - 2 = \dfrac{10}{3}$

The coordinates of the centroid are $\left(2, \dfrac{10}{3}\right)$.

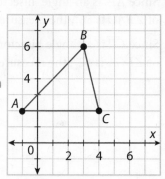

Find the coordinates of the circumcenter of the triangle.

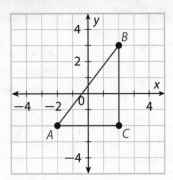

Coordinates: $A(-2, -2)$, $B(2, 3)$, $C(2, -2)$

$$M_{AC} = \left(\frac{-2 + 2}{2}, \frac{-2 + (-2)}{2} \right) = (0, -2)$$

Midpoint of $\overline{AC}$

$\overline{AC}$ is horizontal, so the line perpendicular to it is vertical and passes through the midpoint. The equation is $x = 0$.

Find the equation of the line perpendicular to $\overline{AC}$.

$$M_{BC} = \left(\frac{2 + 2}{2}, \frac{3 + (-2)}{2} \right) = \left(2, \frac{1}{2} \right)$$

Midpoint of $\overline{BC}$

$\overline{BC}$ is vertical, so the line perpendicular to it is horizontal and passes through the midpoint. The equation is $y = \frac{1}{2}$.

Find the equation of the line perpendicular to $\overline{BC}$.

The coordinates of the circumcenter are $\left(0, \frac{1}{2} \right)$.

$\overline{AP}$ **and** $\overline{CP}$ **are angle bisectors of** $\triangle ABC$**, where** P **is the incenter of the triangle. The measure of** $\angle BAC$ **is 56°. The measure of** $\angle BCA$ **is 42°.**

Find the measures of $\angle PAC$ **and** $\angle PCB$**.**

Since $\overline{AP}$ is an angle bisector of $\angle BAC$, the measures of $\angle PAC$ and $\angle PAB$ are equal. Since the measure of $\angle BAC$ is 56°, the measure of $\angle PAC$ is 28°.

Since $\overline{CP}$ is an angle bisector of $\angle BCA$, the measures of $\angle PCB$ and $\angle PCA$ are equal. Since the measure of $\angle BCA$ is 42°, the measure of $\angle PCB$ is 21°.

© Houghton Mifflin Harcourt Publishing Company

EXERCISES

$\overline{DE}$, $\overline{DF}$, and $\overline{EF}$ are midsegments of $\triangle ABC$. Find the lengths of the segments. *(Lesson 23.1)*

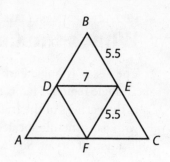

1. $\overline{BD}$ _____

2. $\overline{EC}$ _____

3. $\overline{AF}$ _____

Find the coordinates of the points. *(Lesson 23.2)*

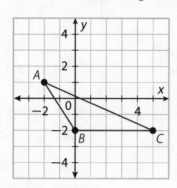

4. Centroid _____

5. Orthocenter _____

Find the coordinates of the points. *(Lesson 23.3)*

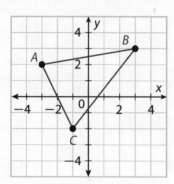

6. Circumcenter _____

$\overline{AP}$, $\overline{BP}$, and $\overline{CP}$ are angle bisectors of $\triangle ABC$, where P is the incenter of the triangle. The measure of $\angle BAC$ is 24°. The measure of $\angle BCA$ is 91°. Find the measures of the angles. *(Lesson 23.4)*

7. $\angle BAP$ _____ **8.** $\angle ABP$ _____ **9.** $\angle BCP$ _____

© Houghton Mifflin Harcourt Publishing Company

What's the Center of the Triangle?

The Texas Triangle Park in Bryan, Texas bills itself as being at the center of the Texas Triangle region. That is the region with the cities of Dallas, Houston, and San Antonio at the vertices of the triangle. The diagram shows a simple representation of the region with San Antonio located at the origin. The point B also gives you coordinates for the location of Bryan. So just how close is Bryan to the center of this triangle?

Before you tackle this problem, decide what you think is the best measure of the triangle's center in this context—the centroid, circumcenter, or orthocenter? Be prepared to support your decision.

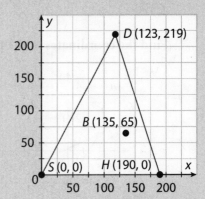

Start by listing in the space below the information you will need to solve the problem. Then use your own paper to complete the task. Be sure to write down all your data and assumptions. Then use graphs, numbers, words, or algebra to explain how you reached your conclusion.

23.1–23.4 Special Segments in Triangles

Segments $\overline{DE}$, $\overline{EF}$, and $\overline{DF}$ are midsegments of $\triangle ABC$
Find the lengths of the indicated segments. *(Lesson 23.4)*

• Online Homework
• Hints and Help
• Extra Practice

1. $\overline{AC}$ _____

2. $\overline{CF}$ _____

3. $\overline{DE}$ _____

4. $\overline{AE}$ _____

5. $\overline{AB}$ _____

6. $\overline{EF}$ _____

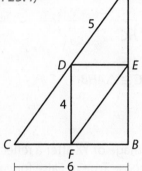

Locate centroids, circumcenters, and incenters. *(Lessons 23.1, 23.2, 23.3)*

7. Find the points of concurrency of $\triangle ABC$.

   a. Determine the coordinates of the centroid of $\triangle ABC$.

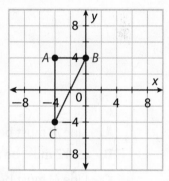

   b. Determine the coordinates of the circumcenter
      of $\triangle ABC$.

   c. In what quadrant or on what axis does the incenter of $\triangle ABC$ lie?

ESSENTIAL QUESTION

8. Describe a triangle for which the centroid, circumcenter, incenter, and orthocenter are the same
point. What features of this triangle cause these points to be concurrent and why?

Assessment Readiness

1. Given △ABC and altitude $\overline{AH}$, decide whether each statement is necessarily true about △AHC. Select Yes or No for A–C.

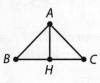

   A. $AH < HC$ ◯ Yes   ◯ No
   B. $AH < AC$ ◯ Yes   ◯ No
   C. △AHC ≅ △AHB   ◯ Yes   ◯ No

2. $\overline{YZ}$ is the image of $\overline{YX}$ after a reflection across line M. Choose True or False for each statement.

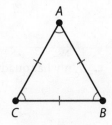

   A. Line M must be the angle bisector of ∠XYZ.   ◯ Yes   ◯ No
   B. ∠XYZ must be acute.   ◯ Yes   ◯ No
   C. Line M must be horizontal.   ◯ Yes   ◯ No

3. Given △ABC is equilateral, what can be determined about its centroid and circumcenter?

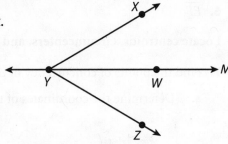

4. $\overline{DE}$, $\overline{EF}$, and $\overline{DF}$ are the midsegments of △ABC. How does the perimeter of △DEF compare to the perimeter of △ABC? Explain.

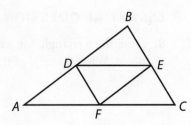

_____

_____

_____

Assessment Readiness

Personal Math Trainer

• Online Homework
• Hints and Help
• Extra Practice

1. Determine whether each pair of angles is a pair of vertical angles, a linear pair of angles, or neither.

   Select the correct answer for each lettered part.

   A. ∠AFC and ∠CFD   ○ Vertical   ○ Linear Pair   ○ Neither

   B. ∠AFB and ∠CFD   ○ Vertical   ○ Linear Pair   ○ Neither

   C. ∠BFD and ∠AFE   ○ Vertical   ○ Linear Pair   ○ Neither

2. Does each transformation map a triangle in Quadrant II to Quadrant I?

   Select Yes or No for A–C.

   A. A rotation of 270°   ○ Yes   ○ No

   B. A translation along the vector $(-2, -2)$ ○ Yes   ○ No

   C. A reflection across the y-axis   ○ Yes   ○ No

3. Are the triangles necessarily congruent?

   Select Yes or No for each statement.

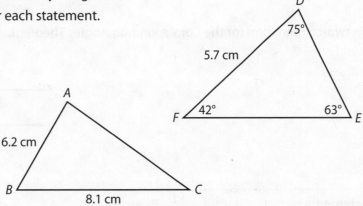

   A. $AC = 5.7$ cm   ○ Yes   ○ No

   B. m∠BAC = 75°, m∠ABC = 63°, and $DE = 6.2$ cm   ○ Yes   ○ No

   C. m∠ACB = 42°, m∠ABC = 63°, and $FE = 8.2$ cm   ○ Yes   ○ No

4. Triangle △ABC is in the second quadrant and translated along (−3, 2) and reflected across the y-axis. Determine if the translation will be in the given quadrant. Select Yes or No for each statement.

A. In the first quadrant after the first transformation   ◯ Yes   ◯ No

B. In the second quadrant after the first transformation   ◯ Yes   ◯ No

C. In the third quadrant after the second transformation   ◯ Yes   ◯ No

5. Given △ABC where A(2, 3), B(5, 8), C(8, 3), $\overline{RS}$ is the midsegment parallel to $\overline{AC}$, $\overline{ST}$ is the midsegment parallel to $\overline{AB}$, and $\overline{RT}$ is the midsegment parallel to $\overline{BC}$, determine if the statements are true or false. Select True or False for each statement.

A. $\overline{ST} = 4$ ◯ True   ◯ False

B. $\overline{RT} = 5$ ◯ True   ◯ False

C. $\overline{RS} = 3$ ◯ True   ◯ False

6. Find each angle measure.

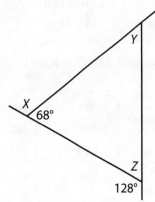

7. Write a proof in two-column form for the Corresponding Angles Theorem.

Given: $\ell \parallel m$

Prove: $m\angle 3 = m\angle 7$

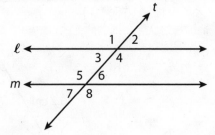

Statements	Reasons

© Houghton Mifflin Harcourt Publishing Company

Performance Tasks

★ **8.** An employee is walking home from work and wants to take the long way to get more exercise. The diagram represents the two different routes, where *A* is the employee's work and *B* is the employee's home. Which route is longer and by how much? Show your work.

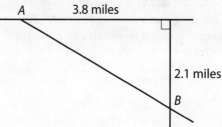

★★ **9.** A student was given the following triangle and asked to find the circumcenter. Find the point and explain the steps for finding it.

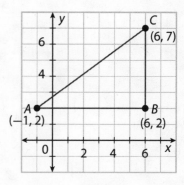

★★★ **10.** While constructing a roof, a construction company built a triangle frame with a base 25 feet long. A cross bar needs to be inserted that connects the midpoints of both sides of the frame. Draw an image to represent the situation and then describe how much wood is needed for the crossbar. Assume the triangle is isosceles. Explain your answer.

© Houghton Mifflin Harcourt Publishing Company

Architect An architect is writing the blueprints for a large triangular building to go in the middle of a city. The building needs to be congruent to a building that is already made, but the blueprints for the previous building were lost. What information will need to be known about each triangular face of the building in order to make sure all faces are congruent, knowing the building does not have any right triangles? Explain each possibility using known triangle congruence theorems and postulates.

Quadrilaterals and Coordinate Proof

MATH IN CAREERS

Urban Planners Urban planners design the way a city looks and functions. Urban planners use math to determine the size and placement of crucial elements in cities, based on factors such as population, industry, and transportation.

If you're interested in a career as an urban planner, you should study these mathematical subjects:

- Algebra
- Geometry
- Calculus
- Statistics
- Linear Algebra

Research other careers that require the use of spatial analysis and statistics to understand real-world scenarios. See the related Career Activity at the end of this unit.

Reading Start-Up

Visualize Vocabulary

Use the review words to complete the chart.

	A formula that finds the distance between two points, written as $(x_2 - x_1)^2 + (y_2 - y_1)^2 = d^2$.
	Two lines that lie in the same plane and never intersect.
	A formula that finds the midpoint of a line segment, written as $M = \left(\dfrac{x_1 + x_2}{2}, \dfrac{y_1 + y_2}{2} \right)$.
	A ratio that is used to determine how steep a line is.
	When two lines intersect, four angles result. This refers to either pair of angles that are not adjacent to each other.

Understand Vocabulary

To become familiar with some of the vocabulary terms in the unit, consider the following. You may refer to the module, the glossary, or a dictionary.

1. A _____ is a quadrilateral with four congruent sides.

2. A _____ is made up of simple shapes, such as triangles and quadrilaterals.

3. A _____ is any quadrilateral whose opposite sides are parallel.

Active Reading

Before beginning the unit, create a booklet to help you organize what you learn. Write a main topic from each module on each page of the booklet. Write details of each main topic on the appropriate page to create an outline of the module. The ability to reword and retell the details of a module will help in understanding complex materials.

Properties of Quadrilaterals

Essential Question: How can you use properties of quadrilaterals to solve real-world problems?

REAL WORLD VIDEO
Check out how architects use properties of quadrilaterals to design unusual buildings, such as the Seattle Central Library.

MODULE PERFORMANCE TASK PREVIEW

How Big Is That Face?

In this module, you will use the geometry of trapezoids and other quadrilaterals to solve a problem related to the external dimensions of the Seattle Central Library. Let's get started and explore this interesting "slant" on architecture!

Are YOU Ready?

Complete these exercises to review the skills you will need for this module.

Congruent Figures

Example 1

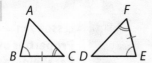

Determine if the pairs of figures are congruent and state the appropriate congruence theorem if applicable.

$\triangle ABC$ is congruent to $\triangle DEF$ via the ASA Congruence Theorem.

1. Determine if the figures are congruent and state the appropriate congruence theorem if applicable.

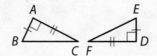

Example 2

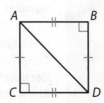

Determine whether the figure contains a pair of congruent triangles and state the appropriate congruence theorem if applicable.

Since $\overline{AD}$ is congruent to $\overline{DA}$ via the Reflexive Property of Congruence, $\triangle ABD$ is congruent to $\triangle DCA$ because of the SSS Congruence Theorem.

2. Determine whether the figure contains a pair of congruent triangles and state the appropriate congruence theorem if applicable.

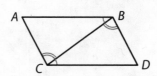

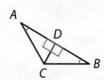

Parallelograms

Example 3

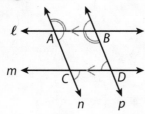

Determine if the figure is a parallelogram.

It is given that lines ℓ and m are parallel. Lines n and p are also parallel because of the Converse of the Corresponding Angles Theorem. Therefore, $ABCD$ is a parallelogram.

3. Determine if the figure is a parallelogram.

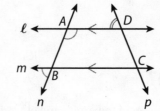

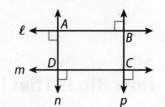

24.1 Properties of Parallelograms

Essential Question: What can you conclude about the sides, angles, and diagonals of a parallelogram?

⊘ Explore   Investigating Parallelograms

A **quadrilateral** is a polygon with four sides. A **parallelogram** is a quadrilateral that has two pairs of parallel sides. You can use geometry software to investigate properties of parallelograms.

(A) Draw a straight line. Then plot a point that is not on the line. Construct a line through the point that is parallel to the line. This gives you a pair of parallel lines.

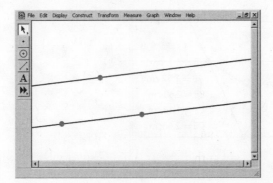

(B) Repeat Step A to construct a second pair of parallel lines that intersect those from Step A.

(C) The intersections of the parallel lines create a parallelogram. Plot points at these intersections. Label the points *A*, *B*, *C*, and *D*.

Identify the *opposite sides* and *opposite angles* of the parallelogram.

Opposite sides: _____

Opposite angles: _____

(D) Measure each angle of the parallelogram.

Measure the length of each side of the parallelogram. You can do this by measuring the distance between consecutive vertices.

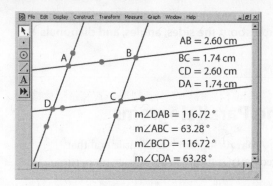

(E) Then drag the points and lines in your construction to change the shape of the parallelogram. As you do so, look for relationships in the measurements. Make a conjecture about the sides and angles of a parallelogram.

Conjecture: _____

_____

(F) A segment that connects two nonconsecutive vertices of a polygon is a **diagonal**. Construct diagonals $\overline{AC}$ and $\overline{BD}$. Plot a point at the intersection of the diagonals and label it E.

(G) Measure the length of $\overline{AE}$, $\overline{BE}$, $\overline{CE}$, and $\overline{DE}$.

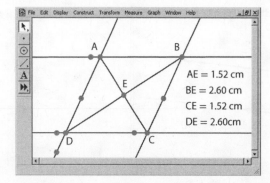

(H) Drag the points and lines in your construction to change the shape of the parallelogram. As you do so, look for relationships in the measurements in Step G. Make a conjecture about the diagonals of a parallelogram.

Conjecture: _____

Reflect

1. *Consecutive angles* are the angles at consecutive vertices, such as ∠A and ∠B, or ∠A and ∠D. Use your construction to make a conjecture about consecutive angles of a parallelogram.

Conjecture: _____

2. Critique Reasoning A student claims that the perimeter of $\triangle AEB$ in the construction is always equal to the perimeter of $\triangle CED$. Without doing any further measurements in your construction, explain whether or not you agree with the student's statement.

_____

_____

⊘ Explain 1 Proving Opposite Sides Are Congruent

The conjecture you made in the Explore about opposite sides of a parallelogram can be stated as a theorem. The proof involves drawing an *auxiliary line* in the figure.

Theorem
If a quadrilateral is a parallelogram, then its opposite sides are congruent.

Example 1 Prove that the opposite sides of a parallelogram are congruent.

Given: *ABCD* is a parallelogram.

Prove: $\overline{AB} \cong \overline{CD}$ and $\overline{AD} \cong \overline{CB}$

Statements	Reasons
1. *ABCD* is a parallelogram.	1.
2. Draw $\overline{DB}$.	2. Through any two points, there is exactly one line.
3. $\overline{AB} \| \overline{DC}, \overline{AD} \| \overline{BC}$	3.
4. $\angle ADB \cong \angle CBD$ $\angle ABD \cong \angle CDB$	4.
5. $\overline{DB} \cong \overline{DB}$	5.
6.	6. ASA Triangle Congruence Theorem
7. $\overline{AB} \cong \overline{CD}$ and $\overline{AD} \cong \overline{CB}$	7.

Reflect

3. Explain how you can use the rotational symmetry of a parallelogram to give an argument that supports the above theorem.

_____

_____

🔑 Explain 2 Proving Opposite Angles Are Congruent

The conjecture from the Explore about opposite angles of a parallelogram can also be proven and stated as a theorem.

Theorem

If a quadrilateral is a parallelogram, then its opposite angles are congruent.

Example 2 Prove that the opposite angles of a parallelogram are congruent.

Given: *ABCD* is a parallelogram.

Prove: ∠A ≅ ∠C (A similar proof shows that ∠B ≅ ∠D.)

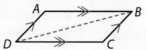

Statements	Reasons
1. *ABCD* is a parallelogram.	1.
2. Draw $\overline{DB}$.	2.
3. $\overline{AB}\|\overline{DC}, \overline{AD}\|\overline{BC}$	3.
4.	4. Alternate Interior Angles Theorem
5.	5. Reflexive Property of Congruence
6.	6. ASA Triangle Congruence Theorem
7.	7.

Reflect

4. Explain how the proof would change in order to prove ∠B ≅ ∠D.

_____

_____

5. In Reflect 1, you noticed that the consecutive angles of a parallelogram are supplementary. This can be stated as the theorem, *If a quadrilateral is a parallelogram, then its consecutive angles are supplementary.*

Explain why this theorem is true.

_____

_____

_____

🔑 Explain 3 Proving Diagonals Bisect Each Other

The conjecture from the Explore about diagonals of a parallelogram can also be proven and stated as a theorem. One proof is shown on the facing page.

Theorem

If a quadrilateral is a parallelogram, then its diagonals bisect each other.

Example 3 Complete the flow proof that the diagonals of a parallelogram bisect each other.

Given: *ABCD* is a parallelogram.

Prove: $\overline{AE} \cong \overline{CE}$ and $\overline{BE} \cong \overline{DE}$

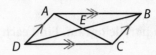

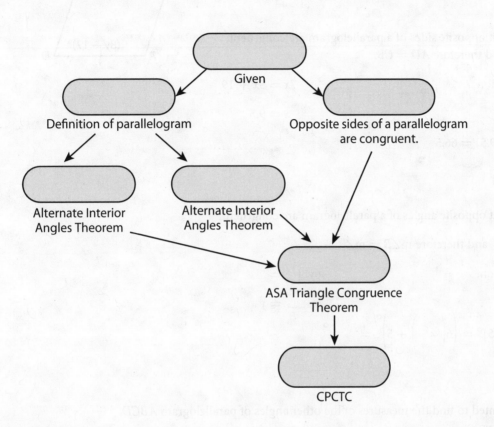

Given

Definition of parallelogram

Opposite sides of a parallelogram are congruent.

Alternate Interior Angles Theorem

Alternate Interior Angles Theorem

ASA Triangle Congruence Theorem

CPCTC

Reflect

6. **Discussion** Is it possible to prove the theorem using a different triangle congruence theorem? Explain.

_____

_____

_____

You can use the properties of parallelograms to find unknown lengths or angle measures in a figure.

Example 4 *ABCD* is a parallelogram. Find each measure.

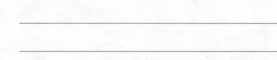

(A) *AD*

Use the fact that opposite sides of a parallelogram are congruent, so $\overline{AD} \cong \overline{CB}$ and therefore $AD = CB$.

Write an equation. $\qquad\qquad\qquad\qquad 7x = 5x + 19$

Solve for *x*. $\qquad\qquad\qquad\qquad\qquad x = 9.5$

$AD = 7x = 7(9.5) = 66.5$

(B) m∠*B*

Use the fact that opposite angles of a parallelogram are congruent,

so $\angle B \cong \angle \boxed{}$ and therefore m∠*B* = m∠$\boxed{}$.

Write an equation. $\qquad\qquad\qquad 6y + 5 = \underline{\qquad\qquad}$

Solve for *y*. $\qquad\qquad\qquad\qquad \underline{\qquad\qquad} = y$

$m\angle B = (6y + 5)° = \left(6\boxed{} + 5\right)° = \boxed{}°$

7. Suppose you wanted to find the measures of the other angles of parallelogram *ABCD*. Explain your steps.

_____

_____

_____

_____

PQRS is a parallelogram. Find each measure.

8. *QR*

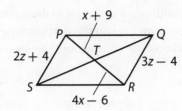

9. *PR*

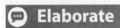

Elaborate

10. What do you need to know first in order to apply any of the theorems of this lesson?

_____

11. In parallelogram *ABCD*, point *P* lies on $\overline{DC}$, as shown in the figure. Explain why it must be the case that $DC = 2AD$. Use what you know about base angles of an isosceles triangle.

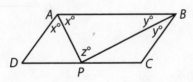

_____

_____

_____

12. **Essential Question Check-In** *JKLM* is a parallelogram. Name all of the congruent segments and angles in the figure.

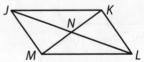

_____

☆ Evaluate: Homework and Practice

• Online Homework
• Hints and Help
• Extra Practice

1. Pablo traced along both edges of a ruler to draw two pairs of parallel lines, as shown. Explain the next steps he could take in order to make a conjecture about the diagonals of a parallelogram.

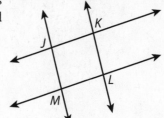

2. Sabina has tiles in the shape of a parallelogram. She labels the angles of each tile as ∠A, ∠B, ∠C, and ∠D. Then she arranges the tiles to make the pattern shown here and uses the pattern to make a conjecture about opposite angles of a parallelogram. What conjecture does she make? How does the pattern help her make the conjecture?

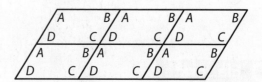

3. Complete the flow proof that the opposite sides of a parallelogram are congruent. Given: *ABCD* is a parallelogram. Prove: $\overline{AB} \cong \overline{CD}$ and $\overline{AD} \cong \overline{CB}$

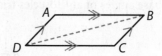

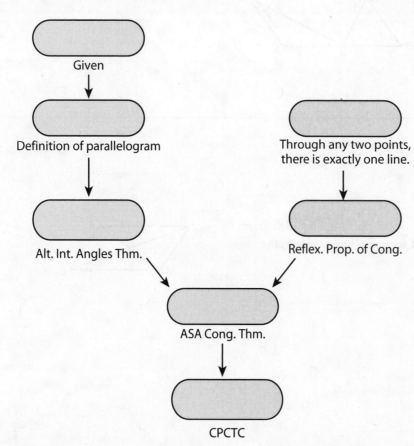

Given

Definition of parallelogram

Through any two points, there is exactly one line.

Alt. Int. Angles Thm.

Reflex. Prop. of Cong.

ASA Cong. Thm.

CPCTC

4. Write the proof that the opposite angles of a parallelogram are congruent as a paragraph proof.

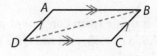

Given: *ABCD* is a parallelogram.

Prove: $\angle A \cong \angle C$ (A similar proof shows that $\angle B \cong \angle D$.)

5. Write the proof that the diagonals of a parallelogram bisect each other as a two-column proof.

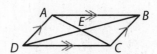

Given: *ABCD* is a parallelogram.

Prove: $\overline{AE} \cong \overline{CE}$ and $\overline{BE} \cong \overline{DE}$

Statements	Reasons
1.	1.

EFGH is a parallelogram. Find each measure.

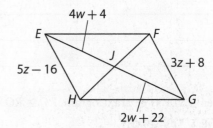

6. *FG*

7. *EG*

ABCD is a parallelogram. Find each measure.

8. m∠*B*

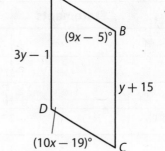

9. *AD*

A staircase handrail is made from congruent parallelograms.
In ▱*PQRS*, *PQ* = 17.5, *ST* = 18, and m∠*QRS* = 110°.
Find each measure. Explain.

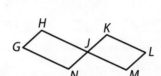

10. *RS*

11. *QT*

12. m∠*PQR*

13. m∠*SPQ*

Write each proof as a two-column proof.

14. Given: *GHJN* and *JKLM* are parallelograms.
   Prove: ∠*G* ≅ ∠*L*

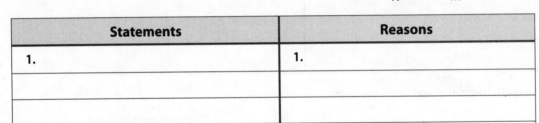

Statements	Reasons
1.	1.

15. Given: *PSTV* is a parallelogram. $\overline{PQ} \cong \overline{RQ}$
   Prove: ∠*STV* ≅ ∠*R*

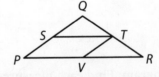

Statements	Reasons
1.	1.

16. Given: *ABCD* and *AFGH* are parallelograms.

Prove: ∠*C* ≅ ∠*G*

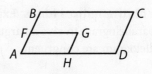

Statements	Reasons
1.	1.

Justify Reasoning Determine whether each statement is always, sometimes, or never true. Explain your reasoning.

17. If quadrilateral *RSTU* is a parallelogram, then $\overline{RS} \cong \overline{ST}$.

18. If a parallelogram has a 30° angle, then it also has a 150° angle.

19. If quadrilateral *GHJK* is a parallelogram, then $\overline{GH}$ is congruent to $\overline{JK}$.

20. In parallelogram *ABCD*, ∠*A* is acute and ∠*C* is obtuse.

21. In parallelogram *MNPQ*, the diagonals $\overline{MP}$ and $\overline{NQ}$ meet at *R* with *MR* = 7 cm and *RP* = 5 cm.

22. Communicate Mathematical Ideas Explain how you can use the rotational symmetry of a parallelogram to give an argument that supports the fact that opposite angles of a parallelogram are congruent.

23. To repair a large truck or bus, a mechanic might use a parallelogram lift. The figure shows a side view of the lift. *FGKL*, *GHJK*, and *FHJL* are parallelograms.

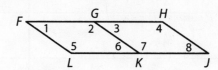

   a. Which angles are congruent to ∠1? Explain.

   b. What is the relationship between ∠1 and each of the remaining labeled angles? Explain.

24. **Justify Reasoning** *ABCD* is a parallelogram. Determine whether each statement must be true. Select the correct answer for each lettered part. Explain your reasoning.

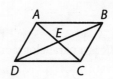

   A. The perimeter of *ABCD* is 2*AB* + 2*BC*.   ◯ Yes   ◯ No

   B. $DE = \frac{1}{2} DB$ ◯ Yes   ◯ No

   C. $\overline{BC} \cong \overline{DC}$ ◯ Yes   ◯ No

   D. ∠*DAC* ≅ ∠*BCA*   ◯ Yes   ◯ No

   E. △*AED* ≅ △*CEB*   ◯ Yes   ◯ No

   F. ∠*DAC* ≅ ∠*BAC*   ◯ Yes   ◯ No

25. Represent Real-World Problems A store sells tiles in the shape of a parallelogram. The perimeter of each tile is 29 inches. One side of each tile is 2.5 inches longer than another side. What are the side lengths of the tile? Explain your steps.

26. Critique Reasoning A student claims that there is an SSSS congruence criterion for parallelograms. That is, if all four sides of one parallelogram are congruent to the four sides of another parallelogram, then the parallelograms are congruent. Do you agree? If so, explain why. If not, give a counterexample. Hint: Draw a picture.

27. Analyze Relationships The figure shows two congruent parallelograms. How are x and y related? Write an equation that expresses the relationship. Explain your reasoning.

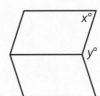

Lesson Performance Task

The principle that allows a scissor lift to raise the platform on top of it to a considerable height can be illustrated with four freezer pop sticks attached at the corners.

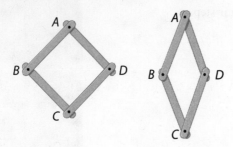

Answer these questions about what happens to parallelogram *ABCD* when you change its shape as in the illustration.

    a. Is it still a parallelogram? Explain.

    b. Is its area the same? Explain.

    c. Compare the lengths of the diagonals in the two figures as you change them.

    d. Describe a process that might be used to raise the platform on a scissor lift.

24.2 Conditions for Parallelograms

Essential Question: What criteria can you use to prove that a quadrilateral is a parallelogram?

Explore   Proving the Opposite Sides Criterion for a Parallelogram

You can prove that a quadrilateral is a parallelogram by using the definition of a parallelogram. That is, you can show that both pairs of opposite sides are parallel. However, there are other conditions that also guarantee that a quadrilateral is a parallelogram.

> **Theorem**
>
> If both pairs of opposite sides of a quadrilateral are congruent, then the quadrilateral is a parallelogram.

Complete the proof of the theorem.

Given: $\overline{AB} \cong \overline{CD}$ and $\overline{AD} \cong \overline{CB}$

Prove: $ABCD$ is a parallelogram.

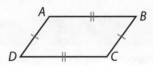

(A) Draw diagonal $\overline{DB}$.

Why is it helpful to draw this diagonal?

_____

_____

(B) Use triangle congruence theorems and corresponding parts to complete the proof that the opposite sides are parallel so the quadrilateral is a parallelogram.

Statements	Reasons
1. Draw $\overline{DB}$.	1. Through any two points, there is exactly one line.
2. $\overline{DB} \cong \overline{DB}$	2.
3. $\overline{AB} \cong \overline{CD}$; $\overline{AD} \cong \overline{CB}$	3.
4. $\triangle ABD \cong \triangle CDB$	4.
5. $\angle ABD \cong \angle CDB$; $\angle ADB \cong \angle CBD$	5.
6. $\overline{AB} \| \overline{DC}$; $\overline{AD} \| \overline{BC}$	6.
7. $ABCD$ is a parallelogram.	7.

It is possible to combine the theorem from the Explore and the definition of a parallelogram to state the following condition for proving a quadrilateral is a parallelogram. You will prove this in the exercises.

Theorem

If one pair of opposite sides of a quadrilateral are parallel and congruent, then the quadrilateral is a parallelogram.

Reflect

1. **Discussion** A quadrilateral has two sides that are 3 cm long and two sides that are 5 cm long. A student states that the quadrilateral must be a parallelogram. Do you agree? Explain.

_____

_____

🔑 Explain 1 Proving the Opposite Angles Criterion for a Parallelogram

You can use relationships between angles to prove that a quadrilateral is a parallelogram.

Theorem

If both pairs of opposite angles of a quadrilateral are congruent, then the quadrilateral is a parallelogram.

Example 1 Prove that a quadrilateral is a parallelogram if its opposite angles are congruent.

Given: $\angle A \cong \angle C$ and $\angle B \cong \angle D$ Prove: $ABCD$ is a parallelogram.

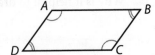

$m\angle A + m\angle B + m\angle C + m\angle D = 360°$ by _____.

From the given information, $m\angle A = m\angle \boxed{}$ and $m\angle B = m\angle \boxed{}$. By substitution,

$m\angle A + m\angle D + m\angle A + m\angle D = 360°$ or $2m\angle \boxed{} + 2m\angle \boxed{} = 360°$. Dividing

both sides by 2 gives _____. Therefore, $\angle A$ and $\angle D$ are

supplementary and so $\overline{AB} \parallel \overline{DC}$ by the _____

A similar argument shows that $\overline{AD} \parallel \overline{BC}$, so $ABCD$ is a parallelogram

by _____.

Reflect

2. What property or theorem justifies dividing both sides of the equation by 2 in the above proof?

_____

🖉 Explain 2 Proving the Bisecting Diagonals Criterion for a Parallelogram

You can use information about the diagonals in a given figure to show that the figure is a parallelogram.

Theorem
If the diagonals of a quadrilateral bisect each other, then the quadrilateral is a parallelogram.

Example 2 Prove that a quadrilateral whose diagonals bisect each other is a parallelogram.

Given: $\overline{AE} \cong \overline{CE}$ and $\overline{DE} \cong \overline{BE}$

Prove: $ABCD$ is a parallelogram.

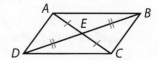

Statements	Reasons
1. $\overline{AE} \cong \overline{CE}, \overline{DE} \cong \overline{BE}$	1.
2. $\angle AEB \cong \angle CED, \angle AED \cong \angle CEB$	2.
3.	3.
4. $\overline{AB} \cong \overline{CD}, \overline{AD} \cong \overline{CB}$	4.
5. $ABCD$ is a parallelogram.	5.

Reflect

3. **Critique Reasoning** A student claimed that you can also write the proof using the SSS Triangle Congruence Theorem since $\overline{AB} \cong \overline{CD}$ and $\overline{AD} \cong \overline{CB}$. Do you agree? Justify your response.

_____

_____

🖉 Explain 3 Using a Parallelogram to Prove the Concurrency of the Medians of a Triangle

Sometimes properties of one type of geometric figure can be used to recognize properties of another geometric figure. Recall that you explored triangles and found that the medians of a triangle are concurrent at a point that is $\frac{2}{3}$ of the distance from each vertex to the midpoint of the opposite side. You can prove this theorem using one of the conditions for a parallelogram from this lesson.

Example 3 Complete the proof of the Concurrency of Medians of a Triangle Theorem.

Given: $\triangle ABC$

Prove: The medians of $\triangle ABC$ are concurrent at a point that is $\frac{2}{3}$ of the distance from each vertex to the midpoint of the opposite side.

Let △ABC be a triangle such that M is the midpoint of $\overline{AB}$ and N is the midpoint of $\overline{BC}$. Label the point where the two medians intersect as P. Draw $\overline{MN}$.

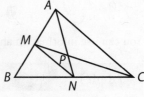

$\overline{MN}$ is a midsegment of △ABC because it connects the midpoints of two sides of the triangle.

$\overline{MN}$ is parallel to _____ and MN = _____ by the Triangle Midsegment Theorem.

Let Q be the midpoint of $\overline{PA}$ and let R be the midpoint of $\overline{PC}$. Draw $\overline{QR}$.

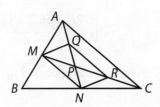

$\overline{QR}$ is a midsegment of △APC because it connects the midpoints of two sides of the triangle.

$\overline{QR}$ is parallel to _____ and QR = _____ by the Triangle Midsegment Theorem.

So, you can conclude that MN = _____ by substitution and that

$\overline{MN} \parallel \overline{QR}$ because _____.

Now draw $\overline{MQ}$ and $\overline{NR}$ and consider quadrilateral MQRN.

Quadrilateral MQRN is a parallelogram because

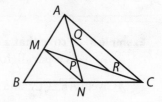

_____.

Since the diagonals of a parallelogram bisect each other, then QP = _____.

Also, AQ = QP since _____.

Therefore, AQ = QP = _____. This shows that point P is located on $\overline{AN}$ at a point that is $\frac{2}{3}$ of the distance from A to N.

By similar reasoning, the diagonals of a parallelogram bisect each other, so RP = _____.

Also, CR = RP since _____.

Therefore, CR = RP = _____. This shows that point P is located on $\overline{CM}$ at a point that is $\frac{2}{3}$ of the distance from C to M.

You can repeat the proof using any two medians of △ABC. The same reasoning shows that the medians from vertices B and C intersect at a point that is also $\frac{2}{3}$ of the distance from C to M, so this point must also be point P. This shows that the three medians intersect at a unique point P and that the point is $\frac{2}{3}$ of the distance from each vertex to the midpoint of the opposite side.

4. In the proof, how do you know that point P is located on $\overline{AN}$ at a point that is $\frac{2}{3}$ of the distance from A to N?

_____

_____

_____

🔑 Explain 4   Verifying Figures Are Parallelograms

You can use information about sides, angles, and diagonals in a given figure to show that the figure is a parallelogram.

Example 4   Show that each quadrilateral is a parallelogram for the given values of the variables.

Ⓐ $x = 7$ and $y = 4$

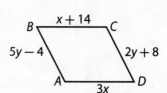

Step 1 Find BC and DA.

$BC = x + 14 = 7 + 14 = 21$

$DA = 3x = 3(7) = 21$

Step 2 Find AB and CD.

$AB = 5y - 4 = 5(4) - 4 = 16$

$CD = 2y + 8 = 2(4) + 8 = 16$

So, $BC = DA$ and $AB = CD$. $ABCD$ is a parallelogram since both pairs of opposite sides are congruent.

Ⓑ $z = 11$ and $w = 4.5$

Step 1 Find $m\angle F$ and $m\angle H$.

$m\angle F = $ _____ $= $ _____

$m\angle H = $ _____ $= $ _____

Step 2 Find $m\angle E$ and $m\angle G$.

$m\angle E = $ _____ $= $ _____

$m\angle G = $ _____ $= $ _____

So, $m\angle F = m\angle$ ☐ and $m\angle E = m\angle$ ☐. $EFGH$ is a parallelogram since

_____

5. What conclusions can you make about $\overline{FG}$ and $\overline{EH}$ in Part B? Explain.

_____

© Houghton Mifflin Harcourt Publishing Company

Your Turn

Show that each quadrilateral is a parallelogram for the given values of the variables.

6. $a = 2.4$ and $b = 9$

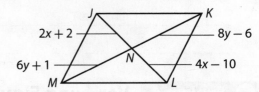

7. $x = 6$ and $y = 3.5$

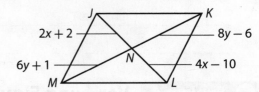

💬 Elaborate

8. How are the theorems in this lesson different from the theorems in the previous lesson, Properties of Parallelograms?

_____

_____

_____

_____

9. Why is the proof of the Concurrency of the Medians of a Triangle Theorem in this lesson and not in the earlier module when the theorem was first introduced?

_____

_____

10. Essential Question Check-In Describe three different ways to show that quadrilateral *ABCD* is a parallelogram.

_____

_____

_____

☆ Evaluate: Homework and Practice

1. You have seen a proof that if both pairs of opposite sides of a quadrilateral are congruent, then the quadrilateral is a parallelogram. Write the proof as a flow proof.

Given: $\overline{AB} \cong \overline{CD}$ and $\overline{AD} \cong \overline{CB}$

Prove: $ABCD$ is a parallelogram.

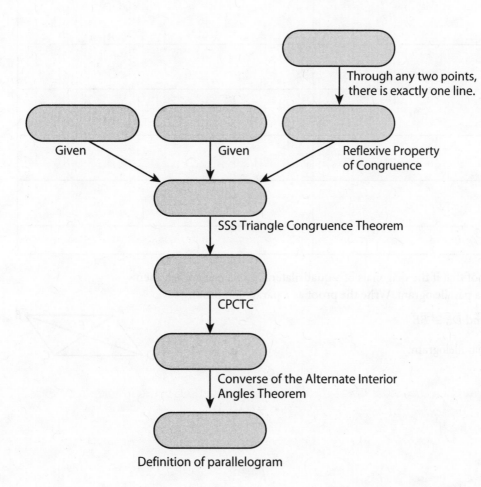

2. You have seen a proof that if both pairs of opposite angles of a quadrilateral are congruent, then the quadrilateral is a parallelogram. Write the proof as a two-column proof.

Given: $\angle A \cong \angle C$ and $\angle B \cong \angle D$

Prove: $ABCD$ is a parallelogram.

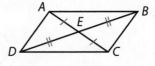

Statements	Reasons
1.	**1.**

3. You have seen a proof that if the diagonals of a quadrilateral bisect each other, then the quadrilateral is a parallelogram. Write the proof as a paragraph proof.

Given: $\overline{AE} \cong \overline{CE}$ and $\overline{DE} \cong \overline{BE}$

Prove: $ABCD$ is a parallelogram.

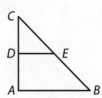

4. Complete the following proof of the Triangle Midsegment Theorem.

Given: D is the midpoint of $\overline{AC}$, and E is the midpoint of $\overline{BC}$.

Prove: $\overline{DE} \parallel \overline{AB}$, $DE = \frac{1}{2}AB$

Extend $\overline{DE}$ to form $\overline{DF}$ such that $\overline{DE} \cong \overline{FE}$. Then draw $\overline{BF}$, as shown.

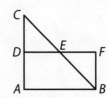

It is given that E is the midpoint of $\overline{CB}$, so $\overline{CE} \cong$ _____.

By the Vertical Angles Theorem, $\angle CED \cong$ _____.

So, $\triangle CED \cong$ _____ by _____.

Since corresponding parts of congruent triangles are congruent, $\overline{CD} \cong$ _____.

D is the midpoint of $\overline{AC}$, so $\overline{CD} \cong$ _____.

By the Transitive Property of Congruence, $\overline{AD} \cong$ _____.

Also, since corresponding parts of congruent triangles are congruent, $\angle CDE \cong$ _____.

So, $\overline{AC} \parallel \overline{FB}$ by _____.

This shows that $DFBA$ is a parallelogram because _____

_____.

By the definition of parallelogram, $\overline{DE}$ is parallel to _____.

Since opposite sides of a parallelogram are congruent, $AB =$ _____.

$\overline{DE} \cong \overline{FE}$, so $DE = \frac{1}{2}\boxed{}$ and by substitution, $DE = \frac{1}{2}\boxed{}$.

Show that each quadrilateral is a parallelogram for the given values of the variables.

5. $x = 4$ and $y = 9$

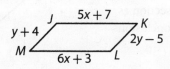

6. $u = 8$ and $v = 3.5$

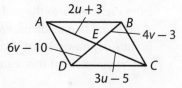

Determine if each quadrilateral must be a parallelogram. Justify your answer.

7.

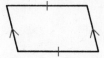

8.

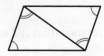

9.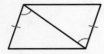

10.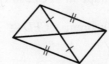

11.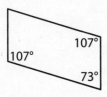

12.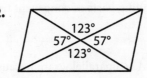

13. Communicate Mathematical Ideas Kalil wants to write the proof that the medians of a triangle are concurrent at a point that is $\frac{2}{3}$ of the distance from each vertex to the midpoint of the opposite side. He starts by drawing $\triangle PQR$ and two medians, $\overline{PK}$ and $\overline{QL}$. He labels the point of intersection as point J, as shown. What segment should Kalil draw next? What conclusions can he make about this segment? Explain.

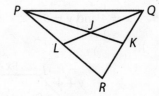

14. Critical Thinking Jasmina said that you can draw a parallelogram using the following steps.

1. Draw a point P.

2. Use a ruler to draw a segment that is 1 inch long with its midpoint at P.

3. Use the ruler to draw a segment that is 2 inches long with its midpoint at P.

4. Use the ruler to connect the endpoints of the segments to form a parallelogram.

Does Jasmina's method always work? Is there ever a time when it would not produce a parallelogram? Explain.

15. Critique Reasoning Matthew said that there is another condition for parallelograms. He said that if a quadrilateral has two congruent diagonals, then the quadrilateral is a parallelogram. Do you agree? If so, explain why. If not, give a counterexample to show why the condition does not work.

16. A parallel rule can be used to plot a course on a navigation chart. The tool is made of two rulers connected at hinges to two congruent crossbars, $\overline{AD}$ and $\overline{BC}$. You place the edge of one ruler on your desired course and then move the second ruler over the compass rose on the chart to read the bearing for your course. If $\overline{AD} \parallel \overline{BC}$, why is $\overline{AB}$ always parallel to $\overline{CD}$?

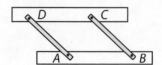

17. Write a two-column proof to prove that a quadrilateral with a pair of opposite sides that are parallel and congruent is a parallelogram.

Given: $\overline{AB} \cong \overline{CD}$ and $\overline{AB} \parallel \overline{CD}$

Prove: *ABCD* is a parallelogram. (*Hint*: Draw $\overline{DB}$.)

Statements	Reasons
1.	1.

Lesson 2

18. Does each set of given information guarantee that quadrilateral *JKLM* is a parallelogram? Select the correct answer for each lettered part.

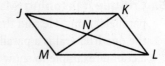

A. *JN* = 25 cm, *JL* = 50 cm, *KN* = 13 cm, *KM* = 26 cm   ○ Yes   ○ No

B. ∠*MJL* ≅ ∠*KLJ*, $\overline{JM}$ ≅ $\overline{LK}$ ○ Yes   ○ No

C. $\overline{JM}$ ≅ $\overline{JK}$, $\overline{KL}$ ≅ $\overline{LM}$ ○ Yes   ○ No

D. ∠*MJL* ≅ ∠*MLJ*, ∠*KJL* ≅ ∠*KLJ*   ○ Yes   ○ No

E. △*JKN* ≅ △*LMN*   ○ Yes   ○ No

H.O.T. Focus on Higher Order Thinking

19. Explain the Error A student wrote the two-column proof below. Explain the student's error and explain how to write the proof correctly.

Given: ∠1 ≅ ∠2, *E* is the midpoint of $\overline{AC}$.

Prove: *ABCD* is a parallelogram.

Statements	Reasons
1. ∠1 ≅ ∠2	**1.** Given
2. *E* is the midpoint of $\overline{AC}$.	**2.** Given
3. $\overline{AE}$ ≅ $\overline{CE}$	**3.** Definition of midpoint
4. ∠*AED* ≅ ∠*CEB*	**4.** Vertical angles are congruent.
5. △*AED* ≅ △*CEB*	**5.** ASA Triangle Congruence Theorem
6. $\overline{AD}$ ≅ $\overline{CB}$	**6.** Corresponding parts of congruent triangles are congruent
7. *ABCD* is a parallelogram.	**7.** If a pair of opposite sides of a quadrillateral are congruent, then the quadrillateral is a parallelogram.

20. Persevere in Problem Solving The plan for a city park shows that the park is a quadrilateral with straight paths along the diagonals. For what values of the variables is the park a parallelogram? In this case, what are the lengths of the paths?

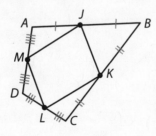

21. Analyze Relationships When you connect the midpoints of the consecutive sides of any quadrilateral, the resulting quadrilateral is a parallelogram. Use the figure below to explain why this is true. (*Hint:* Draw a diagonal of *ABCD*.)

Lesson Performance Task

In this lesson you've learned three theorems for confirming that a figure is a parallelogram.

- If both pairs of opposite sides of a quadrilateral are congruent, then the quadrilateral is a parallelogram.
- If both pairs of opposite angles of a quadrilateral are congruent, then the quadrilateral is a parallelogram.
- If the diagonals of a quadrilateral bisect each other, then the quadrilateral is a parallelogram.

For each of the following situations, choose one of the three theorems and use it in your explanation. You should choose a different theorem for each explanation.

a. You're an amateur astronomer, and one night you see what appears to be a parallelogram in the constellation of Lyra. Explain how you could verify that the figure is a parallelogram.

b. You have a frame shop and you want to make an interesting frame for an advertisement for your store. You decide that you'd like the frame to be a parallelogram but not a rectangle. Explain how you could construct the frame.

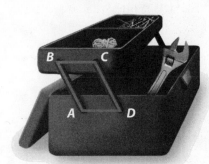

c. You're using a toolbox with cantilever shelves like the one shown here. Explain how you can confirm that the brackets that attach the shelves to the box form a parallelogram ABCD.

© Houghton Mifflin Harcourt Publishing Company

24.3 Properties of Rectangles, Rhombuses, and Squares

Essential Question: What are the properties of rectangles, rhombuses, and squares?

⊘ Explore Exploring Sides, Angles, and Diagonals of a Rectangle

A **rectangle** is a quadrilateral with four right angles.
The figure shows rectangle *ABCD*.

Investigate properties of rectangles.

Ⓐ Use a tile or pattern block and the following method to draw three different rectangles on a separate sheet of paper.

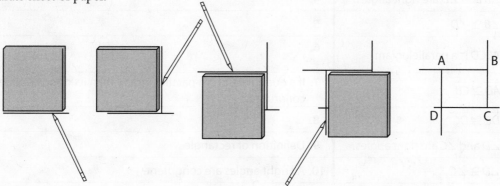

Ⓑ Use a ruler to measure the sides and diagonals of each rectangle. Keep track of the measurements and compare your results to other students.

Reflect

1. Why does this method produce a rectangle? What must you assume about the tile?

_____

_____

_____

2. **Discussion** Is every rectangle also a parallelogram? Make a conjecture based upon your measurements and explain your thinking.

_____

_____

3. Use your measurements to make two conjectures about the diagonals of a rectangle.

Conjecture: _____

Conjecture: _____

Explain 1 **Proving Diagonals of a Rectangle are Congruent**

You can use the definition of a rectangle to prove the following theorems.

> **Properties of Rectangles**
>
> If a quadrilateral is a rectangle, then it is a parallelogram.
> If a parallelogram is a rectangle, then its diagonals are congruent.

Example 1 Use a rectangle to prove the Properties
of Rectangles Theorems.

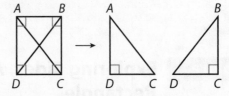

Given: *ABCD* is a rectangle.

Prove: *ABCD* is a parallelogram; $\overline{AC} \cong \overline{BD}$.

(A)

Statements	Reasons
1. *ABCD* is a rectangle.	1. Given
2. ∠*A* and ∠*C* are right angles.	2. Definition of
3. ∠*A* ≅ ∠*C*	3. All right angles are congruent.
4. ∠*B* and ∠*D* are right angles.	4.
5. ∠*B* ≅ ∠*D*	5.
6. *ABCD* is a parallelogram.	6.
7. $\overline{AD} \cong \overline{CB}$	7. If a quadrilateral is a parallelogram, then its opposite sides are congruent.
8. $\overline{DC} \cong \overline{DC}$	8.
9. ∠*D* and ∠*C* are right angles.	9. Definition of rectangle
10. ∠*D* ≅ ∠*C*	10. All right angles are congruent.
11.	11.
12.	12.

Reflect

4. **Discussion** A student says you can also prove the diagonals are congruent in Example 1 by using the SSS Triangle Congruence Theorem to show that △*ADC* ≅ △*BCD*. Do you agree? Explain.

_____

_____

Your Turn

Find each measure.

5. *AD* = 7.5 cm and *DC* = 10 cm. Find *DB*.

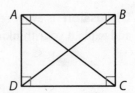

6. *AB* = 17 cm and *BC* = 12.75 cm. Find *DB*.

⚙ Explain 2　Proving Diagonals of a Rhombus are Perpendicular

A **rhombus** is a quadrilateral with four congruent sides.
The figure shows rhombus *JKLM*.

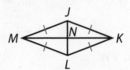

Properties of Rhombuses
If a quadrilateral is a rhombus, then it is a parallelogram. If a parallelogram is a rhombus, then its diagonals are perpendicular. If a parallelogram is a rhombus, then each diagonal bisects a pair of opposite angles.

Example 2　Prove that the diagonals of a rhombus are perpendicular.

Given: *JKLM* is a rhombus.

Prove: $\overline{JL} \perp \overline{MK}$

Since *JKLM* is a rhombus, $\overline{JM} \cong$ ⬚ . Because *JKLM* is also a parallelogram, $\overline{MN} \cong \overline{KN}$ because

_____. By the Reflexive Property of Congruence, $\overline{JN} \cong \overline{JN}$,

so $\triangle JNM \cong \triangle JNK$ by the _____. So, _____ by CPCTC.

By the Linear Pair Theorem, $\angle JNM$ and $\angle JNK$ are supplementary. This means that m$\angle JNM$ + m$\angle JNK$ = ⬚ .

Since the angles are congruent, m$\angle JNM$ = m$\angle JNK$ so by _____, m$\angle JNM$ + m$\angle JNK$ = 180° or

2m$\angle JNK$ = 180°. Therefore, m$\angle JNK$ = ⬚ and ⬚ $\perp \overline{MK}$.

Reflect

7. What can you say about the image of *J* in the proof after a reflection across $\overline{MK}$? Why?

_____

8. What property about the diagonals of a rhombus is the same as a property
of all parallelograms? What special property do the diagonals of a rhombus have?

_____

_____

Your Turn

9. Prove that if a parallelogram is a rhombus, then each diagonal
bisects a pair of opposite angles.

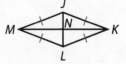

　Given: *JKLM* is a rhombus.

　Prove: $\overline{MK}$ bisects $\angle JML$ and $\angle JKL$;
$\overline{JL}$ bisects $\angle MJK$ and $\angle MLK$.

Explain 3 Using Properties of Rhombuses to Find Measures

Example 3 Use rhombus *VWXY* to find each measure.

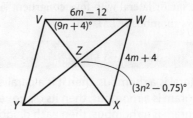

(A) Find *XY*.

All sides of a rhombus are congruent, so $\overline{VW} \cong \overline{WX}$ and $VW = WX$.

Substitute values for *VW* and *WX*. $6m - 12 = 4m + 4$

Solve for *m*. $m = 8$

Sustitute the value of *m* to find *VW*. $VW = 6(8) - 12 = 36$

Because all sides of the rhombus are congruent, then $\overline{VW} \cong \overline{XY}$, and $XY = 36$.

(B) Find $\angle YVW$.

The diagonals of a rhombus are _____, so $\angle WZX$ is a right angle and

$m\angle WZX = $ ⬚.

Since $m\angle WZX = (3n^2 - 0.75)°$, then _____.

Solve for *n*. $3n^2 - 0.75 = 90$

                                                        $n = $ ⬚

Substitute the value of *n* to find $m\angle WVZ$.

                                        $m\angle WVZ = $ ⬚

Since $\overline{VX}$ bisects $\angle YVW$, then _____

Substitute 53.5° for $m\angle WVZ$. $m\angle YVW = 2(53.5°) = 107°$

Your Turn

Use the rhombus *VWXY* from Example 3 to find each measure.

10. Find $m\angle VYX$.   **11.** Find $m\angle XYZ$.

© Houghton Mifflin Harcourt Publishing Company

🖊 Explain 4 — Investigating the Properties of a Square

A **square** is a quadrilateral with four sides congruent
and four right angles.

Example 4 Explain why each conditional statement is true.

(A) If a quadrilateral is a square, then it is a parallelogram.

By definition, a square is a quadrilateral with four congruent sides.
Any quadrilateral with both pairs of opposite sides congruent is a parallelogram,
so a square is a parallelogram.

(B) If a quadrilateral is a square, then it is a rectangle.

By definition, a square is a quadrilateral with four _____.

By definition, a rectangle is also a quadrilateral with four _____.
Therefore, a square is a rectangle.

Your Turn

12. Explain why this conditional statement is true: If a quadrilateral
is a square, then it is a rhombus.

13. Look at Part A. Use a different way to explain why this conditional
statement is true: If a quadrilateral is a square, then it is a parallelogram.

💬 Elaborate

14. Discussion The Venn diagram shows how
quadrilaterals, parallelograms, rectangles, rhombuses,
and squares are related to each other. From this lesson,
what do you notice about the definitions and theorems
regarding these figures?

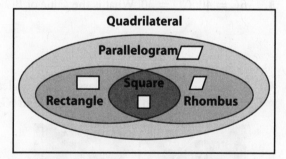

_____

_____

_____

15. Essential Question Check-In What are the properties of rectangles
and rhombuses? How does a square relate to rectangles and rhombuses?

_____

_____

_____

_____

1. Complete the paragraph proof of the Properties of Rectangles Theorems.
   Given: *ABCD* is a rectangle.
   Prove: *ABCD* is a parallelogram; $\overline{AC} \cong \overline{BD}$.

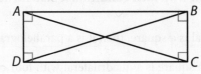

Proof that *ABCD* is a _____ : Since *ABCD* is a rectangle, $\angle A$ and

$\angle C$ are right angles. So $\angle A \cong \angle C$ because _____ .

By similar reasoning, $\angle B \cong \angle D$. Therefore, *ABCD* is a parallelogram because

_____

Proof that the diagonals are congruent: Since *ABCD* is a parallelogram,

$\overline{AD} \cong \overline{BC}$ because _____ .

Also, _____ by the Reflexive Property of Congruence. By the definition of a

rectangle, $\angle D$ and $\angle C$ are right angles, and so _____

because all right angles are _____ . Therefore, $\triangle ADC \cong \triangle BCD$ by the

_____ and ☐ $\cong$ ☐ by CPCTC.

Find the lengths using rectangle *ABCD*.

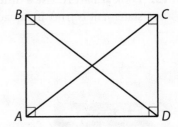

2. $AB = 21$; $AD = 28$. What is the value of $AC + BD$?

3. $BC = 40$; $CD = 30$. What is the value of $BC - AC$?

4. An artist connects stained glass pieces with lead strips. In this rectangular window, the strips are cut so that $FH = 34$ in. Find JG. Explain.

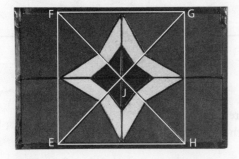

The rectangular gate has diagonal braces. Find each length.

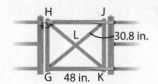

5. Find *HJ*.

6. Find *HK*.

7. Find the measure of each numbered angle in the rectangle.

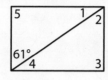

8. Complete the two-column proof that the diagonals of a rhombus are perpendicular.

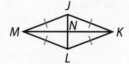

Given: *JKLM* is a rhombus.

Prove: $\overline{JL} \perp \overline{MK}$

Statements	Reasons
1. $\overline{JM} \cong \overline{JK}$	1. Definition of rhombus
2. $\overline{MN} \cong \overline{KN}$	2.
3. $\overline{JN} \cong \overline{JN}$	3. Reflexive Property of Congruence
4.	4. SSS Triangle Congruence Theorem
5. $\angle JNM \cong \angle JNK$	5.
6. $\angle JNM$ and $\angle JNK$ are supplementary.	6.
7.	7. Definition of supplementary
8. $\angle JNM = \angle JNK$	8. Definition of congruence
9. $\boxed{} + \angle JNK = 180°$	9. Substitution Property of Equality
10. $2m\angle JNK = 180°$	10. Addition
11. $m\angle JNK = 90°$	11. Division Property of Equality
12.	12. Definition of perpendicular lines

ABCD is a rhombus. Find each measure.

9. Find *AB*.

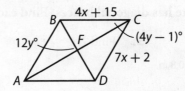

10. Find m∠*ABC*.

Find the measure of each numbered angle in the rhombus.

11.

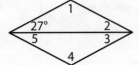

12.

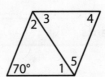

13. Select the word that best describes when each of the following statements are true.
Select the correct answer for each lettered part.

   A. A rectangle is a parallelogram. ◯ always ◯ sometimes ◯ never

   B. A parallelogram is a rhombus. ◯ always ◯ sometimes ◯ never

   C. A square is a rhombus. ◯ always ◯ sometimes ◯ never

   D. A rhombus is a square. ◯ always ◯ sometimes ◯ never

   E. A rhombus is a rectangle. ◯ always ◯ sometimes ◯ never

14. Use properties of special parallelograms to complete the proof.

Given: *EFGH* is a rectangle. *J* is the midpoint of $\overline{EH}$.

Prove: △*FJG* is isosceles.

Statements	Reasons
1. *EFGH* is a rectangle. *J* is the midpoint of $\overline{EH}$.	**1.** Given
2. ∠*E* and ∠*H* are right angles.	**2.** Definition of rectangle
3. ∠*E* ≅ ∠*H*	**3.**
4. *EFGH* is a parallelogram.	**4.**
5.	**5.**
6.	**6.**
7.	**7.**
8.	**8.**
9.	**9.**

15. Explain the Error Find and explain the error in this paragraph proof. Then describe a way to correct the proof.

Given: *JKLM* is a rhombus.

Prove: *JKLM* is a parallelogram.

Proof: It is given that *JLKM* is a rhombus. So, by the definition of a rhombus,
$\overline{JK} ≅ \overline{LM}$, and $\overline{KL} ≅ \overline{MJ}$. If a quadrilateral is a parallelogram, then its opposite sides are congruent. So *JKLM* is a parallelogram.

The opening of a soccer goal is shaped like a rectangle.

16. Draw a rectangle to represent a soccer goal. Label the rectangle *ABCD* to show that the distance between the goalposts, $\overline{BC}$, is three times the distance from the top of the goalpost to the ground. If the perimeter of *ABCD* is 64 feet, what is the length of $\overline{BC}$?

17. In your rectangle from Evaluate 16, suppose the distance from *B* to *D* is $(y + 10)$ feet, and the distance from *A* to *C* is $(2y - 5.3)$ feet. What is the approximate length of $\overline{AC}$?

18. *PQRS* is a rhombus, with $PQ = (7b - 5)$ meters and $QR = (2b - 0.5)$ meters. If *S* is the midpoint of $\overline{RT}$, what is the length of $\overline{RT}$?

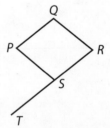

19. Communicate Mathematical Ideas List the properties that a square "inherits" because it is each of the following quadrilaterals.

    a. a parallelogram

    b. a rectangle

    c. a rhombus

H.O.T. **Focus on Higher Order Thinking**

Justify Reasoning For the given figure, describe any rotations or reflections that would carry the figure onto itself. Explain.

20. A rhombus that is not a square

21. A rectangle that is not a square

22. A square

23. Analyze Relationships Look at your answers for Exercises 20–22. How does your answer to Exercise 22 relate to your answers to Exercises 20 and 21? Explain.

Lesson Performance Task

The portion of the Arkansas state flag that is not red is a rhombus. On one flag, the diagonals of the rhombus measure 24 inches and 36 inches. Find the area of the rhombus. Justify your reasoning.

24.4 Conditions for Rectangles, Rhombuses, and Squares

Essential Question: How can you use given conditions to show that a quadrilateral is a rectangle, a rhombus, or a square?

⊘ Explore Properties of Rectangles, Rhombuses, and Squares

In this lesson we will start with given properties and use them to prove which special parallelogram it could be.

Ⓐ Start by drawing two line segments of the same length that bisect each other but are not perpendicular. They will form an X shape, as shown.

Ⓑ Connect the ends of the line segments to form a quadrilateral.

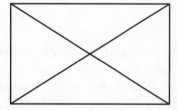

Ⓒ Measure each of the four angles of the quadrilateral, and use those measurements to name the shape.

(D) Now, draw two line segments that are perpendicular and bisect each other but that are not the same length.

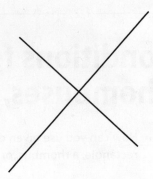

(E) Connect the ends of the line segments to form a quadrilateral.

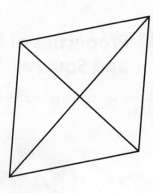

(F) Measure each side length of the quadrilateral. Then use those measurements to name the shape.

_____

Reflect

1. **Discussion** How are the diagonals of your rectangle in Step B different from the diagonals of your rhombus in Step E?

_____

_____

2. Draw a line segment. At each endpoint draw line segments so that four congruent angles are formed as shown. Then extend the segments so that they intersect to form a quadrilateral. Measure the sides. What do you notice? What kind of quadrilateral is it? How does the line segment relate to the angles drawn on either end of it?

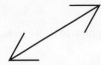

_____

_____

Proving that Congruent Diagonals Is a Condition for Rectangles

When you are given a parallelogram with certain properties, you can use the properties to determine whether the parallelogram is a rectangle.

Theorems: Conditions for Rectangles	
If one angle of a parallelogram is a right angle, then the parallelogram is a rectangle.	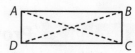
If the diagonals of a parallelogram are congruent, then the parallelogram is a rectangle.	$\overline{AC} \cong \overline{BD}$

Example 1 Prove that if the diagonals of a parallelogram are congruent, then the parallelogram is a rectangle.

Given: $ABCD$ is a parallelogram; $\overline{AC} \cong \overline{BD}$.

Prove: $ABCD$ is a rectangle.

Because _____, $\overline{AB} \cong \overline{CD}$.

It is given that $\overline{AC} \cong \overline{BD}$, and _____ by the Reflexive Property of Congruence.

So, _____ by the SSS Triangle Congruence Theorem,

and _____ by CPCTC. But these angles are _____

since $\overline{AB} \parallel$ ▢. Therefore, m∠BAD + m∠CDA = ▢. So

m∠BAD + ▢ = ▢ by substitution, 2 · m∠BAD = 180°,

and m∠BAD = 90°. A similar argument shows that the other angles

of $ABCD$ are also _____ angles, so $ABCD$ is a _____.

Reflect

3. **Discussion** Explain why this is a true condition for rectangles:
   If one angle of a parallelogram is a right angle, then the parallelogram is a rectangle.

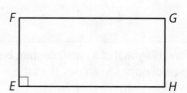

_____

_____

Use the given information to determine whether the quadrilateral is necessarily a rectangle. Explain your reasoning.

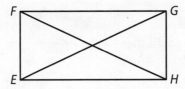

4.   Given: $\overline{EF} \cong \overline{GF}$, $\overline{FG} \cong \overline{HE}$, $\overline{FH} \cong \overline{GE}$

5.   Given: m∠FEG = 45°, m∠GEH = 50°

✪ Explain 2   Proving Conditions for Rhombuses

You can also use given properties of a parallelogram to determine whether the parallelogram is a rhombus.

Theorems: Conditions for Rhombuses	
If one pair of consecutive sides of a parallelogram are congruent, then the parallelogram is a rhombus.	
If the diagonals of a parallelogram are perpendicular, then the parallelogram is a rhombus.	
If one diagonal of a parallelogram bisects a pair of opposite angles, then the parallelogram is a rhombus.	

You will prove one of the theorems about rhombuses in Example 2 and the other theorems in Your Turn Exercise 6 and Evaluate Exercise 22.

© Houghton Mifflin Harcourt Publishing Company

Example 2 Complete the flow proof that if one diagonal of a parallelogram bisects a pair of opposite angles, then the parallelogram is a rhombus.

Given: $ABCD$ is a parallelogram; $\angle BCA \cong \angle DCA$; $\angle BAC \cong \angle DAC$

Prove: $ABCD$ is a rhombus.

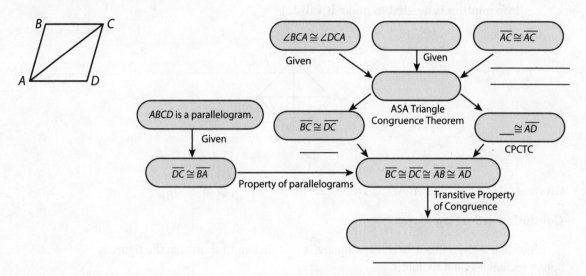

Your Turn

6. Prove that If one pair of consecutive sides of a parallelogram are congruent, then it is a rhombus.

   Given: $JKLM$ is a parallelogram. $\overline{JK} \cong \overline{KL}$

   Prove: $JKLM$ is a rhombus.

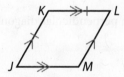

⏺ Explain 3   Applying Conditions for Special Parallelograms

In Example 3, you will decide whether you are given enough information to conclude that a figure is a particular type of special parallelogram.

Example 3   **Determine if the conclusion is valid. If not, tell what additional information is needed to make it valid.**

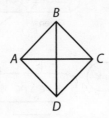

(A)   **Given:** $\overline{AB} \cong \overline{CD}$; $\overline{BC} \cong \overline{DA}$; $\overline{AD} \perp \overline{DC}$; $\overline{AC} \perp \overline{BD}$

Conclusion: *ABCD* is a square.

To prove that a given quadrilateral is a square, it is sufficient to show that the figure is both a rectangle and a rhombus.

Step 1:   Determine if *ABCD* is a parallelogram.

　$\overline{AB} \cong \overline{CD}$ and $\overline{BC} \cong \overline{DA}$ are given. Since a quadrilateral with opposite sides congruent is a parallelogram, we know that *ABCD* is a parallelogram.

Step 2:   Determine if *ABCD* is a rectangle.

　Since $\overline{AD} \perp \overline{DC}$, by definition of perpendicular lines, ∠*ADC* is a right angle. A parallelogram with one right angle is a rectangle, so *ABCD* is a rectangle.

Step 3:   Determine if *ABCD* is a rhombus.

　$\overline{AC} \perp \overline{BD}$. A parallelogram with perpendicular diagonals is a rhombus. So *ABCD* is a rhombus.

Step 4:   Determine if *ABCD* is a square.

　Since *ABCD* is a rectangle and a rhombus, it has four right angles and four congruent sides. So *ABCD* is a square by definition.

　So, the conclusion is valid.

(B)   **Given:** $\overline{AB} \cong \overline{BC}$

Conclusion: *ABCD* is a rhombus.

The conclusion is not valid. It is true that if two consecutive sides of a _____ are

congruent, then the _____ is a _____. To apply this theorem,

however, you need to know that *ABCD* is a _____. The given information is
not sufficient to conclude that the figure is a parallelogram.

7. Draw a figure that shows why this statement is not necessarily true: If one angle of a quadrilateral is a right angle, then the quadrilateral is a rectangle.

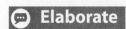

Your Turn

Determine if the conclusion is valid. If not, tell what additional information is needed to make it valid.

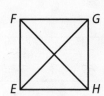

8. **Given:** $\angle ABC$ is a right angle.
   Conclusion: $ABCD$ is a rectangle.

💬 Elaborate

9. Look at the theorem boxes in Example 1 and Example 2. How do the diagrams help you remember the conditions for proving a quadrilateral is a special parallelogram?

10. $EFGH$ is a parallelogram. In $EFGH$, $\overline{EG} \cong \overline{FH}$. Which conclusion is incorrect?

   A. $EFGH$ is a rectangle.

   B. $EFGH$ is a square.

11. **Essential Question Check-In** How are theorems about conditions for parallelograms different from the theorems regarding parallelograms used in the previous lesson?

• Online Homework
• Hints and Help
• Extra Practice

1. Suppose Anna draws two line segments, $\overline{AB}$ and $\overline{CD}$ that intersect at point *E*. She draws them in such a way that $\overline{AB} \cong \overline{CD}$, $\overline{AB} \perp \overline{CD}$, and $\angle CAD$ is a right angle. What is the best name to describe *ACBD*? Explain.

_____

_____

_____

2. Write a two-column proof that if the diagonals of a parallelogram are congruent, then the parallelogram is a rectangle.

Given: *EFGH* is a parallelogram; $\overline{EG} \cong \overline{HF}$.

Prove: *EFGH* is a rectangle.

Statements	Reasons
1.	1.

Determine whether each quadrilateral must be a rectangle. Explain.

3.

Given: $BD = AC$

4.

_____   _____

_____   _____

_____   _____

Each quadrilateral is a parallelogram. Determine whether each parallelogram is a rhombus or not.

5.

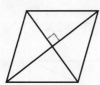

_____

_____

6.

_____

_____

Give one characteristic about each figure that would make the conclusion valid.

7. Conclusion: *JKLM* is a rhombus.

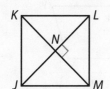

_____

_____

8. Conclusion: *PQRS* is a square.

_____

_____

Determine if the conclusion is valid. If not, tell what additional information is needed to make it valid.

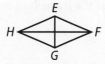

9. Given: $\overline{EG}$ and $\overline{FH}$ bisect each other. $\overline{EG} \perp \overline{FH}$

Conclusion: *EFGH* is a rhombus.

_____

10. $\overline{FH}$ bisects $\angle EFG$ and $\angle EHG$.

Conclusion: *EFGH* is a rhombus.

_____

Find the value of *x* that makes each parallelogram the given type.

11. square

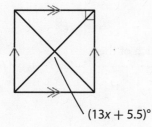

$(13x + 5.5)°$

12. rhombus

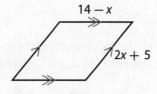

$14 - x$

$2x + 5$

In Exercises 13–16, Determine which quadrilaterals match the figure: parallelogram, rhombus, rectangle, or square? List all that apply.

13. Given: $\overline{WY} \cong \overline{XZ}$, $\overline{WY} \perp \overline{XZ}$, $\overline{XY} \cong \overline{ZW}$

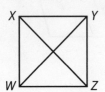

14. Given: $\overline{XY} \cong \overline{ZW}$, $\overline{WY} \cong \overline{ZX}$

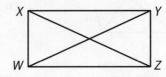

15. Given: $\overline{XY} \cong \overline{ZW}$, $\angle XWY \cong \angle YWZ$, $\angle XYW \cong \angle ZYW$

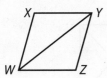

16. Given: $m\angle WXY = 130°$, $m\angle XWZ = 50°$, $m\angle WZY = 130°$

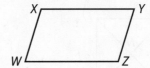

17. Represent Real-World Problems A framer uses a clamp to hold together pieces of a picture frame. The pieces are cut so that $\overline{PQ} \cong \overline{RS}$ and $\overline{QR} \cong \overline{SP}$. The clamp is adjusted so that PZ, QZ, RZ, and SZ are all equal lengths. Why must the frame be a rectangle?

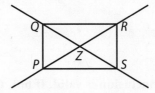

18. Represent Real-World Problems A city garden club is planting a square garden. They drive pegs into the ground at each corner and tie strings between each pair. The pegs are spaced so that $\overline{WX} \cong \overline{XY} \cong \overline{YZ} \cong \overline{ZW}$. How can the garden club use the diagonal strings to verify that the garden is a square?

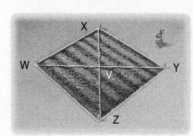

19. A quadrilateral is formed by connecting the midpoints of a rectangle. Which of the following could be the resulting figure? Select all that apply.

  ⭕ parallelogram   ⭕ rectangle

  ⭕ rhombus   ⭕ square

20. Critical Thinking The diagonals of a quadrilateral are perpendicular bisectors of each other. What is the best name for this quadrilateral? Explain your answer.

21. Draw Conclusions Think about the relationships between angles and sides in this triangular prism to decide if the given face is a rectangle.

Given: $\overline{AC} \cong \overline{DF}$, $\overline{AB} \cong \overline{DE}$, $\overline{AB} \perp \overline{BC}$, $\overline{DE} \perp \overline{EF}$, $\overline{BE} \perp \overline{EF}$, $\overline{BC} \parallel \overline{EF}$

Prove: *EBCF* is a rectangle.

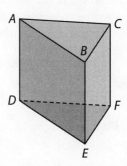

22. Justify Reasoning Use one of the other rhombus theorems to prove that if the diagonals of a parallelogram are perpendicular, then the parallelogram is a rhombus.

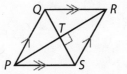

Given: *PQRS* is a parallelogram. $\overline{PR} \perp \overline{QS}$

Prove: *PQRS* is a rhombus.

Statements	Reasons
1. *PQRS* is a parallelogram.	1. Given
2. $\overline{PT} \cong$	2. Diagonals of a parallelogram bisect each other.
3. $\overline{QT} \cong$	3. Reflexive Property of Congruence
4. $\overline{PR} \perp \overline{QS}$	4. Given
5. ∠*QTP* and ∠*QTR* are right angles.	5.
6. ∠*QTP* ≅ ∠*QTR*	6.
7. △*QTP* ≅ △*QTR*	7.
8. $\overline{QP} \cong$	8. CPCTC
9. *PQRS* is a rhombus.	9.

Lesson Performance Task

The diagram shows the organizational ladder of groups to which tigers belong.

a. Use the terms below to create a similar ladder in which each term is a subset of the term above it.

Parallelogram   Geometric figures   Squares

Quadrilaterals   Figures   Rhombuses

b. Decide which of the following statements is true. Then write three more statements like it, using terms from the list in part (a).

If a figure is a rhombus, then it is a parallelogram.

If a figure is a parallelogram, then it is a rhombus.

c. Explain how you can use the ladder you created above to write if-then statements involving the terms on the list.

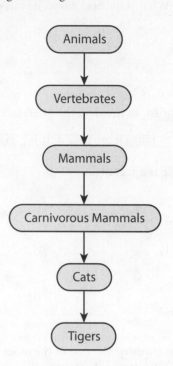

24.5 Properties and Conditions for Kites and Trapezoids

Resource Locker

Essential Question: What are the properties of kites and trapezoids?

Explore Exploring Properties of Kites

A **kite** is a quadrilateral with two distinct pairs of congruent consecutive sides. In the figure, $\overline{PQ} \cong \overline{PS}$, and $\overline{QR} \cong \overline{SR}$, but $\overline{QR} \ncong \overline{QP}$.

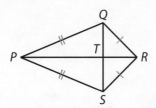

Measure the angles made by the sides and diagonals of a kite, noticing any relationships.

(A) Use a protractor to measure $\angle PTQ$ and $\angle QTR$ in the figure. What do your results tell you about the kite's diagonals, $\overline{PR}$ and $\overline{QS}$?

_____

(B) Use a protractor to measure $\angle PQR$ and $\angle PSR$ in the figure. How are these opposite angles related?

_____

(C) Measure $\angle QPS$ and $\angle QRS$ in the figure. What do you notice?

_____

(D) Use a compass to construct your own kite figure on a separate sheet of paper. Begin by choosing a point B. Then use your compass to choose points A and C so that $AB = BC$.

(E) Now change the compass length and draw arcs from both points A and C. Label the intersection of the arcs as point D.

(F) Finally, draw the sides and diagonals of the kite.

Mark the intersection of the diagonals as point E.

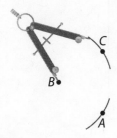

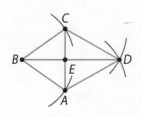

© Houghton Mifflin Harcourt Publishing Company · Image Credits: ©Larry Mulvehill/Corbis

Ⓖ Measure the angles of the kite *ABCD* you constructed in Steps D–F and the measure of the angles formed by the diagonals. Are your results the same as for the kite *PQRS* you used in Steps A–C?

_____

_____

_____

Reflect

1. In the kite *ABCD* you constructed in Steps D–F, look at ∠*CDE* and ∠*ADE*. What do you notice? Is this true for ∠*CBE* and ∠*ABE* as well? How can you state this in terms of diagonal $\overline{AC}$ and the pair of non-congruent opposite angles ∠*CBA* and ∠*CDA*?

_____

_____

2. In the kite *ABCD* you constructed in Steps D–F, look at $\overline{EC}$ and $\overline{EA}$. What do you notice? Is this true for $\overline{EB}$ and $\overline{ED}$ as well? Which diagonal is a perpendicular bisector?

_____

_____

🔑 **Explain 1** **Using Relationships in Kites**

The results of the Explore can be stated as theorems.

Four Kite Theorems
If a quadrilateral is a kite, then its diagonals are perpendicular.
If a quadrilateral is a kite, then exactly one pair of opposite angles are congruent.
If a quadrilateral is a kite, then one of the diagonals bisects the pair of non-congruent angles.
If a quadrilateral is a kite, then exactly one diagonal bisects the other.

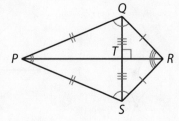

You can use the properties of kites to find unknown angle measures.

Example 1 In kite *ABCD*, m∠*BAE* = 32° and
m∠*BCE* = 62°. Find each measure.

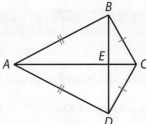

(A) m∠*CBE*

Use angle relationships in △*BCE*.

Use the property that the diagonals of a kite are perpendicular, so m∠*BEC* = 90°.

△*BCE* is a right triangle.

Therefore, its acute angles are complementary.

m∠*BCE* + m∠*CBE* = 90°

Substitute 62° for m∠*BCE*, then solve for m∠*CBE*.

62° + m∠*CBE* = 90°

m∠*CBE* = 28°

(B) m∠*ABE*

△*ABE* is also a right triangle.

Therefore, its acute angles are complementary.

m∠*ABE* + m∠ ☐ = ☐ °

Substitute 32° for m∠ ☐ , then solve for m∠*ABE*.

m∠*ABE* + ☐ ° = ☐ °

m∠*ABE* = ☐ °

Reflect

3. From Part A and Part B, what strategy could you use to determine m∠*ADC*?

_____

_____

Your Turn

4. Determine m∠*ADC* in kite *ABCD*.

🔧 Explain 2 Proving that Base Angles of Isosceles Trapezoids Are Congruent

A **trapezoid** is a quadrilateral with at least one pair of parallel sides.

The parallel sides are called the *bases* of the trapezoid.

The other two sides are called the *legs* of the trapezoid.

A trapezoid has two pairs of *base angles*: each pair consists of the two angles adjacent to one of the bases. An **isosceles trapezoid** is one in which the legs are congruent.

Trapezoid

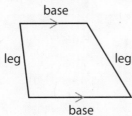

Isosceles trapezoid

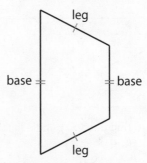

Three Isosceles Trapezoid Theorems

If a quadrilateral is an isosceles trapezoid, then each pair of base angles are congruent.

If a trapezoid has one pair of congruent base angles, then the trapezoid is isosceles.

A trapezoid is isosceles if and only if its diagonals are congruent.

You can use auxiliary segments to prove these theorems.

Example 2   **Complete the flow proof of the first Isosceles Trapezoid Theorem.**

Given: $ABCD$ is an isosceles trapezoid
with $\overline{BC} \parallel \overline{AD}$, $\overline{AB} \cong \overline{DC}$.

Prove: $\angle A \cong \angle D$

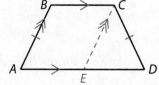

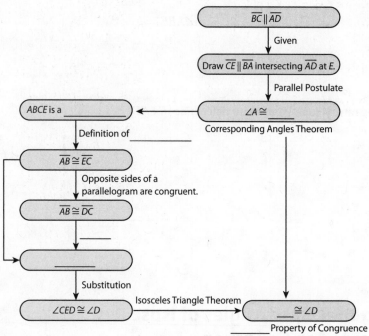

Reflect

5.   Explain how the auxiliary segment was useful in the proof.

_____

_____

_____

6. The flow proof in Example 2 only shows that one pair of base angles is congruent. Write a plan for proof for using parallel lines to show that the other pair of base angles (∠B and ∠C) are also congruent.

_____

_____

_____

Your Turn

7. Complete the proof of the second Isosceles Trapezoid Theorem: If a trapezoid has one pair of base angles congruent, then the trapezoid is isosceles.

Given: $ABCD$ is a trapezoid with $\overline{BC} \parallel \overline{AD}$, $\angle A \cong \angle D$.
Prove: $ABCD$ is an isosceles trapezoid.

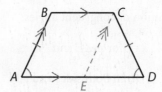

It is given that _____. By the _____, $\overline{CE}$ can be drawn parallel to _____ so that _____ intersects $\overline{AD}$ at E. By the Corresponding Angles Theorem, $\angle A \cong$ _____. It is given that $\angle A \cong$ _____, so by substitution, _____. By the Converse of the Isosceles Triangle Theorem, $\overline{CE} \cong$ _____.

By definition, _____ is a parallelogram. In a parallelogram, _____ are congruent, so $\overline{AB} \cong$ _____. By the Transitive Property. of Congruence, $\overline{AB} \cong$ _____. Therefore, by definition, _____ is an _____.

🔑 Explain 3 Using Theorems about Isosceles Trapezoids

You can use properties of isosceles trapezoids to find unknown values.

Example 3 Find each measure or value.

(A) A railroad bridge has side sections that show isosceles trapezoids. The figure $ABCD$ represents one of these sections. $AC = 13.2$ m and $BE = 8.4$ m. Find DE.

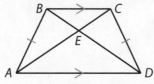

Use the property that the diagonals are congruent.	$\overline{AC} \cong \overline{BD}$
Use the definition of congruent segments.	$AC = BD$
Substitute 13.2 for AC.	$13.2 = BD$
Use the Segment Addition Postulate.	$BE + DE = BD$
Substitute 8.4 for BE and 13.2 for BD.	$8.4 + DE = 13.2$
Subtract 8.4 from both sides.	$DE = 4.8$

Ⓑ Find the value of x so that trapezoid *EFGH* is isosceles.

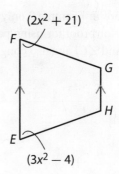
$(2x^2 + 21)$
$(3x^2 - 4)$

For *EFGH* to be isosceles, each pair of base angles are congruent.

In particular, the pair at E and _____ are congruent. $\angle E \cong \angle$ _____

Use the definition of congruent angles. $m\angle E = m\angle$ _____.

Substitute _____ for $m\angle E$ and _____ for $m\angle$ _____.   _____ = _____

Substract _____ from both sides and add _____ to both sides. $x^2 =$ _____

Take the square root of both sides. $x =$ _____ or $x =$ _____

Your Turn

8. In isosceles trapezoid *PQRS*, use the Same-Side Interior Angles Postulate to find $m\angle R$.

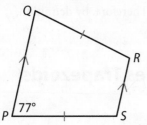
77°

9. $JL = 3y + 6$ and $KM = 22 - y$. Determine the value of y so that trapezoid *JKLM* is isosceles.

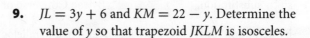

⚙ Explain 4   Using the Trapezoid Midsegment Theorem

The **midsegment of a trapezoid** is the segment whose endpoints are the midpoints of the legs.

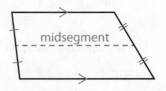
midsegment

Trapezoid Midsegment Theorem

The midsegment of a trapezoid is parallel to each base, and its length is one half the sum of the lengths of the bases.

$\overline{XY} \parallel \overline{BC}, \overline{XY} \parallel \overline{AD}$

$XY = \frac{1}{2}(BC + AD)$

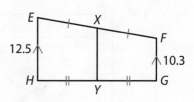

You can use the Trapezoid Midsegment Theorem to find the length of the midsegment or a base of a trapezoid.

Example 4 **Find each length.**

Ⓐ In trapezoid *EFGH*, find *XY*.

Use the second part of the Trapezoid Midsegment Theorem.	$XY = \frac{1}{2}(EH + FG)$
Substitute 12.5 for *EH* and 10.3 for *FG*.	$= \frac{1}{2}(12.5 + 10.3)$
Simplify.	$= 11.4$

Ⓑ In trapezoid *JKLM*, find *JM*.

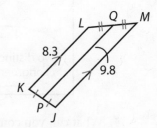

Use the second part of the Trapezoid Midsegment Theorem.	$PQ = \frac{1}{2}(\underline{\quad} + JM)$
Substitute _____ for *PQ* and _____ for _____.	$\underline{\quad} = \frac{1}{2}(\underline{\quad} + JM)$
Multiply both sides by 2.	$\underline{\quad} = \underline{\quad} + JM$
Subtract _____ from both sides.	$\underline{\quad} = JM$

Your Turn

10. In trapezoid *PQRS*, $PQ = 2RS$. Find *XY*.

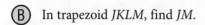

11. Use the information in the graphic organizer to complete the Venn diagram.

Rectangle Four right angles		**Rhombus** Four congruent sides
Parallelogram Two pairs of parallel sides	**Quadrilateral**	**Trapezoid** At least one pair of parallel sides
Square Four right angles and four congruent sides		**Kite** Two distinct pairs of congruent sides

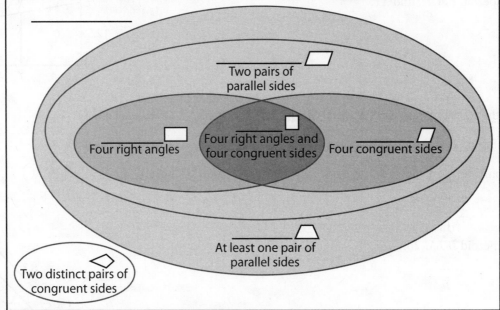

What can you conclude about all parallelograms? _____

_____

12. Discussion The Isosceles Trapezoid Theorem about congruent diagonals is in the form of a biconditional statement. Is it possible to state the two isosceles trapezoid theorems about base angles as a biconditional statement? Explain.

_____

_____

_____

_____

13. Essential Question Check-In Do kites and trapezoids have properties that are related to their diagonals? Explain.

_____

_____

In kite *ABCD*, m∠*BAE* = 28° and
m∠*BCE* = 57°. Find each measure.

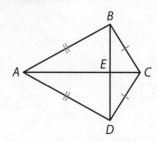

1. m∠*ABE*

2. m∠*CBE*

3. m∠*ABC*

4. m∠*ADC*

Using the first and second Isosceles Trapezoid Theorems, complete the proofs of each part of the third Isosceles Trapezoid Theorem: *A trapezoid is isosceles if and only if its diagonals are congruent.*

5. Prove part 1: If a trapezoid is isosceles, then its diagonals are congruent.

Given: *ABCD* is an isosceles trapezoid with
$\overline{BC} \parallel \overline{AD}$, $\overline{AB} \cong \overline{DC}$.
Prove: $\overline{AC} \cong \overline{DB}$

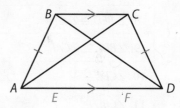

It is given that $\overline{AB} \cong \overline{DC}$. By the first Trapezoid Theorem, ∠*BAD* ≅ _____,
and by the Reflexive Property of Congruence, _____. By the SAS Triangle
Congruence Theorem, △*ABD* ≅ △*DCA*, and by _____, $\overline{AC} \cong \overline{DB}$.

6. Prove part 2: If the diagonals of a trapezoid are congruent, then the trapezoid is isosceles.

Given: *ABCD* is a trapezoid with $\overline{BC} \parallel \overline{AD}$ and diagonals $\overline{AC} \cong \overline{DB}$.

Prove: *ABCD* is an isosceles trapezoid.

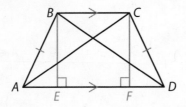

Statements	Reasons
1. Draw $\overline{BE} \perp \overline{AD}$ and $\overline{CF} \perp \overline{AD}$.	1. There is only one line through a given point perpendicular to a given line, so each auxiliary line can be drawn.
2. $\overline{BE} \parallel \overline{CF}$	2. Two lines perpendicular to the same line are parallel.
3. _____	3. Given
4. *BCFE* is a parallelogram.	4. _____ *(Steps 2, 3)*
5. $\overline{BE} \cong$ _____	5. If a quadrilateral is a parallelogram, then its opposite sides are congruent.
6. $\overline{AC} \cong \overline{DB}$	6. _____
7. _____	7. Definition of perpendicular lines
8. $\triangle BED \cong \triangle CFA$	8. HL Triangle Congruence Theorem *(Steps 5–7)*
9. $\angle BDE \cong \angle CAF$	9. _____
10. $\angle CBD \cong$ _____, _____ $\cong \angle CAF$	10. Alternate Interior Angles Theorem
11. $\angle CBD \cong$ _____	11. Transitive Property of Congruence *(Steps 9, 10)*
12. _____	12. Given
13. $\overline{BC} \cong \overline{BC}$	13. _____
14. $\triangle ABC \cong \triangle DCB$	14. _____ *(Steps 12, 13)*
15. $\angle BAC \cong \angle CDB$	15. CPCTC
16. $\angle BAD \cong$ _____	16. Angle Addition Postulate
17. *ABCD* is isosceles.	17. If a trapezoid has one pair of base angles congruent, then the trapezoid is isosceles.

Use the isosceles trapezoid to find each measure or value.

7. $LJ = 19.3$ and $KN = 8.1$. Determine MN.

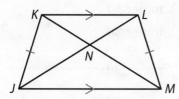

8. Find the positive value of x so that trapezoid $PQRS$ is isosceles.

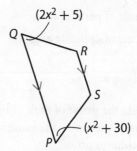

9. In isosceles trapezoid $EFGH$, use the Same-Side Interior Angles Postulate to determine m$\angle E$.

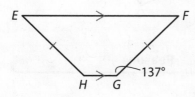

10. $AC = 3y + 12$ and $BD = 27 - 2y$. Determine the value of y so that trapezoid $ABCD$ is isosceles.

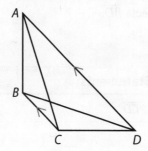

Find the unknown segment lengths in each trapezoid.

11. In trapezoid $ABCD$, find XY.

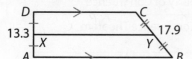

12. In trapezoid $EFGH$, find FG.

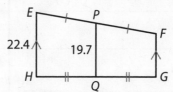

13. In trapezoid $PQRS$, $PQ = 4RS$. Determine XY.

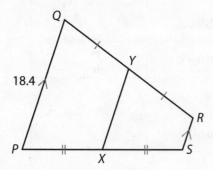

14. In trapezoid $JKLM$, $PQ = 2JK$. Determine LM.

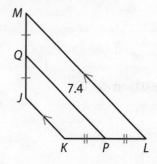

15. Determine whether each of the following describes a kite or a trapezoid. Select the correct answer for each lettered part.

A. Has two distinct pairs of congruent consecutive sides   ◯ kite   ◯ trapezoid

B. Has diagonals that are perpendicular   ◯ kite   ◯ trapezoid

C. Has at least one pair of parallel sides   ◯ kite   ◯ trapezoid

D. Has exactly one pair of opposite angles that are congruent   ◯ kite   ◯ trapezoid

E. Has two pairs of base angles   ◯ kite   ◯ trapezoid

16. Multi-Step Complete the proof of each of the four Kite Theorems. The proof of each of the four theorems relies on the same initial reasoning, so they are presented here in a single two-column proof.

Given: $ABCD$ is a kite, with $\overline{AB} \cong \overline{AD}$ and $\overline{CB} \cong \overline{CD}$.

Prove: (i) $\overline{AC} \perp \overline{BD}$;
       (ii) $\angle ABC \cong \angle ADC$;
       (iii) $\overline{AC}$ bisects $\angle BAD$ and $\angle BCD$;
       (iv) $\overline{AC}$ bisects $\overline{BD}$.

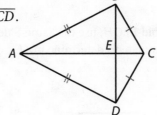

Statements	Reasons
1. $\overline{AB} \cong \overline{AD}$, $\overline{CB} \cong \overline{CD}$	1. Given
2. $\overline{AC} \cong$ _____	2. Reflexive Property of Congruence
3. $\triangle ABC \cong \triangle ADC$	3. _____ (Steps 1, 2)
4. $\angle BAE \cong$ _____	4. CPCTC
5. $\overline{AE} \cong \overline{AE}$	5. Reflexive Property of Congruence
6. _____	6. SAS Triangle Congruence Theorem (Steps 1, 4, 5)
7. $\angle AEB \cong \angle AED$	7. _____
8. $\overline{AC} \perp \overline{BD}$	8. If two lines intersect to form a linear pair of congruent angles, then the lines are perpendicular.
9. $\angle ABC \cong$ _____	9. _____ (Step 3)
10. $\angle BAC \cong$ _____ and _____ $\cong \angle DCA$	10. _____ (Step 3)
11. $\overline{AC}$ bisects $\angle BAD$ and $\angle BCD$.	11. Definition of _____
12. _____ $\cong$ _____	12. CPCTC (Step 6)
13. $\overline{AC}$ bisects $\overline{BD}$.	13. _____

17. Given: *JKLN* is a parallelogram. *JKMN* is an isosceles trapezoid.

Prove: △*KLM* is an isosceles triangle.

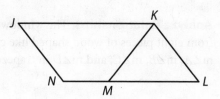

Algebra Find the length of the midsegment of each trapezoid.

18.

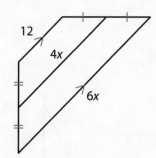

12

4x

6x

19.

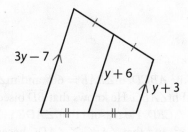

3y − 7

y + 6

y + 3

20. Represent Real-World Problems A set of shelves fits an attic room with one sloping wall. The left edges of the shelves line up vertically, and the right edges line up along the sloping wall. The shortest shelf is 32 in. long, and the longest is 40 in. long. Given that the three shelves are equally spaced vertically, what total length of shelving is needed?

21. Represent Real-World Problems A common early stage in making an origami model is known as the kite. The figure shows a paper model at this stage unfolded.

The folds create four geometric kites. Also, the 16 right triangles adjacent to the corners of the paper are all congruent, as are the 8 right triangles adjacent to the center of the paper. Find the measures of all four angles of the kite labeled *ABCD* (the point A is the center point of the diagram). Use the facts that ∠*B* ≅ ∠*D* and that the interior angle sum of a quadrilateral is 360°.

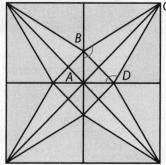

22. Analyze Relationships The window frame is a regular octagon. It is made from eight pieces of wood shaped like congruent isosceles trapezoids. What are m∠A, m∠B, m∠C, and m∠D in trapezoid ABCD?

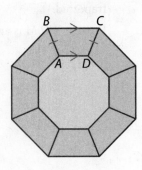

23. Explain the Error In kite ABCD, m∠BAE = 66° and m∠ADE = 59°. Terrence is trying to find m∠ABC. He knows that $\overline{BD}$ bisects $\overline{AC}$, and that therefore △AED ≅ △CED. He reasons that ∠ADE ≅ ∠CDE, so that m∠ADC = 2(59°) = 118°, and that ∠ABC ≅ ∠ADC because they are opposite angles in the kite, so that m∠ABC = 118°. Explain Terrence's error and describe how to find m∠ABC .

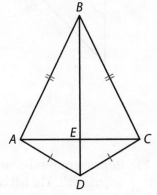

24. Complete the table to classify all quadrilateral types by the rotational symmetries and line symmetries they must have. Identify any patterns that you see and explain what these patterns indicate.

Quadrilateral	Angle of Rotational Symmetry	Number of Line Symmetries
kite		1
non-isosceles trapezoid	none	
isosceles trapezoid		
parallelogram	180°	
rectangle		
rhombus		
square		

25. Communicate Mathematical Ideas Describe the properties that rhombuses and kites have in common, and the properties that are different.

26. Analyze Relationships In kite *ABCD*, triangles *ABD* and *CBD* can be rotated and translated, identifying $\overline{AD}$ with $\overline{DC}$ and joining the remaining pair of vertices, as shown in the figure. Why is this process guaranteed to produce an isosceles trapezoid?

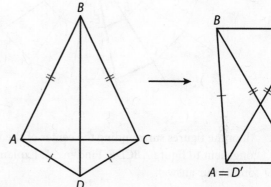

Suggest a converse process, using figures to illustrate your process. What do these processes suggest about the symmetries of kites and isosceles trapezoids? Explain.

Lesson Performance Task

This model of a spider web is made using only isosceles triangles and isosceles trapezoids.

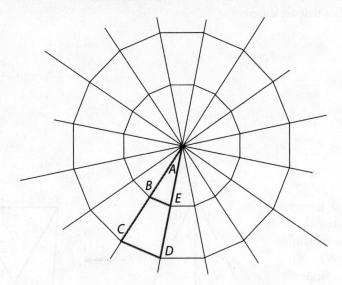

a. All of the figures surrounding the center of the web are congruent to figure *ABCDE*. Find m∠*A*. Explain how you found your answer.

b. Find m∠*ABE* and m∠*AEB*.

c. Find m∠*CBE* and m∠*DEB*.

d. Find m∠*C* and m∠*D*.

Properties of Quadrilaterals

Essential Question: How can you use properties of quadrilaterals to solve real-world problems?

Key Vocabulary

diagonal *(diagonal)*
isosceles trapezoid
   (trapecio isósceles)
kite *(el deltoide)*
midsegment of a trapezoid
   *(segmento medio de un
   trapecio)*
parallelogram
   (paralelogramo)
quadrilateral *(cuadrilátero)*
rectangle *(rectángulo)*
rhombus *(rombo)*
square *(cuadrado)*
trapezoid *(trapecio)*

KEY EXAMPLE   *(Lesson 24.1)*

Given: *ABCD* and *EDGF* are parallelograms.

Prove: $\angle A \cong \angle G$

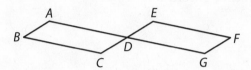

Proof	Reason
ABCD and *EDGF* are parallelograms.	Given
$\angle A \cong \angle C$	Opposite angles of a parallelogram are congruent.
$\overline{AG} \parallel \overline{BC}$	Definition of a parallelogram
$\overline{CE} \parallel \overline{FG}$	Definition of a parallelogram
$\angle C \cong \angle CDG$	Interior angle theorem
$\angle CDG \cong \angle G$	Interior angle theorem
$\angle A \cong \angle G$	Transitive property of congruence

KEY EXAMPLE   *(Lesson 24.2)*

Find the angle and side lengths when *t* is 19 to see if the figure is a parallelogram.

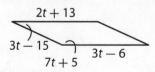

$2(19) + 13 = 51$

$3(19) - 6 = 51$

$3(19) - 15 = 42$

$7(19) + 5 = 138$

The top side is equivalent to the bottom. Also, the top side is parallel to the bottom because the same-side interior angles are supplementary. Therefore, this figure is a parallelogram because the opposite sides are parallel and congruent.

KEY EXAMPLE   *(Lesson 24.3)*

Prove that $\triangle ABE \cong \triangle ADE$ given that $ABCD$ is a rhombus.

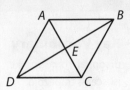

$\overline{AE} \cong \overline{AE}$ by the Reflexive Property.

Since $ABCD$ is a rhombus, $\overline{AB} \cong \overline{AD}$. Since a rhombus is also a parallelogram, $\overline{BE} \cong \overline{DE}$. Therefore, $\triangle ABE \cong \triangle ADE$ via the SSS Congruence Theorem.

KEY EXAMPLE   *(Lesson 24.4)*

Determine which quadrilaterals match the figure: parallelogram, rhombus, rectangle, or square.

Since the figure has four 90° angles and a perpendicular bisector, then the figure is a square. Since the figure is a square, then it is also a rectangle, rhombus, and parallelogram.

KEY EXAMPLE   *(Lesson 24.5)*

Prove that $\triangle ADC \cong \triangle BCD$ given that $ABCD$ is an isosceles trapezoid.

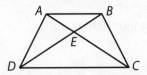

Proof	Reason
$\overline{AD} \cong \overline{BC}$	Definition of an isosceles trapezoid
$\overline{AC} \cong \overline{BD}$	Diagonals of an isosceles trapezoid are congruent
$\overline{DC} \cong \overline{CD}$	Reflexive Property of Congruence
$\triangle ADC \cong \triangle BCD$	SSS Congruence Theorem

EXERCISES

EFGH is a parallelogram. Find the given side length. *(Lesson 24.1)*

1. *EF*

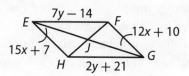

2. *EG*

Determine if each quadrilateral is a parallelogram. Justify your answer. *(Lesson 24.2)*

3.

4.

Find the numbered angles in each rhombus. *(Lesson 24.3)*

5.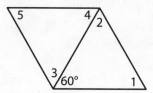

6.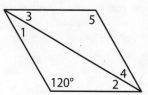

Find the value of *x* that makes each parallelogram the given type. *(Lesson 24.4)*

7. Rectangle

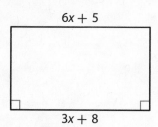

8. Square

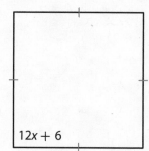

9. A farm, in the shape of an isosceles trapezoid, is putting up fences on its diagonals. If one fence has 16 9-foot segments, how many 8-foot segments will the other fence have? *(Lesson 24.5)*

How Big Is That Face?

This strange image is the flattened east façade of the central library in Seattle, WA, designed by architect Rem Koolhaas. The faces of this unusual and striking building take the form of triangles, trapezoids, and other quadrilaterals.

The diagram shows the dimensions of the faces labeled in feet. What is the total surface area of the east façade?

Use the space below to write down any questions you have and describe how you would find the area. Then use your own paper to complete the task. Be sure to write down all your data and assumptions. Then use numbers, words, or algebra to explain how you reached your conclusion.

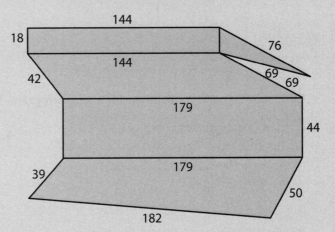

(Ready) to Go On?

24.1–24.5 Properties of Quadrilaterals

- Online Homework
- Hints and Help
- Extra Practice

Find angle measure *x* on each given figure. *(Lesson 24.2)*

1.
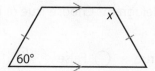

2.
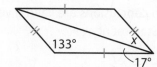

3.
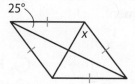

4.
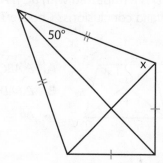

5. Determine whether the trapezoids are congruent. *(Lesson 24.5)*

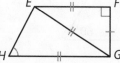

ESSENTIAL QUESTION

6. Name a time when it would be useful to know when a shape is a rectangle or a trapezoid.

MODULE 24
MIXED REVIEW

Assessment Readiness

1. Consider each of the following quadrilaterals. Decide whether each is also a parallelogram. Select Yes or No for A–C.

   A. Trapezoid   ◯ Yes   ◯ No

   B. Rhombus   ◯ Yes   ◯ No

   C. Square   ◯ Yes   ◯ No

2. Which conclusions are valid given that *ABCD* is a parallelogram? Choose True or False for each statement.

   A. $\angle A \cong \angle C$ ◯ True   ◯ False

   B. $\angle A$ and $\angle B$ are complementary.   ◯ True   ◯ False

   C. $\overline{AD} \parallel \overline{BC}$ ◯ True   ◯ False

3. *ABCD* is a trapezoid with $\overline{BC} \parallel \overline{AD}$ and $\angle BAD \cong \angle CDA$. Which of the following statements are valid conclusions? Choose True or False for each statement.

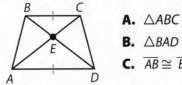

   A. $\triangle ABC \cong \triangle CDA$ ◯ True   ◯ False

   B. $\triangle BAD \cong \triangle CDA$ ◯ True   ◯ False

   C. $\overline{AB} \cong \overline{BC}$ ◯ True   ◯ False

4. Given that *ABCD* is a rhombus, prove that $\triangle ABD \cong \triangle CDB$ and that both triangles are equilateral.

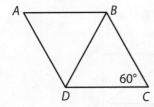

© Houghton Mifflin Harcourt Publishing Company

Coordinate Proof Using Slope and Distance

Essential Question: How can you use coordinate proofs using slope and distance to solve real-world problems?

REAL WORLD VIDEO
Check out how workers use surveying tools and coordinate geometry to measure real-world distances and areas for the construction of roads and bridges.

MODULE PERFORMANCE TASK PREVIEW

How Do You Calculate the Containment of a Fire?

In this module, you will use concepts of perimeter and area to determine the percentage containment of a wildfire. To successfully complete this task, you'll need to master the skills of finding area and perimeter on the coordinate plane. So put on your safety gear and let's get started!

© Houghton Mifflin Harcourt Publishing Company • Image Credits:
©Sportstock/iStockPhoto.com

Are YOU Ready?

Complete these exercises to review the skills you will need for this module.

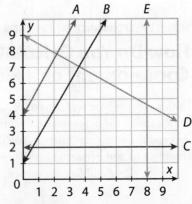

Area of Composite Figures

Example 1

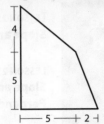

Find the area of the given figure.

Think of the shape as a square and two triangles. The square has sides of length 5 and an area of 25. The top triangle has a height of 4 and a base of 5, so its area is 10. The triangle on the right has a base of 2 and a height of 5, so its area will be 5. Altogether, the area will be 40.

Find the area of the given figure to the nearest hundredth as needed. Use 3.14 for π.

1.

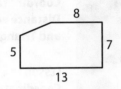

2.

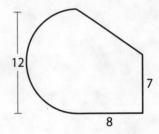

_____

Distance and Midpoint Formula

Example 2 $(3, 3)$ $(5, 6)$

Find the distance and midpoint for each set of ordered pairs.

$$\sqrt{(5-3)^2 + (6-3)^2} = d$$ Set up points in the distance formula.

$$d = \sqrt{13}$$ Simplify.

$$M = \left(\frac{3+5}{2}, \frac{3+6}{2}\right)$$ Set up points in the midpoint formula.

$$M = (4, 4.5)$$ Simplify.

Find the distance and midpoint for each set of ordered pairs, rounded to the nearest hundredth as needed.

3. $(0, 9)$ $(2, 5)$ **4.** $(2, 7)$ $(4, 9)$ **5.** $(1, 8)$ $(3, 8)$

_____   _____   _____

Writing Equations of Parallel, Perpendicular, Vertical, and Horizontal Lines

Example 3   Using the given xy-graph, find the equation of line C in slope-intercept form. The equation for this line is $y = 2$.

Using the given xy—graph, find the equation of the given line in slope-intercept form.

6. E _____

7. B _____

8. A _____

9. D _____

25.1 Slope and Parallel Lines

Essential Question: How can you use slope to solve problems involving parallel lines?

⊘ Explore   Proving the Slope Criteria for Parallel Lines

The following theorem states an important connection between slope and parallel lines.

Theorem: Slope Criteria for Parallel Lines
Two nonvertical lines are parallel if and only if they have the same slope.

Follow these steps to prove the slope criteria for parallel lines.

(A) First prove that if two lines are parallel, then they have the same slope.

Suppose lines m and n are parallel lines that are neither vertical nor horizontal.

Let A and B be two points on line m, as shown. You can draw a horizontal line through A and a vertical line through B to create the "slope triangle," $\triangle ABC$.

You can extend $\overline{AC}$ to intersect line n at point D and then extend it to point F so that $AC = DF$. Finally, you can draw a vertical line through F intersecting line n at point E.

Mark the figure to show parallel lines, right angles, and congruent segments.

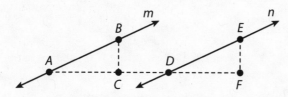

(B) When parallel lines are cut by a transversal, corresponding angles are congruent, so

$\angle BAC \cong$ _____.

$\triangle BAC \cong$ _____ by the _____ Triangle Congruence Theorem.

By CPCTC, $\overline{BC} \cong$ _____ and $BC =$ _____.

The slope of line $m = \dfrac{\boxed{}}{AC}$, and the slope of line $n = \dfrac{\boxed{}}{DF}$.

The slopes of the lines are equal because _____

_____

(C) Now prove that if two lines have the same slope, then they are parallel.

Suppose lines m and n are two lines with the same nonzero slope. You can set up a figure in the same way as before.

Let A and B be two points on line m, as shown. You can draw a horizontal line through A and a vertical line through B to create the "slope triangle," $\triangle ABC$.

You can extend $\overline{AC}$ to intersect line n at point D and then extend it to point F so that $AC = DF$. Finally, you can draw a vertical line through F intersecting line n at point E.

Mark the figure to show right angles and congruent segments.

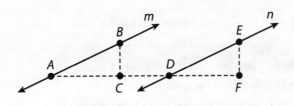

(D) Since line m and line n have the same slope, $\dfrac{\boxed{}}{AC} = \dfrac{\boxed{}}{DF}$.

But $DF = AC$, so by substitution, $\dfrac{\boxed{}}{AC} = \dfrac{\boxed{}}{AC}$.

Multiplying both sides by AC shows that $BC =$ _____.

Now you can conclude that $\triangle BAC \cong$ _____ by the _____ Triangle Congruence Theorem.

By CPCTC, $\angle BAC \cong$ _____ .

Line m and line n are two lines that are cut by a transversal so that a pair of corresponding angles are congruent.

You can conclude that _____ .

Reflect

1. Explain why the slope criteria can be applied to horizontal lines.

_____

_____

2. Explain why the slope criteria cannot be applied to vertical lines even though all vertical lines are parallel.

_____

_____

_____

🔑 Explain 1 Using Slopes to Classify Quadrilaterals by Sides

You can use the slope criteria for parallel lines to analyze figures in the coordinate plane.

Example 1 Show that each figure is the given type of quadrilateral.

(A) Show that *ABCD* is a trapezoid.

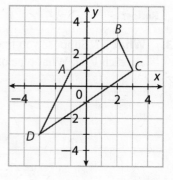

Step 1 Find the coordinates of the vertices of quadrilateral *ABCD*.

$A(-1, 1), B(2, 3), C(3, 1), D(-3, -3)$

Step 2 Use the slope formula to find the slope of $\overline{AB}$ and the slope of $\overline{DC}$.

slope of $\overline{AB} = \dfrac{y_2 - y_1}{x_2 - x_1} = \dfrac{3 - 1}{2 - (-1)} = \dfrac{2}{3}$

slope of $\overline{DC} = \dfrac{y_2 - y_1}{x_2 - x_1} = \dfrac{1 - (-3)}{3 - (-3)} = \dfrac{4}{6} = \dfrac{2}{3}$

Step 3 Compare the slopes.

Since the slopes are the same, $\overline{AB}$ is parallel to $\overline{DC}$.

Quadrilateral *ABCD* is a trapezoid because it is a quadrilateral with at exactly one pair of parallel sides.

(B) Show that *PQRS* is a parallelogram.

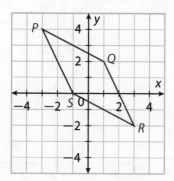

Step 1 Find the coordinates of the vertices of quadrilateral *PQRS*.

$P(-3, 4), Q(1, 2), R\left(\boxed{}, \boxed{}\right), S\left(\boxed{}, \boxed{}\right)$

Step 2 Use the slope formula to find the slope of each side.

$\overline{PQ}: \dfrac{y_2 - y_1}{x_2 - x_1} = \dfrac{2 - 4}{1 - (-3)} = \dfrac{-2}{4} = -\dfrac{1}{2}$

$\overline{QR}: \dfrac{y_2 - y_1}{x_2 - x_1} = \dfrac{\boxed{} - 2}{\boxed{} - 1} = \dfrac{\boxed{}}{\boxed{}} = \boxed{}$

$\overline{RS}: \dfrac{y_2 - y_1}{x_2 - x_1} = \dfrac{\boxed{} - \boxed{}}{\boxed{} - \boxed{}} = \dfrac{\boxed{}}{\boxed{}} = -\dfrac{\boxed{}}{\boxed{}}$

$\overline{SP}: \dfrac{y_2 - y_1}{x_2 - x_1} = \dfrac{4 - \boxed{}}{-3 - \boxed{}} = \dfrac{\boxed{}}{\boxed{}} = \boxed{}$

Step 3 Compare the slopes.

Since the slope of $\overline{PQ}$ is the same as the slope of _____, $\overline{PQ}$ is parallel to _____.

Since the slope of $\overline{QR}$ is the same as the slope of _____, $\overline{QR}$ is parallel to _____.

Quadrilateral *PQRS* is a parallelogram because _____.

Reflect

3. **What If?** Suppose you know that the lengths of $\overline{PQ}$ and $\overline{QR}$ in the figure in Example 1B are each $\sqrt{20}$. What type of parallelogram is quadrilateral *PQRS*? Explain.

_____

_____

_____

Your Turn

Show that each figure is the given type of quadrilateral.

4. Show that *JKLM* is a trapezoid.

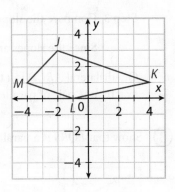

5. Show that *ABCD* is a parallelogram.

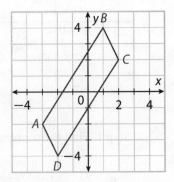

⚙ Explain 2 Using Slopes to Find Missing Vertices

Example 2 Find the coordinates of the missing vertex in each parallelogram.

(A) △ABCD with vertices $A(1, -2)$, $B(-2, 3)$, and $D(5, -1)$

Step 1 Graph the given points.

Step 2 Find the slope of $\overline{AB}$ by counting units from A to B.

The rise from -2 to 3 is 5. The run from 1 to -2 is -3.

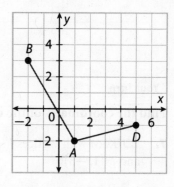

Step 3 Start at D and count the same number of units.

A rise of 5 from -1 is 4. A run of -3 from 5 is 2.

Label $(2, 4)$ as vertex C.

Step 4 Use the slope formula to verify that $\overline{BC} \parallel \overline{AD}$.

$$\text{slope of } \overline{BC} = \frac{4 - 3}{2 - (-2)} = \frac{1}{4}$$

$$\text{slope of } \overline{AD} = \frac{-1 - (-2)}{5 - 1} = \frac{1}{4}$$

The coordinates of vertex C are $(2, 4)$.

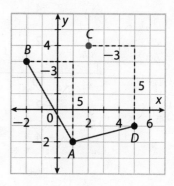

(B) ▱PQRS with vertices $P(-3, 0)$, $Q(-2, 4)$, and $R(2, 2)$

Step 1 Graph the given points.

Step 2 Find the slope of $\overline{PQ}$ by counting units from Q to P.

The rise from 4 to 0 is ☐.   The run from -2 to -3 is ☐.

Step 3 Start at R and count the same number of units.

A rise of ☐ from 2 is ☐.   A run of ☐ from 2 is ☐.

Label $\left(\boxed{}, \boxed{} \right)$ as vertex S.

Step 4 Use the slope formula to verify that $\overline{QR} \parallel \overline{PS}$.

$$\text{slope of } \overline{QR} = \frac{\boxed{} - \boxed{}}{\boxed{} - \boxed{}} = -\frac{\boxed{}}{\boxed{}} \qquad \text{slope of } \overline{PS} = \frac{\boxed{} - \boxed{}}{\boxed{} - \boxed{}} = -\frac{\boxed{}}{\boxed{}}$$

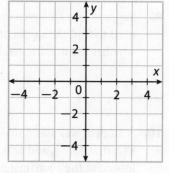

The coordinates of vertex S are $\left(\boxed{}, \boxed{} \right)$.

6. Discussion In Part A, you used the slope formula to verify that $\overline{BC} \parallel \overline{AD}$. Describe another way you can check that you found the correct coordinates of vertex C.

_____

_____

Your Turn

Find the coordinates of the missing vertex in each parallelogram.

7. $\square JKLM$ with vertices $J(-3, -2)$, $K(0, 1)$, and $M(1, -3)$

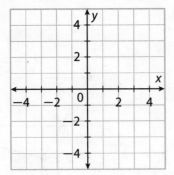

8. $\square DEFG$ with vertices $E(-2, 2)$, $F(4, 1)$, and $G(3, -2)$

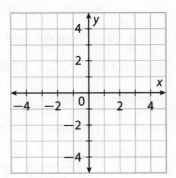

Elaborate

9. Suppose you are given the coordinates of the vertices of a quadrilateral. Do you always need to find the slopes of all four sides of the quadrilateral in order to determine whether the quadrilateral is a trapezoid? Explain.

_____

_____

10. A student was asked to determine whether quadrilateral $ABCD$ with vertices $A(0, 0)$, $B(2, 0)$, $C(5, 7)$, and $D(0, 2)$ was a parallelogram. Without plotting points, the student looked at the coordinates of the vertices and quickly determined that quadrilateral $ABCD$ could not be a parallelogram. How do you think the student solved the problem?

_____

_____

11. Essential Question Check-In What steps can you use to determine whether two given lines on a coordinate plane are parallel?

_____

_____

☆ Evaluate: Homework and Practice

1. Jodie draws parallel lines *p* and *q*. She sets up a figure as shown to prove that the lines must have the same slope. First she proves that $\triangle JKL \cong \triangle RST$ by the ASA Triangle Congruence Theorem. What should she do to complete the proof?

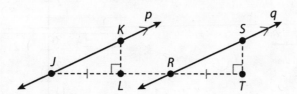

Show that each figure is the given type of quadrilateral.

2. Show that *ABCD* is a trapezoid.

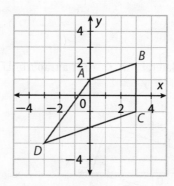

3. Show that *KLMN* is a parallelogram.

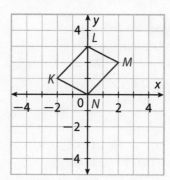

Find the coordinates of the missing vertex in each parallelogram. Use slopes to check your answer.

4. ▱*ABCD* with vertices *A*(3, −3), *B*(−1, −2), and *D*(5, −1)

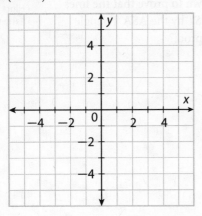

5. ▱*STUV* with vertices *S*(−3, −1), *T*(−1, 1) and *V*(0, 0)

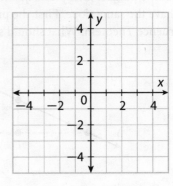

6. Show that quadrilateral *ABCD* is *not* a trapezoid.

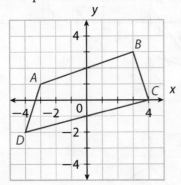

7. Show that quadrilateral *FGHJ* is a trapezoid, but is not a parallelogram.

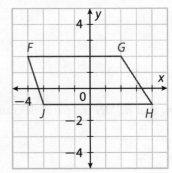

Determine whether each statement is always, sometimes, or never true. Explain your reasoning.

8. If quadrilateral *ABCD* is a trapezoid and the slope of $\overline{AB}$ is 3, then the slope of $\overline{CD}$ is 3.

9. A parallelogram has vertices at $(0, 0)$, $(2, 0)$, $(0, 2)$, and at a point on the line $y = x$.

10. If the slope of $\overline{PQ}$ is $\frac{1}{3}$ and the slope of $\overline{RS}$ is $-\frac{1}{3}$, the quadrilateral *PQRS* is a parallelogram.

11. If line *m* is parallel to line *n* and the slope of line *m* is greater than 1, then the slope of line *n* is greater than 1.

12. If trapezoid *JKLM* has vertices $J(-4, 1)$, $K(-3, 3)$, and $L(-1, 4)$, then the coordinates of vertex *M* are $(2, 4)$.

Explain whether the quadrilateral determined by the intersections of the given lines is a trapezoid, a parallelogram, both, or neither.

13.

Line	Equation
Line ℓ	$y = 2x + 3$
Line m	$2y = -x + 6$
Line n	$y = x - 3$
Line p	$x + y = -3$

14.

Line	Equation
Line ℓ	$y = x + 3$
Line m	$y - x = 0$
Line n	$x + 2y = 6$
Line p	$y = -0.5x - 3$

15.

Line	Equation
Line ℓ	$2y = x + 4$
Line m	$y + 5 = 2x$
Line n	$-2x + y = 2$
Line p	$x + 2y = -6$

16.

Line	Equation
Line ℓ	$3x + y = 4$
Line m	$y + 3 = 0$
Line n	$y = 3x + 5$
Line p	$y = 3$

Algebra Find the value of each variable in the parallelogram.

17.

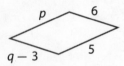

p 6 $q - 3$ 5

18.

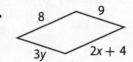

8   9 $3y$ $2x + 4$

19.

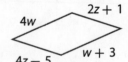

$4w$ $2z + 1$ $4z - 5$ $w + 3$

20. Use the slope-intercept form of a linear equation to prove that if two lines are parallel, then they have the same slope. $\big($*Hint:* Use an indirect proof. Assume the lines have different slopes, m_1 and m_2. Write the equations of the lines and show that there must be a point of intersection.$\big)$

21. **Critique Reasoning** Mayumi was asked to determine whether quadrilateral *RSTU* is a trapezoid given the vertices $R(-2, 3)$, $S(1, 4)$, $T(1, -4)$, and $U(-2, 1)$. She noticed that the slopes of $\overline{RU}$ and $\overline{ST}$ are undefined, so she concluded that the quadrilateral could not be a trapezoid. Do you agree? Explain.

22. Kaitlyn is planning the diagonal spaces for the parking lot at a mall. Each space is a parallelogram. Kaitlyn has already planned the spaces shown in the figure and wants to continue the pattern to draw the next space to the right. What are the endpoints of the next line segment she should draw? Explain your reasoning.

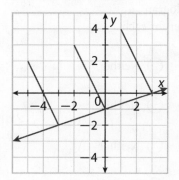

23. Multi-Step Two carpenters are using a coordinate plane to design a tabletop in the shape of a trapezoid. They have already drawn the two sides of the tabletop shown in the figure. They want side $\overline{AD}$ to lie on the line $x = -2$. What is the equation of the line on which side $\overline{CD}$ will lie? Explain your reasoning.

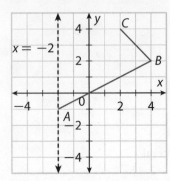

24. Quadrilateral *PQRS* has vertices $P(-3, 2)$, $Q(-1, 4)$, and $R(5, 0)$. For each of the given coordinates of vertex *S*, determine whether the quadrilateral is a parallelogram, a trapezoid that is not a parallelogram, or neither. Select the correct answer for each lettered part.

a. $S(0, 0)$ ◯ Parallelogram   ◯ Trapezoid but not parallelogram   ◯ Neither

b. $S(3, -2)$ ◯ Parallelogram   ◯ Trapezoid but not parallelogram   ◯ Neither

c. $S(2, -1)$ ◯ Parallelogram   ◯ Trapezoid but not parallelogram   ◯ Neither

d. $S(6, -4)$ ◯ Parallelogram   ◯ Trapezoid but not parallelogram   ◯ Neither

e. $S(5, -3)$ ◯ Parallelogram   ◯ Trapezoid but not parallelogram   ◯ Neither

© Houghton Mifflin Harcourt Publishing Company • Image Credits: ©Jetta Productions/Blend Images/Corbis

25. **Explain the Error** Tariq was given the points $P(0, 3)$, $Q(3, -3)$, $R(0, -4)$, and $S(-2, -1)$ and was asked to decide whether quadrilateral $PQRS$ is a trapezoid. Explain his error.

$$\text{slope of } \overline{SP} = \frac{3 - (-1)}{0 - (-2)} = \frac{4}{2} = 2$$

$$\text{slope of } \overline{QP} = \frac{3 - (-3)}{3 - 0} = \frac{6}{3} = 2$$

Since at least two sides are parallel, the quadrilateral is a trapezoid.

26. **Analyze Relationships** Four members of a marching band are arranged to form the vertices of a parallelogram. The coordinates of three band members are $M(-3, 1)$, $G(1, 3)$, and $Q(2, -1)$. Find all possible coordinates for the fourth band member.

27. **Make a Conjecture** Plot any four points on the coordinate plane and connect them to form a quadrilateral. Find the midpoint of each side of the quadrilateral and connect consecutive midpoints to form a new quadrilateral. What type of quadrilateral is formed? Repeat the process by starting with a different set of four points. Do you get the same result? State a conjecture about your findings.

Lesson Performance Task

Suppose archeologists uncover an ancient city with the foundations of 16 houses. The locations of the houses are as follows:

$(2, 2)\ (-5, 6)\ (3, -6)\ (-1, 0)\ (5, -8)\ (3, 5)\ (-3, 3)\ (0, 5)$

$(-8, 1)\ (4, -1)\ (1, -3)\ (-4, -3)\ (8, -7)\ (-5, -4)\ (-2, 8)\ (6, -4)$

a. How could you show that the streets are parallel? Explain.

b. Are the streets parallel?

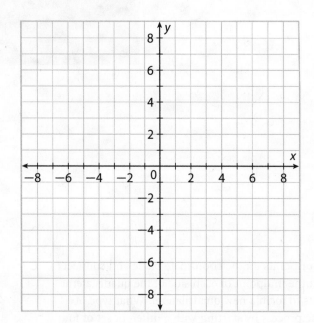

© Houghton Mifflin Harcourt Publishing Company • Image Credits: ©Dmitry Vasilyev/AP Images

25.2 Slope and Perpendicular Lines

Essential Question: How can you use slope to solve problems involving perpendicular lines?

⊘ Explore   Proving the Slope Criteria for Perpendicular Lines

The following theorem states an important connection between slope and perpendicular lines.

> **Theorem: Slope Criteria for Perpendicular Lines**
>
> Two nonvertical lines are perpendicular if and only if the product of their slopes is -1.

Follow these steps to prove the slope criteria for perpendicular lines.

(A) First prove that if two lines are perpendicular, then the product of their slopes is -1.

Suppose lines m and n are perpendicular lines that intersect at point P, and that neither line is vertical. Assume the slope of line m is positive. (You can write a similar proof if the slope of line m is negative.)

Copy the figure on a separate piece of paper. Mark your figure to show the perpendicular lines.

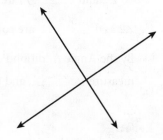

(B) Let Q be a point on line m, and draw a right triangle, $\triangle PQR$, as shown. Which line is this a "slope triangle" for?

_____

Mark the figure to show the perpendicular segments.

(C) Assume that a and b are both positive. The slope of line m is $\dfrac{}{}$.

(D) Rotate $\triangle PQR$ 90° around point P. The image is $\triangle PQ'R'$, as shown.

Which line is $\triangle PQ'R'$ a slope triangle for? _____

Let the coordinates of P be (x_1, y_1) and let the coordinates of Q' be (x_2, y_2).

Then the slope of line n is $\dfrac{y_2 - y_1}{x_2 - x_1} = \dfrac{b}{} = -\dfrac{}{}$.

(E) Now find the product of the slopes.

(slope of line m) · (slope of line n) = $\dfrac{}{} \cdot \left(-\dfrac{}{} \right) = \boxed{}$

Now prove that if the product of the slopes of two lines is −1, then the lines are perpendicular.

Let the slope of line m be $\frac{a}{b}$, where a and b are both positive. Let line n have slope z. It is given that $z \cdot \frac{a}{b} = -1$. Solving for z gives the slope of line n.

$$z = -\frac{\boxed{}}{\boxed{}}$$

(G) Assume the lines intersect at P. Since the slope of m is positive and the slope of n is negative, you can set up slope triangles.

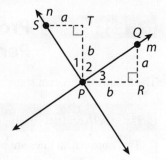

Based on the figure, $\overline{ST} \cong$ _____ and $\overline{PT} \cong$ _____.

Also, $\angle T \cong$ _____ because all right angles are congruent.

Therefore, _____ $\cong$ _____ by the SAS Triangle Congruence Theorem.

(H) By CPCTC, $\angle 1 \cong$ _____.

Since $\overline{TP}$ is vertical and $\overline{PR}$ is horizontal, $\angle TPR$ is a right angle.

So $\angle 2$ and _____ are complementary angles. You can conclude by substitution that

$\angle 2$ and _____ are complementary angles.

By the Angle Addition Postulate, $m\angle 1 + m\angle 2 = m\angle SPQ$, so $\angle SPQ$ must

measure _____, and therefore line m is perpendicular to line n.

Reflect

1. In Step D, when you calculate the slope of line n, why is $x_2 - x_1$ negative?

_____

2. The second half of the proof begins in Step F by assuming that line m has a positive slope. If the product of the slopes of two lines is −1, how do you know that one of the lines must have a positive slope?

_____

_____

3. Does this theorem apply when one of the lines is horizontal? Explain.

_____

_____

🔑 Explain 1 Using Slopes to Classify Figures by Right Angles

You can use the slope criteria for perpendicular lines to analyze figures in the coordinate plane.

Example 1 Show that each figure is the given type of quadrilateral.

(A) Show that *ABCD* is a rectangle.

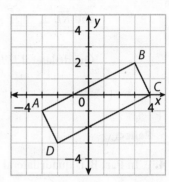

Step 1 Find the coordinates of the vertices of quadrilateral *ABCD*.

$A(-3, -1)$, $B(3, 2)$, $C(4, 0)$, $D(-2, -3)$

Step 2 Use the slope formula to find the slope of each side.

$\overline{AB} : \dfrac{2 - (-1)}{3 - (-3)} = \dfrac{1}{2}$ $\overline{BC} : \dfrac{0 - 2}{4 - 3} = -2$

$\overline{CD} : \dfrac{-3 - 0}{-2 - 4} = \dfrac{1}{2}$ $\overline{DA} : \dfrac{-1 - (-3)}{-3 - (-2)} = -2$

Step 3 Compare the slopes.

$\left(\text{slope of } \overline{AB} \right) \cdot \left(\text{slope of } \overline{BC} \right) = \dfrac{1}{2} \cdot (-2) = -1$

$\left(\text{slope of } \overline{BC} \right) \cdot \left(\text{slope of } \overline{CD} \right) = -2 \cdot \dfrac{1}{2} = -1$

$\left(\text{slope of } \overline{CD} \right) \cdot \left(\text{slope of } \overline{DA} \right) = \dfrac{1}{2} \cdot (-2) = -1$

$\left(\text{slope of } \overline{DA} \right) \cdot \left(\text{slope of } \overline{AB} \right) = -2 \cdot \dfrac{1}{2} = -1$

Consecutive sides are perpendicular since the product of the slopes is -1.

Quadrilateral *ABCD* is a rectangle because it is a quadrilateral with four right angles.

(B) Show that *JKLM* is a trapezoid with two right angles.

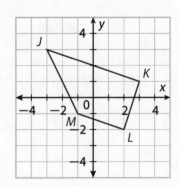

Step 1 Find the coordinates of the vertices of quadrilateral *JKLM*.

Step 2 Use the slope formula to find the slope of each side.

$\overline{JK} : \dfrac{1 - 3}{3 - (-3)} = \dfrac{-2}{6} = -\dfrac{1}{3}$

$\overline{KL} : \dfrac{\boxed{} - 1}{\boxed{} - 3} = \dfrac{\boxed{}}{\boxed{}} = \boxed{}$

$\overline{LM} : \dfrac{\boxed{} - \boxed{}}{\boxed{} - \boxed{}} = \dfrac{\boxed{}}{\boxed{}} = -\dfrac{\boxed{}}{\boxed{}}$

$\overline{MJ} : \dfrac{3 - \boxed{}}{-3 - \boxed{}} = \dfrac{\boxed{}}{\boxed{}} = \boxed{}$

© Houghton Mifflin Harcourt Publishing Company

Step 3 Compare the slopes.

Since the slope of $\overline{JK}$ is the same as the slope of _____ , $\overline{JK}$ is parallel to _____ .

Since the $\left(\text{slope of } \overline{JK}\right) \cdot \left(\text{slope of } \overline{KL}\right) = -\frac{1}{3} \cdot \boxed{} = \boxed{}$ and

$\left(\text{slope of } \overline{KL}\right) \cdot \left(\text{slope of } \overline{LM}\right) = \boxed{} \cdot \left(-\dfrac{\boxed{}}{\boxed{}}\right) = \boxed{}$, $\overline{JK} \perp$ _____

and $\overline{KL} \perp$ _____ .

Quadrilateral $JKLM$ is a trapezoid with two right angles because _____

_____

Reflect

4. In Part B, is quadrilateral $JKLM$ a parallelogram? Why or why not?

_____

_____

Your Turn

Show that each figure is the given type of quadrilateral.

5. Show that $DEFG$ is a rectangle.

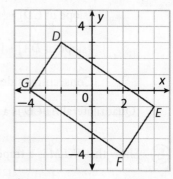

Explain 2 **Using Slopes and Systems of Equations to Classify Figures**

You can use slope to help you analyze a system of equations.

Example 2 A city block is a quadrilateral bounded by four streets shown in the table. Classify the quadrilateral bounded by the streets.

(A)

Street	Equation
Pine Street	$-x + 2y = 4$
Elm Road	$2x + y = 7$
Chestnut Street	$2y = x - 6$
Cedar Road	$y + 8 = -2x$

Step 1 Write each equation in slope-intercept form, $y = mx + b$.

Pine Street equation: $y = \frac{1}{2}x + 2$ Elm Road equation: $y = -2x + 7$

Chestnut Street equation: $y = \frac{1}{2}x - 3$ Cedar Road equation: $y = -2x - 8$

Step 2 Use the equations to determine the slope of each street.

Pine Street: $y = \frac{1}{2}x + 2$, so the slope is $\frac{1}{2}$.

Elm Road: $y = -2x + 7$, so the slope is -2.

Chestnut Street: $y = \frac{1}{2}x - 3$, so the slope is $\frac{1}{2}$.

Cedar Road: $y = -2x - 8$, so the slope is -2.

Step 3 Determine the type of quadrilateral bounded by the streets.

The product of the slopes of consecutive sides is -1.

So, the quadrilateral is a rectangle since it has four right angles.

Step 4 Check by graphing the equations.

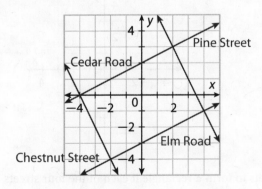

Ⓑ

Street	Equation
Clay Avenue	$3y - 9 = x$
Fresno Road	$2x + y = 3$
Ward Street	$3y = x - 5$
Oakland Lane	$y + 4 = -2x$

Step 1 Write each equation in slope-intercept form, $y = mx + b$.

Clay Avenue equation: $y = \dfrac{\square}{\square}x + \square$

Fresno Road equation: $y = \underline{\hspace{2cm}}$

Ward Street equation: $y = \dfrac{\square}{\square}x - \dfrac{\square}{\square}$

Oakland Lane equation: $y = \underline{\hspace{2cm}}$

Step 2 Use the equations to determine the slope of each street.

Clay Avenue: _____, so the slope is _____.

Fresno Road _____, so the slope is _____.

Ward Street _____, so the slope is _____.

Oakland Lane: _____, so the slope is _____.

Step 3 Determine the type of quadrilateral bounded by the streets.

The slopes of opposite sides of the quadrilateral are _____.

So, the quadrilateral is _____ since _____

Step 4 Check by graphing the equations.

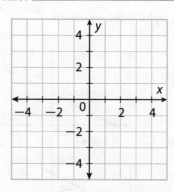

Reflect

6. **Discussion** Is it possible for four streets to form a rectangle if each of the four streets has a positive slope? Explain.

_____

_____

_____

7. A farmers market is set up as a quadrilateral bounded by four streets shown in the table. Classify the quadrilateral bounded by the streets.

Street	Equation
Taft Road	$-2x + 3y = 13$
Harding Lane	$\frac{1}{3}y = -x - 1$
Wilson Avenue	$3y = 2x + 2$
Hoover Street	$3x + y = -14$

💬 Elaborate

8. Suppose line ℓ has slope $\frac{a}{b}$ where $a \neq 0$ and $b \neq 0$, and suppose lines m and n are both perpendicular to line ℓ. Explain how you can use the slope criteria to show that line m must be parallel to line n.

_____

_____

9. Essential Question Check-In What steps can you use to determine whether two given lines on a coordinate plane are perpendicular?

_____

_____

☆ Evaluate: Homework and Practice

Personal Math Trainer

• Online Homework
• Hints and Help
• Extra Practice

1. In the Explore, you proved that if two lines are perpendicular, then the product of their slopes is -1. You assumed that the slope of line m was positive. Follow these steps to complete the proof assuming that the slope of line m is negative.

a. Suppose lines m and n are nonvertical perpendicular lines that intersect at point P. Let Q be a point on line m and draw a slope triangle, $\triangle PQR$, as shown. Write the slope of line m in terms of a and b, where a and b are both positive.

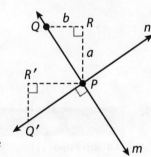

b. Rotate $\triangle PQR$ 90° around point P. The image is $\triangle PQ'R'$, as shown in the figure. Using $\triangle PQ'R'$, write the slope of line n in terms of a and b.

c. Explain how to complete the proof.

Show that each figure is the given type of quadrilateral.

2. Show that *QRST* is a rectangle.

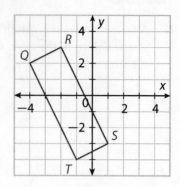

3. Show that *KLMN* is a trapezoid with two right angles.

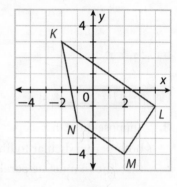

The boundary of a farm consists of four straight roads. Classify the quadrilateral bounded by the roads in each table.

4.

Road	Equation
Lewiston Road	$y - 8 = 2x$
Johnson Road	$2y = -x + 1$
Chavez Road	$-2x + y = -2$
Brannon Road	$x + 2y = -4$

5.

Road	Equation
Larson Road	$y + 1 = 2x$
Cortez Road	$2x + y = 3$
Madison Road	$2x = y + 5$
Jackson Road	$2x + y = -5$

Multi-Step Determine whether the quadrilateral with the given vertices is a parallelogram. If so, determine whether it is a rhombus, a rectangle, or neither. Justify your conclusions. (*Hint*: Recall that a parallelogram with perpendicular diagonals is a rhombus.)

6. Quadrilateral *ABCD* with $A(-3, 0)$, $B(1, 2)$, $C(2, 0)$, and $D(-2, -2)$

7. Quadrilateral *KLMN* with $K(-4, 2)$, $L(-1, 4)$, $M(3, 3)$, and $N(-3, -1)$

8. Quadrilateral *FGHJ* with $F(-2, 3)$, $G(1, 2)$, $H(2, -1)$, and $J(-1, 0)$

Determine whether each statement is always, sometimes, or never true. Explain.

9. If quadrilateral $ABCD$ is a rectangle and the slope of $\overline{AB}$ is positive, then the slope of $\overline{BC}$ is negative.

10. If line m is perpendicular to line n, then the slope of line n is 0.

11. If quadrilateral $JKLM$ is a rhombus and one diagonal has a slope of 3, then the other diagonal has a slope of $\frac{1}{3}$.

12. If k is a real number, then the line $y = x + k$ is perpendicular to the line $y = -x + k$.

13. The slopes of two consecutive sides of a rectangle are $\frac{2}{3}$ and $\frac{3}{2}$.

Algebra **The perimeter of $\square PQRS$ is 84. Find the length of each side of $\square PQRS$ under the given conditions.**

14. $PQ = QR$

15. $QR = 3(RS)$

16. $RS = SP - 7$

17. $SP = RS^2$

18. **Multiple Representations** Line m has the equation $2x + 3y = 6$, line n passes through the points in the table, and line p has the graph shown in the figure. Which of these lines, if any, are perpendicular? Explain.

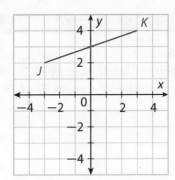

Line n	
x	y
4	5
6	8
8	11

19. Three subway lines run along straight tracks in the city. The equation for each subway line is given. City planners want to add a fourth subway line and want the tracks for the four lines to form a rectangle. What is a possible equation for the fourth subway line? Justify your answer.

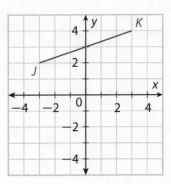

Subway Line	Equation
B	$-2x + y = 4$
N	$2y = -x + 8$
S	$y + 11 = 2x$

20. Quadrilateral $JKLM$ is a rectangle. One side of the rectangle is shown in the figure. Which of the following are possible coordinates for vertices L and M? Select all that apply.

A. $L(4, 1)$ and $M(-2, -1)$

B. $L(5, -2)$ and $M(-1, -3)$

C. $L(4, 7)$ and $M(-2, 5)$

D. $L(5, -2)$ and $M(-1, -4)$

E. $L(3, 0)$ and $M(-3, 0)$

21. Analyze Relationships Quadrilateral *ABCD* is a rectangle. The coordinates of vertices *A* and *B* are *A*(−2, 2) and *B*(2, 0). Vertex *C* lies on the *y*-axis. What are the coordinates of vertices *C* and *D*? Explain.

22. Counterexamples A student said that any three noncollinear points can be three of the vertices of a rectangle because it is always possible to choose a fourth vertex that completes the rectangle. Give a counterexample to show that the student's statement is false and explain the counterexample.

Lesson Performance Task

Each unit on the grid represents 1 mile. A ship is in distress at the point shown. The navigator knows that the shortest distance from a point to a line is on a perpendicular to the line. So, the navigator directs the captain to head the ship on a perpendicular course toward the shoreline.

If the ship succeeds in staying on course, where will it hit land? Explain your method.

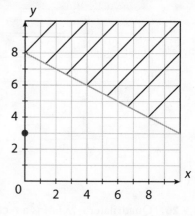

25.3 Coordinate Proof Using Distance with Segments and Triangles

Essential Question: How do you write a coordinate proof?

 **Explore** **Deriving the Distance Formula and the Midpoint Formula**

Complete the following steps to derive the Distance Formula and the Midpoint Formula.

(A) To derive the Distance Formula, start with points J and K as shown in the figure.

Given: $J(x_1, y_1)$ and $K(x_2, y_2)$ with $x_1 \neq x_2$ and $y_1 \neq y_2$

Prove: $JK = \sqrt{(x_2 - x_1)^2 + (y_2 - y_1)^2}$

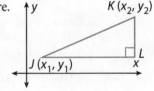

Locate point L so that $\overline{JK}$ is the hypotenuse of right triangle JKL. What are the coordinates of L?

_____

(B) Find JL and LK.

_____

(C) By the Pythagorean Theorem, $JK^2 = JL^2 + LK^2$. Use this to find JK. Explain your steps.

_____

_____

(D) To derive the Midpoint Formula, start with points A and B as shown in the figure.

Given: $A(x_1, y_1)$ and $B(x_2, y_2)$

Prove: The midpoint of $\overline{AB}$ is $M\left(\dfrac{x_1 + x_2}{2}, \dfrac{y_1 + y_2}{2}\right)$.

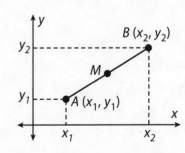

What is the horizontal distance from point A to point B? What is the vertical distance from point A to point B?

_____

(E) The horizontal and vertical distances from A to M must be half these distances.

What is the horizontal distance from point A to point M? _____

What is the vertical distance from point A to point M? _____

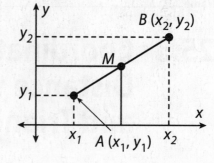

(F) To find the coordinates of point M, add the distances from Step E to the x- and y-coordinates of point A and simplify.

x-coordinate of point M: $x_1 + \dfrac{x_2 - x_1}{2} = \dfrac{2x_1}{2} + \dfrac{x_2 - x_1}{2} = \dfrac{2x_1 + x_2 - x_1}{2} = \dfrac{x_1 + x_2}{2}$

y-coordinate of point M: _____

Reflect

1. In the proof of the Distance Formula, why do you assume that $x_1 \neq x_2$ and $y_1 \neq y_2$?

_____

_____

_____

2. Does the Distance Formula still apply if $x_1 = x_2$ or $y_1 = y_2$? Explain.

_____

_____

_____

3. Does the Midpoint Formula still apply if $x_1 = x_2$ or $y_1 = y_2$? Explain.

_____

_____

_____

Positioning a Triangle on the Coordinate Plane

A **coordinate proof** is a style of proof that uses coordinate geometry and algebra. The first step of a coordinate proof is to position the given figure in the plane. You can use any position, but some strategies can make the steps of the proof simpler.

Strategies for Positioning Figures in the Coordinate Plane

- Use the origin as a vertex, keeping the figure in Quadrant I.
- Center the figure at the origin.
- Center a side of the figure at the origin.
- Use one or both axes as sides of the figure.

Example 1 **Write each coordinate proof.**

Ⓐ **Given:** $\angle B$ is a right angle in $\triangle ABC$. D is the midpoint of $\overline{AC}$.

Prove: The area of $\triangle DBC$ is one half the area of $\triangle ABC$.

Step 1 Assign coordinates to each vertex. Since you will use the Midpoint Formula to find the coordinates of D, use multiples of 2 for the leg lengths.

The coordinates of A are $(0, 2j)$.

The coordinates of B are $(0, 0)$.

The coordinates of C are $(2n, 0)$.

Step 2 Position the figure on the coordinate plane.

Step 3 Write a coordinate proof.

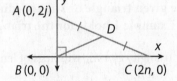

$\triangle ABC$ is a right triangle with height $2j$ and base $2n$.

$$\text{area of } \triangle ABC = \tfrac{1}{2}bh$$
$$= \tfrac{1}{2}(2n)(2j)$$
$$= 2nj \text{ square units}$$

By the Midpoint Formula, the coordinates of $D = \left(\dfrac{0 + 2n}{2}, \dfrac{2j + 0}{2}\right) = (n, j)$.

The height of $\triangle DBC$ is j units, and the base is $2n$ units.

$$\text{area of } \triangle DBC = \tfrac{1}{2}bh$$
$$= \tfrac{1}{2}(2n)(j)$$
$$= nj \text{ square units}$$

Since $nj = \tfrac{1}{2}(2nj)$, the area of $\triangle DBC$ is one half the area of $\triangle ABC$.

Ⓑ **Given:** $\angle B$ is a right angle in $\triangle ABC$. D is the midpoint of $\overline{AC}$.

Prove: The area of $\triangle ADB$ is one half the area of $\triangle ABC$.

Assign coordinates and position the figure as in Example 1A.

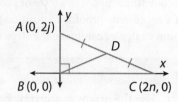

$\triangle ABC$ is a right triangle with height ☐ and base ☐.

area of $\triangle ABC = \frac{1}{2}bh$

$= \frac{1}{2}$ ☐ · ☐

$=$ ☐ square units

By the Midpoint Formula, the coordinates of $D = \left(\dfrac{0 + \boxed{}}{2}, \dfrac{\boxed{} + 0}{2} \right) = \left(\boxed{}, \boxed{} \right)$.

The height of $\triangle ADB$ is ☐ units, and the base is ☐ units.

area of $\triangle ADB = \frac{1}{2}bh = \frac{1}{2}$ ☐ · ☐ $=$ ☐ square units

Since _____, the area of $\triangle ADB$ is one half the area of $\triangle ABC$.

Reflect

4. Why is it possible to position $\triangle ABC$ so that two of its sides lie on the axes of the coordinate plane?

_____

_____

Your Turn

Position the given triangle on the coordinate plane. Then show that the result about areas from Example 1 holds for the triangle.

5. A right triangle, $\triangle ABC$, with legs of length 2 units and 4 units

_____

_____

_____

_____

_____

_____

6. A right triangle, $\triangle ABC$, with both legs of length 8 units

_____

_____

_____

_____

⚿ Explain 2 Proving the Triangle Midsegment Theorem

In Module 8, you learned that the Triangle Midsegment Theorem states that a midsegment of a triangle is parallel to the third side of the triangle and is half as long as the third side. You can now use a coordinate proof to show that the theorem is true.

Example 2 Prove the Triangle Midsegment Theorem.

Given: $\overline{XY}$ is a midsegment of $\triangle PQR$.

Prove: $\overline{XY} \parallel \overline{PQ}$ and $XY = \frac{1}{2}PQ$

Place $\triangle PQR$ so that one vertex is at the origin. For convenience, assign vertex P the coordinates $(2a, 2b)$ and assign vertex Q the vertices $(2c, 2d)$.

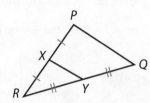

Use the Midpoint Formula to find the coordinates of X and Y.

The coordinates of X are $X\left(\dfrac{0 + 2a}{2}, \dfrac{0 + 2b}{2}\right) = X(a, b)$.

The coordinates of Y are $Y\left(\dfrac{\boxed{} + \boxed{}}{2}, \dfrac{\boxed{} + \boxed{}}{2}\right) = Y\left(\boxed{}, \boxed{}\right)$.

Find the slope of $\overline{PQ}$ and $\overline{XY}$.

slope of $\overline{PQ} = \dfrac{y_2 - y_1}{x_2 - x_1} = \dfrac{2d - 2b}{2c - 2a} = \dfrac{\boxed{} - \boxed{}}{\boxed{} - \boxed{}}$; slope of $\overline{XY} = \dfrac{y_2 - y_1}{x_2 - x_1} = \dfrac{\boxed{} - \boxed{}}{\boxed{} - \boxed{}}$

Therefore, $\overline{PQ} \parallel \overline{XY}$ since _____.

Use the Distance Formula to find PQ and XY.

$PQ = \sqrt{(x_2 - x_1)^2 + (y_2 - y_1)^2}$ $\qquad = \sqrt{(2c - 2a)^2 + (2d - 2b)^2}$

$\qquad = \sqrt{\boxed{} \cdot (c - a)^2 + \boxed{} \cdot (d - b)^2}$ $\qquad = \sqrt{\boxed{} \cdot (c - a)^2 + (d - b)^2}$

$\qquad = \sqrt{\boxed{}} \cdot \sqrt{(c - a)^2 + (d - b)^2}$ $\qquad = \boxed{}\sqrt{(c - a)^2 + (d - b)^2}$

$XY = \sqrt{(x_2 - x_1)^2 + (y_2 - y_1)^2}$ $\qquad = \sqrt{\left(\boxed{} - \boxed{}\right)^2 + \left(\boxed{} - \boxed{}\right)^2}$

This shows that $XY = \dfrac{\boxed{}}{\boxed{}}\, PQ$.

7.   Discussion Why is it more convenient to assign vertex P the coordinates $(2a, 2b)$ and vertex Q the coordinates $(2c, 2d)$ rather than using the coordinates (a, b) and (c, d)?

_____

_____

_____

🔧 Explain 3   Proving the Concurrency of Medians Theorem

You used the Concurrency of Medians Theorem in Module 8 and proved it in Module 9. Now you will prove the theorem again, this time using coordinate methods.

Example 3   **Prove the Concurrency of Medians Theorem.**

Given: $\triangle PQR$ with medians $\overline{PL}$, $\overline{QM}$, and $\overline{RN}$

Prove: $\overline{PL}$, $\overline{QM}$, and $\overline{RN}$ are concurrent.

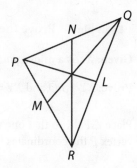

Place $\triangle PQR$ so that vertex R is at the origin. Also, place the triangle so that point N lies on the y-axis. For convenience, assign point N the vertices $(0, 6a)$. (The factor of 6 will result in easier calculations later.)

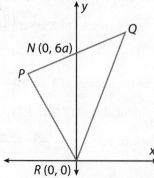

Since N is the midpoint of $\overline{PQ}$, assign coordinates to P and Q as follows.

The horizontal distance from N to P must be the same as the horizontal distance from N to Q. Let this distance be $2b$.

Then the x-coordinate of point P is $-2b$ and the x-coordinate of point Q is _____.

The vertical distance from N to P must be the same as the vertical distance from N to Q. Let this distance be $2c$.

Then the y-coordinate of point P is $6a - 2c$ and the y-coordinate of point Q is _____.

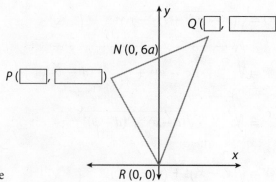

Complete the figure by writing the coordinates of points P and Q.

Now use the Midpoint Formula to find the coordinates of L and M.

The midpoint of $\overline{RQ}$ is $L\left(\dfrac{\boxed{} + \boxed{}}{2}, \dfrac{\boxed{} + \boxed{}}{2}\right) = L\left(\boxed{}, \boxed{}\right).$

The midpoint of $\overline{RP}$ is $M\left(\dfrac{\boxed{} + \boxed{}}{2}, \dfrac{\boxed{} + \boxed{}}{2}\right) = M\left(\boxed{}, \boxed{}\right).$

Complete the figure by writing the coordinates of points L and M.

To complete the proof, write the equation of $\overleftrightarrow{QM}$ and use the equation to find the coordinates of point C, which is the intersection of the medians $\overline{QM}$ and $\overline{RN}$. Then show that point C lies on $\overleftrightarrow{PL}$.

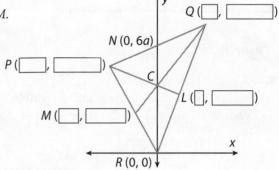

Write the equation of $\overleftrightarrow{QM}$ using point-slope form.

The slope of $\overleftrightarrow{QM}$ is $\dfrac{(6a + 2c) - (3a - c)}{2b - (-b)} = \dfrac{3\boxed{} + 3}{3\boxed{}} = \dfrac{\boxed{} + \boxed{}}{\boxed{}}.$

Use the coordinates of point Q for the point on $\overleftrightarrow{QM}$.

Therefore, the equation of $\overleftrightarrow{QM}$ is $y - \boxed{} = \dfrac{\boxed{} + \boxed{}}{\boxed{}} \cdot \left(x - \boxed{}\right).$

Since point C lies on the y-axis, the x-coordinate of point C is 0. To find the y-coordinate of C, substitute $x = 0$ in the equation of $\overleftrightarrow{QM}$ and solve for y.

Substitute $x = 0$. $\qquad\qquad y - \boxed{} = \dfrac{\boxed{} + \boxed{}}{\boxed{}} \cdot \left(0 - \boxed{}\right)$

Simplify the right side of the equation. $\qquad y - \boxed{} = -2\boxed{}$

Distributive property $\qquad\qquad\qquad y - \boxed{} = -2\boxed{} - 2\boxed{}$

Add $6a + 2c$ to each side and simplify. $\qquad y = \boxed{}$

So, the coordinates of point C are $C\left(\boxed{}, \boxed{}\right).$

Now write the equation of $\overleftrightarrow{PL}$ using point-slope form.

The slope of $\overleftrightarrow{PL}$ is $\dfrac{(6a - 2c) - (3a + c)}{-2b - b} = \dfrac{3\boxed{} - 3}{-3\boxed{}} = \dfrac{\boxed{} - \boxed{}}{-\boxed{}}.$

Use the coordinates of point P for the point on $\overleftrightarrow{PL}$.

Therefore, the equation of $\overleftrightarrow{PL}$ is $y - \boxed{} = \dfrac{\boxed{} - \boxed{}}{-\boxed{}} \cdot \left(x + \boxed{}\right).$

Finally, show that point C lies on $\overleftrightarrow{PL}$. To do so, show that when $x = 0$ in the equation for $\overleftrightarrow{PL}$, $y = 4a$.

Substitute $x = 0$.

$$y - \boxed{} = \dfrac{\boxed{} - \boxed{}}{- \boxed{}} \cdot \left(0 + \boxed{}\right)$$

Simplify right side of equation.

$$y - \boxed{} = -2\boxed{} + 2\boxed{}$$

Add $6a - 2c$ to each side and simplify.

$$y = \boxed{}$$

Reflect

8. A student claims that the averages of the x-coordinates and of the y-coordinates of the vertices of the triangle are x- and y-coordinates of the point of concurrency, C. Does the coordinate proof of the Concurrency of Medians Theorem support the claim? Explain.

_____

_____

_____

_____

Explain 4 — Using Triangles on the Coordinate Plane

Example 4 Write each proof.

(A) **Given:** $A(2, 3)$, $B(5, -1)$, $C(1, 0)$, $D(-4, -1)$, $E(0, 2)$, $F(-1, -2)$

Prove: $\angle ABC \cong \angle DEF$

Step 1 Plot the points on a coordinate plane.

Step 2 Use the Distance Formula to find the length of each side of each triangle.

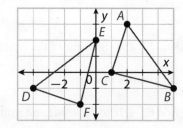

$AB = \sqrt{(5 - 2)^2 + (-1 - 3)^2} = \sqrt{25} = 5$; $BC = \sqrt{(1 - 5)^2 + 0 - (-1)^2} = \sqrt{17}$;

$AC = \sqrt{(1 - 2)^2 + (0 - 3)^2} = \sqrt{10}$; $DE = \sqrt{\left(0 - (-4)\right)^2 + \left(2 - (-1)\right)^2} = \sqrt{25} = 5$;

$EF = \sqrt{(-1 - 0)^2 + (-2 - 2)^2} = \sqrt{1 + 16} = \sqrt{17}$; $DF = \sqrt{\left(-1 - (-4)\right)^2 + \left(-2 - (-1)\right)^2}$

$\qquad = \sqrt{9 + 1} = \sqrt{10}$

So, $\overline{AB} \cong \overline{DE}$, $\overline{BC} \cong \overline{EF}$, and $\overline{AC} \cong \overline{DF}$. Therefore, $\triangle ABC \cong \triangle DEF$ by the SSS Triangle Congruence Theorem and $\angle ABC \cong \angle DEF$ by CPCTC.

B **Given:** $J(-4, 1)$, $K(0, 5)$, $L(3, 1)$, $M(-1, -3)$, R is the midpoint of $\overline{JK}$, S is the midpoint of $\overline{LM}$.

Prove: $\angle JSK \cong \angle LRM$

Step 1 Plot the points on a coordinate plane.

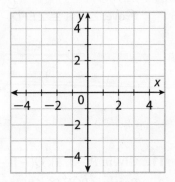

Step 2 Use the Midpoint Formula to find the coordinates of R and S.

$$R\left(\frac{\boxed{} + \boxed{}}{2}, \frac{\boxed{} + \boxed{}}{2}\right) = R\left(\boxed{}, \boxed{}\right)$$

$$S\left(\frac{\boxed{} + \boxed{}}{2}, \frac{\boxed{} + \boxed{}}{2}\right) = S\left(\boxed{}, \boxed{}\right)$$

Step 3 Use the Distance Formula to find the length of each side of each triangle.

$$JK = \sqrt{\left(0 - (-4)\right)^2 + (5 - 1)^2} = \sqrt{16 + 16} = \sqrt{32}$$

$$KS = \sqrt{\left(\boxed{} - 0\right)^2 + \left(\boxed{} - 5\right)^2} = \sqrt{\boxed{} + \boxed{}} = \sqrt{\boxed{}}$$

$$JS = \sqrt{\left(\boxed{} - (-4)\right)^2 + \left(\boxed{} - 1\right)^2} = \sqrt{\boxed{} + \boxed{}} = \sqrt{\boxed{}}$$

$$LM = \sqrt{(-1 - 3)^2 + (-3 - 1)^2} = \sqrt{16 + 16} = \sqrt{32}$$

$$MR = \sqrt{\left(\boxed{} - (-1)\right)^2 + \left(\boxed{} - (-3)\right)^2} = \sqrt{\boxed{} + \boxed{}} = \sqrt{\boxed{}}$$

$$LR = \sqrt{\left(\boxed{} - 3\right)^2 + \left(\boxed{} - 1\right)^2} = \sqrt{\boxed{} + \boxed{}} = \sqrt{\boxed{}}$$

So, $\overline{JK} \cong \boxed{}$, $\overline{KS} \cong \boxed{}$, and $\overline{JS} \cong \boxed{}$. Therefore, $\triangle JKS \cong \boxed{}$ by the SSS Triangle Congruence Theorem and $\angle JSK \cong \angle LRM$

since _____.

Reflect

9. In Part B, what other pairs of angles can you prove to be congruent? Why?

_____

_____

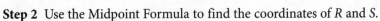

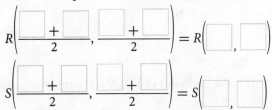

Write each proof.

10. **Given:** $A(-4, -2)$, $B(-3, 2)$, $C(-1, 3)$, $D(-5, 0)$, $E(-1, -1)$, $F(0, -3)$
    Prove: $\angle BCA \cong \angle EFD$

11. **Given:** $P(-3, 5)$, $Q(-1, -1)$, $R(4, 5)$, $S(2, -1)$, M is the midpoint of $\overline{PQ}$, N is the midpoint of $\overline{RS}$.
    Prove: $\angle PQN \cong \angle RSM$

💬 Elaborate

12. When you write a coordinate proof, why might you assign $2p$ as a coordinate rather than p?

13. **Essential Question Check-In** What makes a coordinate proof different from the other types of proofs you have written so far?

1. Explain how to derive the Distance Formula using $\triangle PQR$.

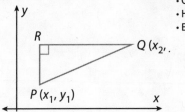

Write each coordinate proof.

2. **Given:** $\angle B$ is a right angle in $\triangle ABC$. M is the midpoint of $\overline{AC}$.

Prove: M is equidistant from all three vertices of $\triangle ABC$.

Use the coordinates that have been assigned in the figure.

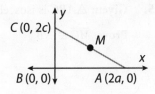

3. **Given:** $\triangle ABC$ is isosceles. X is the midpoint of $\overline{AB}$, Y is the midpoint of $\overline{AC}$, Z is the midpoint of $\overline{BC}$.

Prove: $\triangle XYZ$ is isosceles.

Use the coordinates that have been assigned in the figure.

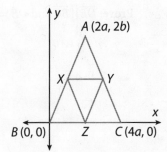

4. **Given:** $\angle R$ is a right angle in $\triangle PQR$. A is the midpoint of $\overline{PR}$. B is the midpoint of $\overline{QR}$.

    Prove: $\overline{AB}$ is parallel to $\overline{PQ}$.

5. **Given:** $\triangle ABC$ is isosceles. M is the midpoint of $\overline{AB}$. N is the midpoint of $\overline{AC}$. $\overline{AB} \cong \overline{AC}$

    Prove: $\overline{MC} \cong \overline{NB}$

6. Prove the Triangle Midsegment Theorem using the figure shown here.

    Given: $\overline{DE}$ is a midsegment of $\triangle ABC$.

    Prove: $\overline{DE} \parallel \overline{BC}$ and $DE = \frac{1}{2}BC$

    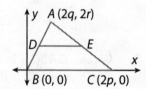

7. **Critique Reasoning** A student proves the Concurrency of Medians Theorem by first assigning coordinates to the vertices of $\triangle PQR$ as $P(0, 0)$, $Q(2a, 0)$, and $R(2a, 2c)$. The student says that this choice of coordinates makes the algebra in the proof a bit easier. Do you agree with the student's choice of coordinates? Explain.

Write each proof.

8. **Given:** $J(-2, 2), K(0, 1), L(-3, -1), P(4, -2), Q(3, -4), R(1, -1)$

   Prove: $\angle JKL \cong \angle PQR$

9. **Given:** $D(-3, 2), E(3, 3), F(1, 1), S(9, -2), T(3, -1), U(5, -3)$

   Prove: $\angle FDE \cong \angle UST$

10. **Given:** $A(-2, 2), B(4, 4), M(-2, -1), N(4, -3), X$ is the midpoint of $\overline{AB}$, Y is the midpoint of $\overline{MN}$.

    Prove: $\angle ABY \cong \angle MNX$

11. **Given:** $J(-1, 4), K(3, 0), P(3, -6), Q(-1, -2), U$ is the midpoint of $\overline{JK}$, V is the midpoint of $\overline{PQ}$.

    Prove: $\angle KVJ \cong \angle QUP$

Prove or disprove each statement.

12. The triangle with vertices $R(-2, -2)$, $S(1, 4)$, and $T(4, -5)$ is an equilateral triangle.

13. The triangle with vertices $J(-2, 2)$, $K(2, 3)$, and $L(-1, -2)$ is an isosceles triangle.

14. The triangle with vertices $A(-1, 3)$, $B(2, 1)$, and $C(0, -2)$ is a scalene triangle.

15. Two container ships depart from a port at $P(20, 10)$. The first ship travels to a location at $A(-30, 50)$, and the second ship travels to a location at $B(70, -30)$. Each unit represents one nautical mile. Find the distance between the ships to the nearest nautical mile. Verify that the port is the midpoint between the two ships.

16. The support structure for a hammock includes a triangle whose vertices have coordinates $G(-1, 3)$, $H(-3, -2)$, and $J(1, -2)$.

   a. Classify the triangle and justify your answer.

   b. **Algebra** Each unit of the coordinate plane represents one foot. To the nearest tenth of a foot, how much metal is needed to make one of the triangular parts for the support structure?

17. Communicate Mathematical Ideas Explain how the perimeter of △*JKL* compares to the perimeter of △*MNP*.

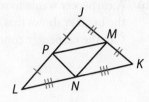

18. The coordinates of the vertices of △*LMN* are shown in the figure. Determine whether each statement is true or false. Select the correct answer for each lettered part.

a. △*LMN* is isosceles. ◯ True ◯ False

b. One side of △*LMN* has a length of 2*c* units. ◯ True ◯ False

c. If *P* is the midpoint of $\overline{LN}$, then $\overline{OP}$ is parallel to $\overline{LM}$. ◯ True ◯ False

d. The area of △*LMN* is 4*cd* square units. ◯ True ◯ False

e. The midpoint of $\overline{MN}$ is the origin. ◯ True ◯ False

H.O.T. Focus on Higher Order Thinking

19. **Explain the Error** A student assigns coordinates to a right triangle as shown in the figure. Then he uses the Distance Formula to show that *PQ* = *a* and *RQ* = *a*. Since *PQ* = *RQ*, the student says he has proved that every right triangle is isosceles. Explain the error in the student's proof.

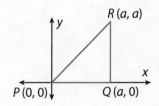

20. A carpenter wants to make a triangular bracket to hold up a bookshelf. The plan for the bracket shows that the vertices of the triangle are $R(-2, 2)$, $S(1, 4)$, and $T(1, -2)$. Can the carpenter conclude that the bracket is a right triangle? Explain.

21. Analyze Relationships The vertices chosen to represent an isosceles right triangle for a coordinate proof are at $(-2s, 2s)$, $(0, 2s)$, and $(0, 0)$. What other coordinates could be used so that the coordinate proof would be easier to complete? Explain.

Lesson Performance Task

A triathlon course was mapped on a coordinate grid marked in 1-kilometer units. The starting point was $(0, 0)$. The triathlon was broken into three stages:

- Stage 1: Contestants swim from $(0, 0)$ to $(0.6, 0.8)$.
- Stage 2: Contestants bicycle from the previous stopping point to $(30.6, 16.8)$.
- Stage 3: Contestants run from the previous stopping point to $(25.6, 28.8)$.

The winner averaged 4 kilometers per hour for Stage 1, 50 kilometers per hour for Stage 2, and 13 kilometers per hour for Stage 3. What was the winner's time for the entire race? (Assume that no time elapsed between stages.) Explain how you found the answer.

© Houghton Mifflin Harcourt Publishing Company • Image Credits: ©Liquidlibrary/Jupiterimages/Getty Images

25.4 Coordinate Proof Using Distance with Quadrilaterals

Essential Question: How can you use slope and the distance formula in coordinate proofs?

⊘ Explore   Positioning a Quadrilateral on the Coordinate Plane

You have used coordinate geometry to find the midpoint of a line segment and to find the distance between two points. Coordinate geometry can also be used to prove conjectures.

Remember that in Lesson 10.3 you learned several strategies that make using a coordinate proof simpler. They are:

- Use the origin as a vertex, keeping the figure in Quadrant I.
- Center the figure at the origin.
- Center a side of the figure at the origin.
- Use one or both axes as sides of the figure.

Position a rectangle with a length of 8 units and a width of 3 units in the coordinate plane as described.

Ⓐ **Method 1** Center the longer side of the rectangle at the origin.

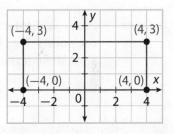

Ⓑ **Method 2** Use the origin as a vertex of the rectangle. Depending on what you are using the figure to prove, one method may be better than the other. For example, if you need to find the midpoint of the longer side, use the first method.

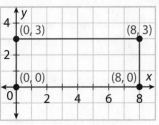

A coordinate proof can also be used to prove that a certain relationship is always true. You can prove that a statement is true for all right triangles without knowing the side lengths. To do this, assign variables as the coordinates of the vertices.

Position a square, with side lengths $2a$, on a coordinate plane and give the coordinates of each vertex.

Ⓒ Sketch the square. Label the side lengths.

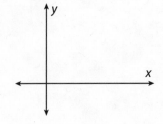

© Houghton Mifflin Harcourt Publishing Company

Ⓓ What are the coordinates of each vertex?

Reflect

1. **Discussion** Describe another way you could have positioned the square and give the coordinates of its vertices.

2. When writing a coordinate proof why are variables used instead of numbers as coordinates for the vertices of a figure?

⚿ Explain 1 Proving Properties of a Parallelogram

You have already used the Distance Formula and the Midpoint Formula in coordinate proofs. As you will see, slope is useful in coordinate proofs whenever you need to show that lines are parallel or perpendicular.

Example 1 Prove or disprove that the quadrilateral determined by the points $A(4, 4)$, $B(3, 1)$, $C(-2, -1)$, and $D(-1, 2)$ is a parallelogram.

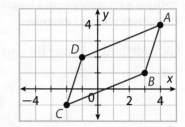

Ⓐ Use slopes to write the coordinate proof.

To determine whether $ABCD$ is a parallelogram, find the slope of each side of the quadrilateral.

Slope of $\overline{AB} = \dfrac{y_2 - y_1}{x_2 - x_1} = \dfrac{1 - 4}{3 - 4} = \dfrac{-3}{-1} = 3$; Slope of $\overline{BC} = \dfrac{y_2 - y_1}{x_2 - x_1} = \dfrac{-1 - 1}{-2 - 3} = \dfrac{-2}{-5} = \dfrac{2}{5}$;

Slope of $\overline{CD} = \dfrac{y_2 - y_1}{x_2 - x_1} = \dfrac{2 - (-1)}{-1 - (-2)} = \dfrac{3}{1} = 3$; Slope of $\overline{DA} = \dfrac{y_2 - y_1}{x_2 - x_1} = \dfrac{4 - 2}{4 - (-1)} = \dfrac{2}{5}$

Compare slopes. The slopes of opposite sides are equal. This means opposite sides are parallel. So, quadrilateral $ABCD$ is a parallelogram.

(B) Use the Distance Formula to write the coordinate proof.

To determine whether $ABCD$ is a parallelogram, find the length of each side of the quadrilateral. Remember that the Distance Formula is length $= \sqrt{(x_2-x_1)^2+(y_2-y_1)^2}$.

$AB = \sqrt{\left(\boxed{} - 4\right)^2 + (1-4)^2}$

$ = \sqrt{(-1)^2 + \left(\boxed{}\right)^2}$

$ = \sqrt{\boxed{}}$

$BC = \sqrt{\left(-2 - \boxed{}\right)^2 + \left(\boxed{} - 1\right)^2}$

$ = \sqrt{(-5)^2 + \left(\boxed{}\right)^2}$

$ = \sqrt{\boxed{}}$

$CD = \sqrt{\left(-1 - \boxed{}\right)^2 + \left(\boxed{} - (-1)\right)^2}$

$ = \sqrt{(1)^2 + \left(\boxed{}\right)^2}$

$ = \sqrt{\boxed{}}$

$DA = \sqrt{\left(4 - \boxed{}\right)^2 + \left(4 - \boxed{}\right)^2}$

$ = \sqrt{\left(\boxed{}\right)^2 + \left(\boxed{}\right)^2}$

$ = \sqrt{\boxed{}}$

Compare the side lengths. The lengths of the opposite sides are _____. By the _____

_____, we can conclude that $ABCD$ is a _____.

Reflect

3. Suppose you want to prove that a general parallelogram $WXYZ$ has diagonals that bisect each other. Why is it convenient to use general vertex coefficients, such as $2a$ and $2b$?

_____

_____

_____

Your Turn

Write a coordinate proof given quadrilateral $ABCD$ with vertices $A(3, 2)$, $B(8, 2)$, $C(5, 0)$, and $D(0, 0)$.

4. Prove that $ABCD$ is a parallelogram.

5. Prove that the diagonals of $ABCD$ bisect each other.

Example 2 Prove or disprove each statement about the quadrilateral determined by the points $Q(2, -3)$, $R(-4, 0)$, $S(-2, 4)$, and $T(4, 1)$.

Ⓐ The diagonals of $QRST$ are congruent.

The length of $\overline{SQ} = \sqrt{(2 - (-2))^2 + (-3 - 4)^2} = \sqrt{65}$.

The length of $\overline{RT} = \sqrt{(-4 - 4)^2 + (0 - 1)^2} = \sqrt{65}$.

So, the diagonals of $QRST$ are congruent.

Ⓑ $QRST$ is a rectangle.

Find the slope of each side of the quadrilateral.

Slope of $\overline{QR} = \dfrac{y_2 - y_1}{x_2 - x_1} = \dfrac{0 - (-3)}{-4 - 2} = \dfrac{3}{-6} = -\dfrac{1}{2}$; Slope of $\overline{RS} = \dfrac{y_2 - y_1}{x_2 - x_1} = \dfrac{\boxed{} - \boxed{}}{\boxed{} - \boxed{}} = \dfrac{\boxed{}}{\boxed{}} = \boxed{}$;

Slope of $\overline{ST} = \dfrac{y_2 - y_1}{x_2 - x_1} = \dfrac{\boxed{} - \boxed{}}{\boxed{} - \boxed{}} = \dfrac{\boxed{}}{\boxed{}} = \boxed{}$;

Slope of $\overline{TQ} = \dfrac{y_2 - y_1}{x_2 - x_1} = \dfrac{\boxed{} - \boxed{}}{\boxed{} - \boxed{}} = \dfrac{\boxed{}}{\boxed{}} = \boxed{}$

Find the products of the slopes of adjacent sides.

$\left(\text{slope of } \overline{QR}\right)\left(\text{slope of } \overline{RS}\right) = \boxed{} \cdot \boxed{} = \boxed{}$; $\left(\text{slope of } \overline{RS}\right)\left(\text{slope of } \overline{ST}\right) = \boxed{} \cdot \boxed{} = \boxed{}$;

$\left(\text{slope of } \overline{ST}\right)\left(\text{slope of } \overline{TQ}\right) = \boxed{} \cdot \boxed{} = \boxed{}$; $\left(\text{slope of } \overline{TQ}\right)\left(\text{slope of } \overline{QR}\right) = \boxed{} \cdot \boxed{} = \boxed{}$

You can conclude that adjacent sides are _____. So, quadrilateral $QRST$ is a _____.

Reflect

6. Explain how to prove that $QRST$ is not a square.

_____

_____

Prove or disprove each statement about quadrilateral *WXYZ*
determined by the points *W*(0, 0), *X*(4, 3), *Y*(9, 3), and *Z*(5, 0).

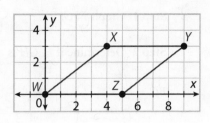

7. *WXYZ* is a rhombus.

8. The diagonals of *WXYZ* are perpendicular.

🔑 Explain 3 Identifying Figures on the Coordinate Plane

Example 3 Use the diagonals to determine whether a parallelogram with the given
vertices is a rectangle, rhombus, or square. Give all the names that apply.

(A) *A*(0, 2), *B*(3, 6), *C*(8, 6), *D*(5, 2)

Step 1 Graph *ABCD*.

Step 2 Determine if *ABCD* is a rectangle.

$$AC = \sqrt{(8-0)^2 + (6-2)^2} = \sqrt{80} = 4\sqrt{5}$$

$$BD = \sqrt{(5-3)^2 + (2-6)^2} = \sqrt{20} = 2\sqrt{5}$$

Since $4\sqrt{5} \neq 2\sqrt{5}$, *ABCD* is not a rectangle. Thus, *ABCD* is
not a square.

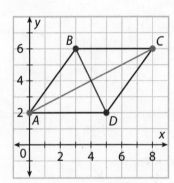

Step 3 Determine if *ABCD* is a rhombus.

Slope of $\overline{AC} = \dfrac{6-2}{8-0} = \dfrac{1}{2}$

Slope of $\overline{BD} = \dfrac{2-6}{5-3} = -2$

Since $\left(\dfrac{1}{2}\right)(-2) = -1$, $\overline{AC} \perp \overline{BD}$. *ABCD* is a rhombus.

Ⓑ $E(-4, -1)$, $F(-3, 2)$, $G(3, 0)$, $H(2, -3)$

Step 1 Graph *EFGH*.

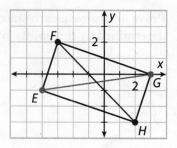

Step 2 Determine if *EFGH* is a rectangle.

$$EG = \sqrt{\left(3 - \boxed{}\right)^2 + \left(0 - \boxed{}\right)^2} = \sqrt{\boxed{}} = \boxed{}$$

$$FH = \sqrt{\left(\boxed{} - (-3)\right)^2 + \left(\boxed{} - 2\right)^2} = \sqrt{\boxed{}} = 5\sqrt{\boxed{}}$$

Since $\boxed{} = 5\sqrt{\boxed{}}$, the diagonals are _____. *EFGH* _____ a rectangle.

Step 3 Determine if *EFGH* is a rhombus.

Slope of _____ $= \dfrac{0 - (-1)}{3 - (-4)} = \dfrac{1}{7}$; Slope of _____ $= \dfrac{-3 - 2}{2 - (-3)} = \dfrac{-5}{5} = -1$

Since $\left(\dfrac{1}{7}\right)(-1) \neq -1$, $\overline{EG}$ is _____ to $\overline{FH}$. So, *EFGH* is not a rhombus

and cannot be a _____.

Your Turn

Use the diagonals to determine whether a parallelogram with the given vertices is
a rectangle, rhombus, or square. Give all the names that apply.

9. $K(-5, -1)$, $L(-2, 4)$, $M(3, 1)$, $N(0, -4)$

10. $P(-4, 6)$, $Q(2, 5)$, $R(3, -1)$, $S(-3, 0)$

💬 **Elaborate**

11. How can you use slopes to show that two line segments are parallel? Perpendicular?

_____

_____

12. When you use the distance formula, you find the square root of a value. When finding the square root of a
value, you must consider both the positive and negative outcomes. Explain why the negative outcome is not
used in the coordinate proofs in the lesson.

_____

_____

13. Essential Question Check-In How can you use slope in coordinate proofs?

_____

_____

_____

_____

⊛ Evaluate: Homework and Practice

• Online Homework
• Hints and Help
• Extra Practice

1. Suppose you have a right triangle. If you want to write a proof about the midpoints of the legs of the triangle, which placement of the triangle would be most helpful? Explain.

   A. Use the origin as a vertex, keeping the figure in Quadrant I with vertices $(0, 2b)$, $(2a, 0)$, and $(0, 0)$.

   B. Center the triangle at the origin.

   C. Use the origin as a vertex, keeping the figure in Quadrant I with vertices $(0, b)$, $(a, 0)$, and $(0, 0)$.

   D. Center one leg of the triangle on the y-axis with vertices $(0, a)$, $(0, -a)$, and $(b, -a)$.

   E. Use the x-axis as one leg of the triangle with vertices $(a, 0)$, (a, b), and $(a + c, 0)$.

2. Describe the position of a general trapezoid $WXYZ$ determined by the points $W(0, 0)$, $X(a, 0)$, $Y(a - c, b)$, and $Z(c, b)$. Then sketch the trapezoid.

Write a coordinate proof for the quadrilateral determined by the points $A(2, 4)$, $B(4, -1)$, $C(-1, -3)$, and $D(-3, 2)$.

3. Prove that $ABCD$ is a parallelogram.

4. Prove that $ABCD$ is a rectangle.

5. Prove that *ABCD* is a rhombus.

6. Prove that *ABCD* is a square.

**Prove or disprove each statement about the quadrilateral determined by the points
$W(-2, 5)$, $X(5, 5)$, $Y(5, 0)$, and $Z(-2, 0)$.**

7. Prove that the diagonals are congruent.

8. Prove that the diagonals are perpendicular.

9. Prove that the diagonals bisect each other.

10. Prove that *WXYZ* is a square.

Algebra Use the diagonals to determine whether a parallelogram with the given
vertices is a rectangle, rhombus, or square. Give all the names that apply.

11. $A(-10, 4)$, $B(-2, 10)$, $C(4, 2)$, $D(-4, -4)$

12. $J(-9, -7)$, $K(-4, -2)$, $L(3, -3)$, $M(-2, -8)$

© Houghton Mifflin Harcourt Publishing Company

Analyze Relationships The coordinates of three vertices of parallelogram *ABCD* are given. Find the coordinates of the fourth point so that the given type of figure is formed.

13. $A(4, -2)$, $B(-5, -2)$, $D(4, 4)$, rectangle

14. $A(-5, 5)$, $B(0, 0)$, $C(7, 1)$, rhombus

15. $A(0, 2)$, $B(4, -2)$, $C(0, -6)$, square

16. $A(2, 1)$, $B(-1, 5)$, $C(-5, 2)$, square

Paul designed a doghouse to fit against the side of his house. His plan consisted of a right triangle on top of a rectangle. Use the drawing for Exercises 17–18.

17. Find *BD*, *CE*, and *BE*.

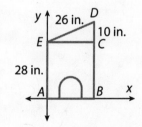

18. Before building the doghouse, Paul sketched his plan on a coordinate plane. He placed *A* at the origin and $\overline{AB}$ on the x-axis. Find the coordinates of *B, C, D,* and *E*, assuming that each unit of the coordinate plane represents one inch.

19. Critical Thinking On the National Mall in Washington, D.C., a reflecting pool lies between the Lincoln Memorial and the World War II Memorial. The pool has two 2300-foot-long sides and two 150-foot-long sides. Tell what additional information you need to know in order to determine whether the reflecting pool is a rectangle. (*Hint*: Remember that you have to show it is a parallelogram first.)

Algebra **Write a coordinate proof.**

20. The Bushmen in South Africa use the Global Positioning System to transmit data about endangered animals to conservationists. The Bushmen have sighted animals at the following coordinates: $(-25, 31.5)$, $(-23.2, 31.4)$, and $(-24, 31.1)$. Prove that the distance between two of these locations is approximately twice the distance between two other locations.

21. Two cruise ships leave a port located at $P(10, 50)$. One ship sails to an island located at $A(-40, -10)$, and the other sails to an island located at $B(60, 110)$. Suppose that each unit represents one nautical mile. Find the midpoint of the line segment connecting the two cruise ships. Verify that the port and the two cruise ships are in a line.

22. A parallelogram has vertices at $(0, 0)$, $(5, 6)$, and $(10, 0)$. Which could be the fourth vertex of the parallelogram? Choose all that apply.

A. $(5, -6)$

B. $(15, 6)$

C. $(0, -6)$

D. $(10, 6)$

E. $(-5, 6)$

H.O.T. **Focus on Higher Order Thinking**

23. **Draw Conclusions** The diagonals of a parallelogram intersect at $(-2, 1.5)$. Two vertices are located at $(-7, 2)$ and $(2, 6.5)$. Find the coordinates of the other two vertices.

24. **Analyze Relationships** Consider points $L(3, -4)$, $M(1, -2)$, and $N(5, 2)$.

  a. Find coordinates for point P so that the quadrilateral determined by points L, M, N, and P is a parallelogram. Is there more than one possibility? Explain.

  b. Are any of the parallelograms a rectangle? Why?

25. **Critical Thinking** Rhombus $OPQR$ has vertices $O(0, 0)$, $P(a, b)$, $Q(a + b, a + b)$, and $R(b, a)$. Prove the diagonals of the rhombus are perpendicular.

26. Multi-Step Use coordinates to verify the Trapezoid Midsegment Theorem which states "The midsegment of a trapezoid is parallel to each base, and its length is one half the sum of the lengths of the bases."

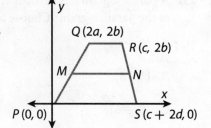

a. M is the midpoint of $\overline{QP}$. What are its coordinates?

b. N is the midpoint of $\overline{RS}$. What are its coordinates?

c. Find the slopes of $\overline{QR}, \overline{PS}, \overline{MN}$. What can you conclude?

d. Find $\overline{QR}, \overline{PS}, \overline{MN}$. Show that $MN = \frac{1}{2}(PS + QR)$.

Lesson Performance Task

According to the new mayor, the shape of City Park is downright ugly. While the parks in all of the other towns in the vicinity have nice, regular polygonal shapes, City Park is the shape of an irregular quadrilateral. On a coordinate map of the park, the four corners are located at $(-3, 4)$, $(5, 2)$, $(1, -2)$, and $(-5, -4)$. The mayor's chief assistant knows a little mathematics and proposes that a special "inner park" be created by joining the midpoints of the sides of City Park. The assistant claims that the boundaries of the inner park will create a nice, regular polygonal shape, just like the parks in all the other towns. The mayor thinks the idea is ridiculous, saying, "You can't create order out of chaos."

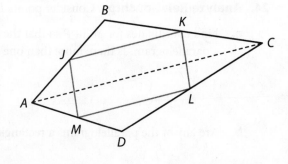

1. Who was right? Explain your reasoning in detail.

2. Irregular quadrilateral $ABCD$ is shown here. Points J, K, L, and M are midpoints.

a. What must you show to prove that quadrilateral $JKLM$ is a parallelogram?

b. How can you show this?

c. If the adjacent sides of $JKLM$ are perpendicular, what type of figure does that make $JKLM$?

25.5 Perimeter and Area on the Coordinate Plane

Essential Question: How do you find the perimeter and area of polygons in the coordinate plane?

⊘ Explore   Finding Perimeters of Figures on the Coordinate Plane

Recall that the perimeter of a polygon is the sum of the lengths of the polygon's sides. You can use the Distance Formula to find perimeters of polygons in a coordinate plane.

Follow these steps to find the perimeter of a pentagon with vertices $A(-1, 4)$, $B(4, 4)$, $C(3, -2)$, $D(-1, -4)$, and $E(-4, 1)$. Round to the nearest tenth.

Ⓐ   Plot the points. Then use a straightedge to draw the pentagon that is determined by the points.

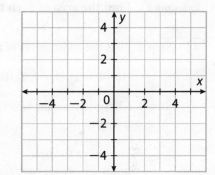

Ⓑ   Are there any sides for which you do not need to use the Distance

Formula? Explain, and give their length(s). _____

_____

Ⓒ   Use the Distance Formula to find the remaining side lengths. Round your answers to the nearest tenth.

Ⓓ   Find the sum of the side lengths.

_____

Reflect

1.   Explain how you can find the perimeter of a rectangle to check that your answer is reasonable.

_____

_____

_____

🎷 Explain 1　Finding Areas of Figures on the Coordinate Plane

You can use area formulas together with the Distance Formula to determine areas of figures such as triangles, rectangles and parallelograms.

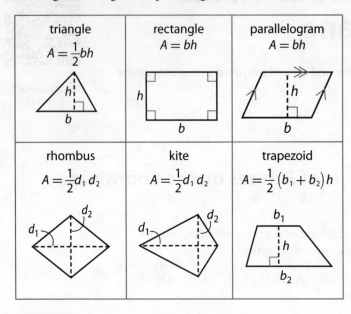

triangle $A = \frac{1}{2}bh$	rectangle $A = bh$	parallelogram $A = bh$
rhombus $A = \frac{1}{2}d_1 d_2$	kite $A = \frac{1}{2}d_1 d_2$	trapezoid $A = \frac{1}{2}(b_1 + b_2)h$

Example 1　Find the area of each figure.

(A)　**Step 1**　Find the coordinates of the vertices of $\triangle ABC$.

$A(-4, -2)$, $B(-2, 2)$, $C(5, 1)$

Step 2　Choose a base for which you can easily find the height of the triangle.

Use $\overline{AC}$ as the base. A segment from the opposite vertex, B, to point $D(-1, -1)$ appears to be perpendicular to the base $\overline{AC}$. Use slopes to check.

slope of $\overline{AC} = \dfrac{1 - (-2)}{5 - (-4)} = \dfrac{1}{3}$; slope of $\overline{BD} = \dfrac{-1 - 2}{-1 - (-2)} = -3$

The product of the slopes is $\dfrac{1}{3} \cdot (-3) = -1$. $\overline{BD}$ is perpendicular to $\overline{AC}$, so $\overline{BD}$ is the height for the base $\overline{AC}$.

Find the length of the base and the height.

$AC = \sqrt{\left(5 - (-4)\right)^2 + \left(1 - (-2)\right)^2} = \sqrt{90} = 3\sqrt{10}$; $BD = \sqrt{\left(-1 - (-2)\right)^2 + (-1 - 2)^2} = \sqrt{10}$

Step 3　Determine the area of $\triangle ABC$.

$\text{Area} = \dfrac{1}{2}bh = \dfrac{1}{2}(AC)(BD) = \dfrac{1}{2} \cdot \left(3\sqrt{10}\right)\left(\sqrt{10}\right) = \dfrac{1}{2} \cdot 30 = 15$ square units

© Houghton Mifflin Harcourt Publishing Company

Step 1 Find the coordinates of the vertices of *DEFG*.

$D(-2, 6)$, $E(4, 3)$, $F(2, -1)$, $G(-4, 2)$

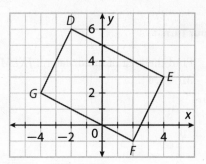

Step 2 *DEFG* appears to be a rectangle. Use slopes to check that adjacent sides are perpendicular.

slope of $\overline{DE}$: $\dfrac{\boxed{} - \boxed{}}{4 - (-2)} = \dfrac{\boxed{}}{6} = \boxed{}$; slope of $\overline{EF}$: $\dfrac{\boxed{} - 3}{2 - \boxed{}} = \dfrac{\boxed{}}{\boxed{}} = \boxed{}$

slope of $\overline{FG}$: $\dfrac{2 - \boxed{}}{-4 - \boxed{}} = \dfrac{\boxed{}}{\boxed{}} = \boxed{}$; slope of $\overline{DG}$: $\dfrac{2 - \boxed{}}{\boxed{} - \boxed{}} = \dfrac{\boxed{}}{\boxed{}} = \boxed{}$

so *DEFG* is a _____ .

Step 3 Find the area of *DEFG*.

$$b = FG = \sqrt{\left(2 - \boxed{}\right)^2 + \left(\boxed{} - 2\right)^2} = \sqrt{\boxed{}} = \boxed{}\sqrt{\boxed{}}$$

$$h = GD = \sqrt{\left(\boxed{} - (-4)\right)^2 + \left(6 - \boxed{}\right)^2} = \sqrt{\boxed{}} = \boxed{}\sqrt{\boxed{}}$$

Area of *DEFG*: $A = bh = \left(\boxed{}\sqrt{\boxed{}}\right)\left(\boxed{}\sqrt{\boxed{}}\right) = \boxed{}$ square units

---

Reflect

2. In Part A, is it possible to use another side of $\triangle ABC$ as the base? If so, what length represents the height of the triangle?

_____

_____

_____

3. **Discussion** In Part B, why was it necessary to find the slopes of the sides?

_____

_____

4. Find the area of quadrilateral *JKLM* with vertices $J(-4, -2)$, $K(2, 1)$, $L(3, 4)$, $M(-3, 1)$.

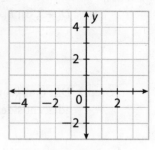

✏️ Explain 2   Finding Areas of Composite Figures

A **composite figure** is made up of simple shapes, such as triangles, rectangles, and parallelograms. To find the area of a composite figure, find the areas of the simple shapes and then use the Area Addition Postulate. You can use the Area Addition Postulate to find the area of a composite figure.

> **Area Addition Postulate**
>
> The area of a region is equal to the sum of the areas of its nonoverlapping parts.

Example 2   **Find the area of each figure.**

(A)   Possible solution: *ABCDE* can be divided up into a rectangle and two triangles, each with horizontal bases.

area of rectangle *AGDE*: $A = bh = (DE)(AE) = (6)(4) = 24$

area of $\triangle ABC$: $A = \frac{1}{2} bh = \frac{1}{2}(AC)(BF) = \frac{1}{2}(8)(2) = 8$

area of $\triangle CDG$: $A = \frac{1}{2} bh = \frac{1}{2}(CG)(DG) = \frac{1}{2}(2)(4) = 4$

area of *ABCDE*: $A = 24 + 8 + 4 = 36$ square units

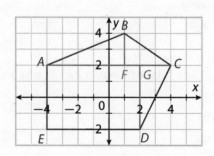

B *PQRST* can be divided into a parallelogram and a triangle.

△*PQT* appears to be a right triangle. Check that $\overline{PT}$ and $\boxed{}$ are perpendicular:

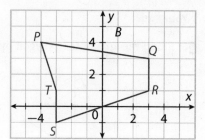

slope of $\overline{PT}$: $\dfrac{1 - \boxed{}}{-3 - \boxed{}} = \dfrac{\boxed{}}{\boxed{}} = \boxed{}$

slope of $\boxed{}$: $\dfrac{\boxed{} - 3}{-3 - \boxed{}} = \dfrac{\boxed{}}{\boxed{}} = \boxed{}$

△*PQT* is a right triangle with base $\overline{PT}$ and height $\boxed{}$.

$$PT = \sqrt{\left(-3 - \boxed{}\right)^2 + \left(1 - \boxed{}\right)^2} = \sqrt{\boxed{}}$$

$$\boxed{} = \sqrt{\left(-3 - \boxed{}\right)^2 + \left(\boxed{} - 3\right)^2} = \sqrt{\boxed{}} = \boxed{}\sqrt{\boxed{}}$$

area of △*PQT*: $A = \frac{1}{2} bh = \frac{1}{2}\left(\sqrt{\boxed{}}\right)\left(\boxed{}\sqrt{\boxed{}}\right) = \boxed{}$

$\overline{QR} \parallel \overline{TS}$ since both sides are vertical.

slope of $\boxed{} = \dfrac{\boxed{} - 1}{-3 - \boxed{}} = \dfrac{\boxed{}}{\boxed{}} = \boxed{}$, so $\overline{QT} \parallel \boxed{}$. Therefore, *QRST* is a

parallelogram.

$\overline{RT}$ is an _____ of △*QRST* and is horizontal. Because $\overline{RT} \perp \overline{RQ}$, △*QRT* is a right

triangle with base $\boxed{}$ and height $\boxed{}$. Therefore, the area of △*QRST* = 2 · (area of △*QRT*).

$RT = \boxed{}$, $QR = \boxed{}$, so the area of △*QRT* = $\frac{1}{2}\left(\boxed{}\right)\left(\boxed{}\right) = 6.$

△*QRST* = 2 · (area of *QRT*) = 2 · $\boxed{}$ = 12

area of *PQRST*: $A = \boxed{} + \boxed{} = \boxed{}$ square units

Reflect

5. Discussion How could you use subtraction to find the area of a figure on the coordinate plane?

_____

_____

_____

6. Find the area of the polygon by addition.

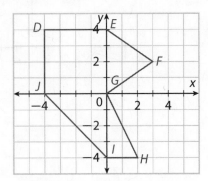

7. Find the area of polygon by subtraction.

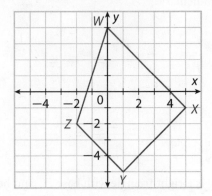

🔑 Explain 3   Using Perimeter and Area in Problem Solving

You can use perimeter and area techniques to solve problems.

Example 3   Miguel is planning and costing an ornamental garden in the a shape of an irregular octagon. Each unit on the coordinate grid represents one yard. He wants to lay the whole garden with turf, which costs $3.25 per square yard, and surround it with a border of decorative stones, which cost $7.95 per yard. What is the total cost of the turf and stones?

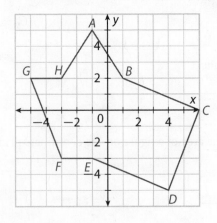

Identify the important information.

- The vertices are $A\left(\boxed{}, 5\right)$, $B\left(1, \boxed{}\right)$, $C\left(6, \boxed{}\right)$, $D\left(4, \boxed{}\right)$, $E(-1, -3)$,

  $F\left(\boxed{}, -3\right)$, $G\left(-5, \boxed{}\right)$, and $H\left(\boxed{}, 2\right)$.

- The cost of turf is $\boxed{}$ per square yard.

- The cost of the ornamental stones is $\boxed{}$ per yard.

Formulate a Plan

- Divide the garden up into _____.

- Add up the _____ of the smaller figures.

- Find the cost of turf by _____ the total area by the cost per square yard.

- Find the perimeter of the garden by adding the _____ of the sides.

- Find the cost of the border by _____ the perimeter by the cost per yard.

- Find total cost by adding the _____ and _____.

 Solve

Divide the garden into smaller figures.

The garden can be divided into square $BCDE$, kite $ABEH$, and parallelogram $EFGH$.

Find the area of each smaller figure.

area of $BCDE$:

slope of $\overline{BC}$: $\dfrac{\boxed{} - 2}{6 - \boxed{}} = \boxed{}$

slope of $\boxed{}$: $\dfrac{\boxed{} - 0}{4 - \boxed{}} = \boxed{}$

Also, $BC = \sqrt{\left(\boxed{} - 1\right)^2 + \left(0 - \boxed{}\right)^2} = \sqrt{\boxed{}}$ and

$CD = \sqrt{\left(4 - \boxed{}\right)^2 + \left(\boxed{} - \boxed{}\right)^2} = \sqrt{\boxed{}}$.

So $BCDE$ is a square, with area $A = s^2 = \left(\sqrt{\boxed{}}\ \text{yd}\right)^2 = \boxed{}\ \text{yd}^2$.

area of kite *ABEH*:

$$HA = \sqrt{\left(-1 - \left(\boxed{}\right)\right)^2 + \left(\boxed{} - 2\right)^2} = \sqrt{4 + \boxed{}} = \sqrt{\boxed{}} \approx \boxed{};$$

$$AB = \sqrt{\left(\boxed{} - (-1)\right)^2 + \left(2 - \boxed{}\right)^2} = \sqrt{\boxed{} + 9} = \sqrt{\boxed{}} \approx \boxed{};$$

$$HE = \sqrt{\left(-1 - \left(\boxed{}\right)\right)^2 + \left(\boxed{} - 2\right)^2} = \sqrt{\boxed{} + 25} = \sqrt{\boxed{}} \approx \boxed{};$$

$$BE = \sqrt{\left(\boxed{} - 1\right)^2 + \left(-3 - \boxed{}\right)^2} = \sqrt{4 + \boxed{}} = \sqrt{\boxed{}} \approx \boxed{};$$

So, $\boxed{} \cong \boxed{}$ and $\boxed{} \cong \boxed{}$. Therefore *ABEH* is a kite.

$b = d_1 = 8, h = d_2 = 4$

$$A = \frac{1}{2}d_1 d_2 = \frac{1}{2}\left(\boxed{}\right)\left(\boxed{}\right) = \boxed{} \text{ yd}^2$$

area of parallelogram *EFGH*:

$\boxed{}$ and $\overline{GH}$ are both horizontal, so are parallel;

slope of $\overline{EH}$: $\dfrac{2 - \boxed{}}{-3 - \boxed{}} = \dfrac{\boxed{}}{\boxed{}} = \boxed{};$ slope of $\boxed{}$: $\dfrac{2 - \boxed{}}{\boxed{} - \boxed{}} = \dfrac{\boxed{}}{\boxed{}} = \boxed{}$

So *EFGH* is a parallelogram, with base $\boxed{} = \boxed{}$ and height. $FH = \boxed{}$.

area of *EFGH*: $A = bh = \left(\boxed{} \text{ yd}\right)\left(\boxed{} \text{ yd}\right) = \boxed{} \text{ yd}^2$

Find the total area of the garden and the cost of turf.

area of garden: $A = \boxed{} \text{ yd}^2 + \boxed{} \text{ yd}^2 + \boxed{} \text{ yd}^2 = \boxed{} \text{ yd}^2$

cost of turf: $\left(\boxed{} \text{ yd}^2\right)\left(\$\boxed{}/\text{yd}^2\right) = \$\boxed{}$

Find the perimeter of the garden.

$EF = 2 \text{ yd}, GH = 2 \text{ yd}$

From area calculations, $BC = CD = DE = \sqrt{\boxed{}} \approx \boxed{} \text{ yd}$, and $AB = AH = \boxed{} \text{ yd}$

$$FG = \sqrt{\left(\boxed{} - \boxed{}\right)^2 + \left(\boxed{} - (-3)\right)^2} = \sqrt{\boxed{}},$$

perimeter of garden $= GH + HA + AB + BC + CD + DE + EF + FG$

$$= \boxed{} + \boxed{} + \boxed{} + \boxed{} + \boxed{} + \boxed{} + \boxed{} + \boxed{} = \boxed{} \text{ yd}$$

Find the cost of the stones for the border.

cost of stones: $\left(\boxed{} \text{ yd}\right)\left(\$\boxed{} \text{ per yd}\right) = \$\boxed{}$

Find the total cost.

total cost: $\$\boxed{} + \$\boxed{} = \$\boxed{}$

Justify and Evaluate

The area can be checked by subtraction:

area of large rectangle $= (11)(10) = 110$ square units

$$\text{area} = (11)\left(\right) - \left(\right)(3) - \frac{1}{2}(2)\left(\right) - \frac{1}{2}\left(\right)\left(\right)$$

$$- (5)\left(\right) - \frac{1}{2}\left(\right)(2) - \frac{1}{2}\left(\right)(5)$$

$$- \frac{1}{2}\left(\right)\left(\right) - \left(\right)\left(\right) - \frac{1}{2}\left(\right)\left(\right)$$

$$= \square - \square - \square - \square - \square - \square - \square - \square - \square = \square$$

The perimeter is approximately the perimeter of the polygon shown:

The perimeter of the polygon shown is $\boxed{}$,

so the answer is reasonable.

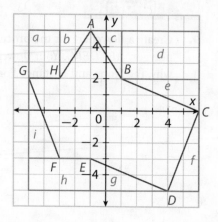

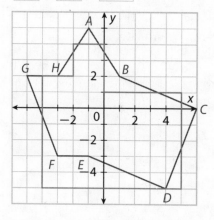

Your Turn

8. A designer is making a medallion in the shape of the letter "L." Each unit on the coordinate grid represents an eighth of an inch, and the medallion is to be cut from a 1-in. square of metal. How much metal is wasted to make each medallion? Write your answer as a decimal.

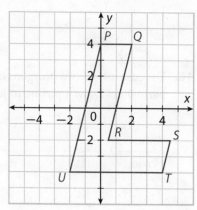

9. Create a flowchart for the process of finding the area of the polygon *ABCDEFG*. Your flowchart should show when, and why, the Slope and Distance Formulas are used.

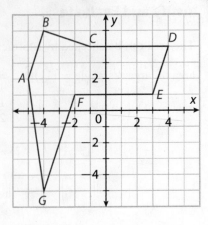

10. **Discussion** If two polygons have approximately the same area, do they have approximately the same perimeter? Draw a picture to justify your answer.

_____

_____

11. **Essential Question Check-In** What formulas might you need to solve problems involving the perimeter and area of triangles and quadrilaterals in the coordinate plane?

_____

_____

_____

_____

Find the perimeter of the figure with the given vertices.
Round to the nearest tenth.

1. $D(0, 1)$, $E(5, 4)$, and $F(2, 6)$

2. $P(2, 5)$, $Q(-3, 0)$, $R(2, -5)$, and $S(6, 0)$

3. $M(-3, 4)$, $N(1, 4)$, $P(4, 2)$, $Q(4, -1)$, and $R(2, 2)$

4. $A(-5, 1)$, $B(0, 3)$, $C(5, 1)$, $D(4, -2)$, $E(0, -4)$, and $F(-2, -4)$

Find the area of each figure.

5.

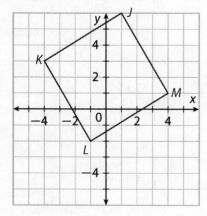

6.

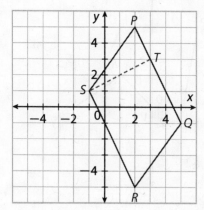

Find the area of each figure by addition.

7.

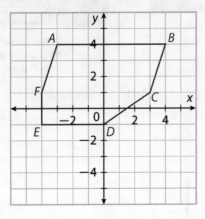

8.

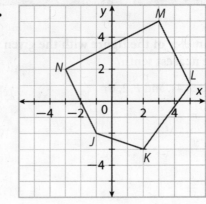

Find the area of each figure by subtraction.

9.

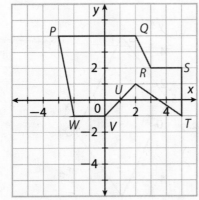

10.

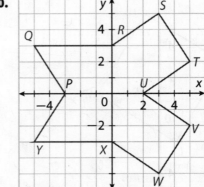

11. Fencing costs $1.45 per yard, and each unit on the grid represents 50 yd. How much will it cost to fence the plot of land represented by the polygon *ABCDEF*?

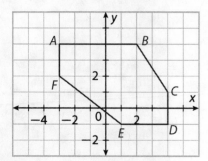

12. A machine component has a geometric shaped plate, represented on the coordinate grid. Each unit on the grid represents 1 cm. Each plate is punched from an 8-cm square of alloy. The cost of the alloy is $0.43/cm², but $0.28/cm² can be recovered on wasted scraps of alloy. What is the net cost of alloy for each component?

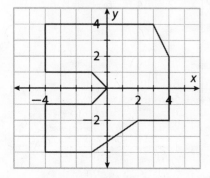

13. $\triangle ABC$ with vertices $A(1, 1)$ and $B(3, 5)$ has an area of 10 units². What is the location of the third vertex? Select all that apply.

A. $C(-5, 5)$

B. $C(3, -5)$

C. $C(-2, 5)$

D. $C(6, 1)$

E. $C(3, -3)$

14. Pentagon *ABCDE* shows the path of an obstacle course, where each unit of the coordinate plane represents 10 meters. Find the length of the course to the nearest meter.

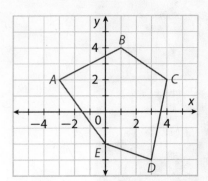

Algebra Graph each set of lines to form a triangle. Find the area and perimeter.

15. $y = 2$, $x = 5$, and $y = x$

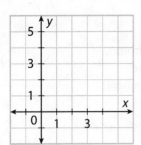

16. $y = -5$, $x = 2$, and $y = -2x + 7$

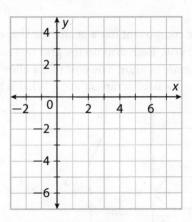

17. Prove that quadrilateral *JKLM* with vertices $J(1, 5)$, $K(4, 2)$, $L(1, -4)$, and $M(-2, 2)$ is a kite, and find its area.

18. **Explain the Error** Wendell is trying to prove that *ABCD* is a rhombus and to find its area. Identify and correct his error. (*Hint:* A rhombus is a quadrilateral with four congruent sides.)

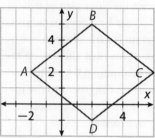

$AB = \sqrt{\left(2 - (-2)\right)^2 + (5 - 2)^2} = \sqrt{25} = 5,$

$BC = \sqrt{(6 - 2)^2 + (2 - 5)^2} = \sqrt{25} = 5$

$CD = \sqrt{(2 - 6)^2 + (-1 - 2)^2} = \sqrt{25} = 5,$

$AD = \sqrt{\left(2 - (-2)\right)^2 + (-1 - 2)^2} = \sqrt{25} = 5$

So $\overline{AB} \cong \overline{BC} \cong \overline{CD} \cong \overline{AD}$, and therefore *ABCD* is a rhombus.

area of *ABCD*: $b = AB = 5$ and $h = BC = 5$, so $A = bh = (5)(5) = 25$

19. **Communicate Mathematical Ideas** Using the figure, prove that the area of a kite is half the product of its diagonals. (Do not make numerical calculations.)

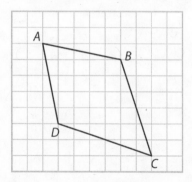

20. **Justify Reasoning** Use the Trapezoid Midsegment Theorem to show that the area of a trapezoid is the product of its midsegment and its height.

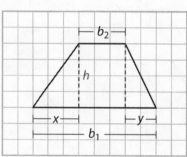

Lesson Performance Task

The coordinate plane shows the floor plan of two rooms in Fritz's house. Because he enjoys paradoxes, Fritz has decided to entertain his friends with one by drawing lines on the floor of his tiled kitchen, on the left, and his tiled recreation room, on the right. The four sections in the kitchen are congruent to the four sections in the recreation room. Each square on the floor plan measures 1 yard on a side.

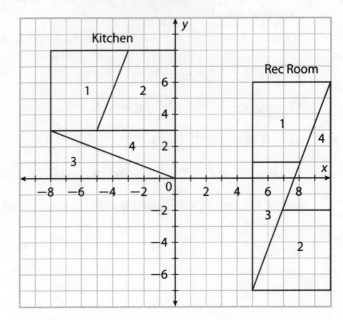

1. Find the area of each of the four sections of the kitchen. Add the four areas to find the total area of the kitchen.

2. Find the area of the kitchen by finding the product of the length and the width.

3. Find the area of the recreation room by finding the product of the length and the width.

4. Describe the paradox.

5. Explain the paradox.

Coordinate Proof Using Slope and Distance

Essential Question: How can you use coordinate proofs using slope and distance to solve real-world problems?

Key Vocabulary
coordinate proof
(prueba coordenada)
composite figure
(figura compuesta)

KEY EXAMPLE (Lesson 25.1)

Show that the figure given by the points $A(2, 4)$, $B(3, 2)$, $C(2, 1)$, and $D(0, 5)$ is a trapezoid.

Determine whether the slopes of $\overline{AB}$ and $\overline{CD}$ are equal to determine whether they are parallel, and whether the figure is a trapezoid.

slope of $\overline{AB} = \dfrac{4 - 2}{2 - 3} = \dfrac{2}{-1} = -2$

slope of $\overline{CD} = \dfrac{5 - 1}{0 - 2} = \dfrac{4}{-2} = -2$

Thus, the figure $ABCD$ is a trapezoid.

KEY EXAMPLE (Lesson 25.2)

Show that $\triangle ABC$ with points $A(-2, 1)$, $B(-3, 3)$, and $C(2, 3)$ is a right triangle.

A right triangle should have a pair of sides that are perpendicular.

slope of $\overline{AB} = \dfrac{1 - 3}{-2 - (-3)} = \dfrac{-2}{1} = -2$

slope of $\overline{BC} = \dfrac{3 - 3}{-3 - 2} = \dfrac{0}{-5} = 0$

slope of $\overline{CA} = \dfrac{3 - 1}{2 - (-2)} = \dfrac{2}{4} = \dfrac{1}{2}$

One pair of slopes has a product of -1, so the triangle is a right.

KEY EXAMPLE (Lesson 25.3)

Prove the triangles $\triangle ABC$ and $\triangle DCB$ are congruent given $A(1, 1)$, $B(3, 1)$, $C(1, 4)$, and $D(3, 4)$.

Note that the triangles share a side. Find the length of each other side.

$AC = \sqrt{(1 - 1)^2 + (4 - 1)^2} = \sqrt{0 + 9} = 3$

$AB = \sqrt{(3 - 1)^2 + (1 - 1)^2} = \sqrt{4 + 0} = 2$

$DC = \sqrt{(3 - 1)^2 + (4 - 4)^2} = \sqrt{4 + 0} = 2$

$DB = \sqrt{(3 - 3)^2 + (4 - 1)^2} = \sqrt{0 + 9} = 3$

$AC = DB$, so $\overline{AC} \cong \overline{DB}$, and $AB = DC$, so $\overline{AB} \cong \overline{DC}$. Additionally, $\overline{CB}$ is congruent to itself by the Reflexive Property.

The triangles have three congruent sides, so are congruent by SSS.

EXERCISES

Determine whether the statement is True or False. *(Lesson 25.1)*

1. The figure given by the points $A(0, -1)$, $B(3, -2)$, $C(5, -4)$, and $D(-1, -2)$ is a trapezoid.

2. The figure given by the points $A(0, 3)$, $B(5, 3)$, and $C(2, 0)$ is a right triangle.

Prove or disprove the statement.

3. $\triangle ABC$ and $\triangle DEF$ are congruent, given $A(-4, 4)$, $B(-2, 5)$, $C(-3, 1)$, $D(-2, -1)$, $E(-1, -3)$, and $F(-5, -2)$. *(Lesson 25.2)*

Find the area of the polygon. *(Lesson 25.3)*

4. $ABCDE$ defined by the points $A(-3, 4)$, $B(-1, 4)$, $C(1, 1)$, $D(-1, 1)$, and $E(-4, -1)$

MODULE PERFORMANCE TASK

How Do You Calculate the Containment of a Fire?

Most news stories about large wildfires report some level of "containment" reached by firefighters. To prevent a blaze from spreading, firefighters dig a "fire line" around its perimeter. For example, if 3 miles of fire line have been dug around a fire that is 10 miles in perimeter, then the fire is said to be 30 percent contained.

The image shows a forest fire. The forest is shown by the shaded square while the fire is shown by the irregular pentagon. The darker lines show where fire lines have been dug. What is the percentage containment of the fire as well as the total area that has been burned?

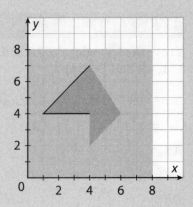

Use your own paper to complete the task. Be sure to write down all your data and assumptions. Then use graphs, numbers, words, or algebra to explain how you reached your conclusions.

(Ready) to Go On?

25.1–25.5 Coordinate Proof Using Slope and Distance

- Online Homework
- Hints and Help
- Extra Practice

Determine and prove what shape is formed for the given coordinates for *ABCD*, and then find the perimeter and area as an exact value and rounded to the nearest tenth. *(Lessons 25.1, 25.2, 25.4, 25.5)*

1. $A(-10, 6), B(-7, 2), C(1, 8), D(-6, 9)$

2. $A(10, -6), B(6, -9), C(3, -5), D(7, -2)$

ESSENTIAL QUESTION

3. When is a quadrilateral both a trapezoid and a parallelogram? Is a quadrilateral ever a parallelogram but not a trapezoid?

Assessment Readiness

1. Does the name correctly describe the shape given by the points $A(2, 2)$, $B(3, 4)$, $C(6, 4)$, and $D(5, 2)$?

   A. Rectangle   ◯ Yes   ◯ No

   B. Parallelogram   ◯ Yes   ◯ No

   C. Square   ◯ Yes   ◯ No

2. Triangle ABC is given by the points $A(3, 2)$, $B(4, 4)$, and $C(5, 1)$. Choose True or False for each statement.

   A. The perimeter of $\triangle ABC$ is 9.9 units.   ◯ True   ◯ False

   B. $\triangle ABC$ is an equilateral triangle.   ◯ True   ◯ False

   C. The perimeter of $\triangle ABC$ is 7.6 units.   ◯ True   ◯ False

3. Triangle DEF is given by the points $D(1, 1)$, $E(3, 8)$, and $F(8, 0)$. Choose True or False for each statement.

   A. The area of $\triangle DEF$ is 25.5 square units.   ◯ True   ◯ False

   B. $\triangle DEF$ is a scalene triangle.   ◯ True   ◯ False

   C. The area of $\triangle DEF$ is 30 square units.   ◯ True   ◯ False

4. What type of triangle is given by the points $D(1, 1)$, $E(3, 8)$, and $F(5, 1)$? Explain how you could find the perimeter of the triangle.

5. For the polygon shown, specify how to find its area using triangles, parallelograms, and rectangles.

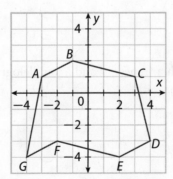

© Houghton Mifflin Harcourt Publishing Company

Assessment Readiness

- Online Homework
- Hints and Help
- Extra Practice

1. Using known properties, determine if the statements are true or not.

   Select True or False for each statement.

   A. If one pair of consecutive sides of a parallelogram is congruent, then the parallelogram is a rectangle. ○ True ○ False

   B. If one pair of consecutive sides of a rhombus is perpendicular then the rhombus is a square. ○ True ○ False

   C. If a quadrilateral has four right angles then it is a square. ○ True ○ False

2. Given the line $y = -\frac{2}{5}x + 3$, determine if the given line is parallel, perpendicular, or neither. Select the correct answer for each lettered part.

   A. $y = \frac{2}{5}x + 7$ ○ Parallel ○ Perpendicular ○ Neither

   B. $5y + 2x = -10$ ○ Parallel ○ Perpendicular ○ Neither

   C. $-5x + 2y = 4$ ○ Parallel ○ Perpendicular ○ Neither

3. Is $\overline{AB}$ parallel to $\overline{CD}$?

   Select Yes or No for each statement.

   A. $A(-5, 12), B(7, 18), C(0, -4),$ and $D(-8, 0)$ ○ Yes ○ No

   B. $A(-6, 2), B(4, 6), C(7, -4),$ and $D(-3, -8)$ ○ Yes ○ No

   C. $A(-6, 2), B(4, 6), C(7, -4),$ and $D(-4, -8)$ ○ Yes ○ No

4. Is $\overline{RS}$ perpendicular to $\overline{DF}$?

   Select Yes or No for each statement.

   A. $R(6, -2), S(-1, 8)$ and $D(-1, 11), F(11, 4)$ ○ Yes ○ No

   B. $R(1, 3), S(4, 7)$ and $D(3, 9), F(15, 0)$ ○ Yes ○ No

   C. $R(-5, -5), S(0, 2)$ and $D(8, 3), F(1, 8)$ ○ Yes ○ No

5. Use the distance formula to determine if $\triangle ABC \cong \triangle DEF$.

   Select Yes or No for each statement.

   A. $A(-5, -7), B(0, 0), C(4, -7), D(-6, -6),$ $E(-1, 1), F(5, -8)$ ○ Yes ○ No

   B. $A(-3, 1), B(1, 1), C(-4, -8), D(1, 1),$ $E(-3, 1), F(4, 8)$ ○ Yes ○ No

   C. $A(-8, 8), B(-4, 6), C(-10, 2), D(4, -4),$ $E(8, -2), F(2, 2)$ ○ Yes ○ No

6. Is Point M the midpoint of $\overline{AB}$? Select Yes or No for each statement.

Select True or False for each statement.

A. $A(1, 2)$, $B(3,4)$, $M(2, 3)$ ◯ Yes   ◯ No

B. $A(0, 8)$, $B(10,-1)$, $M(5, 3.5)$ ◯ Yes   ◯ No

C. $A(-7, -5)$, $B(6, 4)$, $M(-1, -1)$ ◯ Yes   ◯ No

D. $A(4, -2)$, $B(6, -8)$, $M(5, -5)$ ◯ Yes   ◯ No

7. Determine whether the statement about $QRST$ is true or false using the given image.

Select True or False for each statement.

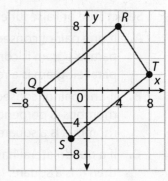

A. The diagonals of $QRST$ are congruent.   ◯ True   ◯ False

B. $QRST$ is a square.   ◯ True   ◯ False

C. $QRST$ is a rectangle.   ◯ True   ◯ False

D. The diagonals of $QRST$ are perpendicular.   ◯ True   ◯ False

8. In trapezoid $JKLM$, determine LM.

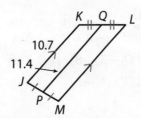

9. The midpoints of an irregular quadrilateral $ABCD$ are connected to form another quadrilateral inside $ABCD$. Explain why the quadrilateral is a parallelogram.

Performance Tasks

★**10.** Streets of a city can be represented by the equations in the given table. Use the equations to find the type of quadrilateral that the streets form. Justify your answer.

Street	Equation
Pine Street	$3x - y = -4$
Danis Road	$3y - x = 4$
Granite Park	$3y = x + 12$
Jason Drive	$y = 3x - 4$

★★**11.** The composite figure shown below represents the design for a new logo. Determine the area of a logo that has twice the area of the image provided. Allow 1 unit to represent two inches. Show your work.

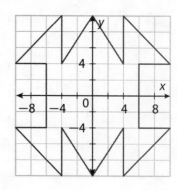

★★★**12.** Each square section in an iron railing contains four small kites. The figure shows the dimensions of one kite. What length of iron is needed to outline one small kite? How much iron is needed to outline one complete section, including the square? Explain how each answer was found.

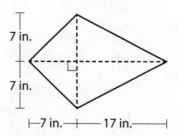

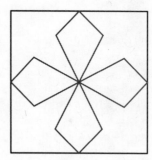

Urban planners A city planner is working to add a new street for the purpose of easing traffic congestion. The current streets can be represented by the image given. Where could the planner add the new street so that the streets form a square? Give the equation and add the line to the drawing.

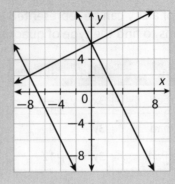

Glossary/Glosario

A

ENGLISH	SPANISH	EXAMPLES
absolute value The absolute value of x is the distance from zero to x on a number line, denoted $\|x\|$. $$\|x\| = \begin{cases} x & \text{if } x \geq 0 \\ -x & \text{if } x < 0 \end{cases}$$	**valor absoluto** El valor absoluto de x es la distancia de cero a x en una recta numérica, y se expresa $\|x\|$. $$\|x\| = \begin{cases} x & \text{si } x \geq 0 \\ -x & \text{si } x < 0 \end{cases}$$	$\|3\| = 3$ $\|-3\| = 3$
accuracy The closeness of a given measurement or value to the actual measurement or value.	**exactitud** Cercanía de una medida o un valor a la medida o el valor real.	
Addition Property of Equality For real numbers a, b, and c, if $a = b$, then $a + c = b + c$.	**Propiedad de igualdad de la suma** Dados los números reales a, b y c, si $a = b$, entonces $a + c = b + c$.	$\begin{aligned} x - 6 &= 8 \\ +6 \quad &+6 \\ \hline x \quad &= 14 \end{aligned}$
Addition Property of Inequality For real numbers a, b, and c, if $a < b$, then $a + c < b + c$. Also holds true for $>$, $\leq$, $\geq$, and $\neq$.	**Propiedad de desigualdad de la suma** Dados los números reales a, b y c, si $a < b$, entonces $a + c < b + c$. Es válido también para $>$, $\leq$, $\geq$ y $\neq$.	$\begin{aligned} x - 6 &< 8 \\ +6 \quad &+6 \\ \hline x \quad &< 14 \end{aligned}$
additive inverse The opposite of a number. Two numbers are additive inverses if their sum is zero.	**inverso aditivo** El opuesto de un número. Dos números son inversos aditivos si su suma es cero.	The additive inverse of 5 is -5. The additive inverse of -5 is 5.
adjacent angles Two angles in the same plane with a common vertex and a common side, but no common interior points.	**ángulos adyacentes** Dos ángulos en el mismo plano que tienen un vértice y un lado común pero no comparten puntos internos.	$\angle 1$ and $\angle 2$ are adjacent angles.
algebraic expression An expression that contains at least one variable.	**expresión algebraica** Expresión que contiene por lo menos una variable.	
alternate exterior angles For two lines intersected by a transversal, a pair of angles that lie on opposite sides of the transversal and outside the other two lines.	**ángulos alternos externos** Dadas dos líneas cortadas por una transversal, par de ángulos no adyacentes ubicados en los lados opuestos de la transversal y fuera de las otras dos líneas.	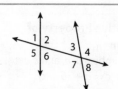 $\angle 4$ and $\angle 5$ are alternate exterior angles.

Glossary/Glosario

alternate interior angles For two lines intersected by a transversal, a pair of nonadjacent angles that lie on opposite sides of the transversal and between the other two lines.

ángulos alternos internos Dadas dos líneas cortadas por una transversal, par de ángulos no adyacentes ubicados en los lados opuestos de la transversal y entre las otras dos líneas.

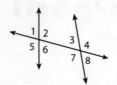

∠3 and ∠6 are alternate interior angles.

---

altitude of a triangle A perpendicular segment from a vertex to the line containing the opposite side.

altura de un triángulo Segmento perpendicular que se extiende desde un vértice hasta la línea que forma el lado opuesto.

AND A logical operator representing the intersection of two sets.

Y Operador lógico que representa la intersección de dos conjuntos.

$A = \{2, 3, 4, 5\}$ $B = \{1, 3, 5, 7\}$
The set of values that are in A AND B is $A \cap B = \{3, 5\}$.

---

angle bisector A ray that divides an angle into two congruent angles.

bisectriz de un ángulo Rayo que divide un ángulo en dos ángulos congruentes.

$\overrightarrow{JK}$ is an angle bisector of $\angle LJM$.

---

angle of rotation An angle formed by a rotating ray, called the terminal side, and a stationary reference ray, called the initial side.

ángulo de rotación Ángulo formado por un rayo rotativo, denominado lado terminal, y un rayo de referencia estático, denominado lado inicial.

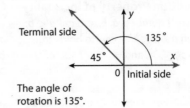

The angle of rotation is 135°.

---

arithmetic sequence A sequence whose successive terms differ by the same nonzero number d, called the common difference.

sucesión aritmética Sucesión cuyos términos sucesivos difieren en el mismo número distinto de cero d, denominado *diferencia común*.

4, 7, 10, 13, 16, …
$+3 \ +3 \ \ +3 \ \ +3$
$d = 3$

---

arrow notation A symbol used to describe a transformation.

notación de flecha Símbolo utilizado para describir una transformación.

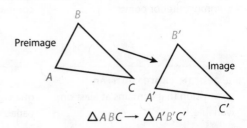

$\triangle ABC \longrightarrow \triangle A'B'C'$

Associative Property of Addition
For all numbers a, b, and c, $(a + b) + c = a + (b + c)$.

Propiedad asociativa de la suma
Dados tres números cualesquiera a, b y c, $(a + b) + c = a + (b + c)$.

$(5 + 3) + 7 = 5 + (3 + 7)$

Associative Property of Multiplication For all numbers a, b, and c, $(a \cdot b) \cdot c = a \cdot (b \cdot c)$.

Propiedad asociativa de la multiplicación Dados tres números cualesquiera a, b y c, $(a \cdot b) \cdot c = a \cdot (b \cdot c)$.

$(5 \cdot 3) \cdot 7 = 5 \cdot (3 \cdot 7)$

ENGLISH	SPANISH	EXAMPLES

asymptote A line that a graph gets closer to as the value of a variable becomes extremely large or small.

asíntota Línea recta a la cual se aproxima una gráfica a medida que el valor de una variable se hace sumamente grande o pequeño.

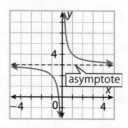

---

auxiliary line A line drawn in a figure to aid in a proof.

línea auxiliar Línea dibujada en una figura como ayuda en una demostración.

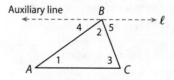

---

axiom *See* postulate.

axioma *Ver* postulado.

B

base angle of a trapezoid One of a pair of consecutive angles whose common side is a base of the trapezoid.

ángulo base de un trapecio Uno de los dos ángulos consecutivos cuyo lado en común es la base del trapecio.

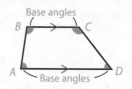

---

base angle of an isosceles triangle One of the two angles that have the base of the triangle as a side.

ángulo base de un triángulo isósceles Uno de los dos ángulos que tienen como lado la base del triángulo.

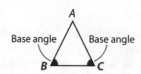

---

base of a power The number in a power that is used as a factor.

base de una potencia Número de una potencia que se utiliza como factor.

$3^4 = 3 \cdot 3 \cdot 3 \cdot 3 = 81$
3 is the base.

---

base of a trapezoid One of the two parallel sides of the trapezoid.

base de un trapecio Uno de los dos lados paralelos del trapecio.

---

base of a triangle Any side of a triangle.

base de un triángulo Cualquier lado de un triángulo.

---

base of an exponential function The value of b in a function of the form $f(x) = ab^x$, where a and b are real numbers with $a \neq 0$, $b > 0$, and $b \neq 1$.

base de una función exponencial Valor de b en una función del tipo $f(x) = ab^x$, donde a y b son números reales con $a \neq 0$, $b > 0$ y $b \neq 1$.

In the function $f(x) = 5(2)^x$, the base is 2.

Glossary/Glosario

Glossary/Glosario

base of an isosceles triangle
The side opposite the vertex angle.

base de un triángulo isósceles Lado opuesto al ángulo del vértice.

---

between Given three points *A*, *B*, and *C*, *B* is between *A* and *C* if and only if all three of the points lie on the same line, and $AB + BC = AC$.

entre Dados tres puntos *A*, *B* y *C*, *B* está entre *A* y *C* si y sólo si los tres puntos se encuentran en la misma línea y $AB + BC = AC$.

---

bisect To divide into two congruent parts.

trazar una bisectriz Dividir en dos partes congruentes.

$\overrightarrow{JK}$ bisects $\angle LJM$.

---

boundary line A line that divides a coordinate plane into two half-planes.

línea de límite Línea que divide un plano cartesiano en dos semiplanos.

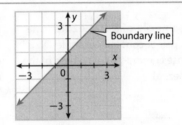

---

box-and-whisker plot A method of showing how data are distributed by using the median, quartiles, and minimum and maximum values; also called a *box plot*.

gráfica de mediana y rango Método para mostrar la distribución de datos utilizando la mediana, los cuartiles y los valores mínimo y máximo; también llamado *gráfica de caja*.

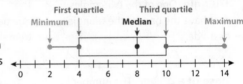

C

categorical data Data that are qualitative in nature, such as "liberal," "moderate," and "conservative."

datos categóricos Datos de índole cualitativa, como "liberal", "moderado" y "conservador".

---

center of rotation The point around which a figure is rotated.

centro de rotación Punto alrededor del cual rota una figura.

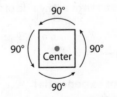

---

centroid of a triangle The point of concurrency of the three medians of a triangle. Also known as the *center of gravity*.

centroide de un triángulo Punto donde se encuentran las tres medianas de un triángulo. También conocido como *centro de gravedad*.

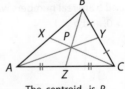

The centroid is *P*.

circumcenter of a triangle The point of concurrency of the three perpendicular bisectors of a triangle.

circuncentro de un triángulo Punto donde se cortan las tres mediatrices de un triángulo.

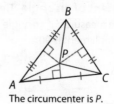

The circumcenter is *P*.

Circumcircle *See* circumscribed circle.

circuncírculo Véase círculo circunscrito.

---

closure A set of numbers is said to be closed, or to have closure, under a given operation if the result of the operation on any two numbers in the set is also in the set.

cerradura Se dice que un conjunto de números es cerrado, o tiene cerradura, respecto de una operación determinada, si el resultado de la operación entre dos números cualesquiera del conjunto también está en el conjunto.

The natural numbers are closed under addition because the sum of two natural numbers is always a natural number.

---

coefficient A number that is multiplied by a variable.

coeficiente Número que se multiplica por una variable.

In the expression $2x + 3y$, 2 is the coefficient of *x* and 3 is the coefficient of *y*.

---

collinear Points that lie on the same line.

colineal Puntos que se encuentran sobre la misma línea.

K, L, and M are collinear points.

---

common difference In an arithmetic sequence, the nonzero constant difference of any term and the previous term.

diferencia común En una sucesión aritmética, diferencia constante distinta de cero entre cualquier término y el término anterior.

In the arithmetic sequence 3, 5, 7, 9, 11, ..., the common difference is 2.

---

common factor A factor that is common to all terms of an expression or to two or more expressions.

factor común Factor que es común a todos los términos de una expresión o a dos o más expresiones.

Expression: $4x^2 + 16x^3 - 8x$
Common factor: $4x$
Expressions: 12 and 18
Common factors: 2, 3, and 6

---

common ratio In a geometric sequence, the constant ratio of any term and the previous term.

razón común En una sucesión geométrica, la razón constante entre cualquier término y el término anterior.

In the geometric sequence 32, 16, 8, 4, 2, ..., the common ratio is $\frac{1}{2}$.

Commutative Property of Addition For any two numbers *a* and *b*, $a + b = b + a$.

Propiedad conmutativa de la suma Dados dos números cualesquiera *a* y *b*, $a \cdot b = b \cdot a$.

$3 + 4 = 4 + 3 = 7$

Commutative Property of Multiplication For any two numbers *a* and *b*, $a \cdot b = b \cdot a$.

Propiedad conmutativa de la multiplicación Dados dos números cualesquiera *a* y *b*, $a \cdot b = b \cdot a$

$3 \cdot 4 = 4 \cdot 3 = 12$

Glossary/Glosario

complement of an angle The sum of the measures of an angle and its complement is 90°.

complemento de un ángulo La suma de las medidas de un ángulo y su complemento es 90°.

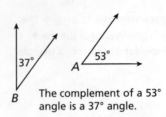

The complement of a 53° angle is a 37° angle.

---

complementary angles Two angles whose measures have a sum of 90°.

ángulos complementarios Dos ángulos cuyas medidas suman 90°.

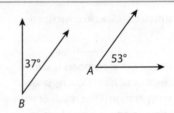

---

component form The form of a vector that lists the vertical and horizontal change from the initial point to the terminal point.

forma de componente Forma de un vector que muestra el cambio horizontal y vertical desde el punto inicial hasta el punto terminal.

The component form of $\overrightarrow{CD}$ is $\langle 2, 3 \rangle$.

---

composition of transformations One transformation followed by another transformation.

composición de transformaciones Una transformación seguida de otra transformación.

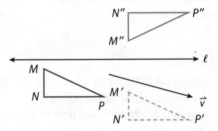

---

compound inequality Two inequalities that are combined into one statement by the word *and* or *or*.

desigualdad compuesta Dos desigualdades unidas en un enunciado por la palabra *y* u *o*.

$x \geq 2$ AND $x < 7$ (also written $2 \leq x < 7$)

0 2 4 6 8

$x < 2$ OR $x > 6$

0 2 4 6 8

---

compound interest Interest earned or paid on both the principal and previously earned interest. The formula for compound interest is $A = P\left(1 + \frac{r}{n}\right)^{nt}$, where A is the final amount, P is the principal, r is the interest rate expressed as a decimal, n is the number of times interest is compounded, and t is the time.

interés compuesto Intereses ganados o pagados sobre el capital y los intereses ya devengados. La fórmula de interés compuesto es $A = P\left(1 + \frac{r}{n}\right)^{nt}$, donde A es la cantidad final, P es el capital, r es la tasa de interés expresada como un decimal, n es la cantidad de veces que se capitaliza el interés y t es el tiempo.

If $100 is put into an account with an interest rate of 5% compounded monthly, then after 2 years, the account will have $100\left(1 + \frac{0.05}{12}\right)^{12\cdot2} = \$110.49$.

---

compound statement Two statements that are connected by the word *and* or *or*.

enunciado compuesto Dos enunciados unidos por la palabra *y* u *o*.

The sky is blue and the grass is green. I will drive to school or I will take the bus.

conditional relative frequency
The ratio of a joint relative frequency to a related marginal relative frequency in a two-way table.

frecuencia relativa condicional
Razón de una frecuencia relativa conjunta a una frecuencia relativa marginal en una tabla de doble entrada.

---

conditional statement A statement that can be written in the form "if p, then q," where p is the hypothesis and q is the conclusion.

enunciado condicional Enunciado que se puede expresar como "si p, entonces q", donde p es la hipótesis y q es la conclusión.

If $x + 1 = 5$, then $x = 4$.
Hypothesis   Conclusion

---

congruence statement A statement that indicates that two polygons are congruent by listing the vertices in the order of correspondence.

enunciado de congruencia Enunciado que indica que dos polígonos son congruentes enumerando los vértices en orden de correspondencia.

$\triangle HKL \cong \triangle YWX$

---

congruent Having the same size and shape, denoted by $\cong$.

congruente Que tiene el mismo tamaño y la misma forma, expresado por $\cong$.

---

congruent angles Angles that have the same measure.

ángulos congruentes Ángulos que tienen la misma medida.

$\angle ABC \cong \angle DEF$

---

congruent polygons Two polygons whose corresponding sides and angles are congruent.

polígonos congruentes Dos polígonos cuyos lados y ángulos correspondientes son congruentes.

---

congruent segments Two segments that have the same length.

segmentos congruentes Dos segmentos que tienen la misma longitud.

$\overline{PQ} \cong \overline{SR}$

---

consecutive interior angles See same-side interior angles.

ángulos internos consecutivos Ver ángulos internos del mismo lado.

---

consistent system A system of equations or inequalities that has at least one solution.

sistema consistente Sistema de ecuaciones o desigualdades que tiene por lo menos una solución.

$\begin{cases} x + y = 6 \\ x - y = 4 \end{cases}$
solution: $(5, 1)$

---

constant A value that does not change.

constante Valor que no cambia.

$3, 0, \pi$

---

constant of variation The constant k in direct and inverse variation equations.

constante de variación La constante k en ecuaciones de variación directa e inversa.

$y = 5x$
↑
constant of variation

construction A method of creating a figure that is considered to be mathematically precise. Figures may be constructed by using a compass and straightedge, geometry software, or paper folding.

construcción Método para crear una figura que es considerado matemáticamente preciso. Se pueden construir figuras utilizando un compás y una regla, un programa de computación de geometría o plegando papeles.

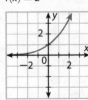

continuous function A function whose graph is an unbroken line or curve with no gaps or breaks.

función continua Función cuya gráfica es una línea recta o curva continua, sin espacios ni interrupciones.

$f(x) = 2^x$

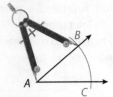

continuous graph A graph made up of connected lines or curves.

gráfica continua Gráfica compuesta por líneas rectas o curvas conectadas.

Angelique's Heart Rate

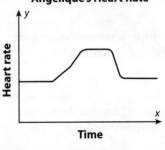

conversion factor The ratio of two equal quantities, each measured in different units.

factor de conversión Razón entre dos cantidades iguales, cada una medida en unidades diferentes.

$\dfrac{12 \text{ inches}}{1 \text{ foot}}$

coordinate plane A plane that is divided into four regions by a horizontal line called the *x*-axis and a vertical line called the *y*-axis.

plano cartesiano Plano dividido en cuatro regiones por una línea horizontal denominada eje *x* y una línea vertical denominada eje *y*.

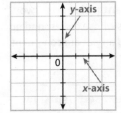

coordinate proof A style of proof that uses coordinate geometry and algebra.

prueba de coordenadas Tipo de demostración que utiliza geometría de coordenadas y álgebra.

coplanar Points that lie in the same plane.

coplanar Puntos que se encuentran en el mismo plano.

corollary A theorem whose proof follows directly from another theorem.

corolario Teorema cuya demostración proviene directamente de otro teorema.

ENGLISH	SPANISH	EXAMPLES
correlation A measure of the strength and direction of the relationship between two variables or data sets.	**correlación** Medida de la fuerza y dirección de la relación entre dos variables o conjuntos de datos.	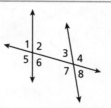
correlation coefficient A number r, where $-1 \leq r \leq 1$, that describes how closely the points in a scatter plot cluster around the least-squares line.	**coeficiente de correlación** Número r, donde $-1 \leq r \leq 1$, que describe a qué distancia de la recta de mínimos cuadrados se agrupan los puntos de un diagrama de dispersión.	An r-value close to 1 describes a strong positive correlation. An r-value close to 0 describes a weak correlation or no correlation. An r-value close to -1 describes a strong negative correlation.
corresponding angles of lines intersected by a transversal For two lines intersected by a transversal, a pair of angles that lie on the same side of the transversal and on the same sides of the other two lines.	**ángulos correspondientes de líneas cortadas por una transversal** Dadas dos líneas cortadas por una transversal, el par de ángulos ubicados en el mismo lado de la transversal y en los mismos lados de las otras dos líneas.	∠1 and ∠3 are corresponding.
corresponding angles of polygons Angles in the same relative position in polygons with an equal number of angles.	**ángulos correspondientes de los polígonos** Ángulos que se ubican en la misma posición relativa en polígonos que tienen el mismo número de ángulos.	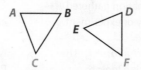 ∠A and ∠D are corresponding angles.
corresponding sides of polygons Sides in the same relative position in polygons with an equal number of sides.	**lados correspondientes de los polígonos** Lados que se ubican en la misma posición relativa en polígonos que tienen el mismo número de lados.	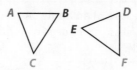 $\overline{AB}$ and $\overline{DE}$ are corresponding sides.
counterexample An example that proves that a conjecture or statement is false.	**contraejemplo** Ejemplo que demuestra que una conjetura o enunciado es falso.	
CPCTC An abbreviation for "Corresponding Parts of Congruent Triangles are Congruent," which can be used as a justification in a proof after two triangles are proven congruent.	**PCTCC** Abreviatura que significa "Las partes correspondientes de los triángulos congruentes son congruentes", que se puede utilizar para justificar una demostración después de demostrar que dos triángulos son congruentes (CPCTC, por sus siglas en inglés).	

Glossary/Glosario

ENGLISH	SPANISH	EXAMPLES

cross products In the statement $\frac{a}{b} = \frac{c}{d}$, bc and ad are the cross products.

productos cruzados En el enunciado $\frac{a}{b} = \frac{c}{d}$, bc y ad son productos cruzados.

$\frac{1}{2} = \frac{3}{6}$
Cross products: $2 \cdot 3 = 6$ and $1 \cdot 6 = 6$

Cross Product Property For any real numbers a, b, c, and d, where $b \neq 0$ and $d \neq 0$, if $\frac{a}{b} = \frac{c}{d}$, then $ad = bc$.

Propiedad de productos cruzados Dados los números reales a, b, c y d, donde $b \neq 0$ y $d \neq 0$, si $\frac{a}{b} = \frac{c}{d}$, entonces $ad = bc$.

If $\frac{4}{6} = \frac{10}{x}$, then $4x = 60$, so $x = 15$.

---

cube root A number, written as $\sqrt[3]{x}$, whose cube is x.

raíz cúbica Número, expresado como $\sqrt[3]{x}$, cuyo cubo es x.

$\sqrt[3]{64} = 4$, because $4^3 = 64$;
4 is the cube root of 64.

---

cumulative frequency The frequency of all data values that are less than or equal to a given value.

frecuencia acumulativa Frecuencia de todos los valores de los datos que son menores que o iguales a un valor dado.

For the data set 2, 2, 3, 5, 5, 6, 7, 7, 8, 8, 8, 9, the cumulative frequency table is shown below.

Data	Frequency	Cumulative Frequency
2	2	2
3	1	3
5	2	5
6	1	6
7	2	8
8	3	11
9	1	12

D

data Information gathered from a survey or experiment.

datos Información reunida en una encuesta o experimento.

---

deductive reasoning The process of using logic to draw conclusions.

razonamiento deductivo Proceso en el que se utiliza la lógica para sacar conclusiones.

---

degree measure of an angle A unit of angle measure; one degree is $\frac{1}{360}$ of a circle.

medida en grados de un ángulo Unidad de medida de los ángulos; un grado es $\frac{1}{360}$ de un círculo.

---

dependent system A system of equations that has infinitely many solutions.

sistema dependiente Sistema de ecuaciones que tiene infinitamente muchas soluciones.

$\begin{cases} x + y = 2 \\ 2x + 2y = 4 \end{cases}$

---

dependent variable The output of a function; a variable whose value depends on the value of the input, or independent variable.

variable dependiente Salida de una función; variable cuyo valor depende del valor de la entrada, o variable independiente.

For $y = 2x + 1$, y is the dependent variable.
input: x output: y

---

diagonal of a polygon A segment connecting two nonconsecutive vertices of a polygon.

diagonal de un polígono Segmento que conecta dos vértices no consecutivos de un polígono.

ENGLISH	SPANISH	EXAMPLES
dimensional analysis A process that uses rates to convert measurements from one unit to another.	**análisis dimensional** Un proceso que utiliza tasas para convertir medidas de unidad a otra.	$12\text{ pt} \cdot \frac{1\text{ qt}}{2\text{ pt}} = 6\text{ qt}$
direct variation A linear relationship between two variables, x and y, that can be written in the form $y = kx$, where k is a nonzero constant.	**variación directa** Relación lineal entre dos variables, x e y, que puede expresarse en la forma $y = kx$, donde k es una constante distinta de cero.	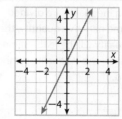
discrete function A function whose graph is made up of unconnected points.	**función discreta** Función cuya gráfica compuesta de puntos no conectados.	
discrete graph A graph made up of unconnected points.	**gráfica discreta** Gráfica compuesta de puntos no conectados.	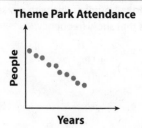

Distance Formula In a coordinate plane, the distance from (x_1, y_1) to (x_2, y_2) is

$$d = \sqrt{(x_2 - x_1)^2 + (y_2 - y_1)^2}.$$

Fórmula de distancia En un plano cartesiano, la distancia desde (x_1, y_1) hasta (x_2, y_2) es

$$d = \sqrt{(x_2 - x_1)^2 + (y_2 - y_1)^2}.$$

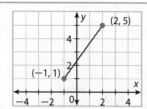

The distance from $(2, 5)$ to $(-1, 1)$ is
$$d = \sqrt{(-1 - 2)^2 + (1 - 5)^2}$$
$$= \sqrt{(-3)^2 + (-4)^2}$$
$$= \sqrt{9 + 16} = \sqrt{25} = 5.$$

distance from a point to a line The length of the perpendicular segment from the point to the line.	**distancia desde un punto hasta una línea** Longitud del segmento perpendicular desde el punto hasta la línea.	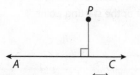 The distance from P to $\overleftrightarrow{AC}$ is 5 units.
Distributive Property For all real numbers a, b, and c, $a(b + c) = ab + ac$, and $(b + c)a = ba + ca$.	**Propiedad distributiva** Dados los números reales a, b y c, $a(b + c) = ab + ac$, y $(b + c)a = ba + ca$.	$3(4 + 5) = 3 \cdot 4 + 3 \cdot 5$ $(4 + 5)3 = 4 \cdot 3 + 5 \cdot 3$
Division Property of Equality For real numbers a, b, and c, where $c \neq 0$, if $a = b$, then $\frac{a}{c} = \frac{b}{c}$.	**Propiedad de igualdad de la división** Dados los números reales a, b y c, donde $c \neq 0$, si $a = b$, entonces $\frac{a}{c} = \frac{b}{c}$.	$4x = 12$ $\frac{4x}{4} = \frac{12}{4}$ $x = 3$

ENGLISH	SPANISH	EXAMPLES
Division Property of Inequality If both sides of an inequality are divided by the same positive quantity, the new inequality will have the same solution set. If both sides of an inequality are divided by the same negative quantity, the new inequality will have the same solution set if the inequality symbol is reversed.	**Propiedad de desigualdad de la división** Cuando ambos lados de una desigualdad se dividen entre el mismo número positivo, la nueva desigualdad tiene el mismo conjunto solución.Cuando ambos lados de una desigualdad se dividen entra el mismo número negativo, la nueva desigualdad tiene el mismo conjunto solución si se invierte el símbolo de desigualdad.	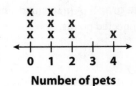 $$4x \geq 12$$ $$\frac{4x}{4} \geq \frac{12}{4}$$ $$x \geq 3$$ $$-4x \geq 12$$ $$\frac{-4x}{-4} \leq \frac{12}{-4}$$ $$x \leq -3$$
domain The set of all first coordinates (or *x*-values) of a relation or function.	**dominio** Conjunto de todos los valores de la primera coordenada (o valores de *x*) de una función o relación.	The domain of the function $\{(-5, 3), (-3, -2), (-1, -1), (1, 0)\}$ is $\{-5, -3, -1, 1\}$.
dot plot A number line with marks or dots that show frequency.	**diagrama de puntos** Recta numérica con marcas o puntos que indican la frecuencia.	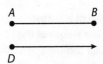

E

elimination method A method used to solve systems of equations in which one variable is eliminated by adding or subtracting two equations of the system.	**eliminación** Método utilizado para resolver sistemas de ecuaciones por el cual se elimina una variable sumando o restando dos ecuaciones del sistema.	
empty set A set with no elements.	**conjunto vacío** Conjunto sin elementos.	The solution set of $|x| < 0$ is the empty set, $\{\ \}$, or $\varnothing$.
endpoint A point at an end of a segment or the starting point of a ray.	**extremo** Punto en el final de un segmento o punto de inicio de un rayo.	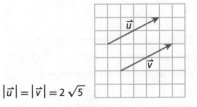
equal vectors Two vectors that have the same magnitude and the same direction.	**vectores iguales** Dos vectores de la misma magnitud y con la misma dirección.	$|\vec{u}| = |\vec{v}| = 2\sqrt{5}$
Equality of Bases Property Two powers with the same positive base other than 1 are equal if and only if the exponents are equal.	**Propiedad de igualdad de las bases** Dos potencias con la misma base positiva distinta de 1 son iguales si y solo si los exponentes son iguales.	If $b > 0$ and, $b \neq 1$, then $b^x = b^y$ if and only if $x = y$.

Glossary/Glosario

ENGLISH	SPANISH	EXAMPLES
equation A mathematical statement that two expressions are equivalent.	**ecuación** Enunciado matemático que indica que dos expresiones son equivalentes.	$x + 4 = 7$ $2 + 3 = 6 - 1$ $(x - 1)^2 + (y + 2)^2 = 4$
equiangular polygon A polygon in which all angles are congruent.	**polígono equiangular** Polígono cuyos ángulos son todos congruentes.	
equiangular triangle A triangle with three congruent angles.	**triángulo equiangular** Triángulo con tres ángulos congruentes.	
equidistant The same distance from two or more objects.	**equidistante** Igual distancia de dos o más objetos.	X is equidistant from A and B.
equilateral polygon A polygon in which all sides are congruent.	**polígono equilátero** Polígono cuyos lados son todos congruentes.	
equilateral triangle A triangle with three congruent sides.	**triángulo equilátero** Triángulo con tres lados congruentes.	
equivalent ratios Ratios that name the same comparison.	**razones equivalentes** Razones que expresan la misma comparación.	$\frac{1}{2}$ and $\frac{2}{4}$ are equivalent ratios.
evaluate To find the value of an algebraic expression by substituting a number for each variable and simplifying by using the order of operations.	**evaluar** Calcular el valor de una expresión algebraica sustituyendo cada variable por un número y simplificando mediante el orden de las operaciones.	Evaluate $2x + 7$ for $x = 3$. $2x + 7$ $2(3) + 7$ $6 + 7$ $\ \ 13$
explicit rule for *n*th term of a sequence A rule that defines the *n*th term a_n, or a general term, of a sequence as a function of *n*.	**fórmula explícita** Fórmula que define el enésimo término a_n, o término general, de una sucesión como una función de *n*.	
exponent The number that indicates how many times the base in a power is used as a factor.	**exponente** Número que indica la cantidad de veces que la base de una potencia se utiliza como factor.	$3^4 = 3 \cdot 3 \cdot 3 \cdot 3 = 81$ 4 is the exponent.

Glossary/Glosario

Glossary/Glosario

exponential decay An exponential function of the form $f(x) = ab^x$ in which $0 < b < 1$. If r is the rate of decay, then the function can be written $y = a(1 - r)^t$, where a is the initial amount and t is the time.

decremento exponencial Función exponencial del tipo $f(x) = ab^x$ en la cual $0 < b < 1$. Si r es la tasa decremental, entonces la función se puede expresar como $y = a(1 - r)^t$, donde a es la cantidad inicial y t es el tiempo.

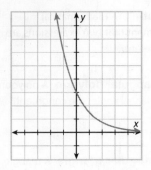

exponential expression An algebraic expression in which the variable is in an exponent with a fixed number as the base.

expresión exponencial Expresión algebraica en la que la variable está en un exponente y que tiene un número fijo como base.

2^{x+1}

exponential function A function of the form $f(x) = ab^x$, where a and b are real numbers with $a \neq 0$, $b > 0$, and $b \neq 1$.

función exponencial Función del tipo $f(x) = ab^x$, donde a y b son números reales con $a \neq 0$, $b > 0$ y $b \neq 1$.

$f(x) = 3 \cdot 4^x$

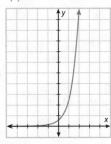

exponential growth An exponential function of the form $f(x) = abx$ in which $b > 1$. If r is the rate of growth, then the function can be written $y = a(1 + r)t$, where a is the initial amount and t is the time.

crecimiento exponencial Función exponencial del tipo $f(x) = ab^x$ en la que $b > 1$. Si r es la tasa de crecimiento, entonces la función se puede expresar como $y = a(1 + r)^t$, donde a es la cantidad inicial y t es el tiempo.

$f(x) = 2^x$

exponential regression A statistical method used to fit an exponential model to a given data set.

regresión exponencial Método estadístico utilizado para ajustar un modelo exponencial a un conjunto de datos determinado.

expression A mathematical phrase that contains operations, numbers, and/or variables.

expresión Frase matemática que contiene operaciones, números y/o variables.

$6x + 1$

exterior angle of a polygon An angle formed by one side of a polygon and the extension of an adjacent side.

ángulo externo de un polígono Ángulo formado por un lado de un polígono y la prolongación del lado adyacente.

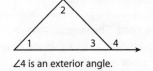

∠4 is an exterior angle.

exterior of an angle The set of all points outside an angle.

exterior de un ángulo Conjunto de todos los puntos que se encuentran fuera de un ángulo.

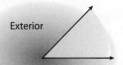

Exterior

ENGLISH	SPANISH	EXAMPLES
exterior of a polygon The set of all points outside a polygon.	**exterior de un polígono** Conjunto de todos los puntos que se encuentran fuera de un polígono.	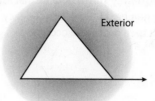 Exterior
extrapolation Making a prediction using a value of the independent variable outside of a model's domain.	**extrapolación** Hacer una predicción con un valor de la variable independiente que esté fuera del dominio de un modelo.	

F

ENGLISH	SPANISH	EXAMPLES
factor A number or expression that is multiplied by another number or expression to get a product. *See also factoring.*	**factor** Número o expresión que se multiplica por otro número o expresión para obtener un producto. *Ver también* factoreo.	$12 = 3 \cdot 4$ 3 and 4 are factors of 12. $x^2 - 1 = (x - 1)(x + 1)$ $(x - 1)$ and $(x + 1)$ are factors of $x^2 - 1$.
factoring The process of writing a number or algebraic expression as a product.	**factorización** Proceso por el que se expresa un número o expresión algebraica como un producto.	$x^2 - 4x - 21 = (x - 7)(x + 3)$
first quartile The median of the lower half of a data set, denoted Q_1. Also called *lower quartile*.	**primer cuartil** Mediana de la mitad inferior de un conjunto de datos, expresada como Q_1. También se llama *cuartil inferior*.	**Lower half** **Upper half** 18, (23,) 28, 29, 36, 42 **First quartile**
flowchart proof A style of proof that uses boxes and arrows to show the structure of the proof.	**demostración con diagrama de flujo** Tipo de demostración que se vale de cuadros y flechas para mostrar la estructura de la prueba.	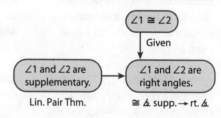
formula A literal equation that states a rule for a relationship among quantities.	**fórmula** Ecuación literal que establece una regla para una relación entre cantidades.	$A = \pi r^2$
frequency The number of times the value appears in the data set.	**frecuencia** Cantidad de veces que aparece el valor en un conjunto de datos.	In the data set 5, 6, 6, 7, 8, 9, the data value 6 has a frequency of 2.

Glossary/Glosario

Glossary/Glosario

frequency table A table that lists the number of times, or frequency, that each data value occurs.

tabla de frecuencia Tabla que enumera la cantidad de veces que ocurre cada valor de datos, o la frecuencia.

Data set: 1, 1, 2, 2, 3, 4, 5, 5, 6, 6, 6, 6
Frequency table:

Data	Frequency
1	2
2	2
3	1
4	1
5	3
6	4

function A relation in which every domain value is paired with exactly one range value.

función Relación en la que a cada valor de dominio corresponde exactamente un valor de rango.

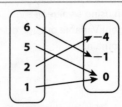

function notation If x is the independent variable and y is the dependent variable, then the function notation for y is $f(x)$, read "f of x," where f names the function.

notación de función Si x es la variable independiente e y es la variable dependiente, entonces la notación de función para y es $f(x)$, que se lee "f de x," donde f nombra la función.

equation: $y = 2x$
function notation: $f(x) = 2x$

function rule An algebraic expression that defines a function.

regla de función Expresión algebraica que define una función.

$$f(x) = \underset{\uparrow}{2x^2 + 3x - 7}$$
function rule

G

geometric sequence A sequence in which the ratio of successive terms is a constant r, called the common ratio, where $r \neq 0$ and $r \neq 1$.

sucesión geométrica Sucesión en la que la razón de los términos sucesivos es una constante r, denominada razón común, donde $r \neq 0$ y $r \neq 1$.

$1, \quad 2, \quad 4, \quad 8, \quad 16, \ldots$
$\cdot 2 \ \cdot 2 \ \cdot 2 \ \cdot 2 \qquad r = 2$

graph of a function The set of points in a coordinate plane with coordinates (x, y), where x is in the domain of the function f and $y = fx$.

gráfica de una función Conjunto de los puntos de un plano cartesiano con coordenadas (x, y), donde x está en el dominio de la función f e $y = f(x)$.

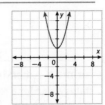

graph of a system of linear inequalities The region in a coordinate plane consisting of points whose coordinates are solutions to all of the inequalities in the system.

gráfica de un sistema de desigualdades lineales Región de un plano cartesiano que consta de puntos cuyas coordenadas son soluciones de todas las desigualdades del sistema.

$(2, 1)$ is in the overlapping shaded regions, so it is a solution.

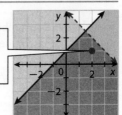

graph of an inequality in one variable The set of points on a number line that are solutions of the inequality.

gráfica de una desigualdad en una variable Conjunto de los puntos de una recta numérica que representan soluciones de la desigualdad.

$x \geq 2$

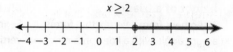

---

graph of an inequality in two variables The set of points in a coordinate plane whose coordinates (x, y) are solutions of the inequality.

gráfica de una desigualdad en dos variables Conjunto de los puntos de un plano cartesiano cuyas coordenadas (x, y) son soluciones de la desigualdad.

$y \leq x + 1$

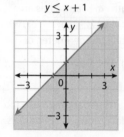

---

greatest common factor (numbers) (GCF) The largest common factor of two or more given numbers.

máximo común divisor (números) (MCD) El mayor de los factores comunes compartidos por dos o más números dados.

The GCF of 27 and 45 is 9.

---

greatest integer function A function denoted by $f(x) = [x]$ in which the number x is rounded down to the greatest integer that is less than or equal to x.

función de entero mayor Función expresada como $f(x) = [x]$ en la cual el número x se redondea hacia abajo hasta el entero mayor que sea menor o igual a x.

---

grouping symbols Symbols such as parentheses ( ), brackets [ ], and braces { } that separate part of an expression. A fraction bar, absolute-value symbols, and radical symbols may also be used as grouping symbols.

símbolos de agrupación Símbolos tales como paréntesis ( ), corchetes [ ] y llaves { } que separan parte de una expresión. La barra de fracciones, los símbolos de valor absoluto y los símbolos de radical también se pueden utilizar como símbolos de agrupación.

$6 + \{3 - [(4 - 3) + 2] + 1\} - 5$
$6 + \{3 - [1 + 2] + 1\} - 5$
$6 + \{3 - 3 + 1\} - 5$
$6 + 1 - 5$
2

H

half-plane The part of the coordinate plane on one side of a line, which may include the line.

semiplano La parte del plano cartesiano de un lado de una línea, que puede incluir la línea.

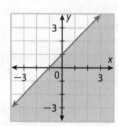

---

height of a figure The length of an altitude of the figure.

altura de una figura Longitud de la altura de la figura.

Glossary/Glosario

ENGLISH	SPANISH	EXAMPLES

height of a triangle
A segment from a vertex that forms a right angle with a line containing the base.

altura de un triángulo
Segmento que se extiende desde el vértice y forma un ángulo recto con la línea de la base.

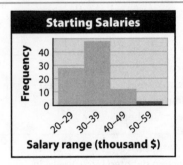

Heron's Formula A triangle with side lengths a, b, and c has area $A = \sqrt{s(s-a)(s-b)(s-c)}$, where s is one-half the perimeter, or $s = \frac{1}{2}(a + b + c)$.

fórmula de Herón Un triángulo con longitudes de lado a, b y c tiene un área $A = \sqrt{s(s-a)(s-b)(s-c)}$, donde s es la mitad del perímetro ó $s = \frac{1}{2}(a + b + c)$.

---

histogram A bar graph used to display data grouped in intervals.

histograma Gráfica de barras utilizada para mostrar datos agrupados en intervalos de clases.

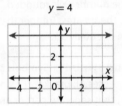

---

horizontal line A line described by the equation $y = b$, where b is the y-intercept.

línea horizontal Línea descrita por la ecuación $y = b$, donde b es la intersección con el eje y.

$y = 4$

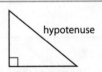

---

horizontal translation (of a parabola) is a shift of the parabola left or right, with no change in the shape of the parabola.

traslación horizontal (de una parábola) Desplazamiento de la parábola hacia la izquierda o hacia la derecha, sin producir cambios en la forma de la parábola.

---

hypotenuse The side opposite the right angle in a right triangle.

hipotenusa Lado opuesto al ángulo recto de un triángulo rectángulo.

hypotenuse

---

hypothesis The part of a conditional statement following the word *if*.

hipótesis La parte de un enunciado condicional que sigue a la palabra *si*.

If $x + 1 = 5$, then $x = 4$.

  Hypothesis

I

---

identity An equation that is true for all values of the variables.

identidad Ecuación verdadera para todos los valores de las variables.

$3 = 3$
$2(x - 1) = 2x - 2$

ENGLISH	SPANISH	EXAMPLES
image A shape that results from a transformation of a figure known as the preimage.	**imagen** Forma resultante de la transformación de una figura conocida como imagen original.	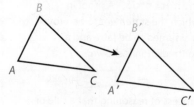
incenter of a triangle The point of concurrency of the three angle bisectors of a triangle.	**incentro de un triángulo** Punto donde se encuentran las tres bisectrices de los ángulos de un triángulo.	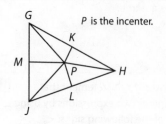 *P* is the incenter.
incircle *See* inscribed circle.	**incírculo** *Véase* círculo inscrito.	
included angle The angle formed by two adjacent sides of a polygon.	**ángulo incluido** Ángulo formado por dos lados adyacentes de un polígono.	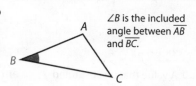 ∠*B* is the included angle between $\overline{AB}$ and $\overline{BC}$.
included side The common side of two consecutive angles of a polygon.	**lado incluido** Lado común de dos ángulos consecutivos de un polígono.	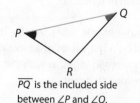 $\overline{PQ}$ is the included side between ∠*P* and ∠*Q*.
inconsistent system A system of equations or inequalities that has no solution.	**sistema inconsistente** Sistema de ecuaciones o desigualdades que no tiene solución.	$\begin{cases} x + y = 0 \\ x + y = 1 \end{cases}$
independent system A system of equations that has exactly one solution.	**sistema independiente** Sistema de ecuaciones que tiene sólo una solución.	$\begin{cases} x + y = 7 \\ x - y = 1 \end{cases}$ Solution: (4, 3)
independent variable The input of a function; a variable whose value determines the value of the output, or dependent variable.	**variable independiente** Entrada de una función; variable cuyo valor determina el valor de la salida, o variable dependiente.	For $y = 2x + 1$, x is the independent variable.
index In the radical $\sqrt[n]{x}$, which represents the nth root of x, n is the index. In the radical $\sqrt{x}$, the index is understood to be 2.	**índice** En el radical $\sqrt[n]{x}$, que representa la enésima raíz de x, n es el índice. En el radical $\sqrt{x}$, se da por sentado que el índice es 2.	The radical $\sqrt[3]{8}$ has an index of 3.
indirect measurement A method of measurement that uses formulas, similar figures, and/or proportions.	**medición indirecta** Método de medición en el que se usan fórmulas, figuras semejantes y/o proporciones.	

Glossary/Glosario

Glossary/Glosario

indirect proof A proof in which the statement to be proved is assumed to be false and a contradiction is shown.

demostración indirecta Prueba en la que se supone que el enunciado a demostrar es falso y se muestra una contradicción.

inductive reasoning The process of reasoning that a rule or statement is true because specific cases are true.

razonamiento inductivo Proceso de razonamiento por el que se determina que una regla o enunciado son verdaderos porque ciertos casos específicos son verdaderos.

inequality A statement that compares two expressions by using one of the following signs: $<$, $>$, $\leq$, $\geq$, or $\neq$.

desigualdad Enunciado que compara dos expresiones utilizando uno de los siguientes signos: $<$, $>$, $\leq$, $\geq$, o $\neq$.

$x \geq 2$

initial point of a vector The starting point of a vector.

punto inicial de un vector Punto donde comienza un vector.

Initial point

input A value that is substituted for the independent variable in a relation or function.

entrada Valor que sustituye a la variable independiente en una relación o función.

For the function $f(x) = x + 5$, the input 3 produces an output of 8.

input-output table A table that displays input values of a function or expression together with the corresponding outputs.

tabla de entrada y salida Tabla que muestra los valores de entrada de una función o expresión junto con las correspondientes salidas.

Input	x	1	2	3	4
Output	y	4	7	10	13

intercept See x-intercept and y-intercept.

intersección Ver intersección con el eje x e intersección con el eje y.

interior angle An angle formed by two sides of a polygon with a common vertex.

ángulo interno Ángulo formado por dos lados de un polígono con un vértice común.

$\angle 1$ is an interior angle.

interior of an angle The set of all points between the sides of an angle.

interior de un ángulo Conjunto de todos los puntos entre los lados de un ángulo.

Interior

interest The amount of money charged for borrowing money or the amount of money earned when saving or investing money. *See also* compound interest, simple interest.

interés Cantidad de dinero que se cobra por prestar dinero o cantidad de dinero que se gana cuando se ahorra o invierte dinero. *Ver también* interés compuesto, interés simple.

Glossary/Glosario

interpolation Making a prediction using a value of the independent variable from within a model's domain.

interpolación Hacer una predicción con un valor de la variable independiente a partir del dominio de un modelo.

---

interquartile range (IQR) The difference of the third (upper) and first (lower) quartiles in a data set, representing the middle half of the data.

rango entre cuartiles Diferencia entre el tercer cuartil (superior) y el primer cuartil (inferior) de un conjunto de datos, que representa la mitad central de los datos.

Lower half   Upper half
18, ⟨23,⟩ 28,   29, ⟨36,⟩ 42
First quartile   Third quartile
Interquartile range: $36 - 23 = 13$

---

intersection The intersection of two sets is the set of all elements that are common to both sets, denoted by ∩.

intersección de conjuntos La intersección de dos conjuntos es el conjunto de todos los elementos que son comunes a ambos conjuntos, expresado por ∩.

$A = \{1, 2, 3, 4\}$
$B = \{1, 3, 5, 7, 9\}$
$A \cap B = \{1, 3\}$

---

inverse of a function The relation that results from exchanging the input and output values of a function.

inverso de una función La relación que se genera al intercambiar los valores de entrada y de salida de una función.

---

inverse operations Operations that undo each other.

operaciones inversas Operaciones que se anulan entre sí.

Addition and subtraction of the same quantity are inverse operations: $5 + 3 = 8, 8 - 3 = 5$
Multiplication and division by the same quantity are inverse operations: $2 \cdot 3 = 6$, $6 \div 3 = 2$

---

inverse relation The relation that results from exchanging the input and output values of a relation.

relación inversa La relación que se genera al intercambiar los valores de entrada y de salida de una relación.

---

inverse variation A relationship between two variables, x and y, that can be written in the form $y = \frac{k}{x}$, where k is a nonzero constant and $x \neq 0$.

variación inversa Relación entre dos variables, x e y, que puede expresarse en la forma $y = \frac{k}{x}$, donde k es una constante distinta de cero y $x \neq 0$.

$y = \frac{8}{x}$
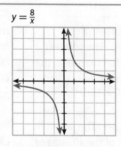

---

irrational number A real number that cannot be expressed as the ratio of two integers.

número irracional Número real que no se puede expresar como una razón de enteros.

$\sqrt{2}, \pi, e$

---

isometry A transformation that does not change the size or shape of a figure.

isometría Transformación que no cambia el tamaño ni la forma de una figura.

Reflections, translations, and rotations are all examples of isometries.

---

isosceles trapezoid A trapezoid in which the legs are congruent.

trapecio isósceles Trapecio cuyos lados no paralelos son congruentes.

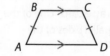

Glossary/Glosario

ENGLISH	SPANISH	EXAMPLES

isosceles triangle A triangle with at least two congruent sides.

triángulo isósceles Triángulo que tiene al menos dos lados congruentes.

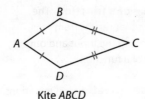

J

joint relative frequency The ratio of the frequency in a particular category divided by the total number of data values.

frecuencia relativa conjunta La línea de ajuste en que la suma de cuadrados de los residuos es la menor.

K

kite A quadrilateral with exactly two pairs of congruent consecutive sides.

cometa o papalote Cuadrilátero con exactamente dos pares de lados congruentes consecutivos.

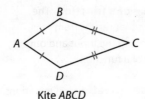

Kite *ABCD*

L

least common denominator (LCD) The least common multiple of the denominators of two or more given fractions or rational expressions.

mínimo común denominador (MCD) Mínimo común múltiplo de los denominadores de dos o más fracciones dadas o expresionnes racionales.

The LCD of $\frac{3}{4}$ and $\frac{5}{6}$ is 12.

least common multiple (numbers) (LCM) The smallest whole number, other than zero, that is a multiple of two or more given numbers.

mínimo común múltiplo (números) (MCM) El menor de los números cabales, distinto de cero, que es múltiplo de dos o más números dados.

The LCM of 10 and 18 is 90.

least-squares line The line of fit for which the sum of the squares of the residuals is as small as possible

línea de mínimos cuadrados La línea de ajuste en que la suma de cuadrados de los residuos es la menor.

leg of a right triangle One of the two sides of the right triangle that form the right angle.

cateto de un triángulo rectángulo Uno de los dos lados de un triángulo rectángulo que forman el ángulo recto.

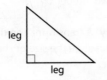

leg of a trapezoid One of the two nonparallel sides of the trapezoid.

cateto de un trapecio Uno de los dos lados no paralelos del trapecio.

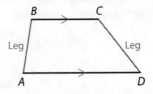

© Houghton Mifflin Harcourt Publishing Company

ENGLISH	SPANISH	EXAMPLES
leg of an isosceles triangle One of the two congruent sides of the isosceles triangle.	**cateto de un triángulo isósceles** Uno de los dos lados congruentes del triángulo isósceles.	
length The distance between the two endpoints of a segment.	**longitud** Distancia entre los dos extremos de un segmento.	$AB = \lvert a - b \rvert = \lvert b - a \rvert$
like terms Terms with the same variables raised to the same exponents.	**términos semejantes** Términos con las mismas variables elevadas a los mismos exponentes.	
line An undefined term in geometry, a line is a straight path that has no thickness and extends forever.	**línea** Término indefinido en geometría; una línea es un trazo recto que no tiene grosor y se extiende infinitamente.	
line graph A graph that uses line segments to show how data changes.	**gráfica lineal** Gráfica que se vale de segmentos de recta para mostrar cambios en los datos.	
line of best fit The line that comes closest to all of the points in a data set.	**línea de mejor ajuste** Línea que más se acerca a todos los puntos de un conjunto de datos.	
line of fit *See trend line.*	**línea de ajuste** *Ver línea de tendencia.*	
line of symmetry A line that divides a plane figure into two congruent reflected halves.	**eje de simetría** Línea que divide una figura plana en dos mitades reflejas congruentes.	
line plot A number line with marks or dots that show frequency.	**diagrama de acumulación** Recta numérica con marcas o puntos que indican la frecuencia.	
line segment *See* segment of a line.	**segmento** *Véase* segmento de recta.	
line symmetry A figure that can be reflected across a line so that the image coincides with the preimage.	**simetría axial** Figura que puede reflejarse sobre una línea de forma tal que la imagen coincida con la imagen original.	

Glossary/Glosario

Glossary/Glosario

Glossary/Glosario

linear equation in one variable
An equation that can be written in the form $ax = b$ where a and b are constants and $a \neq 0$.

ecuación lineal en una variable
Ecuación que puede expresarse en la forma $ax = b$ donde a y b son constantes y $a \neq 0$.

$x + 1 = 7$

---

linear equation in two variables An equation that can be written in the form $Ax + By = C$ where A, B, and C are constants and A and B are not both 0.

ecuación lineal en dos variables Ecuación que puede expresarse en la forma $Ax + By = C$ donde A, B y C son constantes y A y B no son ambas 0.

$2x + 3y = 6$

---

linear function A function that can be written in the form $y = mx + b$, where x is the independent variable and m and b are real numbers. Its graph is a line.

función lineal Función que puede expresarse en la forma $y = mx + b$, donde x es la variable independiente y m y b son números reales. Su gráfica es una línea.

$y = x - 1$

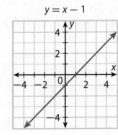

---

linear inequality in one variable An inequality that can be written in one of the following forms: $ax < b$, $ax > b$, $ax \leq b$, $ax \geq b$, or b, where a and b are constants and $a \neq 0$.

desigualdad lineal en una variable Desigualdad que puede expresarse de una de las siguientes formas: $ax < b$, $ax > b$, $ax \leq b$, $ax \geq b$ o $ax \neq b$, donde a y b son constantes y $a \neq 0$.

$3x - 5 \leq 2(x + 4)$

---

linear inequality in two variables An inequality that can be written in one of the following forms: $Ax + By < C$, $Ax + By > C$, $Ax + By \leq C$, $Ax + By \geq C$, or $Ax + By \neq C$, where A, B, and C are constants and A and B are not both 0.

desigualdad lineal en dos variables Desigualdad que puede expresarse de una de las siguientes formas: $Ax + By < C$, $Ax + By > C$, $Ax + By \leq C$, $Ax + By \geq C$ o $Ax + By \neq C$, donde A, B y C son constantes y A y B no son ambas 0.

$2x + 3y > 6$

---

linear regression A statistical method used to fit a linear model to a given data set.

regresión lineal Método estadístico utilizado para ajustar un modelo lineal a un conjunto de datos determinado.

---

literal equation An equation that contains two or more variables.

ecuación literal Ecuación que contiene dos o más variables.

$d = rt$
$A = \frac{1}{2}h(b_1 + b_2)$

---

lower quartile *See* first quartile.

cuartil inferior *Ver* primer cuartil.

M

mapping diagram A diagram that shows the relationship of elements in the domain to elements in the range of a relation or function.

diagrama de correspondencia Diagrama que muestra la relación entre los elementos del dominio y los elementos del rango de una función.

Mapping Diagram

ENGLISH	SPANISH	EXAMPLES
marginal relative frequency The sum of the joint relative frequencies in a row or column of a two-way table.	**frecuencia relativa marginal** La suma de las frecuencias relativas conjuntas en una fila o columna de una tabla de doble entrada.	
mean The sum of all the values in a data set divided by the number of data values. Also called the *average*.	**media** Suma de todos los valores de un conjunto de datos dividida entre el número de valores de datos. También llamada *promedio*.	Data set: 4, 6, 7, 8, 10 Mean: $\frac{4+6+7+8+10}{5} = \frac{35}{5} = 7$
measure of an angle Angles are measured in degrees. A degree is $\frac{1}{360}$ of a complete circle.	**medida de un ángulo** Los ángulos se miden en grados. Un grado es $\frac{1}{360}$ de un círculo completo.	
measure of central tendency A measure that describes the center of a data set.	**medida de tendencia dominante** Medida que describe el centro de un conjunto de datos.	mean, median, or mode
median For an ordered data set with an odd number of values, the median is the middle value. For an ordered data set with an even number of values, the median is the average of the two middle values.	**mediana** Dado un conjunto de datos ordenado con un número impar de valores, la mediana es el valor medio. Dado un conjunto de datos con un número par de valores, la mediana es el promedio de los dos valores medios.	8, 9, ⑨, 12, 15 Median: 9 4, 6, ⑦, ⑩, 10, 12 Median: $\frac{7+10}{2} = 8.5$
median of a triangle A segment whose endpoints are a vertex of the triangle and the midpoint of the opposite side.	**mediana de un triángulo** Segmento cuyos extremos son un vértice del triángulo y el punto medio del lado opuesto.	
midpoint The point that divides a segment into two congruent segments.	**punto medio** Punto que divide un segmento en dos segmentos congruentes.	 Point *B* is the midpoint of $\overline{AC}$.
midsegment of a trapezoid The segment whose endpoints are the midpoints of the legs of the trapezoid.	**segmento medio de un trapecio** Segmento cuyos extremos son los puntos medios de los catetos del trapecio.	
midsegment of a triangle A segment that joins the midpoints of two sides of the triangle.	**segmento medio de un triángulo** Segmento que une los puntos medios de dos lados del triángulo.	
midsegment triangle The triangle formed by the three midsegments of a triangle.	**triángulo de segmentos medios** Triángulo formado por los tres segmentos medios de un triángulo.	

Glossary/Glosario

ENGLISH	SPANISH	EXAMPLES
mode The value or values that occur most frequently in a data set; if all values occur with the same frequency, the data set is said to have no mode.	**moda** El valor o los valores que se presentan con mayor frecuencia en un conjunto de datos. Si todos los valores se presentan con la misma frecuencia, se dice que el conjunto de datos no tiene moda.	Data set: 3, 6, 8, 8, 10 Mode: 8 Data set: 2, 5, 5, 7, 7 Modes: 5 and 7 Data set: 2, 3, 6, 9, 11 No mode
Multiplication Property of Equality If a, b, and c are real numbers and $a = b$, then $ac = bc$.	**Propiedad de igualdad de la multiplicación** Si a, b y c son números reales y $a = b$, entonces $ac = bc$.	$\frac{1}{3}x = 7$ $(3)\left(\frac{1}{3}x\right) = (3)(7)$ $x = 21$
Multiplication Property of Inequality If both sides of an inequality are multiplied by the same positive quantity, the new inequality will have the same solution set. If both sides of an inequality are multiplied by the same negative quantity, the new inequality will have the same solution set if the inequality symbol is reversed.	**Propiedad de desigualdad de la multiplicación** Si ambos lados de una desigualdad se multiplican por el mismo número positivo, la nueva desigualdad tendrá el mismo conjunto solución. Si ambos lados de una desigualdad se multiplican por el mismo número negativo, la nueva desigualdad tendrá el mismo conjunto solución si se invierte el símbolo de desigualdad.	$\frac{1}{3}x > 7$ $(3)\left(\frac{1}{3}x\right) > (3)(7)$ $x > 21$ $-x \leq 2$ $(-1)(-x) \geq (-1)(2)$ $x \geq -2$
multiplicative inverse The reciprocal of the number.	**inverso multiplicativo** Recíproco de un número.	The multiplicative inverse of 5 is $\frac{1}{5}$.

N

negative correlation Two data sets have a negative correlation if one set of data values increases as the other set decreases.	**correlación negativa** Dos conjuntos de datos tienen una correlación negativa si un conjunto de valores de datos aumenta a medida que el otro conjunto disminuye.	
negative exponent For any nonzero real number x and any integer n, $x^{-n} = \frac{1}{x^n}$.	**exponente negativo** Para cualquier número real distinto de cero x y cualquier entero n, $x^{-n} = \frac{1}{x^n}$.	$x^{-2} = \frac{1}{x^2}$; $3^{-2} = \frac{1}{3^2}$
negative number A number that is less than zero. Negative numbers lie to the left of zero on a number line.	**número negativo** Número menor que cero. Los números negativos se ubican a la izquierda del cero en una recta numérica.	-2 is a negative number. 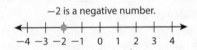
no correlation Two data sets have no correlation if there is no relationship between the sets of values.	**sin correlación** Dos conjuntos de datos no tienen correlación si no existe una relación entre los conjuntos de valores.	

Glossary/Glosario

ENGLISH	SPANISH	EXAMPLES

normal curve The graph of a probability density function that corresponds to a normal distribution; bell-shaped and symmetric about the mean, with the *x*-axis as a horizontal asymptote.

curva normal La gráfica de una función de densidad de probabilidad que corresponde a la distribución normal; con forma de campana y simétrica con relación a la media, el eje *x* es una asíntota horizontal.

normal distribution A distribution of data that varies about the mean in such a way that the graph of its probability density function is a normal curve.

distribución normal Distribución de datos que varía respecto de la media de tal manera que la gráfica de su función de densidad de probabilidad es una curva normal.

nth root The *n*th root of a number *a*, written as $\sqrt[n]{a}$ or $a^{\frac{1}{n}}$, is a number that is equal to *a* when it is raised to the *n*th power.

enésima raíz La enésima raíz de un número *a*, que se escribe $\sqrt[n]{a}$ o $a^{\frac{1}{n}}$, es un número igual a *a* cuando se eleva a la enésima potencia.

$\sqrt[5]{32} = 2$, because $2^5 = 32$.

numerical expression An expression that contains only numbers and operations.

expresión numérica Expresión que contiene únicamente números y operaciones.

O

obtuse triangle A triangle with one obtuse angle.

triángulo obtusángulo Triángulo con un ángulo obtuso.

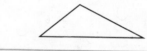

opposite The opposite of a number *a*, denoted −*a*, is the number that is the same distance from zero as *a*, on the opposite side of the number line. The sum of opposites is 0.

opuesto El opuesto de un número *a*, expresado −*a*, es el número que se encuentra a la misma distancia de cero que *a*, del lado opuesto de la recta numérica. La suma de los opuestos es 0.

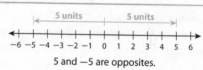
5 and −5 are opposites.

opposite reciprocal The opposite of the reciprocal of a number. The opposite reciprocal of any nonzero number *a* is $-\frac{1}{a}$.

recíproco opuesto Opuesto del recíproco de un número. El recíproco opuesto de *a* es $-\frac{1}{a}$.

The opposite reciprocal of $\frac{2}{3}$ is $-\frac{3}{2}$.

OR A logical operator representing the union of two sets.

O Operador lógico que representa la unión de dos conjuntos.

$A = \{2, 3, 4, 5\}$ $B = \{1, 3, 5, 7\}$
The set of values that are in *A* OR *B* is $A \cup B = \{1, 2, 3, 4, 5, 7\}$.

order of rotational symmetry The number of times a figure with rotational symmetry coincides with itself as it rotates 360°.

orden de simetría de rotación Cantidad de veces que una figura con simetría de rotación coincide consigo misma cuando rota 360°.

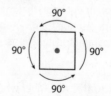
Order of rotational symmetry: 4

Glossary/Glosario

Glossary/Glosario

© Houghton Mifflin Harcourt Publishing Company

Glossary/Glosario

orthocenter of a triangle
The point of concurrency of the three altitudes of a triangle.

ortocentro de un triángulo
Punto de intersección de las tres alturas de un triángulo.

P is the orthocenter.

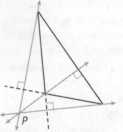

---

outlier A data value that is far removed from the rest of the data.

valor extremo Valor de datos que está muy alejado del resto de los datos.

---

output The result of substituting a value for a variable in a function.

salida Resultado de la sustitución de una variable por un valor en una función.

For the function $f(x) = x^2 + 1$, the input 3 produces an output of 10.

P

parabola The shape of the graph of a quadratic function.

parábola Forma de la gráfica de una función cuadrática.

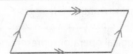

---

paragraph proof A style of proof in which the statements and reasons are presented in paragraph form.

demostración con párrafos Tipo de demostración en la cual los enunciados y las razones se presentan en forma de párrafo.

---

parallel lines Lines in the same plane that do not intersect.

líneas paralelas Líneas en el mismo plano que no se cruzan.

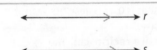

---

parallelogram A quadrilateral with two pairs of parallel sides.

paralelogramo Cuadrilátero con dos pares de lados paralelos.

---

parameter One of the constants in a function or equation that may be changed. Also the third variable in a set of parametric equations.

parámetro Una de las constantes en una función o ecuación que se puede cambiar. También es la tercera variable en un conjunto de ecuaciones paramétricas.

---

perfect square A number whose positive square root is a whole number.

cuadrado perfecto Número cuya raíz cuadrada positiva es un número cabal.

36 is a perfect square because $\sqrt{36} = 6$.

ENGLISH	SPANISH	EXAMPLES
permutation An arrangement of a group of objects in which order is important.	**permutación** Arreglo de un grupo de objetos en el cual el orden es importante.	For objects *A*, *B*, *C*, and *D*, there are 12 different permutations of 2 objects. *AB, AC, AD, BC, BD, CD* *BA, CA, DA, CB, DB, DC*
perpendicular Intersecting to form 90° angles.	**perpendicular** Que se cruza para formar ángulos de 90°.	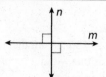
perpendicular bisector of a segment A line perpendicular to a segment at the segment's midpoint.	**mediatriz de un segmento** Línea perpendicular a un segmento en el punto medio del segmento.	 ℓ is the perpendicular bisector of $\overline{AB}$.
perpendicular lines Lines that intersect at 90° angles.	**líneas perpendiculares** Líneas que se cruzan en ángulos de 90°.	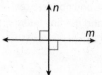
piecewise function A function that is a combination of one or more functions.	**función a trozos** Función que es una combinación de una o más funciones.	
plane An undefined term in geometry, it is a flat surface that has no thickness and extends forever.	**plano** Término indefinido en geometría; un plano es una superficie plana que no tiene grosor y se extiende infinitamente.	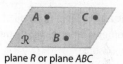 plane *R* or plane *ABC*
point An undefined term in geometry, it names a location and has no size.	**punto** Término indefinido de la geometría que denomina una ubicación y no tiene tamaño.	*P* • point *P*
point-slope form The point-slope form of a linear equation is $y - y_1 = m(x - x_1)$, where *m* is the slope and (x_1, y_1) is a point on the line.	**forma de punto y pendiente** La forma de punto y pendiente de una ecuación lineal es $y - y_1 = m(x - x_1)$, donde *m* es la pendiente y (x_1, y_1) es un punto en la línea.	$y - 3 = 2(x - 3)$
point of concurrency A point where three or more lines coincide.	**punto de concurrencia** Punto donde se cruzan tres o más líneas.	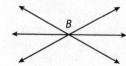
population The entire group of objects or individuals considered for a survey.	**población** Grupo completo de objetos o individuos que se desea estudiar.	In a survey about the study habits of high school students, the population is all high school students.

Glossary/Glosario

Glossary/Glosario

positive correlation Two data sets have a positive correlation if both sets of data values increase.

correlación positiva Dos conjuntos de datos tienen correlación positiva si los valores de ambos conjuntos de datos aumentan.

---

postulate A statement that is accepted as true without proof. Also called an *axiom*.

postulado Enunciado que se acepta como verdadero sin demostración. También denominado *axioma*.

Power of a Power Property If a is any nonzero real number and m and n are integers, then $(a^m)^n = a^{mn}$.

Propiedad de la potencia de una potencia Dado un número real a distinto de cero y los números enteros m y n, entonces $(a^m)^n = a^{mn}$.

$$(6^7)^4 = 6^{7 \cdot 4}$$
$$= 6^{28}$$

Power of a Product Property If a and b are any nonzero real numbers and n is any integer, then $(ab)^n = a^n b^n$.

Propiedad de la potencia de un producto Dados los números reales a y b distintos de cero y un número entero n, entonces $(ab)^n = a^n b^n$.

$$(2 \cdot 4)^3 = 2^3 \cdot 4^3$$
$$= 8 \cdot 64$$
$$= 512$$

Power of a Quotient Property If a and b are any nonzero real numbers and n is an integer, then $\left(\frac{a}{b}\right)^n = \frac{a^n}{b^n}$.

Propiedad de la potencia de un cociente Dados los números reales a y b distintos de cero y un número entero n, entonces $\left(\frac{a}{b}\right)^n = \frac{a^n}{b^n}$.

$$\left(\frac{3}{5}\right)^4 = \frac{3}{5} \cdot \frac{3}{5} \cdot \frac{3}{5} \cdot \frac{3}{5}$$
$$= \frac{3 \cdot 3 \cdot 3 \cdot 3}{5 \cdot 5 \cdot 5 \cdot 5}$$
$$= \frac{3^4}{5^4}$$

---

precision The level of detail of a measurement, determined by the unit of measure.

precisión Detalle de una medición, determinado por la unidad de medida.

A ruler marked in millimeters has a greater level of precision than a ruler marked in centimeters.

---

prediction An estimate or guess about something that has not yet happened.

predicción Estimación o suposición sobre algo que todavía no ha sucedido.

---

preimage The original figure in a transformation.

imagen original Figura original en una transformación.

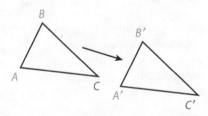

---

prime factorization A representation of a number or a polynomial as a product of primes.

factorización prima Representación de un número o de un polinomio como producto de números primos.

The prime factorization of 60 is $2 \cdot 2 \cdot 3 \cdot 5$.

---

prime number A whole number greater than 1 that has exactly two positive factors, itself and 1.

número primo Número cabal mayor que 1 que es divisible únicamente entre sí mismo y entre 1.

5 is prime because its only positive factors are 5 and 1.

ENGLISH	SPANISH	EXAMPLES
principal An amount of money borrowed or invested.	**capital** Cantidad de dinero que se pide prestado o se invierte.	
Product of Powers Property If a is any nonzero real number and m and n are integers, then $a^m \cdot a^n = a^{m+n}$.	**Propiedad del producto de potencias** Dado un número real a distinto de cero y los números enteros m y n, entonces $a^m \cdot a^n = a^{m+n}$.	$6^7 \cdot 6^4 = 6^{7+4}$ $= 6^{11}$
proof An argument that uses logic to show that a conclusion is true.	**demostración** Argumento que se vale de la lógica para probar que una conclusión es verdadera.	
proof by contradiction *See* indirect proof.	**demostración por contradicción** *Ver* demostración indirecta.	
proportion A statement that two ratios are equal; $\frac{a}{b} = \frac{c}{d}$.	**proporción** Ecuación que establece que dos razones son iguales; $\frac{a}{b} = \frac{c}{d}$.	$\frac{2}{3} = \frac{4}{6}$
Pythagorean Theorem If a right triangle has legs of lengths a and b and a hypotenuse of length c, then $a^2 + b^2 = c^2$.	**Teorema de Pitágoras** Dado un triángulo rectángulo con catetos de longitudes a y b y una hipotenusa de longitud c, entonces $a^2 + b^2 = c^2$.	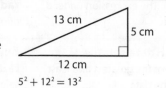 $5^2 + 12^2 = 13^2$ $25 + 144 = 169$
Pythagorean triple A set of three positive integers a, b, and c such that $a^2 + b^2 = c^2$.	**Tripleta de Pitágoras** Conjunto de tres enteros positivos a, b y c tal que $a^2 + b^2 = c^2$.	The numbers 3, 4, and 5 form a Pythagorean triple because $3^2 + 4^2 = 5^2$.

Q

ENGLISH	SPANISH	EXAMPLES
quadrant One of the four regions into which the x- and y-axes divide the coordinate plane.	**cuadrante** Una de las cuatro regiones en las que los ejes x e y dividen el plano cartesiano.	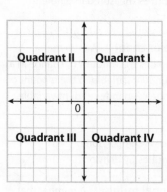
quadrilateral A four-sided polygon.	**cuadrilátero** Polígono de cuatro lados.	
quantitative data Numerical data.	**datos cuantitativos** Datos numéricos.	

Glossary/Glosario

ENGLISH	SPANISH	EXAMPLES
quartile The median of the upper or lower half of a data set. *See also* first quartile, third quartile.	**cuartil** La mediana de la mitad superior o inferior de un conjunto de datos. *Ver también* primer cuartil, tercer cuartil.	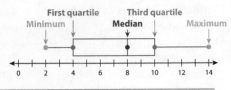
Quotient of Powers Property If a is a nonzero real number and m and n are integers, then $\frac{a^m}{a^n} = a^{m-n}$.	**Propiedad del cociente de potencias** Dado un número real a distinto de cero y los números enteros m y n, entonces $\frac{a^m}{a^n} = a^{m-n}$.	$\frac{6^7}{6^4} = 6^{7-4} = 6^3$

R

radical symbol The symbol $\sqrt{}$ used to denote a root. The symbol is used alone to indicate a square root or with an index, $\sqrt[n]{}$, to indicate the nth root.	**símbolo de radical** Símbolo $\sqrt{}$ que se utiliza para expresar una raíz. Puede utilizarse solo para indicar una raíz cuadrada, o con un índice, $\sqrt[n]{}$, para indicar la enésima raíz.	$\sqrt{36} = 6$ $\sqrt[3]{27} = 3$
radicand The expression under a radical sign.	**radicando** Número o expresión debajo del signo de radical.	Expression: $\sqrt{x+3}$ Radicand: $x + 3$
range of a data set The difference of the greatest and least values in the data set.	**rango de un conjunto de datos** La diferencia del mayor y menor valor en un conjunto de datos.	The data set {3, 3, 5, 7, 8, 10, 11, 11, 12} has a range of $12 - 3 = 9$.
range of a function or relation The set of all second coordinates (or y-values) of a function or relation.	**rango de una función o relación** Conjunto de todos los valores de la segunda coordenada (o valores de y) de una función o relación.	The range of the function $\{(-5, 3), (-3, -2), (-1, -1), (1, 0)\}$ is $\{-2, -1, 0, 3\}$.
rate A ratio that compares two quantities measured in different units.	**tasa** Razón que compara dos cantidades medidas en diferentes unidades.	$\frac{55 \text{ miles}}{1 \text{ hour}} = 55 \text{ mi/h}$
rate of change A ratio that compares the amount of change in a dependent variable to the amount of change in an independent variable.	**tasa de cambio** Razón que compara la cantidad de cambio de la variable dependiente con la cantidad de cambio de la variable independiente.	The cost of mailing a letter increased from 22 cents in 1985 to 25 cents in 1988. During this period, the rate of change was $\frac{\text{change in cost}}{\text{change in year}} = \frac{25 - 22}{1988 - 1985} = \frac{3}{3}$ $= 1$ cent per year.
ratio A comparison of two quantities by division.	**razón** Comparación de dos cantidades mediante una división.	$\frac{1}{2}$ or 1:2
rational number A number that can be written in the form $\frac{a}{b}$, where a and b are integers and $b \neq 0$.	**número racional** Número que se puede expresar como $\frac{a}{b}$, donde a y b son números enteros y $b \neq 0$.	$3, 1.75, 0.\overline{3}, -\frac{2}{3}, 0$
ray A part of a line that starts at an endpoint and extends forever in one direction.	**rayo** Parte de una recta que comienza en un extremo y se extiende infinitamente en una dirección.	$\bullet\!\!\longrightarrow$ D

© Houghton Mifflin Harcourt Publishing Company

Glossary/Glosario

real number A rational or irrational number. Every point on the number line represents a real number.

número real Número racional o irracional. Cada punto de la recta numérica representa un número real.

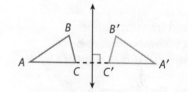

reciprocal For a real number $a \neq 0$, the reciprocal of a is $\frac{1}{a}$. The product of reciprocals is 1.

recíproco Dado el número real $a \neq 0$, el recíproco de a es $\frac{1}{a}$. El producto de los recíprocos es 1.

Number	Reciprocal
2	$\frac{1}{2}$
1	1
-1	-1
0	No reciprocal

rectangle A quadrilateral with four right angles.

rectángulo Cuadrilátero con cuatro ángulos rectos.

recursive rule for nth term of a sequence A rule for a sequence in which one or more previous terms are used to generate the next term.

fórmula recurrente para hallar el enésimo término de una sucesión Fórmula para una sucesión en la cual uno o más términos anteriores se usan para generar el término siguiente.

reflection A transformation across a line, called the line of reflection, such that the line of reflection is the perpendicular bisector of each segment joining each point and its image.

reflexión Transformación sobre una línea, denominada la línea de reflexión. La línea de reflexión es la mediatriz de cada segmento que une un punto con su imagen.

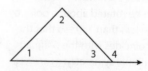

reflection symmetry *See* line symmetry.

simetría de reflexión *Ver* simetría axial.

relation A set of ordered pairs.

relación Conjunto de pares ordenados.

$\{(0, 5), (0, 4), (2, 3), (4, 0)\}$

relative frequency The relative frequency of a category is the frequency of the category divided by the total of all frequencies.

frecuencia relativa La frecuencia relativa de una categoría es la frecuencia de la categoría dividido por el total de todas las frecuencias.

remote interior angle An interior angle of a polygon that is not adjacent to the exterior angle.

ángulo interno remoto Ángulo interno de un polígono que no es adyacente al ángulo externo.

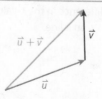

The remote interior angles of $\angle 4$ are $\angle 1$ and $\angle 2$.

resultant vector The vector that represents the sum of two given vectors.

vector resultante Vector que representa la suma de dos vectores dados.

Glossary/Glosario

ENGLISH	SPANISH	EXAMPLES
repeating decimal A rational number in decimal form that has a nonzero block of one or more digits that repeat continuously.	**decimal periódico** Número racional en forma decimal que tiene un bloque de uno o más dígitos que se repite continuamente.	$1.\overline{3},\ 0.\overline{6},\ 2.\overline{14},\ 6.77\overline{3}$
replacement set A set of numbers that can be substituted for a variable.	**conjunto de reemplazo** Conjunto de números que pueden sustituir una variable.	
residual The signed vertical distance between a data point and a line of fit.	**residuo** La diferencia vertical entre un dato y una línea de ajuste.	
residual plot A scatter plot of points whose *x*-coordinates are the values of the independent variable and whose *y*-coordinates are the corresponding residuals.	**diagrama de residuos** Diagrama de dispersión de puntos en el que la coordenada *x* representa los valores de la variable independiente y la coordenada *y* representa los residuos correspondientes.	
rhombus A quadrilateral with four congruent sides.	**rombo** Cuadrilátero con cuatro lados congruentes.	
rigid motion *See* isometry.	**movimiento rígido** *Ver* isometría.	
rigid transformation A transformation that does not change the size or shape of a figure.	**transformación rígida** Transformación que no cambia el tamaño o la forma de una figura.	
rise The difference in the *y*-values of two points on a line.	**distancia vertical** Diferencia entre los valores de *y* de dos puntos de una línea.	For the points $(3, -1)$ and $(6, 5)$, the rise is $5 - (-1) = 6$.
rotation A transformation about a point *P*, also known as the center of rotation, such that each point and its image are the same distance from *P*. All of the angles with vertex *P* formed by a point and its image are congruent.	**rotación** Transformación sobre un punto *P*, también conocido como el centro de rotación, tal que cada punto y su imagen estén a la misma distancia de *P*. Todos los ángulos con vértice *P* formados por un punto y su imagen son congruentes.	
rotational symmetry A figure that can be rotated about a point by an angle less than 360° so that the image coincides with the preimage has rotational symmetry.	**simetría de rotación** Una figura que puede rotarse alrededor de un punto en un ángulo menor de 360° de forma tal que la imagen coincide con la imagen original tiene simetría de rotación.	Order of rotational symmetry: 4
run The difference in the *x*-values of two points on a line.	**distancia horizontal** Diferencia entre los valores de *x* de dos puntos de una línea.	For the points $(3, -1)$ and $(6, 5)$, the run is $6 - 3 = 3$.

Glossary/Glosario

S

same-side interior angles For two lines intersected by a transversal, a pair of angles that lie on the same side of the transversal and between the two lines.

ángulos internos del mismo lado Dadas dos líneas cortadas por una transversal, el par de ángulos ubicados en el mismo lado de la transversal y entre las dos líneas.

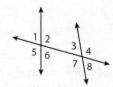

∠2 and ∠3 are same-side interior angles.

---

sample A part of the population.

muestra Una parte de la población.

In a survey about the study habits of high school students, a sample is a survey of 100 students.

---

scale The ratio between two corresponding measurements.

escala Razón entre dos medidas correspondientes.

1 cm : 5 mi

---

scale drawing A drawing that uses a scale to represent an object as smaller or larger than the actual object.

dibujo a escala Dibujo que utiliza una escala para representar un objeto como más pequeño o más grande que el objeto original.

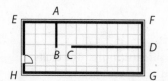

A blueprint is an example of a scale drawing.

---

scale factor The multiplier used on each dimension to change one figure into a similar figure.

factor de escala El multiplicador utilizado en cada dimensión para transformar una figura en una figura semejante.

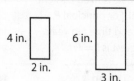

Scale factor: $\frac{3}{2} = 1.5$

---

scale model A three-dimensional model that uses a scale to represent an object as smaller or larger than the actual object.

modelo a escala Modelo tridimensional que utiliza una escala para representar un objeto como más pequeño o más grande que el objeto real.

---

scatter plot A graph with points plotted to show a possible relationship between two sets of data.

diagrama de dispersión Gráfica con puntos que se usa para demostrar una relación posible entre dos conjuntos de datos.

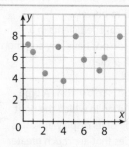

---

second quartile The median of an entire data set, denoted Q_2.

segundo cuartil Mediana de un conjunto de datos completo, expresada como Q_2.

8, 9, ⑨, 12, 15 $Q_2 : 9$

4, 6, ⑦, ⑩, 10, 12

$Q_2 : \frac{7 + 10}{2} = 8.5$

Glossary/Glosario

Glossary/Glosario

segment bisector A line, ray, or segment that divides a segment into two congruent segments.

bisectriz de un segmento Línea, rayo o segmento que divide un segmento en dos segmentos congruentes.

segment of a line A part of a line consisting of two endpoints and all points between them.

segmento de una línea Parte de una línea que consiste en dos extremos y todos los puntos entre éstos.

sequence A list of numbers that often form a pattern.

sucesión Lista de números que generalmente forman un patrón.

1, 2, 4, 8, 16, …

side of an angle One of the two rays that form an angle.

lado de un ángulo Uno de los dos rayos que forman un ángulo.

$\overrightarrow{AC}$ and $\overrightarrow{AB}$ are sides of $\angle CAB$.

significant digits The digits used to express the precision of a measurement.

dígitos significativos Dígitos usados para expresar la precisión de una medida.

simple interest A fixed percent of the principal. For principal P, interest rate r, and time t in years, the simple interest is $I = Prt$.

interés simple Porcentaje fijo del capital. Dado el capital P, la tasa de interés r y el tiempo t expresado en años, el interés simple es $I = Prt$.

simplest form of an exponential expression An exponential expression is in simplest form if it meets the following criteria:
1. There are no negative exponents.
2. The same base does not appear more than once in a product or quotient.
3. No powers, products, or quotients are raised to powers.
4. Numerical coefficients in a quotient do not have any common factor other than 1.

forma simplificada de una expresión exponencial Una expresión exponencial está en forma simplificada si reúne los siguientes requisitos:
1. No hay exponentes negativos.
2. La misma base no aparece más de una vez en un producto o cociente.
3. No se elevan a potencias productos, cocientes ni potencias.
4. Los coeficientes numéricos en un cociente no tienen ningún factor común que no sea 1.

Not Simplest Form	Simplest Form
$7^8 \cdot 7^4$	7^{12}
$\left(x^2\right)^{-4} \cdot x^5$	$\dfrac{1}{x^3}$
$\dfrac{a^5 b^9}{(ab)^4}$	ab^5

skewed distribution A type of distribution in which the right or left side of its display indicates frequencies that are much greater than those of the other side. In a distribution skewed to the left, more than half the data are greater than the mean. In a distribution skewed to the right, more than half the data are less than the mean.

distribución sesgada Tipo de distribución en la que el lado derecho o izquierdo muestra frecuencias mucho mayores que las del otro lado. En una distribución sesgada a la izquierda, más de la mitad de los datos son menores que la media. En una distribución sesgada a la derecha, más de la mitad de los datos son menores que la media.

ENGLISH	SPANISH	EXAMPLES

slope A measure of the steepness of a line. If (x_1, y_1) and (x_2, y_2) are any two points on the line, the slope of the line, known as m, is represented by the equation $m = \frac{y_2 - y_1}{x_2 - x_1}$.

pendiente Medida de la inclinación de una línea. Dados dos puntos (x_1, y_1) y (x_2, y_2) en una línea, la pendiente de la línea, denominada m, se representa con la ecuación $m = \frac{y_2 - y_1}{x_2 - x_1}$.

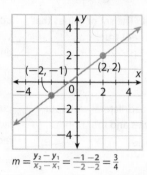

$$m = \frac{y_2 - y_1}{x_2 - x_1} = \frac{-1 - 2}{-2 - 2} = \frac{3}{4}$$

---

slope formula If (x_1, y_1) and (x_2, y_2) are any two points on a line, the slope of the line is $m = \frac{y_2 - y_1}{x_2 - x_1}$.

fórmula de la pendiente Dados dos puntos (x_1, y_1) y (x_2, y_2) en una línea, la pendiente de la línea es $m = \frac{y_2 - y_1}{x_2 - x_1}$.

---

slope-intercept form The slope-intercept form of a linear equation is $y = mx + b$, where m is the slope and b is the y-intercept.

forma de pendiente-intersección La forma de pendiente-intersección de una ecuación lineal es $y = mx + b$, donde m es la pendiente y b es la intersección con el eje y.

$y = -2x + 4$
The slope is -2.
The y-intercept is 4.

---

solution of a linear inequality in one variable A value or values that make the inequality true.

solución de una desigualdad lineal en una variable Valor o valores que hacen que la desigualdad sea verdadera.

Inequality: $x + 2 < 6$
Solution: $x < 4$

---

solution of a linear equation in two variables An ordered pair or ordered pairs that make the equation true.

solución de una ecuación lineal en dos variables Un par ordenado o pares ordenados que hacen que la ecuación sea verdadera.

$(4, 2)$ is a solution of $x + y = 6$.

---

solution of a system of linear equations Any ordered pair that satisfies all the equations in a linear system.

solución de un sistema de ecuaciones lineales Cualquier par ordenado que resuelva todas las ecuaciones de un sistema lineal.

$\begin{cases} x + y = -1 \\ -x + y = -3 \end{cases}$

---

solution of a system of linear inequalities Any ordered pair that satisfies all the inequalities in a linear system.

solución de un sistema de desigualdades lineales Cualquier par ordenado que resuelva todas las desigualdades de un sistema lineal.

$\begin{cases} y \le x + 1 \\ y < -x + 4 \end{cases}$

$(2, 1)$ is in the overlapping shaded regions, so it is a solution.

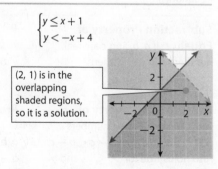

---

solution of an inequality in two variables An ordered pair or ordered pairs that make the inequality true.

solución de una desigualdad en dos variables Un par ordenado o pares ordenados que hacen que la desigualdad sea verdadera.

$(3, 1)$ is a solution of $x + y < 6$.

Glossary/Glosario

ENGLISH	SPANISH	EXAMPLES

solution set The set of values that make a statement true.

conjunto solución Conjunto de valores que hacen verdadero un enunciado.

Inequality: $x + 3 \geq 5$
Solution set: $\{x \mid x \geq 2\}$

-4 -3 -2 -1 0 1 2 3 4 5 6

---

square A quadrilateral with four congruent sides and four right angles.

cuadrado Cuadrilátero con cuatro lados congruentes y cuatro ángulos rectos.

---

square root A number that is multiplied by itself to form a product is called a square root of that product.

raíz cuadrada El número que se multiplica por sí mismo para formar un producto se denomina la raíz cuadrada de ese producto.

A square root of 16 is 4, because $4^2 = 4 \cdot 4 = 16$.
Another square root of 16 is —4 because $(-4)^2 = (-4)(-4) = 16$.

---

standard form of a linear equation $Ax + By = C$, where A, B, and C are real numbers and A and B are not both 0.

forma estándar de una ecuación lineal $Ax + By = C$, donde A, B y C son números reales y A y B no son ambos cero.

$2x + 3y = 6$

---

standard deviation A measure of dispersion of a data set. The standard deviation σ is the square root of the variance

desviación estándar Medida de dispersión de un conjunto de datos. La desviación estándar σ es la raíz cuadrada de la varianza

Data set: $\{6, 7, 7, 9, 11\}$
Mean: $\frac{6+7+7+9+11}{5} = 8$
Variance: $\frac{1}{5}(4 + 1 + 1 + 1 + 9) = 3.2$
Standard deviation: $\sigma = \sqrt{3.2} \approx 1.8$

---

statistics Numbers that describe a sample or samples.v

estadísticas Números que describen una o varias muestras.

---

straight angle A 180° angle.

ángulo llano Ángulo que mide 180°.

---

substitution method A method used to solve systems of equations by solving an equation for one variable and substituting the resulting expression into the other equation(s).

sustitución Método utilizado para resolver sistemas de ecuaciones resolviendo una ecuación para una variable y sustituyendo la expresión resultante en las demás ecuaciones.

Subtraction Property of Equality If a, b, and c are real numbers and $a = b$, then $a - c = b - c$.

Propiedad de igualdad de la resta Si a, b y c son números reales y $a = b$, entonces $a - c = b - c$.

$$\begin{aligned} x + 6 &= 8 \\ -6 &\quad -6 \\ x &= 2 \end{aligned}$$

Subtraction Property of Inequality For real numbers a, b, and c, if $a < b$, then $a - c < b - c$. Also holds true for $>$, $\leq$, $\geq$, and $\neq$.

Propiedad de desigualdad de la resta Dados los números reales a, b y c, si $a < b$, entonces $a - c < b - c$. Es válido también para $>$, $\leq$, $\geq$ y $\neq$.

$$\begin{aligned} x + 6 &< 8 \\ -6 &\quad -6 \\ x &< 2 \end{aligned}$$

---

supplementary angles Two angles whose measures have a sum of 180°.

ángulos suplementarios Dos ángulos cuyas medidas suman 180°.

30° 150°

symmetric distribution A type of distribution in which the right and left sides of its display indicate frequencies that are mirror images of each other.

distribución simétrica Tipo de distribución en la que los lados derecho e izquierdo muestran frecuencias que son idénticas.

---

system of linear equations A system of equations in which all of the equations are linear.

sistema de ecuaciones lineales Sistema de ecuaciones en el que todas las ecuaciones son lineales.

$$\begin{cases} 2x + 3y = -1 \\ x - 3y = 4 \end{cases}$$

---

system of linear inequalities A system of inequalities in which all of the inequalities are linear.

sistema de desigualdades lineales Sistema de desigualdades en el que todas las desigualdades son lineales.

$$\begin{cases} 2x + 3y > -1 \\ x - 3y \le 4 \end{cases}$$

T

term of a sequence An element or number in the sequence.

término de una sucesión Elemento o número de una sucesión.

5 is the third term in the sequence 1, 3, 5, 7, …

---

term of an expression The parts of the expression that are added or subtracted.

término de una expresión Parte de una expresión que debe sumarse o restarse.

$3x^2 + 6x - 8$

Term Term Term

---

terminal point of a vector The endpoint of a vector.

punto terminal de un vector Extremo de un vector.

---

theorem A statement that has been proven.

teorema Enunciado que ha sido demostrado.

---

third quartile The median of the upper half of a data set. Also called *upper quartile*.

tercer cuartil La mediana de la mitad superior de un conjunto de datos. También se llama *cuartil superior*.

Lower half   Upper half
18, 23, 28, 29, (36,) 42
     Third quartile

---

tolerance The amount by which a measurement is permitted to vary from a specified value.

tolerancia La cantidad por que una medida se permite variar de un valor especificado.

---

transformation A change in the position, size, or shape of a figure or graph.

transformación Cambio en la posición, tamaño o forma de una figura o gráfica.

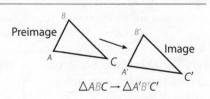

$\triangle ABC \rightarrow \triangle A'B'C'$

---

translation A transformation that shifts or slides every point of a figure or graph the same distance in the same direction.

traslación Transformación en la que todos los puntos de una figura o gráfica se mueven la misma distancia en la misma dirección.

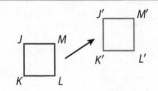

Glossary/Glosario

translation symmetry A figure has translation symmetry if it can be translated along a vector so that the image coincides with the preimage.

simetría de traslación Una figura tiene simetría de traslación si se puede trasladar a lo largo de un vector de forma tal que la imagen coincida con la imagen original.

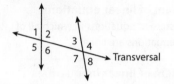

transversal A line that intersects two coplanar lines at two different points.

transversal Línea que corta dos líneas coplanares en dos puntos diferentes.

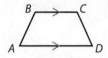

trapezoid A quadrilateral with exactly one pair of parallel sides.

trapecio Cuadrilátero con sólo un par de lados paralelos.

trend line A line on a scatter plot that helps show the correlation between data sets more clearly.

línea de tendencia Línea en un diagrama de dispersión que sirve para mostrar la correlación entre conjuntos de datos más claramente.

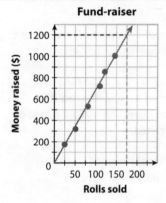

Fund-raiser

triangle A three-sided polygon.

triángulo Polígono de tres lados.

triangle rigidity A property of triangles that states that if the side lengths of a triangle are fixed, the triangle can have only one shape.

rigidez del triángulo Propiedad de los triángulos que establece que, si las longitudes de los lados de un triángulo son fijas, el triángulo puede tener sólo una forma.

two-column proof A style of proof in which the statements are written in the left-hand column and the reasons are written in the right-hand column.

demostración a dos columnas Estilo de demostración en la que los enunciados se escriben en la columna de la izquierda y las razones en la columna de la derecha.

two-variable data A collection of paired variable values, such as a series of measurements of air temperature at different times of day.

datos de dos variables Conjunto de valores variables agrupados en pares, como una serie de mediciones de la temperatura del aire en diferentes momentos del día.

Time	Temperature (°F)
8 A.M.	65
9 A.M.	69
10 A.M.	72

two-way frequency table A frequency table that displays two-variable data in rows and columns.	**table de frecuencia de doble entrada** Una tabla de frecuencia que muestra los datos de dos variables organizados en filas y columnas.	

Preference

Pet		Inside	Outside	*Total*
	Cats	35	15	50
	Dogs	20	30	50
	Total	55	45	100

U

undefined term A basic figure that is not defined in terms of other figures. The undefined terms in geometry are point, line, and plane.	**término indefinido** Figura básica que no está definida en función de otras figuras. Los términos indefinidos en geometría son el punto, la línea y el plano.	
unit rate A rate in which the second quantity in the comparison is one unit.	**tasa unitaria** Tasa en la que la segunda cantidad de la comparación es una unidad.	$\frac{30\text{ mi}}{1\text{ h}} = 30\text{ mi/h}$
unlike terms Terms with different variables or the same variables raised to different powers.	**términos distintos** Términos con variables diferentes o las mismas variables elevadas a potencias diferentes.	$4xy^2$ and $6x^2y$
upper quartile *See* third quartile.	**cuartil superior** *Ver* tercer cuartil.	

V

value of a function The result of replacing the independent variable with a number and simplifying.	**valor de una función** Resultado de reemplazar la variable independiente por un número y luego simplificar.	The value of the function $f(x) = x + 1$ for $x = 3$ is 4.
value of a variable A number used to replace a variable to make an equation true.	**valor de una variable** Número utilizado para reemplazar una variable y hacer que una ecuación sea verdadera.	In the equation $x + 1 = 4$, the value of x is 3.
value of an expression The result of replacing the variables in an expression with numbers and simplifying.	**valor de una expresión** Resultado de reemplazar las variables de una expresión por un número y luego simplificar.	The value of the expression $x + 1$ for $x = 3$ is 4.
variable A symbol used to represent a quantity that can change.	**variable** Símbolo utilizado para representar una cantidad que puede cambiar.	In the expression $2x + 3$, x is the variable.
vector A quantity that has both magnitude and direction.	**vector** Cantidad que tiene magnitud y dirección.	

Glossary/Glosario

vertex angle of an isosceles triangle The angle formed by the legs of an isosceles triangle.

ángulo del vértice de un triángulo isósceles Ángulo formado por los catetos de un triángulo isósceles.

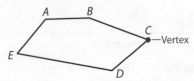

vertex of a polygon The intersection of two sides of the polygon.

vértice de un polígono La intersección de dos lados del polígono.

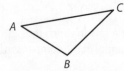

A, B, C, D, and E are vertices of the polygon.

vertex of a triangle The intersection of two sides of the triangle.

vértice de un triángulo Intersección de dos lados del triángulo.

A, B, and C are vertices of △ABC.

vertex of an angle The common endpoint of the sides of the angle.

vértice de un ángulo Extremo común de los lados del ángulo.

A is the vertex of ∠CAB.

vertical angles The nonadjacent angles formed by two intersecting lines.

ángulos opuestos por el vértice Ángulos no adyacentes formados por dos líneas que se cruzan.

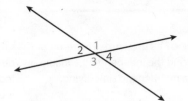

∠**1** and ∠**3** are vertical angles.
∠**2** and ∠**4** are vertical angles.

vertical line A line whose equation is $x = a$, where a is the x-intercept.

línea vertical Línea cuya ecuación es $x = a$, donde a es la intersección con el eje x.

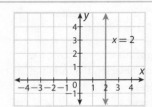

vertical-line test A test used to determine whether a relation is a function. If any vertical line crosses the graph of a relation more than once, the relation is not a function.

prueba de la línea vertical Prueba utilizada para determinar si una relación es una función. Si una línea vertical corta la gráfica de una relación más de una vez, la relación no es una función.

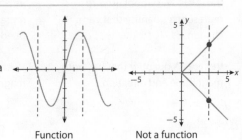

Function   Not a function

Glossary/Glosario

X

x-intercept The x-coordinate(s) of the point(s) where a graph intersects the x-axis.

intersección con el eje x Coordenada(s) x de uno o más puntos donde una gráfica corta el eje x.

The x-intercept is 2.

Y

y-coordinate The second number in an ordered pair, which indicates the vertical distance of a point from the origin on the coordinate plane.

coordenada y Segundo número de un par ordenado, que indica la distancia vertical de un punto desde el origen en un plano cartesiano.

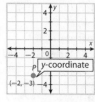

y-intercept The y-coordinate(s) of the point(s) where a graph intersects the y-axis.

intersección con el eje y Coordenada(s) y de uno o más puntos donde una gráfica corta el eje y.

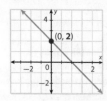

The y-intercept is 2.

Z

zero exponent For any nonzero real number x, $x^0 = 1$.

exponente cero Dado un número real distinto de cero x, $x^0 = 1$.

$5^0 = 1$

Zero Product Property For real numbers p and q, if $pq = 0$, then $p = 0$ or $q = 0$.

Propiedad del producto cero Dados los números reales p y q, si $pq = 0$, entonces $p = 0$ o $q = 0$.

If $(x - 1)(x + 2) = 0$, then $x - 1 = 0$ or $x + 2 = 0$, so $x = 1$ or $x = -2$.

Glossary/Glosario

Index

Index locator numbers are in Module. Lesson form. For example, 2.1 indicates Module 2, Lesson 1 as listed in the Table of Contents.

Index

Index

© Houghton Mifflin Harcourt Publishing Company

Index

Table of Measures

LENGTH

1 inch = 2.54 centimeters

1 meter = 39.37 inches

1 mile = 5,280 feet

1 mile = 1760 yards

1 mile = 1.609 kilometers

1 kilometer = 0.62 mile

MASS/WEIGHT

1 pound = 16 ounces

1 pound = 0.454 kilograms

1 kilogram = 2.2 pounds

1 ton = 2000 pounds

CAPACITY

1 cup = 8 fluid ounces

1 pint = 2 cups

1 quart = 2 pints

1 gallon = 4 quarts

1 gallon = 3.785 liters

1 liter = 0.264 gallons

1 liter = 1000 cubic centimeters

Symbols

$\neq$	is not equal to	π	pi: (about 3.14)
$\approx$	is approximately equal to	$\perp$	is perpendicular to
10^2	ten squared; ten to the second power	$\parallel$	is parallel to
		$\overleftrightarrow{AB}$	line AB
$2.\overline{6}$	repeating decimal 2.66666...	$\overrightarrow{AB}$	ray AB
$\lvert -4 \rvert$	the absolute value of negative 4	$\overline{AB}$	line segment AB
$\sqrt{}$	square root	$m\angle A$	measure of $\angle A$

Formulas

GEOMETRY	
Triangle	$A = \frac{1}{2}bh$
Parallelogram	$A = bh$
Circle	$A = \pi r^2$
Circle	$C = \pi d$ or $C = 2\pi r$
Pythagorean Theorem	$a^2 + b^2 = c^2$

LINEAR EQUATIONS	
Standard form	$Ax + By = C$
Slope-intercept form	$y = mx + b$
Point-slope form	$y - y_1 = m(x - x_1)$
Slope of a line	$m = \frac{y_2 - y_1}{x_2 - x_1}$

SEQUENCES	
Arithmetic Sequence	$a_n = a_1 + (n - 1)d$
Geometric Sequence	$a_n = a_1 r^{n-1}$